NEGOTIATION
Readings, Exercises, and Cases

NEGOTIATION
Readings, Exercises, and Cases

Second Edition

Roy J. Lewicki
The Ohio State University

Joseph A. Litterer
University of Massachusetts

David M. Saunders
McGill University

John W. Minton
Duke University

IRWIN

Burr Ridge, Illinois
Boston, Massachusetts
Sydney, Australia

© RICHARD D. IRWIN, INC., 1985 and 1993

Senior sponsoring editor: Kurt L. Strand
Editorial coordinator: Lisa A. Brennen
Marketing manager: Kurt Messersmith
Project editor: Paula M. Buschman
Production manager: Ann Cassady
Art coordinator: Mark Malloy
Artist: Publisher's Typesetters
Compositor: Carlisle Communications, Ltd.
Typeface: 10/12 Times Roman
Printer: R. R. Donnelley & Sons Company

Library of Congress Cataloging-in-Publication Data

Negotiation : readings, exercises, and cases / Roy J. Lewicki . . . [et al.].—2nd ed.
    p.   cm.
  Includes bibliographical references and index.
  ISBN 0-256-10164-7
  1. Negotiation. 2. Negotiation—Case studies. I. Lewicki, Roy J.
HD58.6.N45 1993
658.4—dc20   92–11882

Printed in the United States of America
     6 7 8 9 0 DOC 9 8 7 6 5 4

Preface

Managers negotiate every day. During an average day, a manager may negotiate with

- The boss, over a budget request.
- Subordinates, over a work deadline.
- A supplier, about a quality problem in the raw materials.
- A banker, over the interest rate of a business loan.
- A government official, regarding compliance with environmental regulations.
- A real estate agent, over the lease on a new warehouse.
- Her/his spouse, over who will walk the dog.
- His/her child, over who will walk the dog (still an issue after losing the previous negotiation).

In short, negotiation is a common, everyday activity that most people use to influence others and to achieve personal objectives. In fact, negotiation is not only a common activity, but an essential activity to living an effective and satisfying life. We all need things—resources, information, cooperation, and support from others. And others have these needs as well. Negotiation is a process by which we attempt to influence others to help us achieve our needs, while at the same time taking their needs into account. It is a fundamental skill, not only for successful management but for successful living.

In 1985, Roy Lewicki and Joseph Litterer published the first edition of this book. As we were preparing that volume, it was clear that the basic processes of negotiation had received only selective attention in both the academic and practitioner literature. Scholars of negotiation had generally restricted examination of these processes to basic theory development and laboratory research in social psychology, to a few books written for managers, and to an examination of negotiation in complex settings such as diplomacy and labor management relations. Efforts to draw from the broader study of techniques for influence and persuasion, to integrate this work into a broader understanding of negotiation, or to apply this work to a broad spectrum of conflict and negotiation settings were only beginning to occur.

In the past seven years this world has changed significantly. There are several new professional associations (the Conflict Management Division of the Academy of Management and the International Association of Conflict Management) that have devoted themselves exclusively to facilitating research and teaching in the fields of negotiation and conflict management. There are several new journals *(Negotiation Journal, International Journal of Conflict Management)* that focus exclusively on research in these fields. There are new funding agencies, such as the National Institute for Dispute

Resolution, whose mission has been to enhance the development of new research and training materials. Finally, through the generosity of the Hewlett Foundations, there are a number of new university centers which have devoted themselves to enhancing the quality of teaching, research, and service in the negotiation and conflict management fields. Many schools now have several courses in negotiation and conflict management—in schools of business, public policy, psychology, social work, education, and natural resources. And development has occurred on the practitioner side as well. Books, seminars, and training courses on negotiation and conflict management abound. And finally, mediation has become an extremely popular process as an alternative to litigation for handling divorce, community disputes, and land-use conflicts. In pragmatic terms, all of this development means that as we assembled this second edition, we have had a much richer and more diverse pool of resources from which to sample. The net result for the student and instructor is a highly improved book of readings and exercises that contains many new articles, cases, and exercises, which represent the very best and most recent work on negotiation and the related topics of power, influence, and conflict management.

For the instructor who was not familiar with the first edition, a brief overview is in order. The first part of the book is organized into 14 sections. The first section introduces the field of negotiation and conflict management with several overview articles; the second describes the basic problems of being in situations of interdependence with other people, and managing that interdependence. The next three sections focus on the basic dynamics of distributive (win-lose) and integrative (win-win) negotiation, and the planning and strategy processes associated with each. Section Six explicitly focuses on negotiation breakdowns, and ways to manage them more effectively. The next five sections contain articles that address some of the subprocesses and specific dynamics of negotiation: persuasion processes, communication processes, the social context of negotiation, sources and use of power, and individual differences ("personality" factors) in negotiation. Section Twelve addresses ways that negotiators can facilitate the resolution of negotiation deadlocks through the assistance of mediators, arbitrators, and other intermediaries. Section Thirteen specifically addresses negotiator ethics. Finally, Section Fourteen contains articles that focus on the challenges of negotiating across international and cultural boundaries. Next, following the readings section, we present a collection of role-play exercises, cases, and self-assessment questionnaires that can be used to teach about negotiation processes. Complete information on the use or adaptation of these materials for all manner of classroom formats is provided in an accompanying Instructor's Manual, which faculty members may obtain from the publisher, Irwin.

For those instructors who were familiar with the first edition, the most visible changes will be in the content and organization of the book, as follows:

1. The content is almost entirely new. Approximately 80 percent of the readings and exercises were either replaced or completely revised for this volume.

2. We have reorganized the book slightly. First, as you will note, we have expanded from 13 to 14 sections in the readings. We have explicitly recognized the importance of cross-cultural differences in negotiation by adding a new sec-

tion on international negotiations. We have also reorganized some of the early sections, by placing the preparation and strategy development section slightly later in the outline and by explicitly addressing techniques for managing negotiation breakdowns. We have also increased the focus of ethics in negotiation and expanded our coverage of individual differences among negotiators.

3. This readings book parallels the structure of a completely revised textbook, *Negotiation,* by Lewicki, Litterer, Minton, and Saunders, also published by Irwin. The books can be used together, and we encourage instructors to contact the publisher for an examination copy.

4. Finally, we have added a large number of new exercises and cases and updated almost every role-play in the book. In addition, to ensure that the exercises can be used without any concern for the security of the confidential role information, *we have decided to publish all confidential role information for the role-playing exercises in the instructor's manual.* Instructors should contact their Irwin representative immediately to receive a copy of this manual. While we recognize that this will require some photocopying costs for instructors, we believe that it will assure greater security in keeping the role-play information confidential and fresh for each new class.

Once again this book could not have been completed without the assistance of many other people. We specifically thank:

- The many authors and publishers who granted us permission to use or adapt their work for this book and whom we have also recognized in conjunction with specific exercises, cases, or articles.
- Many other negotiation teachers and trainers who inspired many of the exercises in this book and gave us excellent feedback on the first edition.
- The staff of Irwin, and particularly Karen Johnson, for their confidence in the project and their continued patience as we completed the project.
- And finally, our families, who continued to provide us with the time and support that we required to finish this project.

Thank you one and all!

Roy Lewicki
Joseph A. Litterer
David M. Saunders
John W. Minton

Contents

Introduction

When most people hear the word "negotiation" they usually think of large, complex, formal deliberations: contract talks between labor and management, discussion of a trade agreement or a treaty between the diplomats of two different nations, or several businesspersons and attorneys meeting to complete a corporate merger or acquisition. Yet these are only a few of the many situations we can call "negotiation." In fact, all of us negotiate every day. Each day we are involved in one or more of the following situations:

- We arrive at an intersection simultaneously with three other cars; somehow, we need to decide who is going to go through the intersection in what order.
- We need to decide how to share a scarce resource—a computer terminal or a library book.
- We must work out an arrangement with other people to share the tasks and chores of daily living—for example, cleaning an apartment, walking the dog, going to the grocery store, or doing the laundry.
- We need to influence someone to change his or her mind—for example, to agree to accept our paper three days after the due date, to waive the fine on our overdue library book, or to give us a pay raise.

The list is endless. Regrettably, however, many of these situations are not often recognized as negotiations. As a result, we may not handle them as effectively as we might. One purpose of this book is to learn how to manage these situations more effectively, by recognizing that they *are* negotiations, and by applying negotiation principles to them.

WHEN IS NEGOTIATION NEEDED?

A negotiation situation is one in which:

- Two or more parties must make a decision about their interdependent goals and objectives.
- The parties are committed to peaceful means for resolving their dispute.
- There is no clear or established method or procedure for making this decision.

1

Like most definitions, this one means the most to those who already understand the nature of what we are trying to define. Let's take an example. Two people who work in the same office want to take their vacation during the first two weeks in July; however, both cannot be away at the same time. In some organizations there are established procedures as to how these decisions will be made: the person with the most seniority gets preference. This procedure may be formalized—that is, it may be part of the company rules or the union contract—or it may simply be an informal tradition in the organization. In any event, there is a rule that can be referred to and used. An alternative way is to refer the decision to a senior manager. But when no senior manager is available or when there are no rules, what are the parties to do? They could flip a coin—but some would feel this decision is too important to be left to chance. They could fight over it—but this hardly seems to be the kind of problem one goes to battle over. At this point, the most reasonable and viable alternative is for the parties to negotiate—that is, discuss their preferences for taking the vacation, attempt to understand each other's preferences, and find a way to settle the problem amicably.

FEAR OF NEGOTIATING

Even after many parties recognize the importance of negotiation as a mechanism for making decisions, solving problems and conflicts, and the prevalence of negotiation in our daily lives, they still back off. They find the prospect of negotiating uncomfortable, even distasteful. They say, "Negotiating isn't for me. I don't negotiate. I don't need to learn anything about negotiation!"

The fact is that we *all* negotiate! In fact, it is impossible *not* to negotiate! Every day we are in situations where we must coordinate our preferences with others', influence other people to our way of thinking, or resolve potential conflicts with others. However, there are several reasons why people believe they can avoid negotiation or find negotiation unpleasant.

First, at the basis of most negotiations is some form of conflict—a conflict of preferences, priorities, or perspectives. Many people are afraid of conflict. Conflict makes them uncomfortable or insecure, and they would prefer to minimize or avoid conflict. Other people want to avoid conflict with the person with whom they must negotiate—a boss, a spouse, a close friend—because they are afraid that they won't perform well, or will endanger their relationship with that person. While these concerns are understandable and very realistic, it is important to understand several things:

• Given all of the situations in which we must be interdependent with others—sharing a scarce resource, coordinating our actions, engaging in give and take—conflict is unavoidable. Daily, we come into contact with people who have preferences and priorities different from our own, and we must learn to live and work together with them and resolve these differences.

• If we truly fear conflict, we will probably either avoid taking any position—and not get what we want—or we will take an arbitrary and (probably) unrealistic position, and still not get what we want.

• Negotiation does not have to be a hostile, bloody, or psychologically intimidating process to be successful. In fact, if it is any of these, it is probably a highly unsuccessful negotiation anyway.

A second reason people fear negotiation is that many of us have the idea that to be successful at negotiation we need to be verbally glib—very articulate, very persuasive, a fast and smooth talker, even a con artist. The stereotypical assumption is that people who get what they want in negotiation tend to be fast talkers, quick-witted, even devious and deceptive. Many of us do not see ourselves as having any of these skills, and wouldn't want them even if we could have them. Thus, if we don't have them, we must not be good negotiators; moreover, we probably could never stand up effectively against those people who, by this definition, *are* good negotiators!

Many people fear negotiation for these reasons and related ones. And their fears do have some basis, for conflict *is* threatening to some people, and some negotiators *are* skilled con artists! But our experience is that these fears—like many other fears—are greatly exaggerated and are compounded by the normal fear one has of learning any new skill. Learning a new skill is a little scary and intimidating—particularly when we have to practice it in public, in front of people who we think are better than we are. But, like so many other things, developing a new skill is far less difficult than we think it is! A purpose of this book—and the related "practice activities" (role plays and simulations)—is to help the student overcome the fear of negotiating. This fear can be overcome through mastery of the concepts presented here and practice of the related skills.

Second, and more important, it is also the purpose of this book to present a comprehensive perspective on effective negotiation. As the reader will discover, effective negotiation is *not* likely to require quick wit, fast talking, and deviousness or deception! In fact, in most of our daily negotiations, these qualities are more likely to get us into trouble than to help us get what we want. Instead, we will show that there are many other, far more important, skills and qualities to effective negotiation—ones we can feel more comfortable with and master very quickly.

Negotiation is a complex human activity. It involves a dynamic interpersonal process. It requires the intellectual ability to understand the key factors that tend to shape and characterize different negotiation situations. It requires skills, both behavioral and analytical, to diagnose negotiation problems and select the correct strategies and approaches. It also requires an understanding of one's own personality and one's system of personal ethics and values, because these will affect how we perceive situations and how we determine the appropriate strategy and tactics. Finally, negotiation is a learnable process. We do not have to be born with the skill. Most of us can improve with a few lessons, a bit of coaching, and some tips on how to do it better. This book provides the tools and resources to learn to negotiate better and to gain greater confidence in one's negotiating ability and potential.

SCOPE OF THIS BOOK

This book represents a compilation of articles on negotiation and related topics: conflict, conflict resolution, power, influence, and persuasion. Most of the articles were selected from newspapers, magazines, and management journals. We chose them because they made very good points, were very readable, and were not unnecessarily theoretical or technical.

The organization of the readings parallels an accompanying textbook (*Negotiation,* 2nd. ed., by Roy J. Lewicki, Joseph A. Litterer, John W. Minton, and David M.

Saunders) and is divided into 14 sections. Section One introduces the general themes of conflict and negotiation, and elaborates many of the points we have made in this introduction. Section Two includes several articles on the general problems that people face when they are interdependent with one another—that is, dependent on each other for their outcomes in various social situations—and explores conflict and negotiation as processes for better managing that interdependence. The articles in Sections Three and Four focus on the two basic approaches to negotiation—distributive and integrative—and discuss the strategies and tactics associated with each approach. Sections Five and Six focus on the planning and preparation needed for negotiation and techniques for "defusing" or redirecting negotiations that might be loaded with conflict and headed for disaster. The articles in Sections Seven through Eleven focus on some of the key elements in the actual give-and-take of negotiation: the persuasion process, the communication process, the impact of a negotiator having a constituency and/or an audience watching the negotiation, ways of understanding differences in negotiator power, and the role and impact of a negotiator's personality. Section Twelve examines the roles played by different types of third parties in helping negotiators to resolve difficult deliberations. In Section Thirteen, we present several articles that address the ethics of negotiation and help negotiators to define what is appropriate (and inappropriate) to do. In the final section (new to this volume), several authors explore the critical factors that affect the negotiation process as it occurs in different cultures around the world.

This comprehensive reading section is followed by a collection of role-play scenarios, simulations, and case material. More will be said about these resources when this section is introduced.

INTRODUCTION TO SECTION ONE: OVERVIEW

The purpose of these articles is to provide a broad introduction to the nature of negotiation as well as to the basic dynamics of conflict and its management. It is these basic dynamics that Leonard Greenhalgh explores in the first article, "Managing Conflict." Greenhalgh begins his article as we did—by pointing out that conflict is inherent in the life of organizations. Conflict occurs whenever there are scarce resources, when people have different interests at stake, or when parties try to limit each other's power to control a situation. Conflict is not necessarily bad or good, but inevitable. And since it is both inevitable and a central part of organizational life, managers must understand how to deal with it effectively. Greenhalgh uses the article to develop a "diagnostic model" of conflict, suitable to be used both by parties to a conflict and by third parties who are evaluating ways to resolve a dispute. He offers seven specific perceptual dimensions of disputes, which provide the foundations of this diagnostic model; the ends of each dimension represent the degree to which a conflict is more or less easy to resolve. The perceptual dimensions include the nature of the issues in question, the magnitude of the stakes, the type of interdependence between the parties, the continuity of the parties' interaction (short term versus long term), the degree of social organization of the parties, the involvement of third parties, and the perceived progress of the conflict (the "balance of power" between the parties). Greenhalgh ends the article by addressing some of the skills necessary to manage conflict effectively in today's organizations.

The second article is a selection from the book *Mediation,* by Jay Folberg and Alison Taylor. In this selection, the authors provide a broader, more theoretical approach to understanding the fundamental nature of conflict. First, the authors explore the functions and dysfunctions of conflict. Second, they make a variety of distinctions among different *definitions* and *types* of conflict (interpersonal versus intrapersonal; latent versus manifest; approach/approach versus approach/avoidance versus avoidance/avoidance). Another key distinction in models of conflict is the notion of a "life cycle" of conflict, in which a conflict episode is divided into stages, phases, or time periods. Receiving particular attention is a model that describes conflict as a helix or continuing spiral, consisting of the stages of latent conflict, conflict initiation, balancing of power, achievement of the balance of power in an equilibrium, and, finally, the disruption of that balance. A second helix, representing the opposite of conflict, or "convergence," is proposed to represent the forces that bring parties together in cooperation and agreement. In this book, the authors use these theoretical bases to examine the nature of mediation as a third-party intervention designed to reduce conflict and enhance negotiation. We will say more about mediation in Section Twelve.

In the third article, we turn from a broader discussion of conflict to a more specific focus on negotiation. In "How to Be a Better Negotiator," Jeremy Main discusses the fundamental shift in strategy being advocated by those who train negotiators to be more effective. For many years, the dominant perspective on negotiating strategy and tactics was to encourage negotiators to "win"—and to use any tactics necessary to achieve that objective. We will call this the "distributive" strategy, and describe it extensively in Section Three. In the past decade, however, a strong countermovement has emerged in negotiation training, which advocates a very different set of strategy and tactics that leads parties to a more cooperative, "win-win" outcome. (Similarly, we will devote our full attention to these "integrative" approaches in Section Four.) Main outlines the major works of Roger Fisher, William Ury, and Gerard Nierenberg in creating the foundational principles for this cooperative approach, and offers a number of examples to highlight the success of the win-win approach.

Finally, Joseph Byrnes offers 10 points of advice for negotiators of all persuasions. A famous study of managers' use of time recently revealed that they spend almost 20 percent of their professional time handling and managing conflicts, frequently through negotiation. Yet managers spend very little time learning how to negotiate more effectively. Byrnes's guidance to managers includes how to prepare better; how to understand the way that conflict shapes and distorts perceptions; how to avoid boxing yourself into a win-lose corner; how to be more creative; how to appreciate the power of silence; how to make trade-offs among alternative settlements; how to help the other side come to mutual agreement; the importance of taking notes and paying attention to deadlines; and how to anticipate the possibility that you and your opponent may not agree, and to deal with that eventuality by cultivating a good alternative option. As we will see later in this book, these sound principles frequently serve as the cornerstones of some of the most popular and powerful models of negotiation effectiveness.

Managing Conflict

Leonard Greenhalgh

Managers or change agents spend a substantial proportion of their time and energy dealing with conflict situations. Such efforts are necessary because any type of change in an organization tends to generate conflict. More specifically, conflict arises because change disrupts the existing balance of resources and power, thereby straining relations between the people involved. Since adversarial relations may impede the process of making adaptive changes in the organization, higher-level managers may have to intervene in order to implement important strategies. Their effectiveness in managing the conflict depends on how well they understand the underlying dynamics of the conflict—which may be very different from its expression—and whether they can identify the crucial tactical points for intervention.

CONFLICT MANAGEMENT

Conflict is managed when it does not substantially interfere with the ongoing functional (as opposed to personal) relationships between the parties involved. For instance, two executives may agree to disagree on a number of issues and yet be jointly committed to the course of action they have settled on. There may even be some residual hard feelings—perhaps it is too much to expect to manage feelings in addition to relationships—but as long as any resentment is at a fairly low level and does not substantially interfere with other aspects of their professional relationship, the conflict could be considered to have been managed successfully.

Conflict is not an objective, tangible phenomenon; rather, it exists in the minds of the people who are party to it. Only its manifestations, such as brooding, arguing, or fighting, are objectively real. To manage conflict, therefore, one needs to empathize, that is, to understand the situation as it is seen by the key actors involved. An important element of conflict management is persuasion, which may well involve getting participants to rethink their current views so their perspective on the situation will facilitate reconciliation rather than divisiveness.

Influencing key actors' conceptions of the conflict situation can be a powerful lever in making conflicts manageable. This approach can be used by a third party

Reprinted from "Managing Conflict" by Leonard Greenhalgh, *Sloan Management Review,* Summer 1986, pp. 45–51, by permission of the publisher. Copyright 1986 by the Sloan Management Review Association. All rights reserved.

intervening in the conflict or, even more usefully, by the participants themselves. But using this perceptual lever alone will not always be sufficient. The context in which the conflict occurs, the history of the relationship between the parties, and the time available will have to be taken into account if such an approach is to be tailored to the situation. Furthermore, the conflict may prove to be simply unmanageable: one or both parties may wish to prolong the conflict or they may have reached emotional states that make constructive interaction impossible; or, perhaps the conflict is "the tip of the iceberg" and resolving it would have no significant impact on a deeply rooted antagonistic relationship.

Table 1 presents seven perceptual dimensions that form a useful diagnostic model that shows what to look for in a conflict situation and pinpoints the dimensions needing high-priority attention. The model can thus be used to illuminate a way to make the conflict more manageable. The point here is that conflict becomes more negotiable between parties when a minimum number of dimensions are perceived to be at the "difficult-to-resolve" pole and a maximum number to be at the "easy-to-resolve" pole. The objective is to shift a viewpoint from the difficult-to-resolve pole to the easy-to-resolve one. At times, antagonists will deliberately resist "being more reasonable" because they see tactical advantages in taking a hard line. Nevertheless, there are strong benefits for trying to shift perspectives; these benefits should become apparent as we consider each of the dimensions in the model.

Issues in Question

People view issues on a continuum from being a matter of principle to a question of division. For example, one organization needed to change its channel of distribution.

TABLE 1   Conflict Diagnostic Model

	Viewpoint Continuum	
Dimension	*Difficult to Resolve*	*Easy to Resolve*
Issue in question	Matter of principle	Divisible issue
Size of stakes	Large	Small
Interdependence of the parties	Zero sum	Positive sum
Continuity of interaction	Single transaction	Long-term relationship
Structure of the parties	Amorphous or fractionalized, with weak leadership	Cohesive, with strong leadership
Involvement of third parties	No neutral third party available	Trusted, powerful, prestigious, and neutral
Perceived progress of the conflict	Unbalanced: One party feeling the more harmed	Parties having done equal harm to each other

The company had sold door-to-door since its founding, but the labor market was drying up and the sales force was becoming increasingly understaffed. Two factions of executive sprung up: the supporters were open to the needed change; the resisters argued that management made a commitment to the remaining sales force and, as a matter of principle, could not violate the current sales representatives' right to be the exclusive channel of distribution.

Raising principles makes conflict difficult to resolve because by definition one cannot come to a reasonable compromise; one either upholds a principle or sacrifices one's integrity. For some issues, particularly those involving ethical imperatives, such a dichotomous view may be justified. Often, however, matters of principle are raised for the purpose of solidifying a bargaining stance. Yet, this tactic may work *against* the party using it since it tends to invite an impasse. Once matters of principle are raised, the parties try to argue convincingly that the other's point of view is wrong. At best, this approach wastes time and saps the energy of the parties involved. A useful intervention at this point may be to have the parties acknowledge that they *understand* each other's view but still believe in their own, equally legitimate point of view. This acknowledgment alone often makes the parties more ready to move ahead from arguing to problem solving.

At the other extreme are divisible issues where neither side has to give in completely; the outcome may more or less favor both parties. In the door-to-door selling example, a more constructive discussion would have ensued had the parties been able to focus on the *economic* commitment the company had to its sales force, rather than on the *moral* commitment. As it was, the factions remained deadlocked until the company had suffered irrevocable losses in market share, which served no one's interests. Divisible issues in this case might have involved how much of the product line would be sold through alternative channels of distribution, the extent of exclusive territory, or how much income protection the company was willing to offer its sales force.

Size of Stakes

The greater the perceived value of what may be lost, the harder it is to manage a conflict. This point is illustrated when managers fight against acquisition attempts. If managers think their jobs are in jeopardy, they subjectively perceive the stakes as being high and are likely to fight tooth and nail against the acquisition. Contracts providing for continued economic security, so-called golden parachutes, reduce the size of the stakes for those potentially affected. Putting aside the question of whether such contracts are justifiable when viewed from other perspectives, they do tend to make acquisition conflicts more manageable.

In many cases the perceived size of the stakes can be reduced by persuasion rather than by taking concrete action. People tend to become emotionally involved in conflicts and as a result magnify the importance of what is really at stake. Their "egos" get caught up in the winning/losing aspect of the conflict, and subjective values become inflated.

A good antidote is to postpone the settlement until the parties become less emotional. During this cooling-off period they can reevaluate the issues at stake, thereby restoring some objectivity to their assessments. If time does not permit a cooling off, an attempt to reassess the demands and reduce the other party's expectations may be possible: "There's no way we can give you 100 percent of what you want, so let's be realistic about what you can live with." This approach is really an attempt to induce an attitude change. In effect, the person is being persuaded to entertain the thought, "If I can get by with less than 100 percent of what I was asking for, then what is at stake must not be of paramount importance to me."

A special case of the high-stakes/low-stakes question is the issue of precedents. If a particular settlement sets a precedent, the stakes are seen as being higher because future conflicts will tend to be settled in terms of the current settlement. In other words, giving ground in the immediate situation is seen as giving ground for all time. This problem surfaces in settling grievances. Thus, an effective way to manage such a conflict is to emphasize the uniqueness of the situation to downplay possible precedents that could be set. Similarly, the perceived consequences of organizational changes for individuals can often be softened by explicitly downplaying the future consequences: employees are sometimes assured that the change is being made "on an experimental basis" and will later be reevaluated. The effect is to reduce the perceived risk in accepting the proposed change.

Interdependence of the Parties

The parties to a conflict can view themselves on a continuum from having "zero-sum" to "positive-sum" interdependence. Zero-sum interdependence is the perception that if one party gains in an interaction, it is at the expense of the other party. In the positive-sum case, both parties come out ahead by means of a settlement. A zero-sum relationship makes conflict difficult to resolve because it focuses attention narrowly on personal gain rather than on mutual gain through collaboration or problem solving.

Consider the example of conflict over the allocation of limited budget funds among sales and production when a new product line is introduced. The sales group fights for a large allocation to promote the product in order to build market share. The production group fights for a large allocation to provide the plant and equipment necessary to turn out high volume at high-quality levels. The funds available have a fixed ceiling, so that a gain for sales appears to be a loss for production and vice versa. From a zero-sum perspective, it makes sense to fight for the marginal dollar rather than agree on a compromise.

A positive-sum view of the same situation removes some of the urgency to win a larger share of the spoils at the outset. Attention is more usefully focused on how one party's allocation in fact helps the other. Early promotion allocations to achieve high sales volume, if successful, lead to high production volume. This, in turn, generates revenue that can be invested in the desired improvements to plant and equipment. Similarly, initial allocations to improve plant and equipment can make a high-quality product readily available to the sales group, and the demand for a high-quality product will foster sales.

The potential for mutual benefit is often overlooked in the scramble for scarce resources. However, if both parties can be persuaded to consider how they can both benefit from a situation, they are more likely to approach the conflict over scarce resources with more cooperative predispositions. The focus shifts from whether one party is getting a fair share of the available resources to what is the optimum initial allocation that will jointly serve the mutual long-run interests of both sales and production.

Continuity of Interaction

The continuity-of-interaction dimension concerns the time horizon over which the parties see themselves dealing with each other. If they visualize a long-term interaction—a *continuous* relationship—the present transaction takes on minor significance, and the conflict within that transaction tends to be easy to resolve. If, on the other hand, the transaction is viewed as a one-shot deal—an *episodic* relationship—the parties will have little incentive to accommodate each other, and the conflict will be difficult to resolve.

This difference in perspective is seen by contrasting how lawyers and managers approach a contract dispute. Lawyers are trained to perceive the situation as a single episode: the parties go to court, and the lawyers make the best possible case for their party in an attempt to achieve the best possible outcome. This is a "no-holds-barred" interaction in which the past and future interaction between the parties tends to be viewed as irrelevant. Thus the conflict between the parties is not really resolved; rather, an outcome is imposed by the judge.

In contrast, managers are likely to be more accommodating when the discussion of a contract is viewed as one interaction within a longer-term relationship that has both a history and a future. In such a situation, a manager is unlikely to resort to no-holds-barred tactics because he or she will have to face the other party again regarding future deals. Furthermore, a continuous relationship permits the bankrolling of favors: "We helped you out on that last problem; it's your turn to work with us on this one."

Here, it is easy, and even cordial, to remind the other party that a continuous relationship exists. This tactic works well because episodic situations are rare in real-world business transactions. For instance, people with substantial business experience know that a transaction is usually not completed when a contract is signed. No contract can be comprehensive enough to provide unambiguously for all possible contingencies. Thus trust and goodwill remain important long after the contract is signed. The street-fighting tactics that may seem advantageous in the context of an episodic orientation are likely to be very costly to the person who must later seek accommodation with the bruised and resentful other party.

Structure of the Parties

Conflict is easier to resolve when a party has a strong leader who can unify his or her constituency to accept and implement the agreement. If the leadership is weak, rebellious subgroups who may not feel obliged to go along with the overall agreement that has been reached are likely to rise up, thereby making conflict difficult to resolve.

For example, people who deal with unions know that a strong leadership tends to be better than a weak one, especially when organizational change needs to be accomplished. A strongly led union may drive a hard bargain, but once an agreement is reached the deal is honored by union members. If a weakly led union is involved, the agreement may be undermined by factions within the union who may not like some of the details. The result may well be chronic resistance to change or even wildcat strikes. To bring peace among such factions, management may have to make further concessions that may be costly. To avoid this, managers may find themselves in a paradoxical position of needing to boost the power of union leaders.

Similar actions may be warranted when there is no union. Groups of employees often band together as informal coalitions to protect their interests in times of change. Instead of fighting or alienating a group, managers who wish to bring about change may benefit from considering ways to formalize the coalition, such as by appointing its opinion leader to a task force or steering committee. This tactic may be equivalent to cooptation, yet there is likely to be a net benefit to both the coalition and management. The coalition benefits because it is given a formal channel in which the opinion leader's viewpoint is expressed; management benefits because the spokesperson presents the conflict in a manageable form, which is much better than passive resistance or subtle sabotage.

Involvement of Third Parties

People tend to become emotionally involved in conflicts. Such involvement can have several effects: perceptions may become distorted, nonrational thought processes and arguments may arise, and unreasonable stances, impaired communication, and personal attacks may result. These effects make the conflict difficult to resolve.

The presence of a third party, even if the third party is not actively involved in the dialogue, can constrain such effects. People usually feel obliged to appear reasonable and responsible because they care more about how the neutral party is evaluating them than about how the opponent is. The more prestigious, powerful, trusted, and neutral the third party, the greater is the desire to exercise emotional restraint.

While managers often have to mediate conflicts among lower-level employees, they are rarely seen as being neutral. Therefore, consultants and change agents often end up serving a mediator role, either by design or default. This role can take several forms, ranging from an umpire supervising communication to a messenger between parties for whom face-to-face communication has become too strained. Mediation essentially involves keeping the parties interacting in a reasonable and constructive manner. Typically, however, most managers are reluctant to enlist an outsider who is a professional mediator or arbitrator, for it is very hard for them to admit openly that they are entangled in a serious conflict, much less one they cannot handle themselves.

When managers remain involved in settling disputes, they usually take a stronger role than mediators: they become arbitrators rather than mediators. As arbitrators, they arrive at a conflict-resolving judgment after hearing each party's case. In most business conflicts, mediation is preferable because the parties are helped to come to an agreement in which they have some psychological investment. Arbitration tends to be more of a judicial process in which the parties make the best possible case to support their position: this tends to further polarize rather than reconcile differences.

Managers can benefit from a third-party presence, however, without involving dispute-resolution professionals per se. For example, they can introduce a consultant into the situation, with an *explicit* mission that is not conflict intervention. The mere presence of this neutral witness will likely constrain the disputants' use of destructive tactics.

Alternatively, if the managers find that they themselves are party to a conflict, they can make the conflict more public and produce the same constraining effect that a third party would. They also can arrange for the presence of relatively uninvolved individuals during interactions; even having a secretary keep minutes of such interactions encourages rational behavior. If the content of the discussion cannot be disclosed to lower-level employees, a higher-level manager can be invited to sit in on the discussion, thereby discouraging dysfunctional personal attacks and unreasonable stances. To the extent that managers can be trusted to be evenhanded, a third-party approach can facilitate conflict management. Encouraging accommodation usually is preferable to imposing a solution that may only produce resentment of one of the parties.

Progress of the Conflict

It is difficult to manage conflict when the parties are not ready to achieve a reconciliation. Thus it is important to know whether the parties believe that the conflict is escalating. The following example illustrates this point.

During a product strategy meeting, a marketing vice president carelessly implied that the R&D group tended to overdesign products. The remark was intended to be a humorous stereotyping of the R&D function, but it was interpreted by the R&D vice president as an attempt to pass on to his group the blame for an uncompetitive product. Later in the meeting, the R&D vice president took advantage of an opportunity to point out that the marketing vice president lacked the technical expertise to understand a design limitation. The marketing vice president perceived this rejoinder as ridicule and therefore as an act of hostility. The R&D vice president, who believed he had evened the score, was quite surprised to be denounced subsequently by the marketing vice president, who in turn thought he was evening the score for the uncalled-for barb. These events soon led to a memo war, backbiting, and then to pressure on various employees to take sides.

The important point here is that from the first rejoinder neither party wished to escalate the conflict; each wished merely to even the score. Nonetheless, conflict resolution would have been very difficult to accomplish during this escalation phase because people do not like to disengage when they think they still "owe one" to the other party. Since an even score is subjectively defined, however, the parties need to be convinced that the overall score is approximately equal and that everyone has already suffered enough.

DEVELOPING CONFLICT MANAGEMENT SKILLS

Strategic decision making usually is portrayed as a unilateral process. Decision makers have some vision of where the organization needs to be headed, and they decide on the nature and timing of specific actions to achieve tangible goals. This portrayal, however, does not take into account the conflict inherent in the decision-making process; most strategic decisions are negotiated solutions to conflicts among people whose interests are affected by such decisions. Even in the uncommon case of a unilateral decision, the decision maker has to deal with the conflict that arises when he or she moves to *implement* the decision.

In the presence of conflict at the decision-making or decision-implementing stage, managers must focus on generating an *agreement* rather than a decision. A decision without agreement makes the strategic direction difficult to implement. By contrast, an agreement on a strategic direction doesn't require an explicit decision. In this context, conflict management is the process of removing cognitive barriers to agreement. Note that agreement does not imply that the conflict has "gone away." The people involved still have interests that are somewhat incompatible. Agreement implies that these people have become committed to a course of action that serves some of their interests.

People make agreements that are less than ideal from the standpoint of serving their interests when they lack the *power* to force others to fully comply with their wishes. On the other hand, if a manager has total power over those whose interests are affected by the outcome of a strategic decision, the manager may not care whether or not others agree, because total power implies total compliance. There are few situations in real life in which managers have influence that even approaches total power, however, and power solutions are at best unstable since most people react negatively to powerlessness per se. Thus it makes more sense to seek agreements than to seek power. Furthermore, because conflict management involves weakening or removing barriers to agreements, managers must be able to diagnose successfully such barriers. The model summarized in Table 1 identifies the primary cognitive barriers to agreement.

Competence in understanding the barriers to an agreement can be easily honed by making a pastime of conflict diagnosis. The model helps to focus attention on specific aspects of the situation that may pose obstacles to successful conflict management. This pastime transforms accounts of conflicts—from sources ranging from a spouse's response to "how was your day?" to the evening news—into a challenge in which the objective is to try to pinpoint the obstacles to agreement and to predict the success of proposed interventions.

Focusing on the underlying dynamics of the conflict makes it more likely that conflict management will tend toward resolution rather than the more familiar response of suppression. Although the conflict itself—that is, the source—will remain alive, at best, its expression will be postponed until some later occasion; at worst, it will take a less obvious and usually less manageable form.

Knowledge of and practice in using the model is only a starting point for managers and change agents. Their development as professionals requires that conflict management become an integral part of their use of power. Power is a most basic facet of organizational life, yet inevitably it generates conflict because it constricts the autonomy of those who respond to it. Anticipating precisely how the use of power will create a conflict relationship provides an enormous advantage in the ability to achieve the desired levels of control with minimal dysfunctional side effects.

The Nature of Conflict

Jay Folberg
Alison Taylor

Psychologists, sociologists, lawyers, diplomats, public servants—all deal in their work with conflict. Conflict, whether between individuals, groups, or nations, has certain basic features. Each discipline and profession has contributed to a better understanding of conflict in specific terms, yet few works have been aimed at understanding conflict as an entity. Fewer still have provided common concepts for those outside of academic circles.

Conflict can be divided into two categories: intrapersonal and interpersonal. The causes and effects of *intrapersonal* conflict, or conflict within the individual, are described in Chapter Four. Mediation is primarily concerned with *interpersonal* conflict—situations that arise between individuals or groups of individuals. The issues discussed during mediation may trigger internal conflict for participants, however, so it is necessary to recognize both kinds of conflict, interpersonal and intrapersonal, and to distinguish between them. We should also note the distinction between conflicts and disputes, though the literature often uses the two terms interchangeably. A *dispute* is an interpersonal conflict that is communicated or manifested. A conflict may not become a dispute if it is not communicated to someone in the form of a perceived incompatibility or a contested claim (Abel, 1973).

Although conflict is not necessarily bad, wrong, or intolerable, our society often views conflict negatively because it is equated with win/lose situations. Conflict can function in important and positive ways: It can help set group boundaries by strengthening group cohesion; it reduces incipient tension by making issues manifest; it clarifies objectives; and it helps establish group norms. (See Coser, 1956, and Mack and Snyder, 1973, for further discussion and references.) Conflict can generate creative energy and improve situations. As Jandt (1973, p. 3) puts it: "Conflict is desirable from at least two standpoints. It has been demonstrated that through conflict man is creative. Further, a relationship in conflict *is* a relationship—not the absence of one. Such a relationship may result in creativity because of its intensity."

Reprinted from Folberg, J., and Taylor, A. *Mediation: A Comprehensive Guide to Resolving Conflicts without Litigation,* 1984, pp. 18–36. © Jossey-Bass and Jay Folberg and Alison Taylor. Used with permission.

Conflict is commonly viewed by the participants as a crisis. A crisis mentality lends itself to destructive processes because people will often rush to use anything they believe will relieve the conflict. Intervention techniques have been developed to help create constructive outcomes from crises, which may result from intrapersonal conflicts. By controlling the perception of what is at stake in a conflict, a mediator can prevent destructive outcomes. This ability to defuse conflict, reframe the issues, and realistically analyze outcomes is an important skill in mediation and is further discussed in many other chapters. Crisis intervention techniques are summarized well by Okun (1982) and are discussed later in the context of crisis mediation.

Kenneth Boulding, in his excellent and seminal work (1962, p. 5), has defined conflict as "a situation of competition in which the parties are *aware* of the incompatibility of potential future positions and in which each party *wishes* to occupy a position which is incompatible with the wishes of the other." Boulding differentiates between static models of conflict and the dynamic or reaction processes of conflict in which the movement of party A affects the subsequent movement of party B, which in turn affects the action of party A, and so on. While others had developed similar dynamic theories using differential equations from physics (Richardson, 1960), Boulding notes that these dynamic processes apply to *all* spheres of human interaction: conflicts between husband and wife, union and management, nation and nation. He views conflict as divisible into three levels: simple conflicts (persons acting for themselves), group conflicts (unorganized subpopulations), and organizational conflicts (representatives).

Boulding believes that conflicts have their own "life cycle" (p. 307). According to his theory, conflicts are spawned, exist for a time, and eventually cease because of their own inherent tendencies, without conflict resolution interventions such as mediation. It may take a long time for unaided conflict to cease, however, as evidenced by the continuation of national and religious feuds spanning decades and even centuries. Boulding's concepts regarding conflict resolution will be discussed later.

Work done by the researchers Dollard and Miller (see the excellent summary of their work by Patterson, 1973) has helped conceptualize three categories of conflicts: approach/approach, approach/avoidance, avoidance/avoidance. While Boulding concentrates on the attributes of the parties in conflict, Dollard and Miller focus on the options for resolution. *Approach/approach* refers to a conflict in which both options for resolving a situation are equally attractive but mutually exclusive—the person can have only one but wants both. *Approach/avoidance* refers to conflicts in which the person desires an option but must not have it for equally strong reasons. Dollard and Miller think this type of conflict is inherent in cases of neurotic repression. The conflict is created by wanting something yet needing to avoid the topic because it is frightening; this conflict leads to repression, a particular type of distortion of reality. *Avoidance/avoidance* conflicts are caused by disliking both of two options yet having to select one of them—as when an employee is told he must either take a 15 percent pay cut or be moved to a less desirable position in an undesirable part of the country.

A comprehensive analysis of conflict is offered by Rummel (1976), who views it as "the clash of power in the striving of all things to be manifest" or as a set of social behavior, an event, or a process. He further defines conflict as "the process of powers meeting and balancing" (p. 238). This definition seems the most universal and applies equally to human and natural sciences. Since mediators work with people, we shall focus on this definition's implications for interpersonal problems.

Rummel differentiates between latent conflict and actual conflict by devising three levels: (1) potentialities, (2) dispositions and powers, and (3) manifestations. He refines the second category even further by making three subcategories. He defines a *conflict structure* as interests that have a tendency to oppose each other; a *conflict situation* refers to opposing interests, attitudes, or powers that are activated. The third level, *manifest conflict,* is the set of specific behavior or actions—demands, threats, assassinations, terrorism, armed aggression, wars—that signal and comprise the conflict. They are the actions that communicate the conflict, thus making it a dispute by our earlier definition.

An illustration of this tripartite system is in divorce, which is inherently a conflict structure insofar as both persons are headed in opposite directions toward separate goals. Divorce may or may not become a conflict situation by Rummel's definition—in other words, a situation where conflict is activated. There are amicable divorces. If conflict is activated, such actions as a threat to withhold custody or one spouse's withdrawal of all the money from the joint savings account would become the manifest conflict in Rummel's terminology.

The life cycle of a conflict can be divided into five phases according to Rummel: (1) the latent conflict, (2) the initiation of conflict, (3) the balancing of power, (4) the balance of power, and (5) the disruption of equilibrium. This five-phase cycle is illustrated in the following example. In environmental issues the interests of the timber industry often diverge from those of conservationists and therefore form a conflict structure (phase 1). This conflict structure may remain latent for many years before a conflict situation emerges, such as the sale of extensive timber rights adjoining a wilderness area (phase 2). After a trigger event, such as a lumber company sending crews to the most sensitive ecological areas for clear-cutting, the conservationists and that company are then in a manifest conflict. This uncertain situation requires each opposing interest to prepare for action. These interests must be balanced through coercive means, such as injunction and adjudication, or through noncoercive methods of conflict resolution, such as mediation (phase 3). The disputants must make accommodations through one of these methods in order to resolve the conflict. After a balance point is reached through a conflict resolution process (phase 4), conditions change over time and the balance of power and equilibrium that had been established will also change. Timber markets may decrease or conservationists may change their view about how much damage clear-cutting does to the adjoining wilderness (phase 5).

Rummel sees these phases as a continuing spiral, a helix, that is set into motion by change but is shaped by the type of power or society (exchange, authoritative, or coercive) in which it is manifested. When the issue has gone through these five phases, it has completed one turn of the helix. These changes in values and norms can affect the sociocultural structure and these changes in turn may produce new latent conflicts (phase 1) or directly create a manifest conflict (phase 2) by serving as a new trigger event, thus repeating the cycle. Empirical studies have shown some validity to his assertion that there are three kinds of manifest conflicts, each a result of the prevailing power system.

Mediation is therefore one of the processes of balancing power in noncoercive ways that will achieve accommodations and result in agreement. The mediation process can be used at two different times in this conflict cycle. It can be started after a trigger event or action has pushed the conflict into the realm of manifestation. Or it can be instituted when the people involved are aware of a conflict structure or conflict situation, thus detouring the usual escalating progression and eliminating the uncertainty and subsequent need for manifested conflict behavior such as threats, denial of rights, or physical violence. In effect, the mediation process can be used to prevent the outbreak of manifest conflict behavior.

Rummel's insightful work sets the conceptual stage for conflict resolution processes such as mediation, while at the same time explaining the scope of conflict within or between societies and nations. Although Rummel's work is more abstract than others cited in this chapter, it provides a conceptual framework for the universal nature of conflict. He points out that the wish to eliminate all three levels of conflict is a desire for a state of unchanging, homeostatic balance, a frozen and fixed reality, which is rare indeed in the natural world and perhaps not even desirable. It is well for mediators to remind themselves and the participants of this observation. In most cases, mediators only attempt to eliminate the manifest conflict behavior and influence the conflict situation. Conflict structure is generally dealt with through political, social, and psychological means that are beyond the scope of the mediation process.

Morton Deutsch (1973) has analyzed the nature of conflict and offers a conceptualization that can be particularly useful in mediation. In Deutsch's terminology, the *manifest conflict* is overt or expressed, whereas the *underlying conflict* is implicit, hidden, or denied. The manifest conflict often involves symbolic components of the underlying conflict but is felt to be "safer." Thus the manifest conflict between father and son over the keys to the car seems safer to dispute than the underlying conflict of who is more powerful. Indian tribes may actively dispute government fishing quotas, while the underlying conflict involves the more fundamental conflict of the white man's control and exploitation of Native American traditions. Others have called this dichotomy between the overt dispute and the hidden conflict the *presenting problem* and the *hidden agenda,* respectively.

Mediators must sort out which issues are manifest and which are underlying in order to develop effective options and outcomes. If the agreements reached in mediation are based only on the manifest conflicts, they are unlikely to last. It is important to remember, however, that dealing with the underlying conflicts may be emotionally painful and can stimulate internal conflict and defensive behavior unless dealt with skillfully.

The constructive and destructive outcomes of conflict have been categorized by Deutsch (1973): mutual loss (lose/lose); gain for one and loss for the other (lose/win); mutual gain (win/win). Walton and McKersie (1965) add two other outcomes: stalemate and compromise. Mediation has a distinct advantage over some other methods of conflict resolution in obtaining constructive outcomes because it promotes resolution of the conflict in the mutual gain or win/win mode.

To summarize the preceding definitions, we find it helpful to regard *conflict* as a set of divergent aims, methods, or behavior. The degree of divergence determines the severity and duration of the conflict and affects the likelihood of successful conflict resolution. Conflicts can be subdivided into various types. We believe Rummel's (1976) description of the conflict process to be the most universal, while Deutsch's definitions of manifested and underlying conflicts appear particularly useful for the mediation process.

We define the opposite of conflict as *convergence:* the aims, processes, methods, or behavior that create order, stability, and unity of direction. An analogy from the natural sciences may be helpful in understanding the nature of conflict and convergence.

Nuclear fission is the ultimate in conflict and divergence; fusion, a merging of diverse elements that produces great energy, is the ultimate in convergence. These two forces—divergence or conflict and convergence or unity—can be visualized as intertwining double helixes (Figure 1).

In effect, then, Rummel's scheme of the conflict process can also be used to describe the opposite of conflict: convergence. Like conflict, convergence can be seen as having an inherent tendency (convergence structure), actualized unity of interests, attitudes, or powers (convergence situation), and specific actions that comprise convergence (manifested convergence). While much attention has been given to conflict, this formulation of its opposite, convergence, has been hampered by simplistic notions that convergence is peace and that peace is the absence of conflict. Delineation of the "life cycle" of convergence is a natural outgrowth of the study of conflict and requires further thought. An understanding of the place of conflict and the processes that promote convergence—the mediation process is one—is essential for mediators.

*   *   *   *   *

FIGURE 1   The Double Helix

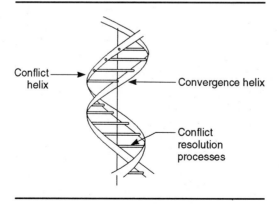

How to Be a Better Negotiator

Jeremy Main

While such notions may seem perfectly obvious to conciliatory souls, they are so novel to many that they've acquired a name of their own. Roger Fisher, director of the Harvard Negotiation Project and high priest of the new cult of negotiation, calls the approach "principled negotiation," presumably to distinguish it from the unprincipled skulduggery that it replaces. Major corporations, government agencies, and unions are applying principled negotiation—or at least some aspects of it—to a growing number of labor disputes, breach-of-contract allegations, patent infringement tiffs, even debates on the location of waste disposal sites.

For example, to get the Public Service Co. of New Hampshire to speed up the conversion of three plants in Portsmouth from oil to coal, the New Hampshire Public Utilities Commission last year chose negotiation rather than a formal adversarial hearing. The controversy arose because hastening the conversion would cost the utility $25 million extra, an amount that it couldn't recover rapidly under the existing rate base. The staffs of the commission and the company had clashed so often at hearings, however, that it seemed unlikely they'd be able to arrive at a solution. The commission turned for help to the New England Environmental Mediation Center, one of several new foundation-supported organizations in this field.

By getting the two staffs to sit down at a table to talk informally and frankly, the center's executive director, William Humm, helped create an atmosphere in which each side actually listened to what the other was saying. "We succeeded eventually in lowering the level of paranoia," says George Gantz of the commission staff. With the burden of mutual distrust lightened, the parties worked out a plan for the utility to recover its costs in five years with a temporary surcharge, compared with the 15 or more years that it would have taken otherwise. Both sides agreed the solution was more innovative and elegant than could have been achieved in a hearing.

For other adversaries, much of the interest in negotiation derives from dissatisfaction with the courts and the ways of lawyers. As the volume of civil cases grows in state and federal courts, and legal fees mount up along with delays, more people are looking for a better way to settle disputes. A deeper impetus may be at work too. Professor Howard Perlmutter of the Wharton School in Philadelphia has made a specialty of the subject of negotiations. He says, "The enormous interest in negotiation today is no accident. The structure of power today means you can't just tell people what to do, even within an organization. The art of negotiation becomes almost the key skill you have."

Whatever the cause of their fascination with the subject, the number of individuals who want to know more has made the teaching of negotiation a minor industry. A book on the subject, *Getting to Yes,* by Roger Fisher and his colleague at the Harvard Negotiation Project, William Ury, has become a best-seller. General Electric has opened up its in-house seminars on negotiation to outsiders—at $1,150 per student, usually for five days. Even diplomats are getting into the act. The Foreign Service Institute—the training arm of the State Department—recently held the first of what may become regular seminars on negotiating.

Gerard I. Nierenberg, 60, senior partner in a small New York law firm, discovered the depth of the interest in negotiation some years ago. As a lawyer, he became dissatisfied in the 1960s with the adversarial nature of the judicial process. "I was winning cases for my clients but destroying their relationships with clients and customers," he says. In 1968 he published a book, *The Art of Negotiating,* and began giving seminars. Both were so successful that he wrote seven more books on the subject and drew all 10 lawyers in his firm, as well as his wife, into the business of teaching negotiating—the practice of law has become peripheral for the firm. Nierenberg, who looks like a slightly pudgy Claude Rains, complete with forelock, gives a theatrical two-day seminar filled with anecdotes and gimmicks. He has no trouble filling spiffy meeting places such as the ballroom at the Plaza Hotel in New York with high-ranking executives, even at a ticket price of $550 a head.

What can be learned from most of the books and seminars on negotiation is so commonsensical and obvious that it is hard to see why negotiators so often go wrong, but go wrong they do, usually right at the start. They fail to learn about the other side and its needs, they pose impossible demands, or they poison the atmosphere with a belligerent, offensive manner.

Theodore Kheel, a veteran New York City labor negotiator, stresses the importance of preparation before you even begin talking—"knowing who is the most important guy on the other team, what is their decision-making process, what are their objectives, style, and communications, what are their egos and image problems." And, of course, the more you know about the business, the background, and the nomenclature, the better.

When you finally do sit down, Gerard Nierenberg stresses, try to create a positive atmosphere. He argues, "If your philosophy says it's a jungle out there, then that is what you create. If your approach to me is adversarial and I respond in that way, then we are liable to end up in a lawsuit. But if you are unreasonable, and I remain reasonable, then I control the climate."

When the parties finally get down to the substance of their meeting, they often go wrong again because they argue the wrong issue. For instance, in a 1983 dispute between a railroad union and Metro-North, the rail line that transports commuters between New York City and Westchester County and Connecticut, talks got hung up because management demanded the right to control crew sizes. By posing the issue this way, the railroad effectively made it nonnegotiable. What union leader who valued his job would yield the union's right to a say in "crew consists," as they're known? What management really wanted was a reduction in crew sizes, which was something that could have been discussed. After a six-week strike, the issue went to mediation.

Negotiators are likely to find themselves stuck in a pointless, dead-end discussion if they try to argue the other side into changing its stated position. Fisher and Ury urge the principled negotiator to instead look for the true interests that lie behind postures and to then try to discuss these interests objectively.

The Conflict Clinic in Cambridge, Massachusetts—a nonprofit mediation service set up by three local universities—is helping a large foreign corporation and its union climb down from positions that have had them at each other's throats for seven years. Among other things, the company had refused to consider changing an around-the-clock schedule of shifts that had been agreed on in a round of bargaining three years earlier. The union now said the schedule was totally unacceptable. Both sides clung to their positions, and a confrontation seemed inevitable. But the Conflict Clinic got them to stop rehashing the same positions and instead to sit down and talk about whatever interests both sides might have in common. After they had talked awhile, it turned out there were other ways for the company to achieve its productivity goals and for the union to secure work schedules that didn't upset family life too much. A joint committee is now working out a new shift schedule. John Murray, head of the Conflict Clinic, says the company and the union have realized that when they share information frankly and sit down as fellow explorers of fact rather than as antagonists, they begin to see solutions that would not have emerged before.

The skilled negotiator watches the other delegation in its entirety. Is it divided or united? It's also a good idea to cast an occasional glance back over your shoulder. The most important part of a negotiation may occur not between parties but inside each party—and the divided party just might be your own. When he negotiated the Panama Canal treaty, Ellsworth Bunker spent more time working on the State Department, the Pentagon, the Senate, and other U.S. bodies than on the Panamanians.

In sorting out what the other side is doing, it's helpful if both sides are using the same guidelines, and each side recognizes that both are. Before settling down to particularly difficult contract talks last year, the Dayton Power & Light Co. and the Utility Workers of America together called in Stephen Schlossberg, former general counsel of the United Auto Workers, to give each side separately his two-day seminar on how to negotiate. The subsequent talks were long and hard—and punctuated by the first layoffs in the company's history—but both sides agree that the seminar helped. First of all, says Dayton Power & Light Vice President Carl Morey, labor and management used the same techniques. Each understood basically what the other was doing. Second, he said, they learned to catch the meaning of body language so they could read signals from the other side—when it was time to ease up, when it was time to take a break. The resulting agreement, says Morey, was more imaginative than what would have come out of the usual adversarial haggling. For example, the agreement establishes new productivity goals; when they are achieved in any month, the workers get 20 cents an hour extra incentive pay in the following month.

The principled negotiator doesn't resort to trickery, but that doesn't mean he naively gives away his position. He doesn't have to reveal what his final best offer will be. Not all principled negotiators agree on just how principled you have to be. "It's OK to mislead the other side as to your intentions,'' Theodore Kheel argues. "You can say I'm not going to give in, and then give in five minutes later. But never give the other side misinformation about the facts.''

Steven Cabot, a Philadelphia lawyer whose specialty of helping corporations deal with labor has earned him a reputation as a union-buster, admits to using fatigue unabashedly as a weapon to wear down the other side. But, warns Theodore Kheel, "suppose you tire out first?" Anger is another risky weapon, though sometimes useful for shaking up the other side. But what if pretended anger becomes real anger or provokes real anger in your adversary? On the other hand, patience is almost always a virtue. "You have to sit on your ass day after day rehashing the issues," says Kheel—not the opening positions, the issues. "Every time the issues are restated, you may get a new insight into how they can be resolved.'' A slight modification of phrasing can have a big effect.

What if the other side resorts to really dirty tricks? Fisher and Ury counsel you not to reply in kind, but to make it clear you have seen the trick. If your adversary puts you in a chair that leaves your chin at tabletop level so that you feel like a little boy among grown-ups, you might say, "I assume we're switching chairs tomorrow.''

And if the other side relies just on the brute strength of the resources behind it? Any party to a negotiation, even a powerful and intransigent one, may eventually come to see that it has reason for wanting talks to succeed. The task for the negotiator is to help the other side see possible disaster ahead while it can still be headed off by a mutually agreeable solution.

In contract talks in the 1950s and 1960s the powerful typographical and long-shoremen's unions in New York City forced employers to accept exorbitant demands. But how much did they really win in the long run? Seven of New York's ten daily newspapers have disappeared, and shipping companies would round the Horn in a blizzard to avoid the city's dying waterfront. When dealing with an overbearing opponent, says Tom Colosi, a vice president of the American Arbitration Association, the key is to look for something the other side cares about, something to create doubts in their minds, so that they see that a solution they dictate is not in their best interest.

The urge to negotiate is even invading the ultimate bastion of adversary proceedings, the practice of law. Of course, lawyers are used to negotiating settlements of cases, but only after prolonging the legal ritual to the point where it may well cost more than the settlement is worth. The idea is catching on that it might be wisest to negotiate from the outset. An amendment to the rules of federal trial procedure that went into effect last month encourages judges to suggest a negotiated settlement at the first pretrial conference rather than waiting until after the legal game has been played out.

The so-called minitrial has become a popular way to escape the cumbersome judicial process. It is not really a trial, but a negotiation between top executives of litigating companies. They listen to their lawyers relatively briefly—presentations are usually limited to four hours or less—and perhaps consult with a lawyer or judge who sits in as adviser or mediator. After hearing both sides' presentations, the judge may tell each how it is likely to fare in court. That can often be sobering, since litigants usually have an inflated idea of the strength of their case. The executives then try to settle the matter between themselves, rapidly and privately. Instead of spending years and hundreds of thousands of dollars in litigation, they can get a solution in a matter of days at a cost of a few thousand dollars. TRW Inc. pioneered the minitrial in 1977 in a complicated patent suit brought by another company. It has used minitrials twice since.

Last year Borden Co. and Texaco were embroiled in a $200-million suit brought by Borden on breach-of-contract and antitrust claims. Lawyers on both sides had worked on the case for thousands of hours; Texaco had produced 300,000 documents in discovery. It was one of those complicated cases that could have run for years more, but finally, at a deposition, the lawyers brought up the idea of a minitrial. The two companies agreed.

An executive vice president from each listened together to the lawyers, who were allotted just one hour on each side plus rebuttal time. After that the executives negotiated. It took a few weeks, off and on, for them to agree, but the agreement they reached was totally unanticipated. Instead of Texaco paying Borden cash, the two companies rewrote a gas supply contract to the benefit of both sides. "That," says Texaco's associate general counsel, Charles F. Kazlaukas Jr., "is truly a win-win situation that we never expected." They shouldn't have been so surprised. Properly done, negotiations can bring out the best, beneficent spirit of commerce—"Let's strike a deal helpful to us both"—instead of letting base instincts decide the issue.

A skillfully negotiated solution offers a lot more than speed and low cost, attractive as these may be. The Japanese talk of building relationships as a cornerstone of business, and they shrink from American-style confrontations. With his competitive drive, the American businessman may seek confrontation and victory. He may win— but he may also leave a beaten opponent who will never want to do business with him again.

Ten Guidelines for Effective Negotiating

Joseph F. Byrnes

Everybody negotiates. Whether it is a child negotiating with her father about the appropriateness of an eight o'clock bedtime, homeowners discussing the assessed valuation of their house with the assessment commission, or a manager submitting the reasons for a pay increase to the boss, the process of persuasion is similar. It is called negotiating.

Negotiation is a discussion between two or more people with a goal of reaching agreement on issues separating the parties when neither side has the power—or the desire to use its power—to get its own way.

We negotiate because we have to or want to. If you do not have the power to get what you want from someone else, you will use negotiations to get at least some of what you want. If you have overwhelming power, as a mother with her young son or a boss with his employees, you are frequently reluctant to simply use your power directly. The son and the employee can be forced to comply, but they may resent being forced or having to hear the too frequently used words, "Do this because I say so." Thus, even when you have the power, you frequently find yourself negotiating with someone else.

Managers typically spend a significant portion of their workday involved in negotiating. In his classic 1973 study, *The Nature of Managerial Work,* Henry Mintzberg identified negotiating as one of the four major aspects of managers' decisional roles.[1] Managers may spend as much as 20 percent of their time dealing with potential and actual conflict and its resolution, primarily through the negotiating process.[2]

While negotiating is a ubiquitous process important in most human endeavors, considerable mystery surrounds the activity. Many works, both popular and academic,

---

Reprinted from *Business Horizons,* May–June 1987, pp. 7–12. Copyright 1987 by the Foundation for the School of Business at Indiana University. Used with permission.

[1]Henry Mintzberg, *The Nature of Managerial Work* (New York: Harper & Row, 1973), pp. 77-94. The other three decision roles Mintzberg assigns to the manager are entrepreneur, disturbance handler, and allocator of resources.

[2]See the estimates of Dennis King, "Three Cheers for Conflict," *Personnel,* January-February 1981: 21; G. G. Shea, *Creative Negotiation* (Boston: DBI, 1983); and R. J. Lewicki and J. A. Litterer, *Negotiation* (Homewood, Ill.: Richard D. Irwin, 1985).

have attempted to shed light on the negotiating phenomenon.[3] It is easy to be over-whelmed by the sheer weight of these volumes. People who are interested in negotiations—not as a life-long study, but as an activity they must frequently perform—find it difficult to grasp the essence of the process.

This article will examine the essentials of effective negotiating by exploring 10 basic and pragmatic guidelines. These 10 guidelines mirror the typical process of negotiating:

1. Preparing for negotiations;
2. Recognizing different perceptions;
3. Avoiding corners;
4. Using creativity and imagination;
5. Appreciating the power of silence;
6. Making trade-offs;
7. Helping the other side to agree;
8. Taking notes;
9. Valuing deadlines; and
10. Anticipating no agreement.

PREPARING FOR NEGOTIATIONS

The first step in the negotiating process is frequently the most neglected. When-ever you anticipate negotiating with some other party, try to carve out enough time to prepare for the bargaining episode.

To more fully appreciate what is involved in preparation, you should ask yourself two basic questions as you get ready for negotiations:

*   What do I want to achieve through negotiations; and
*   Why do I want it?

Be as clear and specific as possible in answering these two key questions. Some-times, this entails some additional digging out of facts and figures to fully develop your negotiating position.

> *Example:* An engineer wants to ask her boss for a raise. She remembers her frustrations the previous year when her supervisor asked her how much she wanted. Her response—"Whatever is fair"—gave her boss the right to determine what raise was fair.
>
> This year, the engineer is determined to ask for a specific raise and have the facts and figures to back it up. This means checking with her friends and with placement agencies

---

[3]See, for example, J. A. Wall, Jr., *Negotiation: Theory and Practice* (Glenview, Ill.: Scott, Foresman, 1985); R. J. Lewicki and J. A. Litterer, *Negotiation: Readings, Exercises, and Cases* (Homewood, Ill.: Richard D. Irwin, 1985); G. I. Nierenberg, *The Art of Negotiating* (New York: Simon and Schuster, 1978); R. E. Walton and R. B. McKersie, *A Behavioral Theory of Labor Negotiations* (New York: McGraw-Hill, 1965).

to determine what the range is for engineers with her education and experience, as well as documenting her achievements in the job this year. She is determined to do her homework.

If possible, ask the same two questions for the other side. What do *they* want to achieve through negotiation, and why do they want it?

> *Example:* The engineering supervisor understands his obligations in salary discussions. He works with the Human Resources Department to identify the going rate for engineers both locally and nationally, differentiated by specialty, industry, performance, and experience. Then he ranks each of his engineers and creates an ideal salary structure for his department. Finally, he assigns tentative pay increases for each of his engineers, based on market factors, ranking, and budget constraints.
>
> He is now ready to talk and probably negotiate with each of his engineers. Of course he leaves himself with some extra budgeted salary money, just in case he feels a need to increase some salaries based on his discussion with the engineers.

It may be impossible to answer these questions before the first meeting, but they certainly can be asked as part of the initial meeting. Of course, if the other side cannot adequately respond to these two questions, it usually means that they have not devoted time and energy to preparation and are consequently less able to bargain effectively.

As a corollary to this guideline, avoid bargaining whenever you are unprepared. Ask for some time to think and prepare. If negotiations commence with a phone call, the caller is usually at an advantage. It is important to avoid making important negotiating decisions on the spot, particularly when the other side is prepared and you are not.

It is not a sign of weakness to ask for more time to prepare adequately for significant negotiations. Common beliefs to the contrary, negotiation is usually a contest of preparation, not a macho battle where contestants are willing to lose rather than admit they are not ready to fight.

RECOGNIZING DIFFERENT PERCEPTIONS

We each view the world in our own way. The way we see a thing can be quite different from how other people see it—or from the way it really is. When you are engaged in negotiations, you should be aware that your perceptions and the perceptions of the other party may be radically different.

Two researchers asked 66 top managers to recall a recent conflict, to state which approach they and the other party used in negotiating this conflict, and to describe how they both behaved during the negotiations.[4] The executives tended to see themselves as *cooperative, collaborative,* and *willing to compromise,* while they perceived the other side as *uncooperative, hostile,* and *hard-nosed.*

When asked to identify specific behaviors, they usually described their own behavior as *informing, suggesting,* and *reminding;* but when describing the behavior of the other side, they frequently used such words as *unreasonable, demanding,* and *refusing.*

---

[4]See K. W. Thomas and L. R. Pondy, "Toward an 'Intent' Model of Conflict Management among Principal Parties," *Human Relations* 30 (December 1977): 1089–1102.

As a general rule, you will perceive yourself as being more reasonable and more accommodating than the other side thinks you are. They will perceive themselves as more reasonable and accommodating than you will perceive them.

These differing perceptions have been the cause of escalating hostilities in both simple and complex negotiations. You say something that you believe is at worst a neutral statement. The other side views it as a nasty remark and they respond in kind. You retaliate with a hostile comment and the battle is joined. All of a sudden, the goal shifts from substantative items to beating the other side.

An awareness of these differing perceptions is the first step toward avoiding the major personal animosities that can develop during negotiations. Beyond awareness, you should pursue two complementary approaches:

- First, never respond to a perceived hostile remark with your own clearly hostile comment. The way to prevent escalation is to break the see-saw process of retaliatory remarks.

- Second, whenever you perceive the other side as hostile or injured, apologize to them. This is difficult for most people, particularly when they are beginning to get annoyed as well. But an apology is the quickest and surest way to de-escalate strong negative feelings.

You need not issue a personal apology. In fact, an apology for the bad situation is usually just as potent.

Example: "I'm sorry that we seem to be having some difficulty on this issue. I know we both have good reasons for our positions. Let's try to look at it from a different angle. I'm having a hard time seeing your point of view. Why don't you try to explain it to me again? I promise not to interrupt you until you're finished."

Beyond breaking the spiral of escalating comments, an apology can also serve to change the other person's perception of you from negative to either neutral or positive. As the other side's perception becomes more positive, you can become more effective in getting across your point of view.

AVOIDING CORNERS

At some point during many negotiations, you may be tempted to box yourself or the other side into a corner. From this corner, there are usually two basic ways out:

- An ignominious defeat; or
- A direct, all too frequent personal battle.

Example: The personnel manager, in the presence of his assistant and the plant manager's assistants, gave the plant manager this alternative: Either remove the safety hazards immediately or Personnel would see to it that the plant was shut down. There could be no compromise on safety. The plant manager's response was short and direct: "Go to hell!"

You can box yourself or the other side into a corner in a variety of ways. It usually involves a public stance of some sort, coupled with a threat or ultimatum. Both sides must then either surrender or fight it out.

An effective negotiator almost never issues an ultimatum and rarely takes a strong public position with no escape route. When you box yourself or the other side into a corner, the negotiation usually swings from an objective, problem-solving process to a personal campaign to beat the other side. This emotional surge normally destroys the desire of both sides to concentrate on the merits of the proposals. Winning at any cost becomes the new objective.

USING CREATIVITY AND IMAGINATION

The best negotiators are always thinking about unusual and creative approaches to bargaining issues. They refuse to follow the line of least resistance, which is simply to split the difference between the parties.

> *Example:* Two sisters quarreled over an orange. They finally agreed to divide the orange in half. The first sister took her half, ate the fruit, and threw away the peel, while the other sister threw away the fruit and used the peel from her half in baking a cake. Too many negotiations end up with half an orange for each side instead of the whole fruit for one and the whole peel for the other.[5]

In a large number of negotiations, the best agreements for all concerned are usually not made because nobody has even thought about them. There is too frequently a rush to be done with the whole thing. Premature criticism and premature closure are the killers of creative thinking.

To preserve creativity and imagination, effective negotiators usually set aside some time during negotiations to examine different and unusual approaches. During this exploration stage, people are encouraged to think out loud, without being committed to any ideas. Criticism, laughter, and ridicule are not permitted. In this way, the more creative ideas are encouraged. Unless time is of critical importance, all negotiations should devote some time to nonjudgmental, creative thinking.

APPRECIATING THE POWER OF SILENCE

Most Americans are uncomfortable with even brief periods of silence. They feel a need to respond quickly, sometimes even before the other side has finished speaking. By their words and behavior, they can give the impression that the words of the other side are unimportant, a mere interruption of their own speech. The absence of active and attentive listening can be a significant disadvantage when negotiating, especially with foreign business people who are accustomed to silence.

[5]This example is taken from R. Fisher and W. Ury, *Getting to Yes* (Boston: Houghton Mifflin Company, 1981), p. 59.

Americans often respond to silence by assuming that their bargaining partners disagree or have not accepted their offer. Moreover, they tend to argue and make concessions in response to silence. This is a particular problem when negotiating with the Japanese, who are quite comfortable with lengthy periods of silence during negotiations.[6]

Negotiators should develop the habit of attentive listening. There is no need to rush to fill a silence that occurs within the bargaining process. If you find silence extremely uncomfortable, try to get the other side to fill it; ask them questions and explore their ideas.

Some people are poor negotiators because they talk too much. As a rule of thumb, if you are talking more than 50 percent of the time, you are talking too much. Try to relax and let the other side do more talking. As one professional negotiator has said, "You never give anything away if you keep your mouth shut."

Silence is a simple but powerful negotiating tool.

MAKING TRADE-OFFS

Never give something for nothing. Even if you cannot get something tangible in return, at least get some goodwill or an IOU for future use. Even if what they obtain is small, the most effective negotiators obtain something for every concession they make.

Example: The supermarket manager was pleased to agree to the end-of-aisle display for the new coffee. He was sure it would do quite well, particularly after the advertising blitz had begun. However, he also requested and received the promise that the salesman would drop by every night during the initial advertising push to restock the display. This would reduce the work load of the night crew.

The essence of excellent bargaining is to trade what is cheap to you, but valuable to another, for what is valuable to you but cheap to another. In this way, both parties are able to more fully satisfy their needs at no enormous cost to the other side. Of course, this is not possible on all issues. However, with a little imagination, such trade-offs are often attainable.

Example: The company finally agreed to an additional personal day for its unionized production workers. But there was a catch. The union, in turn, agreed to the provision that the personal day could be taken only if the employee had no more than two absences in the previous six months. Company officials calculated that the reduced absentee rate would more than offset the cost of the additional personal day.

The give-and-take of negotiations should benefit all parties. When negotiators understand what they really need and what is relatively unimportant, the inevitable trade-offs become more valuable and less costly to both sides. Trading what matters less for what matters more is a highly effective bargaining strategy.

---

[6]For more details of this aspect, see J. Graham, "The Influence of Culture on Business Negotiations," *Journal of International Business Studies* 16 (Spring 1985), pp. 81–96.

HELPING THE OTHER SIDE TO AGREE

Too many negotiators take the old line, "Look out for #1," to a dangerous extreme. They believe they have no responsibility to help the other side. The best negotiators, on the other hand, know it is in their best interests to help the other side and to make it as easy as possible for them to agree.

> *Example:* The general manager knew the town had to allow the rezoning of the land. The new plant would create too many jobs and produce too much tax revenue for the mayor and city council to oppose it. However, the general manager went out of her way to praise these public officials in whatever forum she could find. She wanted to make it as easy as possible for them to agree to the new facility and the accompanying zoning change.

The last thing an effective negotiator does is to undermine the other side by minimizing the gains they achieved through bargaining. Good negotiators make it as easy and pleasant as possible for the other side.

When you represent a larger group, as in labor negotiations or merger talks, there is frequently a need to strongly underline what your counterpart has achieved.

> *Example:* The merger has been agreed to. The acquiring company was able to buy the other firm at a relatively low price. But the chairman of the acquiring company repeatedly emphasized the toughness and shrewdness of the other company's management and the continuing independence of the acquired firm. He wanted many managers and employees in the firm to feel good about the merger and to be willing to stay with the company.

Effective negotiators try hard to put themselves in the other guy's shoes. The best negotiators realize the other party's problem is their problem as well, and they work toward helping their counterparts.

TAKING NOTES

Many managers do not like to take notes or be responsible for paperwork. They reason that keeping notes is secretarial work. In most negotiations, however, the person taking notes and keeping track of the agreements is usually happier with the final results.

The process of most business negotiations needs to be written up in informal notes and then finally summarized in a memo or a report. These are chores that should not be readily delegated to the other side.

> *Example:* The meeting between the sales and operations managers was over. Operations had been quite upset at the recent rash of special orders coming from Sales and wanted to place some limits on these orders. A joint memo to all employees in both departments would be forthcoming.
>
> In spite of the crush of other critical matters, the operations manager volunteered to write up the draft memo. He wanted the wording to be just right, and he knew that he would be happier with the final results if he wrote the draft.

VALUING DEADLINES

Too many negotiations go on interminably. Talk leads to more talk and even more talk. How do effective negotiators break the cycle of words?

Example: The vice president had had enough. Purchasing and Data Processing had been talking about computerized purchasing for over six months now. She brought the two managers from both departments into her office and made them responsible for creating a joint proposal in one month. Both men looked relieved that the negotiations had a definite end point.

Many negotiations within organizations continue much too long because a deadline has not been set. A deadline puts pressure on both sides to be economical in their use of time. It permits negotiators to question the value of a particular discussion and to move on to more productive areas. It also encourages both sides to consider concessions and trade-offs in order to meet the deadline.

Some negotiations—for example, labor negotiations and purchase offers on homes—have built-in deadlines. Wise negotiators will establish deadlines in order to focus efforts and increase efficiency. This is a particularly useful device for departmental and task force meetings, where negotiations can continue indefinitely unless a deadline is set.

ANTICIPATING NO AGREEMENT

Some negotiations do not conclude with an agreement between the parties. Instead, talks break off or, worse, they continue with little chance of an agreement. Wise negotiators are hopeful but realistic and careful. They plan for the worst and figure out ahead of time what they will do if no agreement is forthcoming.

Example: The compensation manager wanted the job of assistant human resources director. She already had talked to the director and tried to convince him she was the right person for the job. But, because she didn't want all her eggs in one basket, she continued her contacts with executive recruiters about generalist human resource positions in other companies.

Effective negotiators prepare for the possibility of no agreement by making their alternative to a negotiated agreement as pleasant and useful as possible. If their alternative to an agreement is attractive, they might reveal it to the other side at a propitious point during the negotiations. If it is not attractive, they keep it to themselves.

Example: The manufacturer wanted to arrange a licensing agreement with the largest and most prestigious firm in South Korea. However, he had made contacts with other firms in South Korea, Taiwan, and Japan in order to have a backup position.
Toward the end of the negotiations, he revealed his contacts with the other companies to the South Korean firm. A satisfactory agreement was concluded shortly thereafter.

Negotiating power develops from the attractiveness of your alternative. The greater your ability to walk away from the negotiations, the stronger is your bargaining position. Always work to develop feasible and satisfactory alternatives to a negotiated agreement with any particular party.

The way to become a better negotiator is to practice using all 10 guidelines. Make a conscious effort to implement these guidelines in every negotiation you undertake.

Because we all negotiate in both our business and personal lives, the opportunities for practice are plentiful. Try to take advantage of them. The payback can be significant.

SECTION TWO

Interdependence

As a people, we treasure independence and autonomy, and believe we have a great deal of it. Politically, we do. But socially? Economically? That is another matter. We may feel we are free to do many things until a truck hits a power line and shuts off our electricity, or the rubbish collectors go on strike, or relatives or friends get sick, or crude oil prices quadruple, or we move to a new community. These sudden breaks in routine events sharply bring home how interdependent we are with others; people (perhaps some we have never seen) and events we have no control over can drastically upset our lives. The number of people we are involved with and the number of ways we are involved is far greater than most of us appreciate.

Even without the major disturbances mentioned above, we are continually adjusting to other people in big and little ways. We almost unconsciously work out who will get on the elevator first; interrupt someone eating to pass us the salt; with a little more effort, we successfully adjust our vacations to fit in with others; or trim a shrub on the border of our property to the mutual satisfaction of us and our neighbor. The very ordinariness of this process is very important, for it shows that many interdependence situations that could lead to conflict do not; instead, with relatively little effort, they almost routinely conclude with success. However, the ease, the ordinariness of this success means we are unlikely to examine what took place in handling this interdependence successfully; so we are not aware of what is involved when the process is not going well. The articles in this section examine various aspects of events and behavior that occur in ordinary, everyday situations and bring out basic processes and structures that need to be used to understand bargaining situations. How can we explain that many of these events go smoothly and others have difficulty?

In the first article in this section, "Strategic Choice," Dean Pruitt and Jeffrey Rubin suggest that there are five basic strategies for managing conflict in an interdependent situation: contending, problem solving, yielding, withdrawing, and inaction. Negotiator preferences for conflict resolution strategies are determined by the strength of two concerns: concern about one's own outcomes and concern about the other person's outcomes. These two concerns are not opposite ends of the same dimension. Rather, the concerns are uncorrelated because their intensity varies independently (knowing the extent to which a negotiator is concerned about his or her own needs tells us nothing about how concerned the person is about the other person's needs, and vice versa). This article clarifies the determinants of preferences for the five strategies for resolving conflict and enables the reader to make these choices with more conscious control.

In their article "Consider Both Relationships and Substance when Negotiating Strategically," Grant Savage, John Blair, and Ritch Sorenson suggest that both relationships and substance need to be considered when using negotiation to resolve conflict. Similar to the dual-concern model presented in the previous article, the importance of substantive outcomes and relationship outcomes are independent. Savage, Blair, and Sorenson suggest that negotiators should consider the other person's evaluation of the relationship and the negotiation outcome before choosing a conflict resolution strategy. Managers are advised to answer four questions (importance of the substantive outcome to me; importance of the substantive outcome to the other party; importance of the relationship to me; importance of the relationship to the other party) before selecting a conflict resolution strategy. The article contains suggested strategies for the 16 possible combinations of answers to the 4 questions, and a good description of tactics for use during different stages of conflict resolution.

In the final article in this section, "The Problem of Cooperation," Robert Axelrod explores why cooperation occurs in situations that appear to have incentives to be selfish. Axelrod presents a clear and cogent description of the Prisoner's Dilemma, a powerful tool for studying how cooperation develops. The Prisoner's Dilemma is a classic problem of interdependence; your outcome is jointly determined by the choices that you and your partner make. While there is no strategy that yields cooperative responses in all Prisoner's Dilemmas, Axelrod does reveal the strategy that is most likely to result in long-term cooperation.

Strategic Choice

Dean Pruitt

Jeffrey Rubin

Peter Colger has to make a decision. For months he has been looking forward to taking his two weeks of vacation at a quiet mountain lodge where he can hunt, fish, and hike to lofty scenic overlooks. Now his wife Mary has rudely challenged this dream. She has told him that she finds the mountains boring and wants to go to Ocean City, Maryland, a busy seaside resort that Peter dislikes intensely. Peter must decide what strategy to employ in this controversy.

Five general strategies are available to Peter. He can engage in *contentious behavior* and try to prevail—for example, by arguing for the merits of a mountain vacation, indicating that he had already made up his mind, threatening to take a separate vacation if Mary does not agree, or even making a large deposit on a room in a mountain hotel. He can take a *problem-solving* approach and try to find a way to go to both places or to a vacation spot that satisfies both sets of interests. He can *yield* to Mary's demands and agree to go to the seashore. He can be *inactive* (do nothing) in the hope that the issue will simply go away. Or he can *withdraw* from the controversy—for example, by deciding not to take a vacation.

The aim of this chapter is to examine the conditions that determine how Peter (and, more generally, anyone facing a conflict) decides among these basic strategies. We will focus mainly on the first three strategies (contending, problem solving, and yielding), which we call the "coping strategies" because they involve active efforts to resolve the controversy.

NATURE OF THE STRATEGIES

Contending refers to any effort to resolve a conflict on one's own terms without regard to the other party's interests. Parties who employ this strategy maintain their own aspirations and try to persuade the other party to yield. Various tactics are available to parties who choose this strategy. They include making threats, imposing pen-

---

Reprinted from Dean Pruitt and Jeffrey Rubin, *Social Conflict* (New York: McGraw-Hill, Inc., 1986). Used with permission of McGraw-Hill, Inc.

alties with the understanding that they will be withdrawn if the other concedes, and taking preemptive actions designed to resolve the conflict without the other's consent (such as making a deposit at a mountain hotel in our example). If the parties are trying to reach a negotiated settlement of the controversy, contending may also involve presenting persuasive arguments, making demands that far exceed what is actually acceptable, committing oneself to an ''unalterable'' position, or imposing a deadline.

By contrast, *problem solving* entails an effort to identify the issues dividing the parties and to develop and move toward a solution that appeals to both sides. Parties who employ this strategy maintain their own aspirations and try to find a way of reconciling them with the other party's aspirations.

The agreement developed in problem solving can take the form of a compromise (an obvious alternative that stands part way between the two parties' preferred positions), or it can take the form of an integrative solution (a creative reconciliation of the two parties' basic interests). The difference between a compromise and an integrative solution is illustrated by two options that were discussed during the Camp David negotiations. A compromise proposal, in which Egypt and Israel would each get half the Sinai, was unacceptable to both sides. The key to settlement was an integrative solution, in which Egypt got the Sinai and Israel got diplomatic recognition and military guarantees.

Various tactics are available to implement the strategy of problem solving. These include risky moves such as conceding with the expectation of receiving a return concession, mentioning possible compromises as talking points, and revealing one's underlying interests. They also include cautious moves such as hinting at possible compromises, sending disavowable intermediaries to discuss the issues, communicating through back channels, and communicating through a mediator.

Although problem solving has been described so far as an individual activity, it can also be a joint enterprise involving both parties. For example, two people can exchange accurate information about their underlying interests, collectively identify new issues in light of this information, brainstorm to seek alternative ways of dealing with the issues, and sometimes even work together to evaluate these alternatives. Joint problem solving is an excellent way to locate mutually acceptable solutions, but it is sometimes impractical because one party is not ready for it or the parties do not trust each other. Hence, individual problem solving must at times be substituted.

Yielding, which involves lowering one's aspirations, need not imply the total capitulation that we saw in the vacation example. It can also imply a partial concession. For example, Peter Colger might decide to foresake his secondary goal of hiking to mountain overlooks in order to make it easier to find a mutually acceptable agreement. He could then engage in problem solving, seeking a quiet resort that permits fishing and hiking where his wife can also accomplish her major goals.

Withdrawing and *inaction* are similar to each other in that they involve termination of efforts to resolve the controversy. They differ in that withdrawing is a permanent termination, whereas inaction is a temporary move that leaves open the possibility of resuming efforts to cope with the controversy. Withdrawing is usually a distinct strategy, but it may at times be hard to distinguish from contending or yielding. For example, if I withdraw from a controversy with my son over the use of my car, I automatically win and thus gain a contentious advantage. If my son withdraws, he is essentially yielding to my viewpoint.

CHOOSING A STRATEGY

There are trade-offs among the five basic strategies, in the sense that choosing one of them makes selecting the others less likely. Inaction and withdrawing are totally incompatible with each other and with the three coping strategies. Though sometimes found in combination with each other, the coping strategies are also somewhat incompatible. There are three reasons for this latter incompatibility. First, the coping strategies are alternative means of moving toward the same end, agreement with the other party. If it is not possible to use one of them, a person is more likely to employ the others. Second, these strategies require different psychological orientations; for example, it does not seem quite right to try to push another party around while yielding to or working with that party. Third, these strategies tend to send out contradictory signals to the other party. Yielding often implies weakness, which is incompatible with putting effective pressure on the other. Contending can undermine the other party's trust, which is an important element of effective problem solving.

Because of these trade-offs, there are indirect as well as direct antecedents of all five strategies. Direct antecedents, as we would expect, directly affect the likelihood of adopting a strategy. Indirect antecedents affect this likelihood by encouraging or discouraging one of the other strategies.

Most of the rest of this chapter is devoted to two theoretical notions about the determinants of choice among the basic strategies. The first, which is summarized in a *dual concern model,* traces strategic choice to the relative strength of concern about own and other's outcomes. The second, which we call the *perceived feasibility perspective,* attributes this choice to the perceived likelihood of success and the cost of enacting the various strategies. These two theoretical notions are complementary in the sense that each deals with issues ignored by the other.

A good deal of evidence will be cited in support of these theoretical notions, most of it derived from laboratory experiments on simulated negotiation. *Negotiation,* a form of conflict behavior, occurs when two parties try to resolve a divergence of interest by means of conversation. Laboratory experiments on this phenomenon place subjects (usually undergraduates) in a simulated negotiation setting and manipulate theoretically relevant variables. Careful measurements of reactions to these variables are taken. A more detailed discussion of this kind of research can be found in Pruitt (1981) and Rubin and Brown (1975).

The chapter ends with a discussion of the forces that determine the vigor with which the three coping strategies are enacted.

THE DUAL CONCERN MODEL

The dual concern model appears in Figure 1. It postulates two types of concerns: *concern about own outcomes,* which is shown on the abscissa, and *concern about the other party's outcomes,* which is shown on the ordinate. These concerns are portrayed as ranging from indifference (at the zero point of the coordinate) to very great concern.

The two concerns in this model are defined as follows: Concern about own outcomes means placing importance on one's own interests—one's needs and values—in the realm under dispute. People with a strong concern about their own outcomes are highly resistant

FIGURE 1   The Dual Concern Model

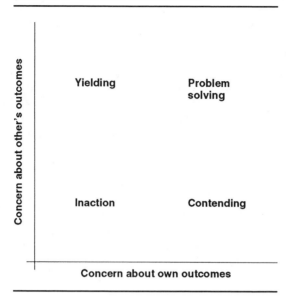

to yielding; in other words, their aspirations tend to be rigid and high.[1] Concern about the other's outcomes implies placing importance on the other's interests—feeling responsible for the quality of the other's outcomes. This concern is sometimes *genuine,* involving an intrinsic interest in the other's welfare. However, it is more often *instrumental,* being aimed at helping the other in order to advance one's own interests. Thus, for example, dependence on another person often encourages efforts to build a working relationship with that person by trying to satisfy his or her needs.

Although this is not shown in Figure 1, it is theoretically possible for people to have negative concerns about the other party's outcomes and even about their own outcomes. In other words, we might have extended the coordinates in the figure downward and to the left. A few points about negative concerns will be made in this chapter but not enough to warrant introducing further complexity into the formal statement of the model.

The dual concern model makes the following predictions about the antecedents of strategic choice: Problem solving is encouraged when there is a strong concern about both own and other's outcomes. Yielding is encouraged by a strong concern about only the other's outcomes. Contending is encouraged by a strong concern about only one's own outcomes. Inaction is encouraged when concern about both parties' outcomes is weak. The model makes no predictions about the antecedents of withdrawing.

The dual concern model has its origins in Blake and Mouton's (1964) managerial grid and has been adapted to the analysis of conflict by various authors (Blake and

---

[1]See Kelley, Beckman, and Fischer (1967) for a sophisticated discussion of the concept of resistance to yielding.

Mouton, 1979; Filley, 1975; Gladwin and Walter, 1980; Rahim, 1983; Ruble and Thomas, 1976; Thomas, 1976). Other labels are sometimes given to the dimensions in this model. For example, concern about own outcomes is sometimes called "assertiveness," and concern about other's outcomes is sometimes called "cooperativeness."

Other versions of the dual concern model (Filley, 1975; Thomas, 1976) postulate a fifth strategy called "compromising," which is ordinarily shown in the middle of the figure because it is viewed as due to a moderate concern about both self and other. We do not take this approach, because we see no need to postulate a separate strategy in order to explain the development of compromises. We see compromises as arising from one of two sources—either lazy problem solving involving a half-hearted attempt to satisfy the two parties' interests, or simple yielding by both parties.

Thomas (1976) notes that the two concerns in the dual concern model are often erroneously reduced to a single dimension, with selfishness (concern about own outcomes) on one end and cooperativeness (concern about other's outcomes) on the other. This is an improper simplification, because it is clear that both concerns can be strong at the same time. People can be both selfish and cooperative (leading them to engage in problem solving in an effort to reconcile both parties' interests). By postulating dual concerns, we are forced to distinguish between two ways of cooperating with the other party, yielding and problem solving. These were not sufficiently separated in a prior theory of strategic choice (Deutsch, 1973), which proposed only a single motivational dimension ranging from competition to cooperation. Postulating dual concerns also forces us to distinguish between two ways of advancing one's own interests, contending and problem solving.

Determinants of Concern about Own Outcomes

The strength of concern about own outcomes differs from situation to situation and from person to person. For example, person A may be relatively indifferent about the location and quality of his or her vacation, whereas this may be a matter of great concern for person B. Person A, on the other hand, may have a much deeper concern about the quality of his or her work on the job.

Concern about own outcomes can be traced to a number of determinants. One is the importance of the values affected by these outcomes. Person B may have an extremely taxing job, which produces a great need for rest and relaxation during his or her vacation, whereas person A may not have such strong needs. When a spouse challenges these vacation preferences, person A is likely to yield or be inactive, whereas person B will make an effort to salvage these preferences via contentious or problem-solving activities.

Another determinant of concern about own outcomes in any one realm is the importance of outcomes in other realms. People do not have an infinite amount of time or energy, so they cannot pursue all of their interests with equal intensity. A strong concern about one issue often leads to a weak concern about others. For example, person A may be relatively indifferent to the issue of quality of vacation because of being wrapped up in his or her job, the campaign for a nuclear freeze, or some other absorbing activity.

Concern about own outcomes also tends to be low when people are afraid of conflict. This is because resistance to yielding, which is produced by a high concern about own outcomes, tends to engender conflict. Fear of conflict is a personality predisposition for some people. It is also produced by certain situations, such as being attracted to—or dependent on—another person but distrustful of the other's opinion of the self (Hancock and Sorrentino, 1980). Situations such as this, which are said to involve "false cohesiveness" (Longley and Pruitt, 1980), are especially common at the beginning of a relationship when people are feeling each other out. Research on newly formed romantic couples suggests that such sentiments can block all forms of assertiveness, including both contentious and problem-solving behavior (Fry, Firestone, and Williams, 1983).

Concern about Own Group's Outcomes.   The forces mentioned so far affect individuals acting on their own behalf. But the parties to conflict are often groups. Hence we must inquire into the antecedents of the concern that is frequently felt by group members about the outcomes achieved by their group.

Especially strong concerns about the fate of the group tend to develop in cohesive groups whose members share a similar life situation and discuss their common fate with one another. This is particularly likely when the members of such groups regard themselves as part of a broader social movement, making common cause with similar groups in other locations (Kriesberg, 1982).

When the parties are groups or organizations, actual conflict behavior is usually carried out by representatives. Research on negotiation (Benton & Druckman, 1973) suggests that representatives are usually more reluctant to yield than are individuals bargaining on their own behalf. This is because they are trying to please their constituents and typically view their constituents as nonconciliatory. The effect disappears in those infrequent cases where the constituent is revealed to have a conciliatory bias (Benton and Druckman, 1974).

Other studies suggest that representatives are especially reluctant to yield under conditions that make them anxious to please their constituents, such as when they have low status in their groups (Kogan, Lamm, and Trommsdorff, 1972), are distrusted by their constituents (Wall, 1975), wish to continue associating with their constituents (Klimoski, 1972), or have female as opposed to male constituents (Forcey, Van Slyck, Carnevale, and Pruitt, 1983). All of these conditions can be viewed as enhancing concern about own side's outcomes.

Accountability to constituents has much the same effect. A representative is accountable to the extent that he or she must report the outcome of the negotiation to powerful constituents. Accountable representatives are especially reluctant to concede in negotiation (Bartunek, Benton, and Keys, 1975), suggesting that they are particularly concerned about group outcomes. As a result, they are more likely to adopt a contentious or problem-solving approach than to yield (Ben-Yoav and Pruitt, 1984b).

Quite often, constituents instruct their representatives to achieve high outcomes and are dissatisfied when they come home with less. This also serves to bolster the concern felt by representatives for their side's outcomes.

Determinants of Concern about the Other Party's Outcomes

As mentioned earlier, concern about the other party's outcomes takes two basic forms: *genuine* concern, based on an intrinsic interest in the other's welfare, and *instrumental* concern, aimed at advancing one's own interests. There is an important difference between these two forms of concern. Because instrumental concern is aimed at impressing the other, it is stronger when the other is more concerned about his or her own outcomes. By contrast, genuine concern aims at serving the other regardless of the other's degree of self-interest.

Genuine concern about the other party's outcomes is fostered by various kinds of interpersonal *bonds,* including attraction (Clark and Mills, 1979), perceived similarity (Hornstein, 1976), and kinship or common group identity (Hatton, 1967). Genuine concern is also fostered by a positive mood (Isen and Levin, 1972) and by taking helpful actions toward someone (not necessarily the party with whom one is now in conflict) in the recent past, especially if there were no clear external incentives for this action (Freedman and Fraser, 1966; Uranowitz, 1975).

Instrumental concern about the other party's outcomes is common whenever one sees oneself as dependent on the other—when the other is seen as able to provide rewards and penalties. An example is the expectation of further negotiation in the future. Dependence leads to the conclusion that it is desirable to build a relationship with the other now. Hence one tries to impress the other with one's concern about his or her welfare.

Dependence is by no means a one-way street. Mutual dependence is quite common and can encourage either mutual yielding or mutual problem solving. The impact on mutual problem solving is illustrated by a case study of mediation between two managers in the same company (Walton, 1969). It was not until both men discovered that they could be hurt by one another that they began trying to solve the problems they were having with each other.

For people to be aware of their dependence on another party, it is often necessary for them to project themselves into the future. This point is important for understanding conflict, because people embroiled in escalating conflicts often lose awareness of the future. They concentrate so hard on winning in the present that they lose track of the importance of maintaining good relations with the other party. In such situations, future perspective can be regained in a number of ways. One is to take time out from the controversy—to become disengaged for a while. Research suggests that such a "cooling off period" enhances cooperativeness in settings where parties are basically interdependent (Pilisuk, Kiritz, and Clampitt, 1971).

Although bonds and dependencies usually foster concern about the other party's outcomes, under certain conditions they can produce exactly the opposite reaction—antagonism toward the other and adoption of contentious tactics. This reaction occurs when people to whom we are bonded—friends, relatives, people we admire—fail to fulfill their minimum obligations or severely frustrate us. Our bonds to these people can actually encourage more anger and aggression than we would otherwise feel, because we believe they owe us preferential treatment. A similar reaction occurs when people on whom we are dependent are unresponsive to our needs (Gruder, 1971). The ordinary reaction to dependence is concern about the other party's needs. But if the other is perceived as taking advantage of this concern, it often seems necessary to reverse gears and retaliate in order to motivate the other to be more responsive. (These reactions are outside the scope of the dual concern model, which deals only with positive concern about the other's outcomes.)

Predictions from the Model

The dual concern model has received support in three recent studies. These studies made use of a laboratory simulation of negotiation in which two participants play the roles of buyer and seller in a wholesale market. Their task is to reach agreement on the prices of three appliances: typewriters, vacuum cleaners, and sewing machines. Each participant has a benefit schedule showing the profit that his or her firm will make at each price level. The participants are allowed to talk about their benefit schedules but not to show them to each other. The benefit schedules are constructed so that there are hidden solutions that provide much greater benefit to both parties than those that are obvious at first, but these solutions can be achieved only if one or both parties engage in problem solving. In all three studies, the two concerns specified in the dual concern model were manipulated independently of each other in a 2 × 2 design. Both subjects in a dyad always received the same combination of concerns.

In the first two studies, concern about own outcomes was manipulated by means of instructions about the lower limit of profit the subjects could achieve. High concern was produced by telling both subjects privately that their firms required them to achieve no less than a particular profit level ($4,600); low concern was produced by telling them nothing about a lower limit on profit. The researchers reasoned that the former condition would encourage more resistance to yielding than the latter.

The first study (Pruitt, Carnevale, Ben-Yoav, Nochajski, and Van Slyck, 1983) involved a manipulation of genuine concern about the other's outcomes. High concern was produced by putting the participants in a good mood, which has been shown to induce a desire to be helpful (Isen and Levin, 1972). Just before the beginning of negotiation, both subjects received gifts from a confederate of the experimenter. There were no gifts in the low-concern condition. The second study (Ben-Yoav and Pruitt, 1984a) involved a manipulation of strategic concern. High concern was produced by giving the subjects an expectation of cooperative future interaction. They were told that they would have to work together toward a common goal on a task following the negotiation. The aim of this instruction was to make them feel dependent on each other and hence desirous of developing a working relationship. In the low-concern condition, they were told that they would be working alone on a subsequent task.

The average joint benefit (sum of the two parties' profits) achieved in the first two studies is shown in Figure 2. In both studies, a combination of high concern about own outcomes and high concern about the other's outcomes (shown in the upper right-hand cell) produced especially high joint benefit. This result is evidence of active problem-solving behavior, as predicted by the dual concern model. Other evidence of problem solving in this condition is the fact that the negotiators were especially likely to give each other information about the entries in their profit schedules. A combination of

FIGURE 2   Joint Benefit Achieved in Studies 1 and 2

	No limit	Limit			No limit	Limit
Positive mood	8540	9890	Expectation of cooperative future interaction		8175	9425
No mood	8900	8960	No expectation of cooperative future interaction		8675	8650
	Study 1				Study 2	

high concern about own outcomes and low concern about the other's outcomes (lower right-hand cell) produced moderately low joint benefit. Contentious statements such as persuasive arguments and threats were especially common in this condition, again supporting the dual concern model. A combination of low concern about own outcomes and high concern about the other's outcomes (upper left-hand cell) produced the lowest joint benefit of all, suggesting the yielding (aspiration collapse) predicted by the dual concern model.

The results of these two studies show that, as predicted by the dual concern model, concern about the other party's outcomes is a two-edged sword. In conjunction with concern about own outcomes, it leads to problem solving and (when both parties share the same concerns) especially high joint benefit. But when concern about own outcomes is weak, concern about the other party's outcomes produces yielding and especially low joint benefit.

In the third study (Ben-Yoav and Pruitt, 1984b), concern about the other party's outcomes was again manipulated by the presence versus absence of an expectation of cooperative future interaction. Concern about own outcomes was manipulated by means of high versus low accountability to constituents. Under high accountability, the constituents (who were confederates) were able to divide the money earned in the negotiation and write an evaluation of the outcomes achieved by their negotiators. Under low accountability, the negotiators divided the money earned, and no evaluations were written:

The results for joint benefit are shown in Figure 3. As predicted by the dual concern model, high accountability in the absence of an expectation of cooperative future interaction encouraged heavy contentious verbalizations and low joint benefit (as shown in the lower right-hand cell). But the impact of accountability was completely reversed when there was an expectation of future interaction. In this condition (upper right-hand cell), accountability encouraged especially high joint benefit, presumably because it fostered heavy joint problem solving.

These results suggest that accountability, and hence concern about own outcomes, is also a two-edged sword. Under normal conditions, it fosters contentious behavior

FIGURE 3   Joint Benefit Achieved in Study 3

	Accountability	
	Low	High
Expectation of cooperative future interaction	8600	9770
No expectation of cooperative future interaction	8840	8300

and low joint benefit. But under conditions that encourage a desire for good relations between the opposing parties, it fosters problem solving and high joint benefit.

In summary, the dual concern model postulates that strategic choice is determined by the strength of two concerns: concern for own outcomes and concern for the other party's outcomes. When both concerns are strong, people prefer problem solving; when the former concern is strong, they prefer contending; when the latter concern is strong, they prefer yielding; and when both concerns are weak, inaction is likely to be found. Concern about own outcomes produces high, rigid aspirations. It tends to be strong when the interests at stake are important, when outcomes in other realms are unimportant, when there is low fear of conflict, when there is high accountability to constituents, and when constituents insist that their representative achieve a high level of benefit. Concern about the other party's outcomes can be either genuine or instrumental (strategic). Genuine concern is fostered by interpersonal bonds of all types and by good mood. Instrumental concern is fostered by a desire to develop a working relationship with a person on whom one is dependent. The predictive value of this model has been demonstrated in three studies.

THE PERCEIVED FEASIBILITY PERSPECTIVE

Choice among the five basic strategies is also a matter of perceived feasibility—the extent to which the strategy seems capable of achieving the concerns that give rise to it and the cost that is anticipated from enacting each strategy. Considerations of feasibility supplement those specified by the dual concern model. The dual concern model indicates the strategies preferred under various combinations of concern about own and other's outcomes. But for a strategy actually to be adopted, it must also be seen as minimally feasible. If not, another strategy will be chosen, even if it is less consistent with the current combination of concerns.

For example, take parties who are concerned about both their own and the other party's outcomes. Problem solving is their preferred strategy. But if this strategy seems infeasible or too risky, they are likely to shift to yielding or contending, their next best alternatives. Which of these is chosen is determined both by the relative strength of the two concerns and by other considerations of feasibility and cost. If the parties are more concerned about the other's outcomes than their own, they adopt a yielding approach, provided that this seems reasonably feasible. If they are more concerned about their own outcomes than the other's, they shift to contentious behavior, also provided that this seems reasonably feasible.

For another example, take parties who are concerned mainly about their own outcomes. Contending is their preferred strategy because it holds the promise of getting something for nothing. But problem solving is a close second if the contentious approach appears infeasible or costly. Indeed, problem solving often seems the most feasible way of pursuing one's own interests.

The next three sections deal with the perceived feasibility of three of the fundamental strategies under consideration in this chapter: problem solving, contending, and inaction.

Perceived Feasibility of Problem Solving

Problem solving seems more feasible the greater the *perceived common ground* (PCG). PCG is a party's assessment of the likelihood of finding an alternative that satisfies both parties' aspirations. The more likely it seems that such an alternative can be found, the more feasible problem solving appears to be. PCG is greater (1) the lower Party's own aspirations, (2) the lower Other's aspirations as perceived by Party, and (3) the greater the perceived integrative potential (PIP)—that is, Party's faith that alternatives favorable to both parties exist or can be devised.

This definition implies that PCG is the mirror image of perceived conflict. As PCG goes up, conflict, in the sense of perceived divergence of interest, goes down.

The reader may be surprised to learn that lower aspirations make problem solving seem more feasible. Superficially, this seems inconsistent with the point made earlier that lack of concern about one's own interests (which produces low aspirations) reduces the likelihood of problem solving. However, these two points are not contradictory. We are talking about two countervailing forces that are simultaneously activated when concern about own interests is low. The one makes problem solving seem more feasible, and the other (by permitting the strategy of yielding) makes problem solving seem less necessary.

Perceived integrative potential (PIP) (a component of PCG) needs further elaboration. At any given point in negotiation, some alternatives are known and the availability of others is suspected. PIP is high when there are known alternatives that provide high benefit to both parties. It is moderately high when it seems probable that such alternatives can be developed—the more definite the prospects for developing such an alternative, the higher is PIP. It is low when there seems little prospect of finding mutually beneficial alternatives.

Greater clarity about the concepts of PIP and PCG is provided by the graphs in Figure 4. The abscissa in these graphs maps Party's own benefits; the ordinate, Party's

FIGURE 4   Four Levels of Perceived Common Ground

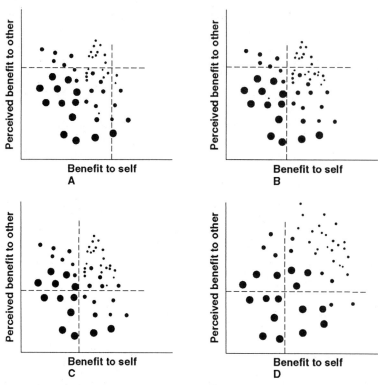

perception of Other's benefits. The heavy points in these graphs refer to known alternatives, the medium points to alternatives that seem potentially discoverable, and the light points to long shots. The location of a point in the space shows the perceived value of that alternative to the two parties. The vertical lines in these graphs refer to Party's own aspirations and the horizontal lines to Other's perceived aspirations.

PCG is greater the more points there are to the northeast (above and to the right) of the intersection of the aspiration lines and the darker these points are. PCG is greater in Figure 4B than in Figure 4A because Party's own aspirations are lower. It is greater in Figure 4C than in Figure 4B because Other's perceived aspirations are also lower. It is greater in Figure 4D than in Figure 4C because of greater PIP—that is, greater perceived likelihood that mutually beneficial alternatives can be developed (as shown by the fact that the darker points are farther from the origin in the northeast direction).

Determinants of Perceived Integrative Potential.   A number of conditions contribute to PIP and hence to the likelihood that problem solving will be employed.

1. *Faith in own problem-solving ability.* Some people are good communi- cators and/or understand well how to devise mutually beneficial alternatives. Hence their experience leads them to see considerable integrative potential in almost any situation. Others, less well endowed, are likely to view conflict as more intractable and to adopt strategies of yielding or contending rather than problem solving.

2. *Momentum.* Momentum refers to prior success at reaching agreement in the current controversy. The more frequent and recent such successes have been, the greater will be Party's faith that these successes can be reproduced in the future and that problem solving is worthwhile. Momentum can sometimes be encouraged by scheduling easier issues earlier in a negotiation agenda, so that a solid foundation of success has been built by the time more difficult issues are encountered.

3. *Availability of a mediator.* Mediators often serve as communication links between the parties, coordinating movement toward compromise or helping to develop integrative solutions. Their availability should make problem solving seem more likely to be successful.

An example of the latter mechanism can be seen in the British reaction to the Argentine occupation of the Falkland Islands in 1982. Yielding was ruled out on the grounds of cost to the British image. Inaction seemed inadvisable because every day of the occupation enhanced the legitimacy of the Argentine action. In short, the choice was between contending and problem solving. At first it appeared that there might be integrative potential; American Secretary of State Alexander Haig was trying to mediate the crisis. Hence the British adopted a problem-solving strat- egy, working with Haig while defending their basic interests by moving their fleet slowly toward South America. However, PIP disappeared with the failure of Haig's mission, making problem solving seem quite infeasible. As a result, the British adopted an exclusively contentious approach, an all-out invasion of the islands.

4. *Other's perceived readiness for problem solving.* Problem solving seems more feasible to the extent that Other seems ready to participate in this process. There are two reasons for this. One is increased PIP, because joint problem solving is usually more efficient than unilateral problem solving. The second is that problem solving seems less risky when Other is not taking a contentious approach, because under those conditions there is less danger in allowing oneself to look weak.

Trust.   The perception that Other is ready for problem solving, and hence that there is integrative potential, is sometimes a function of trust—that is, of Party's perception that Other is concerned about Party's interests. Research (Kimmel, Pruitt, Magenau, and Konar-Goldband, 1980) suggests that trust encourages problem solving when Party is otherwise inclined to adopt this strategy, presumably by making problem solving seem feasible.

Although trust allows people to adopt a problem-solving strategy, it is no guarantee that this strategy will be adopted. Indeed, trust can sometimes have quite the opposite effect, encouraging high, inflexible aspirations defended by contentious behavior.

Whether trust encourages problem solving or contending depends at least in part on Other's perceived resistance to yielding—that is, the apparent firmness of Other's aspirations. A trusted Other whose aspirations do not seem firm will be expected to give in to Party's demands. Hence contentious behavior seems especially feasible. But if Other's aspirations seem firm, trust implies instead that Other will cooperate if and only if Party cooperates. This encourages Party to adopt a problem-solving strategy.

Evidence that problem solving is encouraged by a combination of trust and perceived firmness comes from several bargaining experiments. All of these studies examined bargainer response to helpful actions from the other party, which actions presumably engendered trust. When the other party had been helpful, bargainers were more willing to cooperate if the other also (1) had high threat capacity (Lindskold and Bennett, 1973; Michener, Vaske, Schleifer, Plazewski, and Chapman, 1975), (2) had a tough constituent (Wall, 1977), (3) had been unyielding or competitive in the past (Deutsch, 1973; Harford and Solomon, 1967), or (4) had been unwilling to make unilateral concessions in the past (Komorita and Esser, 1975; McGillicuddy, Pruitt and Syna, 1984). These four conditions presumably enhance Party's perception that Other has firm aspirations.

Trust develops in a number of ways. It is encouraged by a perception that the other party has a positive attitude toward us, is similar to us, or is dependent on us. As an example of the latter point, Solomon (1960) has shown that trust is greater when one sees oneself as having a capacity to punish the other for failing to cooperate.

Trust also tends to develop when one has been helpful toward the other party (Loomis, 1959). This prediction is implied by dissonance (Festinger, 1957) and self-perception (Bem, 1972) theories. It also follows from the assumption that the other will reciprocate one's helpful behavior.

We tend to trust people who have been helpful or cooperative, especially if their help is directed toward us (Cooper and Fazio, 1979) and has occurred recently (Kelley and Stahelski, 1970). Trust is an especially common response when the other's helpful behavior is seen as voluntary and not as a product of environmental forces. Hence we tend to trust others whose helpful behavior is not required by their role (Jones and Davis, 1965) or seems to be costly to them (Komorita, 1973). All of these circumstances encourage problem solving by enhancing perceived integrative potential.

Perceived Feasibility of Contending

Contending seems more feasible the lower the Other's apparent resistance to yielding. There is not much point in putting pressure on an opponent who has ultrastrong feelings, has powerful and resolute constituents, or has already yielded to the bare bone of need. Other tactics, such as yielding and problem solving, are more likely to be adopted. But if the other's aspirations (however high they may be) seem relatively easy to dislodge, contentious behavior gets a boost.

The points just made imply that contentious behavior is often self-liquidating, a victim of both failure and success. If it fails, this indicates that Other's resistance is greater than originally thought, so Party will abandon the tactic. If it succeeds and Other yields, Other's resistance to further yielding is likely to grow because Other will come closer and closer to his or her limit. Again, Party must eventually abandon the tactic.

The feasibility of contending is also a function of Party's apparent capacity to employ contentious tactics and of Other's apparent capacity to counter them. Does Party have good arguments? Does Other have counterarguments? Is Party adept at arguing his or her case? How effective is Other as a debater? Can Party reward or punish Other? How good are Other's defenses against such tactics? Does Party have ways to commit himself or herself credibly? Is Other capable of undoing these commitments?

Capacities such as these are sometimes lumped together under the familiar concepts of "power" and "counterpower." These concepts have some merit in that they allow us to make a few broad generalizations. For example, we can generalize that more powerful people have higher aspirations and make greater use of heavy contentious tactics, regardless of the source of their power. But there is a tendency to overuse these concepts in social science theory, making facile generalizations with little real meaning (see, for example, Morgenthau, 1967). The problem is that there are many kinds of power, each with a different set of priorities (French and Raven, 1959).

In a stable long-term relationship, each party's capacity to employ contentious tactics tends to be matched by the other's level of resistance, so that there is relatively little advantage to either party in employing contentious tactics. Hence, on important issues where the parties cannot easily yield, joint problem solving is most likely to be the strategic choice. This is true even when threat capacity greatly favors one side, as in a relationship between master and slave. Joint problem solving is not uncommon in such relationships, though the outcome is likely to benefit the master far more than the slave. The slave's situation produces aspirations that are so low that his or her resistance to further yielding is strong enough to balance the master's superior threat capacity.

Perceived Cost. Contentious behavior, particularly in its more severe forms, runs the risk of alienating the other party and starting a conflict spiral. There is also some danger of third-party censure. Such considerations can deter contentious behavior, particularly when one is dependent on the other party or on watchful third parties.

Costs are also associated with constituent *surveillance,* which has a complicated relationship to the use of contentious tactics. Surveillance must be distinguished from accountability to constituents. Representatives are accountable to the extent that they can be rewarded or punished on the basis of the outcomes they generate for their constituents. They are under surveillance when their actual conflict behavior (for example, how they negotiate) is being observed. Representatives who are being observed by their constituents usually fear getting out of line with these constituents' expectations. If they believe the constituents favor toughness, they will tend to adopt contentious behavior; if they see the constituents as conciliatory, they will avoid contending. These points are supported by a study of the joint effect of surveillance and sex of constituent (Forcey, Van Slyck, Carnevale, and Pruitt, 1983) on strategic choice. Surveillance by male constituents was found to enhance negotiator contentiousness, whereas surveillance by female constituents was found to diminish contentiousness. This makes sense if we assume that the subjects subscribed to the usual stereotype that men favor a tough approach and women a conciliatory approach to interpersonal relations.

Perceived Feasibility of Inaction

Inaction is obviously the greatest time waster of the strategies. Hence *time pressure* should discourage use of this strategy and, if Party remains engaged in the controversy, encourage the three coping strategies.

There are two sources of time pressure: cost per unit time of engaging in the controversy and closeness to a deadline. In negotiation, time pressure can be due to any cost of continued negotiation, including time lost from other pursuits, the expense of maintaining negotiators in the field, or rapid deterioration of the object under dispute (such as fruits and vegetables). Deadlines are points in the future at which significant costs are likely to be experienced if the controversy has not been resolved. At a strike deadline, the union pulls the workers out of the factory; at a hiring deadline, the job offer is withdrawn. The closer one is to a deadline and the larger the penalty for passing that deadline without agreement, the greater the time pressure and hence the less likely one is to enact the strategy of inaction.

An example of the impact of time pressure on strategic choice can be seen in the 1968 student rebellion in Mexico City, which occurred just before the Olympic Games in that city. As the opening of the games approached, the Mexican government became increasingly concerned about the continuing student disorder. In effect, deadline pressures were increasing, and the existing impasse with the students seemed less and less tolerable. All three of the coping strategies were employed in quick succession. First, the government yielded to a few student demands and then entered into problem-solving discussions. Finding the latter unsuccessful, the government then took the contentious (to say the least) approach of shooting hundreds of students at a rally.

All three coping strategies are possible in the face of time pressure, but research (Pruitt and Drews, 1969) suggests that the favorite strategy is yielding. This is presumably because yielding is the fastest way to move toward agreement. It follows that contending and problem solving are adopted in the face of time pressure only when there is heavy resistance to yielding.

In summary, we have argued that perceived feasibility—assessment of effectiveness and cost—affects strategic choice. This consideration supplements the forces specified in the dual concern model. Thus, for example, problem solving is adopted when one is concerned about both own and other's outcomes provided that there is some perceived possibility of success at a reasonable cost. The perceived feasibility of problem solving is a function of perceived common ground (PCG), the perception that an alternative can be found that satisfied both parties' aspirations. PCG, in turn, is a function of own and perceived other's aspirations and of perceived integrative potential (PIP), the apparent likelihood of identifying mutually beneficial alternatives. Perceived feasibility of contending is a positive function of perceived power and an inverse function of Other's apparent resistance to yielding. Perceived feasibility of inaction diminishes with increased time pressure.

ANTECEDENTS OF WITHDRAWING

The dual concern model and the perceived feasibility perspective are not very useful in understanding the conditions under which people withdraw from a conflict. Hence, we must turn to other considerations.

People decide to withdraw when the benefit they expect from a controversy falls below their limit—that is, their minimal aspiration.

The benefit they expect is determined in part by how far they think the other party will concede. Thus I am unlikely to withdraw from negotiation with an auto dealer if he or she proposes a moderate price for an attractive car and seems willing to go lower. It is also determined in part by perceived integrative potential. If a jointly acceptable package of price, car, and accessories looks easy to devise, I am also unlikely to withdraw.

Logically speaking, the limit should be set at the level of benefit that can be achieved by withdrawing (Fisher and Ury, 1981), and this is often the case. For example, in negotiating with a car dealer, I should set my limit at the lowest price I would have to pay another dealer for a comparable car. However, in actual practice, people often get locked into unrealistic limits through a process of premature commitment. For example, before going to buy a car, I may tell my friends that I intend to pay no more than $6,250, and I may even announce this figure to the dealer as a contentious gambit. Unless I am willing to renege on this commitment, $6,250 becomes my effective limit, and I must withdraw if the dealer does not accept it. (It follows that the contentious strategy of positional commitment is risky unless one is fairly certain about what the other will accept.)

THE VIGOR OF STRATEGIC BEHAVIOR

Implementation of the three coping strategies can be more or less *vigorous*. In the case of contentious behavior, vigor refers to the heaviness of the actions taken. Shouts are more vigorous than persuasive communications, blows more vigorous than shouts, shots more vigorous than blows. In the case of problem solving, vigor refers to the creativity of the problem-solving effort. At the low end of vigor is a simple, dull effort to coordinate the making of concessions toward an obvious compromise. At the high end is an active effort to understand the other's interests and a thoughtful search for a way to reconcile these interests with one's own. In the case of yielding, vigor refers simply to how far one drops one's aspirations. Vigor has no meaning with respect to the strategies of inaction or withdrawing.

There are various determinants of how vigorous a strategy will be. One set of determinants is embodied in the dual concern model (Figure 1). The stronger the concerns specified by this model, the more vigorous will be the predicted strategy. Thus, if concern about own outcomes is weak, greater concern about the other party's outcomes will produce more profound yielding. If concern about the other's outcomes is weak, greater concern about own outcomes will encourage more extreme contentious behavior. If neither concern is weak, problem solving will be more vigorous and creative the stronger are the dual concerns.

It is common for parties who have adopted a coping strategy to begin less vigorously and move toward greater vigor if earlier efforts do not achieve agreement. Such gradualism ensures that no greater costs will be incurred than are necessary to achieve their goals. This point is most obvious in the realm of contentious behavior. Like the United States in the Vietnam War, parties usually begin cautiously and escalate only if they are unsuccessful.

Two of the coping strategies have a paradoxical feature: If they are adopted, the vigor with which they are enacted is a function of some of the same conditions that *discourage* their being adopted in the first place.

One of these strategies is contending. As mentioned earlier, the expectation of resistance from the other party discourages contentious behavior. But suppose that other conditions (such as being a highly accountable representative with no dependence on the other) predispose a party to contend. What is the effect of expected resistance then? Our hypothesis is that it promotes the use of heavier contentious tactics. If the other looks like a pushover, it should be easy to get a concession by simple stone-walling or persuasive argumentation. But if the other's position seems engraved in stone, heavier guns will be needed, in the form of threats or other coercive actions.

Problem solving is the other strategy that exhibits this paradoxical feature. Low PCG discourages problem solving. But it also encourages a creative form of problem solving when this strategy is adopted for other reasons. Suppose, for example, that there is a complete stalemate—both parties are totally unwilling to yield and contentious tactics seem useless. If withdrawing is infeasible and inaction also seems unattractive (perhaps because of time pressure), problem solving is the only possible approach. To the extent that PCG is low (whether because of high aspirations, a perception that the other party has high aspirations, or minimal PIP), it will seem necessary to employ a more creative effort in order to reach agreement.

*   *   *   *   *

CONCLUSIONS

This chapter has presented a preliminary theory about the conditions that affect the choice people make among the five strategies available to them in conflict: contending, problem solving, yielding, inaction, and withdrawing. This theory consists mainly of a dual concern model, supplemented by some ideas about the effect of feasibility considerations. The theory also implies some paradoxical hypotheses about determinants of the vigor with which certain of the strategies are employed . Strangely, the same conditions that make contending and problem solving seem less feasible cause these strategies to be employed with greater vigor if they happen to be adopted.

*   *   *   *   *

Consider Both Relationships and Substance when Negotiating Strategically

Grant T. Savage

John D. Blair

Ritch L. Sorenson

When David Peterson, director of services for Dickerson Machinery, arrives at his office, he notes four appointments on his schedule. With his lengthy experience in negotiating important contracts for this large-equipment repair service, he does not take long to identify the agenda for each appointment.[1]

A steering clutch disk salesman from Roadworks will arrive at 8:30 A.M. Peterson has relied for years on disks supplied by Caterpillar and knows those disks can provide the 8,000 hours of service Dickerson guarantees. Price is an issue in Peterson's selection of a supplier, but more important is a guarantee on the life span of the part.

A meeting is scheduled at 9:30 with a mechanic who has swapped a new company battery for a used battery from his own truck. This "trade" is, of course, against company policy, and the employee has been reprimanded and told his next paycheck will be docked. However, the mechanic wants to discuss the matter.

A representative for Tarco, a large road-building contractor, is scheduled for 10:00 A.M. Peterson has been interested in this service contract for a couple of years. He believes that if he can secure a short-term service contract with Tarco, Dickerson's high-quality mechanical service and guarantees will result in a long-term service relationship with the contractor. The night before, Peterson had dinner with Tarco's representative, and this morning he will provide a tour of service facilities and discuss the short-term contract with him.

Reprinted from *Academy of Management Executive*, February 1989, pp. 37–47. Used with permission.

[1] The incidents reported in this vignette and throughout the article are based on actual experiences in a multistate machinery servicing company.

A meeting with management representatives for union negotiations is scheduled for 1:00 P.M. That meeting will probably last a couple of hours. Peterson is concerned because the company has lost money on the shop undergoing contract talks, and now the union is demanding higher wages and threatening to strike. The company cannot afford a prolonged strike, but it also cannot afford to increase pay at current service production rates. Negotiating a contract will not be easy.

CHOOSING NEGOTIATION STRATEGIES

Peterson's appointments are not unique. Researchers and scholars have examined similar situations. What strategic advice does the negotiation literature offer for handling these four situations?

One of the best developed approaches is *game theory,* which focuses on maximizing substantive outcomes in negotiations.[2] Peterson would probably do well by focusing on only the best possible outcome for Dickerson Machinery in his meetings with the salesman and the employee: He already has a good contract for a steering wheel clutch, but if the salesman can offer a better deal, Peterson will take it; and in the case of the employee, Peterson will hear him out but foresees no need to deviate from company policy.

In contrast, an exclusive focus on maximizing the company's substantive outcomes would probably not work in the other two situations: Tarco may continue being serviced elsewhere unless enticed to try Dickerson; and during the union negotiations, strategies to maximize outcomes for management only could force a strike.

Another well-developed strategic approach is *win-win problem solving.* It is designed to maximize outcomes for both parties and maintain positive relationships.[3] This approach could work in the union negotiation, but the outcome would probably be a compromise, not a true win-win solution.

Win-win negotiation probably is not the best strategy in the other three situations. Either Roadwork's salesman meets the guarantee and beats current prices, or he does not; trying to find a win-win solution would probably be a waste of time. Similarly, because the meeting with the employee will occur after company rules have been applied, a win-win solution is probably not in the company's best interest. Lastly, an attempt to maximize the company's substantive outcomes in a short-term service contract with Tarco could hinder long-term contract prospects.

Any one approach to negotiation clearly will not work in all situations. Executives need a framework for determining what strategies are best in different situations. We believe the best strategy depends on desired outcomes. In this article, we characterize the two major outcomes at issue in the previous examples as *substantive* and *relation-*

---

[2]See H. Raiffa's *The Art and Science of Negotiation,* Cambridge, Mass.: Harvard University Press, 1982, for a discussion of how game theory can help negotiators maximize their substantive outcomes under a diverse set of situations.

[3]Both R. Fisher and W. Ury's *Getting to Yes: Negotiating Agreements Without Giving In* (Boston: Houghton-Mifflin, 1981) and A. C. Filley's "Some Normative Issues in Conflict Management" *(California Management Review,* 1978, 21(2), pp. 61–65) treat win-win problem solving as a principled, collaborative process.

ship outcomes. Although both types of outcome have been discussed in the literature, relationship outcomes have received much less attention. Our contention is that a systematic model of strategic choice for negotiation must account for both substantive and relationship outcomes. In articulating such a model, we suggest that executives can approach negotiation strategically by assessing the negotiation context; considering unilateral negotiation strategies; transforming unilateral into interactive negotiation strategies; and monitoring tactics and reevaluating negotiation strategies.

ASSESSING THE NEGOTIATION CONTEXT

A crucial context for any negotiation is the manager's current and desired relationship with the other party. Unfortunately, in their rush to secure the best possible substantive outcome, managers often overlook the impact of the negotiation on their relationships. This oversight can hurt a manager's relationship with the other party, thus limiting his or her ability to obtain desired substantive outcomes now or in the future.

Each interaction with another negotiator constitutes an *episode* that draws from current and affects future relationships. Intertwined with pure concerns about relationships are concerns about substantive outcomes. Many times negotiators are motivated to establish or maintain positive relationships and willingly "share the pie" through mutually beneficial collaboration. Other negotiations involve substantive outcomes that can benefit one negotiator only at the expense of the other (a fixed pie). These cases often motivate negotiators to discount the relationship and claim as much of the pie as possible.

Most negotiations, however, are neither clearly win-win nor win-lose situations, but combinations of both (an indeterminate pie). Such mixed-motive situations, in which both collaboration and competition may occur, are particularly difficult for managers to handle strategically.[4] The relationship that exists prior to the negotiation, the relationship that unfolds during negotiations, and the desired relationship often will determine whether either negotiator will be motivated to share the pie, grab it, or give it away.

In any case, managers should keep existing and desired relationships in mind as they bid for substantive outcomes. For example, when negotiators are on the losing end of a win-lose negotiation, they should examine the implications of taking a short-term loss. During his third appointment, Peterson's willingness to make only minimal gains in service contracts for the short term may create a positive relationship that will lead to a lucrative, long-term contract with Tarco. The relative importance of possible substantive and relationship outcomes should help executives decide whether and how to negotiate. To guide their decision process, managers should begin by assessing their relative power and the level of conflict between them and the other party. Both are key determinants of their current relationship with the other party.

---

[4]See S. Bacharach and E. J. Lawler's *Lawler's Power and Politics in Organizations: The Social Psychology of Conflict, Coalitions, and Bargaining* (San Francisco, Calif.: Jossey-Bass, 1980) for a recent discussion of mixed-motive negotiation situations.

Exhibit 1 illustrates the negotiation context, showing those aspects of the situation and negotiation episode that shape relationship and substantive outcomes. Existing levels of power and conflict influence (1) the relationship between the executive and the other party and (2) the negotiation strategies they choose. These strategies are implemented through appropriate tactics during a negotiation episode—a one-on-one encounter, a telephone call, or a meeting with multiple parties—and result in substantive and relationship outcomes.

The multiple arrows linking strategies, tactics, and the negotiation episode in Exhibit 1 show the monitoring process through which both the manager and the other party refine their strategies and tactics during an episode. A complex and lengthy negotiation, such as a union contract negotiation, may include many episodes; a simple negotiation may be completed within one episode. Each episode, nonetheless, influences future negotiations by changing the manager's and the other party's relative power, the level of conflict between them, and their relationship.

Relative Power

The relative power of the negotiators establishes an important aspect of their relationship: the extent of each party's dependence on the other. Researchers have found that individuals assess their power in a relationship and choose whether to compete, accommodate, collaborate, or withdraw when negotiating with others.[5] Managers can assess their power relative to the other party by comparing their respective abilities to induce compliance through the control of human and material resources. To what extent do they each control key material resources? To what extent do they each control the deployment, arrangement, and advancement of people within the organization?[6]

These questions will help managers determine whether their relationship with the other party is based on independence, dependence, or interdependence. Additionally, these questions should help executives consider how *and* whether their relationship with the other party should be strengthened or weakened. Often managers will find themselves or their organizations in interdependent relationships that have both beneficial and detrimental aspects. These relationships are called mixed-motive situations in the negotiation literature because they provide incentives for both competitive and cooperative actions.

In his relationship with the Roadwork salesman, Peterson has considerable power. He is satisfied with his current vendor and has other vendors wanting to sell him the same product. The numerous choices available allow him to make demands on the salesman. Similarly, Peterson has more relative power than the mechanic. On the other

---

[5]See L. Putnam and C. E. Wilson's "Communicative Strategies in Organizational Conflicts: Reliability and Validity of a Measurement Scale," in M. Burgoon's (Ed.) *Communication Yearbook 6,* Newbury Park, Calif.: Sage Publications, 1982, pp. 629–52. See also R. A. Cosier and T. L. Ruble, "Research on Conflict Handling Behavior: An Experimental Approach," *Academy of Management Journal,* 1981, 24, pp. 816–31.

[6]Power as the ability to induce compliance is discussed in J. March and H. Simon's *Organizations* (New York: Wiley, 1958) and in P. Blau's *Exchange and Power in Social Life* (New York: Wiley, 1964). Two recent books discussing power from a material-resource perspective are H. Mintzberg's *Power in and Around Organizations* (Englewood Cliffs, N.J.: Prentice Hall, 1983), and J. Pfeffer's *Power in Organizations* (Marshfield, Mass.: Pitman, 1981). A. Giddens' *The Constitution of Society: Outline of the Theory of Structuration* (Berkeley: University of California Press, 1984) discusses power from a critical-theory perspective within the field of sociology, emphasizing how power involves control over human resources.

EXHIBIT 1   Assessing the Negotiation Context

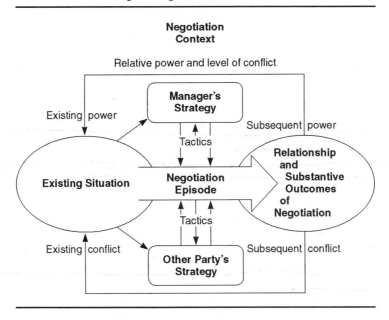

hand, he has relatively little power with Tarco, since the contractor can choose from a number of equipment-service shops. Moreover, Tarco's representative did not make the initial contact and has not actively sought Dickerson's services.

Level of Conflict

The level of conflict underlying a potential negotiation establishes how the negotiators perceive the affective dimension of their relationship—that is, its degree of supportiveness or hostility. Managers can assess the relationship's level of conflict by identifying the differences between each party's interests. On what issues do both parties agree? On what issues do they disagree? How intense and how ingrained are these differences?[7]

Answers to these questions will reveal whether negotiations will easily resolve differences and whether the relationship is perceived as supportive or hostile. These questions, like the questions about relative power, should also help executives consider how *and* whether the relationship should be strengthened or weakened. Very few negotiations begin with a neutral relationship. Indeed, the affective state of the relationship may be a primary reason for negotiating with a powerful other party, especially if the relationship has deteriorated or been particularly supportive.

---

[7]For discussions of conflict intensity and durability, see I. R. Andrews and D. Tjosvold, "Conflict Management under Different Levels of Conflict Intensity," *Journal of Occupational Behaviour,* 1983, 4, pp. 223–28 and C. T. Brown, P. Yelsma, and P. W. Keller, "Communication-Conflict Predisposition: Development of a Theory and an Instrument," *Human Relations,* 1981, 34, pp. 1103–17.

In Peterson's case, neutral to positive relationships exist with the Roadwork salesman and the Tarco representative. However, his relationships with the mechanic and the union are potentially hostile. For example, management and union representatives have already had confrontations. Their conflict may escalate if the relationship is not managed and both sides are not willing to make concessions.[8]

Considering a Unilateral Negotiation Strategy

Before selecting a strategy for negotiation, a manager should consider his or her interests and the interests of the organization. These interests will shape the answers to two basic questions: (1) Is the substantive outcome very important to the manager? and (2) Is the relationship outcome very important to the manager?

Four *unilateral* strategies (see Exhibit 2) emerge from the answers: *trusting collaboration, firm competition, open subordination,* and *active avoidance.*[9] We call these unilateral strategies because in using them, managers consider only their own interests or the interests of their organization, ignoring for the time being the interests of the other party.

The unilateral strategies presented in Exhibit 2 are similar to the conflict management styles suggested by the combined works of Blake and Mouton, Hall, and Kilmann and Thomas.[10] However, while we agree that personalities and conflict-management preferences influence a person's ability to negotiate, our selection of terms reflects our focus on strategies instead of styles. For example, Johnston used the term "subordination" to refer to a strategy similar to the conflict-management style variously termed "accommodation" (Kilmann and Thomas), "smoothing" (Blake and Mouton), or "yield-lose" (Hall).[11] We, however, see using the openly subordinative strategy as more than simply "rolling over and playing dead" or "giving away the store." Rather, this strategy is designed to strengthen long-term relational ties, usually at the expense of short-term substantive outcomes. Our discussion below also

---

[8]See M. Deutsch's *The Resolution of Conflict,* New Haven: Yale University Press, 1973, for a discussion of how spiraling conflicts can be both inflamed and controlled.

[9]For further discussions on these basic strategies, see C. B. Derr's "Managing Organizational Conflict: Collaboration, Bargaining, and Power Approaches," *California Management Review,* 1978, 21, pp. 76–82; Filley, note 3: Fisher and Ury, note 3; R. Johnston's "Negotiation Strategies: Different Strokes for Different Folks." in R. Lewicki and J. Litterer (Eds.). *Negotiation: Readings, Exercises, and Cases,* Homewood, Ill.: Richard D. Irwin, 1985, pp. 156–64; D. A. Lax and J. K. Sebenius. *The Manager as Negotiator: Bargaining for Cooperation and Competitive Gain,* New York: The Free Press, 1986; and D. G. Pruitt's "Strategic Choice in Negotiation," *American Behavioral Scientist,* 1983, 27, pp. 167–94.

[10]For an overview of the contributions by these and other conflict-management researchers, see the special issue on "Communication and Conflict Styles in Organizations," L. L. Putnam (Ed.). *Management Communication Quarterly,* 1988, 1(3), 291–45. See also R. Blake and J. Mouton's "The Fifth Achievement," *Journal of Applied Behavioral Science,* 1970, 6, pp. 413–26; J. Hall's *Conflict Management Survey: A Survey of One's Characteristic Reaction to and Handling of Conflicts Between Himself and Others,* Conroe, Tex.: Teleometrics, 1986: and R. H. Kilmann and K. W. Thomas' "Interpersonal Conflict-Handling Behavior as Reflections of Jungian Personality Dimensions," *Psychology Reports,* 1975, 37, pp. 971–80 and "Developing a Forced-Choice Measure of Conflict-Handling Behavior: The 'Mode' Instrument," *Educational & Psychological Measurement,* 1977, 37, pp. 309–25.

[11]See note 10 above; especially see Johnston.

EXHIBIT 2   Considering a Unilateral Negotiation Strategy

Is the substantive
outcome very important
to the manager?

		Yes	No
		Strategy C1	Strategy S1
Is the relationship outcome very important to the manager?	Yes	**Trustingly collaborate** When both types of outcomes are very important Situation 1	**Openly subordinate** When the priority is on relationship outcomes Situation 2
	No	Strategy P1 **Firmly compete** When the priority is on substantive outcomes Situation 3	Strategy A1 **Actively avoid negotiating** When neither type of outcome is very important Situation 4

goes beyond Johnston's conception, showing how a negotiator can focus the openly subordinative strategy according to his or her substantive goals.

Our view is consistent with research that suggests that individuals adopt different strategies in different relational contexts.[12] We anticipate that managers' success with these unilateral strategies depends on their ability to exhibit a variety of conflict styles. To highlight the role of relationship and substantive priorities, we describe these four unilateral strategies in their most extenuated, ideal form, and articulate their underlying assumptions. In many ways our descriptions are classic depictions of each type of strategy. Two of these strategies—competition and collaboration—are frequently discussed in the conflict and negotiation literature.

1. *Trusting Collaboration (C1)*. In general, if both relationship and substantive outcomes are important to the organization, the manager should consider *trusting collaboration*. The hallmark of this strategy is openness on the part of both parties. By encouraging cooperation as positions are asserted, the executive should be able to

---

[12]M. L. Knapp, L. L. Putnam, and L. J. Davis, "Measuring Interpersonal Conflict in Organizations: Where Do We Go From Here?" *Management Communication Quarterly,* 1988, 1, pp. 414–29; Putnam and Wilson, Endnote 5; and J. Sullivan, R. B. Peterson, N. Kameda, and J. Shimada, "The Relationship between Conflict Resolution Approaches and Trust—A Cross Cultural Study," *Academy of Management Journal,* 1981, 24, pp. 803–15.

achieve important relationship and substantive) outcomes. The executive seeks a win-win outcome both to achieve substantive goals *and* maintain a positive relationship.

Trustingly collaborative strategies generally are easiest to use and most effective when the manager's organization and the other party are interdependent and mutually supportive. These circumstances normally create a trusting relationship in which negotiators reciprocally disclose their goals and needs. In this climate, an effective problem-solving process and a win-win settlement typically result.

2. *Open Subordination (S1)*. If managers are more concerned with establishing a positive relationship with another party than obtaining substantive outcomes, they should openly subordinate. We use the term *subordination* instead of *accommodation* to differentiate this strategic choice from a conflict-management style. An openly subordinative strategy is a yield-win strategy that usually provides desired substantive outcomes to the other party but rarely to the manager. A subordinative strategy may be used regardless of whether the manager exercises more, less, or equal power relative to the other party. Our argument is that subordination can be an explicit strategic negotiation behavior—not simply a reflection of power. If the manager has little to lose by yielding to the substantive interests of the other party, open subordination can be a key way for him or her to dampen hostilities, increase support, and foster more interdependent relationships.

3. *Firm Competition (P1)*. If substantive interests are important but the relationship is not, the manager should consider *firmly competing*. This situation often occurs when managers have little trust for the other party or the relationship is not good to begin with. In such situations, they may want to exert their power to gain substantive outcomes. To enact this competitive strategy, they may also become highly aggressive, bluffing, threatening the other party, or otherwise misrepresenting their intentions. Such tactics hide the manager's actual goals and needs, preventing the other party from using that knowledge to negotiate its own substantive outcomes. Not surprisingly, the credibility of the executive's aggressive tactics and, thus, the success of the firmly competitive strategy often rests on the organization's power vis-á-vis the other party. When following a firmly competitive strategy, the manager seeks a win-lose substantive outcome and is willing to accept a neutral or even a bad relationship.

4. *Active Avoidance (A1)*. Managers should consider *actively avoiding negotiation* if neither the relationship nor the substantive outcomes are important to them or the organization. Simply *refusing* to negotiate is the most direct and active form of avoidance. Executives can simply tell the other party they are not interested in or willing to negotiate. Such an action, however, will usually have a negative impact on the organization's relationship with the other party. Moreover, managers must determine which issues are a waste of time to negotiate. We treat avoidance, like subordination, as an explicit, strategic behavior rather than as an option taken by default when the manager is uncertain about what to do.

However, we recognize that these unilateral strategies are most successful only in a limited set of situations. In the next section we include various *interactive* modifications that make these classic, unilateral strategies applicable to a wider set of negotiation situations.

INTERACTIVE NEGOTIATION STRATEGIES

Before using the unilateral strategies suggested by Exhibit 2, the executive should examine the negotiation from each party's perspective. The choice of a negotiation strategy should be based not only on the interests of the executive or organization, but also on the interests of the other party. The manager should anticipate the other party's substantive and relationship priorities, assessing how the negotiation is likely to progress when the parties interact. This step is crucial because the unilateral strategies described above could lead to grave problems if the other party's priorities differ. For example, when using either trusting collaboration or open subordination, the manager is vulnerable to exploitation if the other party is concerned only about substantive outcomes. When anticipating the other party's substantive and relationship priorities, executives should consider the kinds of actions the other party might take. Are those actions likely to be supportive or hostile? Will they represent short-term reactions or long-term approaches to the substantive issues under negotiation? Are those actions likely to change the party's degree of dependence on, or interdependence with, the organization? The answers will depend on (1) the history of the executive's relations with the other party and (2) the influence of key individuals and groups on the manager and the other party.

In short, executives should take into account both their own and the other party's substantive and relationship priorities in choosing a negotiating strategy. Exhibit 3 is a decision tree designed to help managers decide which strategy to use. The left side represents, in a different form, the analysis in Exhibit 2; thus, Exhibit 3 also shows how the manager's substantive and relationship priorities lead to *unilateral strategies* based solely on the manager's position. The right side illustrates how these unilateral strategies may be continued, modified, or replaced after the manager considers the other party's potential or apparent priorities.[13]

Managers should examine the appropriateness of a unilateral negotiation strategy by accounting for the other party's priorities before they use it. Sometimes such scrutiny will simply justify its use. For example, when both substantive and relationship outcomes are important to an executive, the appropriate unilateral strategy is trusting collaboration. If the manager anticipates that the other party also values both substantive and relationship outcomes (see Exhibit 3, Situation 1), he or she would continue to favor this strategy. At other times, scrutiny of the other party's priorities may suggest some modifications. We discuss next each of the interactive variations of the classic, unilateral strategies.

1. Principled Collaboration (C2). The C1 collaborative strategy assumes that the other party will reciprocate whenever the executive discloses information. However, if the manager negotiates openly and the other party is not open or is competitive, the manager could be victimized. Under such circumstances, the manager should use the

---

[13]We call these strategies *interactive* because they take into account the interactive effect of the manager's and the other party's anticipated or actual priorities concerning substantive and relationship outcomes. Interactive strategies based on anticipating the other party's priorities, as we later discuss in some length, may be changed to reflect more closely the actual priorities of the other party, as revealed through the interaction during a negotiation episode.

EXHIBIT 3   Selecting an Interactive Strategy

Manager's priorities | Other party's priorities

- Is the substantive outcome very important to the manager?
- Is the relationship outcome very important to the manager?

Unilateral strategies

- Is the substantive outcome very important to the other party?
- Is the relationship outcome very important to the other party?

Interactive strategies | Situations

	Situation
C1	1
C2. P2	2
C1	3
S2	4
C2. P2	5
P1. C2	6
P2. C1	7
C2. P2	8
C1	9
S1	10
C1	11
S1	12
C2. P2	13
A3. P1	14
A2	15
A1	16

Suggested strategies

C1: Trusting Collaboration
C2: Principled Collaboration
P1: Firm Competition
P2: Soft Competition
S1: Open Subordination
S2: Focused Subordination
A1: Active Avoidance (refuse to negotiate)
A2: Passive Avoidance (delegate negotiation)
A3: Responsive Avoidance (apply regulations)

modified collaborative strategy of principled collaboration.[14] Rather than relying on only trust and reciprocity, the manager persuades the other party to conduct negotiations based on a set of mutually agreed upon principles that will benefit each negotiator.

2. Focused Subordination (S2). The openly subordinative strategy (S1) assumes that the substantive outcome is of little importance to the organization. Sometimes, however, an organization has both substantive and relationship interests, but the other party has little stake in either interest. By discovering and then acquiescing to those key needs that are of interest only to the other party, the manager can still gain some substantive outcomes for the organization while assuring a relatively positive relationship outcome. Here, managers both create substantive outcomes for the other party and achieve substantive outcomes for themselves or their organization.

3. Soft Competition (P2). Under some circumstances the directness of the firmly competitive strategy (P1) may need to be softened. For example, even though the manager may place little importance on the relationship outcome, this relationship may be very important to the other party. If the other party is powerful and potentially threatening, the manager would be wise to use a competitive strategy that maintains the relationship. Here the executive would avoid highly aggressive and other "dirty" tactics.

4. Passive Avoidance (A2). If the manager does not consider either the relationship or the substantive outcome important but the other party views the negotiation as important for a relationship outcome, the manager probably should *delegate* the negotiation. By passively avoiding the negotiation, the manager allows someone else within the organization to explore possible outcomes for the organization and keep the relationship from becoming hostile. Delegating ensures that possible opportunities are not ignored while freeing the executive from what appears to be a low-priority negotiation.

5. Responsive Avoidance (A3). By contrast, if the manager considers neither the relationship nor the substantive outcome important and the other party considers the substantive outcome important and the relationship unimportant, the manager should *regulate* the issue. Direct interaction with the other party is not necessary; the manager can be responsive but still avoid negotiating by either applying standard operating procedures or developing new policies that address the other party's concern.

Transforming Unilateral Strategies

The model of strategic choice in Exhibit 3 connects unilateral and interactive negotiation strategies. In many instances the interactive strategies are modifications of the unilateral strategies. We base the decision to modify or replace a unilateral strategy almost exclusively on the manager's and other party's differing outcome priorities. Three outcome conditions and three sets of assumptions influence the choice of interactive strategies.

1. Outcome Condition One: The manager may value the relationship, but the other party may not. For example, a manager who assumes that trust and cooperation will result in a fair outcome may be taken advantage of by another party who is concerned

---

[14]See Fisher and Ury, note 3.

with only substantive outcomes.[15] Hence, we suggest either principled collaboration or soft competition for such cases to ensure that the other party does not take advantage of the manager (see Exhibit 3, Situation 2). On the other hand, the manager may simply want to create a long-term business relationship with someone who currently is interested in neither substantive nor relationship outcomes. In these cases the manager should choose to subordinate in a focused fashion—rather than to trustingly collaborate—to establish a relationship with the other party (see Exhibit 3, Situation 4).

2. *Outcome Condition Two: The manager may not value the relationship, but the other party may.* Given only their own substantive priorities, managers would firmly compete or actively avoid negotiation under these circumstances. However, if the other party is interested in the relationship, the manager may not have to compete firmly to obtain desired substantive outcomes. The manager may collaborate or softly compete and still gain substantive goals without alienating the other party (see Exhibit 3, Situations 5–8). Such strategies may also foster a long-term relationship with substantive dividends for the manager.

Similarly, in situations where neither substantive nor relationship outcomes are important to the manager but the relationship is important to the other party, the manager may choose an interactive strategy other than avoidance. The other party is in a position to choose a subordinative strategy and may offer substantive incentives to the manager. If the manager chooses principled collaboration or soft competition, he or she may gain some positive substantive outcomes (see Exhibit 3, Situation 13).

3. *Outcome Condition Three.* Both parties may value the relationship, but the manager may not value substantive outcomes. In these cases, whether or not the other party is interested in substantive outcomes, the manager may choose a trustingly collaborative strategy to maintain positive ties with the other party (see Exhibit 3, Situations 9 and 11).

4. *Transformation Assumptions.* Underlying these three outcome conditions are three sets of assumptions. First, we assume that most relationships will involve some mixture of dependence and interdependence as well as some degree of supportiveness and hostility. Second, we assume that most negotiators will view the relationship outcome as important under four separate conditions—high interdependence, high dependence, high supportiveness, or high hostility—or possible combinations of those conditions. Third, from a manager's perspective, each of the basic strategies has a different effect with regard to power and conflict: (1) collaborative strategies strengthen the interdependence of the manager and the other party while also enhancing feelings of supportiveness, (2) subordinative strategies increase the other party's dependence on the manager while also de-emphasizing feelings of hostility, and (3) competitive strategies decrease the manager's dependence on the other party but may also escalate feelings of hostility.

Thus many of the interactive negotiation strategies in Exhibit 3 seek to enhance interdependent relationships or favorably shift the balance of dependence within a relationship. These same strategies also attempt to dampen feelings of hostility or heighten feelings of supportiveness.

---

[15]See, for example, L. L. Cummings, D. L. Harnett, and O. J. Stevens, "Risk, Fate, Conciliation and Trust: An International Study of Attitudinal Differences Among Executives," *Academy of Management Journal,* 1971, 14, pp. 285–304.

Illustrations of Negotiation-Strategy Transformations

To demonstrate more concretely how Exhibit 3 works, we will examine how Dickerson's Peterson might act if he were to follow the decision tree to choose his negotiation strategies.

1. From Avoidance to Collaboration or Competition. In planning to meet with the steering clutch salesman, Peterson first considers whether the substantive outcome is very important to Dickerson Machinery. Because the company already has a satisfactory source for clutch disks, the substantive outcome is not very important. Second, Peterson considers the importance of the relationship outcome. Given that Dickerson Machinery currently has no ties with Roadworks and Peterson foresees no need to establish a long-term relationship, the relationship outcome is not very important either. Based on Peterson's priorities only, unilateral avoidance strategy (A1) seems appropriate.

However, Peterson now considers the salesman's priorities. First, is the substantive outcome important to the salesman? Obviously, it is—Roadworks is a struggling, new company and needs new clients. Second, is the relationship outcome important to Roadworks? Because the salesman works on a commission with residuals, he probably desires a long-term sales contract, so the relationship outcome is important. The salesman's priorities suggest that he would probably collaborate trustingly (C1).

After answering the questions forming the decision tree in Exhibit 3 (see Situation 13), Peterson has two options for an interactive strategy. Since he is in a position of power, he does not need to make concessions. Moreover, the salesman may have products worthy of consideration. Thus, Peterson can engage in principled collaboration (C2) or softly compete (P2). In other words, he can collaborate based on principles, taking a strong stand on what he expects in a sales contract; or he can softly compete by making product demands that do not offend the salesman.

2. From Collaboration to Subordination. For the situation with the contractor, the relationship outcome is very important to Dickerson Machinery but the immediate, substantive outcome is not. Peterson realizes that Dickerson needs Tarco's business for long-term stability but does not need to make a profit in the short term. Therefore, his unilateral strategy would be to subordinate openly (S1). He decides to change his strategy from the trustingly collaborative (C1) approach he has used in past dealings with Tarco.

As Peterson considers the contractor's priorities, he anticipates that the substantive outcome is important to Tarco but the relationship outcome is not. Tarco's representative has made clear the need for reliable service at the lowest possible price; conversely, Tarco has not responded to Peterson's bids to provide service for more than two years. Peterson recognizes, based on Exhibit 2, that Tarco can compete firmly (P1). After assessing both parties' priorities using the decision tree (see Exhibit 3, Situation 10), he decides he should continue with an interactive strategy of open subordination (S1). Such a strategy is more likely to induce Tarco's representative to offer a contract than the trustingly collaborative strategy he has used previously. For example, he is prepared to subordinate by offering a "winter special" to reduce labor costs by 10 percent, cutting competitive parts costs by 15 percent, and providing a new paint job at 50 percent the normal costs or providing a 6-month deferment on payment, all in addition to paying for the trip to the plant.

3. From Competition to Collaboration. Peterson's analysis of the negotiation with the labor union includes an assessment of the recent history of and level of conflict between the union and the company. Previous episodes in this contract negotiation have led both the union and Dickerson Machinery to change their priorities. During the first few episodes, both parties focused on only substantive outcomes and ignored relationship outcomes, using firmly competitive strategies. Also, during these earlier episodes, both sides' demands hardened to the point where the union threatened to strike and management threatened to give no increases in wages or benefits.

Now, however, Peterson believes that both substantive and relationship outcomes are important to Dickerson. The company wants to find a way to increase productivity without giving much of an increase in pay and benefits. It also does not want to lose good mechanics or stimulate a strike. Dickerson's unilateral strategy under these new conditions should be trustingly collaborative (C1).

From analyzing the union's position, Peterson realizes that both the substantive and relationship outcomes should be important to the union. His informal discussions with union representatives have assured him that both sides are now concerned about maintaining the relationship. Nonetheless, the union clearly wants an increase in pay and benefits even though it also does not want a strike. In short, the union now is likely to trustingly collaborate but could easily shift its priorities and choose to firmly compete.

As he enters the negotiation strategy session this afternoon, Peterson plans to recommend to the management negotiation team the use of a principled collaborative (C2) strategy (see Exhibit 3, Situation 2). Because of the current instability in the relationship, he does not want to provide the union with any opportunity to exploit a perceived weakness that a more trustingly collaborative strategy might create.

Monitoring and Reevaluating Strategies

After implementing their interactive strategy, managers should monitor the other party's tactics. How the other party acts will signal its strategy. Based on the other party's tactics, executives can (1) determine if their assumptions and expectations about the other party's strategy are accurate and (2) modify, if needed, their strategies during this and subsequent negotiation episodes. Exhibit 1 provides an overview of this process. The arrows linking strategies to tactics and the negotiation episode represent how tactics (1) are used to implement a strategy (first arrow), (2) provide information to each party (second, reversed arrow), and (3) may affect the choice of alternative strategies during a negotiation episode (third arrow).

Monitoring Tactics

More specifically, we view tactics in two ways: (1) as clusters of specific actions associated with the implementation of one strategy or another, and (2) as actions that derive their strategic impact from the particular phase of the negotiation in which they are used. In Exhibit 4, we combine these two perspectives to provide executives with descriptions of competitive, collaborative, and subordinative tactics across various phases of negotiation. We suggest that most negotiations go through four phases: (1) the

EXHIBIT 4 Using Tactics across Negotiation Phases

Negotiation Phases	Negotiation Tactics		
	Competitive	Collaborative	Subordinative
The search for an arena and agenda formulation	• Seek to conduct negotiations on manager's home ground • Demand discussion of manager's agenda items; curtail discussions of other party's items • Ignore or discount the other party's demands and requests	• Seek to conduct negotiations on neutral ground • Elicit the other party's agenda items and assert manager's items; incorporate both • Consider other party's demands and requests	• Seek to conduct negotiations on the other party's ground • Elicit the other party's agenda items and subvert manager's items • Concede to the other party's demands and requests
The stating of demands and offers	• Insist other party make initial offers or demands on all items • Respond with very low offers or very high demands • Commit to each item; exaggerate manager's position and discredit other party's	• Alternate initial offers and demands on items with other party • Respond with moderate offers or moderate demands • Indicate reasons for manager's commitment to item outcomes; probe the other party's reasons	• Make initial offers or demands on all other party-relevant items • Make high offers or low demands • Accept the other party's commitments to items; explain manager's commitments
A narrowing of differences	• Demand that other party make concessions; back up demand with threats • Delete, add, or yield only on low manager-interest items • Magnify degree of manager's concessions; downplay other party's	• Seek equitable exchange of concessions with the other party • Delete, add, or yield items if mutual interests converge • Honestly assess manager's and other party's concessions	• Concede to the other party's demands • Delete, add, or yield to any other party-relevant item • Acknowledge the other party's concessions; downplay manager's concessions
Final bargaining	• Seek large concessions from the other party • Concede only minimally on high manager-interest items • Use concessions on low manager-interest items as bargaining chips	• Seek equitable exchange of concessions from the other party • Seek mutually beneficial outcomes when conceding or accepting concessions on items	• Yield to the other party's relevant preferences by accepting low offers and making low demands

search for an arena and agenda formulation, (2) the stating of demands and offers, (3) a narrowing of differences, and (4) final bargaining.[16] Not every negotiation will involve all of these phases. Rather, these phases characterize typical negotiations in mixed-motive situations. Hence, a specific phase may be skipped or never attained.[17]

For example, the search for an arena in which to carry out discussions may be unnecessary for some ongoing negotiations; however, most negotiations will initially involve some Phase 1 interaction about the items to be discussed. During the second phase, both the manager and the other party express their preferences and establish their commitments to specific issues and outcomes. The third phase may be skipped, although it usually occurs if the manager and the other party are far apart in their preferences and commitments. Both sides may add or delete bargaining items or shift preferences to avoid an impasse. The fourth phase completes the negotiation: The manager and the other party reduce their alternatives, making joint decisions about each item until a final agreement is reached.

Exhibit 4 should help managers recognize (1) how using certain tactics during various phases of a negotiation is essential to implementing their strategy and (2) how the tactics of the other party reflect a particular strategic intent. An unanticipated strategy implemented by the other party may indicate that the executive inaccurately assessed the negotiation context or under- or over-estimated the strength of the other party's priorities. Hence, once the manager recognizes the other party's actual strategy, he or she should reassess the negotiation, repeating the process discussed in previous sections to check the appropriateness of his or her strategies.

Sometimes, however, the other party's use of an unanticipated strategy does not mean the executive's assessment of the negotiation context was inaccurate. In Exhibit 3, some combinations of the manager's and other party's priorities result in the listing of two interactive strategies. Managers should normally use the first (left-hand) strategies in these listings. The secondary (right-hand) strategies are suggested as countermoves the executive should use if the other party uses a strategy different from the one expected, but the executive remains convinced that his or her diagnosis is accurate.

Reevaluating Negotiation Strategies

Take, for example, Peterson's appointment with the mechanic who had swapped a battery from a company truck with his own used battery. Going into the negotiation

---

[16]Different researchers offer varying descriptions of negotiation phases. See L. Putnam's "Bargaining as Organizational Communication," in R. D. McPhee and P. K. Tompkins' (Eds.) *Organizational Communication: Traditional Themes and New Directions*, Beverly Hills, Calif.: Sage Publications, 1985, for a summary of this research. Ann Douglas proposed the first three-step model in "The Peaceful Settlement of Industrial and Intergroup Disputes," *Journal of Conflict Resolution,*1957, 1, pp. 69–81. However, this model and subsequent three-stage models do not consider the search for the arena as a component phase of a negotiation. P. Gulliver's *Disputes and Negotiations: A Cross-Cultural Perspective*, New York: Academic Press, 1979, proposes an eight-stage model of negotiation, remedying that oversight. Our proposed four-phase model condenses and draws extensively from Gulliver's work.

[17]Additionally, we view the phases of negotiation as conceptually separate from our notion of negotiation episodes (see Exhibit 1). All four phases may take place during one episode, particularly if the negotiation involves a single issue of low concern to one or another negotiator. On the other hand, during very complex negotiations stretching over a period of months, numerous episodes may constitute each phase.

Peterson decides that his unilateral strategy should be trusting collaboration: The mechanic is highly skilled and would be hard to replace, yet the infraction is a serious matter. He also anticipates that the employee will be interested primarily in retaining a good relationship with Dickerson's management. Hence, Peterson decides to stick with trusting collaboration as his interactive strategy (see Exhibit 3, Situation 3).

However, during the first five minutes of the meeting, Peterson's efforts to discuss returning the battery to the company and removing the infraction from the mechanic's personnel record are repeatedly rebuffed by the employee. Instead, the mechanic threatens to retire early from Dickerson and collect the benefits due him unless Peterson transfers him. Peterson recognizes that the mechanic is employing competitive tactics to set the agenda, which reflects an interest in substantive outcomes but little concern for relationship outcomes.

As the negotiation enters the next phase, Peterson considers the mechanic's apparent priorities and reevaluates his own priorities. Now neither the substantive nor the relationship outcomes are very important to him. He knows that Dickerson has no opening for the mechanic at any other shop; moreover, if the employee wants to leave, the relationship is of little value. Based on this reassessment (see Exhibit 3, Situation 14), Peterson sees that he has two interactive strategic options: He can regulate the matter (A3) by pressing criminal charges or compete firmly (P1) with the employee.

Rather than withdraw from the interaction, Peterson decides to compete firmly and tells the mechanic that unless the battery is returned, he will do everything he can legally do to prevent the mechanic from receiving optimal severance benefits. If the employee refuses to return the battery, Peterson can still request Dickerson's legal department to file criminal charges against him (A3) as a way to publicize and enforce a legitimate regulatory approach designed to help the company avoid this kind of negotiation.

DISCUSSION

Most of the negotiation literature focuses on substantive outcomes without systematically considering the ways negotiations affect relationships. The approach we have taken underscores how negotiation strategies should address both parties' substantive and relationship priorities. Further, we encourage executives proactively to view negotiation as an indeterminate, reiterative, and often confusing process. It requires them to anticipate and monitor the other party's actions. The other party's tactics will inform managers as to whether their assumptions about the other party's priorities and strategy are correct. Based on this assessment, managers can modify their negotiation strategies as needed during current or future episodes.

Managers should need, however, a few caveats about our advice:

1. Underlying the strategic choice model in Exhibit 3 is the assumption that most negotiations are of the mixed-motive sort; that is, the manager and other party usually negotiate over several substantive items. Some items have potential outcomes that can benefit both negotiators; others have potential outcomes that can benefit only one negotiator. Under these conditions, collaborative, competitive, and subordinative strategies may all come into play as the negotiators seek either win-win, win-lose, or yield-win substantive outcomes. Our emphasis in the

model is on win-win substantive outcomes brought about through collaborative strategies (C1 and C2).

2. We assume that most relationships will involve some mixture of dependence and interdependence. Furthermore, we posit that most negotiators will view the relationship outcome as important when it is characterized by either high interdependence or high dependence. Collaborative strategies will strengthen the interdependence of the organization and the other party, subordinative strategies will increase the other party's dependence on the organization, and competitive strategies will decrease the organization's dependence on the other party. Our advice about negotiation strategies is directed particularly toward managers who want to enhance relationships of interdependence or favorably shift the balance of dependence within a relationship.

3. We also recognize that the history and level of conflict between an organization and another party strongly influence each negotiator's attitude toward the existing relationship. Feelings of hostility, we assume, will be escalated by a competitive strategy; in contrast, feelings of hostility will be de-emphasized by a subordinative strategy. Following this same logic, feelings of supportiveness will be enhanced by a collaborative strategy. Several of the strategies suggested in Figure 3—trusting collaboration, soft competition, open subordination, and passive and responsive avoidance—attempt to dampen hostilities and increase supportiveness between the manager and the other party.

4. Our advice to executives is simultaneously well supported and speculative. On one hand, the classic (unilateral) strategies suggested in Exhibit 3 are fairly well supported within the negotiation literature; the link between these strategies and both relationship and substantive outcomes is the special focus of our approach. On the other hand, the effectiveness of the interactive strategies suggested in Exhibit 3 remains open to continuing empirical investigations. We have developed this interactive model of strategic choice by linking our concerns about relationship outcomes with what is currently known about the basic strategies of negotiations.

Although the three sets of assumptions we make about relationships are usually warranted in most organization-related negotiations, executives should carefully consider whether their situations fit with these constraints before using our strategic choice model (Exhibit 3). However, regardless of the situation, we believe that managers will generally be more effective negotiators when they carefully assess both (1) the relationship and the substantive aspects of any potential negotiation and (2) what is important to the other party and what is important to them.

The Problem of Cooperation

Robert Axelrod

Under what conditions will cooperation emerge in a world of egoists without central authority? This question has intrigued people for a long time. And for good reason. We all know that people are not angels, and that they tend to look after themselves and their own first. Yet we also know that cooperation does occur and that our civilization is based upon it. But, in situations where each individual has an incentive to be selfish, how can cooperation ever develop?

The answer each of us gives to this question has a fundamental effect on how we think and act in our social, political, and economic relations with others. And the answers that others give have a great effect on how ready they will be to cooperate with us.

The most famous answer was given over three hundred years ago by Thomas Hobbes. It was pessimistic. He argued that before governments existed, the state of nature was dominated by the problem of selfish individuals who competed on such ruthless terms that life was "solitary, poor, nasty, brutish, and short" (Hobbes 1651/1962, p. 100). In his view, cooperation could not develop without a central authority, and consequently a strong government was necessary. Ever since, arguments about the proper scope of government have often focused on whether one could, or could not, expect cooperation to emerge in a particular domain if there were not an authority to police the situation.

Today nations interact without central authority. Therefore the requirements for the emergence of cooperation have relevance to many of the central issues of international politics. The most important problem is the security dilemma: nations often seek their own security through means which challenge the security of others. This problem arises in such areas as escalation of local conflicts and arms races. Related problems occur in international relations in the form of competition within alliances, tariff negotiations, and communal conflict in places like Cyprus.

The Soviet invasion of Afghanistan in 1979 presented the United States with a typical dilemma of choice. If the United States continued business as usual, the Soviet Union might be encouraged to try other forms of noncooperative behavior later on. On the other hand, any substantial lessening of United States cooperation risked some form of retaliation, which could then set off counterretaliation, setting up a pattern of mutual hostility that could be difficult to end. Much of the domestic debate about foreign policy is concerned with problems of just this type. And properly so, since these are hard choices.

In everyday life, we may ask ourselves how many times we will invite acquaintances for dinner if they never invite us over in return. An executive in an organization does favors for another executive in order to get favors in exchange. A journalist who has received a leaked news story gives favorable coverage to the source in the hope that further leaks will be forthcoming. A business firm in an industry with only one other major company charges high prices with the expectation that the other firm will also maintain high prices—to their mutual advantage and at the expense of the consumer.

For me, a typical case of the emergence of cooperation is the development of patterns of behavior in a legislative body such as the United States Senate. Each senator has an incentive to appear effective to his or her constituents, even at the expense of conflicting with other senators who are trying to appear effective to *their* constituents. But this is hardly a situation of completely opposing interests, a zero-sum game. On the contrary, there are many opportunities for mutually rewarding activities by two senators. These mutually rewarding actions have led to the creation of an elaborate set of norms, or folkways, in the Senate. Among the most important of these is the norm of reciprocity—a folkway which involves helping out a colleague and getting repaid in kind. It includes vote trading but extends to so many types of mutually rewarding behavior that "it is not an exaggeration to say that reciprocity is a way of life in the Senate" (Matthews, 1960, p. 100; see also Mayhew, 1975).

Washington was not always like this. Early observers saw the members of the Washington community as quite unscrupulous, unreliable, and characterized by "falsehood, deceit, treachery" (Smith, 1906, p. 190). In the 1980s the practice of reciprocity is well established. Even the significant changes in the Senate over the last two decades, tending toward more decentralization, more openness, and more equal distribution of power, have come without abating the folkway of reciprocity (Ornstein, Peabody, and Rhode, 1977). As will be seen, it is *not* necessary to assume that senators are more honest, more generous, or more public-spirited than in earlier years to explain how cooperation based on reciprocity has emerged or proved stable. The emergence of cooperation can be explained as a consequence of individual senators pursuing their own interests.

The approach of this [chapter] is to investigate how individuals pursuing their own interests will act, followed by an analysis of what effects this will have for the system as a whole. Put another way, the approach is to make some assumptions about individual motives and then deduce consequences for the behavior of the entire system (Schelling, 1978). The case of the U.S. Senate is a good example, but the same style of reasoning can be applied to other settings.

The object of this enterprise is to develop a theory of cooperation that can be used to discover what is necessary for cooperation to emerge. By understanding the conditions that allow it to emerge, appropriate actions can be taken to foster the development of cooperation in a specific setting.

The Cooperation Theory that is presented in this [chapter] is based upon an investigation of individuals who pursue their own self-interest without the aid of a central authority to force them to cooperate with each other. The reason for assuming self-interest is that it allows an examination of the difficult case in which cooperation is not completely based upon a concern for others or upon the welfare of the group as a whole. It must, however, be stressed that this assumption is actually much less restrictive than it appears. If a sister is concerned for the welfare of her brother, the sister's self-interest can be thought of as including (among many other things) this concern for the welfare of her brother. But this does not necessarily eliminate all potential for conflict between sister and brother. Likewise a nation may act in part out of regard for the interests of its friends, but this regard does not mean that even friendly countries are always able to cooperate for their mutual benefit. So the assumption of self-interest is really just an assumption that concern for others does not completely solve the problem of when to cooperate with them and when not to.

A good example of the fundamental problem of cooperation is the case where two industrial nations have erected trade barriers to each other's exports. Because of the mutual advantages of free trade, both countries would be better off if these barriers were eliminated. But if either country were to unilaterally eliminate its barriers, it would find itself facing terms of trade that hurt its own economy. In fact, whatever one country does, the other country is better off retaining its own trade barriers. Therefore, the problem is that each country has an incentive to retain trade barriers, leading to a worse outcome than would have been possible had both countries cooperated with each other.

This basic problem occurs when the pursuit of self-interest by each leads to a poor outcome for all. To make headway in understanding the vast array of specific situations which have this property, a way is needed to represent what is common to these situations without becoming bogged down in the details unique to each. Fortunately, there is such a representation available: the famous *Prisoner's Dilemma* game.

In the Prisoner's Dilemma game, there are two players. Each has two choices, namely cooperate or defect. Each must make the choice without knowing what the other will do. No matter what the other does, defection yields a higher payoff than cooperation. The dilemma is that if both defect, both do worse than if both had cooperated. This simple game will provide the basis for the entire analysis used in this book.

The way the game works is shown in Figure 1. One player chooses a row, either cooperating or defecting. The other player simultaneously chooses a column, either cooperating or defecting. Together, these choices result in one of the four possible outcomes shown in that matrix. If both players cooperate, both do fairly well. Both get *R,* the *reward for mutual cooperation.* In the concrete illustration of Figure 1 the reward is 3 points. This number might, for example, be a payoff in dollars that each player gets for that outcome. If one player cooperates but the other defects, the defecting player gets the *temptation to defect,* while the cooperating player gets the *sucker's payoff.* In the example, these are 5 points and 0 points, respectively. If both defect, both get 1 point, the *punishment for mutual defection.*

What should you do in such a game? Suppose you are the row player, and you think the column player will cooperate. This means that you will get one of the two outcomes in the first column of Figure 1. You have a choice. You can cooperate as well,

FIGURE 1   The Prisoner's Dilemma

		Column Player	
		Cooperate	*Defect*
	Cooperate	$R = 3, R = 3$ Reward for mutual cooperation	$S = 0, T = 5$ Sucker's payoff, and temptation to defect
Row Player	Defect	$T = 5, S = 0$ Temptation to defect and sucker's payoff	$P = 1, P = 1$ Punishment for mutual defection

Note: The payoffs to the row chooser are listed first.

getting the 3 points of the reward for mutual cooperation. Or you can defect, getting the 5 points of the temptation payoff. So it pays to defect if you think the other player will cooperate. But now suppose that you think the other player will defect. Now you are in the second column of Figure 1, and you have a choice between cooperating, which would make you a sucker and give you 0 points, and defecting, which would result in mutual punishment, giving you 1 point. So it pays to defect if you think the other player will defect. This means that it is better to defect if you think the other player will cooperate, *and* it is better to defect if you think the other player will defect. So no matter what the other player does, it pays for you to defect.

So far, so good. But the same logic holds for the other player too. Therefore, the other player should defect no matter what you are expected to do. So you should both defect. But then you both get 1 point which is worse than the 3 points of the reward that you both could have gotten had you both cooperated. Individual rationality leads to a worse outcome for both than is possible. Hence the dilemma.

The Prisoner's Dilemma is simply an abstract formulation of some very common and very interesting situations in which what is best for each person individually leads to mutual defection, whereas everyone would have been better off with mutual cooperation. The definition of Prisoner's Dilemma requires that several relationships hold among the four different potential outcomes. The first relationship specifies the order of the four payoffs. The best a player can do is get T, the temptation to defect when the other player cooperates. The worst a player can do is get S, the sucker's payoff for cooperating while the other player defects. In ordering the other two outcomes, R, the reward for mutual cooperation, is assumed to be better than P, the punishment for mutual defection. This leads to a preference ranking of the four payoffs from best to worst as $T, R, P,$ and S.

The second part of the definition of the Prisoner's Dilemma is that the players cannot get out of their dilemma by taking turns exploiting each other. This assumption means that an even chance of exploitation and being exploited is not as good an outcome for a player as mutual cooperation. It is therefore assumed that the reward for mutual cooperation is greater than the average of the temptation and the sucker's payoff. This assumption, together with the rank ordering of the four payoffs, defines the Prisoner's Dilemma.

Thus two egoists playing the game *once* will both choose their dominant choice, defection, and each will get less than they both could have gotten if they had cooperated. If the game is played a known finite number of times, the players still have no incentive to cooperate. This is certainly true on the last move since there is no future to influence. On the next-to-last move neither player will have an incentive to cooperate since they can both anticipate a defection by the other player on the very last move. Such a line of reasoning implies that the game will unravel all the way back to mutual defection on the first move of any sequence of plays that is of known finite length (Luce and Raiffa, 1957, pp. 99–102). This reasoning does not apply if the players will interact an indefinite number of times. And in most realistic settings, the players cannot be sure when the last interaction between them will take place . . . . With an indefinite number of interactions, cooperation can emerge. The issue then becomes the discovery of the precise conditions that are necessary and sufficient for cooperation to emerge.

* * * * *

A variety of ways to resolve the Prisoner's Dilemma have been developed. Each involves allowing some additional activity that alters the strategic interaction in such a way as to fundamentally change the nature of the problem. The original problem remains, however, because there are many situations in which these remedies are not available. Therefore, the problem will be considered in its fundamental form, without these alterations.

1. There is no mechanism available to the players to make enforceable threats or commitments (Schelling, 1960). Since the players cannot commit themselves to a particular strategy, each must take into account all possible strategies that might be used by the other player. Moreover, the players have all possible strategies available to themselves.

2. There is no way to be sure what the other player will do on a given move. This eliminates the possibility of metagame analysis (Howard, 1971) which allows such options as "make the same choice as the other is about to make." It also eliminates the possibility of reliable reputations such as might be based on watching the other player interact with third parties. Thus the only information available to the players about each other is the history of their interaction so far.

3. There is no way to eliminate the other player or run away from the interaction. Therefore each player retains the ability to cooperate or defect on each move.

4. There is no way to change the other player's payoffs. The payoffs already include whatever consideration each player has for the interests of the other (Taylor, 1976, pp. 69–73).

Under these conditions, words not backed by actions are so cheap as to be meaningless. The players can communicate with each other only through the sequence of their own behavior. This is the problem of the Prisoner's Dilemma in its fundamental form.

What makes it possible for cooperation to emerge is the fact that the players might meet again. This possibility means that the choices made today not only determine the outcome of this move, but can also influence the later choices of the players. The future can therefore cast a shadow back upon the present and thereby affect the current strategic situation.

But the future is less important than the present—for two reasons. The first is that players tend to value payoffs less as the time of their obtainment recedes into the future. The second is that there is always some chance that the players will not meet again. An ongoing relationship may end when one or the other player moves away, changes jobs, dies, or goes bankrupt.

*   *   *   *   *

The first question you are tempted to ask is, "What is the best strategy?" In other words, what strategy will yield a player the highest possible score? This is a good question, but . . . no best rule exists independently of the strategy being used by the other player. In this sense, the iterated Prisoner's Dilemma is completely different from a game like chess. A chess master can safely use the assumption that the other player will make the most feared move. This assumption provides a basis for planning in a game like chess, where the interests of the players are completely antagonistic. But the situations represented by the Prisoner's Dilemma game are quite different. The interests of the players are not in total conflict. Both players can do well by getting the reward, R, for mutual cooperation or both can do poorly by getting the punishment, P, for mutual defection. Using the assumption that the other player will always make the move you fear most will lead you to expect that the other will never cooperate, which in turn will lead you to defect, causing unending punishment. So unlike chess, in the Prisoner's Dilemma it is not safe to assume that the other player is out to get you.

In fact, in the Prisoner's Dilemma, the strategy that works best depends directly on what strategy the other player is using and, in particular, on whether this strategy leaves room for the development of mutual cooperation. This principle is based on the weight [W] of the next move relative to the current move being sufficiently large to make the future important. In other words, the discount parameter, w, must be large enough to make the future loom large in the calculation of total payoffs. After all, if you are unlikely to meet the other person again, or if you care little about future payoffs, then you might as well defect now and not worry about the consequences for the future.

This leads to the first formal proposition. It is the sad news that if the future is important, there is no one best strategy.

Proposition 1.   If the discount parameter, w, is sufficiently high, there is no best strategy independent of the strategy used by the other player.

*   *   *   *   *

In the case of a legislature such as the U.S. Senate, this proposition says that if there is a large enough chance that a member of the legislature will interact *again* with another member, there is no one best strategy to use independently of the strategy being used by the other person. It would be best to cooperate with someone who will reciprocate that cooperation in the future, but not with someone whose future behavior will not be very much affected by this interaction (see, for example, Hinckley, 1972). The very possibility of achieving stable mutual cooperation depends upon there being a good chance of a continuing interaction, as measured by the magnitude of w. As it happens, in the case of Congress, the chance of two members having a continuing interaction has increased dramatically as the biennial turnover rates have fallen from about 40 percent in the first 40 years of the republic to about 20 percent or less in recent years (Young, 1966, pp. 87–90; Polsby, 1968; Jones, 1977, p. 154; Patterson, 1978, pp. 143–44).

However, saying that a continuing chance of interaction is necessary for the development of cooperation is not the same as saying that it is sufficient. The demonstration that there is not a single best strategy leaves open the question of what patterns of behavior can be expected to emerge when there actually is a sufficiently high probability of continuing interaction between two individuals.

Before going on to study the behavior that can be expected to emerge, it is a good idea to take a closer look at which features of reality the Prisoner's Dilemma framework is, and is not, able to encompass. Fortunately, the very simplicity of the framework makes it possible to avoid many restrictive assumptions that would otherwise limit the analysis:

1. The payoffs of the players need not be comparable at all. For example, a journalist might get rewarded with another inside story, while the cooperating bureaucrat might be rewarded with a chance to have a policy argument presented in a favorable light.

2. The payoffs certainly do not have to be symmetric. It is a convenience to think of the interaction as exactly equivalent from the perspective of the two players, but this is not necessary. One does not have to assume, for example, that the reward for mutual cooperation, or any of the other three payoff parameters, has the same magnitude for both players. As mentioned earlier, one does not even have to assume that they are measured in comparable units. The only thing that has to be assumed is that, for each player, the four payoffs are ordered as required for the definition of the Prisoner's Dilemma.

3. The payoffs of a player do not have to be measured on an absolute scale. They need only be measured relative to each other.

4. Cooperation need not be considered desirable from the point of view of the rest of the world. There are times when one wants to retard, rather than foster, cooperation between players. Collusive business practices are good for the businesses involved but not so good for the rest of society. In fact, most forms of corruption are welcome instances of cooperation for the participants but are unwelcome to everyone else. So, on occasion, the theory will be used in reverse to show how to prevent, rather than to promote, cooperation.

5. There is no need to assume that the players are rational. They need not be trying to maximize their rewards. Their strategies may simply reflect standard operating procedures, rules of thumb, instincts, habits, or imitation (Simon, 1955; Cyert and March, 1963).

6. The actions that players take are not necessarily even conscious choices. A person who sometimes returns a favor, and sometimes does not, may not think about what strategy is being used. There is no need to assume deliberate choice at all.

The framework is broad enough to encompass not only people but also nations and bacteria. Nations certainly take actions which can be interpreted as choices in a Prisoner's Dilemma—as in the raising or lowering of tariffs. It is not necessary to assume that such actions are rational or are the outcome of a unified actor pursuing a single goal. On the contrary, they might well be the result of an incredibly complex bureaucratic politics involving complicated information processing and shifting political coalitions (Allison, 1971).

Likewise, at the other extreme, an organism does not need a brain to play a game. Bacteria, for example, are highly responsive to selected aspects of their chemical environment. They can therefore respond differentially to what other organisms are doing, and these conditional strategies of behavior can be inherited. Moreover, the behavior of a bacterium can affect the fitness of other organisms around it, just as the behavior of other organisms can affect the fitness of a bacterium. . . .

For now the main interest will be in people and organizations. Therefore, it is good to know that for the sake of generality, it is not necessary to assume very much about how deliberate and insightful people are. Nor is it necessary to assume, as the sociobiologists do, that important aspects of human behavior are guided by one's genes. The approach here is strategic rather than genetic.

Of course, the abstract formulation of the problem of cooperation as a Prisoner's Dilemma puts aside many vital features that make any actual interaction unique. Examples of what is left out by this formal abstraction include the possibility of verbal communication, the direct influence of third parties, the problems of implementing a choice, and the uncertainty about what the other player actually did on the preceding move. . . . It is clear that the list of potentially relevant factors that have been left out could be extended almost indefinitely. Certainly, no intelligent person should make an important choice without trying to take such complicating factors into account. The value of an analysis without them is that it can help to clarify some of the subtle features of the interaction—features which might otherwise be lost in the maze of complexities of the highly particular circumstances in which choice must actually be made. It is the very complexity of reality which makes the analysis of an abstract interaction so helpful as an aid to understanding.

. . . The emergence of cooperation [has been explored] through a study of what is a good strategy to employ if confronted with an iterated Prisoner's Dilemma. This exploration has been done in a novel way, with a computer tournament. Professional game theorists were invited to submit their favorite strategy, and each of these decision rules was paired off with each of the others to see which would do best overall. Amazingly enough, the winner was the simplest of all strategies submitted. This was TIT FOR TAT, the strategy which cooperates on the first move and then does whatever the other player did on the previous move. A second round of the tournament was conducted in which many more entries were submitted by amateurs and professionals alike, all of whom were aware of the results of the first round. The result was another victory for TIT FOR TAT! The analysis of the data from these tournaments reveals four properties which tend to make a decision rule successful: avoidance of unnecessary conflict by cooperating as long as the other player does, provocability in the face of an uncalled for defection by the other, forgiveness after responding to a provocation, and clarity of behavior so that the other player can adapt to your pattern of action.

These results from the tournaments demonstrate that under suitable conditions, cooperation can indeed emerge in a world of egoists without central authority. . . . The evolution of cooperation requires that individuals have a sufficiently large chance to meet again so that they have a stake in their future interaction. If this is true, cooperation can evolve in three stages.

1. The beginning of the story is that cooperation can get started even in a world of unconditional defection. The development *cannot* take place if it is tried only by scattered individuals who have virtually no chance to interact with each other. However, cooperation can evolve from small clusters of individuals who base their cooperation on reciprocity and have even a small proportion of their interactions with each other.

2. The middle of the story is that a strategy based on reciprocity can thrive in a world where many different kinds of strategies are being tried.

3. The end of the story is that cooperation, once established on the basis of reciprocity, can protect itself from invasion by less cooperative strategies. Thus, the gear wheels of social evolution have a ratchet.

. . . Note the fascinating case of the "live and let live" system which emerged during the trench warfare of World War I. In the midst of this bitter conflict, the front-line soldiers often refrained from shooting to kill—provided their restraint was reciprocated by the soldiers on the other side. What made this mutual restraint possible was the static nature of trench warfare, where the same small units faced each other for extended periods of time. The soldiers of these opposing small units actually violated orders from their own high commands in order to achieve tacit cooperation with each other. A detailed look at this case shows that when the conditions are present for the emergence of cooperation, cooperation can get started and prove stable in situations which otherwise appear extraordinarily unpromising. In particular, the "live and let live" system demonstrates that friendship is hardly necessary for the development of cooperation. Under suitable conditions, cooperation based upon reciprocity can develop even between antagonists.

While foresight is not necessary for the evolution of cooperation, it can certainly be helpful. . . . From the participant's point of view, the object is to do as well as possible, regardless of how well the other player does. Based upon the tournament results and the formal propositions, four simple suggestions are offered for individual choice: do not be envious of the other player's success; do not be the first to defect; reciprocate both cooperation and defection; and do not be too clever.

SECTION THREE

Distributive Bargaining: Strategy and Tactics

Earlier in this volume, we referred to different types of bargaining situations as different "structures" of bargaining. In this section and the next, we will examine two major structures of bargaining and how they pose different conditions and problems for negotiators.

In distributive bargaining, two parties have different but interdependent goals. When two parties are in a situation where they have incompatible goals, the condition is described as a fixed sum variable share payoff structure, and, sometimes, a win/lose situation. In labor negotiations, labor and management are looking at the profits being made by the company (the sum) and negotiating as to what share the workers will get as a salary increase and how much the firm will keep as profit. There is a clear conflict of interest, and each party is motivated to obtain the largest share. This type of bargaining is also referred to as competitive negotiating, hard bargaining, or win/lose negotiating.

The more one party knows about the other's strategy, the better able that party is to plan negotiations and know what can probably be obtained. Hence, much effort before and during negotiation is directed to getting as much information as possible about the other party. Of course, the same process holds true for the other side; and, hence, it is to each side's advantage to keep its own information as private as possible while trying to learn about the other side. Therefore, in distributive bargaining, we face a situation where both parties are attempting to obtain as much information about the other as possible and, at the same time, give out as little information as they can.

All negotiation strategies and tactics involve risk. While distributive bargaining tactics appear exciting and can yield large gains, they are not without the potential for large losses. Perhaps the largest potential loss involves the negotiator's reputation. Indiscriminate use of "dirty tricks" will eventually be identified in even the smoothest of hard bargainers who use them. The cost of being discovered? An irritated other party who may seek revenge, withdraw his or her business, or cause an unpleasant confrontation. Recipients of dirty tricks have the following options available: ignore them, respond with their own trick, or discuss the tactic and offer to change the bargaining process. Finally, dirty tricks is a loaded term. People draw different ethical boundaries in their lives and when they negotiate. So don't assume that the ethics of the people with whom you negotiate are the same as yours! We'll have more to say about ethics in Section Thirteen.

In the first article in this section, "Winning at the Sport of Negotiation," Kathy Aaronson presents 12 of her favorite bargaining tactics from sales negotiations. For Aaronson, negotiation is a sport where making a good deal is like scoring a touchdown. Given that you are the quarterback, you need to learn the essential plays to win each game. Aaronson discusses how to use some of the classic tactics of distributive negotiation: delay, limited authority, nibbling, and so on. The other message in the article is to label the tactics that you use (and that you see others use) so that your playbook (tactics available) can be as complete as possible for the next game (negotiation).

In the article "Negotiation Techniques," Charles Craver discusses negotiation strategies and tactics that are used by some of the best distributive negotiators: lawyers. Craver divides the negotiation process into three stages (information, competitive, cooperative) and offers important insights about strategies and tactics for each stage. While the article is full of examples from the legal profession, the information contained in the competitive negotiation section of the article is applicable to anyone who wants to sharpen his or her hard bargaining skills.

In the final article in this section, "How to Negotiate Practically Anything," professional negotiator and sports agent Bob Woolf responds to questions posed during an *Inc.* interview. Woolf's philosophy about bargaining is quite clear: one can be honest, fair, and a tough bargainer at the same time. This article contains some critical advice that may initially appear counterintuitive (for instance, Woolf never pushes the other party to concede the last dollar) but in fact forms a cogent part of an eloquent negotiation strategy. This may be distributive bargaining at its best!

Winning at the Sport of Negotiation

Kathy Aaronson

HOW TO TACKLE (AND EMPLOY) THE MOST COMMON BUSINESS NEGOTIATION TACTICS

In order to negotiate successfully and to buffer yourself from experiencing the negotiation emotionally, you must learn to recognize and develop negotiating tactics. Once you have used a tactic or experienced it being used on you, you can *label* it as such. That tactic then becomes just one in a series of possible plays—part of the negotiating game—rather than an attempt to wound or overpower you personally. The following 12 tactics are major negotiating skills.

Tactic 1: Delay

When you have the power, use it; when you don't, delay.

Say you start a job in which you are promised a salary review and the opportunity to make another $1,000 a month after six months on the job. You go into your manager's office and say, "Well, it's my six-month anniversary. Could we please discuss my salary review?"

He says, "I just don't have time now, but I'll get back to you shortly."

A week goes by, and he says, "Give me 10 days—I'm going out of town." Now you're over the moon with frustration, because you've been delayed.

Presidents of companies often can negotiate a contract with an entire foreign country, but cannot negotiate a simple compensation plan with their secretaries. This supervisor may be delaying because he doesn't know how to negotiate with you. He needs to be taught *how* to give you a raise.

When people delay, they frequently need more information to get them "unstuck"—with all the necessary information before them, it will be more difficult to justify a delay.

My suggestion in the case of the salary raise would be for you to go back into the manager's office and say, "I have a feeling you've been delaying this because you need more information from me. And you'd feel more comfortable if I gave you more information about why you should give me a raise."

You might prepare a grid illustrating every month you've been working down the far left side, with the amount of money earned per month. Another sheet would show the number of hours worked per day, the number of accounts and dollar volume of the accounts. On the next page would be another grid, showing in blue the income you've brought into the company, and in the green the income you've earned.

Give your supervisor a copy of this material and say, "I know you have to go through channels, so you could just attach a memorandum to this if you like." You have empowered him with information.

Tactic 2: Silence and Bracketing

Coupled with a tactic called bracketing, silence is very, very powerful. Information gathering is best achieved through silence. When we bracket the attention of the information giver or person we're negotiating with, we direct their concentration to a specific area of the negotiation, then listen aggressively—carefully, silently, and without jumping to respond—to everything they have to say on that subject.

If I simply say, "Let's discuss for a moment a succulent, juicy hamburger," and then I'm silent, you would fill that silence with your gut-level reaction to the specific issue of juicy hamburgers. Your response might be, "Oh, the *best* hamburger I ever had was at Joe's, and now you've got me craving another one." Or, "I don't eat meat, and the very mention of that turns my stomach." Whether your response is positive or negative is not the point: I have *bracketed* your attention to the subject, then used silence for a period to retrieve information regarding how you feel about the subject.

$$* \quad * \quad * \quad * \quad *$$

Tactic 3: Limited Authority

We've all heard this one: "I'll take this upstairs and see what we can do." "I've got to talk to my partner." "My agent makes those decisions." "I've got to send that to my lawyer."

When you've reached a point of closure and are stopped by the limited authority tactic, most likely your prospect *has* the authority, but has discovered some objection to your product, service, or idea that leads him to this point of impasse. Your move is to discover what that objection is by "repackaging" the information for the person of supposedly higher authority.

Example: "You want to review this with your attorney. How does your attorney best like the review information for his approval?"

Your prospect responds: "Well, I send it over, and he reviews it, and sends it back, and we review it together over the phone."

You say: "Well, I'd like to give you the information to present your attorney. What do you suggest I emphasize?" And reposition your presentation so that it removes any mistrust and any misunderstandings that hold potential legal problems. Because you've intuited that what he's said to you is that he doesn't trust your presentation is legally in order.

If you suspect it's the client's accountant who needs to review your proposal, ask "In what format does your accountant prefer to evaluate projects?" Once the person tells you the objections he feels his accountant will have to your presentation, you can reorganize your material as though you were presenting it to the accountant.

You are actually engaging in role-playing. Your prospect takes on the persona of the accountant—or spouse or partner or attorney—and you reorganize your material as though you were presenting it to this invisible third person.

When the invisible objector is "my partner," you ask, "What aspect of the business does your partner oversee?"

"Administration." You would then refocus your presentation as though you were presenting it to an administrator. You may actually even engage in a little outright role-playing: "Let's say you were your partner, and I were presenting this to you. . . ."

Tactic 4: The Bottom Line

This is the point below which you will not go. If the bottom line is that you can't discount a product, all of your energy must be put toward selling it for full value. You've likely heard the adage in sales and marketing: "If you have two aspirin in your pocket and don't know how to sell them, you might as well take them for all the good they'll do you." The bottom line is that you don't waste time redesigning aspirin, you direct your energy toward selling aspirin to people who need aspirin.

Whatever your product, service, or idea, at the bottom line there is a price and there are benefits. The strategy is to identify people or organizations that need it, can afford to pay for it, and can abide by the policies and procedures of the organization that employs you.

When you're negotiating, and you hit your bottom line, you cannot charge any less or redesign your offering. When you accept the bottom line, your creative problem-solving strength is directed toward those prospects who need and want what you are selling.

The bottom line is your scorecard—the description of your product, it's pricing, corporate policy regarding credit terms, volume, availability, delivery time, guarantee, and quality assurance. The configurations of these components determine the bottom line for sales athletes. The key is that you go into negotiations fully understanding what your bottom line is, and prepared to ascertain the bottom line of your prospect.

Imagine a client says his fiscal year ends December 31. The company wants your product but wants you to come back January 1, and here it is October 1. Their unspoken bottom line is that they won't have any money until January 1. Between October 1 and January 1 your competition could come in and usurp this client's enthusiasm for your product. Therefore you may want to talk to your manager and see if you can arrange a purchase order with credit terms—buy now, pay 90 days later.

Or a client company says, "I can get your product cheaper elsewhere, and I must buy on the basis of price only." In fact, you know your product withstands heat, cold, and pressure, or has a benefit above all the other products in the field that justifies its higher price. . . . Your bottom line is that you won't discount, so you use creative problem-solving skills to justify the pricing of your product and close the sale.

Tactic 5: "No"

The great value of getting a "No" from your prospect is that you can ask "Why?" and everything he tells you in response comprises precisely the circumstances under which he will buy. A "No" thus doesn't signal the end—it is the point at which the prospect trusts you enough to tell you he is not going to buy. "No" can be parlayed to a point where true feelings are disclosed, bottom lines are revealed, and where it becomes clear to you what objections you must meet in order to sell your product, service, or idea.

Tactic 6: Nibbling

Children are experts at this. Nibbling is the ability to withdraw and then return, but keep the pressure on:
"May I go to the movie?"
"First clean your room, and I'll think about it."
(Five minutes later) "May I go to the movie, please?"
"Well, did you clean your room?"
"No."
"Clean your room first."
(Ten minutes later) "I *almost* finished cleaning it. Now may I go to the movie?"
In sales, you can use nibbling as a positive negotiating tool to continually keep the subject in front of the prospect until the problem is resolved. The "touchdown" strategy requires nibbling. You can nibble as you relate to your territory like a cop on the beat, continually going back to check on client prospects, seeing them and also being seen.

Tactic 7: Expectation and Control

This is where you say, "This part is not negotiable, but that part is." All of your prospect's energy becomes redirected to the area that is negotiable. You let the prospect know what the product does and does not do, so that the prospect is not blind in his belief about your product. This is positive, clear, friendly, and honest.

Tactic 8: Auction

"I can get it cheaper (better, faster) somewhere else. . . ." This is the single most powerful tool in the hands of a buyer. If you don't know your competition, or don't know what mood they're in today, you're up against the auctioning tactic.

When confronted with this, ask what the cheaper rate is. Give your prospect more details of your presentation. Explain that the price is not negotiable, but that something else is (a better service contract, the color choices, or the delivery time).

You might say, "This is how we do business—we have trucks that work, that send our product out on time, people that stand on the docks to ensure quality control. Our competitors don't. If you're at all concerned that things might shut down or a problem be created for you should our product not arrive, we're going to ask that you consider paying a little more to make sure it does arrive on time."

Tactic 9: Concessions

Concessions, however slight, should be given very carefully, treated like gold, wrapped in silver, and presented like a gift to a monarch. They can be the key to bonding a relationship in negotiating.

*   *   *   *   *

Frequently, a mistake is made in the guise of "inducement closes." A prospect has decided not to buy, and has said something like, "It just doesn't fit." The salesperson then throws in an inducement: "If you buy it by Friday, I'll give you 10 percent off." Meanwhile, the prospect still doesn't think the product or service fits his corporation or his equipment. Salespeople may have a whole list of valuable inducements and just throw them on the prospect's desk in hopes that something will induce a sale.

Use concessions to *build* interest. That way, you can also withdraw them. You say: "If you buy five dozen, you get a display rack." The prospect says: "I'll take three dozen and a display rack." Your response is: "No, I'm sorry, I have to withdraw the rack offer because we have found that if you commit to five dozen you will build repeat business. If you buy only three dozen you won't have the depth of merchandise necessary to generate repeat sales, or to develop a reputation of being a vendor of this item."

You have offered a concession, then taken it away, thereby creating an incentive for buying on your terms and getting the concession back.

Tactic 10: Rationale

If in fact what anyone is looking for in negotiation is satisfaction, recognize that satisfaction doesn't necessarily have to be what the person is asking for.

I divide my time between lecturing and corporations. A very big problem with my work is that when I'm giving a presentation to corporations I can't take phone calls, and when I'm with a corporate client I also can't take phone calls. This means I am not always reachable. Phone calls usually come from people with a problem. At my office, therefore, there must be someone who can handle the callers so that, although they have asked for something (to speak to me) and have not received it, they leave feeling taken care of because they have been given a rationale that satisfies.

If you are to make a mistake in negotiation, it should be that you give too much rationale that satisfies rather than not enough. I once thought someone was absolutely ripping me off. The client said, "Let me break it down for you," and when he gave his rationale, the reality was that I was not being ripped off. I left satisfied even though I did not get what I originally thought I should have gotten.

Frequently, people are remiss with creditors because they are embarrassed that they cannot pay their bills. If, however, they pick up the phone and say, "Listen, there's a strike, I cannot pay in full, but let me work something out" they can negotiate to everyone's satisfaction through rationale.

Tactic 11: Message-Sending

During negotiations, messages will come your way verbally, visually, and in writing. Understanding this tactic is crucial to reading your adversary.

If all of a sudden someone stands up and looks jittery, don't talk through it. Recognize that something has just transpired. Read the nervous laughter, the jiggling foot. If all of a sudden someone starts crying—and that has happened in negotiations— the response to the message would be not to concentrate on price or services, but to move the person from an emotional position back to an intellectual position.

People send written messages, usually of a less dramatic nature but needing to be read with the same sensitivity as visual or verbal cues. A client you've been doing business with for years stops returning your calls—that's a message. Or pays his bills more slowly than usual—that's a message.

Tactic 12: Deadlines

. . . . Frequently deadlines are artificial. They can remove profitability from an account, and when you test them you learn they are in fact there because of the belief that you won't service on time.

"I need it Friday."

"Why?"

"I'm going on vacation for three weeks." That's a deadline.

"I need it Friday."

"Why?"

"We go into production Tuesday." That's a test. To which the response might be, "Well, to get it to you Friday, we will have to FedEx it, which is an extra cost. You'll either have to pay or it will remove the profit from us. Whereas if we send it our usual way, we guarantee it will get there by 9:00 A.M. Monday, which is 24 hours before your production starts."

Those are just the beginnings of a grab bag of tactics you'll see and use in negotiations. Once you begin recognizing and labeling such common moves, you'll see how much fun it is to identify and name your own. Labeling tactics makes them easier to tackle and helps you to buffer yourself from interpreting them emotionally.

*   *   *   *   *

Negotiation Techniques

Charles B. Craver

Practicing lawyers negotiate constantly—with their partners, associates, legal assistants, and secretaries, with prospective clients and actual clients, and with opposing parties on behalf of clients. Although practitioners tend to use their negotiation skills more often than their other lawyering talents, few have had formal education about the negotiation process.

The process consists of three formal phases:

- The information phase, where each party endeavors to learn as much about the other side's circumstances and objectives as possible.
- the competitive phase, where negotiators try to obtain beneficial terms for their respective clients.
- the cooperative phase, where if multiple-item transactions are involved, parties may often enhance their joint interests.

THE INFORMATION PHASE

The focus of this phase is always on the knowledge and desires of the opposing party. It is initially helpful to employ general, information-seeking questions instead of those that may be answered with a yes or no. Expansive interrogatories are likely to induce the other party to speak. The more that party talks, the more he is likely to divulge.

Where negotiators have effectively used open-ended questions to induce the other party to disclose its opening position and its general legal and factual assumptions, they should not hesitate to resort to specific inquiries to confirm suspected details. They can do this by asking the other side about each element of its perceived position. What exactly does that party hope to obtain, and why? What are the underlying motivational factors influencing that side's articulated demands?

Negotiators must try to learn as much as possible about the opposing side's range of potential and actual choices, its preferences and their intensity, its planned strategy,

Reprinted with permission of *TRIAL* (June 1988). Copyright The Association of Trial Lawyers of America.

and its strengths and weaknesses. Bargainers need to be aware that the opponent's perception of a situation may be more favorable to their own than they anticipated. Even the most proficient negotiators tend to overstate their side's weaknesses and overestimate the opposing party's strengths. Only through patient probing of their adversary's circumstances can they hope to obtain an accurate assessment.

The order in which parties present their initial demands can be informative. Some negotiators begin with their most important topics in an effort to produce an expeditious resolution of those issues. They are anxiety-prone, risk-averse advocates who wish to diminish the tension associated with the uncertainty inherent in the negotiation process. They believe they can significantly decrease their fear of not being able to settle by achieving expeditious progress on their primary topics. Unfortunately they fail to appreciate that this approach may enhance the possibility of a counterproductive impasse. If their principal objectives correspond to those of their adversary, this presentation sequence is likely to cause an immediate clash of wills.

Other negotiators prefer to begin bargaining with their less significant subjects, hoping to make rapid progress on these items. This approach is likely to develop a cooperative atmosphere that will facilitate compromise when the more disputed subjects are explored.

Negotiators must decide ahead of time what information they are willing to disclose and what information they must disclose if the transaction is going to be fruitful. Critical information should not always be directly provided. If negotiators voluntarily apprise the other side of important circumstances, this may appear self-serving and be accorded little weight. If, however, they slowly disclose such information in response to opponent questions, what they divulge will usually be accorded greater credibility.

Where an adversary asks about sensitive matters, blocking techniques may be used to minimize unnecessary disclosure. Such techniques should be planned in advance and should be varied to keep the opposing party off balance. A participant who does not wish to answer a question might ignore it, and the other side might go on to some other area.

Where a compound question is asked, a negotiator may respond to the beneficial part of it. Skilled negotiators may misconstrue a delicate inquiry and then answer the misconstrued formulation; they may respond to a specific question with general information or to a general inquiry with a narrow response. On occasion, negotiators may handle a difficult question with a question of their own. For example, if one party asks whether the other is authorized to offer a certain sum, that side may ask about the first party's willingness to accept such a figure.

Many negotiators make the mistake of focusing entirely on their opponents' stated positions. They assume that such statements accurately reflect the desires of the other side. Making this assumption may preclude the exploration of options that might prove mutually beneficial. It helps to go behind stated positions to try to ascertain the underlying needs and interests generating these positions. If negotiators understand what the other party really wants to achieve, they can often suggest alternatives that can satisfy both sides sufficiently to produce an accord.

THE COMPETITIVE PHASE

Once the information phase ends, the focus usually changes from what the opposing party hopes to achieve to what each negotiator must get for his client. Negotiators no longer ask questions about each other's circumstances; they articulate their own side's demands.

"Principled" Offers and Concessions

Negotiators should develop a rational basis for each item included in their opening positions. This provides the other party with some understanding of the reasons underlying their demands, and it helps to provide the person making those demands with confidence in the positions. Successful negotiators establish high, but rational, objectives and explain their entitlement to these goals.

When negotiators need to change their position, they should use "principled" concessions. They need to provide opponents with a rational explanation for modifications of their position.

For example, a lawyer demanding $100,000 for an injured plaintiff might indicate willingness to accept $90,000 by saying that there is a 10 percent chance that the plaintiff might lose at trial or a good probability that the jury in a comparative-negligence jurisdiction will find that the plaintiff was 10 percent negligent. This lets the other party know why the change is being made, and it helps to keep the person at the $90,000 level until he is ready to use a "principled" concession to further reduce the demand.

Argument

The power-bargaining tactic lawyers use most often involves legal and nonlegal argument. Factual and legal arguments are advanced. Public policy may be invoked in appropriate situations. Emotional appeals may be effective in some circumstances. If an argument is to be persuasive, it must be presented objectively.

Effective arguments should be presented in a comprehensive, rather than a conclusionary, fashion. Factual and legal information should be disclosed with appropriate detail. Influential statements must be insightful and carefully articulated. They must not only be fully comprehended, but they must go beyond what is expected.

Contentions that do not surprise the receiving parties will rarely undermine their confidence in their preconceived position. But assertions that raise issues opponents have not previously considered will likely induce them to recognize the need to reassess their perceptions.

Threats and Promises

Almost all legal negotiations involve use of overt or at least implicit threats. Threats show recalcitrant parties that the cost of disagreeing with offers will transcend the cost of acquiescence. Some negotiators try to avoid use of formal "threats," preferring less-challenging "warnings." These negotiators simply caution opponents about the consequences of their unwillingness to accept a mutual resolution.

If threats are to be effective, they must be believable. A credible threat is one that is reasonably proportionate to the action it is intended to deter—seemingly insignificant threats tend to be ignored, while large ones tend to be dismissed. Negotiators should never issue threats unless they are prepared to carry them out, since their failure to do so will undermine their credibility.

Instead of using negative threats that indicate what consequences will result if the opposing party does not alter its position, negotiators should consider affirmative promises that indicate their willingness to change their position simultaneously with the other party. The classic affirmative promise—the "split-the-difference" approach—has been used by most negotiators to conclude a transaction. One side promises to move halfway if only the other side will do the same.

Affirmative promises are more effective than negative threats at inducing position changes, since the first indicates that the requested position change will be reciprocated. A negative threat merely suggests dire consequences if the other side does not alter its position. They are more of an affront to an opponent than affirmative promises, and, as a result, are more disruptive of the negotiation process.

Silence and Patience

Many negotiators fear silence, since they are afraid that they will lose control of the transaction if they stop talking. The more they talk, the more information they disclose and the more concessions they make. When their opponents remain silent, such negotiators often become even more talkative.

When negotiators have something important to say, they should say it and then keep quiet. A short comment accentuates the importance of what they are saying and provides the other party with the chance to absorb what was said. This rule is crucial when an offer or concession is being made. Once such information has been disclosed, it is time for the other side to respond.

Patience can be used effectively with silence. Where the other negotiator does not readily reply to critical representations, he should be given sufficient time to respond. If it is his turn to speak, the first party should wait silently for him to comment. If the first party feels awkward, he should look at his notes. This behavior shows the silent party that a response will be required before further discussion.

Limited Authority

Many advocates like to indicate during the preliminary stages that they do not have final authority from their client about the matter in dispute. They use this technique to reserve the right to check with their client before any tentative agreement can bind their side.

The advantage of a limited-authority approach—whether actual or fabricated—is that it permits the party using it to obtain a psychological commitment to settlement from opponents authorized to make binding commitments. The unbound bargainers can then seek beneficial modifications of the negotiated terms based on "unexpected" client demands. Since their opponents do not want to let such seemingly insignificant items negate the success achieved during the prior negotiations, they often accept the alterations.

Bargainers who meet opponents who initially say they lack the authority to bind their clients may find it advantageous to say they also lack final authority. This will permit them to "check" with their own absent principal before making any final commitment.

A few unscrupulous negotiators will agree to a final accord with what appears to be complete authority. They later approach their opponent with apparent embarrassment and explain that they did not really have this authority. They say that their principal will require one or two modifications before accepting the other terms of the agreement. Since the unsuspecting opponent and his client are now committed to a final settlement, they agree to the concessions.

Negotiators who suspect that an adversary might use this technique may wish to select—at the apparent conclusion of their transaction—the one or two items they would most likely to have modified in their favor. When their opponent requests changes, they can indicate how relieved they are about this, because their own client is dissatisfied. Then they can offer to exchange their items for those their adversary seeks. It is fascinating to see how quickly the opponent will now insist on honoring the initial accord.

The limited-authority situation must be distinguished from the one where an opponent begins a negotiation with no authority. This adversary hopes to get several concessions as a prerequisite to negotiations with a negotiator with real authority.

Negotiators should avoid dealing with a no-authority person, since he is trying to induce them to bargain with themselves. When they give their opening position, the no-authority negotiator will say that it is unacceptable. If they are careless, they will alter their stance to placate the no-authority participant. Before they realize what they have done, they will have made concessions before the other side has entered the process.

Anger

If negotiators become angry, they are likely to offend their opponent and may disclose information that they did not wish to divulge. Negotiators who encounter an adversary who has really lost his temper should look for inadvertent disclosures which that person's anger precipitates.

Negotiators often use feigned anger to convince an opponent of the seriousness of their position. This tactic should be used carefully, since it can offend adversaries and induce them to end the interaction.

Some negotiators may respond with their own retaliatory diatribe to convince their adversary that they cannot be intimidated by such tactics. A quid-pro-quo approach involves obvious risks, since a vituperative exchange may have a deleterious impact on the bargaining.

Negotiators may try to counter an angry outburst with the impression that they have been personally offended. They should say that they cannot understand how their reasonable approach has precipitated such an intemperate challenge. If they are successful, they may be able to make the attacking party feel guilty and embarrassed, shaming the person into a concession.

Aggressive Behavior

Such conduct is usually intended to have an impact similar to that associated with anger. It is supposed to convince an opponent of the seriousness of one's position. It can also be used to maintain control over the agenda.

Those who try to counter an aggressive bargainer with a quid-pro-quo response are likely to fail, due to their inability to be convincing in that role. Negotiators who encounter a particularly abrasive adversary can diminish the impact of his techniques through the use of short, carefully controlled interactions. Telephone discussions might be used to limit each exchange. Face-to-face meetings could be held to less than an hour. These short interactions may prevent the opponent from achieving aggressive momentum.

A few aggressive negotiators try to undermine their opponent's presentation through use of interruptions. Such behavior should not be tolerated. When negotiators are deliberately interrupted, they should either keep talking if they think this will discourage their opponent or they might say that they do not expect their opponent to speak while they are talking.

Uproar

A few negotiators try to obtain an advantage by threatening dire consequences if their opponent does not give them what they want. For example, a school board in negotiations with a teachers' union might say that it will have to lay off one third of the teachers due to financial constraints. It will then suggest that it could probably retain everyone if the union would accept a salary freeze.

Negotiators confronted with such predictions should ask themselves two crucial questions. What is the likelihood that the consequences will occur? and What would happen to the other party if the consequences actually occurred? In many cases, it will be obvious that the threatened results will not occur. In others, it will be clear that the consequences would be as bad or worse for the other side as for the threatened party.

Bargainers occasionally may have to call an opponent's bluff. If union negotiators were to indicate that they could accept the layoffs if the school board would only raise salaries of the remaining teachers by 30 percent, the board representatives would probably panic. They know the school system could not realistically function with such layoffs. They were merely hoping that the union would not come to the same realization.

Settlement Brochures and Video Presentations

Some lawyers, particularly in the personal injury field, try to enhance their bargaining posture through settlement brochures or video presentations. A brochure states the factual and legal bases for the claim being asserted and describes the full extent of the plaintiff's injuries. Video presentations depict the way in which the defendant's negligent behavior caused the severe injuries the plaintiff has suffered.

Brochures are often accorded greater respect than verbal recitations, due to the aura of legitimacy generally granted to printed documents. Use of brochures may bolster the confidence of the plaintiff's lawyer and may enable him to seize control of the negotiating agenda at the outset. If the plaintiff's lawyer is fortunate, the opponent will begin by suggesting that the plaintiff is seeking too much for pain and suffering. This opening might implicitly concede liability, as well as responsibility for the property damage, medical expenses, and lost earnings requested.

Those presented with settlement brochures or video reenactments should not accord them more respect than they deserve. Lawyers should treat written factual and legal representations just as they would identical verbal assertions.

If lawyers are provided with settlement brochures before the first negotiating session, they should review them and prepare effective counterarguments, which they can state during settlement discussions.

Lawyers should not allow their adversary to use a settlement brochure to seize control of the agenda. Where appropriate, they may wish to prepare their own brochure or video to graphically depict their view of the situation.

Boulwareism

This technique gets its name from Lemuel Boulware, former Vice President for Labor Relations at General Electric. Boulware was not enamored of traditional "auction" bargaining, which involves using extreme initial positions, making time-consuming concessions, and achieving a final agreement like the one the parties knew from the outset they would reach. He decided to determine ahead of time what GE was willing to commit to wage and benefit increases and then formulate a complete "best-offer-first" package. He presented this to union negotiators on a "take-it-or-leave-it" basis unless the union could show that GE had made some miscalculation or that changed circumstances had intervened.

Boulwareism is now associated with best-offer-first or take-it-or-leave-it bargaining. Insurance company adjusters occasionally try to establish reputations as people who will make one firm, fair offer for each case. If plaintiff does not accept that proposal, they plan to go to trial.

Negotiators should be hesitant to adopt Boulwareism. The offeror effectively tells the other party that he knows what is best for both sides. Few lawyers are willing to accord such respect to the view of opposing counsel.

Boulwareism deprives the opponent of the opportunity to participate meaningfully in the negotiation process. A plaintiff who might have been willing to settle a dispute for $50,000 may not be willing to accept a take-it-or-leave-it first offer of $50,000. The plaintiff wants to explore the case through the information phase and to exhibit his negotiating skill during the competitive phase. When the process has been completed, he wants to feel that his ability influenced the final outcome.

Negotiators presented with take-it-or-leave-it offers should not automatically reject them simply because of the paternalistic way in which they have been extended. They must evaluate the amount being proposed. If it is reasonable, they should accept it. Lawyers should not permit their own negative reaction to an approach preclude the consummation of a fair arrangement for their clients.

Br'er Rabbit

In *Uncle Remus, His Songs and His Sayings* (1880), Joel Chandler Harris created the unforgettable Br'er Rabbit. When the fox captured Br'er Rabbit, Br'er Rabbit used reverse psychology to escape. He begged the fox to do anything with him so long as he did not throw him in the brier patch. Since the fox wanted to punish the rabbit, he chose the one alternative the rabbit appeared to fear most and flung him in the brier patch. Br'er Rabbit was thus emancipated.

The Br'er Rabbit technique can occasionally be used against win/lose opponents who do not evaluate their results by how well they have done but by an assessment of how poorly their adversary has done. They are only satisfied if they think the other side has been forced to accept a terrible argument.

The Br'er Rabbit approach has risks. Although adroit negotiators may induce a careless, vindictive opponent to provide them with what is really desired, they must recognize that such a device will generally not work against a normal adversary. A typical win/win bargainer would probably accept their disingenuous representations and provide them with the unintended result they have professed to prefer over the alternative that has been renounced.

Mutt and Jeff

In the Mutt and Jeff routine, a seemingly reasonable negotiator professes sympathy toward the "generous" concessions made by the other, while his partner rejects each new offer as insufficient, castigating opponents for their parsimonious concessions. The reasonable partner will then suggest that some additional concessions will have to be made if there is to be any hope of satisfying his associate.

Single negotiators may even use this tactic. They can claim that their absent client suffers from delusions of grandeur, which must be satisfied if any agreement is to be consummated. Such bargainers repeatedly praise their opponent for the concessions being made, but insist that greater movement is necessary to satisfy the excessive aspirations of their "unreasonable" client when their client may actually be receptive to any fair resolution. The opponent has no way of knowing about this and usually accepts such representations at their face value.

Negotiators who encounter these tactics should not directly challenge the scheme. It is possible that their opponents are not really engaged in a disingenuous exercise. One adversary may actually disagree with his partner's assessment. Little is to be gained from raising a Mutt and Jeff challenge. Allegations about the tactics being used by such negotiators will probably create an unproductive bargaining atmosphere— particularly in situations where the opponents have not deliberately adopted such a stratagem.

Those who interact with Mutt and Jeff negotiators tend to make the mistake of directing their arguments and offers to the unreasonable participant to obtain approval when it is often better to seek the acquiescence of the reasonable adversary before trying to satisfy the irrational one. In some instances, the more conciliatory opponent may actually agree to a proposal characterized as unacceptable by his associate. If the unified position of the opponents can be shattered, it may be possible to whipsaw the reasonable partner against the demanding one.

It is always important when dealing with unreasonable opponents to consider what might occur if no mutual accord is achieved. If the overall cost of surrendering to such an adversary's one-sided demands would clearly be greater than the cost associated with not settling, the interaction should not be continued.

Belly-Up

Some negotiators act like wolves in sheepskin. They initially say they lack negotiating ability and legal perspicuity in a disingenuous effort to evoke sympathy and to lure unsuspecting adversaries into a false sense of security. These negotiators "acknowledge" the superior competence of those with whom they interact and say that they will place themselves in the hands of their fair and proficient opponent.

Negotiators who encounter a belly-up bargainer tend to alter their initial position. Instead of opening with the tough "principled" offer they had planned to use, they modify it in favor of their pathetic adversary, who praises them for their reasonableness, but suggests that his client deserves additional assistance. They then endeavor to demonstrate their ability to satisfy those needs. The belly-up participant says the new offer is a substantial improvement, but suggests the need for further accommodation. By the time the transaction is finished, the belly-up bargainer has obtained everything he wants. Not only are his opponents virtually naked, but they feel gratified at having assisted such an inept bargainer.

Belly-up bargainers are the most difficult to deal with, since they effectively refuse to participate in the process. They ask their opponent to permit them to forgo traditional auction bargaining due to their professed inability to negotiate. They want their reasonable adversary to do all the work.

Negotiators who encounter them must force them to participate and never allow them to alter their planned strategy and concede everything in an effort to form a solution acceptable to such pathetic souls. When belly-up negotiators characterize initial offers as unacceptable, opponents should make them respond with definitive offers. True belly-up negotiators often find it very painful to state and defend the positions they espouse.

Passive-Aggressive Behavior

Instead of directly challenging opponents' proposals, passive-aggressive negotiators use oblique, but highly aggressive, forms of passive resistance. They show up late for a scheduled session and forget to bring important documents. When they agree to write up the agreed-upon terms, they fail to do so.

Those who deal with a passive-aggressive opponent must recognize the hostility represented by the behavior and try to seize control. They should get extra copies of important documents just in case their opponent forgets to bring them. They should always prepare a draft of any agreement. Once passive-aggressive negotiators are presented with such a fait accompli, they usually execute the proffered agreement.

THE COOPERATIVE PHASE

Once the competitive phase has been completed, most parties consider the process complete. Although this conclusion might be warranted where neither party could possibly obtain more favorable results without a corresponding loss being imposed on the other party, this conclusion is not correct for multi-issue, nonconstant sum controversies.

During the competitive phase, participants rarely completely disclose underlying interests and objectives. Both sides are likely to use power-bargaining techniques aimed at achieving results favorable to their own circumstances.

Because of the anxiety created by such power-bargaining tactics, Pareto optimal arrangements—where neither party may improve its position without worsening the other side's—are usually not generated. The parties are more likely to achieve merely "acceptable" terms rather than Pareto optimal terms due to their lack of negotiation efficiency. If they were to conclude the process at this point, they might well leave a substantial amount of untapped joint satisfaction at the bargaining table.

Once a tentative accord has been achieved, it is generally advantageous for negotiators to explore alternative trade-offs that might simultaneously enhance the interest of both sides. After the competitive phase, one party should suggest transition into the cooperative phase. The parties can initial or even sign their current agreement, and then seek to improve their joint results.

Each should prepare alternative formulations by transferring certain terms from one side to the other while moving other items in the opposite direction. When these options are shown, each negotiator must candidly indicate whether any of the proposals are preferable to the accord already achieved.

Exploring alternatives need not consume much time. Negotiators may substantially increase their clients' satisfaction through this device, and the negotiators lose little if no mutual gains are achieved.

If the cooperative phase is to work effectively, candor is necessary. Each side must be willing to say whether alternatives are more or less beneficial for it.

On the other hand, this phase continues to be somewhat competitive. If one party offers the other an option much more satisfactory than what was agreed upon, he might merely indicate that the proposal is "a little better." Through this technique, he may be able to obtain more during the cooperative phase than would be objectively warranted.

SATISFYING CLIENTS

Lawyers who understand these common negotiating techniques can plan their strategies more effectively. They can enhance their skill in the information phase, increase the likelihood that they will achieve acceptable agreements during the competitive phase, and endeavor to maximize the gains obtained for their clients in the cooperative phase.

How to Negotiate Practically Anything

If you're like most people, you don't like to negotiate. It's confrontational, unfriendly, sometimes down-right mean. What's more, if you don't do it right you stand to get beat, which will cost you. And you're pretty sure you don't do it right.

Bob Woolf no doubt has mixed feelings about all this. On the one hand, he wants to strip negotiating of its (he thinks) undeserved terror. He's quick to tell you that 95 percent of the folks you'll ever negotiate with feel just as you do: scared. On the other hand, fear of negotiation has made Woolf rich.

Woolf today is perhaps the preeminent sports and entertainment attorney alive. In 1962, 10 years after he began practicing law, Woolf fell into some work for an obscure Boston Red Sox pitcher named Earl Wilson. Wilson referred several of the city's athletes to him, and pretty soon the attorney's practice also included negotiating the contracts and finances of 9 out of 12 members of Bill Russell's legendary Boston Celtics. Later came actors, entertainers, media personalities, eventually even politicians. Woolf traveled with Michael Dukakis last summer, and only Woolf's adept and creative last-second negotiation with Ted Koppel, Roone Arledge, and the Dukakis team saved the candidate's opportunity to do a ''Night-line'' interview one-on-one with the host. (Well, it seemed like a good idea at the time.)

Woolf estimates that he has negotiated more than 2,000 professional contracts plus countless other agreements in the course of managing his clients' personal affairs. Bob Woolf Associates, his Boston firm, handles more than $100 million in contract value annually and has 25 employees. Woolf himself is finishing a book on negotiating called *It Doesn't Hurt to Ask,* due out at the end of the year.

What will the book reveal? Among other things, Woolf's simple but unexpected belief: kindness counts. Forget macho, he says. Forget Machiavelli. What every businessperson should know is that, in negotiating, the race is to the friendly, the honest, and the fair.

Woolf spoke with *Inc.*'s Paul B. Brown and Michael S. Hopkins.

Inc.:

Nothing, you say, is as important to a negotiation as creating the right atmosphere in which to negotiate—having the right attitude yourself and getting the other side to feel the same way. But pleasant though it sounds, a lot of people will find it hard to buy your idea that "nice guys finish first" at the negotiating table. Your argument?

Woolf:

Only that it works. Think about it: why do companies spend millions and millions of dollars on public relations and goodwill advertising to develop a nice relationship with the public? Because they want to do business. They want to create a nice atmosphere. They do it because it works.

Inc.:

Then why do books about winning through intimidation keep showing up on best-seller lists? It seems to us that hardball is in fashion these days.

Woolf:

Maybe, but in fact you don't win through intimidation. The deal doesn't go through. Remember, people are frightened of negotiating to begin with. Who likes confrontation? It's not pleasant to negotiate, whether you're asking your boss for a raise or selling your company. Most people would rather not do it. They're afraid.

So the last thing you want to do is to turn a negotiation into a confrontation. You want to make it a situation of mutual respect. After all, you want the other side to be reasonable, not defensive—to work *with* you. You'll have a better chance of getting what you want. Treat someone the way that you would like to be treated, and you'll be successful most of the time.

Inc.:

But negotiations by definition are adversarial. You want more money from the boss, a better deal from a supplier. . . .

Woolf:

Right, you have a goal. More money, better terms, whatever. That doesn't mean you holler, pound on the desk, or make threats—that's ridiculous. It's just another part of the misconception that people who are dishonest and cunning are going to win. They're not. They're going to lose. That's what I believe. And so does everybody I know who's a professional negotiator, in whatever area.

Granted, there are those who'd like you to believe they know something you don't know. They're the ones who at the racetrack tell you they won the 3d, the 8th, and the 11th race, leaving out the other 8 races they lost. But if you want to win all 11 races, and each time come to an agreement, you'll play fair, work hard to be gracious, and *always* deal in good faith. Your individual wins may not be as big as the other guy's, but they'll be bigger when you add them up.

Inc.:

If it's clear that a good atmosphere produces a good result, why do people hang onto this other view of negotiating?

Woolf:

I don't know. It's crazy. I've been hired by people because they say, "Boy, he is one hard-nosed, rough kind of guy, and that's the kind of guy I want negotiating for me." And I'm thinking, who are they talking about? Not me. I go in every time to set a nice atmosphere. I want to make you happy.

Inc.:

Aren't you afraid the guy across the table will perceive your eagerness to please as weakness and think he can raise the stakes?

Woolf:

Maybe, but I know it's not a weakness, and there are plenty of ways to let him know, nicely, that my pleasantries have nothing to do with the stakes. I just keep reducing his expectations—nicely. He proposes a number and I say, "Gee, that's not really what I was thinking. I never anticipated anything like that. That's kind of way out of line." And I keep on saying it. If I can reduce expectations, things get a heck of a lot easier. It isn't costing me anything to be nice, and it does make the negotiation go better. You can be a tough, hard, efficient negotiator and still be a nice person. And it will help you reach an agreement.

Inc.:

OK, let's say it's time to start the negotiation. Practically speaking, how do you create this atmosphere from the start? You walk into the room. . .

Woolf:

. . . and I let you know what my attitude is. I'm forthright and positive. I tell you I want to make a deal. I tell you I'm not here to outwit you.

Inc.:

You *tell* me?

Woolf:

Right. Straight out. I really am an average guy and I want you to know it. I also ask if you have any particular problems or anything that I should know about that would help me as we talk. Maybe I can work within your needs, maybe I know something that could help you. I try to make it a partnership. You and I have a problem, and we're trying to solve it so you're happy and I'm happy. A successful negotiation isn't one where I get everything and you get nothing.

Inc.:

No? By some standards, that's perfect success.

Woolf:

I don't think so. I haven't done a single contract that I couldn't have gotten more money on. I always leave money on the table.

Inc.:

Forgive us, but people will read that and think you're nuts. Let's assume you can sell a computer system for $220,000. You're saying you'll take $200,000 for it? Why not pick up the extra 10 percent?

Woolf:

Because it's possible to push the price so far, create such antagonism, that the extra 10 percent isn't really worth it. If someone feels you held them up, they're going to take it out on your business or—if it's an employee—on you. In my case, they'll take it out on my client, make him miserable, trade him. Obviously, a negotiation isn't about only money.

You have to give the other people a profit margin and let them live. You want them to thrive and grow. It's only practical: if they go out of business, it doesn't help you any. As they grow, maybe you'll participate in the growth. The idea is to be a deal maker, which means sometimes you'll have to compromise on your demands.

Just never compromise on your principles. You've got to develop a reputation for being smart and honest—so people know you won't renegotiate, you won't play tricks. You can't play tricks, because you'll probably be going back to these people again—or to someone they know. Your good reputation is incredibly important.

Inc.:

You're talking about a negotiation in which there is an ongoing relationship. What about a deal in which you're buying a house, or you're selling your company for cash and moving to Bimini, and you'll never see the other person again?

Woolf:

Look, if someone wants to be a bastard, fine, be my guest, but most people don't. When you buy a car, aren't you just trying to get a fair deal? Or are you trying to prevent the guy from making any profit on the transaction? Would you try to do that? Most people wouldn't.

Inc.:

No. But if I'm negotiating, I don't think it's my job to figure out what's fair for the other guy. Doesn't it make sense to depend on him to protect his interests? And when it comes to leaving money on the table, doesn't it make sense to push for a stiffer deal if it's a onetime relationship?

Woolf:

Well, yes, if it really is a one-time deal then I wouldn't leave as much, but I still wouldn't try for the last dollar. And you're wrong not to judge what's fair from the other side's point of view. If you don't have a pretty good idea before you start talking, then you haven't done your research. You haven't prepared.

In addition to writing my own goals and scenarios before every negotiation I do, I also prepare what I think my counterpart wants. I write down his goals, making believe I'm him. What would I want? What would I give up? I try to figure out what's really important to him.

Inc.:

What exactly do you do before you sit down to talk?

Woolf:

I try to find out everything I can about the person I'm negotiating with, about what's going on in the marketplace, and with my own client—or, if I'm a CEO, about my company and its needs.

Inc.:

How?

Woolf:

There's no formula. Just ask questions. Talk to people who know the person, are around him, deal with him. That includes his secretary and the person he sends to get you at the airport. I want to know everything about who I'm negotiating with. What kind of person is he? What is his reputation? Is he a good negotiator? Is he fair? Does he try to intimidate you? Does he know what he's talking about? Does he have authorization, or will he have to go to someone else to get the deal approved?

Inc.:

So if I'm considering a deal with a new parts supplier, say, I get a list and call his customers. I call the people who sell him his materials. I call people in his town—banks, newspapers, local government officials who might have contact with him. If I'm real serious, I might call civic and social organizations I've discovered he belongs to. . . .

Woolf:

Absolutely. Information is power. And I start the attitude process early, too. If I know someone who's close to the person I'll be negotiating with, often I'll have that person call ahead and say, "Hey, Bob's not a bad guy, believe me, he's going to live up to his contracts." I might call ahead myself just to lay that foundation.

Inc.:

And after you've got the story on the guy?

Woolf:

Then I question myself. I ask whether I'm the right person to do the negotiation. Is my own ego going to get in the way? Is there something about me or the circumstances that will jeopardize the negotiations?

Inc.:

Has the answer ever been yes?

Woolf:

Oh, yeah. Lots of times I know I'm not the right person. For instance, right now I'm trying to help a friend. He's been a sports announcer on television for 27 years, and he asked me to do his contract. He's making just $66,000, but out of friendship I'm trying to do it. The fellow on the other side, however, is antagonistic and offering a $3,000 raise. His posture has nothing to do with my "client." The fellow's just thrilled that I'm calling him, and he's gonna show me. He's gonna beat Bob Woolf. In this case, I'm not the right person to do the negotiation.

You can't let your ego get in the way. After all, you want to accomplish the goal, that's what matters. Sometimes you have to walk away.

Inc.:

That would be hard for me. Here I am all psyched up to do it, and you want me to back away. But this is my company, and this is an important negotiation.

Woolf:

As I'm sure I don't have to tell you, he who represents himself has a fool for a client. The trouble is, you care too much. I, as your attorney, don't. Therefore I can be more objective and keep from getting emotional.

Inc.:

So that means it almost never makes sense for our readers to negotiate for themselves?

Woolf:

Not necessarily. You can do the negotiation if you can keep from getting mad when someone says something you don't like.

Inc.:

OK, say you're the right person, you've set the right tone, and you're prepared. Where does the negotiation take place? Your office, the other side's, or a neutral place?

Woolf:

My office, if possible. I feel more comfortable there. I can be gracious. And on my own turf I have everything I need: files and whatever else I want to show.

Inc.:

Who makes the first offer?

Woolf:

Whenever possible, the other side does. After all, he or she may give me something more than I dreamed of. If not, I'll at least find out what their thinking is like. After the pleasantries are over I might say, "Gee, what did you have in mind? What did you think was fair?"

Inc.:

But of course the other side is going to come back with, "Well, we really don't know, Bob, what would you be happy with?"

Woolf:

Then I'll say, "Well, I don't know what you have in your budget." I always ask that. Has it been a good year for them? I may find out something more than I knew in the beginning, and I still haven't told them anything.

Inc.:

How far will you go to keep from putting the first number down?

Woolf:

As far as I can.

Inc.:

But sometimes you end up having to?

Woolf:

Sometimes I have to. Sometimes they'll say, "Write me a letter and tell me what you want." Remember, I don't always win.

Inc.:

So what is your first offer?

Woolf:

High, of course. But before I make it, I do one more thing. If I'm representing a basketball player, I'll say to the general manager across the table, "Listen, I really don't want to be off base here, so can I check these figures I have for the other salaries on your team? We based our thinking on them, so I'd like you to correct me if they're wrong. I don't want to be out of line with what I'm asking for." I'm not threatening, but they'll know I'm prepared. If I were a businessman cutting a deal with a vendor, I'd be ready to have him check a list of prices he gives to other customers, plus a list of prices his competitors might offer me.

Anyway, my offer on the basketball contract: if everyone of my client's quality and position were getting $600,000, I might ask for $750,000, expecting I can come down to $600,000. Again, I want the other person to feel as though he's accomplished something. It's crucial to the client/team relationship. The same is true of business relationships.

Inc.:

OK, but let's follow that logic all the way through. The $750,000 is higher than what you're expecting. Why not let the other side *really* feel like it's accomplished something by asking for $1 million before coming down?

Woolf:

Well, then it becomes outrageous, and they're not going to believe anything you've said in the first place.

Inc.:

So you have to establish an upper boundary, beyond which trust is gone?

Woolf:

Yes.

Inc.:

Is there a rule that says 30 percent above the norm is OK, but 50 percent is too much?

Woolf:

I've really never looked at it that way. I just use common sense. And all the time I'm asking questions, though I never give away anything myself. I keep asking, "Can you live with this, can you live with that? Will this be all right?" I always encourage the other party to believe that we are going to make a deal. I don't care how far apart we are, that's my attitude. It shows good faith. And when offers are being discussed and terms considered, I'm always staying with *my* numbers. Often I never go down.

Inc.:

How do you deal with things like the split-the-difference gambit? Say you're asking $100,000 for a house and I'm offering $70,000. It looks like we're never going to meet. Finally I get frustrated and say, "We could talk forever. I'm going to be a gentleman and meet you right smack in the middle—$85,000."

Woolf:

Well, if somebody made you that offer, what would you and 99 percent of the people do?

Inc.:

Probably accept it.

Woolf:

Right. But I'd say no. I'd say, "I can't do that, but I *will* take $90,000."

Inc.:

And all of a sudden you've bumped up the floor.

Woolf:

Right. Now, you know you can get $85,000, and probably more—in this situation it will be probably closer to $90,000.

I always come down very slowly if I'm selling, or up very slowly if I'm buying. Let's say that you're asking $100, and I'm offering $40. Just because you come down $10 doesn't mean I have to go up $10. A lot of people think that you have to do what we call tit for tat. That's not so. Maybe I'll go up $5. My theory is to go up slowly or come down slowly and then just continue the negotiation. Keep on talking.

But remember, I don't land every negotiation. You can't win every one. But if you brought it to a head, got an agreement, and you're happy and the other party is happy, then don't second-guess yourself—it's a successful negotiation. Why is it that everyone thinks that if I win, you have to lose? It's just not true.

SECTION FOUR

Integrative Bargaining

Integrative (or collaborative) bargaining occurs when both parties in a negotiation are working together toward common or compatible goals. For integrative bargaining to occur, the parties first must agree on the overall goal that they share. This discovery usually depends on the accurate exchange of information, just the opposite of what is typically sought in distributive (or competitive) bargaining. This need to share, rather than to conceal, information is different from what many normally expect in negotiation. People often find it difficult to accept and do what is necessary for success in integrative bargaining.

This need to share information, though, requires the disputants to collaborate. Barbara Gray, in the reading entitled "Collaboration: The Constructive Management of Differences" (from her 1989 book *Collaborating*) identifies collaboration as a necessary skill, given the failure of more "traditional" individual and collective problem-solving strategies in these turbulent times. Gray sees collaboration as an approach critical to understanding and addressing disputes marked by multiple, often competing, interests. Collaboration, here, is defined as "a process through which parties who see different aspects of a problem can constructively explore their differences and search for solutions that go beyond their own limited vision of what is possible." Gray's chapter goes on to outline the collaboration process, including its benefits, through an example of a truly messy problem—the cleanup following the industrial accident at the Three Mile Island nuclear power plant.

This collaborative/integrative process is placed in an applied setting in Philip Morgan's article "Resolving Conflict through 'Win-Win' Negotiating," in which he asserts that "all managers negotiate; some are better at it than others. What determines whether an outcome is successful or not is the degree of skill of the negotiator." According to Morgan, much of that skill depends on the ability to use a "soft" rather than a "hard" style, involving mutual goal setting and problem solving, the recognition of other parties' legitimate rights and needs, and a spirit of mutual trust based on clear, open communication. Morgan goes on to provide a short list of "dos and don'ts" for the would-be integrative negotiator.

The subject of interests is addressed in more detail by David Lax and James Sebenius in their article "Interests: The Measure of Negotiation." More specifically,

Lax and Sebenius argue for "a more expansive conception of negotiator's interests," and tackle the thorny problem of assessing trade-offs among multiple interests of a subjective or qualitative nature. This entails going beyond the traditional, usually quantitative, "bottom-line" standard often applied to negotiation outcomes. The authors exhort negotiators to "go beyond the obvious and tangible," using a variety of examples to address two critical processes: first, distinguishing among interests, issues, and positions; and second, distinguishing between intrinsic interests (those relative to a specific negotiation) and instrumental interests (those likely to affect subsequent negotiations). This last consideration is central to the role of interparty relationships in the negotiation process.

In this section's last article, "Creative Negotiating," Gordon Shea also criticizes those who see negotiation only as "the act of getting what you want—with no regard as to the cost to the other side." Shea states that "win/lose" outcomes tend to fall apart or backfire over time, turning into "lose/lose" situations. "Win/win" (or integrative) outcomes, though, serve the long-term relationships necessary to business (and other) success in an increasingly competitive world. In lieu of the inevitable cost of cleaning up after faulty negotiations, Shea calls on negotiators to take integrative measures to secure more stable, productive agreements.

Collaboration: The Constructive Management of Differences

Barbara Gray

The world must be kept safe for differences.

Clyde Kuckholn

THE NEED TO MANAGE DIFFERENCES

Our society is at a critical juncture. Constructive approaches for confronting difficult societal problems are essential to managing our global future. The pace at which new problems are generated is rapid, and individual organizations are hard pressed to make effective or timely responses. As a result, problems are piling up; new problems are cropping up daily, while yesterday's problems often go unsolved. Problems range in scope from local (such as allocating water rights for local development) to global (such as preventing deterioration of the ozone layer, which shields our planet from ultraviolet radiation).

This pileup of problems and the inability of organizations to contend with them reflects the turbulence of our environment. Under turbulent conditions organizations become highly interdependent with others in indirect but consequential ways (Emery and Trist, 1965, 1972; Trist, 1977). Under these circumstances it is difficult for individual organizations to act unilaterally to solve problems without creating unwanted consequences for other parties and without encountering constraints imposed by others. Because of this interdependence, the range of interests associated with any particular problem is wide and usually controversial.

Consider the situation in Franklin Township, a rural community adjacent to a growing midwestern university town.

In 1970 Franklin Township was a thriving farming community comprising many large family farms. Over the next 15 years Franklin Township's population increased from 759 to 975 residents as a few scattered tracts of farmland were sold for development. By the mid-1980s, developers began eying the township as a potential bedroom community. When an 80-acre tract of farmland was sold to a local farmer whose family had lived in the area since 1830, township residents breathed a sigh of relief. Development had been coming too fast, creating traffic and excessive demands on the local water system operated by the township's water company.

Local residents were shocked a few months later when the farmer submitted plans to the township supervisors for a development of 80 one-acre lots. The community mobilized quickly, and 57 people showed up at the supervisors' meeting to protest the development. Many residents expressed concerns about overtaxing an already inadequate water supply. They carried a petition demanding the supervisors oppose the development and threatened to sue the water company and the township if they did not. The previous summer these residents had gone without water on several occasions during dry spells, and they feared the situation would worsen when 80 additional faucets were turned on.

A second group of residents, dubbed the "horse people," complained that the development would block their access to the riding trails in the state game lands that abutted the proposed development. These residents requested an easement for public access to the game lands. Objections also came from the residents whose private road was to become the gateway to the new homes and from the fruit farmer whose irrigation system depended on private wells close to the proposed development.

Franklin Township is a simple illustration of a situation in which the interests of multiple parties have become intertwined. The parties in the Franklin Township scenario include a neighbor-turned-developer, part-time township supervisors, local interest groups such as the "horse people," water company authorities, a local commercial farmer, and ordinary citizens concerned about taxes, traffic, and so forth. From many of their perspectives, the solution to the problem seems black-and-white—either support or oppose the development. Yet, for the township supervisors, the problem is more complex. They are faced with several questions: How should the township supervisors handle the developer's request for permits? How should they respond to the opposition from homeowners? What is the developer's responsibility to the community? Are the residents' concerns legitimate? Is it prudent to expect the water system to accommodate the new level of demand? What if other farmers followed suit and similar developments were proposed?

The township supervisors have several options. One is the "ostrich approach." They can postpone making a decision for as long as possible and hope the problem will go away. That outcome is, of course, unlikely since township ordinances usually mandate a specific response period. A second option is to take sides with one or more of the parties. There are several possible consequences of this choice, including escalation of the conflict, as township supervisors in North Salem, New York, recently discovered (Foderaro, 1988). In North Salem a developer sued the supervisors, charging that a new zoning ordinance was exclusionary. Dissension among the supervisors over development also caused one to resign and another to lose a bid for reelection.

Other options are available to the supervisors in Franklin Township. They can adopt a "hands off, let the experts decide" approach in which they rely on legal or engineering advisers to make the decisions for them. A fourth option, the traditional approach, involves holding public hearings in which interested parties can vent their concerns. These, however, frequently churn up issues and raise community expectations, often well beyond what responsible public officials can reasonably deliver. Though well intended, both of these options also often lead to less than satisfactory solutions.

One reason the solutions are unsatisfactory is that they are often not accepted by the public. For highly controversial issues, it is likely at least some of the public will not accept the decision of public officials, even when these officials decide only after conscientiously gathering and weighing information from all interested parties. Often, these officials must spend countless future hours justifying their decision after the fact. This problem occurs because parties who gave input do not know if or how their interests were considered during decision making (Delbecq, 1974; Wondolleck, 1985). Because parties are not privy to the process by which their interests and those of others are evaluated, those who gave input initially often feel betrayed when the final solution does not satisfy their requests (Carpenter and Kennedy, 1988). The problem of acceptance increases if the decision threatens basic values or creates a situation of high perceived risks for some stakeholders (Klein, 1976).

Seasoned public officials often become thick-skinned, shrugging off the conflict with the adage "you can't please everyone." Unfortunately, heated issues do not die easily and often reemerge in an escalated form.

Additionally, there is growing evidence that for complex problems of this type, individual and collective efforts to solve them are often suboptimal because even well-intended decision makers do not really understand the interests they are trying to reconcile (Fisher and Ury, 1981; Wondolleck, 1985; Lax and Sebenius, 1986). Research has shown, for example, that it is often possible to improve on an agreement through a procedure called postsettlement settlement (Raiffa, 1985). In this procedure, parties reach a preliminary agreement and then invite a third party to review it and recommend improvements that benefit all of the parties. Often these opportunities for joint gains lie in trade-offs that the parties were unable to recognize for themselves (Lax and Sebenius, 1986). Procedures that encourage parties to search for these joint gains have the potential to produce better agreements and to prevent escalation.

In light of this, consider a fifth option available to the Franklin Township supervisors. They can assemble a representative sample of the stakeholders (those with a stake in the problem) and let them work out an agreement among themselves. The stakeholders in this case include the developer, the commercial fruit farmer, the township supervisors, the "horse people," the water company board, the homeowners concerned about water, and the homeowners concerned about traffic. This option has the advantage of dealing with interrelated issues in the same forum, since the township supervisors do not have jurisdiction over the water company but do have authority to approve or disapprove the rest of the development plan. Getting all the stakeholders together to explore their concerns in a constructive way allows them to search for a solution they can all accept and averts the potential for escalation of the conflict. Additionally, the supervisors do not abdicate their responsibility, because they must agree to any decision that is reached. This approach is called collaboration.

COLLABORATION AS AN ALTERNATIVE

Collaboration is a process through which parties who see different aspects of a problem can constructively explore their differences and search for solutions that go beyond their own limited vision of what is possible. Collaboration is based on the simple adages that "two heads are better than one" and that one by itself is simply not good enough! Those parties with an interest in the problem are termed stakeholders. Stakeholders include all individuals, groups, or organizations that are directly influenced by actions others take to solve the problem. Each stakeholder has a unique appreciation of the problem. The objective of collaboration is to create a richer, more comprehensive appreciation of the problem among the stakeholders than anyone of them could construct alone. The term *problem domain* will be used here to refer to the way a problem is conceptualized by the stakeholders (Trist, 1983).

A kaleidoscope is a useful image to envision what joint appreciation of a domain is all about. As the kaleidoscope is rotated, different configurations of the same collection of colored shapes appear. Collaboration involves building a common understanding of how these images appear from their respective points of view. This understanding forms the basis for choosing a collective course of action.

Collaboration is not really a new concept. It is not unlike the town meeting concept, which is a cornerstone of the democratic process. Town meetings turn on the principles of local participation and ownership of decisions. Collaboration reflects a resurgence of interest in those fundamental principles. Any one of the stakeholders in Franklin Township could suggest that they try collaboration. Because of their responsibility for rendering a permit decision, however, the township supervisors are in the best position to initiate a collaborative dialogue. Their role in such a process would be to help the parties articulate their interests and to facilitate a reconciliation.

Questions like those facing the supervisors and residents of Franklin Township are being asked in communities around the world. In some, like Franklin Township, the issues are controversial. In other cases, such as those concerning the cleanup of toxic dumps or the destruction of the ozone layer, the issues are scientifically and politically complex, involve many interested parties, and are often hotly contested.

Not all occasions for collaboration are conflict induced. In some cases, parties may have a shared interest in solving a problem that none of them alone can address. The opportunity for collaborating arises because stakeholders recognize the potential advantages of working together. They may need each other to execute a vision that they all share. Managing a joint business venture is a good example. Addressing the problem of illiteracy in a community is another. Parties come together because each needs the others to advance their individual interests. Opportunities for collaborating are arising in countless arenas in which business, government, labor, and communities are finding their actions interconnected with those of other stakeholders. In the next section, several public- and private-sector opportunities for constructive collaboration are considered.

OPPORTUNITIES FOR COLLABORATING

Situations that provide opportunities for collaborating are many and varied. They include joint ventures among selected businesses, settlement of local neighborhood or environmental disputes, revitalization of economically depressed cities, and resolution of major international problems. These opportunities can be classified into two general categories: resolving conflicts and advancing shared visions.

Resolving Conflict

Collaboration can be used effectively to settle disputes between the parties in multiparty conflict. Collaboration transforms adversarial interaction into a mutual search for information and for solutions that allow all those participating to ensure that their interests are represented. Often, parties in conflict are motivated to try collaboration only as a last-ditch effort when other approaches have reached impasse or have produced less than acceptable outcomes. Parties will try collaboration only if they believe they have something to gain from it. In protracted stalemates, for example, the cost to all parties of inaction may be a sufficient incentive to induce collaboration.

Collaboration has been used to settle hundreds of site-specific environmental disputes (Bingham, 1986), important product liability cases, intergovernmental disputes, and many other community controversies involving transportation, housing, and mortgage lending. Within the environmental area, Bingham (1986) has identified six broad categories within which collaborative solutions to disputes have been sought: land use, natural resource management and public land use, water resources, energy, air quality, and toxics.

The potential for collaboration in international affairs also appears promising. Within the last year a number of major political conflicts have moved from stalemate to early dialogue, signaling a growing potential to search for alternatives to violence. In addition, the list of major global issues in which the interests of several nation-states, nongovernmental organizations (NGOs), and multinational corporations intersect continues to grow. Salient issues include a variety of property rights issues related to the use of the seas and exploration in Antarctica, global environmental issues such as the future of rain forests and control of acid rain, and transnational technology issues such as the management of international telecommunications. For problems of this scope, international collaboration is essential for finding solutions.

The chlorofluorocarbons treaty reached in Montreal in March 1987 provides one model of successful international collaboration. The treaty is historical because it is the first international agreement designed to avert a global disaster (Benedick, 1988). The treaty restricts the production of chemicals (chlorofluorocarbons and others) that erode the stratospheric ozone layer, which protects the earth from the sun's damaging ultraviolet rays. Stakeholders included chlorofluorocarbon producers in several countries, NGOs such as environmental groups and the United Nations Environment Program, members of the scientific community, and governments from the North and the South. Forty-eight countries have signed the treaty, and it is awaiting formal ratification by the countries involved. In addition to the freeze on production, the treaty paves the way for discussions of longer-term strategies to preserve the ozone layer.

Advancing Shared Visions

Collaborations induced by shared visions are intended to advance the collective good of the stakeholders involved. Some are designed to address socioeconomic issues such as illiteracy, youth unemployment, housing, or homelessness, which cut across public- and private-sector interests. Collaborating is also becoming increasingly crucial to successful business management, as companies see advantages in sharing research and development costs (Dimancescu and Botkin, 1986) and exploring new markets through joint ventures (Perlmutter and Heenan, 1986). The proliferation of joint ventures in the auto industry alone has surprised analysts, who a decade ago were predicting a major shakeout in that industry would force many automakers to go out of business (Holusha, 1988).

Public-private partnerships that have sprung up to address deteriorating conditions in U.S. cities are illustrative of collaborative efforts across sectors to advance shared visions. In these partnerships, public and private interests pool their resources and undertake joint planning to tackle economic redevelopment, education, housing, and other protracted problems that have plagued their communities. In the area of education, for example, representatives of industry, labor, and schools have teamed up to deal with youth unemployment and juvenile crime (Elsman and The National Institute for Work and Learning, 1981). These and other partnerships such as the Boston Compact, the Greater Baltimore Committee, the Newark Collaboration, and the Whittier Alliance in Minneapolis began with stakeholders articulating a desirable future they collectively wanted to pursue.

Successfully advancing a shared vision, whether in the public or the private sector, requires identification and coordination of a diverse set of stakeholders, each of whom holds some but not all of the necessary resources. To be successful, coordination must be accomplished laterally without the hierarchical authority to which most managers are accustomed. These circumstances require a radically different approach to organizing and managing, especially for international joint ventures.

> The challenge of managing these coalitions is staggering, given the complexity of the stakeholder network that often involves at least two foreign governments. As a result, interorganizational relations must be carefully worked through in order to gain the advantages of such a union [Heenan and Perlmutter, 1979, p. 82].

Even when parties agree initially on a shared vision, collaboration among them is not necessarily free of conflict. Conflicts inevitably ensue over plans for how the vision should be carried out. And further problems typically arise when stakeholders try to implement their agreements. Overcoming the barriers created by different institutional cultures is frequently a formidable task. Getting the business community and a major urban school district to work together on problems of youth employment, for example, requires considerable adaptation on the part of each. Similar obstacles must be overcome by Japanese and American managers who are trying to implement a management system for a new joint venture (Holusha, 1988).

Nature of Collaborative Problems

It should be clear by now that there is no shortage of problems for which collaboration offers a decided advantage over other methods of decision making. The characteristics of these problems can be described generally as follows:

- The problems are ill defined, or there is disagreement about how they should be defined.
- Several stakeholders have a vested interest in the problems and are interdependent.
- These stakeholders are not necessarily identified a priori or organized in any systematic way.
- There may be a disparity of power and/or resources for dealing with the problems among the stakeholders.
- Stakeholders may have different levels of expertise and different access to information about the problems.
- The problems are often characterized by technical complexity and scientific uncertainty.
- Differing perspectives on the problems often lead to adversarial relationships among the stakeholders.
- Incremental or unilateral efforts to deal with the problems typically produce less than satisfactory solutions.
- Existing processes for addressing the problems have proved insufficient and may even exacerbate them.

Problems with these characteristics have been dubbed "messes" (Ackoff, 1974) or metaproblems (Chevalier, 1966). What is needed to deal constructively with problems of this type is an alternative model of how to organize to solve them. This book proposes a model of organizing based on collaboration among the parties rather than on competition, hierarchy, or incremental planning (Trist, 1977). This book offers a comprehensive treatment of collaborative dynamics in the hope that potential parties will appreciate how they can use collaboration to successfully address multiparty problems. Let us turn now to an in-depth look at what collaborating entails.

DYNAMICS OF COLLABORATION

Collaboration involves a process of joint decision making among key stakeholders of a problem domain about the future of that domain. Five features are critical to the process: (1) the stakeholders are interdependent, (2) solutions emerge by dealing constructively with differences, (3) joint ownership of decisions is involved, (4) stakeholders assume collective responsibility for the future direction of the domain, and (5) collaboration is an emergent process.

Collaboration Implies Interdependence

Collaboration establishes a give and take among the stakeholders that is designed to produce solutions that none of them working independently could achieve. Therefore, an important ingredient of collaboration is interdependence among the stakeholders. Initially, the extent of interdependence may not be fully appreciated by all the parties. Therefore, the initial phase of any collaboration usually involves calling attention to the ways in which the stakeholders' concerns are intertwined and the reasons why they need each other to solve the problem. Parties in conflict especially lose sight of their underlying interdependence. Heightening parties' awareness of their interdependence often kindles renewed willingness to search for trade-offs that could produce a mutually beneficial solution. In the collaborations investigated in this book, external events often propel reexamination of taken-for-granted interdependencies.

Solutions Emerge by Dealing Constructively with Differences

Respect for differences is an easy virtue to champion verbally and a much more difficult one to put into practice in our day-to-day affairs. Yet differences are often the source of immense creative potential. Learning to harness that potential is what collaboration is all about.

Consider the parable of the elephant and the blind men. Several blind men walking through the jungle come upon an elephant. Each approaches the elephant from a different angle and comes into contact with a different part of the elephant's anatomy. The blind man who contacts the elephant's leg declares, "Oh, an elephant is like a tree trunk." Another, who apprehends the elephant's tail, objects to the first's description, exclaiming, "Oh, no, the elephant is like a rope." A third, grasping the elephant's large, floppy ear, insists, "You are both wrong; the elephant is like a fan." Clearly, each man, from his vantage point, has apprehended something important and genuine about the elephant. Each one's perception of elephant is accurate, albeit limited. None of the blind men, through his own inquiries, has a comprehensive understanding of the phenomenon called "elephant." Together, however, they have a much richer and more complete perspective.

Like the blind men, most of us routinely make a number of assumptions that limit our ability to capitalize on this creative potential. One assumption that we frequently make is that our way of viewing a problem is the best. Best to us may mean the most rational, the fairest, the most intelligent, or even the only way. No matter what the basis, we arrive at the conclusion that our way is superior to any other. Thus we lose sight of the possibility that multiple approaches to the elephant yield multiple perceptions about what is possible and what is desirable.

Even if we grant that multiple perceptions are possible, we can easily fall prey to another common assumption; that is, we conclude that different interpretations are, by definition, opposing interpretations. But here we need to distinguish between interpretations that differ from each other and those that are truly opposed. As Fisher and Ury have aptly pointed out, "Agreement is possible precisely because interests differ" (1981, p. 44). Without differing interests, the range of possible exchanges between parties would be nonexistent. Because parties' interests do vary, as do the resources and skills they have to solve a problem, they are able to arrange trade-offs and to forge mutually beneficial alliances.

It is also frequently the case that as we strive to articulate our differences, we discover that our underlying concerns are fundamentally the same. These shared concerns may have been masked by the different ways we described or framed the problem or may have been obscured by strong emotions that deafened us to the messages coming from the other parties. Parties in conflict are known to engage in selective listening and to pay more attention to information that confirms their preconceived stereotypes of their opponents. Stereotypes cause us to discount the legitimacy of the other's point of view and cause both sides to ignore data that disconfirm their stereotypes (Sherif, 1958). Stereotypes also restrict the flow of information between the parties: Without this exchange of information, the parties cannot discover clues about their shared or differing interests that may contain the seeds of an agreement.

Stereotyping figures prominently in the type of complex multiparty disputes addressed in this book. Frequently the parties have had a long history of interaction, fighting out their differences in legislative and judicial arenas. Working on opposite sides in these arenas allows the parties to continually reconfirm their stereotypic impressions with hard evidence (about the other side's motives, values, and willingness to reach accommodation). Collaboration operates on the premise that the assumptions that disputants have about the other side and about the nature of the issues themselves are worth testing. The premise is that testing these assumptions and allowing a constructive confrontation of differences may unlock heretofore disguised creative potential. Through such exploration stakeholders may discover new options that permit constructive mergers of interests previously unimagined or judged infeasible.

Collaboration Involves Joint Ownership of Decisions

Joint ownership means that the participants in a collaboration are directly responsible for reaching agreement on a solution. Unlike litigation or regulation, in which intermediaries (courts, regulatory agencies, legislators) devise solutions that are imposed on the stakeholders, in collaborative agreements the parties impose decisions on themselves. They set the agenda; they decide what issues will be addressed; they decide what the terms will be. Any agreements that are reached may be free-standing contracts, or they may serve as input to a legal or a public policy process that ratifies, codifies, or in some other way incorporates the agreements. Clearly where matters of public policy are under consideration, collaboration cannot serve as a substitute for constitutional decision-making processes. However, it can "provide a sense of direction, smooth social conflict, and speed formal processes" (Dunlop, 1986, p. 24).

When collaboration occurs, the various stakeholders bring their idiosyncratic perceptions of the problem to the negotiations. Each holds assumptions, beliefs, and viewpoints that are consistent with their independent efforts to confront the problem. Through collaboration these multiple perspectives are aired and debated, and gradually a more complete appreciation of the complexity of the problem is constructed. This more complete appreciation forms the basis for envisioning new alternatives that take into account the stakeholders' multiple interests. Thus, the outcome of collaboration is a weaving together of multiple and diverse viewpoints into a mosaic replete with new insights and directions for action agreed on by all the stakeholders. Three key steps in reaching a joint decision include (1) the joint search for information about the problem, (2) the invention of a mutually agreed upon solution about the pattern of future exchanges between stakeholders, and (3) ratification of the agreement and plans for implementing it.

Stakeholders Assume Collective Responsibility for Future Direction of the Domain

One outcome of collaboration is a set of agreements governing future interactions among the stakeholders. Trist (1983) refers to this as self-regulation of the domain. During collaboration a new set of relationships among the stakeholders is negotiated as they address the problem at hand. The process of collaborating essentially restructures the socially accepted rules for dealing with problems of this type. The negotiations may also restructure the rules governing how stakeholders will interact with respect to the problem in the future. That is, formal or informal contracts about the nature of subsequent exchanges among the stakeholders are forged during collaboration. Collaboration may lead to increased coordination among the stakeholders, although that is not a necessary outcome of the process.

Collaboration Is an Emergent Process

Collaboration is essentially an emergent process rather than a prescribed state of organization. By viewing collaboration as a process, it becomes possible to describe its origins and development as well as how its organization changes over time. Hence, collaboration can be thought of as a temporary and evolving forum for addressing a problem. Typically, collaborations progress from "underorganized systems" in which individual stakeholders act independently, if at all, with respect to the problem (Brown, 1980) to more tightly organized relationships characterized by concerted decision making among the stakeholders.

Collaboration as it is defined here should be distinguished from the terms *cooperation* and *coordination* as used by Mulford and Rogers (1982). They use these terms to classify static patterns of interorganizational relations. Coordination refers to formal institutionalized relationships among existing networks of organizations, while cooperation is "characterized by informal trade-offs and by attempts to establish reciprocity in the absence of rules" (Mulford and Rogers, 1982, p. 13). While these distinctions may be useful for distinguishing formal and informal relationships, they do not capture the dynamic evolutionary character of the phenomenon described in this book. To presume that the parties in a collaborative effort are already part of an organized relationship underrepresents the developmental character of the process and ignores the delicate prenegotiations that are often necessary to bring stakeholders together initially.

Both cooperation and coordination often occur as part of the process of collaborating. The process by which reciprocity is established informally in the absence of rules is as important to collaboration as the formal coordination agreements that eventually emerge. Skillful management of early interactions is often crucial to continued collaboration, since these informal interactions lay the groundwork for subsequent formal interactions.

Once initiated, collaboration creates a temporary forum within which consensus about the problem can be sought, mutually agreeable solutions can be invented, and collective actions to implement the solutions can be taken. Understanding how this process unfolds is critical to successfully managing the kinds of multiparty and multiorganizational relations described earlier in the chapter.

Envisioning interorganizational relations as processes rather than as outcomes in which stakeholders assume decision-making responsibility for their collective future permits investigation of how innovation and change in currently unsatisfactory exchange relationships can occur. If collaboration is successful, new solutions emerge that no single party could have envisioned or enacted. A successful example can best illustrate the dynamics of collaboration.

SUCCESSFUL COLLABORATION

Pernicious stereotypes and misinformation precipitated a major conflict between government agencies and citizens in the community surrounding Three Mile Island Nuclear Reactor. The conflict surfaced over plans for cleanup of the reactor, which was badly damaged during a catastrophic accident in 1979. Through an unprecedented intervention, called the Citizens' Radiation Monitoring Program, local residents and the federal and state governments collaboratively generated credible information to assuage residents' fears about radiation exposure during the initial phase of the cleanup (see Gricar and Baratta [1983] for a more detailed description).

Citizens' Radiation Monitoring Program

The accident at Three Mile Island (TMI) in March 1979 released small but significant levels of radioactivity into the atmosphere, exposing residents of the area surrounding TMI to a maximum radiation dosage twice that of average yearly background levels. Despite reports of no immediate or long-term health effects from the accident, many residents were concerned about the risks associated with radiation exposure. These concerns were heightened when Metropolitan Edison (the operator of Three Mile Island) proposed releasing low levels of radioactive krypton gas into the atmosphere as the first step in the proposed cleanup of the reactor. The full extent of damage to the reactor could not be determined until the gas it contained was removed. The staff of the Nuclear Regulatory Commission (NRC) had determined that the purge would not endanger the health and safety of the public (TMI Support Staff, 1980).

At the time public trust in Met Ed and the NRC was seriously eroded because of the widespread belief that these agencies had deliberately misled the public about radiation levels during the accident. The NRC's own special inquiry into the accident attributed what it called "public misconceptions about risks" to "a failure to convey credible information regarding the actual risks in an understandable fashion to the public" (Rogovin, 1980). This mistrust prompted several communities to appeal to the governor and to the President for independent sources of information about radiation levels. Concern about the risks grew to extreme proportions in March 1980 during public meetings on the environmental impact of the purge. Public opposition to the proposed purge was so fierce that it drowned out the NRC's announcement that a community monitoring program was under way.

In February, the U.S. Department of Energy (DOE) assembled a team of representatives (called the Technical Working Group) from the Environmental Protection Agency, the Pennsylvania Department of Environmental Resources (DER), the Pennsylvania State University, and EG&G Idaho (a technical consultant to Met Ed) to design and implement the Citizens' Radiation Monitoring Program. The program's purpose was to ensure that citizens in the vicinity of TMI received accurate and credible information about radiation levels during the purge. The program was based on the premise that citizens were more likely to believe information generated by themselves or by their neighbors than by government officials, whose credibility they considered questionable. Through the program, local citizens conducted routine monitoring of radiation levels using equipment provided by the Department of Energy.

The Technical Working Group (TWG) sought input on the design of the program from officials of three counties and twelve municipalities that fell within a five-mile radius of TMI. Each community nominated four citizens to serve as monitors. The monitors included teachers, secretaries, engineers, housewives, police officers, and retirees. They ranged in age from early twenties to senior citizens. Their political persuasions about nuclear power ran the gamut from pro- to antinuclear. The monitors were given an intensive "crash course" on radiation and its effects and detection methods, and were given hands-on training so that they could operate the monitoring equipment and interpret the measurements for their fellow citizens.

Each participating community drew up its own monitoring schedule and selected the locations for its monitoring equipment. The citizen monitors posted daily results of the monitoring in the townships, and the TWG disseminated the results to the local media and to the participating agencies.

The Citizen's Radiation Monitoring Program represents a dramatic departure from typical government efforts to communicate with the public. In this case, traditional efforts by government agencies to disseminate public information were grossly ineffective and only increased public mistrust of the agencies. Following months of technical review of Met Ed's proposal for the purge, the NRC tried at public meetings to present a rational argument in support of the purge. Both the meetings and the environmental assessment itself focused exclusively on the technical aspects of reactor decontamination. Rational arguments, however, meant little to citizens whose calculation of the risks involved was much more personal. The accident clearly had left social and psychological scars on the community (Scranton, 1980; Kemeny, 1979; Brunn, Johnson, and Ziegler, 1979) and had created widespread uncertainty about safety. Because of general unfamiliarity with radiation and its effects, the lack of credible information, and the imperceptible nature of radiation itself, the public had little basis for judging either the level of danger or its seriousness. With no precedents to consider, it is not surprising that public fears about potential risks were running high.

Perceptions by public officials that those who resisted were troublemakers or fanatics only fueled the controversy. By underestimating the degree to which emotional concerns for safety shaped public attitudes, these officials reduced their own credibility and further escalated public mistrust.

Collaboration in this case occurred among the Department of Energy, the other agencies involved in the Technical Working Group, and the local municipalities and counties.

Let us examine this case with respect to the five features of collaboration described above. First, how were the stakeholders interdependent? The stakeholders in this case were interdependent because neither Met Ed nor the community could afford not to begin cleanup of the reactor. Leaving the krypton gas inside the reactor posed an unknown risk to the public and prevented Met Ed from determining the extent of damage from the accident. Thus safe but timely decontamination of the reactor was critical.

Second, how were differences handled? Initially in this case there were very different perceptions about safety and about the credibility of those agencies disseminating safety information. Prior to the monitoring program, Met Ed and the government agencies had relied on a rational, technocratic approach to educate the public and had dismissed the citizens' concerns as irrational. The monitoring program was an acknowledgment that these differing perceptions of risk needed to be addressed, not ignored. Enlisting local citizens as monitors was a novel and unprecedented step by these agencies, which typically relied on narrow, technically oriented solutions.

Third, were the stakeholders jointly involved in decision making? The initial proposal for citizen monitoring came from the mayor of one of the affected communities. Exploratory meetings involved several, but not all, stakeholder groups. Once the DOE made the decision to go ahead, decision making was shared among several agencies in the TWG, and, to a lesser extent, the local communities and their citizen monitors participated in making decisions about the execution of the program. Met Ed, a key stakeholder, was purposely excluded from the group because its participation would likely have damaged the credibility of the entire effort. Thus, this process did not provide for full participation by all the stakeholders, but it did incorporate widespread representation in the overall planning.

Fourth, who assumed responsibility for the future direction of the domain? This case graphically illustrates how responsibility for ensuring that credible information about radiation levels was available to the communities surrounding TMI was shared among the stakeholders. The DOE supplied the financial resources; EG&G Idaho, the EPA, and the DER contributed technical expertise and staff; the university designed the equipment and provided training and organizational expertise; and the citizens donated their time and talent to carry out the monitoring.

Finally, to what extent was the collaboration emergent? The process of collaborating grew out of a major public controversy. At the outset, mechanisms for managing the differing interests and coordinating a viable plan of action were underdeveloped. The Citizens' Radiation Monitoring Program emerged through a series of steps. It began with the citizens' opposition to the venting and their plea for credible information. This was followed by the formation of the TWG, involvement of the communities, creation of the training program, and, finally, the monitoring itself. Because of the urgency of the situation, the entire collaborative process lasted only five months.

The consequences of this collaborative effort are summarized below:

- Met Ed was allowed to execute a critical first step in the reactor cleanup process.
- Residents in the community received information they could trust to judge their own levels of radiation exposure. A survey conducted before and after the training indicated a significant increase in the monitors' belief that they could get accurate information about radiation levels and that they had sufficient information to make a judgment about their own safety (Gricar and Baratta, 1983).

- Residents who participated as monitors gained a deeper appreciation for the technical issues associated with nuclear power and engaged in rational dialogue and debate with each other on contested topics during the training program.

In addition to the above outcomes, the Citizens' Radiation Monitoring Program demonstrated that government, communities, and the private sector often hold very different perceptions about a problem. Without a frank and open dialogue characterized by reason and respect, these perceptions cannot be examined. Had the NRC proceeded with the purge without community guarantees about credible information, the conflict would only have escalated, probably to the level of violence.

BENEFITS OF COLLABORATING

When collaboration is used to address multiparty problems, several benefits are possible (see Table 1).

First, collaboration increases the quality of solutions considered by the parties because solutions are based on a broad, comprehensive analysis of the problem. The collective capacity to respond to the problem is also increased as stakeholders apply a variety of complementary resources to solving it. Collaboration also offers a way to reopen negotiations when impasse imperils more traditional processes. More important, use of collaboration early in a multiparty conflict can minimize the possibility that impasse will occur.

The process of collaborating builds in certain guarantees that each party's interests will be protected. It does so by continually remanding ownership of the process and any decisions reached to the parties themselves. Parties often assume that by collaborating they will lose any individual leverage they have over the problem. This concern about loss of control is deceptive, however. It is rare in any multiparty conflict that any party satisfies 100 percent of their interests and incurs no costs while the other

TABLE 1   The Benefits of Collaboration

- Broad comprehensive analysis of the problem domain improves the quality of solutions.
- Response capability is more diversified.
- It is useful for reopening deadlocked negotiations.
- The risk of impasse is minimized.
- The process ensures that each stakeholder's interests are considered in any agreement.
- Parties retain ownership of the solution.
- Parties most familiar with the problem, not their agents, invent the solutions.
- Participation enhances acceptance of solution and willingness to implement it.
- The potential to discover novel, innovative solutions is enhanced.
- Relations between the stakeholders improve.
- Costs associated with other methods are avoided.
- Mechanisms for coordinating future actions among the stakeholders can be established.

parties gain nothing. Collaborative processes protect each party's interests by guaranteeing that they are heard and understood. In addition, the processes are structured to ensure that ownership of the solution remains with the participants since ratification hinges on their reaching agreement among themselves.

> Instead of trying to restrict participation, a common tactic, the professional manager gains more control over the situation by ensuring that all the necessary parties are there at the table, recognizing that parties in a dispute often engage in adversarial behavior because no other approach is available to protect their interests [Carpenter and Kennedy, 1988, p. 26].

Parties retain control during collaboration precisely because *they* must be the ones to adopt or reject the final agreement.

Ownership of the process and of the outcomes generates two additional benefits. The parties themselves, who are most familiar with the problem, not their agents, fashion the solution. Additionally, commitment to the solution is generally high as a result of collaboration. Investment in a process of building a comprehensive appreciation of the problem and designing a solution jointly enhances the parties' acceptance of the solution and their commitment to carry it out (Delbecq, 1974).

By focusing on interests and encouraging the exploration of differences, the potential to discover novel, innovative solutions like the Citizens' Radiation Monitoring Program is enhanced. Even when parties are unable to reach closure through collaboration, some benefits from collaborating are still possible. Collaborating usually leaves parties with a clearer understanding of their differences and an improved working relationship. These outcomes permit the parties to amicably "agree to disagree" or to accept a decision imposed by a traditional dispute resolution forum in lieu of reaching a collaborative agreement. Sometimes parties reach agreement on all but one or two areas and turn to a judicial or administrative agency to resolve the remaining disagreements.

Collaboration also has the potential to reduce the costs parties incur from acting alone or the costs associated with protracted conflict among the stakeholders. Although it is difficult to make reliable comparisons (of the cost of collaborating versus not doing so), it is reasonable to assume that collaboration can reduce the cost of hiring intermediaries (such as attorneys in legal disputes), the cost of research and development (R&D) expenditures for partners in R&D consortia, and a myriad of social costs stemming from protracted inaction on critical social and international problems.

Finally, through collaboration stakeholders can develop mechanisms to coordinate their future interactions. Through this coordination, stakeholders take concerted rather than disconnected actions to manage the problem domain, and interdependencies become more predictable.

REALITIES OF COLLABORATING

Just as it is important to articulate the benefits of collaborating, it is equally important to dispel the notion that collaboration is a cure for all evils. There are many circumstances in which stakeholders are unable or unwilling to engage each other in this way. Collaboration is not always an appropriate alternative. For example, when one party has unchallenged power to influence a domain, collaboration does not make sense. . . .

Nor is collaboration an idealistic panacea. Realistically, collaboration involves difficult issues that have often eluded simple solutions in the past. Many multiparty problems are political in nature because they involve "distributional" issues. In distributional disputes the stakeholders are concerned about the allocation of funds, the setting of standards, or the siting of facilities. Groups in distributional disputes are contesting "a specific allocation of gains and losses" (Susskind and Cruikshank, 1987, p. 19). Allocating gains and losses, however, involves the allocation of risks that, as the Three Mile Island case illustrated, are perceived very differently by different stakeholders. Moreover, perceptions of risk often have deep psychological and emotional roots. Dealing with these emotional attachments is a tricky business. Success depends as much on the process of legitimizing parties' interests as on the substantive outcomes. The design of meetings between stakeholders is crucial to success. Many well-intended efforts to involve the public in government decisions, for example, are exercises in frustration and often exacerbate rather than improve the situation because careful attention to the process of managing differences is neglected (Wondolleck, 1985; Carpenter and Kennedy, 1988).

Thus, solving complex multiparty problems requires more than sound economic policies and technological breakthroughs. It also demands careful attention to the process of making decisions. Successful collaborations are not achieved without considerable effort on the part of the participating stakeholders and usually not without the skill and forbearance of a convening organization and/or a skilled third party. Often parties perceive real risks to collaborating, if only because the process is unfamiliar and the outcomes are uncertain. Unless issues like these and more serious ones such as concerns about cooptation or lack of fairness are dispelled up front, attempts at collaboration will not succeed. It is often the convener or third party who initially proposes the possibility of collaborating and who then shepherds the parties through a collaborative process. Hence, for collaboration to occur, someone must introduce a mind-set, a vision, a belief in the creative potential of managing differences, and must couple this mind-set with a constructive process for designing creative solutions to complex multiparty problems.

. . . Negotiation is not used here to denote specific tactics of positional bargaining, which are often associated with collective bargaining or buyer-seller transactions. Instead, negotiation is used in the broader sociological sense used by Strauss (1978). Through their talk, stakeholders try to arrive at collective interpretations of how they see the world. These interpretations form the basis for actions. Negotiation, therefore, refers to conversational interactions among collaborating parties as they try to define a problem, agree on recommendations, or design action steps. In this way they create a negotiated order . . .

Not all collaborations lead to agreements for action, but when agreements are reached, they are arrived at by consensus. Consensus is achieved when each of the stakeholders agrees they can live with a proposed solution, even though it may not be their most preferred solution. Both consensus building and negotiation . . . refer to the process of constructing agreements among the stakeholders.

Collaboration can occur with or without the assistance of a third party who serves as a mediator or facilitator. The task of the third party is not to render a decision (in the way that a judge does, for instance) but to help structure a dialogue within which the parties can work out their differences. The term *mediator* will generally be used here to refer to this third-party role. . . .

Resolving Conflict through "Win-Win" Negotiating

Philip I. Morgan

Recently, during a short stay in a hotel, a leak developed in the shower stall above my room causing water to drip from a hole in the ceiling. I immediately called the manager, and he quickly agreed to provide me with another room that same day when one became available. Afterwards, however, I reflected that it would be inconvenient for me to move since I was comfortably settled. Besides, the leak was more of an inconvenience than a real nuisance. The real source of my discomfort was the *price* I was being charged for the room! I then looked at the situation from the hotel manager's viewpoint and reflected that since the hotel was full, it would mean a loss of revenue to him since the room couldn't be rented while the ceiling was being repaired. Wasn't there a better solution, one that would meet both our needs? I called the manager back, explained my real problem with the room, and he quickly offered to substantially reduce the rental price for the room. Both of us were happy with this outcome.

Since people generally want different things and must compete for scarce resources, conflict is inevitable. Whether the conflict is over hotel room prices, wages, working conditions, layoffs, grievances, procedures, or budgets, it's important to learn to deal with it constructively. This usually means learning how to develop effective negotiating skills.

All managers negotiate; some are better at it than others. What determines whether an outcome is successful or not is the degree of skill of the negotiator.

HARD VERSUS SOFT NEGOTIATORS

Not all negotiated agreements end so amicably as the one above. What typically happens is that the parties become locked into ways of thinking and operating predicated on a set of faulty value assumptions. These positions can be characterized on a continuum of "Hard" versus "Soft" negotiating styles. (see Figure 1).

FIGURE 1   Hard versus Soft Negotiators

Hard Negotiators	Soft Negotiators
Open with high demands.	Open with modest proposals.
Stick to their guns.	Are flexible, make many concessions.
Make a few trivial concessions and reduce even these as negotiations proceed.	Make large concessions.
Appear unconcerned about the threat of deadlock.	Are terrified of deadlock (and show it).
Emphasize winning.	Emphasize the relationship (that is, say "Let's be friends").
Make threats.	Make more concessions.

Being a hard negotiator is generally more certain to get someone what he or she wants, provided that person "hangs tough" and provided he or she is dealing with a soft negotiator. However, if the person meets with an equally hard adversary, the result is usually a refusal to negotiate and deadlock. Even if both sides get *some* of what they want, the relationship invariably deteriorates.

Hard negotiators will always win over soft negotiators where one emphasizes "winning" and the other "relationship." What typically happens is "Soft" will make a concession to "Hard" to set an example, but the only response from "Hard" is to increase his or her demands. And every concession made by "Soft" unwittingly reinforces "Hard's" behavior by rewarding him for being hard.

Fortunately, there is an alternative.

THE INTEGRATIVE SOLUTION

The reason the hotel situation was resolved so amicably was because the negotiated settlement followed certain guidelines common to all successful negotiations. Primarily, it was an example of an *integrative* solution. An integrative solution is one where both parties' needs are met. Obviously not all problems can be resolved in this way. Nevertheless, the integrative approach seems to offer a better alternative to the more common adversarial one practiced by most managers.

For an integrated solution to work, certain preconditions must exist. First, the parties must be motivated to collaborate rather than to compete. Both parties must perceive that they have a common stake in this situation and that there is more to be gained by negotiating than by *not* negotiating. One way to encourage such thinking is for each party to prepare by setting goals and objectives for himself or herself.

Once the negotiation process gets underway, superordinate goals can be emphasized; for example, that the company should make a profit or stay in business. Usually there's little argument here. It's only when deciding the means to these ends that there is disagreement. Therefore, generating many alternatives in a mutual problem-solving, "brainstorming" process may be motivating and may facilitate the negotiating process. Once the problem is separated from the personalities involved, both parties can then become involved in *mutual goal setting and problem solving.*

Second, rather than downplaying the other party's needs and wants as unacceptable, each party must recognize the other's *legitimate* right to seek his or her own best interests.

Finally, a spirit of *mutual trust* should be developed between the parties. This is difficult to accomplish, but without it the integrative approach will fail. The absence of trust engenders defensiveness, withdrawal, and suspicion of the other's motives. To build trust, it's important to share information about oneself as openly as one judges appropriate. The parties must each state their needs and work at understanding by *listening* to the other's point of view and also clarifying issues. This doesn't mean being indiscriminately open and trusting. It does, however, mean that each should share his or her concerns with the other party and work toward a mutual agreement.

The following are a few further dos and don'ts to follow in seeking an integrative solution. Even when the integrative approach is not immediately apparent, the following guidelines should enable a manager to become a more skillful negotiator. They should also create a climate where an integrative solution can at least be considered.

SOME DON'TS

First, some things to avoid:

Either/Or–Win/Lose Thinking.   The major feature of hard versus soft negotiating is that both parties become locked into an either-or style of thinking. The assumption is that one side must win and the other must lose. For example, "Hard" may say, "Look, this is my final offer; take it or leave it!" This usually induces in "Soft" a false sense that this is the only choice left. The way out of this faulty dilemma is to recognize that there are nearly always other alternatives and that an attempt should be made to search for the commonalities in the situation.

Bargaining Based on Positions.   Typically in negotiation parties take *positions* on certain issues and attempt to bargain from this standpoint. Much time is wasted in posturing. People become ego-involved with their pet positions and are fearful of losing face if they are seen to have to give in to the other side's demands. As both sides tend to paint themselves into a corner from which there is little room to maneuver, the result is deadlock.

Selling Short.   Sometimes people will do this to avoid hassles. For example, they may say, "I just want to get it over," "I was glad to get *anything* at all," or "I gave in to get a quick settlement." There may be some legitimate reason for "giving in" under certain circumstances. However, when this behavior becomes habitual, a person may simply be taking the easiest way out.

Such behaviors come from the mistaken assumption that one alone is under pressure. We may forget that other people may be under even greater pressure and assuming they're not merely strengthens their hand and weakens our own.

SOME DOS

Now here are a few things one should actively do:

Adequately Prepare.   Poor negotiators begin negotiating before objectives are set or adequate alternatives are considered. The attitude seems to be one of, "Let's see what the other side has to say for itself, then we'll develop our strategy as we go along." The problem with playing it by ear is that the initiative is lost and, at best, each side simply muddles along.

Consider Alternatives.   Roger Fisher and William Ury in *Getting to Yes* suggest that before one even begins to negotiate, one should develop what they call one's BATNA—"Best Alternative to a Negotiated Agreement." They suggest that it's important to know beforehand what one intends to do if one doesn't reach agreement. They believe that if someone knows what his or her best alternative is, every negotiation will be successful in the sense that the outcome will be better than the *best* alternative. Otherwise, it needn't be accepted.

One should also consider the other side's BATNA. What can they do if there is no negotiation?

Set Objectives and Establish Criteria.   Setting realistic objectives and establishing criteria are one and the same since objectives determine how successful or unsuccessful one has been in negotiating. However, one should be sure the objectives are realistic and measureable. "To get as much as we can for as little as we can give away" may be a nice ideal, but it won't take a manager very far since he or she has no way of measuring any settlement from the negotiation process.

In setting objectives, one should begin by making a list of *all* one's objectives; for example, to survive in business, to make a profit, and to avoid a price war. Next, one should divide the objectives into two lists, one titled "likes," the other "musts." "Likes" are things that would be *nice* to have but that could be done without. "Musts" are those items one absolutely must have for the negotiations to be successful. As negotiations progress, a manager may find himself or herself abandoning many of the "likes" since these items consist of the least important objectives. The "must" objectives are those he or she really *aims* to achieve and is willing to bargain for.

"Must" objectives are the manager's "bottom line" or limits. If he or she doesn't achieve these objectives, the manager is willing to forego bargaining. Naturally, both kinds of objectives aren't as set in concrete as may be implied here. Circumstances may dictate that the objectives or their order changes. So a continuous review process is necessary.

Insist on Objective Standards.   Negotiations should be based on a set of principles. For example, using fairness, the golden rule, equal treatment, or the going rate for a job makes it easier to reach agreement.

When selling a car, for example, one doesn't arbitrarily set a price for it. Instead, one generally decides on the price based on the "Blue Book" market rate for the particular car, year, and other comparables. Arguing from a set of principles makes it easier to reach agreement since reasoning is based on objective standards, not subjective ones.

Clarify Interests and Values.   Is it money? Ethical principles? The working relationship with the other side? Job security? Next, one needs to determine what actions are likely to enhance or jeopardize these concerns. It is important, too, to decide what the other side really cares about. The tendency is to assume that the other side wants the exact opposite of what one wants. But that isn't always so.

Only by actively listening to the other side can both parties' interests and values be clarified.

Get Closure on Agreement.   When the negotiation session ends, it's a good idea to obtain closure by summarizing what has been agreed on in writing. Many negotiations have gone wrong on just this final point because perception is such an individual thing. It's important that one state specifically just what it is to which one is agreeing. It may even be necessary to paraphrase what the other party says to the individual's satisfaction before leaving the bargaining table.

Interests: The Measure of Negotiation

David A. Lax

James K. Sebenius

People negotiate to further their interests. And negotiation advisers urge attention to interests—often solemnly, as if the suggestion were original and surprising. Yet Socrates' admonition to "Know Thyself" surely scoops any late twentieth century advice of this sort. So, academic compulsiveness aside, why write an article on interests or, more to the point, why read one?

The answer, in part, is that negotiators often focus on interests, but conceive of them too narrowly. We will argue for a more expansive conception of negotiator's interests. Moreover, interests often conflict, and simply listing them without understanding the trade-offs among them is a bit like writing out a recipe without including the proportions. In addition to determining interests, negotiators need ways to assess the relative importance of those various interests. We will try to clarify the logic of assessing trade-offs.

As hard as it may be to sort out one's own interests, understanding how others see theirs—*their* subjective scheme of values as perceived through *their* peculiar psychological filters—can be extraordinarily difficult. Obviously, suggesting a stretch "in the other person's shoes" is good advice; equally obviously, it is only a starting point. In this article we will try to go further.

AN EXPANSIVE CONCEPTION OF A NEGOTIATOR'S INTERESTS

In evaluating the interests at stake, a typical negotiator might focus on commodities that can be bought and sold or on concrete terms that can be written into a contract or treaty. And, negotiators definitely have such interests: the crippled plaintiff desperately wants compensation; a sales manager cares intensely about prices, profit margins,

Reprinted with permission from David A. Lax and James K. Sebenius, "Interests: The Measure of Negotiation," *Negotiation Journal*, January 1986, pp. 73–92.

return on investment, and personal compensation; managers may derive value from seeing their particular product sweep the market or furthering some vision of the public interest.

Throughout this article, we assume that negotiators want to do well for themselves. Of course, "doing well" is only measured with respect to the things they care about, whether out of direct self-interest or concern for the welfare of others. Thus, doing "better" in a negotiation need not imply pressing for more money or a bigger share; rather, it means advancing the totality of one's interests, which may include money and other tangibles as well as fairness, the well-being of one's counterparts, and the collegiality of the process. For instance, furthering Robert's interests may mean taking less money to obtain a fair settlement by a friendly process: by the same token, Helen may want only to publicly humiliate her counterpart and extract from him the very biggest check.

It is especially common in business negotiations, however, to assume that interests extend only to the bottom line. Yet imagine holding rigidly to this assumption when negotiating with the number two executive of a technical products company from the upper half of the Fortune 500. He echoed his firm's philosophy when he stated:

> Our most important goal is to do a good job. We don't have a specific growth target, but what we want to do is make a contribution. Not just a "me too" thing, but to develop technically superior products. Another goal is to earn our way, to grow from our own resources. A third goal is to make this an interesting and satisfactory place to work. The fourth goal . . . there must be a fourth goal. I mentioned it also in a speech at [a nearby university]. Oh yes, the fourth goal is to make a profit. (Donaldson and Lorsch, 1984, p. 85)

Negotiators' interests can go beyond the obvious and tangible. Take for example the almost universal quest for social approval or the simple pleasure one derives from being treated with respect, even in a one-time encounter. A stockbroker may want to build a relationship with a customer because of the future business it may bring; or a plaintiff, anxious at the thought of a trial, may be willing to take a reduced settlement to avoid courtroom trauma. Negotiators have good reasons to be concerned with their reputations. A person who is widely known never to recede from a position may rarely be called on for concessions. Fisher and Ury (1981) argue that a negotiator should seek to be known for reaching agreements only by means of "objective" principles; once achieved, among other effects, such a "principled" reputation may reduce the need to haggle.

Beyond concerns about reputation, relationship, and process, negotiators often care about subtle aspects of precedent. For example, Luther—a product manager in a fast-growing medical devices firm—confronted his colleague Francoise for the second time with a vigorous demand for priority use of the firm's advertising department—even though Francoise had informally "reserved" this block of the ad department's time for her people. After analyzing her interests in this unexpected negotiation, Francoise balked at a few seemingly reasonable settlements that Luther suggested. Why? Francoise sought to avoid two undesirable precedents: first, in the *substance* of the issue (*her* division needed to count absolutely on future ad department reservations); and second, in the *procedure* set for raising a whole range of similar matters (she wanted to bolster the use of established policies). Concern with both types of precedent abounds in organizations and elsewhere.

Strategic interests are often at stake for managers. By this, we refer to the alignment of a particular decision with the manager's long-term personal or institutional strategy. Suppose that a prompt investment in the capacity to manage mutual funds appears likely to have high short-term potential for a firm whose long-term plan has been to develop expertise in real estate investments. Would a key manager's proposal now to devote substantial energy to mutual funds research and investment be wise? Recourse to strategic rather than short-term financial analysis may unravel the firm's best interests in this case.

Through actions in one negotiation, a manager may have an interest in reducing the cost of later encounters and in affecting their outcomes. A manager may thus strive to create in subordinates the impression that explicit bargaining is impossible and that commands must be obeyed. Perhaps the back-and-forth process has become too costly and inefficient for the task at hand. In such cases, paradoxically, a prime managerial interest in routine dealings may actually be to drive out future overt bargaining. It is exceedingly ironic that a powerful interest to be achieved through a determined pattern of negotiation may be to establish an impregnable image of rigid hierarchy, potent command, and iron control—that brooks *no* conscious negotiation. Especially in early encounters, say, between a freshly hired vice president and others in the firm, the new officer may regard the establishment of a favorable pattern of others' automatic deference to "suggestions" as of central interest. Or the new officer may strongly weigh the effects on his or her perceived track record or esteem as an expert so that others may be more likely to show deference in the future.

Comparing obvious, "bottom line" interests with "others"—reputation, precedent, relationships, and the like—a very detailed study of corporate resource allocation in a multidivisional chemical company noted:

> These are the dimensions a manager takes into account when he makes his decisions. In some instances they far outweigh the importance of the substantive issues in his assessment of decision-making priorities.
>
> It is worth pausing to emphasize this point. There is a very strong tendency in financial or decision-making treatments of capital budgeting to regard the personal status of managers as noise, "a source of bias." . . . Theoreticians do not consider the problem a rational manager faces as he considers committing himself to a project over time. He has made other commitments in the past, other projects are competing for funds and engineering at the division level, and other managers are competing for the jobs he seeks. At the same time those same managers are his peers and friends. Whatever he does, he is more than likely going to have to live with those same men for a decade or more. While only some projects are technically or economically interdependent, all are organizationally interdependent. (Bower, 1972, p. 302)

It is not always easy to know how to evaluate interests; sometimes they may derive from interactions too complex to understand directly. In such cases, carefully chosen *proxy interests* may help. For example, the President of the United States cannot possibly predict the effects of any particular negotiated outcome on all of his substantive interests over the course of his term or beyond. Taking account of this, Richard

Neustadt, in his classic bargaining manual, *Presidential Power* (1980), counsels him to evaluate his dealings in terms of three particular interests. The first is obvious: his interest in the *substance* of the immediate issue.

Second, however, the President's *professional reputation* can heavily affect the reactions of important Washingtonians to his later concerns and actions. The President needs the resources and cooperation of these Washingtonians to carry out his programs. Thus, beyond the substance of the issue, Neustadt suggests, the effect of the current negotiation on the President's professional reputation among Washingtonians should be a proxy interest reflecting, in part, his ability to get the Washingtonians to act in accord with his subsequent desires.

Third, Neustadt argues that the President should evaluate the effect of his actions on his *popular prestige*. High prestige reflects the strength of his mandate and influences Washingtonians. It is, in part, a proxy interest; actions that enhance his public prestige improve his chances favorably to influence subsequent outcomes of direct concern. A President may also value popular prestige for its own sake. As negotiator, the President may well have to trade these interests off against each other; for example, he may yield somewhat on his substantive interest in the immediate issue to enhance his reputation and prestige elsewhere. In many positions less complex than that of the President, negotiators' interests are difficult to enumerate because the link between actions and eventual outcomes is hazy. In such cases, a negotiator may benefit by finding simplified proxy interests that predict outcomes either directly or indirectly, by predicting the negotiator's subsequent influence on outcomes of concern.

In short, interests include anything that the negotiator cares about, any concerns that are evoked by the issues discussed. Clarifying interests, however, can sometimes be difficult. We have often found that two distinctions can help.

TWO HELPFUL DISTINCTIONS

Interests, Issues, and Positions

Negotiators seek to reach agreement on specific *positions* on a specific set of *issues*. For example, a potential employee may initially demand $36,000 (the position) for salary (the issue). The job seeker's underlying *interests* may be in financial security, enhanced lifestyle, organizational status, and advanced career prospects. Or, the desire of a Midwestern utility company to build a dam may collide with farmers' needs for water and environmentalists' concern for the downstream habitat of endangered whooping cranes. Increased economic return, irrigated crops, and preserved species are the relevant *interests;* they conflict over the *issue* of the dam's construction, *positions* on which are pro and con.

Negotiators often assume that issues directly express underlying interests. Of course, many different sets of issues may reflect the same interests: a country might seek to serve its interest in mineral development through negotiations over *issues* as varied as simple royalty concessions, joint ventures, or service contracts. Conceivably, the country's interest could be equally satisfied by different terms on each of these alternative issues. The issue at hand, however, may be only a proxy for imperfectly related interests. For example, the United States in the Paris Peace talks may have insisted on a round table and the North Vietnamese a rectangular one. The relevant compromise would hardly have been oval. The real interests were far from the rectangular versus round issue.

Many negotiators retard creativity by failing to distinguish the issues under discussion from their underlying interests. When the issues under discussion poorly match the interests at stake, modifications of the issues sometimes enable all parties to satisfy their interests better. For example, recall the conflict between the midwestern utility company, the farmers, and the environmentalists. After several years of costly and embittering litigation, the parties came to a resolution by a shift to issues that matched their underlying interests in a more fruitful manner. By moving from positions ("yes" and "no") on the issue of the dam's construction to discussions about the nature of downstream water guarantees, the amount of a trust fund to protect the whooping crane habitat, and the size of the dam, the parties reached an agreement that left all of them better off.

Negotiators who mistakenly see their interests as perfectly aligned with their positions on issues may be less likely to shift issues creatively. They might even suspiciously oppose proposals to modify the issues. Indeed, in attempting to protect their perceived interests, such negotiators may dig their heels in hard to avoid budging from their desired positions. In the "dam versus no dam" conflict, positions could have hardened to a point where the grim determination of each side to prevail over the other—whatever the cost—would have ruled out any real search for preferable options. At a minimum, such rigid dealings can be frustrating and time-consuming: impasses or poor agreements often result.

The prevalence of hard-fought, time-consuming, unimaginative "positional" negotiations led Fisher and Ury (1981, p. 11) to propose a general rule: "Focus on interests, not positions." While we think that negotiators should always keep the distinction clearly in mind, focusing exclusively on interests may not always be wise. When parties have deep and conflicting ideological differences, for example, satisfactory agreements on "smaller" issues may only be possible if ideological concerns do not arise. In such cases, the negotiations should focus on the issues or on a much narrower set of interests—not the full set of underlying interests. Two hostile but neighboring countries embroiled in tribal, religious, or ideological conflict may be best off handling a sewage problem on their common border by only dealing with this more limited issue. Or leftist guerilla leaders, each with an underlying interest in ruling the country, might unite on the issue of overthrowing the rightist dictator; an agreement that attempted to reconcile their underlying interests would likely be more difficult to achieve. Moreover, a negotiator may choose to focus on an issue that, for legal or other reasons, provides greater leverage than do discussions of underlying interests. The nature-loving group that has an abiding interest in preventing development may develop a sudden attachment to the issue of wetlands protection if the Wetlands Preservation Act provides the strongest grounds for negotiating with and deterring developers.

At times, a tenacious focus on positions may yield desirable results. With a group of landowners, the CEO of a major mining company had negotiated the general outlines of a contract along with a few critical particulars. Then the CEO turned the rest of the negotiations over to a company lawyer to finish in short order—before a hard-to-obtain environmental permit expired. One provision that the second group of negotiators inherited had not been extensively debated before. Yet, its tentative resolution, while barely acceptable to the landowners, clearly would confer great benefits on the company. Though the landowners' representatives sought to focus on "interests" and "fairness" in order to undo the provision, the company's lawyer made a powerful commitment to it and turned a completely deaf ear to all argument, urging instead that they get on with "unresolved" matters. Though this tactic risked negative repercussions on the other issues, the lawyer's firm commitment to a position was an effective means of claiming value in this instance.

Thus interests should be distinguished from issues and positions.[1] Focusing on interests can help one develop a better understanding of mutual problems and invent creative solutions. But such a focus may not always be desirable when, for example, underlying interests are diametrically opposed or when a focus on particular issues or positions provides leverage. Whatever the focus, however, interests measure the value of any position or agreement.

Intrinsic and Instrumental Interests

It should be clear that negotiators may have many kinds of interests: money and financial security, a particular conception of the public interest, the quality of products, enhancing a reputation as a skilled bargainer, maintaining a working relationship, precedents, and so on. However, one distinction—between intrinsic and instrumental interests—can provide an economical way to capture some important qualities of interests, call negotiators' attention to often-overlooked, sometimes subtle interests, and lead to improved agreements.

One's interest in an issue is *instrumental* if favorable terms on the issue are valued because of their effect on subsequent dealings. One's interest in an issue is *intrinsic* if one values favorable terms of settlement on the issue independent of any subsequent dealings. Thus, a divorcing parent's interest in gaining custody of his or her child, the farmer's interest in water rights, or a country's interest in secure borders can usefully be thought of as intrinsic interests. Such interests need not have any obvious or agreed-upon economic value. For example, Charles, a 60-year-old venture capitalist, was negotiating the dissolution of a strikingly successful technology partnership with Marie, a young, somewhat standoffish woman whom he had brought on as a partner two years before. At first Charles bargained very hard over the financial terms because he viewed them as indicating who had really contributed important ideas and skills to the venture's success. When Marie belatedly acknowledged her genuine respect for his ideas and contributions, Charles became much less demanding on the financial issues. In this instance, it happened that the venture capitalist also had a strong intrinsic interest in psychic gratification from acknowledgement of his role as mentor and father-figure.

Most issues affect both intrinsic and instrumental interests. Dealings with a subordinate who wants to hire an assistant can arouse an intrinsic interest in the overall size of the budget as well as a concern with the perceived precedent the hiring will set in the eyes of the subordinate's peers—an instrumental interest. Recognizing the distinction may lead to improved agreements; the subordinate who can create a justifiable device to prevent decisions about his or her staff support from setting precedents may well receive authorization to hire a new assistant.

One of the main reasons we focus on the intrinsic-instrumental distinction is for the light it sheds on three often-misunderstood aspects of negotiation: interests in the process, in relationships, and in principles.

"Process" Interests—Intrinsic and Instrumental. Analysts often assume that negotiators evaluate agreements by measuring the value obtained from the outcome. Yet, negotiators may care about the *process* of bargaining as well. Even with no prospect of further interaction, some would prefer a negotiated outcome reached by pleasant, cooperative discussion to the same outcome reached by abusive, threat-filled dealings. Others might even derive value from a strident process that gives them the satisfied feeling of having extracted something from their opponents. Either way, negotiators can have intrinsic interests in the character of the negotiation process itself.

Beyond such intrinsic valuation, an unpleasant process can dramatically affect future dealings; the supplier who is berated and threatened may be unresponsive when cooperation at a later point would help. Indeed, negotiators often have strong instrumental interests in building trust and confidence early in the negotiation process in order to facilitate jointly beneficial agreements.

"Relationship" Interests—Intrinsic and Instrumental. Negotiators often stress the value of their relationships; this interest sometimes achieves an almost transcendent status. For example, Fisher and Ury (1981, p. 20) say that "every negotiator has two kinds of interests: in the substance and in the relationship." Many negotiators derive intrinsic value from developing or furthering a pleasant relationship. Moreover, when repeated dealings are likely, most negotiators perceive the instrumental value of developing an effective working relationship. After studying hundreds of managers in many settings, John Kotter (1985, p. 40) sensibly concluded:

> Good working relationships based on some combination of respect, admiration, perceived need, obligation, and friendship are a critical source of power in helping to get things done. Without these relationships, even the best possible idea could be rejected or resisted in an environment where diversity breeds suspicion and interdependence precludes giving orders to most of the relevant players. Furthermore, since these relationships serve as important information channels, without them one may never be able to establish the information one needs to operate effectively.

Of course, in the dissolution of a partnership or the divorce of a childless couple with few assets, the parties may find no instrumental value in furthering their relationship; that is, the parties would not be willing to trade substantive gains on, say, financial terms, to enhance their future dealings. In fact, a bitter divorcing couple may actually prefer a financial outcome that requires absolutely no future contact over another that is better for both in tax terms but requires them to deal with each other in the future. Similarly, a division head with two valuable but constantly warring employees may have a keen interest in separating them organizationally to prevent *any* active relationship between them. And, when dealing with an obnoxious salesperson who has come to the door or by the office, one's interest in the "relationship" may mainly be to terminate it.

Interest in "Principles"—Intrinsic and Instrumental.   Negotiators may discover shared norms or principles relevant to their bargaining problem. Such norms may include equal division, more complex distributive judgments, historical or ethical rationales, objective or accepted standards, as well as notions that simply seem fair or are represented as such. (Gulliver, 1979; Fisher and Ury, 1981). Acting in accord with such a norm or principle may be of intrinsic interest to one or more of the parties; for example, a settlement of $532—arrived at in accord with the mutually acknowledged principle that each party should be paid in proportion to time worked—may be valued quite differently than the same dollar figure reached by haggling. Of course, an acknowledged norm need not be an absolute value in a negotiation: it may be partly or fully traded off against other interests.

Even when none of the parties derive intrinsic value from acting in accord with a particular principle, it may still guide agreement. Principles and simple notions often serve as naturally prominent focal points for choosing one settlement within the range of possible outcomes (Schelling, 1960). For example, equal division of a windfall may seem so irresistibly natural to the partners in a small firm that they would scarcely consider negotiation over who should get more.

The principles that guide agreement in the first of many related disputes may set a powerful precedent. Thus, negotiators may work hard to settle the first dispute on the basis of principles that they believe will yield favorable outcomes in subsequent disputes. They may take a loss with respect to intrinsic interests in the first negotiation in order to satisfy their instrumental interests in the principles used to guide the agreement.

In short, with many less tangible interests—such as process, relationships, or fairness—a negotiator should ask why they are valued. Distinguishing between their instrumental and intrinsic components can help. But even with these components sorted out, how can a negotiator go about assessing their "relative importance?" More generally, what logic guides setting priorities among conflicting interests?

THINKING ABOUT TRADE–OFFS

Listing one's own interests as well as a best guess at those of other parties is certainly useful. But difficult questions tend to arise in negotiations that force one to make sacrifices on some interests in order to gain on others: How much of a trade is desirable? In buying a seller-financed house, how should Ralph evaluate higher purchase prices compared to lower mortgage interest rates? How much more should a manufacturer be willing to pay for the next quality grade of components? How much should a sales manager trade on price for the prospects of a better relationship? How much should a manager be willing to give up on substance to secure a favorable precedent?

Thinking about trade-offs is often excruciatingly difficult and badly done. Yet, whether or not negotiators choose to ponder priorities, they effectively make trade-offs by their choices and agreements in negotiation. Because we believe that negotiators benefit by being self-conscious and reflective about their interests and the trade-offs they are willing to make, we propose several methods to illuminate trade-offs. These methods draw primarily on judgment about interests, not about negotiating. The methods we consider help to convert developed substantive judgments into forms useful for analysis and practice (e.g., Raiffa, 1982, Keeney and Raiffa, 1976; Barclay and Peterson, 1976; or Greenhalgh and Neslin, 1981). Finally, although these techniques have formal origins rooted in management science and technical economics, we find that their prime value comes in their contribution to clear thinking rather than from their potential for quantification. While negotiators may often choose not to quantify their trade-offs, they may benefit greatly by employing the same style of thought in comparing interests.

Certain trade-offs are easy to specify. The present value or total cost of a loan is a well-known mathematical function of the amount and duration of the loan and the interest rate. Thus, beginning with a given price and interest rate for the seller-financed home, Ralph can calculate precisely the benefit of a 1 percent decrease in interest rate and how much of a price increase he would be willing to accept before he became indifferent to the original price and interest rate. Yet other trade-offs may seem much harder to think about, especially ones that involve "intangibles" like principles, anxiety about a process, or the relationship.

Assembling Trade-offs among Seemingly Intangible Interests.   Seemingly intangible trade-offs can also be dealt with an analogous ways. For instance, consider Joan, a plaintiff crippled in a car accident who wishes to negotiate an out-of-court settlement with an insurance company that is better than her alternative of a full court trial. Suppose that, only taking trial uncertainties and legal fees into account, Joan would be willing to accept a settlement of $300,000. But this analysis leaves her uncomfortable. The trial would cause her great anxiety, and her analysis so far does not take this anxiety into account. How should she consider the anxiety factor in her preparation for negotiation? Perhaps she should lower her minimum requirements, but by how much? How can she even think about this?

After several anxious, inconclusive struggles with this assessment, a friend asks Joan to imagine the anxiety she would feel during a trial. The friend then asks her to imagine that a pharmacist offered to *sell* her a magic potion that would completely eliminate the feeling of anxiety from court proceedings. What would be the most she would pay for the potion before the trial? Would she pay $10? "That's silly. Of course." Would she pay $100? "Sure." $100,000? "Certainly not, that's one-third of my minimum settlement!" What about $50,000? "Probably not." $1,000? "I think so." $10,000? "Well, that's a tough one. But, if push came to shove, the trial would be an awful experience. So probably yes." $25,000? "Maybe not, but I'm not sure." . . . And so on.

We want to stress our opinion that the important point in making such assessments is not quantitative precision. An absolutely precise cut-off would seem artificial. What is important is to get a sense of the order of magnitude of the value Joan places on avoiding anxiety. Here we see that she would pay between $10,000 and $25,000 or a little more to eliminate the anxiety. Thus, she should be willing to reduce her minimum settlement requirements by that amount because a negotiated settlement would avoid the anxiety. She should, of course, strive for more, but she can feel more comfortable knowing that her minimum requirements now roughly reflect her interest in avoiding trial anxiety.

Similarly, Mr. Acton, the insurance company executive, may feel that going to trial against a plaintiff who evokes such sympathy will harm his firm's reputation. How should he value this reputation damage and how should it affect his approach to the negotiation? As described in this thumbnail sketch, in comparing the court alternative to possible negotiated agreements, the executive sees two interests at stake: money and reputation. Action could try to value the reputation damage directly by estimating the number of present and future customers he would lose and the financial loss this would create. If he finds such direct assessment difficult, he could attempt, like the plaintiff, to place a monetary value on the "intangible" interest. What is the most he would be willing to pay a public relations firm to completely undo the reputation damage? If the most he would be willing to pay is $20,000, Acton could modify his maximum acceptable settlement and take this into account when negotiating with the plaintiff.

In some instances, concerns with precedent, prestige, anxiety, reputation, and similar interests loom large; negotiators focus on them and, because such interests are difficult to weight, feel paralyzed with respect to their choices as a negotiator. After fretting inconclusively, the negotiators may ask themselves how much they would be willing to pay to have the prestige conferred upon them by other means. They might discover that they value the prestige possibilities little relative to possible substantive gains. Or, by similar analytical introspection, they might discover that they would be willing to pay only a small sum to avoid an undesirable precedent. In such cases, the negotiators would have learned a great deal. First, the intangible interest is a second or third order concern rather than a first order one as they originally feared; they can now feel freer to make concessions on the less important interest if necessary. Second, unless the choice between packages becomes close, they may need to pay little attention to this interest. In short, much of the purpose of such assessments is more to discover the relative importance of different interests rather than to be painstakingly precise about monetary or other valuations.

In other instances, interests in precedent or reputation overwhelm the possible improvements in substantive outcome. Suppose that Jeff, a lawyer working on a highly publicized class action suit against a corporation, has an interest in his financial compensation and in the reputation he might develop by exceeding expectations for how favorable a settlement he can get for his clients. Even if Jeff finds the range of possible financial compensation paltry, he may see that his interest in enhancing his reputation and political ambitions is extremely well-served by every increment he can obtain in the settlement. Thus, he may bargain tenaciously on his client's behalf. In this case, the nonmonetary interest was the first order concern. In other instances, simple self-assessment may suggest that the monetary and nonmonetary issues are roughly comparable concerns or that the monetary aspects predominate.

A More General Approach for Assessing Trade-offs.   The judgment that one "cares more about quality than price" cannot be made independently of the *range* of possible values of quality and price. That is, in the abstract, a manufacturer may say that it cares more about quality than about price. However, while the total increment in technologically feasible quality may be small, the price differential necessary to achieve it may be undesirably high. Relative to the feasible range of qualities, the manufacturer actually places greater weight on price. Similarly, the management negotiator who professes to care more about obtaining productivity-enhancing changes in work rules than about wages must analyze the ranges of work rules and wages that are possible outcomes from this negotiation. Wages might range from a minimum of $10 an hour to a maximum of $13 an hour—and this increment would have a significant impact on the competitiveness of the negotiator's firm. Yet if the increment from the worst to best possible work rules was small and would only marginally affect the firm's competitiveness, the negotiator should give greater weight or importance to wages. The trade-off rate should result from comparing the valuation of the wage increment between $10 and $13 with the valuation of the benefit of moving from the worst to best work rules—not on the judgment that the negotiator "cares more" about one or the other issue in general.

This leads to a straightforward method for such assessments. Like the preceding examples, the purpose of this method is to help organize one's subjective judgments to get a clearer sense of the relative importance of various interests. Again, we are concerned with orders of magnitude rather than precise quantification. To illustrate the central elements of this approach, we shall work through the thought process in a highly stylized, simplified, example and then discuss the more general lessons for thinking about trade-offs.

Assessing Lisa's Interests

Consider Lisa, a 34-year-old second level manager who has been offered a position in another division of her firm as the supervisor of a soon-to-be created department. She must soon negotiate with William, a long-time engineer who moved into senior management ranks seven years ago and has cautiously but steadily improved his division's results. Lisa has narrowed the issues she will have to negotiate to three: the salary, vacation time, and the number of staff for the new department. We will ask her to analyze her interests and then draw on her subjective judgment to assign 100 points to the issues in a way that reflects their relative importance to her. To begin, she should assess the range of possibilities for each issue. Based on a variety of discussions with William, with others in the firm, and on the results of numerous feelers, Lisa has concluded that the salary could plausibly run from $32,000 to $40,000, the vacation from two to four weeks, and the staff size from 10 to 20. Suppose that her current job pays her $32,000, gives her four weeks of vacation, and assigns her a staff of 10 (See Table 1).

Lisa should start by imagining the least appealing scenario: $32,000, two weeks of vacation, and a staff of 10. Her next task is to assess her relative preferences on each issue. To do this, she must decide which one of the three incremental improvements she values most. That is, would she feel best with (a) $40,000 salary but only two weeks vacation and 10 subordinates; (b) four weeks vacation but only $32,000 salary and 10 subordinates; or (c) 20 subordinates but only $32,000 salary and two weeks of vacation? In making this evaluation, she examines her interests in money and the effects of

TABLE 1 Lisa's Negotiation: Issues and Ranges

Issues	Range
Salary	$32-40,000
Vacation	2-4 weeks
Staff	10-20 people

a higher salary on her satisfaction, as well as the peace of mind and pleasure from longer vacations. On further reflection, Lisa realizes that she must also consider her ability to do her job effectively and thus to improve her subsequent career prospects. A bigger staff could help her effectiveness directly; enhanced organizational status from a big staff and high salary may independently bolster her job prospects as well as add to her effectiveness. Suppose that after contemplating her interests in this way, Lisa decides that she prefers the salary increment to the other two increments, and, of the other two, she prefers the staff increment to the vacation possibilities.

Now comes a harder part. She must allocate 100 points—importance weights—among the three increments in a way that reflects her underlying subjective feelings. Would she prefer the package with the largest salary increment but minimum vacation and staff to the package with the lowest salary but maximum staff and vacation? If so, she should allocate more than 50 points to the salary increment. If she is indifferent between the two packages, she should allocate exactly 50 points to the salary increment.

Lisa decides that she slightly prefers the salary increment and assigns an importance weight of 60 points to the salary increment. Now, she can either assign importance weights to the staff and vacation increments or she can think about the relative value she places on each of the possible salaries. She begins with the latter and again compares ranges. How does she compare the salary increment from $32,000 to $35,000 with the increment between $35,000 and $40,000? The first increment would improve her housing and thus enhance her life in direct and important ways; the second increment although larger, would go toward luxuries and saving. She thus feels indifferent between the first, smaller increment and the second, larger increment. In other words, she gives 30 of the 60 importance points to the increment between $32,000 and $35,000 and 30 to the remaining increment.

Table 2 presents importance scores that reflect Lisa's preferences for salary; Figure 1 shows a plot of them. Interpreting this assessment, Lisa would get 0 points if she receives a salary of $32,000, 30 points if she manages to receive $35,000, 60 points if she is able to get a salary of $40,000. She must now assign points reflecting her comparative valuations of the vacation and staff increments. Naturally, making an assessment like this can feel like comparing apples and oranges—but Lisa will end up doing it either explicitly or implicitly.

She can assess her valuations of the other two issues by comparing their increments directly, or by comparing one of the increments with her salary assessments. For example, how does the increment from 10 to 20 subordinates compare with the salary increment from $32,000 to $35,000? If Lisa is indifferent, she should assign 30 importance points to the staff increment and, thus, the remaining 10 points to the vacation

TABLE 2   Lisa's Assessment of the Value of
Different Salaries

Salary($)	Importance Points Assigned
$32,000	0
$33,000	10
$34,000	20
$35,000	30
$36,000	36
$37,000	42
$38,000	48
$39,000	54
$40,000	60

FIGURE 1   Lisa's Assessment of the Value of
Different Salary Levels

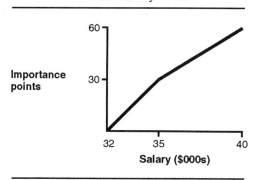

increment. She decides and continues in this manner, finishing the assessment by as-
signing 20 of the 30 importance points to the increment between 10 and 15 subordinates
and 10 points to the remaining increment. Lastly, she assigns eight of the 10 vacation
points to getting the third week of vacation and two points to the remaining week.

Table 3 shows a scoring system that reflects this assessment. From the table, a
$35,000 salary, three weeks of vacation, and 15 subordinates would be values at 58
points (30 + 8 + 20) whereas a salary of $37,500, two weeks of vacation and 16
subordinates would be valued at 67 points (45 + 0 + 22). It is worth noting that all
the scoring is relative to an arbitrarily chosen zero point. That is, the "worst"
agreement—$32,000, two weeks of vacation and 10 subordinates, the bottom of the
range for each issue—receives a score of zero. All other possible agreements are
scored relative to this "worst" agreement. The important comparison, though, is with
Lisa's current job which, at a salary of $32,000, four weeks of vacation, and 10

TABLE 3   Lisa's Assessment of the Importance of Salary, Vacation, and Staff Size

Salary ($000)	Importance Points	Weeks of Vacation	Importance Points	Staff Size	Importance Points
32	0	2	0	10	0
33	10	3	8	15	20
34	20	4	10	20	30
35	30				
36	36				
37	42				
38	48				
39	54				
40	60				

subordinates is valued at 10 points. Although any such scoring system is necessarily rough. Lisa can use it to evaluate possible agreements and to understand the trade-offs she may have to make.

Comparing different increments can be difficult, but a few tricks can sometimes facilitate the process. For example, Lisa might construct one package of $32,000, two weeks of vacation, and 20 subordinates and another of $32,000, four weeks of vacation, and 10 subordinates. But, to compare them? Lisa might imagine that the phone rings and the call eliminates one of the options. Which option would feel worse to lose? Or, suppose that a coin flip will determine the choice of packages. Is a 50-50 chance of losing each appropriate? Or, would she prefer 60-40 chances favoring one of the packages?

In helping Lisa construct this scoring system, we assumed that the value of an increment on one issue did not depend on how other issues were resolved; thus, scoring a package simply involves adding the points obtained on each issue. In some situations, though, the value of the outcome on one issue depends on how other issues are resolved.[2] For example, suppose that with a high salary Lisa would like a larger number of subordinates. With a low salary, however, she might feel aggrieved; a larger staff would mean more responsibility for which she was not compensated. Thus, how she values staff size could depend on her salary level. Such interdependent preferences could be assessed using more elaborate techniques, but the general logic of defining and comparing increments would remain roughly analogous.

Assessing William's Interests

Lisa, in addition to assess her own interests, must also do the same for her negotiating counterpart and potential supervisor, William. Her preliminary investigations had fairly confidently bounded the ranges of the issues, but now the question becomes how *he* sees *his* real interests in them. Tentative discussions with William left Lisa little doubt that he would prefer to pay less, allow shorter vacations, and get by with as few new staff as possible. In fact, during a meeting in which he enthusiastically offered her the job "in principle," William sketched the terms he felt were appropriate: "a bit over $30,000, a few weeks vacation, and only the staff you really need." More than a little daunted by this less than forthcoming stance, Lisa feels a strong need to develop a much deeper understanding of William's interests.

Asking around, she discovers that William is generally not at ease with "personnel" matters and that he tends to seek out whatever firm "policy" he can find for guidance. Fortunately for Lisa, little in the firm would be directly comparable to the new department she would head. But a few discreet inquiries turn up the fact that the supervisor of the firm's largest department makes around $39,000. Since the new department is an important endeavor, Lisa feels fairly certain that salary money will not be too tight, but that the other supervisor's compensation will make any salary above $39,000 very uncomfortable for William to consider.

In trying to ferret out William's feelings about vacation. Lisa discovers that he has been a hard worker, seldom taking more than a few days or a week each year. Also he has mentioned the extreme importance of dedication and long hours during the uncertain start-up of this new organizational unit. Lisa infers that the prospect of her taking extended vacations early on, while not at all uncommon elsewhere in the firm, would not sit at all well with William.

Finally, on the matter of staffing, Lisa recalls some comments William made during a long lunch they had together to explore the possibilities of her heading the new department. In the course of their conversation, he had mentioned two significant incidents from his career. First, he recalled extreme pressure on the engineering group some years ago to come up with a new design. The group was simply too small to produce the needed results in time. Quality of work and quality of life "needlessly suffered" and, to William's mind, that kind of "economizing" makes no business or personal sense. Yet William also recounted an agonizing experience some years later when the engineering group had greatly expanded. A mild economic downturn and the loss of a major customer had forced him to lay off nearly a quarter of the group's engineers. Recalling the pain of that experience, he noted that things would have been much better if most of those let go had never been hired in the first place; instead, others already in the department should have worked somewhat longer hours. To Lisa, the implications of these incidents seemed obvious: William would have little problem giving her the staff that he believed she really needed, but would be allergic to any perceived excess.

Lisa could then make this assessment much more precise, estimating importance weights for William. Already, however, the contours of a possible approach have begun to emerge as she considers her interests (recall Table 3) together with her insights into William's concerns. Lisa expects to press fairly hard for a salary in the $39,000 range, perhaps conceding a few weeks of vacation time for the last few thousand dollars. Money, she reasons, is most valuable to her and relatively "cheap" to William; in addition, he cares a great deal about avoiding too much time off and two extra weeks of vacation are not crucial to her. From her analysis of the new department's mission so far, Lisa has become increasingly sure that the job can be done with 15 people, though 20 would certainly be nice. She plans to devote a great deal of time to developing and presenting justification of the need for 15.

We will not go further in exploring how William's interests might be more formally assessed or how his and Lisa's preferences could be better dovetailed.[3] And, of course, this rough assessment of an artificially simplified set of issues only starts the process. As Lisa learns more, relative valuations may be revised, issues may be reformulated, and new options invented. For example, her interests in "salary" could be expanded to include stock options, bonuses, fringe and in-kind benefits. "Vacation" might encompass time to be taken in later years, a generous policy of accumulating unused vacation or turning it into salary, or leaves for various purposes like education. "Staff" may mean direct employees of various backgrounds and levels, "loans" from other departments, consultants, temporary help, or equipment to enhance the productivity of a given number of staff. But throughout, constant probing of each party's interests is the sine qua non of creating value by designing good negotiated agreements.

General Lessons for Assessing Interests

The most important lessons from this kind of assessment are those that help one think more clearly about the qualitative judgments that negotiators implicitly make all the time. Such evaluations are often made with respect to nominal issues rather than directly on underlying interests. Lisa's interests in money, lifestyle, peace of mind, career prospects, and organizational status are not perfectly aligned with the issues of salary, vacation limits, and staff size. When thinking about how well different packages satisfy her interests, the negotiator may discover reformulations that align more closely with her interests. If some of these "new" issues are easier to grant, they may form the basis for a better agreement.

During the process, the negotiator may learn about and change her perceptions about how well different positions on the issues serve her interests. As she learns, the relative importance of the increments on the issues may shift. If so, she should modify her assessments.

In contrast to the apparent crispness of the issues, interests are often vaguer. There may be no apparent scale with which to measure, for example, precedent or organizational status. Yet, the same logic that is useful for making issue trade-offs can apply to assuring the relative impact of interests. The generic steps are as follows:

- Identify the interests that may be at stake.
- For each interest, imagine the possible packages that serve it best and worst; for example, imagine the range of precedents that might follow from the negotiation. This roughly defines the *increment*.
- As with Lisa's job negotiations, the importance of each interest depends on the relative importance of its *increment* compared to those of the other interests; how does the gain from the worst to the best possible precedent compare with the gain from the worst to the best possible monetary outcome?

The currency of negotiation generally involves *positions* on *issues* but the results are measured by how well underlying *interests* are furthered. As such, it is helpful to shuttle constantly between often abstract interests and more specific issues, both to check for consistency and to keep real concerns uppermost in mind.

Assessing the Interests of Others

Finally, it goes almost without saying that negotiators should constantly assess their counterparts' interests and preferences. Obviously, careful listening and clear communication help this process. Uninvolved third parties can render insights not suspected by partisans wrapped up in the negotiation. And some negotiators find that, as part of preparing for the process, actually playing the other party's role can offer deepened perspectives. In various management programs at Harvard, for example, senior industrialists have been assigned the parts of environmentalists and vice versa. To simulate arms talks, high-level U.S. military officers and diplomats have been assigned to play Russian negotiators in intensive simulations. Palestinians and Israelis have had to swap places. After some initial discomfort and reluctance, the most common reaction of participants in these exercises is surprise at how greatly such role-playing enhances their understanding of each side's interests, of why others may seem intransigent, and of unexpected possibilities for agreement.

Beyond various ways of trying to put oneself in the other's shoes, assessment of another's interests may be improved by investigating:

- Their past behavior in related settings, both in style and substance.

- Their training and professional affiliation: engineers and financial analysts will often have quite different modes of perception and approaches to potential conflict from, say, lawyers and insurance adjusters.

- Their organizational position and affiliation. Those in the production department will often see long, predictable manufacturing runs as the company's dominant interest while marketers will opt for individual tailoring to customer specs and deep inventories for rapid deliveries. This is but one example of the old and wise expression "where you stand depends on where you sit."

- Whom they admire, whose advice carries weight, and to whom they tend to defer on the kind of issues at stake.

In the end, interests are bound up with psychology and culture. Some settings breed rivalry; others esteem the group. Some people are altruists; others sociopaths. To some, ego looms large; to others, substance is all. Airport bookstore wisdom names Jungle Fighters, Appeasers, Win-Winners, and Win-Losers. Professionals diagnose personality Types A and B and victims of cathected libido. Others have developed such classes, sometimes wisely, but for now we stress that *perceived* interests matter, that perceptions are subjective. Thus, to assess interests is to probe psyches.

INTERESTS AND ISSUES ARE VARIABLE

Many academic treatments of negotiation take the issues and interests at stake as unchanging over the course of the negotiation. Yet both the issues under discussion and the interests perceived to be at stake can change.

The link between issues and interests is often unclear; the negotiator faced with a set of issues must figure out which of his or her interests are at stake. For example, getting a corner office might enhance prestige and status, but how much would this affect various dealings and decisions?

Because these links are often vague and complex, perceptions of the links can be influenced or manipulated. One may shape the "face" that any issue wears (Neustadt, 1980); presenting food stamps as a means to increase demand for agricultural products rather than as a welfare program may win agricultural state representatives' support for the program. Similarly, by portraying a new project that in reality departs sharply from a firm's past strategy as a direct extension of current projects, a subordinate may both obtain funding and avoid a review of the project's fit with broader strategic goals.

One may attempt less drastic changes in an individual's perception of the relationship between the issue at hand and the underlying interest. Thus, the mining company negotiator may attempt to persuade a small country's Finance Minister that high royalty rates, although they appear to further the country's interest in revenues, will actually be worse than lower royalty rates. The mining company might argue, "once rates reach a certain level, we will invest less, other companies will be scared off, and you will end up losing in terms of your monetary interests." If persuaded, the country's evaluation of how its interests would be satisfied by different potential agreements would change.

Certain other tactics may effectively expand or contract the interests evoked, often in ways not intended by the negotiator. "Take-it-or-leave-it" offers, forced linkages, commitment moves, threats, and preemptive actions all have potential to elicit strong negative reactions that may overwhelm the original issues at stake. Concern for one's reputation or self-esteem may predominate. A trade union's motivation for strikes, for instance, may shift over time from the strictly economic to a desire for revenge. Likewise, wars can escalate out of all proportion to the possible substantive gains for either side. The sudden Argentine occupation of the Falkland Islands in 1982 and the British response quickly came to involve weighty, irreconcilable interests such as national "honor" and the "right" response to aggression.

In many circumstances threats, commitments, and deterrent moves are effective and can be analyzed in terms of values for the immediate issues involved (Tedeschi, Schlenker, and Bonoma, 1973). In other cases, such tactics can induce anger, loss of "face," and aggression (Deutsch and Kraus, 1962; Rubin and Brown, 1975). That is, the tactics bring new and often unhelpful interests into the negotiation. Counter-tactics may well bring in additional interests and a spiral begins. Conflicts are more likely to escalate when disputants attribute their concessions to their own weakness; similarly, escalation is less likely when concessions can be attributed to something impersonal, such as a budgeting system, a formal procedure, or a widely accepted norm (Bacharach and Lawler, 1981).

The essence of some tactics is to add new interests. For example, one may make a commitment to a position by invoking an interest that the other negotiator cannot satisfy and that would not otherwise be part of the process; in holding to a position, the insurance claims adjuster may invoke a strong interest in maintaining a reputation as a tough bargainer for subsequent claims negotiations. The potential house buyer who announces that one's spouse would be tremendously angry if the purchase price were to exceed $150,000 adds a new interest to the negotiation: the relationship between husband and wife.

Other tactics, in contrast, may eliminate interests. Flipping a coin or submitting a dispute to arbitration may remove implications of weakness, strength, coercion, or tactical advantage.

Thus, interests can change even when issues remain fixed. The reverse is also true. Because the relation between issues and interests may be unclear, negotiators may reformulate the issues. During negotiations over deep seabed mining in the Law of the Sea negotiations, for example, many of the different nations' underlying interests remained fairly constant. However, as the negotiations evolved, the issues changed dramatically—from whether mining should be done by private firms at all or by an international mining entity to the nitty-gritty aspects of mining contracts for private firms and the financing mechanism for the first operation of a new international mining entity. Trying to pin down the precise nature of the final issues at stake occupied a great deal of the negotiators' time, perhaps more than it took ultimately to resolve the issues (Sebenius, 1984).

PRESCRIPTIVE SUMMARY

As a summary for analysts and practitioners, we have converted the main observations of this paper into the following prescriptive checklist:

Assessing Which Interests are at Stake

- Beyond the obvious tangible interests that may be affected by issues to be discussed, consider subtler interests in reputation, precedent, relationships, strategy, fairness, and the like.

- Distinguish underlying interests from the issues under discussion and the positions taken on them.

- Distinguish between intrinsic and instrumental reasons for valuing interests, especially some of the subtler ones.

- In seeking to understand other's interests, remember that interests depend on perceptions, that perceptions are subjective, and thus that to assess interests is to probe psyches. This process can be aided by clear communication, the advice of third parties, role-playing, and taking into account past behavior, training, professional affiliation, and organizational position, as well as those to whom the other defers.

- Keep in mind that interests and issues can change on purpose or accidentally as the parties learn, events occur, or certain tactics are employed.

Assessing Trade-offs

- Trade-offs are as important to interests as proportions are to recipes.

- To assess trade-offs among intangible interests, it is sometimes helpful to imagine services one could buy otherwise to satisfy the same interests.

- To assess trade-offs among issues:
  —Specify the worst and best possible outcomes on each issue to define the possible increments.

—Compare the increments by thinking hard about underlying interests and which increments are most valued.

—Break the increments into smaller pieces and similarly compare their relative evaluation.

—Change assessments with learning about how different positions on the issues affect interests.

—Assess interest trade-offs using the same logic.

When to Focus on Interests and When on Issues

- Focus the negotiation on interests to enhance creativity and break impasses by reformulating issues to align better with underlying interests.

- Focus the negotiation on positions, issues, or a narrower set of interests when underlying conflicts of ideology make agreement difficult or when a restricted focus is more advantageous for claiming value.

Negotiation is a process of potentially opportunistic interaction in which two or more parties with some conflicting interests seek to do better by jointly decided action than they could otherwise. The alternatives to negotiated agreement or what the parties could do alone define the threshold of value that any agreement must exceed. The potential of negotiation is bounded only by the quality of agreement that can be devised. But, for evaluating alternatives and creating agreements, interests are the measure and raw material of negotiation.

ENDNOTES

We would like to thank Arthur Applbaum, Mark Moore, Howard Raiffa, Lawrence Susskind, and Thomas Weeks for helpful and friendly comments. A number of the ideas in this paper have been stimulated by the work of, and discussions with, Roger Fisher and William Ury, whom we also thank. Support from the Division of Research at the Harvard Business School and the Sloan Foundation Program of Research in Public Management is gratefully acknowledged. Much of this article is drawn from material prepared for a chapter of our book, *The Manager as Negotiator* (New York: The Free Press, forthcoming).

1. More technically minded readers may find the following formulation helpful: Let us represent a negotiator's multiattribute utility function; the attributes of u are the negotiator's interests. Let p be a vector of positions taken on the issue vector $i(.)$. Let f be a vector-valued function that reflects the negotiator's beliefs about how well an agreement with position p on issues i advances his interests. Thus, an agreement p gives the negotiator utility $u(f(i(p)))$. Typically, of course, the negotiator will be uncertain about the relationship between issues and interests, which we might model by letting w represent the random variable reflecting relevant and uncertain events and letting $f(i(p),w)$ reflect the negotiator's beliefs about the relationship between issues and interests conditional on w. Thus, we might say that the negotiator wants to choose p to maximize

$E_w[u\,(f\,(i\,(p),w))]$, where E_w is the expectation over the negotiator's subjective beliefs about w.

2. The "additive scoring rule" constructed in this example is a simple case of a multiattribute value or utility function. When interdependencies exist, non-additive, multiattribute utility functions (see Keeney and Raiffa, 1976) can be used in this assessment.

3. Or for that matter, how to take the twin scoring systems for Lisa and William's values to produce a Pareto frontier. For a discussion of how to do this, see Raiffa (1982) or Barclay and Peterson (1976).

REFERENCES

Barclay S. B. and Peterson, C. "Multi-attribute Utility Models for Negotiators," *Technical Report 76–1,* McLean, Virginia: Decisions and Designs, Inc., 1976.

Bower, J. L. *Managing the Resource Allocation Process.* Homewood, Ill.: Richard D. Irwin, 1972.

Deutsch, M. and Kraus, R. M. "Studies of Interpersonal Bargaining," *Journal of Conflict Resolution* 6 (1962), pp. 52–76.

Donaldson, G. and Lorsch, J. W. *Decision Making at the Top.* New York: Basic Books, 1984.

Fisher, R. and Ury, W. L. *Getting to YES: Negotiating Agreement without Giving In.* Boston: Houghton-Mifflin, 1981.

Greenhalgh, L. and Neslin, S. A. "Conjoint Analysis of Negotiator Preferences." *Journal of Conflict Resolution* 25 (1981) pp. 301–27.

Gulliver, P. H. *Disputes and Negotiations: A Cross Cultural Perspective.* New York: Academic Press, 1979.

Keeney, R. and Raiffa, H. *Decisions with Multiple Objectives.* New York: Wiley, 1976.

Kotter, J. *Power and Influence.* New York: Free Press, 1985.

Neustadt, R. E. *Presidential Power,* 4th ed. New York: Wiley, 1980.

Raiffa, H. *The Art and Science of Negotiation.* Cambridge, Mass.: Harvard University Press, 1982.

Rubin, J. Z. and Brown, B. R. *The Social Psychology of Bargaining and Negotiation.* New York: Academic Press, 1975.

Schelling, T. C. *The Strategy of Conflict.* Cambridge, Mass.: Harvard University Press, 1960.

Sebenius, J. K. *Negotiating the Law of the Sea.* Cambridge, Mass.: Harvard University Press, 1984.

Tedeschi, J. T., Schlenker, B. R., and Bonoma, T.V. *Conflict, Power, and Games.* Chicago: Aldine, 1973.

Creative Negotiating

Gordon Shea

As a young team leader and project engineer I had just completed negotiating my largest contract with a supplier and was enthusiastically describing my "victory" to the purchasing agent.

"Does your agreement leave him with a satisfactory profit?" he asked.

I was taken aback. "How do I know? That's his worry."

"No," he stated firmly, "that's our worry, too."

Watching the evening news or reading the front page of the daily paper, we constantly encounter evidence of the proliferation of negotiations and of the importance to us—on every level from the personal to the international—of the outcomes of these negotiations. With so much at stake and with negotiation becoming more widely acceptable as a form of intervention, you may automatically assume that the techniques of the skill of negotiation are widely taught and practiced.

However, the one-sided view of the negotiating process that I demonstrated in my handling of the contract with the supplier is not an unusual one. Traditionally, negotiation is looked at as "the art of getting what you want"—with no regard as to the cost to the other side. The success of an agreement is often measured in terms of gains made by your side and concessions forced from the other side. I call these one-sided agreements "win-lose" agreements—and win-lose agreements have a tendency to backfire somewhere down the road, becoming lose-lose agreements. As life becomes increasingly complex, and the consequences of unresolved conflicts increasingly dire, the benefits of *creative* negotiation become clearer.

Negotiation is an intimidating word for many people. Some connect it with the formal give and take between diplomats or corporate executives, something far removed from the lives of ordinary people. But situations that can benefit from effective creative negotiation run the gamut from international disputes to labor-management conflicts, community clashes, and family confrontations.

The problems involved in organizing a household in which both parents work can lead to bitterness, chaos, or disruption—or they can be dealt with according to the principles of creative negotiation, which provides a set of healthy, productive techniques for resolving conflict and for reaching "win-win" agreements.

Reprinted from *Creative Living* magazine, with permission of Northwestern Mutual Life Insurance Company.

151

In like manner, a corporate takeover can be an opportunity for meeting mutual needs and experiencing successful cooperation—or, mismanaged, can lay the groundwork for years of production, personnel, and management headaches.

The key to a creative negotiation is that the negotiators must focus on the needs of *all* participants. As the purchasing agent patiently explained to me:

"Unless our suppliers also think they have a reasonable deal, we may come up short. The other side could lose interest in our order. They could fail to ship parts on time, thus causing your assembly lines to be down. To prosper in business *long term,* look at the whole relationship with another firm, not just the immediate gains you can make from a fast deal. We need our suppliers and in this business you don't win alone.

"You don't get high performance from people who feel beaten or abused. If you need a low price for something, ask for the other side's help in creatively lowering costs or see what you can do for them in return. Use your imagination."

I gradually gained an understanding of his way of looking at business negotiations and over the years I have found it far superior to the alternative—business as jungle fighting.

I now see negotiating as one of the highest human arts, a skill that offers an opportunity to improve the relationships and transactions among all of us for mutual and beneficial gain. And *creative* negotiation can bring about even greater gains. It involves efforts on all sides and at all stages to provide innovative solutions that enable *everyone* to profit substantially, often far beyond expectations. This win-win consequence enhances relationships and prepares the participants for greater cooperation in the future. Someone once described the process of creative negotiating this way: "Instead of dividing up the apples, we both shake the tree to get more apples."

Let's take a look at a situation in which creative negotiating successfully produced a win-win solution.

A chemical company employed several students, evenings, to do cleanup work. At exam time, they would work faster, finish their work early, and do some studying toward the end of their shift. The supervisor was satisfied that the work was done up to standard but was criticized one night by his manager for "letting the students loaf." "They're paid to work—not to read books," was his pronouncement.

The supervisor called a meeting of the students and stated his needs: "To get my boss off my back about them reading on the job; to continue to get the work done well; and to keep the high morale and cooperative attitude of the group intact." He didn't propose solutions.

The group identified their needs: "To help the supervisor meet his needs and to get some time to study without lessening the work output." They then "brainstormed" the problem and the supervisor recorded the ideas produced. They came up with 27 possibilities, six of which had considerable merit and were implemented by the supervisor.

Their ideas included a better way to distribute work assignments, formation of group work teams on some assignments, and more productive ways to use their break time. The primary solution, however, was that each person would read his lessons aloud into a tape recorder and then play the tapes back at exam time with the help of a "walkman" type system.

In Preparation
___

Priming the other side

- State your intent to negotiate creatively and invite your counterparts to participate.
- Explain that you want to reach an agreement that will meet their needs as fully as possible and that you expect your own needs to be met equally well.
- Explain that creative negotiating is different from bargaining—that it is a creative effort to enlarge the pie so that everyone gets more than they might normally expect.
- Listen carefully to your counterparts' responses. Avoid taking their remarks personally and acknowledge their feelings and concerns without judging them.
- Offer to explain the process and potential of the method.
- Allow your counterparts to talk out any negative feelings they may have about your proposal.
- Provide information on procedures as needed. It is best to wait until they ask for it, but they may not do so.
- Make an open-ended statement of your needs and invite your counterparts to talk about theirs. Dig deep until the needs of all concerned have been heard.
- List basic needs of both parties so that they are known to all and avoid dealing initially with proposed solutions.
- If possible, gradually lead your counterparts into the process of win-win negotiation, taking plenty of time to talk out procedural problems as they occur.
___

Since their work was quite routine and their hands were now free when studying, they gave their supervisor eight hours of work every evening and they all had time to study. The net effect was a modest increase in productivity, high morale, and a significant improvement in the average grades of each student.

A more conventional way to approach this problem would have been for the supervisor to lay down the law—the students were to keep working all night—most likely resulting in rapid turnover, low morale, ''stretching'' the work, and a concomitant drop in the the quality of work. Instead, he stated his needs and encouraged the other ''party'' to do the same.

The brainstorming technique used here is particularly effective for group negotiations. During a brainstorming session, ideas are thrown out for consideration without restraint. The key to effective brainstorming is the suspension of all evaluation during the idea-generating session—no criticism, spoken or implied, is allowed.

This example proves that negotiation can be more than a contest of relative power. But whether or not creative negotiation will work depends on the participants' *perception* of two important facets. Is the problem viewed as a source of struggle or as an opportunity for growth and development? Do the participants think that each got a half share (compromise as opposed to win-win solution) or that the pie to be divided was made larger by group efforts? A positive attitude on these two points is a prerequisite for creative negotiating.

Conflict is inevitable. It is how you choose to respond to situations of conflict that will determine whether they will be constructive learning experiences or exercises in futility.

In business, I've always been interested in what really worked *without negative side effects.* I got tired of accepting a lot of so-called "agreements" that presumably solved problems, only to have trouble crop up again and again, often in different guises. Policing bad agreements costs time and energy and keeps us from creative thought. Unless an agreement is at least reasonably win-win, it produces marginal results. Creatively meeting each other's needs is an essential ingredient in negotiating a high-performance agreement.

At one time I was given an ideal opportunity to reverse the tendency to go for a win-lose solution and put creative negotiating techniques into practice. When I took over as supervisor of a department in a large company, I inherited a long-standing problem.

Marvin was a quiet, pleasant man who worked alone, conducting studies and issuing analytical reports to government agencies and to customers. Marvin was largely self-taught and, though his work was highly praised by outsiders, no one in the company knew exactly what he did or how he worked out the details.

Marvin had been a good employee for many years, meeting all deadlines even though he had been sick a great deal lately. He would be eligible for retirement shortly, although he could remain with the firm for many more years if his work continued to be satisfactory.

My predecessors had been unsuccessful in convincing Marvin to train someone else to do his job. His former supervisors described Marvin as "stubborn," "scared of losing his job," and "trying to be the indispensable man."

After thinking about the problem I came to three conclusions:

I didn't want to solve this problem at the expense of creating another one. I had been told that I could fire Marvin if he didn't come around. But firing is a "solution" that would cost us a hard-working, conscientious employee and probably hurt the product Marvin prepared. And I had no assurance that I'd get a better employee to replace him. That simplistic win-lose solution would almost certainly produce a lose-lose situation.

Marvin was best qualified to solve this problem. He knew the work and he was the only one who would know why he was resisting the prospect of training someone else.

I wanted to eliminate the presumption of badness that we often project on people when they fail to meet our needs. Mutual problems are best solved when we assume that the other person has his own reasons for doing what he is doing. Most often our assumption of badness develops because we fail to realize that people may not be resisting *what* we need them to do as much as they are resisting the *way* we are telling them to do it. Allow for flexibility.

Therefore, on Monday I applied the following methodology:

1. *Acknowledge the positive elements in the situation.* I expressed appreciation for Marvin having met the deadlines despite having been sick. This was honest positive stroking.

2. *Acknowledge the problem and introduce the win-win concept.* I told Marvin that I had a problem and that I needed his help to solve it. I said frankly that the problem involved both of us and that I wanted to reach a resolution that would be satisfactory to both of us.

3. *Define the problem in terms of needs—both mine and Marvin's.* I told Marvin my needs by way of example, but I hastened to add that I was interested in having him state *his* needs. I said that I needed to continue to get his job done on an ongoing basis. I said that I was responsible for organizational continuity.

Marvin thought a minute and then said, "I don't know exactly what you mean by needs, but I know I need this job for another 28 months." I asked why he specified 28 months. He said that by then his place in Florida would be paid for and he could retire *if he had to.*

At that point I felt it important to state that I hoped he would be with us longer than that. I also said that we'd try to work things out if he got sick again, but that his illness was the source of my concern. By making this clear, I probably met his need for security (as well as I could), if that issue was bothering him.

After Marvin agreed that my concern about his illness was valid, we began the real problem-solving process.

Using a "needs agenda" approach we listed our needs and then worked on developing ways to meet each one of them. Often I go item by item, but there is no reason not to jump around if something occurs to you that would meet a need somewhere down the list. For instance, Marvin said that he worked best alone and found it distracting to have to explain complex procedure to a "green kid." He also expressed discomfort at the idea of training someone, saying, "I don't know anything about training people." We listed his needs on a flipchart and taped it to my wall so that we could look at it together. His needs were (as he stated them):

- Continued employment for 28 months minimum.
- Not to be distracted by someone asking him questions while he worked.
- Either not to have to train someone or to learn how to train.

My list had only the one item at that time (which was also posted so as to be visible to both of us): To continue getting Marvin's job done now and in the future. As we moved on toward generating problem-solving solutions, new needs were revealed.

"Training someone wouldn't necessarily give you what you want anyway," Marvin said. "If that person got sick, quit, or dropped dead after I left, you still wouldn't be able to get my job done. And if the person stayed, you might wind up with another Marvin," he grinned.

At one point Marvin proposed that he write out, step-by-step, everything he did to analyze the data, stating the basis of all the decisions that he made. "If you had an exact procedure anyone could do my job."

At this, I thought of all the supervisors before me who had locked themselves into a single solution: "Have Marvin teach someone his job," something that wouldn't necessarily have met their long-term needs anyway.

"How can we be sure that the procedures are really complete once you've finished?" I asked.

"We'll need someone to check it carefully," Marvin responded. "Someone to think it through and see if it makes sense. It might be a good idea for someone to check out the procedure by going through it step-by-step."

We agreed to use one of the newest and least knowledgeable people in the department. If that person could follow each procedure, almost anyone could—that was to be our test for efficiency and comprehensibility.

My encounter with Marvin embodied all the basic precepts of creative negotiation. Although one of the requirements, of course, is flexibility, it is helpful to keep a standard formula in mind. The approach outlined below is a modification of John Dewey's problem-solving methodology with an infusion of creative techniques.

Define the problem in terms of participant needs (rather than in terms of solutions). People almost invariably leap to their solutions (or state their positions) even before they begin to think about what they *need* out of the current situation. Needs are open-ended, solutions are closed. Trying to impose solutions is not a way to win friends or resolve conflicts.

Get the useful facts. Do not overelaborate or deal with constraints. People need facts in problem solving but they often overdo it. The best facts are those that are objectively true (not judgmentally true). Avoid creating obstacles!

Generate solutions (suspend critical evaluation during this step). Here a variety of idea-generating techniques, such as brainstorming and the needs agenda, can be used to develop innovative solutions.

Select solutions that meet the needs of all participants to formulate the agreement. If a need is not adequately met, more creative idea generation may be needed.

Implement solutions. It's usually a good idea to plan the "how" separately from the "what." An agreement should clearly spell out who will do what to carry out the solution.

Monitor results. The agreement can specify its own monitoring devices that tell you early when things are going wrong so that they can be corrected. Focus on creative problem solving (not blame) when new or unanticipated problems arise and don't let them fester.

Adjust the agreement if necessary. Change is often the hallmark of a viable agreement. If the parties reached an agreement they can also change it. An agreement should be a living thing that adapts as the participants grow and develop new needs and as the future unfolds.

My experience with Marvin is not an isolated instance. I've witnessed several hundred major examples of creative negotiating that vastly improved interpersonal and intergroup relationships, and that proved to be good business to boot. The potential is promising.

I've seen a company and union merge their interests and resources, after years of fighting, strikes, and name calling, to the point where workers increased their productivity an average of 7 percent a year during the first five years, substantially reduced operating costs and spearheaded the drive for company technological innovation. Management learned a whole new way to deal with the union, overcame its tendency to manage arbitrarily (and to block employee suggestions), and significantly altered the company culture and its organizational structure. This firm went from being a company that was virtually on the rocks to being a solid leader in its field.

Creative negotiation is not easy, especially when you are new at it. But I have found over and over again that when people really decide to blaze new trails in business with creative approaches to negotiating win-win agreements, there seems to be almost no limit to the positive results that can be created.

SECTION FIVE

Strategy, Planning, and Preparation

Successful professional negotiators agree on one thing: the key to success in negotiation is preparation and planning. Persuasive presentation, skillful communication, nimble shifting of position, and a host of other skills used during actual negotiations are important, but they cannot overcome the disadvantage created by poor planning, nor can they help negotiators who lock themselves into untenable positions before or during the early stages of negotiation. Further, while interpersonal skills during negotiation can reap the most from a strategy, a well-laid plan has its own strength, and even modest skills can see it through to an acceptable conclusion. The previous two sections discussed two major types of negotiation, distributive and integrative (win/lose and win/win). This section addresses the operational and strategic process of planning and preparing for negotiations of either sort.

There are at least two levels or stages of preparation for negotiation. One involves getting ready for a specific negotiation, when we want to learn more about the other party, the situation we face, and so on. The other involves making ourselves ready to negotiate at any time. Professional runners prepare for the next race, but they have also been preparing themselves all year, in fact for many years, to run races. Given that we are all going to face negotiation situations regularly, we need to know how to prepare properly.

Conflict is a part of life, welcomed by some, regretted by others, but present nonetheless. Nowhere is this more so than in negotiation. Some bargaining is obviously competitive, as when two parties have different and mutually exclusive objectives (such as haggling over the price of something). Even in integrative bargaining, when the parties are working toward joint or convergent goals, there may still be substantial conflict about how much each will contribute or how much each will benefit. Hence conflict, while varying in intensity, is inherent in any negotiation situation and needs to be planned and prepared for.

Preparation and planning may imply that negotiation is inherently systematic, rational, and predictable. Preparation and planning do pay off, but not in such a deterministic fashion. There is no inherently proper way of determining the best settlement in negotiation; settlements are always arbitrary. In addition, negotiations are rarely completely cool, harmonious, or generous and mutually supportive. There is frequently a troublesome trade-off between individual and joint interests. These conditions may be accentuated and multiplied when one or, perhaps, both parties perceives the relationship as competitive, as an effort to win at the other party's expense. Doing this, of course, engenders defensiveness, distrust, and counteroffensiveness, usually resulting in a less satisfactory outcome for both parties. One key message has been that these conditions can be reduced and subordinated by structuring the relationship as collaborative, wherein parties work together on joint or mutually supportive goals, work to trust each other, and find ways to cooperate.

In earlier discussions we may have misled by suggesting that in integrative bargaining there is cooperation, while in distributive bargaining cooperation does not exist. Even in distributive bargaining, there must always be a certain minimal level of cooperation. Suppose that you are selling a used car and drive a hard bargain, getting as much as the buyer can possibly pay, while withholding special features such as an extra set of stereo speakers, snow tires, and so on. You may have "won" in the sense of getting as much as possible from the situation; and the other party may have "lost" as much as possible because they did not get any concessions from you in what was a heated, highly competitive negotiation. Yet, you will have nothing if the other party does not cooperate and go through with the deal. In most states, for a limited amount of time after a deal has been reached, people can walk away from an agreement to purchase a house, a car, and most major appliances. In less legal types of arrangements, like an adjustment made between two managers about the transfer of materials between their departments, both parties have to continue to perceive an advantage for the agreement to work. These aspects of negotiation may be difficult to understand fully at first. The readings in this section should help to that end.

Robert Kuhn's article "How to Plan the Strategies" (from his 1988 book, *Dealmaker*) differentiates between incremental and strategic thinking. While both are appropriate and necessary, the former involves "satisficing," or reacting to contingencies; the latter involves a more proactive, creative approach to the future. Specifically, strategic thinking must deal with surprise, with the unforeseen and the unanticipated. Kuhn states that a good strategy defines one's approach, linking goals to tactics while searching for competitive advantages and distinct competencies. He cautions, though, against putting too much faith in strategy as an inviolable process, stating that "the mirage of control is the problem of strategy." He also warns against focusing on gimmicks or tricky tactics in lieu of solid strategizing.

Philip Sperber's "Prenegotiation Planning for the Business Pro" (from his 1983 book *Fail-Sale Business Negotiating*) suggests that negotiation success begins with developing an understanding of the many, sometimes hidden, reasons that negotiations occur. The main thrust of Sperber's advice is contained in a five-step process for researching the other side—including a strong case in favor of role-playing important negotiations before actually conducting them. In addition, recognizing the importance of nonlinear thinking in prenegotiation planning, Sperber's article includes self-administered measures of abstract and creative thinking abilities for readers seeking more insight as to their skill in these areas.

Continuing with the preparation theme, Bill Scott's "Preparing for Negotiations" (from his 1981 book *The Skills of Negotiating*) builds on preparation, subject to three assumptions: the negotiation planners have "done their homework" regarding the other side, that they know the rules "governing the territory" of the negotiation, and that the negotiation will be a simple one (that is, that it will be accomplished in just a few meetings). Scott suggests that the conduct of negotiation preliminaries attend to the purpose, plan, pace, and place of the negotiation, and to making it a positive experience for the other party.

The last article in this section, Len Leritz's "The No-Fault Formula: Five Easy Steps," is a chapter from his 1987 book entitled *No-Fault Negotiating*. Leritz's "formula" consists of a regimen he proposes for structuring the strategic thinking process, covering what the planner sees or hears, assumes, feels, needs, and wants or will do. The article lists the benefits of the process, giving examples for framing questions and statements for each of the five steps, and an illustration of the formula in application.

How to Plan the Strategies

Robert Kuhn

STRATEGY IS MORE THINKING THAN DOING

Strategy is an ancient term derived from warfare. It depicts the fighting plans of battlefield commanders. One can envision generals hunched over detailed relief maps, moving armies as if pawns. One can visualize wars being won and lost by subtle shifts of thrust, parry, and feint.

Strategy in deal making is a directed plan. It defines the approach. It links overall goals with operational tactics. It has specific, clear-cut objectives and describes the actions and reactions of decision makers to the shifts and changes of conditions. Strategy for a dealmaker is like a hammer for a carpenter or a bat for a baseball player. It is the tool that gets the job done. The better your strategy, the better your deals.

In this sense, strategy is the search for *competitive advantage,* for areas of relative strength that can coax, coddle, or coerce favorable outcomes. Competitive advantage seeks to capitalize on your *distinctive competencies,* those aspects of the deal-making process where your side excels or can excel compared with the other side.

Assessing mutual strengths and weaknesses is the key to devising the best deal-making strategy. Compare your strengths and weaknesses to those of your opponent in the context of the deal issues. The result of this assessment is a series of alternative strategies. These various options for deal-making direction are then evaluated for probable outcomes, and the best are chosen to put into action.

Creativity promotes strategy formulation.

Consistency directs strategy evaluation.

Structure controls strategy implementation.

There is, however, a dark side to strategy. Its presence can fool dealmakers into thinking they've got a good grip on a situation when they haven't got a handle on anything. The more the strategic sophistication, at times the stronger the strategic illusion. The mirage of control is the problem of strategy.

From Robert Kuhn, *Dealmaker* (New York: John Wiley & Sons, Inc., 1988), pp. 64–72. Reprinted by permission of John Wiley & Sons, Inc.

It has been said that corporate strategy is like a ritual rain dance. It has no effect on the weather that follows, of course, but it makes those who do it feel they are in complete charge. Often when we use strategic planning, we are laboring to improve the dancing, not the weather.

WAYS OF THINKING: INCREMENTAL VERSUS STRATEGIC

Strategic planning is not sorcery; strategic hocus-pocus will not conjure up instant deal closing. Strategic planning is just a way of thinking about a transaction. It can be best understood in contrast to its opposite, incremental planning. The best dealmakers function well in both modes. While the strategic process leads to original thinking in devising alternative options, the incremental mode can be fertile soil for the spontaneous sprouting of "aha" insights.

Incremental Thinking

Operating in the incremental mode, the dealmaker begins *reactively* by recognizing an immediate problem, some unexpected shock, whether opportunity or threat. The dealmaker then searches selectively through a restricted variety of potential solutions, making marginal movements from the status quo, evaluating each tiny step in order. Deviations from current policy are considered sequentially and widened progressively until the first satisfactory solution is found. Such an agreeable answer is accepted immediately and all other alternatives, even if potentially better, are ignored.

Herbert Simon's idea of *bounded rationality* controls here.[1] Dealmakers can't ever know *everything;* so if they want to do *anything,* they must replace *optimizing,* finding the best answer, with *satisficing,* finding an acceptable answer. According to bounded rationality, problems in the real world need only be solved satisfactorily, not perfectly.

Strategic Thinking

Operating in the strategic mode, dealmakers begin *proactively* by defining general goals and setting specific objectives. They scan the deal-making environment seeking opportunities and threats and analyze both sides for relative strengths and weaknesses. The key here is deal-making strengths and weaknesses in the light of the opportunities and threats in a search for competitive advantages.

What emerges from this dynamic, creative process[2] is a set of alternatives. Each is evaluated for probable consequences. Strategic choice is made with the guideline of internal consistency: Which set of strategies best matches goals and strengths? Implementation (including step and time sequencing), feedback, and review complete the process.

It is a common misconception to judge incremental decision making bad, and strategic decision making good. Each is good, but in its own arena. One would not

---

[1]Herbert Simon, *Administrative Behavior* (New York: Free Press, 1976).
[2]See Deal Secret 30 for specific techniques for generating creative alternatives.

resolve an ugly personality clash in the strategic mode, just as one would not formulate a comprehensive plan in the incremental mode. Learn when to stay incremental and when to jump strategic.

STRATEGY AND SURPRISE

Strategic thinking, to be truly strategic, must deal with surprise. The unanticipated must be anticipated; the unforeseen, seen. If everything is assumed to be known, if your deal-making future is expected to emulate your deal-making past, then the process is simple extension (trending), and strategy is playing no part. Strategic deal making must be concerned with radical change, discontinuity, sharp breaks with the past, even violent twists from current paths. Dealmakers must plan for the unplanned.

SCOPE OF STRATEGY

Strategic thinking works for individuals as well as for companies. People can apply the thought processes for making personal decisions and planning personal deal making. For example, you can use the strategic method to resolve whether to push for a still higher salary at a prospective job or to negotiate a better position at your current job.

An honest assessment of your strengths and weaknesses in light of the employment opportunities and threats (e.g., the prospective versus current job) can be a critical part of the process. Careful consideration of diverse alternatives in light of overall lifetime goals is certainly worth the effort. (One would not, of course, need strategic thinking to make the vast majority of daily deals. Lifetime goals are irrelevant for buying a car or settling time-to-bed arguments with kids.)

WHEN PLANNING STRATEGY

What to do first when planning your strategy? When negotiating or structuring a deal, do *not* focus on conjuring up tricky tactics. Gimmicks do not achieve. Plots sicken as they thicken.

Devising the plan must come first. Where do you want to go, and how will each step of the process help get you there? See ends from beginnings. Have a clear vision of the proposed path—even though that path will twist and turn often. Keep ultimate results in current focus. After each step of the deal, try to reconstruct your objectives. Are you proceeding on target? Or have you drifted? If you've strayed off course, can you get back on? Or should you now consider altering your objectives to conform to the new reality? Negotiating deals is a continuous series of course corrections and target shifts.

STRATEGIC ATTITUDES

There are three general kinds of strategic attitudes in deal making. They are: (1) simple and direct, (2) press and push, and (3) cool and aloof.

Simple and Direct

Come right to the point. Say what you mean. The straightforward approach may be startlingly effective, disarming the other side and driving to quick resolution. Go simple and direct when

You've worked with the other side before.

The deal is bogging down.

Immediate closure is a goal.

Press and Push

Here's where the shoving starts. Sensitive points are squeezed. To be effective, the pressing and pushing should be subtle. If the other side thinks that you are twisting arms they will become resentful. Pressure is not some evil, alien torture. It is often the mechanism to get a deal closed.[3] Press and push when

Your side is stronger.

The other side needs a quick close.

You want to assess limits.

Cool and Aloof

This approach uses reverse psychology. Play hard to get. Let the other side sell themselves. It can be marvelously effective. If you give points too quickly, if you're too compromise minded, the other side may worry that they've undershot their potential. (I've been there, kicking myself when the positive response came a mite too easily.) Avoid tempting your opponents: Awakening latent greed is not smart. The key here is making the other side work when exacting the concession. Be cool and aloof when

The other side is stronger.

Your side is under time pressure.

You have other alternative deals.

TACTICS TO CONSIDER

Attitudes and approaches to negotiating vary. In some situations, the "drip" is preferred, letting out demands little by little so as not to scare off the other side. In different situations, the "drop" is preferred, with the whole load being dumped at once. The following 12 tactics are used commonly in negotiations. They give flavor for

---

[3]On arrival in the United States, my father-in-law had to be pressured and tricked by a real estate agent to make an excellent purchase of a small apartment building. Having been buffeted by the business ways of his old country, my father-in-law was highly skeptical of everyone. There's no doubt that, left unpressured and untricked, he would have never bought anything. His investment of $15,000 grew to over $400,000 in 15 years, not to mention all the years of income, free rent, and meaningful work.

the 40 Deal Secrets in Part II. If you choose to use them, know how to thrust. If they're used against you, know how to parry. Consistency is vital here: Tactics must be matched to strategy.

1. *Patience.* You wait. However anxious, you don't show it. Patience is a devastating weapon when the other side is highly volatile. When you set the pace, you control the deal.

2. *Slow agony.* The deal moves at a crawl. Every issue takes inordinate amounts of time. Delays are frequent. Slow agony never says "no"; the deal never actually stalls. This is an interesting defense against high pressure.

3. *Apathy.* Overt concern is minimal. Whether the deal goes or blows appears immaterial. You request without energy and respond without passion. Apathy defends against high pressure.

4. *Empathy/sympathy.* Concern is shown for the other side. This is a powerful tactic for breaking deadlocks and bridging gaps. Such feelings should be genuine. Do not feign personal concern; compassion as a ruse is off limits. Use empathy/sympathy when you mean it.

5. *Sudden shifts.* Whim and caprice do not build solid reputation. Consistency is important, but sometimes it equals sluggishness, even obstinacy. When talks are turgid and momentum has dissipated, unexpected changes can dislodge blockage and overcome obstacles. You have nothing to lose by shaking the tree.

6. *Faking.* Dealmakers are like football halfbacks, able to feint one way and run the other. Faking is more trading than lying. Fake when you want to protect a particular point. For example, you might insist on all cash in selling your home (or business) just to be able to maintain your price when you finally "concede" some seller financing—which you planned to concede all along.

7. *Walking.* Closing your briefcase and leaving the room. A dead deal. This tactic is less extreme than it looks. After all, you can always reopen negotiations (though some of your credibility is lost). Walking works when the other side has more basic power and has pushed too hard too long. Quitting is the ultimate leveler.

8. *Fait accompli.* The threat to take unilateral action. The deal, or something about it, would be irrevocably changed. For example, when a financially troubled company negotiates with creditors, each side can threaten to file bankruptcy proceedings—which would put all decisions in the hands of the court. Use fait accompli when you control a critical issue—but use it cautiously.

9. *Salami.* Cut a little here, a little there, and soon the salami is all gone. Some negotiators grind for small gain—but they never stop. The deal's never done. You must stop these people. Strict limits are the antidote for salami tactics.

10. *Limits.* Allow the other side to go so far but no farther. Setting boundaries can be imposing, even riveting. Don't do it often, but always make it count. Set your limits once and stick to them. Use this tactic when the other side keeps pushing.

11. *Deadlines.* Countdowns are contentious. Calendar pressure is trouble-some. One must never make a hasty decision under time constraint. Try to force yourself to go even a bit slower than normal. If the deal evaporates, it evaporates. It's far better to pass a dozen good deals than to make one bad one.

12. *Antagonism.* Not a good tactic. More is accomplished by seeking per-sonal harmony even during professional disputes. Nonetheless, people are antag-onistic, some deliberately as a technique, others because that's just the way they are. Disarm the antagonism by sidesteps, not body blocks, by leveraged angles, not frontal assaults. Direct confrontation rarely works. Try gentle correction, tinged with humor. "I see the new day hasn't brought forth a new attitude." "I can't toughen my position because you can't get more upset."

WHAT TO DO?

You are a buyer negotiating to buy a new home. You currently rent an apartment and have no pressure to move quickly. The sellers, however, have serious concerns. They have moved to a new city and have already bought another home. What to do?

Time is a strength to you and a weakness to them. Draw up a series of alternatives related to time. You might give a short deadline for your offer if you feel pressure is the right tactic. Conversely, you might grant extra time to the sellers. Evaluating the different options requires careful analysis of the personalities of the people. The high-pressure strategy might be more effective if the sellers are unable to maintain two mortgages or cannot be bothered with unfinished business in their old city. The sym-pathetic strategy would be more effective if the sellers show appreciation by making an easier agreement. It is also possible to hedge your bets: Try one approach, and if it doesn't work, shift to the other. (Think carefully about the order.)

Prenegotiation Planning for the Business Pro

Philip Sperber

UNDERSTANDING THE HIDDEN BUSINESS REASONS FOR NEGOTIATION

The reasons for negotiating must be carefully analyzed before you can even begin to establish your maximum concessions and minimum requirements. This advice is so basic that most people tend to gloss over it. Too often, even in simple bargaining situations, only the initial motive for entering into the negotiation is emphasized. Other primary and secondary reasons are thought of haphazardly or not at all. One study showed that 46 percent of corporate managers did not really know what they wanted.

Let's take the situation where a chemical company develops a new compound useful as an insecticide. Although the chemical does not kill insects any better than what is on the market at present, it appears to be significantly safer as far as human exposure is concerned. The hitch is that the company has never been in insecticides and feels that it would be too costly and too risky to try to grab a significant share of the market away from the companies entrenched in the area.

Assume the chemical company president is your boss and tells you that the new compound does not fit in with the company's long-range product-market plans. You are assigned the task of "spinning off" this R&D (research and development) by-product as profitably as possible.

You promptly research the insecticide market, as well as those companies that appear to be potential entrants. With the aid of technical personnel, you prepare a prospectus on the benefits and potential of your company's new compound. You then contact your prospects and offer the product development to the highest bidder.

Unfortunately, the firms with the large market shares have a lot of money invested in their existing insecticides and are not too enthusiastic about another insecticide that does not have a dramatic improvement in killing power. The potential entrants to the insecticide market show interest in the product but are worried about the risk of competing with the well-known brands. As a result, you sell the rights to the product

From Philip Sperber, *Fail-Safe Business Negotiating* (Englewood Cliffs, N.J.: Prentice Hall, 1983), pp. 10–21. Reprinted with permission of Doreen F. Sperber.

for only $20,000, notwithstanding the fact that the research and development costs were $200,000. After all, you did the best you could under the circumstances.

Nothing of the sort! Before implementing any negotiation strategy, the business reasons for entering into negotiation must be viewed as a set of problems to be solved. The facts and assumptions pertinent to the situation should be assimilated. The problem or problems should be defined. All alternative solutions, no matter how unlikely they appear on the surface, should be listed. The benefits and disadvantages of each should then be analyzed. Finally, the best solution to the problem should be selected, at which time the appropriate negotiating strategy will become apparent. Other attractive solutions should be kept in mind as negotiation proceeds. They may have to be implemented should the ideal solution become impractical or be opposed.

In the preceding example, the most attractive solution was to recoup the company's R&D expense and make a profit. When it became apparent that this goal was not feasible, another desirable alternative to sale should have been considered.

The candidates for product purchase were, for one reason or another, not willing to put up a great deal of front money. In the end, it was one of the entrenched firms with a large market share that finally bought the product development for $20,000. The alternative of licensing one of the potential entrants should have been considered. Unlike the entrenched firm that already had an insecticide on the market, the potential entrant would have the incentive to introduce the new product and compete with the entrenched firms. If this firm were successful, the royalties generated by sales from the new insecticide would greatly exceed the $200,000 investment made by the chemical company.

As a matter of fact, your president wanted to spin off the product because of the cost and risk of commercialization, not because the product was incompatible with company operations. In view of this, analysis of the business reasons would have indicated that it might be possible to strike a bargain for both royalties and the future right to commercialize the product. Although the product is of little interest now, the licensee might be successful in capturing a healthy share of the market by creating demand for a product that is safer. The insecticide venture might eventually represent a profitable low-risk option your president would like to exercise.

It is vital that you understand and analyze the reasoning for initiating a negotiation. If you evaluate the various negotiating alternatives and their consequences for meeting business objectives, you can enter the negotiation with flexibility and foresight and change emphasis on issues and concessions under the pressure of the firing line. You then can be confident of shooting for the best deal during each different bargaining situation. To further illustrate the benefits of proper business preparation, let us assume you persuade a company to pay you a healthy royalty on sales of the insecticide to be commercialized. The only issue is whether the product patent and trade secret rights are sold outright or are merely licensed. You are assured that the firm will agree to a diligence clause requiring them to spend at least a minimum effort in terms of facilities, personnel, and money in a good faith attempt to successfully commercialize the insecticide. Therefore, there is no reason for you to keep title to the product rights. Secretly, you feel there is great value in keeping open the option of entering the market at some future point in time. You therefore tell the company that a written guarantee will not suffice. You are only willing to grant a license for exclusive manufacture and sale of the insecticide, with the reservation of rights in your company to also make and sell the insecticide if you feel that the licensee is not being diligent or aggressive enough in the marketplace. The other firm reacts negatively to the threat of future competition from you and refuses to agree to this without a reduction in royalties. You assent, provided they agree to a final concession of granting you a nonexclusive license to make and use any improvements they develop in the insecticide area.

The agreement in principle has been reached, and you shake hands and agree to have your attorneys work out the details for execution. The other party leaves happy with the knowledge that front money is not required and resources can be used solely for the investment necessary to commercialize the product. The royalty rate decrease is also a matter of personal satisfaction for the other negotiator. You leave happy because your company will be receiving much more money than the nominal lump-sum purchase price that was offered if the licensee is successful. You are also happy because you have the right to jump on the bandwagon after the other company does the spade work in obtaining market acceptance. And finally, you are happy because you will also have access to their insecticide improvements so that your company will not be at a disadvantage if it later decides to compete with the superior insecticide they develop.

TECHNIQUES OF RESEARCHING THE NEGOTIATOR AND THE COMPANY

There are five main considerations in researching the negotiator and his or her company. First, the company with which you are about to negotiate a deal and the specific individuals you meet at the bargaining table should be thoroughly investigated. In order to plan the negotiation, you must have a good understanding of their business and psychological needs, how they think and react and their negotiation procedure, tactics, and strategy. With these data, you will be prepared and will have an edge in the bargaining process.

Second, the simplest method of learning about the other firm, its past history and its present policies, and learning about its individual negotiators is to research the published literature. A good picture of the business can be obtained by studying annual reports, press releases, institutional advertising, reports of security analysts, government agency records, stock market guides, clipping services, credit information, and litigation reports. Information about the individuals with whom you will be negotiating can be obtained from biographies in *Moody's, Standard & Poor's,* and *Dun & Bradstreet,* speeches and articles, and *Who's Who* directories.

Third, more sophisticated sources of information can include interviewing other parties involved in litigation or settlements of disputes with the company with which you are about to deal—especially parties who have unsuccessfully negotiated with the company and those who presently have some type of business relationship with it. To obtain unpublished personal information about the individual with whom you will be negotiating, it will be necessary to speak to former classmates, acquaintances, friends, co-workers in previous employment, and fellow members of clubs, professional societies, and trade associations.

In some sensitive situations, it may even be necessary to use a private investigator. The information that can be obtained in this manner is invaluable in determining the negotiator's status socially and within the company, authority to make commitments, integrity, prior tactics, strengths and weaknesses, emotional needs, and even religion, race, and IQ, all of which play a role in how he or she will approach the negotiation. Sometimes, even mannerisms, voice modulation, or other personal characteristics, if known prior to confrontation at the bargaining table, will tip you off about the negotiator's thinking and reactions enough to give you an edge.

Unfortunately, there are many executives who use an investigator for tasks that are unethical and even illegal. One expert estimates that $800 million is annually spent on industrial spying. Using an insider, a wiretap, or a bug to find out what the party's real bottom line is, the sincerity of its assurances, and its actual reasons for entering into the deal is an invasion of privacy.

Fourth, if the deal is of major importance to your company's business in the future, then the prenegotiation research can be taken even one step further by going through one or more dry runs with the second- or third-choice candidates. This will give you a better feel for the kind of deal that can be reached. You will have a better understanding of what concessions the first-choice candidate will expect. You will also have the flexibility of falling back on the second or third choice, should your first choice be unreasonable.

Fifth, when you are about to negotiate a deal with your first-choice candidate, you should consider making further use of all the research data you have gathered and analyzed. This can be accomplished using the technique of role playing, a combination of business gaming and brainstorming. Your negotiating team is split so that one or more persons represent the other party, and the team acts out the entire negotiation.

Role playing will introduce the members of your negotiating team to the facts and issues with dramatic impact. It transforms the intellectual and logical exercise of forecasting and formulating strategy into an emotional experience that your negotiating team will both feel and hear.

After the role playing, your negotiating team can have an in-depth discussion as to what took place, the difficulties that arose, the mistakes that were made, the behavior to be changed, and new issues and points of view that were not anticipated. Probably the greatest benefit of role playing is bringing human behavior into the laboratory where you can put yourself into the other party's shoes in order to experience the different emotions. Role playing even has the advantage of giving the junior members of your negotiating team the chance to play devil's advocate in the role of the other party, allowing them to say how they actually feel about your strategy and tactics instead of what they think you want to hear.

To sum up, role playing is a valuable research tool that enables you to discover problem areas you have overlooked or ignored and correct and polish your presentation and strategy. Based on responses I have received from thousands of seminar attendees, there is less than a 10 percent chance that you have participated in role playing in preparation for a negotiation. You will be making a valuable contribution to your company by introducing role playing for major deals.

SECRETS OF THE CREATIVE NEGOTIATOR

A creative idea, plan, or solution to a problem almost always involves using a principle or relationship that everyone knows but everyone also didn't remember and relate. Creative negotiators aren't more intelligent. They simply have a way of using their memory and cognitive and perceptual abilities far more effectively than others. These individuals put their subconscious to work in addition to applying abstract thought and analytical skills, and their insight comes after relaxing and stepping away from the problem. There are six basic steps to the personality trait of creative thinking, and you can adopt them:

1. Formulate the problem to be solved and possible alternative solutions.

2. Gather all the data considered relevant to defining the problem and clarifying conflicting approaches to solving it.

3. Organize, study, and digest these data in the context of the problem to be solved.

4. Put the problem aside consciously, and wait for the subconscious mind to act upon it and "report back."

5. Act on the feedback from the subconscious, which will come in the form of a sudden idea or hunch.

6. Rigorously test the solution chosen.

In Step 1, before you can gather information and facts relevant to the matter being considered, you must define the problem and possible alternative solutions. Alfred P. Sloan, former chairman of General Motors, often would postpone making a decision until there was sufficient disagreement among the executives considering the problem. Only then would he look at the facts to see which of the approaches and opinions were practical and desirable. He would not tolerate starting out with a conclusion and then looking for facts to support it.

Write down the aspects and characteristics of the problem from the first moment it has become of interest. And keep writing, writing, writing as you go along. Putting information, ideas, and other people's opinions down in written form is an essential part of abstract thinking, recognized by virtually all problem solvers. Never be without paper, pencil, or pen. Ideas strike at any hour and under any circumstance, and those that aren't immediately translated into an appropriate notation almost always vanish back into the subconscious. Memory behaves in the same fashion.

Once you honestly start the writing process, you'll find that it leads into a sharp focus on the task undertaken, reduces wasted motion—both intellectual and physical—and brings practical guidelines into existence as if by magic. Even if you are not a strong abstract thinker (test yourself in the following section), you will greatly improve your creativity by disciplining yourself to use the approach outlined in this chapter.

Step 2 should continue until you have much more data than can possibly apply to the problem. Even then, you'll probably realize you stopped too soon and will need to gather more data before finishing Step 3.

For the mass of data to be useful, it must be arranged pursuant to Step 3 in some scheme that is appropriate. One of the best approaches is to key the various notes, reports, books, transcripts, and so on into an outline, a chart, or some similar schematic or graphic representation of your objective (or the problem).

It is important to rearrange and regroup the data, trying different combinations, trade-offs, and basic changes in the model and considering all alternative approaches suggested by the data until you are convinced you have exhausted all the realistic possibilities. Then, and only then, when you honestly believe there are no other new realignments worth considering, should you move to the next phase of this problem-solving technique.

Forget it all in Step 4. With the first three steps properly completed, you are ready to turn the problem over to the subconscious—where the full intellectual resources can be applied. Drawing upon memory, which has recorded every scrap of information, every concept, every impression ever heard, seen, thought, or otherwise received, your subconscious can tremendously augment the available data in the areas you have been deliberately "stirring up" while sorting the information gathered consciously. In a process that can only be called synthesis, cross-linkages are established, often between products and principles that have seemed totally unrelated. New frames of reference form, and unsuspected causal relationships are activated. All this goes on while the conscious mind is otherwise occupied—a condition that one must establish and maintain.

This is the incubation period or gestation phase of the creative cycle. Generally speaking, its length cannot be predicted. Its outcome, however, is completely predictable. There will be a "report" to the conscious mind, and that report will most likely be the solution to the problem.

In the interim between conscious commitment to the subconscious domain and the flash of revelation, it is imperative that you "forget" the problem completely.

The subconscious flash will come. It may be in a whisper, a hesitant thought that hardly seems worth noting or as increasingly happens with those who are "veterans" in the technique, a stunning hunch that literally wipes the mind clean and makes the hands tremble. It will come in many instances at the least expected or welcome time: You may be driving off the first tee, staring out the window of a bus or plane, or waiting for a court to play tennis.

At any time, in any situation, you may suddenly think again of the problem deliberately put aside. If you ignore the thought, you may have "blown" the solution. It is most unlikely that the subconscious will ring again on the particular matter. Step 5 opens with an invitation—strong or subdued—but its characteristics are unmistakable: All of a sudden, you will be seeing the problem from a new perspective and with new ideas.

When the invitation comes, it must be accepted immediately for Step 5. Record every idea received. Be noncritical. Judgment must be withheld until you are sure no more ideas or hunches are forthcoming. There may be times when you experience an "avalanche effect." Ideas come in a flood, perhaps including the clear-cut solution of a difficult problem.

There is a tendency for people, especially conformists, to dismiss wild ideas. (Test your degree of open-mindedness and creativity in the following section.) Record them all. Remember that information is blind to the use to which it may be put by its possessor. Ideas that are totally unrelated may emerge. There's no way of predicting the subconscious linkages that will be established during mental synthesis. Failure to record them all could cost you the solution to the problem in the near or distant future. Put down everything that comes into your mind at this time.

Now the first five steps of the creative process have done the work. Chances are, you'll have the solution to the immediate problem before you. Step 6 is to prove it workable in practice and undertake whatever further experimentation, discussion, consultation, or other follow-up is required.

Now is the time to apply judgment—rigorously—to the ideas and hunches that have come to you. Rate them as well as you can according to difficulty of implementation, costs, conformance with organizational policies, and time required to find out whether the approach will be satisfactory. This done, work should be resumed, perhaps by a team of investigators if there are enough approaches.

Just as important as presenting your creative plan or solution are the form and substance of your answers and explanations in response to questions stemming from your proposal. If you present a new idea or solution to a problem without adequate evaluation, thorough examination of all the negative consequences that could result, and a full and organized comprehension of all the supporting arguments and reasons, a few pointed questions could place you in a defensive position. You must be able to communicate your position so that it will withstand close scrutiny from people who are looking for every little way in which your proposal can damage them or be misconstrued to their detriment. In fact, questions give you an extra opportunity to make your ideas even more attractive, logical, and personal.

In addition to the dry runs and role playing already discussed, you must analyze expected areas of resistance and counterarguments. You must go even further and be ready to counter rebuttals to your explanations by addressing counterarguments. You will appear confident, intelligent, and strong even if your proposal is shot down. This rigorous exercise of being one step ahead of the other party also facilitates catching your own mistakes before you make them.

You must closely examine all of the effects each of the best solutions and approaches will have on the parties and individuals involved. Will their financial, personal, and other goals be promoted or retarded? Who will be misled or confused? How will each person and party be motivated, and what reaction can be expected? Who can you expect an objection from, and what will that objection be? How will your plan affect the future? Will additional financing be needed? Will improvements or modifications be required? Will additional personnel be needed? Will the other party be happy with your solution over the long run?

ARE YOU A STRONG ABSTRACT AND CREATIVE THINKER?

Abstract thinking and creative thinking are two important skills for the successful negotiator. To see how strong your skills are in these areas, rate yourself by responding to the following two lists of statements.

First, to evaluate your abstract thinking skills, rate yourself from 0 to 5 for each of the following statements, with 0 being *no* and 5 being *yes*. Put down your true feelings, not what you think the ratings should be, because there are no correct answers. See the end of this section for an interpretation of your responses.

1. I do not play by the book.
2. I frequently seek comfort and protection.
3. The overall effect art has on my emotions is important to me.
4. I am not a doer.
5. I find new solutions to problems.
6. I do not take care of others.
7. Detail and realism in art are not important to me.
8. I am a misty-eyed romantic.
9. I like dreaming and planning.
10. I do not control my emotions effectively.

Now, to see how creative you are, rate yourself from 0 to 5, for the following statements, with 0 being *no* and 5 being *yes*. Again, put down your true feelings, not what you think the ratings should be, because there are no correct answers.

1. Nonfiction books can be a waste of time. If you want to read, read novels.
2. You have to admit that some criminals are very smart.
3. There are more important things to do than trying to be a fastidious dresser.
4. I do not have very strong convictions. What's right is not always right; what's wrong is not always wrong.
5. It doesn't bother me when my boss gives vague instructions.
6. Business before pleasure is not a hard-and-fast rule in my life.
7. Taking a different route to work can be fun, even if it takes longer.
8. Most rules and regulations can be broken under the right circumstances.
9. Playing with a new idea is fun, even if it doesn't come to anything.
10. When people are nice to me, I don't care why.
11. I do not try to avoid unusual words and word combinations when writing.
12. Detective work sounds like a fun job.
13. Crazy people can have good ideas.
14. I write letters to friends even though there are so many clever greeting cards available.
15. Pleasing myself means more to me than pleasing others.
16. You will not find the true answer to many questions no matter how long you dig.
17. A logical, step-by-step method is not best for solving problems.
18. It's not a waste of time to ask questions if I have no hope of obtaining answers.
19. I am often uncertain that I'm following the correct procedures for solving a specific problem.

20. I concentrate harder on what interests me than do most people.
21. When trying to solve a problem, I spend a great deal of time analyzing it.
22. I occasionally voice opinions that seem to turn people off.
23. I waste little time thinking about what others think of me.
24. Complex situations interest me because they are challenging.
25. It is more important to do what is right than to win acceptance of others.
26. People who seem unsure and uncertain about things have my respect.
27. More than others, I want things to be interesting and exciting.
28. On occasion, I get overly enthusiastic on the job.
29. I often get my best ideas when doing nothing in particular.
30. I rely on hunches or a "gut" feeling that I am right when moving toward solving a problem.
31. I sometimes enjoy doing things I'm not supposed to do.
32. I dislike hobbies that involve collecting things.
33. I have capacities that have not been tapped yet.
34. Daydreaming helps me on the way to many important projects.
35. I dislike people who are objective and rational.
36. I am more enthusiastic and energetic than most people.
37. I get along more easily with people in the same social and business class as myself.
38. I have a high degree of aesthetic sensitivity.
39. I have a good capacity for self-instruction.
40. I dislike people who are very sure of their conclusions.
41. Inspiration is important for solving problems.
42. In an argument, I feel that it would be great for the person who disagrees with me to become a friend, but not at the price of sacrificing my point of view.
43. I do not avoid situations in which I might feel inferior.
44. The source of information is more important to me than the content.
45. I get a certain enjoyment from things being uncertain and unpredictable.
46. My self-respect is more important than the respect of others.
47. People who strive for perfection are wise.
48. I prefer to work solo rather than in a team effort.
49. Creativity can be utilized in any field of endeavor.
50. It is unimportant to have a place for everything and everything in order.
51. I never think other people can read my thoughts.
52. The trouble with people is that they often take things too lightly.
53. I am a self-starter.

54. I am curious and playful.

55. My motivation and enthusiasm for my projects stay even in the fact of obstacles or opposition.

56. People who are willing to entertain ''crackpot'' ideas are practical.

57. What could be, rather than what is, is the important question.

58. After I've made up my mind, I often can change it.

59. I think the statement ''Ideas are a dime a dozen'' is a misconception.

60. I don't mind asking questions that show ignorance.

61. Sometimes ideas come to me as if from some external source.

62. There are times when I have an ''avalanche'' of ideas.

63. I look for ways of converting necessities into advantages.

64. It is a good idea not to expect too much of others.

65. I cannot change my interests to pursue a job or career as easily as I can change a job to pursue my interests.

66. Many breakthroughs are due to chance.

67. People who are theoretically oriented are no less important than those who are practical.

68. It is important to understand the motives of people you deal with.

69. I see things in terms of their potential.

70. When brainstorming, I come up with more ideas and come up with them faster than most others in the group.

71. I am not ashamed to express interest in the opposite sex if so inclined.

72. I tend to rely more on my first impressions and feelings when making judgments than on a thorough analysis.

73. I frequently anticipate solutions to my problems.

74. I rarely laugh at myself for my quirks and peculiarities.

75. Clever thinkers resort to metaphors and analogies.

76. When someone gets ahead of me in line, I usually point it out to him or her.

77. Problems that do not have clear answers interest me.

78. I usually work things out for myself rather than get someone to show me.

79. I let my feelings guide me through experiences.

80. I frequently begin work on a problem that I remotely sense and cannot yet express.

81. I frequently tend to forget names of people, streets, and towns.

82. I tolerate frustration more than the average person.

83. During adolescence I liked to be alone to pursue my own interests and thoughts.

84. I feel that the adage ''Do unto others . . .'' is less important than ''To thine own self be true.''

85. Things obvious to others are not so obvious to me.

86. I feel I will make important contributions to society.

87. I have more problems than I can handle and more work than there is time for.

Your abstract thinking and planning abilities are strong if the sum of your ratings in the first list of statements exceeds 25 and get stronger as you approach 40.

You are probably exceptionally creative if the sum of your ratings in the second list exceeds 375, very creative if it is above 300, above average in creativity if it is above 225, average if it is above 175, below average if it is above 125, and noncreative if it is below 125.

BOTTOM-LINE STRATEGY

Even the most complex business negotiation boils down to one of two situations: *One,* you are trying to sell a product or service to somebody, or vice versa. *Two,* you have been wronged in some manner and are looking for reparation, or vice versa.

How the other side views its position in these two broad negotiating situations may always be analyzed in dollars and cents. If a competitor is making false statements about your project in its advertising, your ability to persuade the competitor to cease and desist is dependent primarily upon the economics of the situation. The money the competitor has spent on the inventory of promotional literature containing the false statements, the money lost from cancelling advertising at the last minute, and the expense of printing new advertising will be weighed against the persuasiveness of your demand. If you threaten to sue, then your competitor will also have to weigh the cost of the defense against the cost of complying with your demands. If your competitor is getting a lot of mileage and is capturing a substantial share of the market by using the false statements, it may feel that its success is worth the cost of defending a lawsuit. If you counteract the false advertising with your own ads and successfully repulse the inroads being made by your competitor, this may be more economically costly for the competitor than a lawsuit and might result in a stand-off where it makes sense to cease the false advertising. As we see, although many of the issues involve intangibles and actions, everything can be viewed in terms of dollars and cents in analyzing your competitor's needs.

Prior to each negotiation, you should conduct an objective economic analysis of what the other party would like to realize from the negotiation, what the party would be willing to settle for, and what the party's bottom line is. Thus, if you wish to construct chemical process facilities for a potential customer, you must determine their current per-unit-volume profit, their return-on-investment and payback period expectations, and their desire to modernize existing facilities. Based on the answers to these questions and your own knowledge of the profit per unit volume that can be anticipated after planned start-up, you will have a fairly good feel for your customer's bottom-line settlement figure for the construction price as well as the low figure at which the customer will aim.

Once you go through the economic analysis of perceiving the other side's business needs, you will have a relatively good idea of what that side's reasonable goals

FIGURE 1   Prenegotiation planning

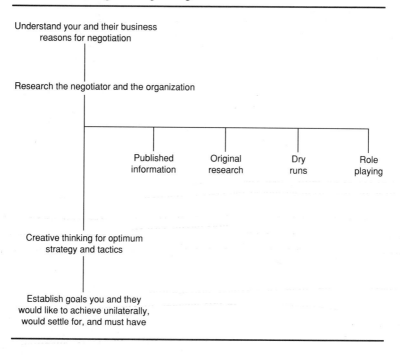

should be. Based on this information, you will be able to determine whether the goals you would like to achieve, the goals for which you would settle, and the bottom-line goals you must have overlap with those of the other party. If the reasonable goals each of you would settle for more or less coincide, then you should continue bargaining until you reach that point, at which time the negotiation can be closed. However, if your bottom-line goals (the least for which each of you would settle) are far apart, you probably will not conclude an agreement that is mutually acceptable unless unexpected circumstances that alter the assumptions of your goal analysis are found during the negotiation. By establishing a three-tier level of goal analysis, as described above (and shown in Figure 1), you will know how unreasonable others' initial demands are and whether they are being sincere in setting forth their reasons.

Preparing for Negotiations

Bill Scott

It is critically important, when one's strategy is towards cooperation to mutual advantage, to build firm foundations at the start of the negotiation meeting. But before we can lay firm foundations, we must have a good job of preparing the ground.

Time after time, one finds negotiators having two cries. On the one hand, "We just didn't have time to do our preparation properly before the meeting." On the other hand, after the meeting, "Well, that has certainly taught me that I ought to be more careful about the way I prepare."

There is no substitute for adequate preparation.

We shall deal with the subject in this chapter, making three sets of assumptions:

1. That the negotiator will have done his homework on the content issues for negotiation. That is, the buyer will have researched all specifications, quantities, market competition, market prices, etc. The banker will be aware of the availability of funds, the appropriate rate of interest, the status of the client, etc.
2. That the negotiator is familiar with the rules governing the negotiating territory. The company rules for purchasing or for selling, the trade and/or international rules that apply, the essential legal matters.
3. We assume that the deal is one which can be settled within one or two meetings.

This chapter will give suggestions about:

- Conducting the preliminaries.
- A general approach to the planning of negotiations.
- The essence of the negotiating plan.
- Physical preparation.

CONDUCTING THE PRELIMINARIES

Other Party comes to a meeting bringing with him not only knowledge of the basic facts. He brings also his own way of conducting negotiations, his expectations about the way that our Party will behave, and his counterintentions.

Reprinted from Bill Scott, *The Skills of Negotiating* (Brookfield, Vt.: Gower Publishing Co., 1981), pp. 77–87. Used with permission of Gower Publishing Co., Old Post Road, Brookfield, VT 05036.

Whether he has done his preparations systematically or not at all, he will bring impressions and opinions which will influence his conduct.

To help him to bring the right attitudes and information, we need to have explored beforehand as far as possible the purpose of the meeting and the agenda of items which we will discuss. This may have been done through correspondence or by telephone or even, for major negotiations, through preliminary meetings between representatives.

A great deal of Other Party's basic values are deeply engrained. We cannot much influence them during the preliminaries, but we can and do influence his opinions of us and his expectations about the way we shall behave, which in turn influence the way he will prepare to behave with us.

In part his expectations will be based on factors outside our control, such as the stories he has heard about us, the sort of relationship he would expect with a different Party in our situation, and the experience he has had with other organizations in our own industry and culture.

He may have more direct evidence about us. Evidence from dealings which he or his colleagues have had with our organization, evidence of the manner in which we negotiate and of the effectiveness with which we have implemented previous deals.

There remain however the preliminaries through which we can ourselves influence him. The manner in which we communicate beforehand needs to reflect our interest in dealing with him; our integrity; our co-operativeness. To create the most positive expectations, we need to apply the basic ground rules for communication between people distant from one another: to be prompt and polite, clear, concise, and correct.

We need also to be sensitive in the volume of our preliminary work. Sometimes we have to deal with businesses which seem virtually to resist paperwork. Such organizations always appreciate some brief statement on paper, covering issues like purpose, time, and estimated duration; but with them, anything more than one sheet of paper is irritating and counterproductive.

For other organizations, where formality rules strongly, there is a need for meticulous detail in preliminary exchanges. Indeed, the preliminaries can escalate, almost to become the most important part of the negotiating process.

To summarize: it is important in the way we conduct the preliminaries to help the Other Party to prepare himself for the negotiations, and to ensure he enters the negotiating room looking forward to a desirable relationship.

GENERAL APPROACH TO PLANNING

In principle, preparations for negotiation should lead to a plan which is simple and specific, yet flexible.

It must be sufficiently simple for the negotiator himself easily to carry the headlines in his own thinking. He must have these headlines, these principles of his plan, very clear in his mind; so clear, that he can handle the heavy on-going content of the negotiation with Other Party (making great demands on his conscious energy), yet at the same time subconsciously be able to relate to his plan.

Such simplicity is hard to achieve.

The plan must be specific: it cannot be simple without being very specific. No room for reservations or elaborations.

Yet it must be flexible. The negotiator must be able to listen effectively to Other Party; to see the relationship of Other Party's thinking to his own plans; and to adjust flexibly.

So the aim of our preparation is to produce a plan which is simple and specific, yet flexible.

That is the ideal, but the reality is usually very different. The negotiator hunts out the information, reads through the correspondence in the files, talks to half a dozen colleagues with interest in the negotiation—each putting a different picture—and is under pressure to be on his way to the motorway or the airport with very little time to form this ragged mass of impulses into any coherent pattern.

His need now is for a discipline; for a general approach which he can use quickly and which he can apply to many different types of negotiation.

The general approach we use is in three stages:

Ideas stage.

Thesis sentence.

Analysis stage.

The aim of the *ideas stage* is to make a quick review of the area for negotiation and at the same time to clear one's own mind. It corresponds to the brainstorming stage in "Preparation of information," but is now in two steps. Step one is quickly to jot down all one's jumbled ideas about the negotiation. . . . Step two is to jot down our thoughts about Other Party on another sheet of paper. What they do, where they are, what they look like, what we know of the individuals, what we know they want from the negotiation, what we guess they want, and what else we would like to know. Again, random thoughts (Figure 1).

This ideas stage has led us to the production of two sheets of paper. One with random ideas on the subject and one with random ideas on the Other Party. Having been filled in, having got our minds cleared, these sheets have already largely served their purpose. They should now be put away (not necessarily thrown away—they just might serve some useful purpose later in our preparations).

Our conscious energy is now free to prepare our plans, uncluttered by the jumble of thoughts that was previously there; and the first step in this *analytical stage* is to prepare a thesis sentence.

This thesis sentence is a statement in general terms of what we hope to achieve from the negotiation process. It is a statement for our own guidance, and may sometimes differ from the general purpose of the negotiation as defined to/agreed with Other Party.

The thesis sentence needs to be simple, so we should try to specify it within a maximum of 15 to 20 words. If it takes more, the negotiator has not sufficiently simplified his thinking about why he is entering the negotiating process.

It is critical that his thinking should be so sharp. If he finds it difficult to state his purpose within 20 words, then he needs to spend more time on clearing his mind, drafting his thoughts about the purpose of the meeting, then pruning and modifying until he gets inside the maximum of 20 words (Figure 2).

Continuing the analysis stage the second step is to develop a plan for handling the negotiation meeting.

FIGURE 1   Random Thoughts about Other Party

Jensen Electric Supply

30 years relationship
Annual golf match
Good customers
Tough but fair
Enjoy dealing
Probably see Alf
Hope not Doug
Are they in trouble?
Maybe need help
Maybe we need to
            protect
Is whole region in
      trouble
Or just them?

Know our
    processes
Keep it friendly

The need now is to produce an ordered approach to the conduct of the negotiation, together with a statement of one's opening position.

THE ESSENCE OF THE PLAN

The control of any meeting hinges on three of the 'Four P's' . . . : the Purpose of the meeting, the Plan for the meeting, and the Pace of the meeting. (The Personalities element, the introduction of the people and their roles, should be a routine, not a part of the plan specific to any one meeting.) Our preparation must cover those 3 Ps.

FIGURE 2   Thesis Sentence

Jensen – Generator Contract

Thesis.   To ensure goodwill, check
their business strength,
and get best compensation.

The *Purpose* spelt out in one sentence which can be offered to Other Party as "our view of the purpose of this meeting." It should be "our declared view" of the purpose, not necessarily the same as the thesis sentence. The *Plan* or agenda must be kept simple. The human brain has the ability to keep a clear image of only a few agenda topics throughout a negotiation meeting. About four main items. If in the preparation one tries to give equal significance to say seven or eight main points—then the brain is overstretched. It cannot later have a sharp recollection of so many main points. It cannot easily, during the negotiation, relate all that is going on to the prepared plan.

So at the analysis stage we are concerned to prepare our plans for the negotiation meeting under about four main headings.

The *Pace*—in terms of "how long"—should also be estimated.

The practical way to go about this preparation is—after going through the brainstorming stage and preparing the thesis sentence—to plan the agenda. Aim for the ideal of *four* main agenda points, subheading each if need be.

In negotiations "Towards Agreement," a sequence I regularly find useful is — "Ours — Theirs — Creative possibilities — Practical actions." "Ours" may, in one session, be "what we hope for from the negotiation," with the corresponding "theirs" being what they hope for; then the creative possibilities for the two of us working together; and finally — what we should do before we meet again.

In a later session, the same sequence might become—"our offer—their offer—overlaps and problems—action needed to resolve problems."

And for the next meeting—"Where we'd got to and what we each had to do — our new position — their new position — what is agreed and what remains to be done."

Having got the plan worked out, we should "top" it with a statement of Purpose (already considered when building our Thesis Sentence, though not necessarily to be repeated verbatim); and we should "tail" it with an estimate of the time we shall need (Figure 3).

Finally, the plan needs reducing to key words printed on a postcard.

FIGURE 3   Plan for Meeting

Jensen – Generator Contract

Purpose   Agree settlement

Plan   Their reasons/our problems
Any creative possibilities?
How to settle?
What settlement?

Pace   11·00 – 12·00

The purpose of this final stage of planning is to provide a document which the negotiator can have in front of him in the negotiating room. He then needs the key statements prominent and visible at one glance of the eyes. He needs them as prompters for his subconscious, so that he can still control the negotiating process, even when his conscious energy is absorbed in the content of the negotiation (Figure 4).

In addition to this procedural preparation for a negotiation, there is another item to which we have already attached much importance. This is the Opening Statement to be made at the outset of the negotiating process.

Following this preliminary work the negotiator goes into the negotiating room properly prepared both to control the process of negotiating, and to present his own position.

What about the room he is going into?

THE PHYSICAL PREPARATION

In this section we shall look briefly at the negotiating room, the layout of the room and the need for services.

The negotiating room itself needs to have the obvious facilities—light, heating, air, noiseproofing.

More contentious are the furnishing and the layout of the room. Negotiators seem to need a table at which to be seated—they seem to feel defenseless without a table between them. But what sort of table? A rectangular table—or the typical business-

FIGURE 4 Prompter for Control of
Negotiation

Generator Contract

To Agree Settlement

Reasons/Problems
Creative?
How Settle?
How Much?

11·00 - 12·00

---

man's desk—leads to parties being seated opposite to one another. This immediately creates a head-on physical confrontation.

Negotiators recognize that they feel differently on the rare occasions when they sit at round tables. In any poll of negotiators there will be a hefty majority who find it more comfortable and more constructive to use a round table than to use either a rectangular or a square one.

Should negotiators, whether at round or rectangular tables, split into their respective teams or should they intermix? It depends on the mood and style of the negotiations.

Where the parties are relaxed and collaborative, then the relaxation and collaboration is heightened by intermixing. At the extreme this would lead to each negotiator in a team being seated between two negotiators from the Other Party; but that would be contrived only by a formal approach to seating positions. Within an agreement-oriented group, the ice-breaking period leads to informality in the choice of seating positions. It is a purely random matter as to whether one walks up to the table with and sits beside a member of Own or of Other Party.

Where the negotiation process is more conflicting, then it is natural that the parties will gather together, probably on opposite sides of the table. This is both for psychological and for practical reasons. Psychologically, the mood is of "all together against them." Practically, either Party may want to refer to papers which they want to keep obscured from Others (impracticable if Others are neighbors) or they may want to sit together so that they can pass notes within their team.

Incidentally neither the regular reference to secret papers nor the passing of notes are symbols of good negotiators. Energy is needed for the exchanges with Other Party and not for private transactions. It is more skillful to take a recess, either to check on the private papers, or to handle private communication with colleagues.

It is not only the shape of table that is important—it is also size. There is a comfortable distance at which individuals or groups of individuals may sit from one another. If the parties are sitting a little closer, then the atmosphere becomes warmer. If they are sitting a lot closer then they become uncomfortable and heated. If the distance apart is, on the other hand, too much, then the parties become remote and the discussion becomes academic.

Apart from the question of the room and the furnishing, the host needs to make suitable provisions for sustenance and for the well-being of Other Party. A special courtesy is in providing Other Party with a room which they can use for recesses, together with such other facilities as typing, telex, and telephone.

SUMMARY

1. The preparation for a negotiation meeting needs discipline. It needs time and the regular use of the same approach.

2. We suggest a disciplined approach of:

   a. Brainstorming.

   b. Thesis sentence.

   c. Planning.

3. The preparation needs to cover purpose, plan, and pace of the meeting.

4. The Opening Statement should be prepared equally carefully.

5. Physical arrangements influence the form of the subsequent negotiations.

The No-Fault Formula:
Five Easy Steps

Len Leritz

IT'S MAGIC

The No-Fault Formula gets more of what you want, more often, from more people. Simple and effective, the No-Fault Formula provides a five-step process for:

1. Creating a safe environment.
2. Shifting your focus from problems to relationship conflicts, process, or criteria issues.
3. Creating mutual understanding instead of pitted battles.
4. Attending to the obvious.

The formula also helps you to avoid getting stuck in your negotiations. By using the Formula, you will recognize blocks as they arise. When you do get stuck, the Formula provides a means of moving the negotiation forward.

In short, it is the way to effectively implement everything presented in this book. You may not be able to create miracles, but this formula will provide a good bit of magic. *It works.*

More than just another quick trick (although it is that), it is a way of thinking. It is a way to stay clear and focused on the important issues. My experience, and the experience of many others who have learned to think in terms of these five steps, is a sharp increase in both the quality and the quantity of the results we want.

You'll be surprised how well it works. It's even easy. It just takes a little practice.

THE FIVE STEPS

The formula has five steps:

1. I See/Hear—The Data

Identify and describe, without judgment, the specific behavior or events which have occurred or are occurring. Be clear about what has been and is going on, or about the conditions that exist.

For example:

"I noticed you . . ."

"I hear you saying . . ."

"My data is . . ."

"The facts are . . ."

What facts do I have? What happened? What do we know about the situation? Do others have data that might be useful? What data do we need in order to understand the problem fully? What are they doing? Saying? What am I doing? Saying?

2. I Assume—Interpreting the Data

Identify and possibly share my assumptions or interpretations of the above events or behaviors. Search out possible causes for the problem or conflict. Why do I think these events are occurring? What am I saying to myself about the data?

For example:

"My assumptions about your behavior are . . ."

"It seems to me that . . ."

"I believe/am concluding that . . ."

"I think the reasons are . . ."

"I feel that this has occurred because . . ."

3. I Feel—The Cost or Impact

The cost can be time, money, relationships, productivity, or emotions.

Describe what you are experiencing emotionally. Describe how the above events and behavior are affecting you and others. What is it costing you or the organization financially, or in terms of productivity, time, or use of resources?

For example:

"I am angry, frustrated, concerned, etc. . . ."

"The client is feeling . . ."

"As a result, the other staff members are . . ."

"As a result, we lost the contract."

"As a result, we have missed our target date."

4. I Need—The Alternative Desired Results or Conditions

The needs are what you want but are not currently getting.

Describe your internal needs or what you need that is different from what you are getting. Needs may be stated in terms of individual or organizational goals and objectives.

For example:

"My preference is to resolve this issue, meeting your needs and mine, if possible."

"I need to feel that my concerns are being heard."

"I need to have a contract I can take back and sell to my Board."

"Our objective in this situation is to . . ."

5. I Want/Will—The Plan of Action

The "Wants" are what you want behaviorally from the other person in response to your needs. This is the proposed solution or answer. It is what you want others to do and what you are willing to do in order to create the results or conditions you need (Step 4). The plan of action always refers to behavior—what we are going to do.

For example:

"I want you to . . ."

"I want you to give me a report by Friday, and I will let you know then what I have found out."

"What I need from you is . . ."

"Will you go with me to the store?"

"I am willing to listen, and I need you to talk."

UNDERSTANDING THE FORMULA: WHY IT WORKS

STEP 1: I SEE/HEAR

How to Gather Your Data

In the first step of the Formula, you describe the specific behaviors, events, or conditions about which you are negotiating. This is an attempt to identify and clarify for yourself and for the other party the substantive/problem issues as well as the triggering events that tell you there is a problem. You may describe behaviors or events which have occurred in the past or which currently exist. You may also need to describe any environmental factors that are affecting the current situation. You describe your data—the data that tells you a problem or conflict exists. It means getting an overview of the situation.

The value of this step is that it gives you greater clarity about the context from which you are drawing your perceptions. It is the first step in beginning to define the issues. This step is also useful as a reality check. As you share the data you have with the other person, you are able to check whether you have all the facts. If you do not have all the facts, the other person probably will fill in with the additional pieces they have. Getting agreement about the facts is an essential first step in any negotiation.

Often it is useful to have two opposing parties in a negotiation gather data together so they have a common database. I have used combined labor/management or marketing/production committees to research and collect data prior to or during a negotiation.

How to Get to the Real Issues

Describing your data is how you implement the principle of Attending to the Obvious. You do it by paying attention to what is immediately, obviously going on before you and describing that data to the other party.

Observing and listening to what the other person is saying and doing during a negotiation gives us the immediate, ongoing data we need to move toward a successful resolution. Usually, what we begin talking about in a negotiation is not what we end up talking about. We often begin with symptoms and move toward clarifying the real issues. We clarify the real issues by paying attention to what is immediately going on before us and by identifying underlying needs.

Attending to the obvious also means being conscious about what we know— whether it is the past and current behavior of the other party or current environmental conditions. Again, only by consciously focusing on present reality, not on our fantasies, do we reach the real issues.

How to Clarify Double Messages

To stay with foreground, we actively listen to what the other person is saying and doing during the negotiation process. We feed back to them what we are observing and taking in. Active listening to foreground behavior is important because the other person often gives us incongruent or double messages. Active listening is a way to point out inconsistencies in what is said and done. It is a way to stay focused on the real issues and not be put off by the other person's denials and games.

Other Party:

No, I'm not angry!

Your Response:

I hear you say you're not angry, but your tone of voice and the look in your eyes tell me you are.

or

Other Party:

No, I did not do it!

Your Response:

I hear you say you didn't do it, but I also know that you were the only one in the office last night.

Attending to the other person's double messages alerts us to potential blocks as they arise. Paying attention makes us conscious of changes in our relationship with the other person, at the same time we are aware of the content of the discussion.

Make Them Accountable

This step provides us with a tool for being persistent. By feeding back the data we are receiving, we can consistently bring the data we have into the open. Thus, we are able to hold the other party accountable.

For example, you may have a salesperson who promises results but does not get the job done. When you confront her, she says, "No problem, I can do it," in her best rah, rah! cheerleader voice. By attending to the obvious, you can point out that past experiences together with her tone of voice make you doubt that she will do it. You may need to repeat this several times until you can get her to address the underlying problems that are blocking her performance.

Create a Safe Environment

Describing our data by actively listening is a primary means by which we create safe environments. Active listening slows down the process of negotiating. For an extrovert, active listening means having the opportunity to think out loud. For introverts, it means having more time to process what is happening.

In addition, as the pace of a discussion speeds up, people become increasingly threatened and defensive. Taking the time to let them know that you heard them slows the pace 100 percent. Making them do the same slows the pace 200 percent and keeps both of you grounded in reality.

Active listening also helps create safe environments by allowing other people to know they are being accurately heard and understood. When other people feel understood, their capacities expand and they become less defensive.

Describe, Don't Judge

As we point out our data, it is important that we describe rather than judge. We need to be specific about our facts and avoid the temptation of making broad, sweeping generalizations. For example, "I've noticed we have gotten four complaints about the billings this month" is a nonjudgmental statement compared to "You always do a sloppy job on the billings." "They would not make a commitment during the meeting" is descriptive versus "They are resistive and stubborn."

STEP 2: I ASSUME

How to Interpret Your Data

In the second step of the formula, you let the other person know how you are interpreting the data. You share your assumptions and perceptions.

Sharing your assumptions is valuable for two reasons. First, it helps the other person understand you, what you are thinking and why. He is better able to understand and accept why you have responded behaviorally in certain ways. It helps him make sense of you.

Second, it allows you to check out the validity of your assumptions. One of the primary causes of unnecessary conflict in negotiations is false assumptions and failing to check them out. Checking out your assumptions is often one of the quickest ways your conflicts can get resolved.

I have a bittersweet example of this: A client called me and complained bitterly because his partner had not shown up at the office for two days. He called me because I had been mediating some conflicts in their relationship. He assumed his partner was being passive-aggressive, and dumping everything on him to pay him back, and in his anger, he walked out to "even the score" and didn't come back for two days.

As it happened, my client's partner had been in an automobile accident and was in the hospital. In the family's concern and confusion, no one had thought to call my client, and he in turn had not bothered to call his partner to check out his assumptions. So much for false assumptions.

Distinguish between Assumptions and Judgments

It is important to distinguish between sharing our assumptions and judging the other person. For example, we might have an employee who has arrived late at work. We might ask that employee if he came late because he is angry about the performance review he received the day before. Or, we might tell him we think he has a bad attitude (judgment). These are different types of statements. Sharing our assumptions encourages increased understanding. Sharing our assumptions encourages increased understanding. Judging other people constricts their capacities and encourages them to become defensive.

When sharing assumptions, we try to make specific statements about specific behaviors. The intent is to clarify the motives behind the other person's behavior or to understand why certain events have taken place. It is a step in defining further the causes for the conflict or problem.

In judging the other person, we tend to make broad, sweeping statements. The intent is to "beat" the other person, to get them to admit they are wrong, or to try to make them feel guilty. Judging is nonproductive. It creates unnecessary blocks in the negotiating process.

Useful and Nonuseful Questions

One way to avoid making judgmental statements is to phrase our comments as tentative questions rather than as dogmatic truths. We check out our perceptions rather than condemning the other person.

If you do use questions to check out your assumptions, make sure they are factual questions. Avoid using rhetorical questions designed to make the other person admit he is wrong. Again, the purpose of checking out assumptions is to enhance understanding, not to make the other person more defensive. For example:

"I'm wondering . . ."

"When you do that, I assume . . ."

"Did you not call because you were angry?"

"Do you assume I'm not interested?"

Nonuseful statements and questions:

"I think you deliberately did that to sabotage the meeting."

"When you do that, you make a fool out of yourself."

"How do you think I felt when you didn't call?"

"Do you think you're the only one interested in the outcome of this case?" (This is a judgment couched as a rhetorical question.)

"Why did you do that (Stupid)?" (This is another rhetorical question.)

As this last question illustrates, "Why" questions are usually sneaky judgments. Translate your "Why" questions to "What" and drop the superior dismissal and sarcasm from your voice, if you do not want to come across as judgmental.

STEP 3: I FEEL

How to Clarify the Impact

In this third step, your intent is to help the other person understand how events or behaviors are affecting you, and possibly others, perhaps even the organization. Your purpose is to clarify the effect on yourself and others.

It is important that you make the other party feel your presence. Failure to make your presence felt encourages him to relate to you as an object rather than a real person. It allows him to avoid you, ignore you, deceive you, and dismiss you. Other people need your help to bring you into focus.

Good Negotiators Know What They Are Feeling

Sharing emotional impact is very important and often avoided. But being clear about what you are experiencing emotionally is important to you and the other person. It is important to you because getting clear about what you are specifically feeling tells us what you are specifically needing. This is particularly true of feelings of vulnerability.

Anytime we get angry, it is because we feel diminished or devalued as a person or because we are threatened. Our anger is our natural self-defense, an internal message that says we need to stand up for ourselves. Underneath our anger is always some feeling of vulnerability. We get angry because we are frightened or embarrassed or dismissed or misunderstood. If we listen to the feelings of vulnerability beneath our anger, they will tell us what we need.

If we are frightened, we need more safety or assurance. If we are embarrassed, we need more protection. If we are dismissed or misunderstood, we need to be taken seriously and be listened to.

Listening to our emotions is important because they tell us when we have a conflict which needs to be addressed. When we feel attacked or dismissed, when we feel as though we are fighting with the other person rather than dancing with them, we know we have a conflict as well as a problem.

Communicating what we are experiencing emotionally is important for us to be understood. Sharing our feelings with the other person gives him more personal data about us. If we want to be understood, we must be willing to let the other person know what we are feeling and what we are thinking.

Sharing our feelings invites other people to see us as a flesh and blood person like themselves. To share only what we are thinking invites other people to objectify us, to see us as different from them rather than like them. When we are sharing only our thoughts in a negotiation, the other person is more likely to perceive us as an object to be beaten rather than as a person to be understood.

By sharing what we are experiencing emotionally, we are more likely to see how we are alike and what we have in common. Sharing emotions moves both persons toward a cooperative relationship.

Our tendency is to avoid sharing our emotions. We find it easier to tell the other person what we are thinking, to share our opinions. Sharing our emotions is more personal and, therefore, more vulnerable.

Don't Confuse "I Feel" with "I Feel That"

We often give the appearance of sharing our emotions, when in reality we are judging the other person. This is evident when we use the term "I feel that . . ." or "I feel like . . ." followed by the pronoun "you."

"I feel that . . ." is not a statement of feelings. It is a statement of what we think. It is usually a sneaky way to judge the other person. Translated, "I feel that . . ." really means "I think you are wrong, stupid, selfish, misguided, etc." "I feel that you . . ." statements are about the other person, not our own experience.

Statements of our personal emotional experience are synonymous with the verb "to be." "I *am* angry" (or overwhelmed or excited or frustrated) is a statement about us, not the other person. This is a subtle but important linguistic point. We often think we are sharing our experience and wonder why the other person is becoming constricted and defensive.

When we find the other person becoming defensive, we need to stop and get honest with ourselves. We need to verify whether we are really sharing our emotional experience to increase understanding and cooperation between us. Usually we are subtly trying to "beat" the other person, to point out to them how they are wrong. We do it in a sneaky way so they cannot come back on us.

Rule of Thumb: Eliminate such statements as "I feel that you . . ." and/or "I feel as if you . . ." from your negotiating vocabulary. They are rarely productive.

Organizational Impacts

In addition to personal or emotional impact, a situation often has organizational effects as well. Current events or conditions may be affecting whether the organization is:

- Fulfilling its mission.
- Living out of its values.
- Achieving its goals and objectives.
- Managing itself effectively.
- Creating a quality work environment.
- Making it in the marketplace.

To identify organizational effects, the following questions are helpful:

1. Is the organization fulfilling its stated mission? Are we doing what we are supposed to be doing?
2. Are we acting congruently with our espoused values? In what ways are we living up to our criteria for success? In what ways does our behavior contradict our values?
3. Are we achieving our goals and objectives? Are we on track and on time?
4. What effect is the current situation having on:
   - Our reporting relationships?
   - How we make decisions and solve problems?
   - The flow of information in all directions in the organization?
   - How people are being rewarded?
5. What effect is the current situation having on:
   - Individual productivity?
   - Individual attitudes?
   - Internal relationships?
   - The psychological climate. Is it positive? Cynical? Stressed? Overwhelmed? Trusting? Energetic? Resigned? Negative?
6. What effect is the current situation having on:
   - Our relationships with our clients?
   - Our share of the marketplace?
   - Our relationships with our competitors?

These questions provide a framework for determining the impact of problems and conflicts on your organization.

STEP 4: I NEED

How to Identify Alternate Needs and Desired Outcomes

Needs are internal to people and organizations. Personally, they have to do with the quality of our physical and psychological existence. We need food and shelter and rest. We need to feel valuable and worthwhile. We need to feel adequate and capable.

We need to feel as though we belong and that we are not alone. We need to make sense out of our lives. This is the stuff of any negotiation. We know what we need when we listen to what we are experiencing emotionally.

Organizationally, needs have to do with the effectiveness and efficiency of the organization in fulfilling its mission. It is what the organization needs to accomplish its business—its reason for existence.

If the purpose of all negotiation is to get other people to do what we want, to cooperate with us, then stating what we need is the heart of the negotiating process. This is the step which is most often skipped over. We seem to find it easier to tell others what we want them to do and how we want them to be different than to tell them what we need.

Again, the reason for this is that we are afraid of being too vulnerable. We are afraid of being taken advantage of if we let them know what we need, personally or organizationally.

Ironically, the whole purpose of negotiating is to meet individual or organizational needs. If we do not state what we need, we are not likely to get our needs met. To tell another person what we want from them without stating our underlying needs makes it difficult for them to understand us. They are much more likely to respond in the ways we desire when they understand why. To state what we need and why gives validity to our particular requests. It lets the other person know we are not making arbitrary demands.

And again, ..., the *requirements that I need* are different from *my solutions*—what it is I want others to do to help me meet my needs.

Having made a case for stating our needs, let's add a word of caution. Sometimes it is foolish to tell the other person what we need when the other person is obviously out to take advantage of us. In these cases, we need to proceed more slowly. We need to use common sense about when we are unnecessarily giving ourselves away by being too open. We may need to get agreement about fair criteria for a settlement before stating our needs.

To tell a prospective employer that I desperately need the job and do not have any other offers is probably not to my best advantage. If our corporation is in serious financial trouble and everyone in top management is in survival mode, it is probably a fair assumption that the other drowning rats are not particularly concerned with my needs. If I know a buyer is trying to put the squeeze on me, I'm not going to tell him how badly I need to sell the property.

At the same time, most negotiating does not take place in Enforcer environments. More often, it will be to your advantage to make a clear presentation of your needs.

STEP 5: I WANT/WILL

How to Develop Your Plan of Action

What we want in a negotiation is always some change in the external conditions or a change in the behaviors of the other person. What we want is what we perceive to be the solution to our problem or conflict.

People often have difficulty distinguishing between what they need for themselves and what they perceive as their best solutions—what they *want others* to do to help them meet their needs. Again, needs are the results, outcomes, or conditions necessary for our physical, fiscal, psychological, or relational existence. *Wants* (solutions) are what we want others to do to help us meet our needs. They are the ways we are both going to achieve our needs. Our needs and our wants (solutions) are separate but related realities.

I need to be treated fairly and I want (the solution) you to agree to fair criteria for settling my insurance claim.

I need to be respected by my staff, and I want (the solution) you to respect me by not confronting me in front of them.

I need to be understood and I want (the solution) you to listen to me and not walk away.

I need to get pressure off of me; therefore I want (the solution) you to get the project brought up-to-date.

I need to know my teenager is safe, and I want (the solution) her home by midnight.

Quite simply, the importance of stating what we want (the solution) is that:

1. We let the other person know clearly what it is we are asking from them behaviorally.
2. We clarify what must happen if we are to achieve our goals.

Negotiations often fail or are hampered because we do not state what we want. To tell someone I am angry with them or that I am disappointed in their performance without telling them specifically what I want them to do leaves them hanging. To tell you that I don't trust you and then not tell you what you could do so I would trust you is a Gotcha! I cannot expect others to read my mind. If I do expect that, I'm likely to be disappointed.

ELEVEN BENEFITS OF THE NO-FAULT FORMULA

You can use the Formula for many purposes. It is a process to:

1. Keep you in Generative capacities for thinking so you can see the whole picture accurately without getting defensive.
2. Help you move the other party into Generative capacities and out of self-protective behavior.
3. Identify what the real issues are that need to be addressed.
4. Stay on track and not get off on tangents.
5. Prepare for negotiations before you move into them—to lay out your strategy.
6. Expand your capacities for empathy so you accurately understand the needs of the other party.
7. Analyze conflicts, performance problems, or organizational problems.

8. Confront others about their behavior—including performance problems.

9. Improve your listening skills.

10. Clarify your internal needs.

11. Develop plans of action to solve personnel or organizational problems.

THE FIVE STEPS ILLUSTRATED

The following example illustrates using the five steps as an analytical tool:

I see/hear

I'm aware that Martha is shifting in her chair. Her voice sounds tentative, and she is avoiding eye contact. I also know she has been having problems with her staff. They are frustrated because she has procrastinated confronting her division manager about his performance.

I assume

I'm assuming she is not comfortable with what I am proposing to do in the staff retreat. I think she is afraid that she will be confronted publicly by some of her staff members.

I feel

I feel concerned that she may veto the retreat or dilute the process so that nothing significant happens.

I need

I need to find a way to help her feel safe with the process and to trust me.

I want/will

I want her (the solution) to tell me what she is feeling and thinking right now. I want to understand her specific fears so we can create a process that will be nonthreatening and effective. I want her to tell me what she needs to be able to trust me.

In this example, I have both a problem and a conflict to address.

Negotiation Breakdowns:
Causes and Cures

It is inevitable that some negotiations go awry. Since the cost of a failed or faulty negotiation can be high in many different ways, a strong negotiator needs to try to understand why negotiations break down and to have a "tool kit" for repairing them when they do. The causes of negotiation breakdown can be internal or external to the negotiation—that is, under the control of the participating negotiators or not. Problems based on external factors are addressed elsewhere in this book—for example, see the Downie article on third-party intervention in Section Twelve. The focus of the present section is internal breakdown factors. Additionally, since many breakdowns are related to poor communication, readers should refer to the following Section (Seven) on communication during negotiation.

The first article in this section is Max Bazerman's "Why Negotiations Go Wrong," a diagnostic piece based on a wealth of observations collected and analyzed by Bazerman and his colleagues. Bazerman identifies five mistakes commonly made by negotiators, such as failure to view things from the other side's perspective and failure to recognize and manage the tendency for commitment to escalate and drag negotiators toward untenable positions and inadvisable outcomes. The fact that these mistakes are often interrelated accentuates the damage caused by them individually.

The theme of mistakes and entrapment is explored further by Jeffrey Rubin in his article, "Psychological Traps." A psychological trap is an outlook or mental set which works to our disadvantage and which we find difficult to stop. A common trap in negotiation occurs when people set goals to put the other party down or to "win" by achieving some arbitrary standard. Some auto salespeople boast that they always sell a "loaded" car; that is, one with stereo, better-grade upholstery, and so on. What these salespeople do not mention is the number of people who do not buy a car from them because they left when they felt they were being pushed into something they did not want. It is all too easy in negotiation to want to get more than the other person and, in the process, actually get less than might have been attained. There are other traps, such as wanting to complete a negotiation (at any cost) once it has been started. Determination to see something through is a virtue, but there are times when we continue with a process when it would be to our advantage to stop. The appearance of "giving up" is something that many people find difficult to cope with. It is hard to get out of a trap even when one is aware of it. Regrettably, we often are unaware of the traps we create for ourselves. Rubin identifies common traps and suggests some ways to prepare to avoid them.

The last two articles in this section focus on opposing parties' behaviors. Frank Acuff and Maurice Villere, in their article "Games Negotiators Play," suggest that some negotiators actively and intentionally play "games," and that some of these games are really destructive communication rituals. This view draws on the theory of transactional analysis (TA), an approach to understanding individual psychological behavior in social interaction. TA creates a framework for examining interactive communication patterns between individuals and for determining whether those interactive patterns are productive or destructive to each party's aims. Acuff and Villere identify a number of destructive games in the communication-negotiation process, each with an identifiable format and scenario leading to an unproductive outcome. Using TA, negotiators can learn to assess how destructive communication games occur and how these processes can be counteracted to turn negotiations toward more productive ends.

The final article in this section, "Taking the Bull Out of the Bully", is from Len Leritz's book *No-Fault Negotiating*. Leritz presents and explains methods for managing what he calls "enforcer" types of negotiators: bullies, avoiders, withdrawers, high rollers, and wadshooters. Each type is described, behavioral examples are provided, and appropriate responses are set forth. Dealing with bullies, for instance, starts with getting their attention—drawing them up short, so that they must question (and hopefully abandon) their bullying behaviors. Many of the remedial behaviors Leritz suggests are useful against a variety of enforcer behaviors, and he offers examples of behavior sets that might be effective in different situations.

Why Negotiations Go Wrong

Max H. Bazerman

On the eve of the Revolutionary War, English political philosopher Edmund Burke eloquently exhorted members of the House of Commons to head off the coming conflict by negotiating with the upstart colonials:

"All government—indeed, every human benefit and enjoyment, every virtue, and every prudent act—is founded on compromise and barter."

His observation is at least as accurate today, when negotiation is woven into the daily fabric of our lives. On the personal level, we buy and sell houses and cars, jointly decide where to eat dinner, and bargain over salaries. On a larger scale, unions and management negotiate contracts, and nations arrange treaties and trade agreements. Failed negotiations may produce anything from minor inconveniences to nuclear holocaust.

In studying why negotiations fail, I have built on what other researchers have learned about decision making in general, concentrating on the biases that can undermine negotiations. I will describe five common cognitive mistakes negotiators make and suggest some strategies for avoiding them.

EXPANDING THE FIXED PIE

Two sisters have a single orange to share. One wants to make orange juice. The other wants the peel to make a cake. After much discussion, they agree to a distributive compromise. They each take half the orange, and end up with a very small glass of juice for one sister and a very small cake for the other.

In this example, first presented by Mary Follett many years ago, the sisters overlooked an integrative solution to their problem: One sister takes all the juice and the other takes all the peel. This way, each gets exactly what she wants and twice as much as she actually received. Such integrative solutions reconcile the parties' interests and yield a higher joint benefit than is possible through simple compromise. Unfortunately, too many negotiators have the same "fixed-pie" bias that kept the sisters fighting over the orange: They assume that there is only a fixed amount of profit or gain in what is being negotiated and that in order for them to win something, the other party must necessarily lose it.

This is true in some negotiations, of course, but too often we assume it is without trying to think integratively. I believe this comes from our highly competitive society. We experience so many real win-lose situations—in athletics, in admission to college, in job promotion—that we apply the lessons learned indiscriminately. Faced with negotiations that require both competition and cooperation, as most do, we think only of the competitive aspects. This orientation produces a distributive rather than an integrative approach to bargaining.

Psychologists Dean Pruitt and Jeffrey Rubin describe the Camp David talks this way in their new book, *Social Conflict:* "When Egypt and Israel sat down to negotiate at Camp David in October 1978, it appeared that they had before them an intractable conflict. Egypt demanded the immediate return of the entire Sinai Peninsula; Israel, which had occupied the Sinai since the 1967 Middle East war, refused to return an inch of this land. Efforts to reach agreement, including the proposal of a compromise in which each nation would retain half of the Sinai, proved completely unacceptable to both sides."

As long as the dispute was defined in terms of what percentage of the land each side would control, no agreement could be reached. However, once both realized that what Israel really cared about was the security that the land offered, while Egypt was primarily interested in sovereignty over it, the stalemate was broken. The two countries were then able to reach an integrative solution: Israel would return the Sinai to Egypt in exchange for assurances of a demilitarized zone and Israeli air bases in the Sinai.

The fixed-pie assumption reduces our ability to negotiate matters of day-to-day existence as well as those of international politics. Consider a Friday evening dinner and a movie. You and your date like each other's company, but you have different tastes in restaurants and movies. Instead of haggling about each issue separately, see if one of you cares more about the restaurant and the other more about the movie. If you do, you can work out an integrative trade-off—one picks the restaurant and the other the movie—in which you both get what is most important to you.

Similarly, while purchasing goods is usually thought of in win-lose terms, another approach is sometimes possible. For example, a retailer may be willing to cut the price if payment is made in cash—especially, in some cases, if you don't ask for a receipt or other documentation the IRS might find of interest.

DEHEXING THE WINNER'S CURSE

While on vacation in a foreign country, you spot a very attractive ruby in a jewelry store window. You know something about rubies, but you are far from being an expert. After some preliminary discussion, you make the merchant an offer that you think is on the low side. He quickly accepts and the sale is made. How do you feel as you walk out the door?

If you are like most people in this situation, you find yourself suffering from "the winner's curse," a sinking feeling that you've been taken. Why else would the merchant have accepted your offer so quickly?

My research with economist William Samuelson suggests that a key factor in the winner's curse is that one side has much better information than the other. A good negotiator must consider the knowledge and likely strategy of the other side, but this is hard to do when our opponents know something we don't and can use the information to selectively accept or reject our offer. This quandary was expressed humorously by Groucho Marx, when he said he didn't care to belong to any club that would accept him as a member. Its willingness to take him—to accept his offer—suggested that its standards were so low that the club wasn't worth joining.

Although we are all familiar with the saying, "Let the buyer beware," we seem to have difficulty putting it into practice. We consistently undervalue the importance of looking at a situation from the opponent's standpoint and getting comparable information before we complete a transaction: a good mechanic's evaluation of a used car, an inspector's assessment of a house we are considering buying, a jeweler's assessment of a coveted gem. To protect yourself in negotiations of any sort, you need to develop or borrow the expertise to balance the quality of information. If you can't get such information before making an offer, ask yourself, "Will I be happy if the offer is accepted quickly?" If not, reconsider your offer.

DE–ESCALATING CONFLICT

The Professional Air Traffic Controllers Organization (PATCO) strikes to obtain a set of concessions from the government. When the government refuses to meet the demands, PATCO has two options: to back off and return to work under the old conditions or to continue the strike, despite the threat of dismissal.

Shortly after the strike started, it became clear to objective observers that, faced with an unyielding administration, PATCO had a weak negotiating position. Rational analysis would have led its leaders to end the strike or at least reduce their demands before its members were fired. Instead, PATCO acted just as individuals, organizations, and countries so often do in this situation. It increased its commitment to the strike to justify the earlier decision to proceed with it.

In negotiations, both sides often start with extreme demands, expecting to compromise somewhere in the middle. But they get caught up in the struggle, feel they have too much time, money, and ego invested to back off and take a hard line instead of adopting a conciliatory or problem-solving approach.

Why does this happen, when rational outsiders realize that continuing or escalating the conflict is a mistake? There are at least four complementary reasons. First, once negotiators make an initial commitment to a position, they are more likely to notice information that supports their initial evaluation of the situation. Second, their judgment is biased to interpret what they see and hear in a way that justifies their initial position. Third, negotiators often increase their demands or hold out too long to save face with their constituency. They may even act against their constituents' best interest to "look strong" to them.

Finally, the competitive context of the negotiation adds to the likelihood of escalation. Unilaterally giving up or even reducing demands seems like defeat, while escalating commitment leaves the future uncertain. It is easy for negotiators to see this uncertain future as more desirable than the certain loss of concession. After all, the other side may be ready to cave in.

This last point is illustrated by a game known as the Dollar Auction (see "Psychological Traps," *Psychology Today,* March 1981). Someone offers to auction off a dollar bill to the highest bidder. The highest bidder will get the dollar, but the second-highest must also pay what he or she bid and receive nothing.

The bidding typically starts out fast and furious until it reaches the 50-to-75-cent range, at which point everyone except the two highest bidders normally drops out of the auction. What usually follows is an escalating pattern in which both end up bidding far more than a dollar, since neither is willing to quit and accept a loss. People escalate their commitment both to justify their earlier bids and to prevent the financial and ego loss of coming in second.

No specific bid is clearly wrong, since it is rational to bid "just another 10 cents," if the other party is about to quit bidding. But when both parties think this way, an escalatory spiral emerges that is very reminiscent of the Vietnam War and other international and industrial failures in which both competitors get trapped by their previous commitments.

To prevent this kind of escalation, negotiators must be aware of their tendency to justify past actions and must constantly evaluate the costs and benefits of continuing along the same lines. Being aware of the tendency to escalate can also be very helpful in anticipating how opponents are likely to think and act. People usually hold out when they have too much invested in their position psychologically to give in. This suggests that a negotiator should avoid pushing opponents into a corner, getting them angry, or otherwise making them feel that they can't afford to give up the struggle.

UNDERCUTTING OVERCONFIDENCE

After a baseball player is in the major leagues for two years (three years, starting in 1987), he may choose arbitration if he and his team are unable to agree on a contract. Under the system of final-offer arbitration, the two sides submit offers and the arbitrator must accept one or the other, not a compromise. The challenge for each side is to come just a little closer than the opposition to what the arbitrator thinks is appropriate.

Let's say the player's agent estimates that the team owner will offer $400,000 per year. The agent believes his player is worth twice that but estimates the arbitrator will think $600,000 is right. What amount should the agent propose?

A naïve analysis would suggest an offer of, say, $775,000, a bit closer to $600,000 than the expected $400,000 offer of the team. This reasoning illustrates a fourth common negotiator error. Individuals are consistently overconfident of the reasonableness of their position and of the likelihood that an objective third party will agree with them. In this case, if the arbitrator's assessment of the appropriate wage turns out to be $550,000 rather than $600,000, the agent's overconfident offer of $775,000 will cost the client hundreds of thousands of dollars when the arbitrator accepts the team's offer because it is closer to his estimate.

Colleague Margaret Neale and I demonstrated this error in several experiments in which negotiator overconfidence showed itself in two areas. In simple two-party negotiations, negotiators consistently expected the other side to concede more than objective analysis would suggest; and under final-offer arbitration, negotiators overestimated the likelihood that their final offer would be accepted.

For example, while obviously only half of all final offers can be accepted in final-offer arbitration, the people in our experiments estimated, on the average, a 65 to 68 percent probability that their offer would win out. This overconfidence reduces the incentive to compromise, while a less optimistic assessment makes a negotiator more uncertain and thus more likely to compromise further. In our studies, negotiators who were simply appropriately confident were consistently more willing to compromise and more successful in negotiations than their overconfident fellows.

Negotiators seem to follow the intuitive rule, "When in doubt, be overconfident." To avoid this, negotiators should try to obtain objective assessments from outside experts to temper overconfidence and overestimation.

REFRAMING NEGOTIATIONS

You bought your house in 1982 for $60,000. It is now on the market for $109,000, with a real target of $100,000, which you estimate is the true market value. You receive an offer of $90,000. Does this represent a $30,000 gain (compared to the original price) or a $10,000 loss (compared to your target price)?

Both answers are correct. But which way you think of the situation strongly affects your attitude toward the offer. Research by psychologists Daniel Kahneman and Amos Tversky suggests that there are important differences in how people respond to problems depending on whether they are framed in terms of losses or gains. In a series of experiments covering situations as diverse as risking lives and risking money, they demonstrated that if a situation is presented in terms that make it seem like a choice between a small sure gain and a risky larger gain, most will take the sure thing. But if exactly the same situation is presented in a way that makes it seem like a choice between a sure smaller loss and a possible larger loss, most prefer to gamble.

Neale and I extended this finding to the area of negotiations when we analyzed this hypothetical situation:

The union claims it needs a raise to $12 an hour and that, considering inflation, anything less would represent a loss to its members. Management argues that the company can't remain competitive if it pays more than $10 an hour; anything more would be an unacceptable loss. What will happen if both sides must choose between settling for $11 an hour (a certain settlement) or going to binding arbitration (a risky settlement, since both sides must agree to abide by whatever figure the arbitrator decides on)?

If both labor and management continue to view the matter in terms of what they have to lose, they are likely to choose the risky road of arbitration. But if each side reframes the situation positively—the union seeing anything above $10 an hour as a gain and management seeing anything under $12 an hour as a gain—then caution will rule and a negotiated settlement of $11 is more likely.

Neale, Thomas Magliozzi, and I confirmed the finding that people who frame the outcomes of negotiation in terms of gains or profit are more willing to make concessions to obtain the sure outcome available in a negotiated settlement. In contrast, negotiators who think in terms of losses or costs are more likely to take the risk-seeking action of holding out and possibly losing all in an attempt to force further concessions from their opponent.

Negotiators need to be aware of how framing affects the decision process. If you are evaluating a negotiation in terms of what you can lose, make sure you also consider what you can gain, and vice versa. Otherwise, your behavior may reflect the distortion of framing rather than your actual preference for a particular action.

The framing effect also suggests that a negotiator should try to present information in a way that leads the opposition to see what they have to gain from a risk-free settlement. Finally, when third parties are trying to get others to compromise, they should strive to frame suggestions in ways that show what both sides will gain from a settlement.

I have presented these common negotiator errors as separate problems, but clearly they overlap. To mention just a few examples, negotiators who don't start out with a fixed-pie bias find it easier to avoid escalating demands and to reframe their thinking and proposals in a positive way. Negotiators who try to understand an opponent's thinking are less likely to feel overconfident in their judgment or to escalate demands needlessly. Negotiators who are aware of the tendency to be overconfident in their judgment are more likely to consider what opponents are thinking and to reframe their perceptions in positive terms.

Psychological Traps

Jeffrey Z. Rubin

You place a phone call and are put on hold. You wait. And then you wait some more. Should you hang up? Perhaps. After all, why waste another second of your valuable time? On the other hand, if you hang up you'll only have to call again to accomplish whatever business put you on the phone in the first place. Anyway, you've already spent all this time on hold, so why give up now? So you wait some more. At some point you finally resign yourself to the likelihood that you've been left on hold forever. Even as you hang up, though, your ear remains glued to the receiver, hoping to the bitter end that all the time spent waiting was not in vain.

Almost all of us have spent too much time caught in little traps like that. Even when it no longer makes sense, we continue to spend money on a failing automobile or washing machine, on an aging and decrepit house, a risky stock investment, or a doubtful poker hand. We simply do not know when to cut our losses and get out. And the same goes for more serious situations. Some of us remain longer than we should in a marriage or love relationship, a job or career, a therapy that is yielding diminishing returns. On a grander scale, entrapment is part of the dynamic in political controversies—Abscam, Watergate, the war in Vietnam.

A common set of psychological issues and motivations underlies all such situations, a process of entrapment that shares many of the characteristics of animal traps and con games and has been studied in a variety of laboratory and natural settings. As researchers, we are attempting to describe the properties of psychological traps: what they have in common, where they lurk, whom they tend to snare, and how they can be avoided.

When I was growing up in New York City there was a cunning little device that we called the Chinese Finger Trap—a woven straw cylinder about three or four inches long, with an opening at each end just large enough for a child's finger to be inserted. Once you put a finger into each end, the trap was sprung. The harder you tugged in opposite directions in an effort to get free, the more the woven cylinder stretched and pulled tight around each finger. Only by pushing inward, by moving *counter* to the direction in which escape appeared to lie, could you get free. So it is with entrapping situations. The tighter one pulls, the greater the conflict between the lure of the goal and the increasing cost of remaining in pursuit of it. And the tighter one pulls, the greater the trap's bite. Only by letting go at some point can the trap be escaped. Or, as the Chinese philosopher Lao-tzu put it: "Those who would conquer must yield; and those who conquer do so because they yield."

To understand psychological entrapment, we must first understand the simplest traps of all—physical traps for animals. Sometime rather early in the evolution of our species, human beings came to understand that the active pursuit of quarry by hunting was often impractical or undesirable. Thus, trapping was invented. A trap allows hunters to outwit their quarry, to offset any advantage that the quarry may have by virtue of its greater power, speed, or the limited destructive capacity of the hunters' weapons. An animal trap accomplishes these ends in a strikingly simple and clever way: it brings the quarry to the hunter rather than the other way around. Instead of continuing to hunt for quarry, often in vain and at considerable cost, trappers get the quarry to catch itself. Once set, the animal trap takes on a life of its own, a surrogate hunter waiting with infinite patience for the quarry to make an unwise choice. The consequence of having this surrogate is that hunters' limited resources can now be devoted to other pursuits, including the construction of additional traps.

Ingenious devices, these animal traps, devilishly clever and efficient—and utterly sinister in their effect on the victims who fall prey to them. What properties, then, make them work?

First of all, an effective trap must be able to lure or distract the quarry into behaving in ways that risk its self-preservation. Often this important first step is accomplished with some form of bait that is so tantalizingly attractive, so well suited to the quarry's particular needs, that the animal is induced to pursue it, oblivious to the trap's jaws.

Second, an effective animal trap permits traffic in one direction only. It is far easier for a lobster to push its way through the cone-shaped net into the lobster trap than, once in, to claw its way out. The bait that motivated the quarry to enter the trap in the first place obscures the irreversibility of that move. Doors that yield easily, inviting the quarry's entry, slam shut with a vengeance.

Third, an effective trap is often engineered so that the quarry's very efforts to escape entrap it all the more. The bear's considerable strength, applied in an effort to pull its paw from a trap, only sinks the trap's teeth deeper into its flesh. A fish's tendency to swim away from anything that constrains its free movement only deepens the bite of the hook. An effective trap thus invites the quarry to become the source of its own entrapment or possible destruction.

Finally, an effective animal trap must be suited to the particular attributes of the quarry it is designed to capture. One cannot catch a guppy with a lobster trap or a mosquito with a butterfly net. Consider the awful and awesomely effective 19th-century American wolf trap. The simplicity and frightening elegance of this trap is that it depends on the wolf's appetite for the taste of blood. A bloodied knife blade was left to freeze in the winter ice. While licking the knife, the wolf would cut its tongue and begin to bleed. It would then start to lick at the knife all the more, which in turn led to a greater flow of blood—and the wolf's ultimate undoing. The animal's blood attracted the victim and, eventually, one another. Thus a whole pack of wolves could be destroyed with just one trap.

Confidence games are psychological traps for capturing people and are remarkably similar to self-entrapment. Like animal traps, they rely for their effectiveness on the trapper's (con artist's) ability to lure the quarry (mark) into a course of action that becomes entrapping. The lure is typically based on the mark's cupidity; the fat, wriggling worm is the tempting possibility of getting something for nothing, a big killing that appears to happen at the expense of someone else.

The effective con also depends on the mark's willingness to cheat another person in order to reap large and easy profits. As a result, the mark's progressive pursuit of the lure tends to obscure the fact that the path taken is not easily reversible. With the con artist's kind assistance, the mark is increasingly rendered a coconspirator in a crime against another, a bit like Macbeth: "I am in blood/stepp'd so far that, should I wade no more,/Returning were as tedious as go o'er."

In addition, the mark's very efforts to escape—by making a quick, glorious, and final big killing before quitting once and for all—only lead to deeper entrapment. The more money the mark is persuaded to put up in this effort, the more carefully he or she is apt to guard the investment—and to justify it through the commitment of additional resources.

Finally, just as an animal trap is tailored to its quarry, so must a con be geared to the brand of avarice and dishonesty of the mark. "Different traps for different saps" is the rule.

There are two kinds of cons: so-called short cons, such as Three-Card Monte or the Shell Game, in which the mark is fleeced for a few dollars on the spot; and big cons, in which the mark is directed to a "big store"—a place where the con is played out. Big cons reached their heyday around the turn of the 19th century in this country and lined the pockets of skilled con artists with hundreds of thousands of dollars. Big cons include the Rag, the Pay-Off, and the Wire, the last of these made famous by Paul Newman and Robert Redford in *The Sting*. In that con, a mark was persuaded that horse-race results had been delayed long enough for him to place a bet *after* the race had been run, thereby betting on a sure thing. The con took place in a large ground-floor room, rented for the week as the big store. All the roles in the drama, save that of the mark, were played by confederates, creating an elaborate and complex ruse.

The steps or stages involved in most big cons are remarkably consistent:

1. "Putting the mark up"—finding the right person to fleece.
2. "Playing the con"—befriending the mark and gaining the mark's confidence.
3. "Roping the mark"—steering the victim to the "inside man," the person who is in charge of running the big store.
4. "Telling the tale"—giving the inside man an opportunity to show the mark how a large sum of money can be made dishonestly.
5. "Giving the convincer"—allowing the mark to make a substantial profit in a test run of the swindle.
6. "Giving the breakdown"—setting the mark up to invest a large sum of money for the final killing.
7. "Putting the mark on the send"—sending the mark home for that amount of money.

8. "The sting"—fleecing the mark in the big store.

9. "Blowing the mark off"—getting the mark out of the way as quickly and quietly as possible.

In psychological entrapment, one person may simultaneously play the role of roper, inside man, and mark. In so doing, we manage to ensnare ourselves. As with physical and psychological devices for capturing others, these traps only work when people are, first and foremost, interested in—and distracted by—the lure of some goal. Final victory in Vietnam, a happy marriage, a big killing at the gambling table, or simply the return of the person who pushed the hold button: all may be viewed as worthy goals—or as bait that conceals a dangerous hook. In entrapping situations, marks initially look in one direction only—forward—as they pursue the mirage of a goal that lies just beyond their grasp.

In their single-minded rush toward the objective, marks neglect the possibility that they are being sucked into a funnel from which escape may prove remarkably difficult. The first stage of entrapment—eager, forward-looking pursuit of one's goal—is thus followed by attention to the costs that have been unwittingly incurred along the way. The compulsive gambler's drive for a killing is inevitably followed by attention to the mounting costs of the pursuit, costs that in turn need to be justified by greater commitment. Similarly, when our personal or professional lives are disappointing—and our efforts to achieve a turnaround do not pay off quickly enough—we may decide to justify the high cost by renewing our commitment and remaining on the treadmill.

But notice that the more resources committed to attaining the goal, the greater the trap's bite. Each additional step toward a rewarding but unattained goal creates new and greater costs, requiring greater justification of the course of action than ever before. With each additional year that a person remains in a dissatisfying job, hoping it will take a turn for the better, he or she feels more compelled to rationalize the time invested by remaining in the job even longer.

In certain entrapping situations, those in which several people are competing with one another, reward pursuit and cost justification are followed by a third stage, in which people try to make sure that their competitors end up losing at least as much—if not more—than they. Like two children in a breath-holding contest or two nations in an arms race, many entrapping situations evolve to the point where each side's focus is no longer on winning or even on minimizing losses, but on getting even with the adversary who engineered the mess.

In the last major stage of entrapment, marks must finally let go, either because their resources are gone, because they are rescued by another person, or because they recognize the desperation of the pursuit. Just as the Chinese Finger Trap can be escaped only by pushing inward, entrapment can be avoided only by letting go.

One devilishly simple and effective example of entrapment is a game known as the Dollar Auction, invented about 10 years ago by Martin Shubik, an economist at Yale. As his proving ground, Shubik allegedly used the Yale University cocktail-party circuit. Anyone can make some money—but perhaps lose some friends—by trying it out at a party.

Take a dollar bill from your pocket and announce that you will auction it off to the highest bidder. People will be invited to call out bids in multiples of five cents until no further bidding occurs, at which point the highest bidder will pay the amount bid and win the dollar. The only feature that distinguishes this auction from traditional auctions, you point out, is the rule that the *second-highest* bidder will also be asked to pay the amount bid, although he or she will obviously not win the dollar. For example, Susan has bid 30 cents and Bill has bid 25 cents; if the bidding stops at this point, you will pay Susan 70 cents ($1 minus the amount she bid) and Bill, the second-highest bidder, will have to pay you 25 cents. The auction ends when one minute has elapsed without any additional bidding.

If my own experience is any indication, the game is likely to follow a general pattern. One person bids a nickel, another bids a dime, someone else jumps the bidding to a quarter or so, and the bidding proceeds at a fast and furious pace until about 50 or 60 cents is reached. At around that point, the number of people calling out bids begins to decrease, and soon there are only three or four people still taking part. The bidding continues, at a somewhat slower pace, until the two highest bids are at about $1 and 95 cents. There is a break in the action at this point, as the two remaining bidders seem to consider what has happened and whether they should continue. Suddenly the person who bid 95 cents calls out $1.05, and the bidding resumes. Soon the two remaining bidders have escalated matters so far that both bids are over $4. Then one of the guests suddenly escalates the bidding by offering $5, the other (who has already bid $4.25 or so) refuses to go any higher, and the game ends. You proceed to collect $4.25 from the loser and $4 from the ''winner.''

Several researchers have had people play the Dollar Auction game under controlled laboratory conditions and have found that the participants typically end up bidding far in excess of the $1 prize at stake, sometimes paying as much as $5 or $6 for a dollar bill. The interesting question is, of course, why. What motivates people to bid initially and to persist in a self-defeating course of action?

Thanks primarily to the extensive research of Allan Teger, a social psychologist at Boston University, the question has been answered. Teger found that when Dollar Auction participants were asked to give reasons for their bidding, their responses fell into one of two major motivational categories: economic and interpersonal. Economic motives include a desire to win the dollar, a desire to regain losses, and a desire to avoid losing more money. Interpersonal motives include a desire to save face, a desire to prove one is the best player, and a desire to punish the other person.

Economic motives appear to predominate in the early stages of the Dollar Auction. People begin bidding with the hope of winning the dollar bill easily and inexpensively. Their bids increase a little bit at a time, in the expectation that their latest bid will prove to be the winning one. If the other participants reason the same way, however, the bidding escalates. At some subsequent point in the Dollar Auction, the bidders begin to realize that they have been drawn into an increasingly treacherous situation. Acknowledging that they have already invested a portion of their own resources in the auction, they begin to pay particular attention to the amount they stand to lose if they come in second. As the bidding approaches $1—or when the amount invested equals the objective worth of the prize—the tension rises. At this stage, Teger has found, the participants experience intense inner conflict, as measured by physiological measures of anxiety and nervousness; about half of them then quit the game.

People who remain in the auction past the $1 bid, however, typically stick with it to the bitter end—until they have exhausted their resources or their adversary has quit. Interpersonal motives come to the fore when the bid exceeds the objective value of the prize. Even though both players know they are sure to lose, each may go out of his or her way to punish the other, making sure that the other person loses even more, and each may become increasingly concerned about looking foolish by yielding to the adversary's aggression. Teger found that this mutual concern occasionally leads bidders to a cooperative solution to the problem of how to quit without losing face: a bid of $1 by one player, if followed by a quick final raise to $2 by the second, allows the first person to quit in the knowledge that both have lost equally.

If entrapping situations are as ubiquitous and powerful as I have suggested, how do people ever avoid getting into them? What, if anything, can people do to keep from getting in deeper? Over the past six years or so, I have been working with a research group at Tufts University to find some answers to these questions. We have conducted most of our research in the laboratory, using the Dollar Auction and several other procedures. We have begun to study entrapment in naturalistic settings, by holding contests in which residents of the Boston area, chosen at random, are invited to solve a series of increasingly difficult problems that require more and more of their time.

In one experimental model, people were invited to pay for the ticks of a numerical counter in the hope that they would obtain a jackpot—either by reaching a number that had been randomly generated by computer or by outlasting an adversary. A second laboratory paradigm challenged people to solve a jigsaw puzzle correctly within a limited period; if they succeeded, they received a cash jackpot, but if they failed, they had to pay for the number of pieces they had requested. Finally, in a third type of experiment, undergraduates were instructed to wait for an experimenter or another participant to arrive at the laboratory so that they could receive a research credit; naturally, the experimenter was always late, and the subjects had to continually decide how much longer they would wait.

In one such experiment, Tufts undergraduates were seated in individual rooms, given $2.50 in cash for agreeing to come to our laboratory, and invited to win an additional $10 jackpot by solving a crossword puzzle. The puzzle consisted of 10 words of varying difficulty, eight or more of which had to be correctly solved in order to win the jackpot. Each student was given three "free" minutes to work on the puzzle; after that, 25 cents was deducted from the initial $2.50 stake for each additional minute. People could quit the experiment at any point and leave with their initial stake—minus 25 cents for each minute they remained in the study past the first three. If they remained in the study after 13 minutes had passed, they had to begin paying out of their own pockets, since their initial stake was exhausted at that point. The study was stopped after 15 minutes.

Almost everyone found the puzzle too difficult to solve without the aid of a crossword-puzzle dictionary, which they were told was available on request. Participants were also told that because there were two people working on the puzzle and only one dictionary, it would be available on a first-come, first-served basis. (No such dictionary was actually available.) When students requested the dictionary, they had to turn their puzzles face down, so they were not able to wait for the dictionary and work on the puzzle at the same time. Surprisingly, nearly 20 percent of the students stayed in the experiment the full 15 minutes.

We investigated several important influences on the entrapment process here. First, we created either a competitive or noncompetitive relationship between the participants by telling the students either that the $10 jackpot would be awarded to the first person who solved the puzzle or that it would go to anyone who was able to do so. We found that students who believed they were in a competition became more entrapped—they played the game far longer and spent more of their money—than those not in competition.

We also studied the nature of the investment process by giving participants different instructions about quitting the experiment. Some were told that they could quit at any time. Others were advised that the experimenter would ask them every three minutes if they wished to continue. We expected that the experimenter's intervention would serve as an indirect reminder of the cost of continued participation and that those students who were spoken to would become less entrapped than the others. That is exactly what happened. Students who were not asked if they wished to continue remained in the experiment far longer and, as a group, lost more than twice as much money.

In all of our experiments, as in the one described above, we encourage subjects to move toward some rewarding goal, while we increase the time or money they must invest in it and give them the option to quit at any time. Both our research and Teger's reveal certain repeating themes in the behavior of the participants, which I can summarize in the form of some advice on how to avoid entrapment:

- *Set limits on your involvement and commitment in advance.* We find that people who are not asked to indicate the limits of their participation become more entrapped than those who do indicate a limit, especially publicly. Depending on the entrapping situation you are in, you may wish to set a limit based on your past experience (for example, the average time you've spent waiting on hold); your available resources (the amount of time or money you have left to spend); the importance of reaching your goal on this occasion (you may be able to call later to make a plane reservation); and the possibility of reaching your goal in some other way (using a travel agent to make the reservation).

- *Once you set a limit, stick to it.* We all play little games with ourselves—we flip a coin to make a decision and then when we don't like the result, decide to make the contest two out of three flips. We set limits that are subsequently modified, shaded, and shifted as we get close to the finish. Each new investment, like the addition of an AM/FM radio to a new car that has already been decked out with extras, tends to be evaluated not in relation to zero (the total cost of the investment) but in relation to that inconsequential, minuscule increment above and beyond the amount we've already agreed to spend. If you're the sort of person who has trouble adhering to limits, get some help. Find a friend, tell him or her the limit you wish to set, and have your friend rope you in when you get to the end of your self-appointed tether. Ulysses used that method to resist the deadly temptation of the Sirens' wail.

- *Avoid looking to other people to see what you should do*. It's one thing to use a friend to rope you in, and it's another matter entirely to deal with your uncertainty about what to do by sheepishly following others. Given the uncertainty in entrapping situations, it is tempting to look to others for clues about the appropriateness of one's own behavior. Our research indicates that the presence and continued involvement of another person in an entrapping situation increases one's own entrapment, and that this occurs even when the behavior of each person has no effect on the other's fate. Proprietors of Las Vegas gambling casinos know what they're doing when they use shills to "prime the pump" and get the gambler's competitive juices flowing. Similarly, one is far more likely to continue waiting for a bus that has not yet arrived—and even wait for an outrageous, irrationally long time—if other people are also waiting.

- *Beware of your need to impress others*. Other people are not only a source of information about what to do in entrapping situations; they are also a critically important source of praise or disapproval for our behavior. We all want to be liked, loved, and respected by people whose opinions matter to us. This motive is perfectly healthy and often appropriate, but not in entrapping situations. Our research shows that people become more entrapped when they believe their effectiveness is being judged and scrutinized by others. This is particularly powerful when the perceived evaluation occurs early in the game, and diminishes in importance if evaluative observers are introduced later on. We also find that people who are especially anxious about their appearance in the eyes of others and who feel that they have something to prove by toughing things out get more entrapped than their less anxious counterparts.

- *Remind yourself of the costs involved*. Our research indicates that people are less likely to become entrapped when they are made aware early on of the costs associated with continued participation. Even the availability of a chart that depicts investment costs is sufficient to reduce entrapment. The net effect of such information about costs is to offset the distracting, shimmering lure of the goal ahead—especially if the cost information is introduced right away. If you don't start paying attention to the costs of your involvement until fairly late in the game, you may feel compelled to justify those costs by investing even more of your resources.

- *Remain vigilant*. Entrapping situations seem to sneak up on us. People who understand and avoid one brand of trap often manage to get caught in others with surprising frequency and ease. Just because you knew when to bail out of that lousy stock investment doesn't mean that you will have the good sense to give up on an unsatisfactory relationship or a profession in which you feel you have too much invested to quit. Obviously, people who are told about entrapment and its dangers are less likely to become entrapped. Our studies also show that being forewarned about one kind of trap, moreover, can put people on guard against other kinds of traps.

Although very little is known at this point about the kinds of people who tend to get entrapped, we have recently begun to study this issue and can therefore engage in a bit of informed speculation. First, people who go for bait are also likely to end up hooked. Those who are exceptionally ambitious or greedy or unusually self-confident and self-assured about their ability to reach a goal must tread warily. There may be icebergs lurking in those calm and glassy seas ahead. Second, the sort of person who believes that he should—indeed must—profit according to his efforts may also be ripe for the plucking. Those who tend to trust excessively in a just world, who think that people get what they deserve and deserve what they get, may end up caught in a version of the Chinese Finger Trap. They use their belief in justice to rationalize continued investments—and so tighten the noose all the more. Finally, the man or woman who tends to get swept up in macho ideology, who feels that nothing else applies, is also especially vulnerable to entrapment. Such people may be willing to invest more and more in order to avoid some small embarrassment—only to suffer greater humiliation in the final reckoning.

Despite cautionary advice, we all still manage to get ourselves entrapped. When the inevitable happens, when you find yourself asking "What have I done?," remember there are times when the wisest course may be to quit, not fight. There may just not be a way of salvaging the time, effort, money, even the human lives that have gone into a particular sinking ship. Know when to give it up, when to push rather than pull those fingers, when to yield and wait for victory another day. For there is almost always another day, despite our proclivity for ignoring that fact.

Games Negotiators Play

Frank L. Acuff

Maurice Villere

The process and outcome of negotiations can have an enormous impact not only upon the parties involved, but on third parties and the public interest itself. For example, a recent transit strike in a large metropolitan area completely shut down mass transit operations in the city for over three months. This strike affected not only the salaries of the union employees and the profits of management, but the industries and individuals dependent on mass transit—primarily retail establishments and the poor.

Much of the delay in settling disputes is attributable to the negotiating practices of the parties involved. Some practices are efficient and effective in meeting the goals of all concerned. Other practices lead to long and tedious dickering which brings severe hardship to many who should not be involved and many who cannot bear such a hardship.

Many of the examples to be discussed in this article are drawn from labor negotiations for illustration purposes, but have an applicability to many other personnel or business transactions. Whether an attempt by junior to get dad's car keys or a diplomatic strategy to obtain pivotal concessions of international impact, the negotiating process is a pervasive one to all of us. Moreover, productive negotiations will become even more imperative as industries and institutions become larger and more complex.

One poor negotiating practice which is present in all types of negotiations (regardless of the nature of the business or the parties involved), and which is a major deterrent to effective and efficient settlements, is game playing.

"Game" is defined here in the terms of transactional analysis (TA). According to TA, a game is an implicit interactional strategy where the outcome is negative. By implicit, we mean that in a game a person appears to be doing something agreeable and profitable on the surface while the actual motive is negative and is disguised ulteriorly.[1] The negative payoff is usually in the form of a subtle or not so subtle put-down or negative stroke addressed toward an opposing party. In the terminology of TA, games arise out of "not OK" positions. In the negotiating setting, the position is often I'm

---

Reprinted from *Business Horizons*, February 1976. Copyright 1976 by the Foundation for the School of Business at Indiana University. Used with permission.

[1]Eric Berne, *Games People Play* (New York: Grove Press, 1964).

OK but my opponent is a not OK enemy to be dealt with. For those not familiar with TA terms, see the accompanying box of definitions.

A classic example of a game in TA terminology is NIGYSOB, or Now I've Got You, You Son of a Bitch. In negotiating, this game may come about, for instance, when one party uses a trivial error (tardiness) of the opponent's as a basis for belittling the opponent's overall considerateness and sincerity. A thus has an excuse to show displeasure against B and is actually delighted to have a vehicle from which to vent pent-up feelings.

A: Excuse me, Fred, what time do you have?

B: About ten fifteen.

A: Didn't we agree to meet at ten on the nose?

B: Right, I'm sorry. One of the team got a phone call at the last minute.

A: Let's stick to our word, then, Fred, and not keep the members of my committee away from all their other obligations. I should certainly hope these negotiations are as high a priority for you as they are for us.

The joy A gains from such self-righteous anger may easily overshadow the original provocation. The problem with game playing is that, in the end, nobody wins. One may get the temporary feeling that he is one up on someone else (that he has really put someone else down, for example, by making him feel foolish), but in the long run nothing is accomplished. Certainly, the demeanor of mutuality and cooperation, the basis for effective negotiating, is severely jeopardized. In fact, often an atmosphere of hostility replaces the previously cooperative one. Now rather than attempting to pull in harness toward just terms, hurt parties will become primarily concerned with protecting their egos and getting even. As a consequence, games prevent honest and open relationships, promote distrust, destroy rapport, and, in the final analysis, inhibit the attainment of objectives.

NEGOTIATING GAMES

In order to deal effectively with game players, one must first be aware that a game is in progress. A prime way to achieve this awareness is to become familiar with typically played negotiating games. The following 10 games appear to be typical in a multitude of negotiating settings. Though obviously not complete, these games should introduce the reader to games generally played during negotiating sessions.

Expertise

The apparent purpose of this game is to establish that one has a knowledge of the facts affecting the negotiations. Expertise is usually played early in the negotiations, thus trying to achieve a position of credibility by giving the impression one's homework has been done.

Transactional Analysis Principles

Transactional Analysis (TA) divides the individual's personality into three ego states. An ego state is defined as a consistent pattern of thinking and feeling attached to a pattern of behaving. The three states are defined as follows.

Parent—that part of the personality dealing mainly with values, opinions, and how-to prescriptions. It may be expressed two ways. First is the critical parent state, which only accepts the individual if he follows instructions very closely. This state is the prime dispenser of negative strokes. Second is the nurturing parent, the supportive type of authority which accepts the individual unconditionally.

Adult—the rational part of the personality. Rather than being concerned with outdated parental dictums, the adult part of us acts as a computer by digesting current factual data for problem-solving purposes. The adult often plays the role of executive of the personality, utilizing parent and child data for decision making and permitting the activation of the other ego states where appropriate.

Child—the emotional part of the personality. It may be expressed through: (a) free child, the source of straightforward feelings, creativity, and spontaneity; or (b) adapted child, which expresses itself as rebelliousness or oversubmissiveness—the "yes man" in all of us.

Parent Cues (Verbal)	*Adult Cues* (Verbal)	*Child Cues* (Verbal)
Shoulds	Who?	I need
Oughts	What?	I feel
Do's	Now?	Wow
Don'ts	Why?	Gee
Be like me.	Let's consider this.	I want it my way.

A: We have been able to determine the economic factors affecting this negotiation through the prodigious efforts of our resident economist, Dr. Adam Smith, and the cooperation granted us by the U.S. Bureau of Labor Statistics.

B: We likewise have gathered the data necessary to assess the economic needs and strains in force upon the parties through the use of a fourth-generation computer and the most advanced systems analysis and programming available in data processing.

A: Advanced data processing techniques are fine, but unless these are based on useful information, the output will be of little use to us. "Garbage in, garbage out," as they say.

B: We agree. That is why that instead of depending on a single individual who is interpreting governmental statistics perhaps irrelevant to our own situation, we would enlist the help of DP techniques that would make a great deal of information immediately relevant.

This game appears to be played only on the adult-adult level, since the tool of this game is purportedly "the facts," or an easy access to them. Actually, however, A's ego state is closer to that of the critical parent whose purpose is to demean B's competence through A's "superior" grasp of the subject matter.

Snow Job

This game is similar to Expertise in that purported facts and figures are its main tool and its use may be that of trying to establish credibility. Snow Job is played by A and B trying to overwhelm the other with facts and figures, a game often played throughout the negotiations process.

A: It is clear that by your proposal the 30 percent increase affects the lower 72 percent of the workers with gains of less than 9 percent increase, and the top 10 percent wage earners with gains of $.67 per hour, a proportion our membership can hardly tolerate, particularly when the whole package represents 7 percent less than the average real wages now paid by (X competitor), and 15 percent less than (Y competitor) pays its middle 18 percent of the wage earners.

B: I really didn't understand all that. Could you please summarize the details?

A: I don't think that's necessary. It's obvious that any one of those facts will tell you we must have a 57 percent increase.

So What?

This game is played by the parties immediately after a concession has been won at the bargaining table. Regardless of the priority given the item prior to concession, the postconcession posture is that the item really wasn't important in the first place.

The winning position is to de-emphasize the conceded item so that the party gaining the concession can maintain leverage for gaining other concessions. In other words, "What you gave us was small potatoes, now let's get on to the biggies." The party granting the concession will attempt, of course, to escalate the importance of the concession. The transaction might look like this.

A: The parties then agree that one company-paid holiday per year will be added.

B: Right. Now, let's get on to some of the demands central to these negotiations.

A: What could be more central than this one holiday? You've been stressing this issue since the last negotiations. We've spent several hours this week negotiating an item which will have a major cost and scheduling impact on our operations. This concession should wash out some of the remaining negotiable items.

B: Hardly. This is something we really shouldn't have had to bargain over in the first place.

Wheat and Chaff

This game has perhaps the longest life span of any negotiating game. It is established early and nurtured throughout negotiations. Wheat and Chaff is played by putting in chaff (minutiae or not really priority items) in order to obtain the wheat (priority items). The idea is to pad the demands with items you can give away. Ideally, this course of action leads to the position, "We've given so much (chaff disguised as wheat) but gotten so little (wheat)," or "We're doing all the giving." B naturally responds that what they have received are really items of low priority (chaff). While B stresses the lack of *quality* (wheat) in the concessions A has made, A will continue to emphasize the *quantity* of items conceded.

Wheat and Chaff may be played for political reasons, espousing the multitude of items the rank and file wishes voiced during negotiations. Wheat and Chaff, therefore, may serve the purpose of at least introducing these items if not resolving them. In this way those represented will know that their representatives have "fought the good fight."

Wooden Leg

The thesis of this game is "What would you expect of a man with a wooden leg?" A argues that he is suffering from a limitation that makes him unresponsible for his action. Examples in everyday life are a headache and drunkenness in order to avoid doing a full day of productive work. This game is played from A's child ego state, and is complemented by B's parent.

A: We haven't been able to show the real impact of your counterproposal because we are lacking representation from each of the subdepartments affected.

B: That would bring your committee size to 27. Our sessions would be unmanageable.

A: True, but we're at a severe disadvantage without having full representation from all groups.

A wooden leg often used by both company and union negotiators are the respective constituents whom they represent—management and the rank and file. A, for example, contends that B's proposal is on its face acceptable, but the unruly mob back at the union hall or the management team just won't buy it at this time.

A popular wooden leg of union negotiating teams is a purported lack of financial resources and staffing with which to prepare for negotiations. Being careful not to infringe upon the Expertise game, the union will stress that it has not been blessed with the wealth of resources possessed by management's negotiating team.

Between a Rock and Hard Place

In this game, A argues, "I hear you, I know what you need, and I'd like to give it to you, but I can't win for losing." Like Wooden Leg, a purported helplessness abounds. Separation appears to be momentarily established between A and his constituents. Ostensibly a strong attempt is made by A to establish an empathy and identification, and even temporary coalition with B. Actually, however, A is creating a noncompromising posture by claiming to be caught in a dilemma.

Sandbagger

In this game, A attempts to negotiate from a position of strength by establishing his own weaknesses. A creates, or feigns the degree of his wounds and weaknesses in order to exaggerate the relative strength of the opponent. By emphasizing his own weakness, A hopes to gain relative strength by preying upon B's sympathy or uncautiousness.

A, for example, may claim that negotiating is a new experience, and ask for B's patience and understanding. Or, A may state that even though he lacks the eloquence which comes from B's formal education and training, A will nevertheless attempt to struggle on. A will argue that such an imbalance is but yet another example of the uphill battle which "simple earnest men" must fight.

A: Tell me, none of us have had much of a chance to look into the world of high finance. I notice in the newspaper that your stock rose ninety-three points last year. What does that mean?

B: The points are equivalent to dollars.

A: Is it good that the points increased?

B: Certainly our shares are now worth more. Investors have increased confidence in our business.

A: Interesting. What would cause all these points, as you call them, to increase so much?

B: Largely because of our record year of profits.

A: You don't say! It doesn't really matter, I was just curious.

A's own weaknesses are created or magnified in both Sandbagger and Wooden Leg. In the former, A is more likely to be cognizant of the degree of his exaggeration, whereas in the latter, the actual or imagined weakness is more likely an unconscious crutch. In Sandbagger, the con man in all of us is at work.

Boredom

The game is best played during a time when the opponent is making his most salient and forceful points. Body language is often an important supporting device, courteously notifying the opponent that his points fail to impress. A often plays boredom during points which B is reiterating. By such reiteration, B risks terminating the game if actual ennui sets in.

If It Weren't for You

This game shields A from acknowledging his own inadequacies. A union-initiated game might look like this:

A: If it weren't for your narrowminded views on each of the issues, our rank and file wouldn't be so discontented.

B: Your excessive demands have made the rank and file unduly optimistic.

A: Our demands are in fact great because of the substandard base on which the rank and file has been living.

Presumably, all would be well with the rank and file if only B would bow to demands. If, in fact, B presented A with no differences on the various bargaining issues, there would be nothing left to bargain about. A's constituents might question the effectiveness, and even the necessity, of their leadership—there are no battles to be won if there are no battles. B has thus performed a service for A by providing opposition.

"Yes, But"

In the "Yes, But" game one individual appears to be seeking advice from another. In fact, his true purpose is to give negative strokes by discounting all the advice given. Every time a solution is suggested for solving his problem, he derides it with a "yes, but . . ."

A: We very much feel the need to negotiate next week, but our schedule looks awfully tight for our regular morning sessions. Any suggestions as to when to get together?

B: Well, instead of our usual morning meetings, let's try afternoons.

A: Yes, we would, but it looks like full agendas for every afternoon next week except Friday.

B: Okay, let's shoot for Friday afternoon. We can at least discuss remaining items on through—

A: Yes, but do you really think we could accomplish anything in just one afternoon?

B: Well, we've met at night in the past. Perhaps the afternoon meeting combined with one or two evening meetings.

A: Yes, but we've often questioned the real utility of bargaining when tired. Why don't we shoot for week after next?

COUNTERACTING GAMES

A number of general strategies can be used to counteract or avoid game playing.

Be Aware

Sometimes it is difficult to know if you are in a game because of the subtle nature of games. However, if you feel discounted or believe you are not getting anywhere in the negotiating, you are probably in a game.

Cultivate Openness

You and the other party are in the negotiating process together. If you both do not pull together in a straightforward manner, you will be pulling apart. As a result, costly negotiating time will be prolonged and, in the end, key issues and facts may be left out of the final contract—issues and facts which might mean the difference between a fair and livable settlement and an ineffective and unpopular one.

Give an Unexpected Response

Games are between at least two people and require cooperation to be successfully completed. Completion of a game is not possible if the second party does not give the proper response that will lead to the negative stroke. The critical parent, the main stroke dispenser, is trying to put down an adapted child. Similarly, the adapted child is setting himself up to be put down by a critical parent or be rescued by a nurturing parent.

By responding from an ego state other than that of the adapted child, critical parent, or nurturing parent, one will be much more successful in getting out of the game.

Stop Exaggerating

Games involve one-upmanship. *I am better or stronger than you* is their implied meaning. Games can be terminated or avoided by getting down to the facts and by resisting the temptation to impress or depress the other party. Egotists and masochists are often on the receiving end of most negative strokes. If a negotiator comes to the bargaining table to prove something about himself, his organization, or the other parties involved rather than for the purpose of equitably settling a dispute, that's game playing.

POSITIVE STROKES

The payoff of any game is a negative stroke or a put-down. When disputes become defensively charged or frustrating, it is easy to push the blame off on someone else in the form of a negative stroke. Attacking the other party closes, rather than opens, further communications. The following are examples of converting negative game strokes into positive, cooperative statements.

Negative Game Stroke: "That statement doesn't make any sense."

Positive Version: "Could you explain fully what you mean?"

Negative Game Stroke: "Do you really think you can get away with that?"

Positive Version: "We are more optimistic in meeting other demands than we are with this one."

AVOID VICTIM/PERSECUTOR ROLES

The persecutor dishes out the negative strokes and the victim collects them. Do not put yourself in the role of the victim by coming to the bargaining table unprepared with poorly researched information. By the same token, it is profitable to avoid the role of persecutor. You may have to negotiate tomorrow with the party you put down today. Supplant a spirit of persecution or hostility with one of cooperation. Cooperation has a way of being contagious. It is also the spirit which leads to effective and efficient results.

Game Inducing Stimulus	Game Perpetuating Response	Unexpected Game Disrupting Response
"This whole interchange is irrational." (Critical Parent)	"What's the use of arguing with you. You're going to get your way anyway." (Adapted Child)	"Any suggestions for getting us back on the track?" (Adult)
"I know you're not prepared only because you've had a lot of other problems at the office. No problem." (Nurturing Parent)	"I've got so many other things on my mind that I'm no good to anybody today." (Adapted Child)	"Based on the information I brought with me, let's see in what areas we can move forward." (Adult)
"Your demands are unrealistic!" (Critical Parent)	"You're the one who's unrealistic." (Critical Parent)	"Why?" (Adult)

Taking the Bull Out of the Bully

Len Leritz

Negotiating would be easy if we didn't have to deal with problem people—if everyone would be reasonable and see things our way. The reality, however, is that much of the time we are dealing with problem people. Much of the time we are negotiating with people who look like adults on the outside but are thinking like kids on the inside.

ENFORCER TYPES: BULLIES, AVOIDERS, WITHDRAWERS, HIGHROLLERS, AND WADSHOOTERS

1. *Bullies*—Bullies will verbally or physically attack, use threats, demand, or otherwise attempt to intimidate and push others around. Their basic approach is to use force. You hear them say things like:

"That's a stupid thing to say!"

"Do you expect me to respond to that?"

"If you don't, I will . . .!"

"I want it, and I want it now!"

"Move it!"

"You can't do that!"

"You better shape up!"

We read daily newspaper accounts of Bully behavior:

- Bus Drivers Walk Out
- Tutu's Son Jailed for Insulting Police
- Nigerian Leader Overthrown
- TWA Airliner Highjacked
- Corporation Dismembered after Hostile Takeover

And we don't have to read the newspapers to find Bullies. They have a way of popping up in our own lives. A few years ago, one of my boys had a soccer coach who had a high need to win and who assumed the best way to improve athletic performance was by berating kids. He also assumed that no one had a right to question his style of coaching. I did . . . he showed up at my front door using the same bully behaviors. He wasn't able to hear me when I talked in a normal tone of voice. It required the filing of a formal complaint against him with the soccer board to get his attention.

On another occasion, I was representing a client in the dissolution of a business partnership. My client was tired of fighting and wanted to retire. His partner knew that and used it as a leverage to renege on an earlier agreement and to demand an additional $100,000.

In Response: The first rule in negotiating with Bullies is that you have to get their attention. You have to draw a boundary of consequence. They need to believe that if they proceed on their present course, you will create negative consequences that will outweigh the benefits they hope to gain. You have to draw a boundary and you have to mean it.

Sometimes our tone of voice is enough of a boundary. When I say to you, "I will not tolerate your attempt to take advantage of me," and mean it, my words and voice tone may be enough to get your attention. Other times, tone of voice is not enough and we need to use stronger measures to get their attention.

In the previous example, we did a little research and found two important leverages. The first was that we found two prospective buyers for the business.

When we met with him again, we offered to buy him out based on the same formula he was requesting. At first he refused. We then hauled out our second lever, which was that the three key employees who made the business work had agreed to quit if he refused a reasonable settlement and would set up a competing business financed by my client. At that point, he committed to our earlier agreement. We had succeeded in getting his attention. This example also points out the importance of creating as many options as possible. *Your power is in direct proportion to how many options you have.*

2. *Avoiders*—Avoiders will physically avoid or procrastinate, hide out, or refuse to negotiate out of fear of losing. You'll hear them say things like:

"I'll do it tomorrow."

"We don't have anything to talk about."

"I don't have time."

"That's not my problem."

In Response: In negotiating with Avoiders, you must identify what their fear is and find a way to make it safe enough for them to stop running away.

My friend, Rob, had an office manager he needed to fire. After procrastinating for four months, he brought the issue up over breakfast one morning, saying that he had several major contracts coming up and a new person would not be able to cover all the bases quickly enough.

I invited him to do two things. One was to make a detailed list of all his performance requirements and find out from an employment agency how hard it would be to find a replacement. The second was to estimate what his manager's mistakes had cost him over the last six months.

Rob then came up with another concern. His manager had formed friendships with several of his key clients. He was afraid that it might damage him if he fired her. My response: check it out.

Rob did all three assignments and had a new person in place functioning at 30 percent better productivity within three weeks. So much for our fears.

3. *Withdrawers*—Withdrawers will emotionally withdraw, get confused, go dumb and numb, or become paralyzed with fear. You'll hear them say things like:

"I don't understand."

"That doesn't make sense."

"I don't know."

In Response: The appropriate response toward someone who is withdrawing is much the same as with someone who is avoiding. Your task is to make it safe enough so the person does not have to withdraw or become confused. You need to ask yourself what it is that you might be doing that is contributing to the other person's fear. You may be closing the person down by your tone of voice, your persistent questions, your position in the organization, your threats, or your silence.

Some possible verbal responses might be:

"What is it that is confusing you?"

"What don't you know?"

"What do you need to be clearer about this?"

4. *High Rollers*—High Rollers will attempt to shock and intimidate their opposition by making extreme demands.

"You have until five o'clock to comply."

"I want $50,000 for my car."

"I want it all done by noon."

In Response: When responding to High Rollers, insist on fair principles or invite them to explain how they arrived at their position. Both of these strategies are explained in the next section of this chapter.

"Can you tell me your criteria for that price?"

"I want to respond to your request, but I will need to do it in a manner that is also reasonable for me."

5. *Wad Shooters*—Wad Shooters assume an all-or-nothing, take-it-or-leave-it stance.

"That's my bottom line."

"If you don't want it, forget it."

"Either you agree to all five points or I'm leaving now."

"Take it or leave it."

In Response: Your possible responses are to ignore their statements, take a break, use silence, or insist on fair principles. All of these are described below.

WHAT TO DO WITH THEM

Enforcer behaviors tend to be uncomplicated and obvious. Consequently, certain responses tend to work effectively with most Enforcer behavior. As we move into describing the upper or more sophisticated levels of thinking, we'll see that more individualized responses are needed.

The above examples of responses were brief. The following is a more developed list of useful responses for countering the various types of Enforcer behavior just described. These strategies will be carried out most effectively if you are operating from the Generative style of thinking.

1. Get Their Attention

The first step in dealing with Enforcers is to get their attention. Until you get their attention you are wasting your time. Nothing constructive will happen until you do.

When you recall Enforcers' limited emotional capacities for empathy, you'll understand why it is essential to first get their attention. At this stage, you are not a flesh and blood person to them. You are simply an object to be eliminated, beaten, or avoided. Enforcers, being egocentric, are prisoners within their own bodies. *Who are you and what you need does not exist for them.*

Enforcers have no capacity to understand the effects of their behavior on you. To be passive or aggressive with them is nonproductive. To respond to them with aggression will scare them more and further constrict their ability to think. They will become more aggressive or more withdrawn. To respond passively will not get the Avoider's attention and will encourage Enforcers to push on since aggression appears to be working. To turn the other cheek to an Enforcer is suicidal.

Instead, you need to assertively get their attention. You need to shock them out of their self-centered stance and let them know that you mean business—that you intend to be taken seriously. You need to make them feel your presence.

You will get their attention by drawing a boundary. The intention in drawing a boundary is not to punish the other person. The purpose is simply to let them know what you will and will not tolerate. *The purpose is to create a negative consequence that will outweigh whatever benefit they are deriving from their current behavior.*

How you draw your boundary will differ in each situation. You need to ask yourself what it is that will get the other person's attention—what is important to them. You may do it by physical action, by shouting at them, by walking out, by filing for divorce, by initiating legal litigation, or by telling them in a quiet and firm voice what you will and won't accept.

The key to drawing a boundary is that you have to mean it. If you don't mean it, you're wasting your energy. The other person almost always knows whether you are serious in backing up your boundary. When you mean it, they know it. No one crosses your boundary when you mean it.

Here is an example of what I call the "Skillet Approach" to dealing with Enforcers. I once had a client who had been physically abused by her husband for years. On her part, she whined and nagged at him. When he couldn't stand it any longer, he'd let her have it. She had threatened to leave him for years, but he knew she didn't mean it.

One night she finally decided to mean it. He had pushed her around earlier in the evening. She waited until he went to sleep and then went to the kitchen and got her biggest cast-iron skillet. She woke him up while holding the skillet over his head. "If you ever hit me again, I'll kill you in your sleep," she told him.

This time she meant it and he believed her. Though he had trouble sleeping for a while, the abusive behavior stopped. The woman had gotten her husband's attention by creating a consequence (the skillet), and she meant it. She said it in a quiet, firm voice, not a whining nag.

Ask yourself what "skillet" you need to use—and mean it when you use it. When you don't mean it, you are reinforcing the behavior you don't want. If you don't mean it, don't draw the boundary. And remember, if you don't draw the boundary, nothing is likely to change.

2. Explicitly Identify Their Behavior

The second step after getting the other person's attention is to explicitly identify the behavior and invite him to do something more constructive. Explicitly identifying his behavior will help him become conscious of what he is doing and will often take the power out of it. This is especially true if others are involved and the Enforcer feels embarrassed. Suggesting other options at this point will help him save face and will keep the negotiations moving. For example:

> "Your repeated attacks are not getting us any closer to an agreement. I'd like to suggest that we each try to explain what we need, then work together to brainstorm some ways that we might both get what we need."

3. Help Them Feel Safer

Help Enforcers feel safer so their capacities expand and they can move into more cooperative behaviors. You can help them feel safer by not becoming defensive and by looking behind their behavior to their underlying needs and interests.

"Would you be more comfortable if we met in your office?"

Respond to the needs in their internal kids, not to their external behavior.

"I can see how you feel frustrated."

Actively listen to them so they feel understood.

"What I hear you saying is . . ."

Help them create safe conditions by asking them what they need.

"What do you need to be willing to stay here and talk this out?"

Meet on their territory. Be aware of their constituency and to whom they need to look good.

> "I want you to be able to go back to your department and feel proud of what we accomplished."

Above all, do not attack in return. Remember, the more aggressive the bully, the more frightened the internal kid. Helping bullies feel safer is usually the last thing you think of doing. And that's precisely what you need to do to get them on your level.

4. Insist on Fair Principles

Bullies, High Rollers, and Wad Shooters will attempt to force you to accept unreasonable agreements. When this happens, refuse to negotiate except on the basis of fair principles. Refuse to be pressured. Instead, insist on fair criteria for both the process and the final settlement. In getting their attention, firmly make it clear that you will continue negotiating only on this basis.

> "I refuse to be pressured into an agreement. I am only willing to continue the negotiation if we can agree to some fair procedures that we will both honor."

> "Let's check with some other suppliers and see what they are charging."

> "The bluebook price for my car is $400 higher. I want to trade cars, but I am not willing to accept an unfair price for my car."

5. Invite Them to Explain

When the other person takes extreme stands and makes extreme demands, ask them to explain how they arrived at their position. Point out that you need to better understand their underlying needs. This strategy throws the ball back to them to justify themselves and allows them to be heard. Demands that cannot reasonably be justified lose their power.

> "In order to understand your demands, I need to hear more from you about how you arrived at those points."

> "Your price is a little higher than I expected. I want to pay you fairly for your work. Explain to me what you will need to do to complete the job."

6. Use Silence

Silence can be one of your most powerful strategies. When the other person is being aggressive or unreasonable, don't respond verbally. Just sit there and look at them calmly. Silence gives them nothing to push against. Calm silence communicates power. The other person will feel uncomfortable with the power of your silence and will probably begin to fill it in—often by backtracking and becoming more reasonable. You have nothing to lose by letting them do the talking at this point.

A variation of using silence is to walk away. "I'm willing to talk about this whenever you are willing to stop attacking me. Until then, we have nothing to talk about."

7. Sidestep/Ignore

Sidestepping or ignoring can be an effective response to personal attacks, extreme demands, and take-it-or-leave-it challenges. Instead of responding directly, act as if you didn't hear them. Change the topic and/or refocus the discussion on the underlying problem or conflict at hand.

Corporate Attorney: "I can't believe they pay you a professional salary."

Opposing Attorney: "I think we still have four issues we have not settled. Let's look at them one at a time."

Film Supplier: "The price is $10,000 per segment. Take it or leave it."

Production Manager: "Your tone of voice sounds angry. Do you feel as if we have not been fair to you in the past?"

or

"How many segments did you say you had?"

or

"What do you think would be fair criteria for deciding what the price should be?"

8. Don't Become Defensive or Invite Criticism

Becoming defensive and justifying your position or needs encourages the other party to step up their attack. If you become defensive, they know that they have you on the run. Invite their criticism and refocus it as an attack on the problem needing to be solved. Invite them to explain how their comments will help solve the problem or conflict.

Magazine Editor: If you were committed to this magazine, you would have been here last week.

Art Director: (Defensive Reply) I couldn't help it. I was burned out and needed the time off.

(Non-Defensive Reply) I know you are under a lot of pressure and last week was frustrating. What do you think we need to do so we don't get caught in that kind of last-minute bind in the future?

9. Refuse to Be Punished

Anyone has a right to be angry from time to time, but no one has the right to punish you. You do not deserve to be punished. You will know you are being punished when:

The other person keeps repeating their attack.

The other person vents their anger but refuses to tell you what they want from you behaviorally in response.

Refuse to be punished. Draw a boundary by asking the other person what they want from you. If their response is "I don't know," inform them that you are willing to continue the discussion when they do know. In the meantime, you're not willing to be punished.

10. Ask Questions

Making statements in which you take a stand will make the other person defensive. Instead, ask questions. Asking questions doesn't give them an object to attack and it invites them to justify their position or to vent their feelings. Asking questions gives you more information about the other party.

When asking your questions, ask "what" questions rather than "why" questions. "What" questions invite factual responses. "Why" questions are usually sneaky judgments that make the other party defensive. Listen to whether you want to make the other person feel guilty or whether you really want information. "What" questions will keep the negotiation moving. "Why" questions will tend to lead you to battle positions.

(Attacking) Why did you think you could do that?

(Information-seeking) What was your motivation for doing that?

(Attacking) Why did you do that?

(Information-seeking) What are the assumptions behind your actions?

11. Point Out Consequences

When the other person refuses to agree to a reasonable settlement, point out the consequences for them if you fail to reach an agreement. Try to present it as a statement of 'inevitable consequences' rather than as a threat.

"The reality is, if our company shows a loss again in the fourth quarter due to the strike, we will have no choice but to lay off five hundred union workers."

SUMMARY

In this chapter we have seen some common Enforcer behavior patterns and a number of options for responding to them. Keep in mind the importance of getting the Enforcer's attention before anything else constructive is likely to happen. And remember, the bigger the bully, the more frightened the internal kid. Don't let yourself be bluffed by bullies. If they were really all that strong, they would be operating from a posture of quiet strength rather than trying to push you around.

Communication

At the heart of the negotiation process is communication. Without communication no additional information would be provided to support a bid or offer, nor would there be information as to why that bid or offer was unacceptable. Without more information there would be no reason, other than the passage of time, for parties to make concessions. In short, there would be no negotiation. In addition, as mentioned in the introduction to Section Six (Negotiation Breakdowns), faulty negotiation can often be traced to faulty or inappropriate communication.

The readings in this section provide several interesting viewpoints on communication during bargaining. In the first article, "Bargaining and Communication," Fred Ikle addresses concerns about both the economic and communicative aspects of bargaining. He highlights the fundamental tension created by negotiators' common versus competing interests and the need for communication as a process to resolve the tension. This tension between negotiators leads to critical negotiating dilemmas and dynamics. One dilemma centers on the nature of truthful communication in negotiation. On the one hand, the parties need to communicate with each other accurately in order to explore their true preferences and priorities. On the other hand, they need to recognize that there are incentives for not being completely truthful with their opponent—for example, for not disclosing their true "bottom line." Bluffing, deception, and concealment of minimally acceptable preferences can be advantageous to negotiators in obtaining more desirable outcomes. Bargainers thus have to choose between the advantages of being deceptive in communication, at the risk of not being believed, and the advantages of being completely truthful, at the risk of putting themselves at a disadvantage.

A second common communication problem is that negotiation frequently involves misunderstandings and miscommunications. Ikle argues that many people attribute breakdowns in negotiation to miscommunication—and that if the parties somehow communicated more accurately or more fully, negotiating problems would be more easily resolved. While this argument may frequently be true, better communication is not necessarily the best solution to all negotiating problems. Enhanced communication *can* reduce the possibility of misunderstanding and improve the relationship between parties over the long term, but stalled negotiations frequently also require more structural approaches to bring the parties closer together.

As a third point, Ikle discusses the function of ambiguous communications. Just as it has been assumed that negotiation would be improved if the parties eliminated misunderstanding and miscommunication, so has it been commonly assumed that communication in negotiation should be as clear and accurate as possible. Ikle identifies the circumstance under which ambiguous communication, both in verbal expression and the specificity versus vagueness of agreements reached, actually may be functional.

Finally Ikle examines the role of rhetoric and propaganda in negotiation. Negotiators, particularly when they are accountable to larger organizations, governments, or institutions, often need to employ rhetoric and propaganda in the negotiation process. The function of this propaganda is only partially directed toward influencing the actual outcome. Its more immediate purpose is to persuade or influence constituencies, bureaucracies, or outside observers that the negotiator is taking a "hard-line" position. As Ikle states, the more rhetorical and propagandistic the communication is, the more polarizing it is likely to be, and the less likely it is to be helpful within the negotiation in terms of achieving jointly acceptable outcomes.

The article "Meta-Talk: The Art of Deciphering Everyday Conversations," by Gerard Nierenberg and Henry Calero, shows that the way we use words, particularly everyday expressions and phrases, has a distinct psychological effect on the listener. If negotiators can effectively understand how to use these expressions, with their desired impact, then they can more effectively prepare the receiver for the message to be sent. These authors' insights into the nature of communication are useful and demonstrate how attention to communication detail can strongly shape the basic message that negotiators want to send. To use communication in negotiation successfully, we need to know what contributes to clarity and understanding, and also to know when we want, or do not want, to achieve clarity and understanding.

The last two items in this section are short "checklists" for negotiators who want to facilitate communication in bargaining settings. "Some Communication Freezers," by Mary Tramel and Helen Reynolds, is a list of statements and "openers" that tend to close down, or at least detract from, the communication process. To check the veracity of their advice, ask yourself what thoughts and reactions you might experience if you were on the receiving end of the examples on the list. The other item here, the "Ten Commandments of Good Communication," recognizes that, in negotiation as elsewhere, communication is a two-way process. Skill in sending information is of limited value when not accompanied by skill in receiving it. Similar in many ways to the prescriptions provided by those who advocate "active listening," this checklist covers behaviors and tactics that will increase your reception and retention of incoming information, with the likely admirable side effect of convincing other negotiating parties that their ideas, needs, and rights are legitimate and worth consideration. Both of these pieces should be invaluable when planning, role playing, conducting, or reviewing negotiations where communication is a critical part of the process.

Bargaining and Communication

Fred Charles Ikle

All bargaining requires communication. In fact, almost all the action in bargaining consists of communication if the term *communication* is defined broadly enough to include everything that a party does to make its opponent aware of its wishes, intentions, and interpretations of the adversary relationship. In everyday interpersonal bargaining, opponents communicate with words, signals, or gestures. In international negotiations, the parties may also communicate through their many postures, economic measures, and policy changes. Even such moves as personnel changes can be used to communicate in a bargaining situation: for instance: the placement of a "dove" by a "hawk" in a government position can convey a threat.

THE ESSENCE OF BARGAINING

Bargaining can be defined as a process of interaction between two or more parties for the purpose of reaching an agreement on an exchange, or an agreement to satisfy a common interest where conflicting interests are present. The agreement may be explicit (for instance, expressed in a contract) or tacit (i.e., an unspoken mutual understanding). Agreement, by definition, is the coincidence of offer and acceptance, both of which are acts of communication. Three conditions are necessary for bargaining to occur:

1. The parties must have some common interests, which means that they jointly prefer certain outcomes over other possible outcomes (e.g., the joint preference that war not break out, or that a sale take place).

2. The parties must have conflicting interests, which means that some of the jointly preferred outcomes are better for one party whereas others are better for the other party (e.g., divergent preferences regarding the conditions under which a conflict is settled short of war, or regarding the price of a sale).

3. The parties must be able to communicate somehow.

It is useful to distinguish between *negotiation* as a form of bargaining where explicit proposals are being put forward, and *tacit bargaining* where the parties do not explicitly propose terms or explicitly consent to a settlement. Note, however, that in negotiation the explicit exchanges are only part of the bargaining process. In international negotiation, especially, the most important moves are often tacit, while the verbal exchange is secondary.

Bargaining can also be examined in terms of economic variables alone. Indeed, for many real-life bargaining situations, the essentials are explainable with the concepts and language of economics (Cross, 1969). Yet, the role of communications in bargaining tends to be oversimplified in such approaches, and other social and psychological aspects, of course, fall outside an economic analysis.

The basic moves in bargaining and negotiation are commitments and threats. A *commitment* can be defined as an action whereby one party changes his *own* incentives in order to alter the opponent's expectations about his future conduct. That is, one party seeks to convince his opponent that he will carry out some prediction (such as holding firm or implementing a threat) by making it more difficult for himself not to do so—in other words, by committing himself.

A *threat* can be defined as a special kind of conditional prediction that a party addresses to his opponent. To threaten is to let one's opponent know that, should he fail to comply with your position, you will make a special effort to inflict a certain damage on him (Ikle, 1964, 1968).

Since the nuclear era, the concept of the threat has been extensively analyzed in writings on military strategy and disarmament. Nuclear deterrence, of course, is based on a threat. A key question about threats is their credibility: Will they be carried out if the opponent fails to comply, or will the first party be "caught bluffing"? To make threats more credible, they are usually buttressed by commitments.

THE FUNCTION OF LYING AND TRUTHFULNESS

As seen by the opponents in a bargaining situation, communication ordinarily serves to convey some truthful information as well as to give false information (or at least to conceal the truth). If one or both parties conveyed either only false or only truthful information, bargaining would tend to atrophy. Thus, if a party became known to give information that is almost invariably false, its threats and commitments would lose credibility, while its offers to agree would lose all value. If, on the other hand, a party consistently conveyed truthful information, its explicit commitments and threats would become highly rigid. With complete truthfulness, every explicit threat would be carried out whenever the opponent failed to comply, and every explicit commitment would be upheld. For instance, if a completely truthful seller argued that he would not accept a lower price, he would in fact be predicting with certainty that a sale at a lower price will never take place.

If the definition of truthfulness is extended to mean that the parties not only abstain from knowingly making false statements but also fully reveal their intended moves and their own (cardinal) preferences, the process of bargaining atrophies to a "game with complete information" (in the mathematical game-theory sense of the term). The outcome is then given by the parties' payoff structure. Stated in this form, the fact that bargaining is incompatible with completely truthful communication sounds like a truism. However, in many proposed "rules" for negotiators, the requirement for and complexity of *partial* truthfulness is lost sight of.

To exploit the common interests in a bargaining situation, the parties can often benefit from mutual frankness. Of course, the more they are like partners engaged in common enterprises—rather than like hostile antagonists—the better can they jointly search for common interests. This search takes the form of discovering, or inventing, outcomes that leave both parties better off—a process that will be facilitated if the parties reveal their true preferences. Thus, bargaining can become partly common problem solving (Walton & McKersie, 1965, pp. 356—57; Shure & Meeker, 1969).

MISUNDERSTANDINGS AND LONG-TERM CONDITIONS

The possibility for exploring common interests is related to the notion that conflict frequently stems from misunderstandings. The valid core of this notion must be separated from unwarranted extensions. Of course, the proposition that conflict would be eliminated if people (or nations) understood each other better can become tautologically true, depending on the definition of "understanding." But the view that people and nations would overcome their conflicts if only they could better communicate their objectives and intentions to each other is based on too rosy a picture of the world. Indeed, one can easily find illustrations where a full communication of antagonistic objectives would only have deepened existing conflicts. Also, evidence from experiments in interpersonal bargaining indicates that the opponents would have been unable to converge on certain mutually advantageous outcomes had they had more complete information about each other's payoffs (Shure & Meeker, 1969).

One of the interesting features of the "prisoner's dilemma" games is the very fact that the parties' knowledge of the opponent's payoff matrix does not help in resolving the conflict. Indeed, one can invent "prisoner's dilemma" games where misinformation between the parties would help both sides to achieve a better outcome. If communication between the parties cannot be blocked or used for misinformation, the mutually deleterious outcomes of a "prisoner's dilemma" will be avoided only if the parties remain concerned about a long-term "super game," that is to say, if they expect and plan for recurrent conflicts of the "prisoner's dilemma" type.

The valid core of the notion that conflict can be reduced through better communication has several elements:

First, there is the before-mentioned possibility that through frank discussion the parties can discover new outcomes that are to their mutual advantage.

Second, if the actual differences between parties have been exaggerated, better communication will help to reduce antagonistic feelings.

Third, clear communication of a commitment or threat can help to deter the opponent from an initiative that would exacerbate the conflict. That is to say, if a party really means to carry out its threat or to stick with a commitment, and if the opponent will yield if he learns of this determination, communicating firmness obviously helps to prevent a clash. Since World War II, this thought has found wide expression in the literature on international relations and nuclear deterrence. For instance, it has often been argued that the Communist attack on South Korea would not have taken place had the United States made it clear that it would come to South Korea's help.

Fourth, communication in bargaining serves what might be called a "systemic" purpose; that is, the purpose of altering the long-term relationship with the opponent rather than the outcome of a particular negotiation. Indeed, the full implications of threats and commitments cannot be ascertained realistically without reference to long-term expectations among the parties. In simulation experiments in bargaining, where subjects (say, college students) take the role of parties, it is most difficult, if not impossible, to introduce realistically these long-term expectations and the processes by which they change. This is one reason why the results of simulation studies of threats are difficult to apply to real-life situations.

Another reason for the limited applicability of game experiments is the richness and importance of the context of bargaining situations, which modifies the nature and functioning of threats and commitments. As one reviewer of the extensive literature on such games observed:

> Game experiments on "threat" have shown most clearly the futility of posing psychological hypotheses containing terms like "threat" in a way that suggests the existence of a "theory of behavior under threat." Hypotheses so formulated cannot be tested, because the "threat conditions" set up by different investigators may have little in common except a designation as such (*Journal of Conflict Resolution*, 1970, p. 65).

Even if the researcher is prepared to disregard the long-term context (or "super game") in his gaming experiments, he will find it difficult to operationalize the concept of threat. Several otherwise interesting experiments have been criticized on this score (Kelley, 1965).

Since full communication of a threat or commitment is required to make it effective, the opponent, whose bargaining position is supposed to be softened by such moves, may have an interest in not receiving this communication. The efficacy of this "burning of communications bridges" has been observed in the way children bargain with parents, in day-to-day bargaining among adults, and even in labor-management negotiations (Schelling, 1960, pp. 17–18, 146–150; Walton & McKersie, 1965, pp. 113–15). It has much less application in international negotiations for the simple reason that modern governments cannot convincingly pretend that they do not hear messages that the opponent broadcasts to them. (Sometimes governments refuse to accept a diplomatic note that a messenger from a foreign embassy attempts to deliver. This occasional practice has symbolic meaning only: it conveys strong disapproval or disdain regarding the content of the note, or underlines the lack of diplomatic relations with the sender country; but it cannot mean that the message has not been heard.)

AMBIGUITY VERSUS SPECIFICITY

Ambiguity has several important effects in negotiation. On the one hand, ambiguous agreements can lead to a reopening of the conflict later on. On the other hand, an attempt to introduce specificity might prolong negotiation or even prevent agreement altogether. Hence, parties often tolerate ambiguous agreement deliberately, thereby postponing the residual points of disagreement—perhaps in the hope that these would never lead to conflict. Ambiguity in an agreement can also be unintended, resulting from inadequate communication between the parties regarding each other's understanding of the terms on which they converge.

In international negotiation, particularly in East-West conferences, a great deal of time is sometimes spent in disputes about how specific an agreement should be made. These disputes are essentially a symptom of disagreement about the substance of the settlement, not about its form. If there were agreement on the substance of the settlement, there should, on the one hand, be no objection to spelling it out in detail and, on the other, little interest in recording the details. If a party objects to giving an agreement greater specificity, this is usually a concealed way of communicating that there is continuing disagreement. Sometimes, disputes about how specific an agreement should be can stem from different preferences as to how much latitude future mediators should have (Ikle, 1964, pp. 8–15).

Ambiguity in conveying commitments or threats serves to soften these moves. Thus, an ambiguous threat is unspecific concerning either the occasion when the threatened action would occur or the content of that action. From the point of view of the threatening party, an ambiguous threat has the disadvantage of being less credible, but the advantage of allowing more freedom to react mildly without proving oneself a bluffer. Moreover, the opponent might give in (or stay deterred) regardless, since he, too, faces uncertainty.

PROPAGANDA AND RHETORICAL DEBATE

If the bargaining parties are not private individuals, but organizations or institutions (such as governments or labor unions), the communication flow affects third parties as well as the internal bureaucracy of each party. Consequently, much of what is said in negotiations may be addressed to (1) outsiders, in the hope that they in turn would influence the opponent (for instance, through propaganda to affect "world opinion"); or (2) one's own internal bureaucracy. Representatives of labor unions have to make statements for the benefit of rank-and-file membership; government delegates at international conferences may have to address themselves to interagency conflicts back home or to domestic public opinion. Indeed, such internal audiences are often the only justification for the negotiator's rhetoric.

The exchange of words across the conference table thus is only partly relevant to the outcome and, even when relevant to the outcome, is often effective indirectly through third parties. This limited relevance can be analyzed in more detail:

1. Weak rhetoric at the conference table may lead to weak delegation reports to the home government. The delegate at the conference site, as a result of his ineffectiveness in debating tactics, may get the impression that his government's position is difficult to defend and that the opponent is unlikely to budge. Hence, he will report to his government that the opponent's position is firm and advise making a concession. (This hypothesis might be tested by correlating weak defenses at the conference table with the recommendations that the delegation sends back home afterwards.) The same applies to the conference talk between delegates of nongovernmental organizations, such as labor unions and business corporations.

2. Weak rhetoric at the conference makes it easier for "soft" allies to maneuver a party into concessions. If the opposing ideas are strong adversaries, the rhetorical aspects of the debate will have little direct effect on their positions, since the relationship between such opponents cannot be affected much by words alone. However, *within* a team of close allies (such as the United States and the United Kingdom in the nuclear test ban negotiations), where words *are* used to settle differences, the "rhetorical loss" of a point with the common opponent might lead to the "forensic loss" of the same point in the private debate with an ally who prefers to soften the common allied position. Thus, while the rhetoric in long-winded negotiations may have little effect on "world opinion" because the news media will have long ceased to pay attention to it, debating defeats might, nonetheless, be exploited by allies (the ever-present witnesses at the green table) in the private forum where the interallied policy is hammered out.

3. In a protracted conference where little real bargaining occurs, the formal debates may nonetheless generate major themes that become part of the agenda or the negotiating position for subsequent bargaining. This may be a deliberate tactic of one or the other party, or it may be inadvertent. In the 1957 London Disarmament Conference, principal aspects of the nuclear test ban—such as the moratorium and the isolation from other arms controls—were already raised to such a status during the prolonged debates that it would have been hard to reject them out of hand when the real negotiations started a year later (Zoppo, 1961).

4. Sometimes negotiators at the conference table—like human beings in other situations—talk without really knowing what they wish to accomplish with their words. That is, communication during bargaining situations may serve no bargaining purpose at all—or, at the most, may serve merely to fill the time until new conditions lead to a change in the position of one or the other side.

One of the advantages of mediation is that it tends to do away with the largely dysfunctional rhetoric so common in direct negotiations. Part of the function of a mediator is to facilitate, as well as to filter, communication between opponents. Proposals and counterproposals conveyed through a mediator are more tentative, since the mediator can be more easily disavowed than an official delegate. Also, a mediator, not being part of the bureaucracies of either side, does not have to insert statements addressed to these home constituencies.

SUMMARY

The many functions of communication in bargaining situations can be grouped as follows:

1. Communication, especially of the explicit, verbal types, serves to convey or to accept offers. When an offer is made very precisely and explicitly, or when an acceptance is final, the statements of the negotiator become, in part, "performative sentences" (in J. L. Austin's meaning of this term). That is, the very saying of the sentence is also the act described in this sentence: e.g., "my government offers, . . ." "I accept" (Austin, 1965).

2. Communication, explicit as well as tacit, is used to change the opponent's expectations as to the probable outcome from the time bargaining begins until agreement is reached or contact is broken off.

   a. Expectations are changed through the terms of offers and counteroffers (they convey the range of the outcome), as well as through commitments (they indicate the probability that a position will be maintained) and through threats (they alter the expected loss in the event no agreement is reached).

   b. In addition, the way in which offers are conveyed and the language used to describe the issues can highlight one particular outcome within a range. The communications signal a "focal point" toward which the opponent's (and perhaps one's own) expectations regarding the outcome are being guided (Schelling, 1960, pp. 111–13).

3. Communications between the opponents can also accomplish changes in the way in which they *evaluate* alternative outcomes. In interpersonal bargaining, this may take the form of direct persuasion. In international negotiations, direct persuasion between opposing governments occurs rarely. Nonetheless, in prolonged international negotiations, a similar, although somewhat more indirect, process can be of prime importance. The ways in which the parties evaluate their own payoffs and those of their opponent can be changed gradually, not because diplomats are such persuasive people, but because these evaluations are highly complex, often result from intricate intragovernmental compromises, and involve a great deal of uncertainty. Hence, the gain and loss calculations regarding specific outcomes tend to be uncertain and can be modified by the casualness or reluctance with which a concession is given, the way in which a certain outcome is labeled, the boundaries that are drawn around the bargaining issues, and other ways of defining or describing the situation (Ikle, 1964, Chap. 10).

   This change in the evaluation of a specific outcome should not be confused with a change in expectations as to the characteristics of possible outcomes. (The former, for instance, would be the view that a certain territorial settlement means a loss or a gain. The latter would be the expectation that agreement can be reached that the 18th or 19th parallel will become the new boundary.) Incidentally, diplomatic histories tend to neglect the fact that such a change in evaluations often results from the communications flow in prolonged negotiations.

4. Finally, communication between negotiators serves to reveal new outcomes. The parties, by exchanging information about their preferences and about various constraints and opportunities regarding the issues under negotiation, might help each other to discover or to invent outcomes that would leave both sides better off than with the outcomes initially sought.

REFERENCES

Austin, J. L. 1965. *How to Do Things with Words*. New York: Oxford University Press.

Cross, John G. 1969. *The Economics of Bargaining*. New York: Basic Books.

Ikle, Fred C. 1964. *How Nations Negotiate.* New York: Harper & Row.

———— 1968. "Negotiation." *International Encyclopedia of the Social Sciences,* ed. David L. Sills. Vol. 11. New York: Macmillan, pp. 117–20.

Journal of Conflict Resolution. 1970. "Editorial Comments." *Journal of Conflict Resolution* 14:65.

Kelley, Harold H. 1965. "Experimental Studies of Threats in Interpersonal Negotiations." *Journal of Conflict Resolution* 9:79–105.

Schelling, Thomas C. 1960. *The Strategy of Conflict.* Cambridge, Mass.: Harvard University Press.

Shure, Gerald H., and Robert J. Meeker. 1969. "Bargaining Processes in Experimental Territorial Conflict Situations." *Peace Research Society (International) Papers,* ed. Walter Isard and Julian Wolpert. Vol. II. Philadelphia: Peace Research Society, pp. 109–22.

Walton, Richard E., and Robert B. McKersie. 1965. *A Behavioral Theory of Labor Negotiations.* New York: McGraw-Hill.

Zoppo, Ciro E. 1961. *The Issues of Nuclear Test Cessation at the London Disarmament Conference of 1957: A Study in East-West Negotiation.* RM-2821-ARPA. Santa Monica, Calif.: RAND Corporation (September).

ADDITIONAL READINGS

Borah, Lee A., Jr. "The Effects of Threat in Bargaining: Critical and Experimental Analysis." *Journal of Abnormal and Social Psychology* 66 (1963): 37–44.

Hermann, Margaret, and Nathan Kogan. "Negotiation in Leader and Delegate Groups." *Journal of Conflict Resolution* 12 (1968):332–344.

Rapoport, Anatol, and A. M. Chammah. *Prisoner's Dilemma: A Study in Conflict and Cooperation.* Ann Arbor: University of Michigan Press, 1965.

Shubick, Martin. "Some Reflections on the Design of Game Theoretic Models for the Study of Negotiation and Threats." *Journal of Conflict Resolution* 7 (1963):1–12.

————. *Games of Status.* Santa Monica, Calif.: The RAND Corporation, August 1968.

Meta-Talk: The Art of Deciphering Everyday Conversation

Gerard I. Nierenberg
Henry H. Calero

"In daily life, our conversation says both much more and much less than is intended," write Gerard I. Nierenberg and Henry H. Calero. *"For these meanings behind our ordinary talk, we have coined the word 'meta-talk.'"* Their book, Meta-Talk, *analyzes a lot of language that is all too familiar in the offices of top executives and the corridors of middle management.*

FALSE HUMILITY

Recently an expert was asked to testify regarding the possibility of anticipating earthquakes along the San Andreas fault in California. He started his testimony with the expression "In my humble opinion . . . ," which drove the person asking the question into a rage. He shouted, "We are not interested in your false humility, we are seriously concerned about future earthquakes and determining where and when they may occur. Please tell us what you believe to be the best approach to the problem."

The expert, visibly shaken, squirmed in his seat, adjusted his pants, sat up straight, and replied sternly, "At present, no one can accurately predict where or when an earthquake will occur on the surface of this planet."

Variants on "In my humble opinion" are: "I do the best I can" and "Far be it from me to say." All are clichés of false humility.

False humility is also present in the use of the expressions "As you are aware" and "As you well know." These phrases seem to suggest that the speaker is not taking any chances of insulting the listener's intelligence by saying something he is already aware of. This is often not the case. For example, a scientist while telling his colleagues about his newest discovery may say, "As you are aware," knowing full well they are *not* aware. Rather than softening the blow, he draws sharp attention to their ignorance and sets himself apart from them.

SOFTENERS

Most of us at some time have prefaced our words with an expression intended to influence the listener in a positive manner. We call them "softeners." In such situations we might say, "It goes without saying . . ." (attempting to get agreement before

---

Reprinted from *MBA Magazine*, January 1974. Used with permission of the author. **245**

stating something); "What I'm about to tell you . . ." (usually a disclosure that must be handled very carefully and involves the listener); "I venture to say," "Don't take me seriously," "off the top of my head" or "at first blush" are sometimes used to mean the same thing.

"Would you be kind enough to . . ." is a softener that attempts to influence another with praise or flattery. "I'm sure someone as intelligent as you . . ." strokes a person's ego, as does "You're very perceptive about . . ." "What is your expert opinion of my . . ." asks for concurrence, not censure, as the individual who tells that speaker he disagrees will soon learn. No one uses such expressions looking for negative responses. The meta-talk means: "I've scratched your back and you should scratch mine."

"You are right but . . ." attempts to avoid conflict by feigned agreement. Acceptance statements often are followed by the incongruous qualifiers—"but," "yet," "however," and "still." They communicate that the person doesn't think you are right, but would like to soften the blow. A husband arguing with his wife about his conduct at a social gathering says, "You are right, I shouldn't have done that, but . . ." then he explains the logic and reason behind his behavior. Instead of contrition, justification is the theme. Seldom do we encounter someone who says, "You are right," and lets it go at that. Even less seldom do we find a person who follows "You are right" with "What should I have done?"

FOREBODERS

Often we put listeners in a negative, anxious frame of mind with the use of "foreboders," as when we say, "Nothing is wrong" ("There *is* something wrong. However, I don't want to talk about it").

Similar foreboders that have a negative effect on the listener are: "It really doesn't matter" (it sure does); "Don't worry about me" (please do); and a statement Oliver Hardy used to make to Stan Laurel, "I have nothing more to say," before lashing out at him verbally and physically.

INTERESTERS

Some statements and questions attempt to arouse the interest of the listener.

"And do you know what he said?" is a strong plea for interest and is used to get undivided attention. Used once or twice it is very effective, but eventually it no longer creates interest but rather boredom or even distaste. We begin to anticipate the question, no longer listening but waiting for its repetition. This phrase often becomes a verbal tic, revealing the speaker's feeling of insecurity.

"Guess what happened?" When this question is used the listener is being told to ask, "What?" so that in complicity with the speaker he will share an unimportant bit of information. The question does not give the listener a choice—it demands his attention and reveals that the speaker is uncertain that he has anything relevant or interesting to say.

"What do you think of . . .?" This query calls for interest and agreement. But the question is often used to insist on agreement with the speaker's opinions. For the meta-talk expert, then, "What do you think of . . .?" is followed by insights into the foibles and prejudices of the person who uses it.

"I could say something about that." This statement can cause both interest and conflict. In a discussion between two persons, a long-suffering soul who resists disclosing his true feelings may utter this expression only after a long sigh to demonstrate his patience. Yet the person who dislikes conflict attempts not to fuel arguments by using such trite phrases, remaining silent instead. On the other hand, the I-don't-want-to-cause-trouble-but-will-anyway type tends to use this expression. He draws attention to a conflicting statement or issue by seeming to avoid a confrontation. "I could say something about that" may provoke the response, "Well, why don't you?" Then the fight is on.

DOWNERS

Downers are used intentionally to put the listener in a defensive state of mind.

"How about . . ." is used in numerous negotiating situations to arouse tension in an otherwise cooperative environment. Most of us have the emotional stability to handle one, two, or even three "How abouts." However, when the phrase is repeated again and again, the cumulative effect serves to make us defensive, angry, and sometimes irrational. "How about" serves to stimulate our opposition to the person uttering it.

"Don't be ridiculous!" heads the list of commands beginning with "Don't." The person saying it is authoritarian, incapable of seeing any colors except black and white. Very few listeners would resent a command that makes sense ("Don't walk on the grass"; "Don't smoke in bed.") But, "Don't be ridiculous!"? Is one supposed to abjectly renounce all his characteristic ways to please the person making the demand? Not likely. "Don't be ridiculous!" usually prompts the question, "What do you mean by ridiculous?" This continues the downward spiral of the conversation that will probably end in angry words or blows. A popular variation is "Don't be unreasonable."

"Needless to say" is a phrase often used to impose an opinion. "Needless to say, we would all like to be handsome and rich." Or would we? Sometimes we project our own feelings and needs on others by using this phrase. Because we feel very strongly about something we want others to share our feelings and we take the liberty of assuming they do. A similar device appeals for consensus by threatening ostracism from the group: "I think we all agree that . . ." These phrases and statements may unconsciously express contempt for the listener.

Self-doubt is revealed in the many expressions that plead with the listener to accept without question the veracity of everything that the speaker has to say. "Believe me," "I'm not kidding," "I have to tell you," "I wouldn't lie to you" have little value except as communication stoppers. Probably everything that follows is going to be a lie or a half-truth.

Hostility in communication often indicates weakness. "Mind your own business," "Stay out of this," "The matter is closed," "I don't want to hear any more," and other abrupt attempts to terminate a conversation can frequently be traced to the fact that the speaker feels he has lost an argument. He tries to regain control of the situation by displaying his power to choose what will or will not be discussed.

Denial is a device often used by people to pretend that things are better than they actually are. An example is the man who asks, "You don't think something's happened, do you?" when he means, "I think something's happened!"

Uncertainty about our ability to do a job well may produce meta-talk that indicates we cannot do it at all. An individual who has been asked to undertake a difficult assignment may reply, "I'll do my best" or "I'll try." The boss may wonder about such statements. Does "I'll do my best" mean "My best is none too good," "I can't do it," "I'm not sure I can do it," or what? The same is true of "I'll try." Either statement can prompt the anxious question: "Don't you think you can do it?" That is because the statements are rationalizations that prepare for failure. The lower the aspirations of an individual, the more probable it will be that he will anticipate failure. Those who are more highly motivated "try" less and "do" more.

Others prepare for failure by using "if-then" statements: "If you will grant X, Y, and Z, then I'll be able to . . ." This can be a perfectly legitimate statement if X, Y, and Z are realistic requests. Often they are not. They merely serve to interrupt communications and try to place blame for the failure on the other person. The meta-talk here is, "Play the game my way or I won't play well and it will be your fault."

Concealed aggression is a common element in many adult conversations. Polite prefaces are often used to soften penetrating questions or abrupt statements: "Do you mind if I ask you . . ." or "Have you ever considered doing . . ." These and similar phrases if used sparingly can grease the wheels of communication but if overused they tend to build up resentment by pressing a point of view too hard.

META-TALK IN BUSINESS

The hot air of talk is as important to a salesman as a cool breeze is to the yachtsman: neither can make his landing without some wind. Some salesmen, however, have learned to minimize the use of small talk and have become outstanding listeners. They realize that many prospective purchasers can talk themselves into buying.

Questions are vital, of course, to the buyer-seller relationship. However, people have become very sophisticated and a deal can be destroyed if questions are too frequently answered with questions. "How much will it cost me?" brings the reply, "How much do you think it should cost you?" This device to avoid saying "I don't know" can quickly degenerate into a downward spiral of increasingly hostile questions and evasive answers.

When a buyer or seller says he will "try" to do something, he is often signaling that you should be prepared for his future inability to produce. If you are confronted with a promise to "try" to get certain terms on a deal, be ready to hear sometime later, "Well, I tried" (and failed). Frequent cost overruns on defense contracts would indicate that this and similar clichés ("I'll see what I can do." "We will make every effort") are used far too often in government contract dealings. On the individual level as well as the corporate, "trying" is the meta-talk of one preparing to be an underachiever.

"Trying" puts a distance between the subject and the desired object because the infinitive "to do" is much weaker than the active use of the verb, "I will do it."

Similarly the person who relates well to others in a buyer-seller situation will avoid other indications of distance.

Not all such distance-putting verbal devices are the result of injured pride. Many of us try to soften criticism by putting a string of words between "I" or "we" and the complaint: "I don't know how to say this . . ." "I am doing this for your own good . . ."; "We've done business for a long time . . ."; "I wish I didn't have to say this, but . . ." All of these clichés leave an impression that there is something not quite right about offering criticism. Yet it is often necessary to straighten out a relationship that has taken a wrong turn. Many successful executives are very aggressive and seldom waste time in softening criticism. So long as the criticism is valid and is kept impersonal this may be a good way for them to handle the problem. A frank revelation of feelings can actually improve a relationship by removing the "polite" distance between two people.

Meta-talk abounds in relationships between superiors and subordinates, particularly those characterized by a lack of openness. An aware employee would recognize at once that if his boss says, "I want there to be complete frankness between us at all times," he may really be saying, "Don't tell me anything I don't want to hear." No superior can obtain frankness or any other quality from an employee merely by requesting it. He may get a semblance of frankness or honesty in this way. To achieve an open relationship, however, trust must first be established. Similarly, statements such as "This is the way I'd like to see it done" can really mean, "You are incapable of thinking for yourself. *I'm* the only one who thinks around here." The boss who signals this through his meta-talk is not getting as much as he should from his employee. No intelligent person enjoys a relationship that limits his creative ability to come up with alternatives to problems, and "This is the *only* way" certainly does that.

If employees confident of their abilities resent such signals from their superiors, less confident subordinates employ meta-talk to beg for reassurance while denying any weakness in their performance. "On the whole . . ." and "Under the circumstances . . ." often introduce these self-serving statements: "On the whole I'm satisfied with the job I did"; "Under the circumstances, I don't see how I could have done anything differently." The meta-talk of these statements is, "I don't have any specific strong points to bring out, so I'll generalize."

An employer may say, "On the whole, your idea sounds all right." If he follows up with, "Let me sleep on it," chances are he doesn't think it is important enough to keep him awake. The employee who eagerly awaits the next day to get the verdict is in for a jolting disappointment.

Quite naturally, money and its allocation produce a great deal of meta-talk in superior-subordinate relationships. Oddly some employees can be quite forthright and aggressive about getting every penny of a proposed departmental budget, let us say, and yet be very reluctant to discuss their personal financial needs for fear of being rebuffed. Asking for raises and forestalling such requests provide cartoonists with limitless material. They also can be time-consuming in offices where there is no open communication between employee and boss. One seemingly open conversation with a superior might go like this: "Dave, this company is confronted by a strong competitive market dominated by buyers. In order to survive, we must minimize all costs in order to compete." The subordinate has no difficulty translating this. It means, "Don't expect any increase in pay" or "You're not going to get the increase I promised you last year." For some timid souls the meta-talk is enough, but a more desperate one might venture: "I was wondering how you felt about considering giving me a raise?" Note the distance put between "I" and "raise." It almost becomes an abstract speculation. Therefore, if it is answered with a terse "lousy!" the employee can gracefully but quickly take cover.

A stronger person might preface his request with what he hopes are rhetorical questions: "Do you like my performance?" or, "Have you found any significant weaknesses in my department?" If the answers are favorable he can then proceed with, "In view of that fact . . ." or, "Considering that . . ." both are meta-talk for "I am too good to refuse." The superior may simply acknowledge that fact or say, "I'll tell you what . . ." meaning "You're not going to get a pay increase that easily." A negotiating situation at least has been set up.

Some employees say only what they know will please the boss. Often they preface their remarks with, "Tell me if I'm wrong." This is a perfectly safe thing to say since any boss who can be taken in by this ruse is also probably not going to be critical of his own ideas. This situation is destructive. Words are used as weapons, not as instruments for transmitting and sharing ideas.

There are certain "buzz" words that have become clichés. These are used to obtain feedback and may have a limited positive use. However, when used to excess, such expressions as "Right?" "Is that clear?" "Okay?" "Check?" "Do you follow?" are verbal tics that unconsciously express a doubt that the listener is capable of clearly understanding anything. They also become unreliable guides since they practically demand an affirmative answer. The speaker assumes he will get one and rushes on, ignoring verbal and nonverbal feedback. There is a hidden assumption that for every problem there is but one correct and one incorrect solution. Most of life's problems do not lend themselves to such a simplistic approach. No successful businessman can afford to come up with "the" solution. Generally, there are many alternatives, one of which seems especially appropriate in a given time and place. It often takes time and a supportive relationship to come up with an appropriate answer. Clichés only hamper the process.

Some executives try to conceal their sense of self-importance with statements that minimize their ability or power: "May I make a modest suggestion?" or "If I may venture an idea . . ." Probably no one is fooled by such preliminary statements, but subordinates are alerted that a "great thought of Western man" is about to make its appearance and they had better like it.

A well-intentioned friend, determined to "help" an out-of-work executive, begins to offer "off the top of his head" (meaning, "I'm a genius, I can turn out ideas like popcorn") solutions to his employment problem. Suddenly, the executive interrupts with "Now wait a minute!" What does the meta-talk mean? The friend has made the hidden assumption that the executive is over the hill and incapable of making a decision for himself. He must be "told" what to do. The "Wait a minute" is a protest from the victim who is being talked to, not communicated with. The conversation has added to his problems and increased his self-doubts.

In a supportive relationship, this would not happen. The priorities would be reversed: instead of the friend offering solutions to assumed problems, the problems would be thoroughly analyzed and, more important, the executive's aims and aspirations for the future would shape proposed solutions to the problems. The term *Job's comforters* means those who discourage or depress while seeming to give consolation. These abound in both business and social situations. Don't be one. Communicate.

Communication Freezers

Mary Tramel

Helen Reynolds

1. Telling the other person what to do—for example:
   "You must . . ."
   "I expect you to . . ."
   "You cannot . . ."

2. Threatening with "or else" implied:
   "You had better . . ."
   "If you don't . . ."

3. Telling the other person what he ought to do:
   "You should . . ."
   "It's your duty to . . ."
   "It's your responsibility to . . ."

4. Making unasked-for suggestions:
   "Let me suggest . . ."
   "It would be best if you . . ."

5. Attempting to educate the other person:
   "Let me give you the facts."
   "Experience tells us that . . ."

6. Judging the other person negatively:
   "You're not thinking straight."
   "You're wrong."

7. Giving insincere praise:
   "You are an intelligent person."
   "You have so much potential."

8. Putting labels on people:
   "You're a sloppy worker."
   "You really goofed on this one!"

Reprinted from Mary Tramel and Helen Reynolds, *Executive Leadership* (Englewood Cliffs, N.J.: Prentice Hall, 1981), pp. 208–9. Used with permission of the authors.

9. Psychoanalyzing the other person:
   "You're jealous."
   "You have problems with authority."

10. Making light of the other person's problems by generalizing:
    "Things will get better."
    "Behind every cloud there's a silver lining."

11. Giving the third degree:
    "Why did you do that?"
    "Who has influenced you?"

12. Making light of the problem by kidding:
    "Think about the positive side."
    "You think *you've* got problems!"

Ten Commandments of Good Communication

Prepared by the staff of the Executive Communication Course, American Management Association

As a manager, your prime responsibility is to get things done through people. However sound your ideas or well-reasoned your decisions, they become effective only as they are transmitted to others and achieve the desired action—or reaction. Communication, therefore, is your most vital management tool. On the job you communicate not only with words but through your apparent attitudes and your actions. For communication encompasses all human behavior that results in an exchange of meaning. How well you manage depends upon how well you communicate in this broad sense. These 10 commandments are designed to help you improve your skills as a manager by improving your skills of communication—with superiors, subordinates, and associates.

I. **Seek to clarify your ideas before communicating.** The more systematically we analyze the problem or idea to be communicated, the clearer it becomes. This is the first step toward effective communication. Many communications fail because of inadequate planning. Good planning must consider the goals and attitudes of those who will receive the communication and those who will be affected by it.

II. **Examine the true purpose of each communication.** Before you communicate, ask yourself what you *really* want to accomplish with your message— obtain information, initiate action, change another person's attitude? Identify your most important goal and then adapt your language, tone, and total approach to serve that specific objective. Don't try to accomplish too much with each communication. The sharper the focus of your message the greater its chances of success.

III. **Consider the total physical and human setting whenever you communicate.** Meaning and intent are conveyed by more than words alone. Many other factors influence the over-all impact of a communication, and the manager must be sensitive to the total setting in which he communicates. Consider, for example, your sense of *timing*—i.e., the circumstances under which you make an an-

---

nouncement or render a decision; the *physical setting*—whether you communicate in private, for example, or otherwise; the *social climate* that pervades work relationships within the company or a department and sets the tone of its communications; *custom and past practice*—the degree to which your communication conforms to, or departs from, the expectations of your audience. Be constantly aware of the total setting in which you communicate. Like all living things, communication must be capable of adapting to its environment.

IV. *Consult with others, where appropriate, in planning communications.* Frequently it is desirable or necessary to seek the participation of others in planning a communication or developing the facts on which to base it. Such consultation often helps to lend additional insight and objectivity to your message. Moreover, those who have helped you plan your communication will give it their active support.

V. *Be mindful, while you communicate, of the overtones as well as the basic content of your message.* Your tone of voice, your expression, your apparent receptiveness to the responses of others—all have tremendous impact on those you wish to reach. Frequently overlooked, these subtleties of communication often affect a listener's reaction to a message even more than its basic content. Similarly, your choice of language—particularly your awareness of the fine shades of meaning and emotion in the words you use—predetermines in large part the reactions of your listeners.

VI. *Take the opportunity, when it arises, to convey something of help or value to the receiver.* Consideration of the other person's interests and needs—the habit of trying to look at things from his point of view—will frequently point up opportunities to convey something of immediate benefit or long-range value to him. People on the job are most responsive to the manager whose messages take their own interests into account.

VII. *Follow up your communication.* Our best efforts at communication may be wasted, and we may never know whether we have succeeded in expressing our true meaning and intent, if we do not follow up to see how well we have put our message across. This you can do by asking questions, by encouraging the receiver to express his reactions, by follow-up contacts, by subsequent review of performance. Make certain that every important communication has a "feedback" so that complete understanding and appropriate action result.

VIII. *Communicate for tomorrow as well as today.* While communications may be aimed primarily at meeting the demands of an immediate situation, they must be planned with the past in mind if they are to maintain consistency in the receiver's view; but, most important of all, they must be consistent with long-range interests and goals. For example, it is not easy to communicate frankly on such matters as poor performance or the shortcomings of a loyal subordinate—but postponing disagreeable communications makes them more difficult in the long run and is actually unfair to your subordinates and your company.

IX. *Be sure your actions support your communications.* In the final analysis, the most persuasive kind of communication is not what you *say* but what you *do.* When a man's actions or attitudes contradict his words, we tend to discount what he has said. For every manager this means that good supervisory practices— such as clear assignment of responsibility and authority, fair rewards for effort, and sound policy enforcement—serve to communicate more than all the gifts of oratory.

   X. *Last, but by no means least: Seek not only to be understood but to understand—be a good listener.* When we start talking we often cease to listen—in that larger sense of being attuned to the other person's unspoken reactions and attitudes. Even more serious is the fact that we are all guilty, at times, of inattentiveness when others are attempting to communicate to us. Listening is one of the most important, most difficult—and most neglected—skills in communication. It demands that we concentrate not only on the explicit meanings another person is expressing, but on the implicit meanings, unspoken words, and undertones that may be far more significant. Thus we must learn to listen with the inner ear if we are to know the inner man.

SECTION EIGHT

Persuasion

In the previous section, we stated that communication is the heart of negotiation, and that breakdowns in communication are a frequent cause of negotiation ineffectiveness. Linked closely to communication is the process of persuasion. How arguments are constructed, and how they are joined together into a persuasive message, is another important element in understanding the dynamics of successful negotiation.

Many of the important elements of the persuasion process have been covered in the earlier discussion of distributive and integrative bargaining processes. We noted previously that information, per se, may be the strongest possible persuasive force in negotiation; each of these strategic approaches uses information for different motivational ends. However, there are a variety of other factors to be considered in constructing a persuasive message, and in understanding how receivers are persuaded by various verbal and nonverbal elements. The articles in this section focus specifically on the more subtle, nonverbal, and tactical approaches to persuasion that can be used in negotiation, and examine the impact of these particular approaches.

In the first article in this section, "The Tactics and Ethics of Persuasion," Philip Zimbardo reviews a variety of tactics that can be used to change another party's attitudes. This article was prepared to help social activists learn how to be more persuasive in promoting attitude change on important social issues—that is, antiwar issues, environmental issues, social issues. Zimbardo suggests that one's tactics can be organized into three major categories: preparing the initial contact, gaining access to the person to be persuaded, and maintaining and directing the relationship. While many of his examples are drawn from simple persuasion situations in which college students or other social activists seek to change individual attitudes regarding major social issues, the basic elements and process relate to most negotiation situations. The article also examines the ways that police use persuasion strategies to extract confessions or compliance from people who are arrested, and explores some of the more "Machiavellian strategies" for obtaining compliance or change in another's point of view. Zimbardo believes that using some of these strategies may raise ethical concerns for the persuader and addresses this question in discussing the tactics.

In the second article in this section, Icek Ajzen presents an overview of the Elaboration Likelihood Model of Persuasion that was developed by Richard Petty and John Cacioppo. Ajzen notes that this model has revolutionized social psychologists' understanding of how and why persuasion works. The model posits that there are two

257

routes to persuasion: a *central* route that involves thoughtful processing, and a *peripheral* route where little attention is paid to logical arguments. Ajzen discusses the factors that influence persuasion along both routes. The effective negotiator needs to prepare his or her persuasive approach in light of both routes.

In the article "How to Increase Your Influence", David Berlew discusses the limitations of logical persuasion strategies. Berlew argues that logical persuasion strategies are least effective when neither party has clear expertise and both parties have strong self-interest (a common negotiation situation). Rather than pursue a logical persuasion strategy in these circumstances, Berlew suggests that an exchange strategy should be used. The article discusses the three components of an effective exchange strategy and presents cautions about how and when it should be used.

In the final article in this section, "The Effects of Anger on Negotiations over Mergers and Acquisitions", Joseph Daly examines the influence of anger on persuasion. Daly notes that anger has two types of effects on negotiations. First, anger appears to influence how people process information about negotiating; for instance, angry negotiators perceive fewer outcome options in negotiations than do less angry negotiators. Second, angry negotiators are more likely to pursue intangible goals such as revenge or retaliation than are less angry negotiators. Daly concludes the article with a discussion of the strategic implications of anger, how to use it as a persuasive tactic, the use of intermediaries, and how to restore relationships disrupted by anger.

The Tactics and Ethics
of Persuasion

Philip G. Zimbardo

The police interrogator is recognized by society as an agent of change whose job it is to persuade witnesses and suspects to give evidence, admissions, and confessions of guilt. When he is successful, the individual may lose his freedom or life, but society is presumed to be the beneficiary of this loss. The salesman's effective persuasion may or may not benefit either the "target" of his sales attempt or the society, but it certainly brings personal gain to the salesman and those he represents. What is similar about both is that they are "formal" persuasive communicators insofar as their goal to effect a specified change is explicitly formulated and their tactics often are laid down in training manuals used in their initiation. Examination of their tactics reveals a further basis of similarity—a willingness to employ virtually any means to achieve their goals. Indeed, for one, it has been necessary to establish Supreme Court rulings to limit the use of third-degree physical brutality and excessive psychological coercion; for the other, the Better Business Bureaus and Ralph Nader are needed to limit the excessive exploitation of the consumer.

Every social interaction, however, carries the burden of being a potential attitude change encounter. The ethical issues raised by deceptive business practices or police coercion are often ignored in other equally compelling influence situations. Parents, educators, priests, and psychotherapists, for example, represent some of the most powerful "behavioral engineers" in this society. It is rare that the appropriateness of evaluating what they do in ethical terms is even considered. This is largely because they are not perceived as formal agents of attitude and behavior change. They function with the benefits of socially sanctioned labels which conceal persuasive intent: parents "socialize," teachers "educate," priests "save souls," and therapists "cure the mentally ill."

There are two other characteristics of the influence situations in which they operate which minimize any issue of unethical, deceptive, or coercive persuasion. First, there is an illusion that the goal of the situation is defined in terms of the best interests of the target person: the child, student, sinner, sick patient. Second, an

---

Reprinted from *Attitudes, Conflicts and Social Change*, Bert King and Elliot McGinnes (eds.), 1972, pp. 81–99. Copyright ©1972 Academic Press. Used with permission of Academic Press and the author.

attribution error process typically occurs by which we judge that the individual could have resisted the pressures brought to bear upon him. One would want to believe that people change only when they want to or when they are subjected to overwhelming *physical* forces. The extent to which behavior is controlled by external social and psychological forces is denied in favor of the presumed strength of individual will power to resist. Given these three characteristics, then, the most persuasive communicators are not acknowledged as such, or are not recognized as exerting a potentially negative effect on the individuals with whom they interact.

Upon closer analysis, however, these underpinnings of this naive view of such attitude-change agents lose some of their foundation. For example, all of them can be viewed as "salesmen" for the established *status quo* with the best interest of society placed before the best interest of the individual. "Socialization" to be a Hitler *Jungn,* "socialization" to repress impulses, to be a good child, to do what one is told, to be seen and not heard, to be patriotic, to be polite, not to question elders, and so forth are goals of the adults in the society, which may be at odds with the child's personal growth. "Education" can mean to bias, to present prejudiced opinion as scientific or accepted fact, to perpetuate preferred ways of thinking. For example, the Russians teach the doctrine of Lysenko, some U.S. schools reject Darwinism, teachers can be models of racial prejudice, and the like. To save sinners may involve making people feel guilt, shame, anxiety—deny the pleasure of physical contact; accept the poverty and *status quo* of this world for a pie in the sky when you die. To cure the mentally ill sometimes involves communicating what the person must do in order that society not label him a "deviant" and cast him out into a madhouse. Psychotherapy can be seen as conformity training in which there is a unilateral influence attempt to make the patient's "abnormal" behavior "normal" (like everyone else's) again.

Such a predisposition to make the attribution error of overestimating internal relative to external causality is seen repeatedly in those phenomena which most intrigue and fascinate us. Hypnosis, voodoo deaths, brainwashing, placebo effects, Asch's conformity, and Milgram's obedience findings all share this property. Dramatic changes in behavior occurs in others, which we believe we personally could resist. The strength of the situational forces are not appreciated, while our own ability not to be tender minded, or weak willed, or suggestible, or controlled by words is magnified.

Research from many disparate areas clearly reveals how easy it is to bring behavior under situational control. Hovland (1954) has noted that it is almost impossible *not* to get positive attitude change in a laboratory study of attitude change. Orne (1962) despairs at being able to find a task so repulsive and demeaning that "experimental subjects" will *not* perform it readily upon request. Milgram (1963) shows that the majority of his subjects engage in extremely aggressive behavior in a situation which psychiatrists had believed would only have a weak effect in inducing blind obedience. We comply, conform, become committed, are persuaded daily in the endless procession of influence situations that we enter, yet each of us continues to maintain an illusion of personal invulnerability. It is only when the situational forces become so obviously unfair—so physically suppressive or psychologically repressive—that we question the ethics of the change situation.

In this sense, then, one may talk about the politics of persuasion since an influence attempt backed by society is persuasion sanctioned by established policy. If a *communicator* advocates change which is not acceptable to the power structure controlling the resources of the society, then pressure is applied to change the communicator. Attempts are made to bring him back in line or, failing this, to reject him through relabeling as a "revolutionary," "radical," or "traitor."

Society in the United States is now in a state of confusion because agents of change whose persuasive influence once was sanctioned by society are no longer granted dispensation to use the approved labels "educator," "pediatrician," and so forth, or to be immune from persuasion attempts themselves. It then becomes obvious to former "targets" that there was previously an implicit contract of complicity and that there still is with other agents. When people become aware of this duplicity and cognizant of the hidden situational forces, they lose trust in parents, educators, politicians, and all those who now reveal themselves as undercover agents of change. They become cynical toward a system which professes to function for the people when, in fact, it functions for the communicator and his powerful backers, the "Society." Finally, when the illusion of individual assertiveness, resistance, and willpower disintegrates under the realization of the overwhelming forces operating to keep even their "personal" communicators in line, then feelings of hopelessness come to the surface.

If a society, through its political power base, wanted to make war and not peace, and most of its traditional communicators have supported this view (or did not openly oppose it), how could the society ever be changed? The two alternatives are revolution, which destroys the established base of power, or persuasion, which redirects available knowledge and tactics and utilizes former "targets" as new agents of communication.

The remainder of this paper presents one attempt to apply the research findings of social psychology and the salesman's intuition to just this problem. Can "students" and young people effectively persuade adults, who collectively have the power to change the system, to use their voting power in an effort to promote peace?

Tactics and strategies designed to achieve this goal will be formulated explicitly, and then, for purposes of comparison, the tactics of the police interrogator will be outlined. The ethical issues involved in attempting "to turn a society around" by working through its system will not be discussed, but the question of using "Machiavellian" techniques on an individual in order to do so will be raised.

PERSUADING FOR NEW POLITICS

Preparing for the Initial Contact

A. Be Informed.   Get as much accurate, up-to-date, reliable evidence as you can. Commit important facts, arguments, statistics, and quotations to memory so they are "natural" when you need them. You should see yourself as more expert on the particular issue of concern than the people you will try to persuade. Your perceived competence is a very important source trait. However, *do not use information as a put-down*. Do not overkill. Hold your storehouse in reserve and select only the facts you need.

B. Learn as Much as You Can about Those You Will Engage.   Be familiar with their neighborhood, local issues, basic values, language style (use of diction, clichés, homilies), source of local pride and discontent, the nature of usual influence media, attitudes on the issue in question, and the like. You can obtain this information from local businessmen (barbers, cab drivers, grocery store employees, bartenders, and others), salesmen, letters to the newspaper, and distinguishing characteristics of the neighborhood or the individual home. You can also encourage people to state their opinions on preliminary telephone surveys. When you are in this learning phase, do not try to exert influence.

C. Actively Role-Play with a Friend the Anticipated Situation. Imagine and then work through as realistically as possible the persuasion situation in which you will operate. If available, tape-record or videotape such dress rehearsals and then critically analyze your performance. Switch roles and try to be the target person in the situation where he is experiencing the pressure to comply to a request for some commitment.

D. Do a Critical Self-Appraisal. Analyze your own personal strengths and weaknesses, your appearance, and discuss any source of fear, anxiety, anticipated embarrassment, and so forth with one or more persons with whom you feel comfortable before you actually start out.

E. Be Confident. Expect that you will be effective more often than not. You must expect some setbacks, but you must be dedicated to winning, to making the "sale." If you do not handle the situation carefully, you may produce the undesirable effect of increasing the person's resistance to any further influence attempts by others, or you may generate a backlash effect yourself. If you blow it once or twice, or if you get doors slammed in your face before you even start talking (this will surely happen in some neighborhoods), keep trying. If you lose your confidence, however, or you get negative results in a variety of neighborhoods with a variety of techniques, then perhaps you are not suited for face-to-face confrontations and your talents could be put to better use elsewhere.

F. Be Sensitive to the Varied Reasons Underlying the Attitude(s) in Question. Attitudes are formed and maintained because of needs for information, for social acceptance by other people, or for ego protection from unacceptable impulses and ideas. Deeply held attitudes probably have all three of these motivational bases. *Information per se* is probably the least effective way of *changing* attitudes and behavior. Its effectiveness is maximum at the attitude-formation stage when the person has not yet taken a stand and put his ego on the dotted line. Your general approach must acknowledge that the individual is more than a rational, information processor— sometimes he is irrational, inconsistent, unresponsive to social rewards, or primarily concerned about how he appears to himself and to others.

G. Even as a Stranger You Can Exert Considerable Influence. You can be an effective agent for change by serving as a model for some behavior by publicly engaging in it, selectively reinforcing some opinions rather than others, and providing a new source of social contact, recognition, and reward for many people.

Gaining Access to and Establishing the Contact

A. Before you can persuade, you must get the person to acknowledge your presence, to attend to you and to follow your presentation. People are wary of an assault on their privacy and "life space" by an unknown person on their doorstep. You might want to consider an initial phone call or letter to contacts to be made at home.

B. If you are making a home contact, be aware of the particular situation you have encountered. Be sure that the person is willing to give you the required time. You might be interrupting dinner, a phone call, a family quarrel, a visit with guests, or some bad news. You do not want the dominant motivation of the homeowner to be to get rid of you as soon as possible.

C. Although strangers can influence everyday behavior, persuasion is enhanced when the target perceives some basic similarity with the source. This "strategy of identification" (practiced by all good entertainers and politicians) involves finding something in common between you. Physical similarity is the most obvious: age, sex, race, ethnic features, dress (distribution of hair). In addition, similarity is inferred from voice dialect, regionalisms, and appropriate slang, jargon, or group-membership-identifying phrases (for example, "such a lot of *chutzpah* he's got, that vice president," or "People like us who work for a living have callouses on their hands; a politician like X who talks about working for the people, probably has them only on his mouth.") Canvassing should be arranged to optimize this perceived similarity by selecting neighborhoods and locations which are approximately matched to the available canvassers. The canvasser should try to uncover as many points of similarity as possible because similarity breeds familiarity, which breeds liking and enhances credibility and greater acceptance of the message.

D. Students are not seen as credible sources on most issues that concern them directly, and to be effective, it is important that they increase their source credibility. This may be accomplished in a number of ways:

1. Impress the audience with your expertise, concern, and dedication, being forceful but not overbearing.
2. Make some points which are against your own best interest: indicate the sacrifices you have made and would be willing to make.
3. Have a respected person introduce you, make the contact for you.
4. Begin by agreeing with what the audience wants to hear, or with whatever they say first.
5. Minimize your manipulative intent until you ask for the commitment.

E. Avoid group situations where the majority are known or expected to be against you, since they will provide support for each other and their cohesion might make salient the group norm that you appear to be attacking (which they never cherished so much before your attack).

Maintaining, Intensifying, Directing the Interpersonal Relationship

Once you have managed to get the person to receive you, then you must hold this attention, while trying to get your message (and yourself) accepted.

A. You have the power to reinforce many behaviors of the target person, a power you should use judiciously but with conscious awareness of what and how you are reinforcing.

1. Listen attentively to what the other person has to say about anything of personal interest. This not only "opens up" the person for a dialogue, and helps in establishing what are the primary values, beliefs, and organization of his (or her) thinking, but establishes you as someone open to what others have to say. (The opportunity to tell a college student where to get off is very rewarding for many people.)

2. Maintain eye contact with the person and as close physical proximity as seems acceptable to the person.

3. Individuate the person, by using names (with Mr. or Mrs. or titles where there is an age or status discrepancy). Make the person feel you are reacting to his uniqueness and individuality—*which you should be*—and are not reacting in a programmed way to your stereotyped conception of a housewife, blue-collar worker, etc. Similarly, help the other person to individuate you, to break through the categorization and pigeonholing process which makes you just an anonymous canvasser. At some point, describe something personal or unique about your feelings, background, interests, and so forth (which you expect will be acceptable). However, once accomplished, then do not allow yourself to be the exception to the stereotype—say, "most other students are like me in how we feel about X."

4. Reinforce specific behaviors explicitly and immediately, by nodding, saying "good," "that's an interesting point," and the like. Reinforce more general classes of behavior by smiling, and by making it obvious you enjoy the interaction and by being impressed with the person's openness, sensitivity, intelligence, or articulateness. As a student with a lot of "book learning" you can still learn a lot from people who have gone to the "school of hard knocks," who have "real-life learning" and "street savvy" to offer you. Let them know that this is how you feel when talking to someone who has not had the benefit of your degree of education.

5. The person must perceive that you personally care about and are enthusiastic about the item(s) under discussion; moreover he/she must perceive that *you* as a person really care about the complaint act—at a personal level and not merely as part of your role.

6. Your reinforcement rate should increase over the course of the interaction, so that ideally, at the end of the time, the person is sorry to see you leave.

B. Be aware of sources of resentment against you for what you represent by your physical appearance, group membership (as a student), and the like; work first to differentiate those biased and often unfounded feelings and reactions from those reactions you want to elicit by your influence attempt.

Working class people in particular will resent you for having an easy life. They have worked with their hands, strained their backs, calloused their knees, scrubbing, lifting, sweating, struggling, eking out a measly subsistence, while you (as they see it) sit on your butt and have every need catered to. You can blunt this resentment in at least two ways: (1) by showing respect, even awe, for how hard they work, acknowledging that you found it really tough that summer you worked as a hod-carrier, and so forth; (2) by offhandedly noting what a sweat you had studying for that last calculus exam, that while other students may have a lot of money, *you* don't and you don't know whether you can afford to make it through college, and the like—whatever you can honestly say to undercut the perception that you are privileged and spoiled.

In contrast, middle-class office workers are likely to resent you for a different set of reasons: that (according to the stereotype) you do not show respect for your elders, that you are an uncouth, dirty, disruptive, pot-smoking libertine, and so forth. A neat appearance and considerate, respectful manner will do much to combat this stereotype.

C. Plan the organization of your approach well enough so that it seems natural and unplanned, and be flexible enough to modify it as necessary.

1. Do not surround your best arguments with tangential side arguments or a lot of details. Arguments that come in the middle of a presentation are remembered least well. Put your stronger arguments first if you want to motivate or interest uninvolved people.

2. Draw your conclusions explicitly. Implicit conclusion drawing should be left for only very intelligent audiences.

3. Repeat the main points in your argument, and the major points of agreement between you and the target person.

D. Tailor your approach to the target person.

1. Do not put him on the defensive, or even encourage or force a public defense of (and thus commitment to) any position against you. Opposing beliefs are seen as providing the opportunity for open discussion, and as a starting point to find areas of common agreement. If the person is for you, then get a public commitment early, and try to make that commitment more stable and more extreme than it was originally.

2. If possible, have the person restate your ideas and conclusions for himself, in his own words (encourage active participation).

3. If the person appears to be very authoritarian in manner and thinking, then he will probably be more impressed by status sources, decisiveness, and one-sided generalizations than by informational appeals, expert testimony, unbiased presentation of both sides of the issue, and so forth. Make any approach responsive to the dominant personality and social characteristics of the person to whom you are talking.

4. Work in pairs. Although a more personal relationship can be established in a two-person interaction, there is much to be gained from teamwork. Working in pairs provides each student with social support, lowers apprehension about initiating each new contact, and allows one of you to be "off the firing line" appraising the situation, to come in when help is needed, to refocus the direction, or respond to some specific trait detected in the target person. There are several ways in which teams can be composed to produce interesting effects. There is a general principle covering them all; namely, *the two members of the team should differ in some obvious characteristic, such as temperament, age, or sex.* There are two reasons behind this

principle: first, it maximizes the chances that either one or the other member will be similar to the target person and therefore can gain a persuasive advantage at the appropriate moment; second, it promotes that subtle idea that even when people differ in outward characteristics, they can still agree on the important issue of peace—therefore, the target person, who may differ from both persuaders, can be encouraged to agree also. The obverse of this "team difference" principle is also important: *it is very inefficient for similar canvassers to accompany each other.*

Getting the Commitment and Terminating the Contract

Do not insist that the person accept and believe what you have said before he makes a behavioral commitment. Get the behavioral commitment anyway, and attitude change will follow. The ideal conclusion of the contact will also leave the person feeling that the time spent was worthwhile and his self-esteem will be greater than it was before you arrived.

A. Do not overstay your welcome or be forced to stay longer than is worthwhile according to your time schedule. Timing is essential both in knowing when to ask for the commitment and in knowing when to quit with an intractable person. For a person who needs more time to think, encourage him if you get a promise to allow you to come back.

B. Provide several levels of possible behavioral alternatives for the person: pushing the most extreme is likely to get a greater level of compliance even if the extreme is rejected.

C. Be clear as to what actions are requested or what has been agreed upon or concluded.

D. Use a "bandwagon" effect, if called for, to indicate prestigious others who have joined in the action.

E. When you believe the target person is about to make the commitment (or after a verbal agreement is made), stress the fact that the decision is his own; it involves free choice, no pressure. This maximizes the dissonance experienced by the decision made and forces the individual to make his behavior internally consistent by generating his own intrinsic justification for his behavior. Each person is his own best persuader. After the final commitment, honestly and openly thank the person and reinforce his behavior.

F. Broaden the contact in two ways. First, get the name of one or more neighbors who would agree with that person's position—you will talk to them too and use the person's name if that is O.K. with him. Second, honestly react to something about his person which is irrelevant to the main social/political issue at hand—the house, decor, hair, clothes, and avocation mentioned, or a favor which you can do related to something mentioned.

G. Extend your influence if you can get the target person also to be an agent of influence. Try to enlist his aid in getting at least one other person to agree to do what he has just done. He should be motivated to proselytize at this time, especially if he is an outgoing person good at persuading others. If he convinces others, that will reduce his own doubts about whether he has done the right thing.

MACHIAVELLIAN STRATEGIES

Just how far should you go to make the "sale," to get the commitment? The answer to such a question depends ultimately on a complex interplay of ethical, ideological, and pragmatic issues. Each individual must establish his own set of weighting coefficients to determine how much pressure he is willing to exert. Assuming that your approach will achieve your purpose, is it "right," "proper," "decent," "humane," "moral" for you to deceive someone, to hit him below his unconscious, to arouse strong negative feelings of guilt, anxiety, shame, or even positive feelings of false pride? Behaving unethically for whatever reason pollutes the psychological environment by replacing trust, understanding, and mutual respect with deceit, lies, and cynicism.

Police interrogation manuals state: "When you break a man by torture, he will always hate you. If you break him by your intelligence he will always fear and respect you" (Kidd, 1940, p. 49). This generalization may hold only when he does not realize that you, in fact, have broken him by intention. When deception techniques are employed by a sophisticated, trained practitioner, the "victim"—be he a criminal subject, collegiate experimental subject, or "mark" in a pool hall hustle—does not realize he has been conned. But *you* always know what your intention was and that you "broke a man" thus. What effect does such knowledge have upon you? Do you respect yourself more because of it? Do you begin to depersonalize other human beings as they become notches on your gun handle, "hits/misses," "easy cases/tough customers"? Thus, you must reflect upon the psychological effects of behaving unethically, both upon the target person and upon yourself. If you are so ideologically committed to your cause or goal that any ends justify the means, then ethical issues will get a zero weighting coefficient. But that alone should give you pause.

a. Will it be possible to restore ethical precepts after your ends have been achieved?

b. If you have been converted to such an extreme view, can others be similarly moved without recourse to deception?

c. Have you not been duped into the extreme position you now hold?

d. Are you being honest with yourself in recognizing that you are about to be dishonest with others, and are not covering up the fact with rationalizations about "the other side did it first" (if that's true then the poor victim gets it from both ends).

Finally, if you cast ethics to the wind, yet proceed firmly convinced that Goodness, Justice, and Truth are what you stand for, then ask one more practical question: "Is it likely to work?" How much effort, training, staging, and time will it take to carry off the caper? Are you the type of person who can be effective at this game? What happens if the person discovers the gimmick? Will each "miss" turn into a "boomerang" or a backlash that will actively work against your cause? Will you then get only the immediate, small behavioral compliance, but blow the hoped-for bigger subsequent commitment and attitude change? Have you "ruined" the person for further persuasion attempts (or experiments) by your colleagues?

Having posed and answered such questions to your own satisfaction, and if you still want to go for broke, then the time has come to go Machiavellian. Once such a decision has been made, your only concern is to find the weak points of the target person, and learn what conditions to manipulate and how best to exploit the unsuspecting victim.

Before describing several concrete examples of how Machiavellian tactics can be utilized in even such an incongruous situation as a "peace campaign," let us see how they are already effectively being used.

The Police Interrogator Misrepresents a Little Bit

Confessions are often obtained by either minimizing the seriousness of the offense and allowing the suspect a "face-saving" out, or by the opposite through misrepresenting and exaggerating the seriousness of the crime.

The first approach can be accomplished through "extenuation"—in which the investigator reports that he does not take too seriously a view of the subject's indiscretion, since he has seen thousands of others in the same situation. Or he may "shift the blame" to circumstances, the environment, or a subject's weaknesses, any of which might lead anyone to do what the suspect did. A more morally acceptable motive may be suggested for the crime, such as self-defense, an accident, a mistake, heat of passion, and so forth. In order to "open up" a suspect, it is recommended that good "bait" is to blame anyone who might be associated with the crime other than the suspect; for example, an accomplice, a fence, a company, loan sharks, or even the victim.

Some provocative examples of the way in which experts use this approach in order to misrepresent the nature of the crime to the suspect in order to get him to talk about it are:

1. A 50-year old man accused of having taken "indecent liberties" with a 10-year-old girl was told:
   "This girl is well developed for her age. She probably learned a lot about sex from the boys in the neighborhood and from the movies and TV; and knowing what she did about it, she may have deliberately tried to excite you to see what you would do" (Inbau & Reid, 1962, p. 45).

2. Or, in forcible rape cases, "where circumstances permit, the suggestion might be offered that the rape victim acted like she might be a prostitute . . . that the police knew she had been engaged in acts of prostitution on other occasions" (Inbau & Reid, 1962, p. 46).

3. "During the interrogation of a married rape suspect, blame may be cast upon the subject's wife for not providing him with the necessary sexual gratification. "When a fellow like you doesn't get it at home, he seeks it elsewhere' " (Inbau & Reid, 1962, p. 51).

Once the suspect is in a state of emotional confusion, then "he is unable to think logically and clearly, since his sense of values has been disturbed and his imagination is distorting his perspective. It is possible for the investigator to obtain admissions or even a confession from the suspect by further misrepresenting the picture" (O'Hara, 1956, p. 105).

This misrepresentation can take the form of a "knowledge bluff"—revealing a few known items and pretending to know more, or lying to the suspect that his fingerprints, blood, etc. were found at the scene of the crime (even show him falsified samples and records). In some cases of murder, it might be stated that the victim is not dead or, as happened in Minneapolis, a youthful offender, John Biron, might be told that he will be tried as a juvenile when it was known that he is legally an adult (see *Time Magazine,* December 3, 1965, p. 52; April 29, 1966, p. 65).

Since modern interrogation involves establishing "rapport" or a meaningful interpersonal relationship between the suspect and the interrogator, it must involve a distortion of the social-psychological situation. Even before the questioning begins; the interrogator is urged to role-play the position of the subject in order to be able to respond to him—"man to man, not as policeman to prisoner" (Inbau & Reid, 1962, p. 19).

Under this category would fall all the appeals which depend upon the interrogator being friendly, kind, sympathetic, understanding, "a Dutch uncle," or an older brother. He is the one who provides social approval and recognition, who accords the suspect status, and is aware of and able to manipulate the suspect because of his social values, feelings of pride, and class or group membership.

The police manuals recognize that "It is a basic human trait to seek and enjoy the approval of other persons." Therefore, it is wise to flatter some subjects, for example, by complimenting an accused driver of a getaway car for his maneuvering and "cornering," or by comparing a juvenile with his movie idol, or a member of a racial group with a respectable, outstanding member of that group. This approach apparently works best with "the uneducated and underprivileged," since they "are more vulnerable to flattery than the educated person or the person in favorable financial circumstances."

A slightly different approach is needed for the white-collar first offender, which includes clerks, managers, cashiers, office workers, professionals, and teachers—in short, most of the audience of this book. Since these people traditionally subscribe to orthodox ethical principles and conventional moral standards, the calm, dignified approach of the physician is respected and effective. One police manual author states rather boldly: "The character of a person in this category is weak and must be exploited fully" (O'Hara, 1956).

To create rapport, the interrogator could pat the suspect on the shoulder, grip his hand, or offer to do a favor for him—get water, talk to his wife, employer, etc. O'Hara says (1956): "Gestures of this type produce a very desirable effect. They import an attitude of understanding and sympathy better than words."

For suspects who have pride in their family, if an attempt to get their parents to cooperate fails, their attention is called to a (faked) circular being prepared for broadcast and distribution throughout the country. It not only describes the fugitive, but lists all of his known relatives' names and addresses as possible leads for approaching him. Cooperation quite often is obtained in this way.

The reader may recall that in the famous case of George Whitmore, Jr. (who confessed to the slaying of two society girls in New York in 1963), he gave a 61-page typed confession after 20 hours of interrogation. He virtually sentenced himself to death or life imprisonment with this confession—which later was proved false and coerced when the true murderer was subsequently exposed.

MAKING MACHIAVELLI WORK FOR PEACE

The following hypothetical examples do not have the time-tested validity of those reported in the police interrogator's literature; rather, they merely illustrate how such tactics can be adapted to suit virtually any cause. The content of our cause will be related to "canvassing for peace," but one could imagine an adversary who could use them to canvass for war.

A. Mutt and Jeff.   The so-called Mutt and Jeff technique of police interrogation involves a sneaky one-two punch in grilling suspects. A rough analog of this tactic in political persuasion can be devised. One persuader is militant in style and extreme in his position; the second persuader is moderate and reasonable as if to save the listener from the excess of the first, but in fact exacts a considerable concession by virtue of his soothing performance.

A very skilled and aggressive antiwar debater, who is dying to be turned loose but who may sometimes turn people off, can be paired with a sympathetic gentlemanly type who can gently chide him in the presence of the listener with remarks such as, "My friend may be overdoing it a little because he feels so strongly about the war, but what I would say on this point is that the war is much too expensive. I think that this is a position with which most hard-headed Americans can agree." Thus, the "moderate" brings the listener over to his side by using the "militant" as a foil.

This technique at best must be used very delicately and sparingly. It is double-edged. Too much "Mutt" militance on the doorstep will drive the listener up the wall, and both may get thrown out before Jeff can intervene. Furthermore, it takes a couple of good ham actors to carry it off, and too much "con" in the canvassing operation would be unfortunate, especially if neighbors compare notes.

B. The Stigmatized Persuader.   Recent research has found that a person with a visible stigma (such as blind or crippled) elicits a mixed reaction. There is sympathy and a tendency to want to help in some way, but also considerable tension from guilt, revulsion, and resentment (the disabled person has intruded himself upon the complacent life space of the individual). These basic motives to help and to ignore can both be elicited by having a person with a real or faked stigma appear on the doorstep (for example, a pretty girl with a scar, a boy on crutches, a team of whom one member is apparently blind). After the general introduction, the person with the stigma clearly states the level of commitment desired and then suggests that if the person does not want to act on it now, they could perhaps spend some time together talking it over. Embarrassed sympathy will make it difficult to terminate the interaction brusquely, but if an easy way out is provided by the canvasser, it will be the preferred way of resolving the conflict. They may sign now to avoid facing the stigmatized of the world any more than is necessary.

C. The "Overheard" Communication.   It is a well-known result of studies of persuasive communication that a message accidentally overheard can be more effective than when the speaker is aware of the listener's presence. In the "accidental" case, the listener has no reason to be suspicious that the speaker is trying to manipulate him.

The following setup tries to utilize this advantage of overhearing. Since it is an artifice, it is not recommended for widespread use.

In a possible one-person version, a coed enters a busy laundromat with a basket of laundry, puts the clothes in the machine, and asks another customer for change of a quarter to make a phone call to her mother. While pretending to call Mom she describes the chores she is doing and checks on the groceries she is to buy at the supermarket. "A daughter like that, I should only have," is the kind of thought running through the heads of the women there. "Good Daughter" then proceeds to talk to her mother briefly about the war and agree with her mother that it is awfully important to end this terrible war very soon and that she is happy that the mother has written to her congressman, and hopes she will also vote for Candidate X. She talks loudly enough to let the target audience hear, but goes about her business when she is finished, unless someone in the audience initiates a conversation.

Variations on this idea can be adapted for use in bus stations, drugstores, barber shops, and other such places, although this technique suffers from the general difficulty that the same person cannot wash the same bundle repeatedly, call the same Mom over and over, or get more than a few hair cuts a day without seeming very peculiar indeed.

The two-person version is more practical. This can be enacted when riding back and forth on crowded subways or buses, never traveling the same line at the same hour of a weekday. A student and an older person (his uncle or Dad, presumably) make the ideal team. The two get into a spirited argument about today's mood of campus protest. Even though they argue, it is obvious that they have a great deal of affection for each other, and the student (or son) slips in references to good behaviors ("When I was fixing our sink last night with that rusty drainpipe, I was thinking down the drain, down the drain, boy, all the money we're spending in Vietnam is just going right down the drain, totally wasted"). Their voices are raised just enough so that people can hear, but not enough to be obnoxious. The Dad complains that students aren't working hard like he did in his day (avoid references to riots, drugs, and the like—the most intense antistudent issues). The son agrees that this may be true, but the reason is that they are disillusioned because America is fighting an expensive, faraway war when there are all these problems that need working on at home. The Dad tentatively offers a few lukewarm arguments in favor of present war policy, but soon changes his mind when the student confidently (but not arrogantly) cites facts and arguments for quick withdrawal. The Dad agrees to write against the war to his congressman, but counterattacks with gusto on the issue of student laziness. The son now concedes this point (it would not leave a good taste with the listeners if the cocky son triumphed completely over the wishy-washy Dad). The son resolves to get back to his campus and get all his buddies more involved in their own education and in constructive action. He complements his Dad on his understanding and on all he has done all these years for his son. They now chat amiably about other things.

POSTSCRIPT

The fundamental thesis of this paper is reflected in Bandura's (1969) perceptive concern for the potential misuse of the therapist's influence in his one-way power relation with those labeled "patients."

As behavioral science makes further progress toward the development of efficacious principles of change, man's capacity to create the type of social environment he wants will be substantially increased. The decision process by which cultural priorities are established must, therefore, be made more explicit to ensure that "social engineering" is utilized to produce living conditions that enrich life and behavioral freedom rather than aversive human effects. [p. 112].

REFERENCES

Bandura, A. *Principles of Behavior Modification.*New York: Holt, 1969.

Hovland, C. I. "Reconciling Conflicts Results Derived from Experimental and Survey Studies of Attitude Change," *American Psychologist* 14, 1954, pp. 8–17.

Inbau, F. E., and J. E. Reid, *Criminal Interrogation and Confessions.* Baltimore: Williams & Wilkins, 1962.

Kidd, W. R. "Police Interrogation," *The Police Journal.* New York, 1940.

Milgram, S. "Behavioral Study of Obedience," *Journal of Abnormal and Social Psychology* 67, 1963, pp. 371–78.

Mulbar, H. *Interrogation.* Springfield, Ill: Charles C. Thomas, 1951.

O'Hara, C. E. *Fundamentals of Criminal Investigation.* Springfield, Ill: Charles C. Thomas, 1956.

Orne, M. "On the Social Psychology of the Psychological Experiment: With Special Reference to Demand Characteristics of Their Implications," *American Psychologist* 17, 1962, pp. 776–85.

Time Magazine, December 3, 1965, p. 52.

Time Magazine, April 29, 1966, p. 65.

A New Paradigm in the Psychology of Persuasion

Icek Ajzen

Social psychologists probably have expended more time, effort, and ingenuity on the study of persuasion than on the study of any other single issue. Communication and persuasion was one of the first problems to be submitted to systematic investigation in the social psychological laboratory, and despite mounting frustrations, social psychologists have never lost interest in the topic. Until only a few years ago, much of the work on persuasion was guided by a conceptual framework developed in the 1950s by Hovland and his associates at Yale University. Although this framework made reference to the processing of information contained in a persuasive communication, particularly to questions of attention, comprehension, and acceptance, most of the empirical research that was generated had little to do with processes of this kind. In fact, the contents of persuasive messages and the receiver's reaction to the information they contain were largely neglected. Instead, the approach taken by Hovland and his associates encouraged research on a variety of other factors, external to the message, which were thought to influence the effectiveness of a given communication. These factors concerned the characteristics of the communicator, such as his or her credibility; the characteristics of the receiver, such as the receiver's intelligence or involvement; and the general features of the situation, such as the amount of fear generated by the message or forewarning of persuasive intent. In the course of more than 30 years, virtually thousands of empirical and theoretical papers were published on these issues; yet despite this massive effort, the outcome was singularly disappointing. As many reviewers of this literature have noted, the Hovland approach produced an accumulation of largely inconsistent and often contradictory research findings that yielded few, if any, generalizable principles of effective communication.

It is against this backdrop of failure that Petty and Cacioppo's theoretical and empirical work on the "elaboration likelihood model" must be evaluated. In the past 10 years, these investigators have almost single-handedly fostered a revolution in the study of communication and persuasion. In stark contrast to the frustratingly incon-clusive results of earlier efforts, the prolific output from Petty and Cacioppo's labo-ratories has begun to produce a sensible and coherent body of knowledge related to persuasive communication. Their latest book, *Communication and Persuasion: Central and Peripheral Routes to Attitude Change,* provides a general, up-to-date overview of their approach. It presents the elaboration likelihood model in some detail and summarizes the current status of empirical research designed to test and validate the theoretical framework, research generated primarily by the authors and their students.

Petty and Cacioppo's secret of success, if there is a secret, lies in their rejection of the view of persuasion implicit in the Hovland school of thought. Variables related to the source, receiver, and the context of a persuasive communication, termed peripheral cues, are ac-corded secondary importance. Of primary importance is the extent to which receivers of a persuasive communication carefully and thoughtfully assess and elaborate on the central merits of the advocated position. Central processing of this kind is expected to change attitudes in the advocated direction to the extent that issue-relevant thoughts produced are predominantly favorable. It is thus the nature of the receiver's thoughts that is held primarily responsible for attitude change. Only when the receivers are not motivated or are incapable of elaborating on the arguments contained in the message may attitude change proceed along the peripheral route, without much attention to the merits of the arguments. Under those conditions, receivers' attitudes may be influenced by "affect transfer" from situational stimuli to the message (i.e., by classical conditioning) or by simple cognitive heuristics (e.g., "if an expert advocates a certain position, it must be right").

As might be expected, therefore, much of the research reported in the present monograph is concerned with the likelihood that message elaboration will take place and with the evaluative direction of such elaboration. Among the factors found to increase elaboration likelihood are high involvement of the receiver, low distraction, moderate message repetition, more than one message source, and high need for cog-nition on the part of the receiver. The thoughts generated under high message elabo-ration are found to be predominantly favorable when the message contains strong, cogent arguments and to be predominantly unfavorable when the message contains largely weak arguments. Moreover, elaboration can be biased, usually in the direction of the receiver's initial position, depending on such factors as amount of prior knowl-edge and forewarning of persuasive intent.

The peripheral route to persuasion, emphasized by the Hovland school of thought, is also integrated into the elaboration likelihood model. When involvement is low or dis-traction is high, receivers are unlikely to generate many message-relevant thoughts. Under these conditions, attitude change is shown to be affected by the expertise and likability of the source, by the number of arguments contained in the message, by pleasant background music, and by other peripheral cues. Petty and Cacioppo thus confirm the importance of some of the variables studied in the past, but they also show that these variables become important only under conditions of low elaboration likelihood. In this manner, they manage to account for many conflicting findings of past research.

In a comparison of the two roads to persuasion—reliance on central processing or on peripheral cues—the central road is the overwhelming favorite. It produces attitude change that is more lasting, more resistant to counterpropaganda, and more predictive of future behavior.

Clearly, Petty and Cacioppo and their elaboration likelihood model have achieved a great deal in a relatively short period of time, not all of which could be mentioned in this short review. Nevertheless, much work remains to be done. Any discussion of fear appeals in persuasion, a hotly debated topic in the field, is conspicuously absent. What is the likely effect of fear arousal on message-relevant thoughts and therefore on attitude change? Similarly, the present monograph has little to say about the question of humor in persuasion, an issue that has generated considerable interest in recent years. Another area that deserves greater attention in future work on the model are changes in cognitive structure that are postulated to result from message elaboration. To what extent are the new thoughts that are generated by a message incorporated into the receiver's system of salient beliefs? The present monograph makes little distinction between thoughts generated by a message and beliefs held as a result of message elaboration. Instead, it is assumed without question that any new thoughts will be automatically integrated into the existing belief system.

But these are really minor points that should not detract from the importance of the present volume. Although not polished in style and perhaps a bit difficult for the unsophisticated reader, this book provides a wealth of useful and important information for applied and theoretical purposes. Partial overviews and summaries are available elsewhere, but the present monograph is the best and most complete source of information about the elaboration likelihood model and the research it has generated. This book should be required reading for all students and professionals interested in the psychology of persuasion.

How to Increase Your Influence

David E. Berlew

Negotiation is nothing more than a process for reaching agreement when there are conflicting interests. The basis of negotiation is exchange: every party gains and gives concessions until they reach agreement. Negotiation appears to be the most effective process for this purpose, but unfortunately it is complex and difficult to do well. In every negotiation course I have taught, an overdependence on logical persuasion has been the biggest obstacle to effective negotiating. To understand why, it is necessary to examine what I will call the logical persuasion influence strategy.

To pursue a logical persuasion strategy, the influencer makes a proposal or suggestion and supports it with facts or reasons. If the "influence target" is inclined to resist, he or she will challenge the weakest of the influencer's supporting arguments by offering counterarguments. The influencer refutes the target's weakest counterargument. And so it goes, back and forth, until one party concedes or both become weary. With each round of argument and counterargument is the danger of getting farther and farther away from the influencer's objective.

Logical persuasion works best when one party is acknowledged as having more expertise than the other, and when neither party has a vested interest in the position. By this I mean that they have something to gain if their own proposal is accepted, and something to lose by accepting the other party's proposal.

Logical persuasion is least effective as a strategy for reaching agreement when expertise is balanced or unrecognized, and when each party has a vested interest in his or her position.

Let us examine a typical line-staff interaction. A training manager proposes to a senior line manager that the latter identify the training and development needs of his management and professional staff using a new needs assessment methodology just developed by the training department. To support the proposal, the training manager gives three reasons: it will give the line manager more detailed information about the development needs of his staff than the informal method used previously; the new needs assessment methodology is state of the art; and a standardized methodology will provide comparable data regarding development needs across the entire organization.

The senior line manager rejects the training manager's proposal, giving the following reasons: the informal method he used in the past is quite adequate; new state-of-the-art systems are never reliable until they have been field-tested for at least one year; and comparable data are unnecessary because the work his unit does and his staff's development needs are unique in the organization.

The training manager probably will challenge the weakest of the line manager's three reasons, beginning an argument/counterargument spiral. Given this start, reaching a mutually satisfactory agreement quickly, if at all, is unlikely. To get her needs assessment study done, the training manager will have to get support from a higher level. This is not surprising, since we can assume that each party has a vested interest in the position he or she has taken. If the line manager will not adopt the new technology, the training manager will experience a severe setback in her new program. If the line manager agrees to use the new methodology, time and resources he would prefer to use elsewhere will be required. The training manager's technical expertise will have little impact on the line manager.

Another dynamic at work here can reduce further the effectiveness of a logical persuasion strategy. To paraphrase an oriental saying: "An idea that has to be defended is least likely to change." When the training manager pushes against the line manager with logical arguments, the line manager almost instinctively mobilizes his energy, in the form of counterarguments, to push back. Every argument elicits a counterargument, every force an equal and opposite force. This dynamic increases the probability that the logical persuasion strategy will lead to an extended debate or argument.

So what can you do when persuasion doesn't work? One alternative is to use an exchange strategy of influence: a simplified form of the negotiation process. At the most basic level it involves three elements: know what you want, ask for it, and be prepared to pay for it.

In behavioral terms, using an exchange strategy requires that you state exactly what you want or need (expectation), ask about and then listen carefully to any problems your request causes for the other person (active listening), and find ways to resolve those problems or satisfy additional needs the other person may have in order to gain his or her cooperation (offering incentives).

In our example, the training manager might use an exchange strategy this way:

Training Manager:

I would like you to use this new needs assessment technology in your division this year. (expectation) What kind of problems would that cause you? (active listening).

Line Manager:

Well, it sounds like extra work. We know how to do the informal needs assessment and it takes very little of our time.

Training Manager:

So it would take extra resources, which are limited. I know that your division is very busy. Would it cause you any other problems? (active listening)

Line Manager:

(Beginning to trust the training manager who is "pulling" rather than "pushing") Well . . . frankly, I am somewhat intimidated by the complexity of the new method. I know we can turn out a good report the old way, but if we use the new methodology we might produce a poor report, especially if we don't have enough manpower to put on it. It is a risk I would prefer not to take if I can avoid it.

Training Manager:

Since you haven't had any experience with the new methodology, you are concerned that you might not turn out a first class report, and that your division's reputation might be damaged. Is that it? (active listening)

Line Manager:

Yes, that's right. I can't think of anything else. But as you can see, it would be quite inconvenient for me to do what you ask right now.

Training Manager:

Yes, I know what I am asking is inconvenient for you. But I would really like you to do it. (expectation) Let me propose an exchange that might work for both of us. If you will agree to help me by being the first division to use the new needs assessment methodology, I will spend whatever time necessary working with you and your staff to collect the data and prepare the report. That way, you will have an extra pair of hands, and I can guarantee that your division's report will be first class. (offering incentives) Is that agreeable to you?

Line Manager:

That takes care of my problems. Under those conditions I think I can cooperate with you.

The training manager simply told the line manager what she wanted, acknowledged that it might be inconvenient for the line manager to comply, and indicated her willingness to give something to get what she wanted. By doing so, she successfully avoided a time-consuming discussion about the relative advantages of the old and new methodologies.

The power of the exchange strategy of influence stems from several sources. First, the way the training manager opened the conversation discouraged a debate on the merits of the new technology. Second, by accepting rather than questioning or refuting the problems raised by the line manager, the training manager avoided "pushing back" and thereby creating resistance. This also encouraged the line manager to be more open about his real concern. Finally, because the training manager acknowledged that what she wanted might inconvenience the line manager, he was able to let his guard down in anticipation of a balanced agreement.

Used skillfully, the exchange strategy usually results in an agreement that is fair and acceptable to both parties. The line manager did not have to accept the training manager's offer; he could have asked for more, or even refused if the training manager could not or would not offer him enough to compensate him for his inconvenience. The training manager would have to decide how important the line manager's cooperation was to her, and what she was willing to give in order to get it.

This third basic element of the exchange strategy of influence—being prepared to pay for what you want—deserves special attention. Thinking of incentives (things you can give to get what you want) as currencies of exchange is useful. In our example, the line manager had the prime currency: his agreement to cooperate. The training manager used two alternative currencies of exchange to obtain the line manager's agreement to use the new technology: her time and the guarantee of a first class report.

But what if the training manager had no time that she could give to the line manager to gain his agreement? What other incentives or currencies might she exchange? "I do not have much to offer," is a common lament of staff personnel, as well as managers trying to exert influence laterally and upward. Is that true in the training manager's case?

Let us begin with the problems the training manager is creating for the line manager by requesting his cooperation: extra work and extra risk. Type 1 currencies are anything the influencer can do that will help alleviate any problems or inconvenience that his or her request will cause the other person. If we brainstormed we might come up with several viable currencies our training manager might offer, such as:

- The assistance of one of her subordinates.
- A training session for the line manager's staff who will prepare the report.
- A "fool-proof" report format: just fill in the numbers.
- The training manager's gratitude (an intangible currency).

Although we can identify potential currencies in advance, we cannot accurately assess their value until we find out from the influence target exactly how they expect to be inconvenienced by our request.

The influencer can offer Type 2 currencies to satisfy other needs the influence target may have, that is, needs or problems other than those the influencer has caused by his or her request or expectation. In our example, possible Type 2 currencies are:

- Special training for the line manager's staff (unrelated to needs assessment).
- Rescheduling standard training sessions to the convenience of the line manager.
- Informal publicity that the line manager is enlightened and avant-garde with respect to training and development.
- Extra counseling for the line manager's problem employees.
- Consultation for the line manager on a specific problem, by the training manager or one of her colleagues from personnel.

Again, we can anticipate potential Type 2 currencies, but their exchange value is determined by the influence target's needs.

For most of us, the exchange strategy of influence is less natural and more difficult to use than a logical persuasion strategy. Logical persuasion is tolerant of imprecision; it never hurts to modify a proposal. To use the exchange strategy successfully, influencers must be clear about their basic need, and know how much they are willing to give up to satisfy it. If they ask for too little and the other party agrees, they are stuck with an unsatisfactory agreement. This would have been the case if our training manager, in her opening statement, had asked the line manager to *consider* using the new technology, and he had replied, "I would be happy to consider it," and walked away. Conversely, if the influencer asks for too much, he or she is perceived as unreasonable and loses credibility.

The exchange strategy can have negative results if it is not carried out thoughtfully and with skill. Badly implemented, it sounds like attempted bribery. Skillfully executed, it produces an agreement that both parties can accept and carry out. It leaves the impression that the influencer is a person who knows what he or she wants, and is also sensitive to the needs of the other person.

The Effects of Anger on Negotiations over Mergers and Acquisitions

Joseph P. Daly

Although emotions have been found to constitute a fundamental aspect of conflict as the involved parties perceive it, very little research has been done on the effect that emotion has on behavior in conflict situations (Pinkley, 1988). The study that forms the basis for this article focuses on a specific emotion, anger, in a specific setting, negotiations over mergers and acquisitions. The focus of the study is anger because of its potential role as a key emotion in negotiations due to its relationship to "fairness judgments." Averill (1982) found evidence indicating that anger is frequently triggered when a person feels he has been treated unfairly. Fairness is thought to be an important criterion that parties base decisions upon in settings where goods or services are exchanged (see Homans, 1961) and in dispute resolution settings (see Ury, Brett, and Goldberg, 1989). My study draws upon interviews with individuals who negotiate transactions over corporate ownership and addresses three questions:

- What triggers anger in negotiations?
- What effect does anger have on negotiation process and outcomes?
- Once we have a sense of the causes and effects of anger, what are some implications of that knowledge for negotiation practice?

The principal lesson that emerges from the interviews is that anger tends to have two types of effects on an angered negotiator's behavior, an "information processing effect" and a "goal orientation effect." The information processing effect inhibits the angered negotiator's ability as a decision maker to search effectively for mutually agreeable solutions. The goal orientation effect is a shift that tends to occur in the angered individual's priorities; instead of pursuing profit maximization goals, the angered individual tends to more readily pursue profit maximization goals, the angered individual tends to more readily pursue goals that involve punishing or retaliating against the

Reprinted from Joseph Daly, "The Effects of Anger on Negotiations over Mergers and Acquisitions," *Negotiation Journal*, January 1991, pp. 31–39. Used with permission of Plenum Publishing Corporation and the author.

offending party. Both types of effect are likely to inhibit problem-solving behavior in negotiations. However, the information processing effect of anger is likely to be common to all emotions. While all emotions may have predictable effects on a person's goal orientations, the effects of anger are not likely to be the same as for other emotions.

For the study, interviews were conducted with 10 individuals who participate in negotiating merger and acquisition transactions. Six were corporate managers, two were investment bankers, one an in-house corporate attorney; and one an accountant who had both advised merger clients and negotiated his own accounting firm's merger with another firm.

I chose the mergers and acquisitions context because it is a setting where financial incentives are relatively great and where the values and training of the participants encourage them to focus on the financial aspects of the deal. Therefore, emotional issues are not generally a factor at the outset of the negotiations. If emotional conflicts do occur, they will be more noticeable in the financial market context than in negotiation settings where personal relationships are involved, such as divorce mediation.

Obviously, the choice of the mergers and acquisitions context necessarily limits our ability to make generalizations about the causes and effects of anger. The conditions that trigger anger in mergers and acquisitions negotiations are unlikely to be the same as those that trigger anger in negotiation settings such as divorce mediation because of fundamental differences in the nature of the relationship between the parties. Anger tends to be triggered by violations of normative expectations, that is, expectations that are driven by shared values (Averill, 1982). Normative expectations are distinct from simple predictions of behavior in that they are seen to have moral force to them. For example, I may expect you in a negotiation to follow a given pattern of offers and counteroffers and there may be any number of reasons—including your reputation, my past experience in bargaining, etc.—behind that expectation. When an expectation has moral force to it, when that expectation does not merely specify "party B will likely do X" but goes beyond that to take on the form, "party B is obligated to do X," the expectation is value-driven. As Rousseau (1989) points out, the nature of the parties' expectations in an exchange relationship is likely to depend on the nature of the interdependence between the parties. In relationships where interdependence is limited to economic issues—such as is usually the case in mergers and acquisitions— the parties are likely to have fewer normative expectations of each other than do the parties in relationships where interdependence extends to noneconomic issues. As a consequence, anger is likely to be triggered less often, and by different types of behavior, in mergers and acquisitions negotiations than it is in negotiation settings where the parties tend to have a more personal relationship.

A further difference between the mergers and acquisitions context and contexts such as divorce mediation is that in the divorce mediation setting anger is often "built in" to the conflict: the behaviors that have generated the conflict, in many cases, have also generated anger on one or more sides. In the mergers and acquisitions setting, by contrast, anger is more likely to be a by-product of the parties' interaction when it occurs.

In situations where anger is built in, the allegedly unfair behaviors that initially trigger anger may be primary elements of the bargaining agenda and thus relatively difficult to resolve because fairness is not quantifiable. Issues of fairness are symbolic issues that, as Gallo (1968, cited from Rubin and Brown, 1975) points out, are less amenable to concession making because they are difficult to trade off against economic issues. In settings such as those of mergers and acquisitions, when anger is generally not built in to the conflict, economic issues are more likely to dominate the agenda. Economic issues, being quantifiable, are more easily traded off against one another.

EMOTIONS

Emotions are psychological states in which an individual's evaluative judgments of a person or situation are accompanied by arousal of the autonomic nervous system, that part of the nervous system normally not under our conscious control. We cannot directly control our heartbeat, for example, which is among the functions that are affected when we get emotional. According to Mandler (1984), emotions frequently are produced by unexpected events. The unexpected event may be the disconfirmation of your image of a person or situation or it may be the interruption of your "script" for a particular situation.

Specific emotions may have "restorative action plans" associated with them. Restorative action plans are means of resolving the discrepancy that triggered the emotion in the first place. Restorative action plans may be innate (e.g., fleeing as a response to fear) or may be prescribed by cultural norms (e.g., duelling as a response to an insult among 18th century European aristocrats).

Instigating Anger

The interviewees in the study were asked to describe events that occurred during the negotiations which they observed to have triggered anger—in themselves, in members of their negotiating team, in the other party's negotiating team, or in parties they had advised. A list of the conditions described by the interviewees as likely to trigger anger appears in Table 1. These conditions are consistent with exploratory findings by Averill (1982) that anger is triggered in a person who believes that another person or group has intentionally violated an important value-laden expectation held by the angered individual. In addition, the violation must have caused harm to that person.

The Effects of Anger

As already noted, two parallel sets of effects of anger on human judgment have been observed: information processing effects and goal orientation effects. Information processing effects occur when people are in situations of decision making under uncertainty and they are highly aroused emotionally. Under those conditions, decision makers often focus their attention very narrowly on the circumstances that triggered their arousal and limit their search for decision alternatives. These effects do not occur only as a result of anger; they can occur as a result of any strong emotion. Goal orientation effects occur when angered individuals change their objectives in the situation, adopting goals that may or may not be compatible with the goals they were pursuing before they were angered. The tendency for emotionally aroused individuals

TABLE 1   Behaviors Reported as Triggering Anger in Negotiations

Misrepresentation
   Lying: Direct misrepresentation through verbal communication
   Indirect misrepresentation: Giving false impressions through verbal communication
   Nonverbal deception

Making excessively high demands

Overstepping the bounds of one's authority

Insulting the other party

Causing the other party to lose face

Showing personal animosity toward the other party in a professional relationship

Falsely accusing the other party of wrongdoing

Failing to honor agreements, both formal and informal

Failing to reciprocate the other party's concessions

Failing to adequately prepare and/or organize for the negotiation

Lacking commitment to achieving an agreement (failure to bargain in good faith)

Questioning a representative's authority to negotiate the deal

Seeking to undermine a representative's authority by "going over his or her head" to
   negotiate with his or her constituents directly

Showing excessive concern for unimportant details without putting them in the perspective of
   the larger deal

---

to make predictable changes in goals may be common to all emotions. However, the specific changes in goal orientation that emotional people make are likely to depend on the emotion that they are experiencing (e.g., whereas angry people may try to harm the persons who triggered their anger, grateful people may try to do something helpful for the persons who triggered their gratitude).

Averill (1982) believes that anger is a functional emotion because it upholds socially acceptable ways of behaving. When a standard of socially acceptable behavior is violated, Averill claims, the person(s) most directly affected by the violation are expected by others to get angry. Averill's notion of the role that norms of anger play is consistent with Fincham and Jaspers' (1979) notion that man acts as an intuitive jurist. Averill assumes that social norms provide guidelines for responding when anger is triggered just as statutory and common law provide guidelines to decision makers in legal contexts.

Depending on the circumstances surrounding the instigation of anger, and on the nature of the relationship between the violator and victim, anger can serve one of three specific purposes, according to Averill. Anger can be used to break off a relationship, to strengthen a relationship, or to vent one's feelings. The angered person's objective in responding to anger may be constructive (taking action to ensure that the violation is not repeated) or destructive (taking action to retaliate against or punish the violator).

Consistent with Averill's (1982) findings, interviewees in the study I conducted indicated that when anger is instigated in negotiation situations, the angered party's motives in the situation often shift—goal orientation effects of anger. The shift is one from evaluating the alternatives in terms of personal benefit to evaluating them in terms of how effectively they will ensure that the violation is not repeated or that there will be retaliation for the injury. Interviewees indicated that an angered negotiator was likely to shift his or her focus from evaluating the benefits of the deal to that of "teaching them a lesson":

> I think that [anger] takes you from a position of viewing the acquisition as more of a partnership—an effort by both parties to meld their assets so that everybody comes away with some benefit—to a more adversarial perspective. I might be more likely to maximize whatever advantage we had in terms of the deal than I would were the situation more friendly. I might be more likely to press for a tougher deal, something that might be less advantageous to them.

Punishment and retaliation are among the responses described by Averill's (1982) respondents as ones they had resorted to when angered (other responses included talking the situation over with the instigator or with a neutral third party). Retaliation was a response frequently used by angry negotiators in a study of face-saving behavior in bargaining by Brown (1968). Brown found that negotiators who suffered a loss of face were more likely to retaliate against the offending party and at greater cost to themselves than those who did not suffer such a loss.

When punishment or retaliation is used by angered parties in bargaining, as for example, by subjects who were trying to save face in Brown's (1968) study, it may be that the information processing effect of inducing well-learned responses encourages more aggressive responses such as punishment and retaliation. The less aggressive responses to anger described by Averill's (1982) respondents—talking the situation over with the instigator or with a neutral party—are likely to require more extensive use of judgment in many situations than does retaliation. To the extent that information processing abilities are reduced due to anger, less aggressive responses may be more difficult to implement.

As can be seen in interviewees' accounts, the effect of shifts in goal orientation is to encourage the angered negotiator to pursue contending strategies of negotiation as opposed to problem-solving strategies (Pruitt, 1981). Contending strategies are means by which one negotiator acts to maximize his or her own profit at the expense of the other party. Pruitt's problem-solving strategies are means by which a negotiator works cooperatively with the other party so that one party can gain, without the other losing, profit. Pruitt (1981, 1983) argues that problem-solving negotiators are much more likely to reach integrative solutions than are contending ones. Two necessary elements of problem-solving, according to Pruitt (1981, 1983) and Pruitt and Rubin (1986), are trust and creativity in the fashioning of trade-offs.

The information processing effects of anger are associated with a narrowing of focus that is likely to inhibit problem solving by inhibiting creative exploration of more integrative alternative solutions. The goal orientation effects of anger are likely to be associated with an inhibition of problem solving according to the Pruitt framework because a breakdown of trust often accompanies anger in exchange relationships. As Rousseau (1989) points out, when expectations are violated in exchange relationships, the victimized party tends to become more distrustful of the offending party because trust in another party is generally based on expectations regarding that party's future behavior.

IMPLICATIONS FOR NEGOTIATION PRACTICE

Several implications for negotiation practice can be drawn from our understanding of anger as it has been described here. Three such implications are: using anger as a persuasive tactic, restoring a relationship disrupted by anger, and using intermediaries to avoid negative consequences of anger.

Anger as a Persuasive Tactic

In negotiation, anger can be used to persuade the other party not to pursue a manipulative tactic or to take a hard-line stance on the grounds that the behavior in question is normatively unacceptable. The practice of using anger to emphasize issue importance may itself be ethically questionable if the negotiator who makes use of anger in this way is actually feigning anger rather than allowing himself or herself to show true anger.

Anger is only one of several means that a negotiator can use to emphasize an issue's importance. However, using anger to emphasize one's position on an issue has certain advantages. One advantage is that anger can be a very compelling influence on the other party's behavior. Growing angry at an unreasonable tactic or offer shows that the angered negotiator believes the other party ought to abandon that tactic or position as a matter of principle. Etzioni (1988) maintains that, for most people, the performance of moral commitments and duties tends to take precedence over the pursuit of economic gain. Growing angry at the other party's behavior in negotiations also has the advantage of functioning as an unspecified threat. Anger is often preliminary to aggression (Averill, 1982). When a negotiator's interests are threatened, angry responses can perform a function for the angered negotiator similar to that of growling for a dog whose meal is being targeted by another animal: they convey an open-ended threat. For a negotiator, anger may be used to indicate that negative consequences (such as an impasse) may ensue if an unreasonable tactic or position is pursued, without specifically committing the negotiator to such a course of action. Angry responses may also lend credence to a stated threat.

One of the interviewees in my study, a corporate manager, recommended that negotiators allow themselves to show anger when trying to emphasize the importance of a specific issue to the other party. However, he recommended that such displays of anger be used prudently. Two cautions he urged were: (a) do not overuse anger to emphasize issue importance to the point where the other party no longer takes you seriously or calls off the deal and (b) wait until the other party has something invested in the negotiation process before you use anger in this way. As the manager put it:

> You take it far enough along, you put enough structure on it that you're comfortable with it, and then you start drawing the line. If you draw those lines too early, people may hit the eject button and then you're out of it.

Restoring Disrupted Relationships

As mentioned above, Averill (1982) maintains that anger is triggered when an individual perceives that another person intentionally committed a wrong that has caused harm to him or her. Anger for Averill performs the function of upholding socially acceptable ways of behaving by providing mechanisms for noting and correcting such behavior. Averill's conception of anger suggests that, if one is accused of having committed such a wrong, there are at least three means of reducing that person's level of anger: (1) persuade the accuser that the act was not intentional; (2) persuade the accuser that the harm that was done was relatively slight; and (3) take responsibility for the act and promise it will not happen again.

These three approaches to reducing another's anger correspond to three types of "social accounts"—arguments offered in defense of perceived wrongdoing—described by Bies (1987). They are: (1) causal accounts, explanations that absolve the alleged offender from responsibility for the act; (2) referential accounts, comparisons between the outcome of the action and the outcomes received by others in similar situations to show that the harm done was relatively slight; and (3) penitential accounts, or apologies. As Bies (1987) points out, however, merely providing such an argument does not guarantee that it will be effective. In order for an account to have the effect of reducing another's anger, it must be perceived as adequate, truthful, and sincere by the angered party. Causal accounts, therefore, should be used only when the explanation in question is true, is believable, and truly does absolve one of wrongdoing. Apologies must be sincere; if offenses are repeated in the future, subsequent apologies are likely to be wholly ineffective.

Using Intermediaries

Not surprisingly, both investment bankers interviewed for the study credit intermediaries with preventing anger from killing a deal. Both claimed that by keeping the parties physically separated at times, serving as communication channels, and filtering out relationship-threatening messages, intermediaries are able to consummate deals that would not have taken place had the parties negotiated face-to-face. As one investment banker put it:

> If people don't feel that another party is negotiating with them in good faith, they'll break off negotiations. Emotion will take over and rationality will be left behind. That is to some extent the role we play. We are the buffer. If we manage the process right, we'll minimize the risk that the two parties will disturb each other . . . Because if you don't have that process and you've got a lot of different parties, some more anxious than others, anger can be a disastrous thing.

The form of "rationality" that the investment banker refers to is what Etzioni (1988) calls "instrumental rationality." It is a rationality of means, not of ends. It is a rationality that assumes that what the parties in a negotiation desire is to consummate a profitable deal. Etzioni (1988) also identifies a different form of rationality, a "normative rationality of ends." According to Etzioni, decision makers want to do what is right in addition to doing what is in their best interests.

It is necessary to maintain the distinction between instrumental rationality and normative rationality if we are to evaluate the role of emotions in conflict situations. Are emotions such as anger "bad" in negotiations, as the investment banker above maintains? From the perspective of instrumental rationality, anger is likely to have a negative effect on negotiations. As we have seen, anger is likely to inhibit the total profitability of a negotiation through its effects on the information processing capabilities on either side. Anger is also likely to be disruptive in terms of instrumental rationality due to its goal orientation effects: if the initial goals of a party are toward profit maximization, the shifts in goal orientation that are likely to occur toward punishing the other party or ensuring that the violation is not repeated will tend to result in lower performance when performance is measured by profitability. From the standpoint of instrumental rationality, therefore, the investment banker makes a valid point when he argues that anger should be avoided in negotiations and that intermediaries can aid the progress and profitability of negotiations by keeping anger to a minimum. The same belief is echoed by Rubin and Sander (1988), who recommend that when the negotiating climate between the parties is adversarial, it may be better to manage the conflict through intermediaries who can be buffers between the parties.

However, the investment banker's argument ignores important questions that can be posed from the standpoint of normative rationality. A specific question is: Is it really that important for a negotiator to achieve a profitable agreement? Perhaps one could agree to a profitable resolution with a party who is deceptive, abusive, or manipulative—but would it be worth it? Long-term considerations can also enter into the decision to accept or reject an offer. For example, if the offended party is the buyer in an acquisition, that party has to consider to what extent the behavior of the offending party will affect them in the future (e.g., if the offending party is slated to head up the new acquisition). Anger serves a normatively rational purpose, according to Averill (1982), by upholding socially acceptable ways of behaving. Averill proposes responses to anger that, unlike aggressive responses, are socially constructive: talking over the anger-instigating incident with the other party or with a neutral third party, for example. It is possible, therefore, that by expressing anger in the proper ways, relationships disrupted by anger actually may be strengthened and parties who unwittingly harm another will be made aware of the effect their behavior has had. Further research is needed to identify the conditions under which anger tends to be beneficial in negotiations from the perspectives of both instrumental and normative rationality.

CONCLUSION

The practical implications that have been drawn from this analysis of anger in mergers and acquisitions negotiations are just a few of the many that could be identified and further developed from future research. Future studies of conflict behavior can profitably go beyond the narrow focus on anger used here to consider other emotions and related states, such as fear, resentment, gratitude, guilt, or stress. Scholars and negotiators should be mindful not to ignore emotional factors in negotiation simply because emotions and their causes are complex. As I pointed out earlier, emotions are an integral part of the way human beings approach many conflict situations. Those of us who are interested in resolving disputes can only benefit by gaining a better understanding of emotions, the factors that trigger them, and their consequences.

REFERENCES

Averill, J. (1982). *Anger and aggression*. New York: Springer-Verlag.

Bies, R. J. (1987). "The predicament of injustice: The management of moral outrage." In *Research in organizational behavior* 9, edited by L. L. Cummings and B. M. Staw. Greenwich, CT: JAI Press.

Brown, B. (1968). "The effects of need to maintain face on interpersons bargaining." *Journal of Experimental Social Psychology 4:* 107-22.

Etzioni, A. (1988). *The moral dimension: Towards a new economics*. New York: Free Press.

Fincham, F. and Jaspers, J. (1979). "Attribution of responsibility: From man the scientist to man as lawyer." In *Advances in experimental social psychology,* edited by L. Berkowitz. New York: Academic Press.

Gallo, P. (1968). "Prisoners of our own dilemma?" Paper presented to the Western Psychological Association, March.

Homans, G. C. (1961). *Social behavior: Its elementary forms*. New York: Harcourt, Brace, and World.

Mandler, G. (1984). *Mind and body: The psychology of emotion and stress*. New York: W. W. Norton.

Pinkley, R. (1988). "Cognitive interpretations of conflict: A multidimensional scaling analysis." Unpublished doctoral dissertation. Department of Psychology, University of North Carolina at Chapel Hill.

Pruitt, D. (1981). *Negotiation behavior:* New York: Academic Press.

————. (1983). "Achieving integrative agreements." In *Negotiating in Organizations,* edited by M. Bazerman and R. J. Lewicki. Beverly Hills, Calif.: Sage.

Pruitt, D., and Rubin, J. (1986). *Social conflict: Escalation, stalemate and settlement*. New York: Random House.

Rousseau, D. M. (1989). "Psychological and implied contracts in organizations." *Employee Responsibilities and Rights Journal 2:* 121–139.

Rubin, J. Z. and Brown, B. R. (1975). *The social psychology of bargaining and negotiation*. New York: Academic Press

Rubin, J. Z., and Sander, F. E. A. (1988). "When do we use agents? Direct vs. representative negotiation." *Negotiation Journal 4:* 395–401.

Ury, W., Brett J., and Goldberg S. (1989). *Getting disputes resolved*. San Francisco: Jossey-Bass.

This study was supported by a grant from the Dispute Resolution Research Center (DRRC) at Northwestern University. An earlier version of the paper appeared in the DRCC's working paper series as Working Paper Number 43.

The author is indebted to the following for their suggestions on the research and writing of this paper: Bob Bies, Denise Rousseau, Jerry Fox, Tom Tripp, and Max Bazerman.

The Social Context of Negotiation

A significant element contributing to the dynamics in any complex negotiation is whether there are more than two parties in the negotiation. Thus far, we have devoted almost all of our attention to negotiation as a dyadic process—the dynamic interaction between negotiator and opponent. And some negotiations *are* exclusively conducted by two parties: a buyer and a seller, a husband and wife, or a boss and subordinate. But many more negotiations—particularly those that occur in organizations—involve other parties. The negotiators themselves may be representing groups of people who are not at the table but are affected by the outcome. A union leader represents the rank and file; a diplomat represents the country's government and leadership; a manager represents the senior leadership and owners of the company. Negotiators who represent these "constituencies" are usually given instructions as to how to negotiate and what objectives are to be achieved; in addition, they are held accountable by their constituencies for achieving these objectives. In addition, there may also be other parties, such as third parties or audiences to the negotiation, who may or may not be directly affected by the negotiations themselves, and who may or may not be able to observe and participate in the process.

When constituencies, third parties, and audiences become involved in the negotiation, their very presence changes the nature of the negotiating dynamics. Experienced negotiators know how to assess the impact and consequences of these other actors on the negotiation process. Moreover, by understanding this impact, they can effectively employ constituencies, audiences, and third parties, either to protect themselves from undue pressures or to increase the pressures on their opponent.

The articles in this section outline the nature of this larger social dynamic. In the first article, "A Core Model of Negotiation," Thomas Colosi notes that while a great deal of the popular writing on negotiation depicts it as a one-on-one process, much of actual negotiation is, in fact, a rich and complex social interaction. Many negotiators function in teams rather than alone. Moreover, negotiating teams seldom agree among themselves as to their positions on issues. Individuals play different roles within these teams, which often has the consequence of protracting a dispute rather than facilitating its resolution. Finally, as the negotiating team is often constituted with organization members who have different job titles and levels of seniority, deliberations within and outside the team are likely to occur across hierarchical levels in the organization. The "reality," as painted by Colosi, shows how actual negotiations in organizations are often far more complex than the one-on-one dynamics described in many articles or artificially simulated in class role plays.

The second article, by Jeffrey Rubin and Frank Sander, addresses a key question in the larger social dynamic of negotiation: When is it better for the key party to be represented by an ''agent,'' rather than to be directly involved? The authors argue that using an agent inevitably complicates a negotiation, because the number of possible interactions (between the parties themselves, between party and agents, and between agents) increases from one to six. The advantages of using an agent are that an agent may have greater expertise (in a specific issue or the negotiation process), may be more emotionally detached, and may offer an opportunity for the party to employ various tactical ploys that could not be used on one's own. However, it is possible that each of these ''good reasons'' can backfire if the party is not careful about how an agent is chosen or used. The authors emphasize that parties do not often exercise enough control over how agents are selected or monitored, and that negotiations may actually suffer rather than prosper because of the use of agents. The article concludes by proposing some general principles as to when agents are desirable and when the parties ought to represent themselves in negotiation.

In the third article, ''Saving Face,'' Bert Brown focuses on an individual predisposition—''face,'' or one's social image and reputation—which is significantly enhanced in the complex social environment of negotiation. Negotiators—like most people in public social environments—want to maintain a good public image/reputation, and are very concerned about losing that public image/reputation. When people (negotiators) are told that they look weak and foolish, and when that information is presented to them by observers who have had a chance to evaluate their behavior, negotiators will change their negotiating strategy and engage in behaviors specifically intended to save or regain that lost ''face.'' Face-saving motivations usually lead negotiators to take tough and unyielding stands in order to appear strong, even when those stands are costly and unproductive for the long-term economic success of the negotiations. Thus, face saving is a social dynamic that has high social value for the individual negotiator, but may also have great economic costs. We can frequently observe these behaviors among politicians, labor leaders, and other public negotiators who appear to be far more concerned with their public image and reputation than the substantive issues they are advocating.

In the fourth article, David Kuechle offers advice to important parties—in this case, company presidents and key spokesmen—who must ''negotiate'' with a public opinion that is angry and antagonistic. These events occur under conditions of crisis, when their companies are usually enmeshed in some highly unpopular or controversial activity. Kuechle discusses three well-known examples: Union Carbide's handling of the public reaction to the leak of poison gas in Bhopal, India; Nestlé's handling of a problem with the use of its powdered infant formula in Third World countries; and Arthur D. Little's agreement to test a deadly nerve gas for the U.S. government. By examining the ways that the CEOs of these organizations managed the public reaction to each business problem, Kuechle proposes some important principles for effectively managing public outrage and anger. He also shows how, in several of the cases, the chief executive did not follow this advice, and the consequences produced for them and their organizations.

While Kuechle's article largely focuses on the ''public'' as a liability that must be effectively managed to keep from adding to a negotiator's problems, Margo Vanover suggests that the social environment of our negotiations can also serve as an important ally in helping us achieve our objectives. This assistance occurs by organizing, mobilizing, and enlisting coalitions of support. Vanover emphasizes the importance of coalitions and offers a number of specific, useful suggestions for building broad support and focusing this coalition of support on the key opponent. Her suggestions include ways to choose a leader, guidelines for making a coalition successful, and a valuable list of 20 tips for making coalitions work.

A Core Model of Negotiation

Thomas Colosi

THE CONVENTIONAL PERCEPTION OF BILATERAL NEGOTIATION

Negotiations are typically depicted as involving one group sitting across a bargaining table from a second. One side presents its demands or proposals to the other, and a discussion or debate follows. Counterproposals and compromises are offered. When the offers are eventually accepted on both sides, the dispute is settled and an agreement is signed.

Within this model, all the interesting and relevant action is presumed to occur back and forth between the two sides. The model assumes that each party is monolithic, even if represented by bargaining teams. The way in which the participants are billed—labor versus management, prisoners versus guards, environmentalists versus industry—reflects the same monolithic assumption; that is, that all team members share the same set of demands, agree on a strategy for handling the opposition, and have come to the table with equal enthusiasm for the negotiating process.

Unfortunately, the conventional model of negotiation obscures much of the richness and complexity of the bargaining process. In practice, bargaining teams are seldom monolithic. Team members often have conflicting goals and values; some sort of consensus must develop internally before agreement can be reached with the other side. While some students of negotiation have recognized the importance of this internal bargaining, conventional models do not explain their relationship to the functioning of the larger process. By contrast, the model developed in this article attempts to incorporate this dimension and thus to present a richer and more realistic view of negotiation.

For the sake of simplicity, the model presented below assumes—at this point—just two bargaining teams. Later in the article it is expanded to incorporate multiparty situations; conceivably it might also be applied to cases involving just two individuals. In any event, the model is intended to describe the structure or core of negotiation, regardless of the particular issues at stake, the identity of the parties, or the sector (public or private) in which the dispute takes place.

STABILIZERS, NONSTABILIZERS, AND QUASI MEDIATORS

Within each team, negotiators usually hold quite different attitudes. Some negotiators tend to settle at any cost. They may be called *stabilizers*. They seek agreement with the other side to avoid the disruptive consequences of nonsettlement, particularly such lengthy, expensive, or disruptive alternatives as litigation, strikes, demonstrations, riots, and wars. A second general type, the *nonstabilizers,* do not particularly like the negotiation process. Nonstabilizers tend to disagree with most of the proposals of their own team and all of the counterproposals of the other side. They would rather see disruption through raw contests of will and power than compromise on a given position. The terms nonstabilizers would accept are far more stringent than those to which the stabilizers would agree.

Finally, in the middle is a third type, the *quasi mediator,* who plays several roles. He or she is usually the spokesperson charged with the success of the effort. To those sitting across the table, the quasi mediator may simply look like another negotiator, but within a team he or she often acts as a kind of mediator between the stabilizers and the nonstabilizers. As will be shown later, the quasi mediator can also be a mediator between the team and its own constituents or clients.

HORIZONTAL, INTERNAL, AND VERTICAL NEGOTIATIONS

Although most conventional models limit their analysis to the bargaining that goes on across the table, relatively little true negotiating goes on horizontally. Instead, speeches are made, symbols and platitudes are thrown out, and emotions are displayed. If the communication is healthy, the two teams use this time constructively to educate each other: They explain proposals and counterproposals, compare data, show videotapes, share printouts, and present experts. Except for this opportunity to educate and to learn, however, all of this may be less important than the real activity going on internally.

The standard model also misses another important dimension of negotiation: the interchanges that occur between a bargaining team and its vertical hierarchy. A team is rarely independent of a larger constituency. It is at the bargaining table because it has been sent to accomplish something. In the context of private sector labor negotiation, for example, management's vertical hierarchy is the company's leadership; for the union's bargaining committee, it is the international union and, most times, ultimately the membership who must vote on a proposed contract. Almost always, important negotiations must take place between a team and its vertical hierarchy at one point or another in the bargaining.

Since negotiators are continually being reeducated through the horizontal negotiations occurring at or near the bargaining table, they are frequently far more advanced in their thinking than are their constituents back home. The resulting gap can be a dangerous trap for all concerned. Part of the art and skill of being a negotiator is recognizing how far from the constituents the bargaining team has moved. The negotiator must also know when and how to go back and educate his or her own constituents.

Sometimes the vertical hierarchy will tell a negotiator what should be achieved at the bargaining table, but after several sessions with the other side, the negotiator may come to believe that these goals cannot be reached. It is within this context that negotiation between the team and its own vertical hierarchy takes place. The quasi mediator is often responsible for negotiating with the hierarchy of the team's parent organization. In labor-management negotiations, for instance, the spokesperson or quasi mediator on the union team may wind up intellectually positioned between the local's viewpoint on an issue and management's last known position. In such a case, the union spokesperson not only tries to get management to go along with labor's point of view but may also have to try to get the rest of the union team to accept management's view on some points.

INTERNAL TEAM NEGOTIATIONS

Resolving differences between the stabilizers and nonstabilizers may be a prerequisite for effective negotiation with the other side, as well as one for reaching accommodation with the team's own vertical hierarchy if settlement is the objective. Unless some means exist for coordinating positions and goals over time, there will be serious problems. When a team is considering making an offer, for example, the stabilizers likely will want to present a generous package, while the nonstabilizers will not want to offer anything. The quasi mediator must begin to explore with the stabilizers why the concessions might be excessive. At the same time, of course, the quasi mediator must discuss with the nonstabilizers why the proposal may be good and why the team should not be so rigid. In the same way, when a team receives an offer from the other side, the quasi mediator must show the nonstabilizers why the team should not hold out for more while checking the stabilizers' tendency to grab the offer too quickly. Much like a neutral mediator, the quasi mediator may meet jointly and separately with the stabilizers and nonstabilizers. If the team is not well disciplined, these discussions unfortunately may take place at the table. Ideally, they should take place in a separate caucus, away from the other side.

RAISING AND MAINTAINING DOUBTS TO FOSTER SETTLEMENT

In a sense, this internal team negotiation process is a microcosm of the larger negotiations that occur across the table. Similar aspects of bargaining positions come into play; the same kinds of negotiation skills are required. As in across-the-table bargaining, the most important efforts are those directed at changing the minds of parties who do not want to settle.

It is reasonable to ask why the focus should be on those who oppose settlement: Perhaps those who are anxious to settle—to sell the farm—should be challenged with at least as much force. The answer lies in the true essence of negotiation. Negotiations are not squabbles or battles between two sides. The goal of the process is not for one team to extract huge concessions from the other. Instead, the essence of negotiation is to provide an opportunity for parties to exchange promises through which they will resolve their differences with one another. A settlement thus is no more—and no less—than an expression of an exchange of promises. Because the emphasis in negotiations is on the resolution of differences through the exchange of promises, the process is oriented in favor of settlement. Attention is naturally focused on parties who seem to stand in settlement's way.

Settlement is fostered through the raising and maintaining of doubts. In all negotiations, parties that want to reach some settlement (e.g., the stabilizers and quasi mediators) work to raise or maintain doubts in the minds of others as to the viability of their particular positions, as well as doubts about the consequences of nonagreement. This effort is focused on nonstabilizers and the team across the table. The nonstabilizers are asked to consider the implications of nonsettlement, what it would mean to them personally, or to their organization, objectives, ideals, and reputations. Thus, the same techniques and strategies teams may use to raise and maintain doubts in the minds of parties across the table are also appropriate internally with the nonstabilizers. By the same token, of course, the nonstabilizers engage in a parallel effort to raise doubts in the minds of stabilizers and the quasi mediator about the consequences of settlement.

Because a particular settlement may not be in the interests of the nonstabilizer, he or she frequently must be convinced to accept a settlement through some method other than fostering doubts. Negotiators have an additional tool when dealing with a nonstabilizing teammate: the discipline of the parent organization. This discipline, which might rely upon power, title, prestige, or majority rule, operates within the team. The decision-making process is normally carried over from the parent organization through the chief spokesperson or team leader, which reinforces the roles and relationships of the vertical hierarchy. For instance, an organization that makes most of its important decisions by a majority vote will probably be represented in negotiations by a team that also makes its decisions by majority vote.

According to most practitioners, negotiation is a consensual process. The negotiators come to agreement precisely because they find settlement preferable to nonagreement. But it is erroneous to conclude, as some have, that everyone wins or gains from a negotiated agreement. The notion of "win-win" outcomes is another reflection of the limits of the conventional model of negotiation. Both sides across a table may appear to win, but within each team—where so much more bargaining goes on—there are often nonstabilizers who may view themselves as definite losers in the process.

TARGETING UNDERLYING CONCERNS

The creation and maintenance of doubts about the consequences of nonagreement (or one decision versus another) is central to inducing skeptics to settle. This is true whether they are nonstabilizers within a team or nonstabilizers across the table. But where should this effort be directed?

Fisher and Ury (1981) observe that a negotiator can move the opposite side closer to settlement by convincing it to participate in joint problem solving. This may be accomplished by separating the opposing side's *position* from its underlying *interests*.

Although positions are usually explicit, the interests that underlie them often are left unstated. For example, a community coalition might oppose the establishment of a home for mentally retarded adults in its neighborhood. Yet what is its true interest? Frequently, the community feels that the retarded adults would make the neighborhood less safe. Preserving safe streets may be the real interest at stake. A sophisticated advocate of the home would try to raise doubts about whether the community's stated position will actually satisfy its interests: ''Might not additional numbers of sincere, capable adults contribute to community safety? Look at their abilities as well as their problems.'' An educational process showing that the retarded adults would pose no danger to neighborhood residents—and in fact might improve their security—could foster doubts in the minds of the neighbors about their flat refusal to consider the proposal. Even if opponents are not convinced on this particular score, identifying safety as their prime interest allows the parties to explore mitigating measures.

Education can be the most effective way to raise doubts. It is used, therefore, in every phase of negotiation: across the table, within a team, and between a team and its constituents. The plan of attack is to move the opponent to a more agreeable position.

As Fisher and Ury observe, the effective negotiator aims for the underlying interests that form the foundation of the adversary's position. What happens, however, if a negotiator cannot identify the opponent's interests? Where else can doubts be targeted to get others to adopt a more flexible stance? An answer requires a closer look at the different levels of concern that are often negotiated: issues, proposals, problem definitions, and assumptions.

ISSUES, PROPOSALS, PROBLEMS, AND ASSUMPTIONS

The negotiator's job is to raise and maintain doubts on all four levels of concern. Consider, for example, a proposal to site a hazardous waste management facility that requires the approval of a community board. If there is local opposition, it probably will be based on the assumption that such facilities are inherently dangerous. If that assumption cannot be questioned, no basis exists for negotiations between the community and the developer. As a consequence, the facility will be blocked.

Moreover, even if the project sponsors can convince the community that such facilities are not necessarily dangerous, they may encounter a different obstacle—that of problem definition. For example, the community might contend that its opposition is not to treatment facilities in general but to the proposed location of this particular plant. (It might be near a flood plain.) Casting the problem in these terms obviously would affect proposed solutions. The range of proposals could include the following: having no facility at all, putting the facility at another site, using control technologies to make the facility fit the site, or making the site more acceptable for the proposed use. The issues to be discussed in negotiation would be tied to such proposals. For example, discussion might focus on the need for such a facility, the reasons for (and against) this particular location, and the cost-effectiveness of various mitigating measures.

The task of the facility sponsor would be to raise doubts about the viability of any unacceptable proposals or issues. As assumptions and problem definitions are revealed—which is much more likely than the disclosure of an opponent's real interests—the sponsor would also question them. Since the issues and proposals are derived from the problems and assumptions, the sponsor would probably try to move the negotiations into discussions of the latter before considering specific issues and proposals. In short, the sponsor would focus on the underlying concerns.

EXPANDING THE CORE MODEL

Multilateral Negotiations

The core model that has been described above includes five axes of negotiation: one horizontal, two internal, and two with vertical hierarchies. This model was based on the simplifying assumption that only two teams are at the table. While there are many instances of two-party negotiation, in other cases—particularly those that arise in the public sector—many more parties may be involved. How must the core model be expanded to accommodate additional parties?

The most important difference between two-party and multiparty negotiation is that the latter opens up the possibility of coalition. For example, three parties—A, B, and C—may come to full agreement or no agreement, but they also may be able to forge alternative side deals. Any two parties may strike a deal that leaves the third out. Were A negotiating with just one other party, he could simply weigh any proposed settlement against the consequences of nonagreement. Here, however, he must also compare a possible settlement with both B and C with the advantages of different agreements with B alone or C alone. The addition of each new party at the bargaining table greatly increases the number of theoretical alliances. The introduction of additional parties, necessary as they might be, greatly complicates the negotiation process. Some coalitions may hold for the entire negotiation, but often alliances shift with various issues. Moreover, the lineup of coalitions may shift over time as events, personalities, and loyalties change. Consensus building is always a delicate balancing act.

Finally, the presence of so many parties at the table usually will mean that much more business must be transacted. The important education process usually requires much more time, as the negotiators at the table have the burden of carrying far more information back through their vertical hierarchy. Perhaps we should not be surprised that so many public disputes seem to take months—even years—to negotiate.

The Solitary Negotiator

When only two individuals are negotiating, each acting on his or her own behalf, the conventional model with its emphasis on two independent units bargaining across the table may afford understanding. Yet perhaps even here it is an oversimplification if we do not look at the negotiation that occurs within each of us. Individuals often have mixed feelings and competing priorities. People must admit (to themselves at least) that they sometimes vacillate between accepting a settlement and holding out for more.

Speculation as to whether stabilizing, nonstabilizing, and mediating impulses may exist in one mind is best left to psychiatrists, psychologists, behaviorists, neurologists, and theologians. It does seem true, however, that even in one-on-one bargaining, there can be distinct and contradictory attitudes toward a particular settlement. One strength of the model developed here is that it recognizes the stabilizing and nonstabilizing forces within each bargaining unit (be it a team or an individual), and attempts to understand the means by which they may be integrated.

Quasi Mediators and Mediators

Outside mediators enter disputes for a very specific reason: to fill a trust vacuum that exists at an impasse among and within the parties. The quasi mediator and mediator play separate, yet related, roles: Both use the creation and maintenance of doubts to move other negotiators closer to settlement. The quasi mediator, like the other negotiators, has personal, organizational, and institutional stakes in the outcome of the negotiation process. The truly neutral mediator does not. The quasi mediator also has some power to make decisions about substantive and procedural issues. Whatever power the mediator might enjoy is procedural.

When Should We Use Agents? Direct versus Representative Negotiation

Jeffrey Z. Rubin
Frank E. A. Sander

Although we typically conceive of negotiations occurring directly between two or more principals, often neglected in a thoughtful analysis are the many situations where negotiations take place indirectly, through the use of representatives or surrogates of the principals. A father who speaks to his child's teacher (at the child's request), two lawyers meeting on behalf of their respective clients, the foreign service officers of different nations meeting to negotiate the settlement of a border dispute, a real estate agent informing would-be buyers of the seller's latest offer—each is an instance of negotiation through representatives.

In this brief essay, we wish to build on previous analyses of representative negotiation[1] to consider several key distinctions between direct and representative negotiations, and to indicate the circumstances under which we believe negotiators should go out of their way either to choose *or* to avoid negotiation through agents.

The most obvious effect of using agents—an effect that must be kept in mind in any analysis of representative negotiation—is complication of the transaction. As indicated in Figure 1, if we begin with a straightforward negotiation between two individuals, then the addition of two agents transforms this simple one-on-one deal into a complex matrix involving at least four primary negotiations, as well as two subsidiary ones (represented by the dashed lines in Figure 1). In addition, either of the agents may readily serve as a mediator between the client and the other agent or principal. Or the two agents might act as comediators between the principals. At a minimum, such a complex structure necessitates effective coordination. Beyond that, this structural complexity has implications—both positive and negative—for representative negotiation in general. Let us now review these respective benefits and liabilities.

Reprinted from Jeffrey Z. Rubin and Frank E. A. Sander, "When Should We Use Agents? Direct versus Representative Negotiation," *Negotiation Journal*, October 1988, pp. 395–401. Used with permission of Plenum Publishing Corporation and the authors.

[1] See, in particular, the concise and insightful discussion by Lax and Sebenius (1986) in Chapter 15 of their *The Manager as Negotiator*.

FIGURE 1   Possible Relations among Two Principals (P1 and P2) and Their
Respective Agents (A1 and A2) (A solid line denotes an actual
relation, a dashed line a potential one)

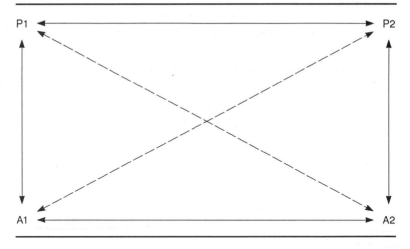

EXPERTISE

One of the primary reasons that principals choose to negotiate through agents is
that the latter possess expertise that makes agreement—particularly favorable
agreement—more likely. This expertise is likely to be of three different stripes:

Substantive Knowledge.   A tax attorney or accountant knows things about the
current tax code that make it more likely that negotiations with an IRS auditor will
benefit the client as much as possible. Similarly, a divorce lawyer, an engineering
consultant, and a real estate agent may have substantive knowledge in a rather narrow
domain of expertise, and this expertise may redound to the client's benefit.

Process Expertise.   Quite apart from the specific expertise they may have in
particular content areas, agents may have skill at the negotiation *process,* per se,
thereby enhancing the prospects of a favorable agreement. A skillful negotiator—
someone who understands how to obtain and reveal information about preferences,
who is inventive, resourceful, firm on goals but flexible on means, etc.—is a valuable
resource. Wise principals would do well to utilize the services of such skilled negotiators, unless they can find ways of developing such process skills themselves.

Special Influence.   A Washington lobbyist is paid to know the "right" people,
to have access to the "corridors of power" that the principals themselves are unlikely
to possess. Such "pull" can certainly help immensely, and is yet another form of
expertise that agents may possess, although the lure of this "access" often outweighs
in promise the special benefits that are confirmed in reality.

Note that the line separating these three forms of expertise is often a thin one, as in the case of a supplier who wishes to negotiate a sales contract with a prospective purchaser, and employs a former employee of the purchaser to handle the transaction: the former employee, as agent, may be a source of both substantive expertise *and* influence.

Note also that principals may not always know what expertise they need. Thus, a person who has a dispute that seems headed for the courts may automatically seek out a litigator, not realizing that the vast preponderance of cases are settled by negotiation, requiring very different skills that the litigator may not possess. So, although agents do indeed possess different forms of expertise that may enhance the prospects of a favorable settlement, clients do not necessarily know what they need; it's a bit like the problem of looking up the proper spelling of a word in the dictionary when you haven't got a clue about how to spell the word in question.

DETACHMENT

Another important reason for using an agent to do the actual negotiation is that the principals may be too emotionally entangled in the subject of the dispute. A classic example is divorce. A husband and wife, caught in the throes of a bitter fight over the end of their marriage, may benefit from the "buffering" that agents can provide. Rather than confront each other with the depth of their anger and bitterness, the principals (P1 and P2 in Figure 1) may do far better by communicating only *indirectly,* via their respective representatives, A1 and A2. Stated most generally, when the negotiating climate is adversarial—when the disputants are confrontational rather than collaborative—it may be wiser to manage the conflict through intermediaries than run the risk of an impasse or explosion resulting from direct exchange.

Sometimes, however, it is the *agents* who are too intensely entangled. What is needed then is the detachment and rationality that only the principals can bring to the exchange. For example, lawyers may get too caught up in the adversary game and lose sight of the underlying problem that is dividing the principals (e.g., how to resolve a dispute about the quality of goods delivered as part of a long-term supply contract). The lawyers may be more concerned about who would win in court, while the clients simply want to get their derailed relationship back on track. Hence the thrust of some modern dispute resolution mechanisms (such as the mini-trial) is precisely to take the dispute *out* of the hands of the technicians and give it back to the primary parties.[2]

Note, however, that the very "detachment" we are touting as a virtue of negotiation through agents can also be a liability. For example, in some interpersonal negotiations, apology and reconciliation may be an important ingredient of any resolution (see, e.g., Goldberg, Green, and Sander, 1987). Surrogates who are primarily technicians may not be able to bring to bear these empathic qualities.

---

[2] Compare in this connection the unfortunate recent decision of the United States Court of Appeals for the Seventh Circuit to the effect that a federal district court judge has no power to compel principals with settlement authority to attend a settlement conference, *G. Heileman Brewing Co.* v. *Joseph Oat Corp.,* 848 F. 2d 1415 (7th Circuit 1988).

TACTICAL FLEXIBILITY

The use of agents allows various gambits to be played out by the principals in an effort to ratchet as much as possible from the other side. For example, if a seller asserts that the bottom line is $100,000, the buyer can try to haggle, albeit at the risk of losing the deal. If the buyer employs an agent, however, the agent can profess willingness to pay that sum but plead lack of authority, thereby gaining valuable time and opportunity for fuller consideration of the situation together with the principal. Or an agent for the seller who senses that the buyer may be especially eager to buy the property can claim that it is necessary to go back to the seller for ratification of the deal, only to return and up the price, profusely apologizing all the while for the behavior of an "unreasonable" client. The client and agent can thus together play the hard-hearted partner game.

Conversely, an agent may be used in order to push the other side in tough, even obnoxious, fashion, making it possible—in the best tradition of the "good cop/bad cop" ploy—for the client to intercede at last, and seem the essence of sweet reason in comparison with the agent. Or the agent may be used as a "stalking horse," to gather as much information about the adversary as possible, opening the way to proposals by the client that exploit the intelligence gathered.

Note that the tactical flexibility conferred by representative negotiations presupposes a competitive negotiating climate, a zero-sum contest in which each negotiator wishes to outsmart the other. It is the stuff of traditional statecraft, and the interested reader can do no better than study the writings of Schelling (1960) and Potter (1948), as well as Lax and Sebenius (1986). To repeat, the assumption behind this line of analysis is that effective negotiation requires some measure of artifice and duplicity, and that this is often best accomplished through the use of some sort of foil or alter ego—in the form of the agent. But the converse is not necessarily true: Where the negotiation is conducted in a problem-solving manner (cf., Fisher and Ury, 1981), agents may still be helpful, not because they resort to strategic ruses, but because they can help articulate interests, options, and alternatives. Four heads are clearly better than two, for example, when it comes to brainstorming about possible ways of reconciling the parties' interests.

Offsetting—indeed, typically *more* than offsetting—the three above apparent virtues of representative negotiation are several sources of difficulty. Each is sufficiently important and potentially problematic that we believe caution is necessary before entering into negotiation through agents.

EXTRA "MOVING PARTS"

As indicated in Figure 1, representative negotiations entail greater structural complexity, additional moving parts in the negotiation machinery that—given a need for expertise, detachment, or tactical flexibility—can help move parties toward a favorable agreement. Additional moving parts, however, can also mean additional expense, in the form of the time required in the finding, evaluating, and engaging of agents, as well as the financial cost of retaining their services. And it can mean additional problems, more things that can go wrong. For instance, a message intended by a client may not be the message transmitted by that client's agent to the other party. Or the message received by that agent from the other party may be very different from the one that that agent (either deliberately or inadvertently) manages to convey to his or her client.

At one level, then, the introduction of additional links in the communication system increases the risk of distortion in the information conveyed back and forth between the principals. Beyond that lies a second difficulty: the possibility that eventually the principals will come to rely so extensively on their respective agents that they no longer communicate directly—even though they could, and even though they might well benefit from doing so. In effect (See Figure 1), P1, in order to reach P2, now invariably goes through the A1-A2 chain, even though such maneuvering is no longer warranted. Consider, for example, the case of a divorcing couple who, in explicit compliance with the advice of their adversary lawyers, have avoided any direct contact with each other during the divorce proceedings. Once the divorce has been obtained, will the parties' ability to communicate effectively with each other (e.g., over support and custody issues) be adversely affected by their excessive prior reliance on their attorneys?

Yet another potentially problematic implication of this increasingly complex social machinery is that unwanted coalitions may arise that apply undue pressure on individual negotiators. Thus A2, in performing a mediatory function between P2 and the other side (P1 and A1) may be prone to become allied with the opposing team—or at least to be so viewed by P2. Greater number does not necessarily mean greater wisdom, however, and the pressures toward uniformity of opinion that result from coalition formation may adversely affect the quality of the decisions reached.

In sum, the introduction of agents increases the complexity of the social apparatus of negotiation, and in so doing increases the chances of unwanted side effects. A related problem should be briefly noted here: the difficulty of asymmetry, as when an agent negotiates not with another agent but directly with the other principal. In effect, this was the case in 1978 when Egypt's Sadat negotiated with Israel's Begin at Camp David. Sadat considered himself empowered to make binding decisions for Egypt, while—at least partly for tactical purposes—Begin represented himself as ultimately accountable to his cabinet and to the Israeli parliament. While this "mismatched" negotiation between a principal (Sadat) and an agent (Begin) *did* result in agreement (thanks in good measure to President Carter's intercession as a mediator), it was not easy. The asymmetry of role meant that the two sides differed in their readiness to move forward toward an agreement, their ability to be shielded by a representative, and their willingness/ability to guarantee that any agreement reached would "stick."[3]

Different dynamics will characterize the negotiation depending on whether it is between clients, between lawyers, or with both present. If just the clients are there, the dealings will be more direct and forthright, and issues of authority and ratification disappear. With just the lawyers present, there may be less direct factual information, but concomitantly more candor about delicate topics. Suppose, for example, that an

---

[3] Compare in this connection Rule 4.2 of the American Bar Association's Model Rules of Professional Conduct, which prohibits a lawyer from dealing directly with the opposing principal, if that principal is represented by an attorney.

aging soprano seeks to persuade an opera company to sign her for the lead role in an upcoming opera. If she is not present, the opera's agent may try to lower the price, contending that the singer is past her prime. Such candor is not recommended if the singer is present at the negotiation!

PROBLEMS OF "OWNERSHIP" AND CONFLICTING INTERESTS

In theory, it is clear that the principal calls the shots. Imagine, however, an agent who is intent on applying the *Getting to YES* (Fisher and Ury, 1981) approach by searching for objective criteria and a fair outcome. Suppose the client simply wants the best possible outcome, perhaps because it is a one-shot deal not involving a future relationship with the other party. What if the agent (a lawyer, perhaps) *does* care about his future relationship with the other *agent,* and wants to be remembered as a fair and scrupulous bargainer? How *should* this conflict get resolved and how, in the absence of explicit discussion, *will* it be resolved, if at all? Conversely, the client, because of a valuable long-term relationship, may want to maintain good relations with the other side. But if the client simply looks for an agent who is renowned for an ability to pull out all the stops, the client's overall objectives may suffer as the result of an overzealous advocate.

This issue may arise in a number of contexts. Suppose that, in the course of a dispute settlement negotiation,[4] a lawyer who is intent on getting the best possible deal for a client turns down an offer that was within the client's acceptable range. Is this proper behavior by the agent? The Model Rules of Professional Conduct for attorneys explicitly require (see Rules 1.2(a), 1.4) that every offer must be communicated to the principal, and perhaps a failure to do so might lead to a successful malpractice action against the attorney if the deal finally fell through.

Another illustration involves the situation where the agent and principal have divergent ethical norms. Suppose that a seller of a house has just learned that the dwelling is infested with termites, but instructs the agent not to reveal this fact, even in response to specific inquiry from the buyer. How should these tensions be fairly resolved, keeping in mind the fact that the agent may be subject to a professional code of conduct that gives directions that may conflict with the ethical values of the client?[5] There may, of course, be artful ways of dealing with such dilemmas, as, for example, slyly deflecting any relevant inquiry by the buyer. But preferably these problems should be explicitly addressed in the course of the initial discussion between agent and principal. To some extent, the problem may be resolved by the principal's tendency to pick an agent who is congenial and compatible. But, as we pointed out before, principals are not always aware of and knowledgeable about the relevant considerations that go into the choice of an agent. Hence, if these issues are not addressed explicitly

---

[4] See Sander and Rubin (1988) for a discussion of the differences between dealmaking and dispute settlement negotiation.

[5] See, for example, Rule 4.1 of the ABA's Model Rules of Professional Conduct, prohibiting attorneys from making materially false statements.

at the outset, termination of the relationship midstream in egregious cases may be the only alternative.

Differing goals and standards of agent and principal may create conflicting pulls. For example, the buyer's agent may be compensated as a percentage of the purchase price, thus creating an incentive to have the price as high as possible. The buyer, of course, wants the lowest possible price. Similarly, where a lawyer is paid by the hour, there may be an incentive to draw out the negotiation, whereas the client prefers an expeditious negotiation at the lowest possible cost.

While these are not insoluble problems, to be sure, they do constitute yet another example of the difficulties that may arise as one moves to representative negotiations. Although in theory the principals are in command, once agents have been introduced the chemistry changes, and new actors—with agenda, incentives, and constraints of their own—are part of the picture. Short of an abrupt firing of the agents, principals may find themselves less in control of the situation once agents have come on the scene.

ENCOURAGEMENT OF ARTIFICE AND DUPLICITY

Finally, as already noted, the introduction of agents often seems to invite clients to devise stratagems (with or without these agents) to outwit the other side. Admittedly, there is nothing intrinsic to the presence of representatives that dictates a move in this direction; still, perhaps because of the additional expense incurred, the seductive lure of a ''killing'' with the help of one's ''hired gun,'' or the introduction of new, sometimes perverse incentives, representative negotiations often seem to instill (or reflect) a more adversarial climate.

CONCLUSION

It follows from the preceding analysis that, ordinarily, negotiations conducted directly between the principals are preferable to negotiation through representatives. When the principals' relationship is fundamentally cooperative or informed by enlightened self-interest, agents may often be unnecessary; since there is little or no antagonism in the relationship, there is no need for the buffering detachment afforded by agents. Moreover, by negotiating directly, there is reduced risk of miscoordination, misrepresentation, and miscommunication.

On the other hand, representative negotiation *does* have an important and necessary place. When special expertise is required, when tactical flexibility is deemed important and—most importantly—when direct contact is likely to produce confrontation rather than collaboration, agents *can* render an important service.

Above all, the choice of whether to negotiate directly or through surrogates is an important one, with significant ramifications. It therefore should be addressed explicitly by weighing some of the considerations advanced above. And if an agent *is* selected, careful advance canvassing of issues such as those discussed here (e.g., authority and ethical standards) is essential.

REFERENCES

Fisher, R. and Ury, W. L. (1981). *Getting to YES: Negotiating agreement without giving in.* Boston: Houghton Mifflin.

Goldberg, S. Green, E. and Sander, F. E. A. (1987). "Saying you're sorry." *Negotiation Journal* 3: 221–224.

Lax, D. A. and Sebenius, J. K. (1986). *The manager as negotiator.* New York: The Free Press.

Potter S. (1948). *The theory and practice of gamesmanship: The art of winning games without actually cheating.* New York: Holt.

Sander, F. E. A. and Rubin, J. Z. (1988). "The Janus quality of negotiation: Dealmaking and dispute settlement." *Negotiation Journal* 4: 109–113.

Schelling, T. (1960). *The strategy of conflict.* Cambridge, Mass.: Harvard University Press.

We thank Michael Wheeler for the many constructive comments, suggestions, and conversations that preceded this article; and we gratefully acknowledge the helpful comments of Stephen B. Goldberg on an earlier draft of this manuscript.

Saving Face

Bert R. Brown

Some time ago a newspaper article described the achievement pressures put on students at the Harvard Business School. One young man, explaining why he and his peers worked unusually hard, said: "Fear of embarrassment is the great social motivator. There are a hundred people who can annihilate you in those classes. You don't want to look like a yo-yo in front of a hundred guys."

On April 30, 1970, President Nixon defended his decision to send troops into Cambodia by saying: "If when the chips are down the world's most powerful nation . . . acts like a pitiful, helpless giant, the forces of totalitarianism and anarchy will threaten free nations. . . . I would rather be a one-term President . . . [than] . . . see this nation accept the first defeat in its proud 190-year history."

Bibb Latané of Ohio State and John Darley of Princeton did an experiment to discover when people will help in a crisis [*P.T.*, December 1968]. They found that individuals were less likely to intervene to help a person in distress when other persons were nearby and that the likelihood of intervention decreased as the number of others present increased. The researchers noted that some of the subjects were concerned not to make fools of themselves by overreacting.

Need. The student, the President, and the bystander all illustrate, in diverse ways, a universal psychological mechanism: the need to save face. Ten years ago, Erving Goffman identified this pervasive need, suggesting that it motivates us (1) to appear capable and strong whenever possible, and (2) to avoid situations that would make us look foolish in front of others. "Face" is thus heavily dependent on one's supposed status, prestige, or recognition in the eyes of others. Goffman was first to observe that individuals will guard against loss of face even if it becomes very costly for them to do so.

With introspection, we can see the face-saving mechanism at work in our everyday lives, when we often go to elaborate, contorted extremes to offset embarrassment, avoid looking foolish, and protect our fragile self-esteem. And if we look around us, we see increasing evidence of the important role that this motive has had historically:

for example, in the alignment of nations in the First and Second World Wars, in the Korean War and subsequent negotiations, in the Cuban missile crisis, in the Arab-Israeli conflict, and of course in our current involvement in Indochina.

Smoke.   Because of the fundamental nature of face-saving, and because it can have so many serious real-world repercussions, I have become interested in learning more about this motive: when it is likely to occur, what situational factors are likely to provoke it. If we can answer these questions, I reasoned, we might be better able to deal constructively with the smoke screen that face saving sets up between friends and governments alike.

The first step was to define the motive in specific, behavioral terms. *The need to maintain face is expressed in the sacrifice of tangible rewards to avoid looking foolish or incompetent in public.* This definition includes two essential points: the motive (1) is *costly;* the need to preserve or restore self-esteem outweighs opportunities for financial gain; and (2) requires the presence of an *audience,* real or imagined.

Two components of the need to maintain face are *face saving* and *face restoration.* The former is designed to prevent a loss of face before it actually occurs. We may construct extravagant facades to protect ourselves in situations that might be embarrassing; we withdraw from experiences that might prove humiliating. In this sense, face saving is anticipatory. Face restoration, by contrast, occurs after one has suffered humiliation. In such cases the individual tries to counteract his loss of face, by either retaliation or reassertion. Armed with this definition, we have conducted a number of laboratory experiments to explore the situational factors that affect face-saving. We have primarily used two paradigms: a bargaining game that involves aggressive exchanges between players and an embarrassing performance situation.

We based the bargaining task on a two-person trucking game originally devised by Morton Deutsch and Robert Krauss. Each player operates a trucking company, Acme or Bolt, and he must move his truck over a road system to his destination. The faster he completes the trip, the more money he will earn. Of course there is a dilemma: one must choose between two routes to the finish—a short, direct route and a longer, more circuitous one. A portion of the short route narrows to a one-lane pathway; if both trucks attempt passage at the same time they will collide, causing both players to lose time and money. One player, then, has to yield. The longer route has no common pathway but is twice as long; its use permits a player to avoid encounters with his opponent, but it automatically limits the amount he can earn. In order for each to win the maximum amount, therefore, the opposing players must cooperate.

To complicate the game further, each player also controls a tollgate at one end of the common pathway on the short route, through which his opponent's truck must pass. In each trial we required players either to charge one of several specified tolls or to grant free passage. If a truck refuses to pay a demanded toll, it must then back out of the common pathway and take the longer route.

Feedback.   In our first experiment, 60 male subjects played this game with a stooge (Bolt) who had sole use of the tollgate and who systematically exploited them during the first round of 10 trials. That is, the stooge charged high tolls, causing subjects to lose much of their initial stake. At the end of this round, subjects got written feedback from—we told them—an audience of peers who had been observing.

Half of the subjects received evaluations that derogated them for allowing themselves to be exploited: e.g., "Bolt was out to beat Acme and he really made Acme look like a sucker," or, "Bolt played tricky. He ran rings around Acme and made him lose a lot. Acme looked pretty bad." The rest of the subjects read comments that commended them for playing fair: e.g., "Bolt was rough and tricky but Acme came out okay because he played it straight," or "Bolt was out to beat Acme and made him look like a sucker, but Acme played fair and looked good."

Now the subjects played another round of 10 trials, and this time they, not the stooge, had control of the toll gate. We gave them the following toll schedule:

Toll you may charge:						
00	10	15	20	30	40	50
Costs to self:						
00	00	00	10	25	40	60

In other words, subjects could retaliate against the stooge by charging high tolls, or increase their own earnings by charging lesser ones. The more severe the retaliation, the smaller one's own gains became.

Revenge. The results were clear. Students who had received the sucker feedback from their audience were far more likely to retaliate against their opponents than subjects who had received favorable feedback. More importantly, the first group retaliated at high personal cost; they were willing to lose money in order to restore face with their opponents. The second group, who did not feel that they had played foolishly, went on to maximize their profits.

It is possible, of course, that these results can be explained by revenge—the desire to inflict harm on one's opponent—rather than by the face-saving motive. We do not think that simple revenge was the primary factor here, since the "not-foolish" group was far less retaliatory than the "foolish" group, though all had been objectively victimized in the same way. Our post-experimental questionnaire also showed that subjects who felt humiliated were more concerned with appearing strong to the stooge than were the other subjects. We concluded that young men will try to reassert capability and strength after being made to look foolish—even if it is costly.

The price one pays for such sweet retaliation, however, must not be known to one's enemy. If X is aware that Y must sacrifice money for the pleasure of defeating him, Y's ability to restore face is greatly reduced. A variation of the bargaining experiment showed that the costs one willingly incurs to save face (or restore it) are likely to be greater when one knows that those costs will not be publicized. We told half of our subjects that before the second 10 trials their costs for retaliation—the toll schedule—would be shown to their opponents, while the rest thought that these costs would remain private. The latter group retaliated more frequently, tending to lose more money than the former.

Pacifier.   We next turned to a different experimental paradigm: public embarrassment. We told subjects, 48 freshman males, that they were participating in a perception study. Their task was to form detailed impressions of an object during a three-minute "sensing period"—but using only one prescribed sense. Each student sat in a private cubicle, blindfolded ("so as not to confound visual perception with other forms of perception being studied," we told them).

In the "embarrassing" condition, we gave each of one group of subjects a four-inch rubber pacifier (sterilized, in a cellophane packet) and told him to "sense it orally": "suck, bite and lick the object to form detailed impressions of it." Each remaining subject got a four-inch rubber soldier; we told him to "touch and feel the object with your hands to form detailed impressions."

It appears that there is almost nothing more embarrassing to a freshman male than sucking a baby pacifier, except perhaps having to describe the experience. After the "sensing" part of the experiment, we gave each subject the choice of discussing his impressions before a panel of evaluators (to increase a monetary reward) or of declining public exposure (thereby forfeiting the reward). Subjects who had to suck the pacifiers sacrificed far more money, on the average, than those who had had the less embarrassing task. The pacifier group said that they simply didn't want to look foolish.

The evaluative role of the audience is important in face saving, too. In a similar experiment, subjects had to perform the same embarrassing task. But half of them believed that the audience was convened specifically to evaluate them as they discussed the experience; the rest thought that the audience was only a casual gathering of visitors, convened merely by coincidence. Subjects declined public discussion much more often in the first case.

Sing.   Our most recent set of experiments has explored the influence of felt incompetence, audience acquaintanceship, and expected feedback on face saving. We used a different sort of embarrassment in this series.

We asked our subjects—72 freshman males—to sing "Love Is a Many-Splendored Thing" privately, after which they received apparently objective computer evaluations of their vocal abilities: "competent" or "incompetent." We selected that song for its high embarrassment potential, having discovered that most college students are willing to blunder their way through folk songs and easy ballads without undue embarrassment.

After receiving their voice evaluations, subjects sang the same song to a panel of evaluators (ostensibly sitting behind a one-way mirror). We explained that the purpose of the study was to compare the computer evaluations with those made by the audience. Further, we would pay the freshmen according to the length of time they continued to sing—the longer they kept going, the more they would earn.

Expectations.   We hypothesized that singing time would be: (1) shorter (and monetary sacrifice greater) in the "incompetent" group than in the "competent" group; (2) shorter when subjects expected to get feedback on their performances than when feedback was not expected; (3) longer before an audience of strangers than before acquaintances or friends. The results supported the first and third predictions.

In further support of the face-saving concept, the most common reason the freshmen gave for declining to sing was the desire to avoid looking foolish or incompetent. "I seriously did not feel it worth my time to stand there and croak like a frog, which is what my voice is like," explained one student. "I don't need the money particularly, and my embarrassment overcame my dedication to science," another rationalized. "I stopped because I couldn't remember the rest of the song and I know I can't sing so I felt really stupid," said a third.

Contrary to several theories and common sense, close friends do not liberate individuals from face-saving. Quite the reverse. Our subjects were more likely to withdraw from public performance in front of their friends than in front of strangers, and similarly they sacrificed more money before strangers they expected to meet later than before strangers whom they would not meet. Knowledge about future dealings with one's audience, therefore, evokes the motive to save or restore face.

Sex.   Thus far we had used males in most of our research, since we wanted first to get hold of the situational factors involved in face-saving. We suspected that there would be differences *between* the sexes in face-saving, and also *within* each sex group depending on the sex of the audience. After reviewing the research on sex differences in several related areas (embarrassment, blushing, empathy, and status-associated sex), we predicted that:

1. Women would be more prone to face saving than men.
2. Among women, face saving would increase in the presence of males, but among males face saving would decrease in front of females.
3. Overall, a male audience would be more likely to induce face saving than a female audience would.

We used the public-singing situation to test these predictions, asking males and females to sing "Love is a Many-Splendored Thing" before male or female evaluators. The primary measure of face saving was length of singing time in front of the audience (subjects were paid for each five seconds they sang). The results:

Average Singing Time (In seconds)

	Sex of Subjects		
Sex of Audience	Male	Female	Overall
Male	77	65	71
Female	90	16	53
Overall	84	41	

This shows: (1) that females sang for significantly shorter periods of time than males, regardless of the sex of the audience, and (2) that face saving was most pronounced among women who had to sing to a female audience. Recall that the less one sang, the greater the face saving.

Mix.   We next tried to understand the reason for the increased face-saving in the female-female condition. Answers to a postexperimental questionnaire showed that women expected a female audience to be more critical than a male audience. They also attributed greater singing ability to women, and this increased their embarrassment—which in turn made them stop singing sooner. Interestingly, this process was not at work among the males; the sex of the audience had no significant effect on their singing times.

This finding suggested that for women the expertise of the audience has an important effect on the need to save face. To test this, we did an experiment with women only, using the same singing paradigm. We informed subjects that the (female) audience consisted of either "excellent" or "poor" singers. The results were clear: women who had to perform in front of the excellent group sang, on the average for 32 seconds; those who sang for the poor group carried on for an average of 119 seconds.

Points.   Taken together, these two studies of sex differences tell us, not so much that men and women are unlike in their needs to maintain face, but that they differ in their responses to particular situations. All of us use face saving to keep from looking foolish, but some circumstances make us feel more foolish than others.

From our research we can draw six conclusions about the nature of face-saving:

1. Face saving is heightened when one's audience gives him derogatory feedback rather than supportive feedback.
2. The costs one will incur to save (or restore) face are far greater when one is sure that only he will know those costs.
3. Face saving, by withdrawal from the public eye, is a likely response to public embarrassment even if this involves high cost to oneself. We are not motivated solely by rational, economic interests.
4. Face saving increases when one's audience has an evaluative role.
5. Face saving is likely to occur if one feels personally incompetent, and if this incompetence threatens to become publicly visible.
6. Individuals are more likely to save face in front of friends or strangers they will meet later, than before acquaintances or strangers they will never meet.

Peace.   These findings point to a generalized strategy to cope with the need to save face in settling conflicts. For example, if derogatory feedback increases face saving, mediators should encourage negotiators to be supportive of each other. Compromises can be rationalized by pointing out that disputants are being wise, not weak, in making them. In short, mediators should be interpersonally skillful as well as impartial, and should be attuned to the strength and subtlety of the motive to maintain face.

Perhaps if the universality of this motive is brought into the open and better understood, we can learn to control it, negotiate around it, and not let it get in the way of our best interests. Students could study out of the motivation to learn; governments could admit to mistakes, however tragic; and we would be less likely to let the Kitty Genoveses die because we are embarrassed to intervene.

Negotiating with an Angry Public: Advice to Corporate Leaders

David Kuechle

Shortly after midnight on December 3, 1984, poison gas seeped from an underground storage tank in Bhopal, India, and formed a deadly white cloud over a 25-square-mile area. By morning the leaking gas had killed more than 1,200 people, and 50,000 others had been injured. Most of those who died had been sleeping. They suffocated as the gas attacked their lungs and bloodstreams.

The gas, methyl isocyanate, was the principal ingredient in pesticides used by Indian farmers and fruit growers. The pesticides were produced in a factory owned by the Indian subsidiary of Union Carbide Corporation.

Upon receiving word of the disaster at corporate headquarters in Danbury, Connecticut, company officials called an immediate worldwide halt to the production and shipment of methyl isocyanate, and dispatched a doctor and four technicians to India to discover the causes of the leak. The next day, Warren M. Anderson, Union Carbide's chairman, flew to Bhopal for a firsthand investigation. By Friday, December 7, over 2,000 Bhopal residents had died. More than 200,000 others were sick or injured.

Meanwhile, members of the news media, representatives of environmental groups, politicians, and so-called ''experts'' on poisonous gases descended on Bhopal and Union Carbide. Stories about the tragedy hit the headlines and prime-time news broadcasts within hours, and stayed there for more than a month. Union Carbide officials were besieged with questions, the answers to which were largely unknown for several days. Nonetheless, the news gaps were filled by persons who speculated on causes of the disaster, on design of the safety systems at Union Carbide's plant, on the advisability of working with deadly chemicals in heavily populated areas, on the likelihood of extensive damage claims against the company, and on corporate responsibility in general.

In short, Union Carbide Corporation found itself surrounded by concerned, sometimes angry, members of the public. And the anger escalated rapidly as people de-

Reprinted from David Kuechle, ''Negotiating with an Angry Public: Advice to Corporate Leaders,'' *Negotiation Journal,* October 1985, pp. 317–30. Used with permission of Plenum Publishing Corporation and the author.

manded to know the answers to such questions as: What happened? Why? What's being done about it? What's the likely impact?

The Bhopal disaster underlines the special negotiation problems faced by corporate executives whose companies are involved in a crisis. In most cases of this nature there's been an accident: possibly an airplane crash, a derailment of a train carrying hazardous chemicals, or a large tanker run aground and leaking oil onto the beaches. Or there's a threat of catastrophe, causing widespread alarm, often fueled by sensational and irresponsible comments, followed by urgent demands for information and explanations. Usually the company involved is on the defensive, required to explain, to provide a story. The responses can have a far-reaching impact. In some cases these responses have been handled badly, leading to boycotts of the company's products, monumental lawsuits, damage to the company's image, and demands for resignations by corporate executives.

This article examines crises faced recently by three multinational corporations: Nestlé S.A. of Switzerland, Arthur D. Little Inc. of Cambridge, Massachusetts, and Union Carbide in the Bhopal incident. In particular, it focuses on the actions of corporate executives, and derives some important negotiation principles for dealing with a concerned, angry public. Effective leadership in such instances can help temper the inevitable anger and, sometimes, even convert those who voice anger into enthusiastic supporters.

NESTLE CORPORATION AND THE
INFANT FOOD CONTROVERSY[1]

Nestlé S.A. has produced and marketed infant weaning formulas since 1867. These were promoted through the years by doctors in European colonies which later became independent Third World countries.

From the beginning the formula products were considered by Nestlé to be lifesaving: something that the company was proud to produce and sell. However, in 1973, two British doctors reported that there was widespread misuse of Nestlé's formula products among impoverished, mostly illiterate, families where there was a tendency for mothers, trying to save money, to use less-than-necessary quantities of formula powder by diluting it with more water than recommended. The water was frequently contaminated; as a result, the children became increasingly susceptible to diarrheal diseases and were handicapped in their ability to assimilate nutrients because their stomachs and intestines did not work properly. This, in turn, could lead to malnutrition and death.

The report was widely reprinted, and during the next five years the situation escalated as Nestlé became the target of special interest groups, politicians, and journalists from around the world.

---

[1] Material in this account was taken mostly from teaching cases titled *Nestlé and the Infant Food Controversy* (A) and (B), prepared by Aylin Hunt under the supervision of Professors George Taucher and Christopher Gale from IMEDE (International Management Development Institute, Lausanne, Switzerland) and Professor Michael R. Pearce from the University of Western Ontario, School of Business Administration.

In June of 1974, the Third World Action Group, located in Bern, Switzerland, published a booklet titled *Nestlé Kills Babies,* asserting that the company's sales promotion practices for infant formulas were unethical, and charging the company with responsibility for death or permanent physical and mental damage to babies. In particular, its authors castigated Nestlé's sales representatives, who dressed like nurses in order to give a scientific appearance.

In response to *Nestlé Kills Babies,* the corporation brought suit in Bern against 13 members of the Third World Action Group and two newspapers that carried articles about the booklet. The company charged criminal libel.

Meanwhile, other special interest groups became involved. Among these was the U.S. Interfaith Center on Corporate Responsibility (ICCR), an organization sponsored by the National Council of Churches. In 1975, ICCR sponsored a half-hour film titled *Bottle Babies,* produced by Peter Krieg, a well-known German film maker. Most of the camera work was done in Kenya in "documentary" style, picturing malnourished children, the mixing of formula products with polluted water, hospitals where infants were being treated, and infant graves—one with a used can of Nestlé formula in the position of a headstone. The film was shown to gatherings of church groups, and typically was followed by an impassioned plea for viewers to write letters of protest to company management and elected officials.

In June of 1977 a group called Third World Institute, led by Douglas Johnson at the University of Minnesota, formed the Infant Formula Action Coalition (INFACT). Johnson, encouraged by ICCR and others, felt that significant progress could not be made until Nestlé was pressured to change. He believed that legal or shareholder action against a foreign-based company would be useless. So, on July 4, 1977, INFACT announced a consumer boycott against all infant formula companies whose marketing practices INFACT found to be improper; Nestlé was the largest and most prominent among them.

Nestlé became a symbol of all that was under attack when a demonstration, marking the start of the boycott, was staged in front of the company's Minneapolis, Minnesota, headquarters. There were about 100 participants, urging consumers to boycott over 40 Nestlé products.

Actions by INFACT, ICCR, and other pressure groups drew attention and support from other well-known U.S. activists. These included Cesar Chavez, Ralph Nader, Dr. Benjamin Spock, and Gloria Steinem. In 1978, Senator Edward Kennedy, Chairman of the Senate's Subcommittee on Health and Scientific Research on Infant Nutrition, scheduled public hearings on the infant food controversy. CBS produced a television report on the issue that included portions of the Kennedy hearings.

In particular, the CBS report focused on Senator Kennedy's badgering attack on Dr. R. Oswaldo Ballarin, President and Chairman of Nestlé, Brazil. The incident took place when Kennedy interrupted Dr. Ballarin as the latter delivered a prepared statement charging that the boycott of Nestlé products was "an indirect attack on the free world's economic system."

Kennedy stated that the boycott was a recognized tool in a free economic, democratic society, adding that various groups which had staged the boycott were, in part, sponsored by the National Council of Churches. Then the senator questioned Ballarin extensively concerning the company's practices, ending with the following exchange:

Senator Kennedy: What do you feel is your corporate responsibility to find the extent of the use of your product in the developing part of the world?

Dr. Ballarin: We cannot have that responsibility, sir . . . How can I be responsible for the water system?[2]

ARTHUR D. LITTLE, INC.[3]

In June, 1982, Arthur D. Little, Inc. (ADL), the international consulting firm, entered into contracts with the U.S. Department of Defense to perform experiments on deadly nerve gases and blister agents in order to develop ways to identify such substances, to devise means for handling them safely, and, eventually, to detoxify them.

The substances, developed during World War II for use in chemical warfare, had been stored underground since then in steel drums. The exact locations were secret, but there had been instances in recent years when the storage containers had begun to crack. The gases leaked into the ground and seeped upward, causing the death of animals grazing on the land above. In at least one such instance, an entire flock of sheep had been destroyed on the range of a midwestern U.S. farmer, and nerve agents were blamed. According to scientists the nerve gases are so lethal that an accidental release could kill anywhere from 10 to 30 persons instantly if dispersed into the atmosphere.[4]

In order to perform work on these substances, the company had constructed a new analytic chemistry laboratory at its headquarters property in Cambridge, Massachusetts. The laboratory, its equipment, and procedures were subsequently inspected and approved by the Chemical Security Office of the U.S. Department of the Army, by two independent consultants, and by the Massachusetts Department of Public Health.

As the laboratory was being built, rumors regarding its purpose began to spread in the community. These were fueled by a perceived reluctance on the part of the company spokespersons to talk about the laboratory and by conflicting stories emanating from ADL headquarters.

The first delivery of nerve and blister agents came to ADL in a U.S. army truck that was escorted by armed military personnel carriers and police cruisers, an unusual, almost threatening sight. When asked, a company spokesperson confirmed that the truck was, indeed, carrying nerve and blister agents, and this information increased alarm among members of the Cambridge community. Their concerns were promptly taken up by the Cambridge City Council, which scheduled the first of two open meetings to which ADL executives were invited.

The executives attempted to explain and justify their work, but they were largely unsuccessful, as demonstrated by subsequent efforts by the City Council to halt ADL's work through issuance of a general order prohibiting testing, storage, transportation, and disposal of nerve and blister agents within the city.

---

[2] Material quoted in this section was taken from the transcript of U.S. Senate Subcommittee Hearings, May 1978, pp. 126–39.

[3] Material in this account was taken from published sources and internal documents provided by Arthur D. Little, Inc.

[4] *The Boston Globe,* August 2, 1985, p. 13.

ADL, in turn, obtained a temporary court injunction preventing enforcement of the city's order. This spurred further action by the city, as the Council appointed a Citizens' Advisory Committee to study the situation and make recommendations. The committee, consisting of 17 residents of Cambridge and adjoining communities—many of whom were distinguished scientists from major universities in the area—delivered a draft report on July 18, 1984, stating that "the benefits of research with these chemicals [did] not justify lethal risks to the general public." These risks, according to the majority of the Advisory Committee, were unacceptable.[5]

Despite the committee's report and widespread opposition within the community, the company continued its work. Meanwhile media attention mounted, and at least six public interest groups were formed with purposes ranging from the stimulation of community debate to outright barring of ADL from further testing.

On December 14, 1984, Middlesex County Superior Court Judge Robert Hallisey ruled that the City of Cambridge's ban on testing was "valid and enforceable." The company promptly appealed, but this ruling, coupled with increased pressure group activity, caused ADL to announce on February 28, 1985, that it had "voluntarily" stopped testing nerve and blister agents until it could sort out the court decisions.

On August 1, 1985, the Massachusetts Supreme Judicial Court affirmed Judge Hallisey's ruling. This apparently put an end to the controversy as Alma Triner, the company's Vice President for Public Relations, said that the company was surprised and disappointed by the decision but would obey the law and stop the testing.[6]

AN ANGRY PUBLIC

When a business faces a crisis, its leaders inevitably find themselves facing a concerned public consisting of political leaders, special interest groups, neighbors, employees, customers, members of the financial community, curious onlookers, and journalists.

Some of the interested parties are frightened. Some are confused. Some see an opportunity to enhance their own parochial causes. And some seek newsworthy stories. Business leaders who fail to seize control of the situation—to build a solid foundation that enables them to be heard and trusted—will almost certainly cause the initial concern to escalate into anger.

If answers are not forthcoming—if executives refuse comment, defer to their public affairs departments, or defy credibility by providing incomplete or conflicting information—others will quickly fill the gaps. This happened when *New York Times* investigative reporters went to work in Bhopal immediately after the disaster and uncovered embarrassing information about Union Carbide's safety practices. In turn, their stories provided impetus for concerned readers to become angry tormentors. It happened to Nestlé S.A. and Arthur D. Little, Inc. as pressure groups formed and became increasingly active after learning about their activities.

---

[5] See *Draft Report to the City Manager,* Cambridge Scientific Advisory Committee, July 18, 1984, p. 2.

[6] *The Boston Globe,* August 2, 1985, p. 13.

Sometimes business leaders themselves help turn concerned questioners into active adversaries and angry tormentors when they react to questions by thrashing about, impugning motives of their adversaries, and filing lawsuits.

The three cases in this study provide examples of business leaders taking effective action to avert or quell anger. They also provide examples of leaders making mistakes during crises. For this reason, the cases give readers an intimate opportunity to learn—to derive insights that can help develop negotiating skills for dealing with crisis situations and, often, for converting a disaster into an opportunity to build understanding, to enlist support of would-be detractors, and even to enhance a company's image.

Four broad-based, interrelated principles for effective negotiation in crises emerge from these cases. They are: (1) Take the initiative. Make news! (2) Identify and speak to the affected audiences. (3) Focus attention on shared objectives. (4) Use a wide-angle lens. Each of these principles will be described and discussed in turn, drawing on evidence from Nestlé S.A., Arthur D. Little, Inc., and Union Carbide Corporation.

Take the Initiative. Make News!   Most of the time corporations go about their businesses in unheralded fashion, turning out products and delivering services as a matter of course. Consequently, their activities are not generally newsworthy, and most corporate executives do not develop skills in the art of *making* news. By contrast, political leaders and members of special interest groups are generally well trained in making news, and they respond enthusiastically when there are opportunities for them to be heard. They especially covet the limelight when commonly perceived villains are involved, such as large, multinational corporations and their top executives.

Journalists, constantly hunting for good stories, naturally seek out newsmakers when crises strike. If corporate executives fail to provide good stories, the journalists will certainly turn to others. A statement, *any* statement with a "good," controversy-provoking quote, is often sufficient to satisfy media representatives. As a result, reporters often put considerable pressure on business executives to say something, anything, even if all the facts are not yet known.

Union Carbide officials were immediately viewed as villains in the Bhopal catastrophe. This image was sharpened as they scrambled desperately to gather information, putting off reporters as the pressures mounted. Meanwhile scientists and engineers, not connected with the company, willingly speculated about possible causes of the accident, and medical experts offered opinions about the long-term physical effects of methyl isocyanate on human organs. Members of the legal profession also became involved, speculating about the potential liability of Union Carbide for the deaths and injuries suffered at Bhopal. Many of the resulting news stories were acknowledged by reporters to be unconfirmed reports. But even so, they made headlines, and at the expense of Union Carbide.

Union Carbide took the initiative in the Bhopal crisis faster than either Arthur D. Little regarding the nerve-gas controversy or Nestlé regarding infant formula usage. If it had waited as long as either of the other two companies before taking control, Union Carbide might have perished as a corporate entity. First, the trip to India by Chairman Warren Anderson was, itself, newsworthy. Later, he was arrested in India along with two Union Carbide executives from India, and this event made headlines, resulting in some expressions of sympathy for Anderson. Subsequent announcements by the corporation—that disaster aid was being made available and that the Bhopal factory would not reopen without Indian approval—helped give the corporation additional control over the news. All of these actions served to dull the swords of would-be adversaries and to cool passions of those who otherwise might have taken extreme action.

It was nearly six months after the first expressions of concern by Cambridge citizens before Arthur D. Little (ADL) began to take initiative in the nerve gas crisis. On March 19, 1984, President John Magee appeared alone before the City Council and, like Anderson of Union Carbide, injected himself—a living, breathing person—into the situation. In so doing, he created an image that was sympathetic for some when he said:

> I am no absentee landlord trying to foist something on someone else. The laboratory is not far from my office. If there were an accident my fellow employees and I would be the first to suffer.

In addition, Magee distributed a concise, clearly written position paper prior to the meeting, thereby providing journalists with some easily understood, highly quotable paragraphs, any of which could be used alone or in conjunction with any others. In short, ADL had already done most of what the journalists would be required to do, thus making their work considerably easier. At the same time the position paper helped Magee control the ensuing agenda by outlining topics for questioning.

Nestlé, on the other hand, did not take initiative for nearly five years following the October 1973 report that brought the infant formula issue into focus. Up until the summer of 1978, when Nestlé executives held a massive conference with journalists from around the world at its headquarters in Switzerland, the company, like Arthur D. Little, had been reacting to others who were making news. Once Nestlé executives decided to speak—before the Kennedy Investigating Committee, then in the press conference—they thrashed about, impugning motives of their perceived tormentors, and even lashing out against Senator Kennedy and CBS for their treatment of Dr. Ballarin.

There are many ways to *make* news when crisis situations arise. The first, and most obvious, is to provide complete information to political leaders, employees, neighbors, customers, journalists, and others who are likely to be interested—in *anticipation* of their questions. Indeed news making can defuse a potential confrontation before it has a chance to develop. In the initial stages of a crisis, if the company itself breaks the story, it is the company that shapes the information.

For ADL, there were warnings as early as the fall of 1983 that members of the community were concerned about the firm's activities. Until then, ADL's executives might have been reluctant to release information regarding their pending work, lest they frighten people unnecessarily. However, when it became clear that political leaders and neighbors were concerned, the company should have seized the initiative by inviting journalists and community leaders to a press conference wherein they disclosed the nature of their work, identified and described the properties of the chemicals to be tested, and provided details on how those chemicals would be transported and treated within and outside the laboratory.

As it turned out, the company did do all this—five months later. In the meantime, the firm's image suffered, and people became angry. The anger was accelerated when the company refused to comply with the City Council's order that testing be stopped.

Even in a fast-breaking crisis like Bhopal, it is possible to take early initiatives. Union Carbide did this on the day of the disaster by calling a press conference at the Danbury (Connecticut) Hilton Hotel. The conference room was jammed with reporters, and much of the questioning was speculative. But all of it was urgent, because journalists were under pressure to produce stories, and to do so quickly. Union Carbide was able to tell journalists that it was sending help to India: medical supplies, respirators and the like, and a doctor with extensive knowledge of methyl isocyanate's effects. Later the same day, the firm announced that it was sending a team of technical experts to examine the plant and determine what went wrong. The next day the company resumed the initiative by announcing that it would deplete stocks of methyl isocyanate in storage at their plants in Woodbine, Georgia, Cubatao, Brazil, and Beziers, France, by turning them into products.[7]

Nestlé S.A., on the other hand, had several years to take the initiative. If Nestlé's managing director had personalized the situation like Union Carbide's Anderson—perhaps by firsthand visits to hospitals in Kenya or Ethiopia, where infants were reported to be suffering—this could have made news. Likewise, if Nestlé's executives had expressed concern over the suffering of infants in developing nations as a result of ignorance, poverty, and malnutrition, or even possibly from having used Nestlé products, this, too, could have made news. As it was, the media focused on the following public comment of Nestlé's Managing Director, Dr. Arthur Furer:

> We accept no responsibility for the hygienic conditions in these countries and for the lack of knowledge of writing and reading . . .[8]

This often quoted comment cast Dr. Furer as a noncaring, irresponsible corporate leader whose prime concerns centered on sales and profits. The image was far from the truth about the man. Nonetheless, for many viewers and listeners, the image *was* the truth.

*   *   *   *   *

Corporate executives who face crisis situations usually seek guidance from attorneys before taking action or making statements. Often attorneys caution against doing or saying anything that could be interpreted as an admission of liability or fault. From a strictly legal viewpoint this may be good advice. In terms of the public's perception of the corporation, however, this stance can appear to be self-serving and uncaring. There is a fine line between observing caution for purposes of enhancing one's position in a court of law and displaying reluctance to speak when the corporate image is at stake. Failure to speak is often viewed as a plea of *nolo contendere.*

Identify and Speak to the Affected Audience.   Successful political leaders know and speak to their audiences whenever possible—often using the media for that purpose and sometimes using business executives who face crisis situations as their

---

[7] See "Union Carbide: Coping with Catastrophe," *Fortune*, January 7, 1985.

[8] This quotation was taken from the British Broadcasting Corporation's (BBC) news program of 1978 titled *Panorama*, anchored by Michael Cochran.

pawns. Senator Edward Kennedy did this with great effectiveness at the expense of Dr. Oswaldo Ballarin of Nestlé. Kennedy was not talking to Ballarin when he interrupted the Nestlé executive. Rather, he took advantage of the situation to address members of his own voting constituency: church members, the disadvantaged, advocates of the free enterprise system, and those who exercise their rights to protest through consumer boycotts.

Later Kennedy sought to ingratiate himself further with his audience by posing "trap" questions to Dr. Ballarin:

> . . . would you agree with me that your product should not be used where there is impure water?

> Yes or no?

> . . . do you think that your product ought to be used where there is illiteracy, vast illiteracy?

These questions were virtually impossible for Dr. Ballarin to answer in a few short sentences. The Nestlé official hesitated and asked Kennedy to repeat the questions. But, by doing so, he appeared inept and confused, and this image was conveyed by television and radio into millions of homes around the world.

The audiences affected by crisis situations are varied. However, the largest, and often most influential, audience consists of readers, viewers, and listeners who are generally reluctant to immerse themselves in details, examine all available facts, and arrive at independent conclusions about events in the news. Rather, these are people who respond to images more than facts, who appreciate brevity, not thoroughness. Journalists who address this audience seek stories that are brief, devoid of technical language, and, ideally, possess emotional appeal. They know that impressions are often formed during brief television appearances, by newspaper headlines, and by slick-covered magazines with lots of pictures. Senator Kennedy knew this too and, playing on his image as champion of the disadvantaged, scored points at the expense of Dr. Ballarin, a compassionate, decent man who had been cast in the role of villain.

Political leaders and spokespersons for special interest groups are acutely aware of the propensities of mass media audiences. For this reason, demonstrations against Nestlé were staged outside the company's offices in Los Angeles, the world's film capital, where media artistry abounds. And that is why Alice Wolfe, Cambridge City Councilor, pitted Arthur D. Little, Inc. against "defenseless" residents of Cambridge when she made the following, oft-quoted, comment:

> We have more to lose than Arthur D. Little has. They lose a little money but we have the potential for a disaster.[9]

Most corporate executives are understandably reluctant to engage in exchange of pithy comments with politicians or representatives of interest groups. Yet, by preparing 15-second statements that focus on commonly shared emotions, they can do a great

---

[9] This statement was made at a public hearing of the Cambridge City Council on March 19, 1984.

deal to enhance the image of their organization. Chairman Anderson of Union Carbide, after being released by Indian officials following his arrest, did so when he said:

> My immediate concern is to get the people affected immediate disaster relief.[10]

Nestlé and Union Carbide had greater reason than ADL to be concerned about communicating effectively with mass media audiences during their respective crises, because a large percentage of their customers were members of these audiences. Consumer boycotts and other negative reactions against their products could have immediate impact on their income statements. For this reason, they had greater need than ADL to communicate their positions effectively to a mass audience.

Arthur D. Little's customers were mostly professionals, persons who were likely to demand facts and expertise, not images, and who were more likely to continue doing business with ADL because of the firm's unique scientific capabilities and reliability— not for its ability to create popular images before the television viewing audience. Thus, ADL made it clear in its early actions and statements that the firm was obligated to its customers, even if this meant fighting in the courts. To do otherwise could have put ADL customers on notice that the company could not be counted on to undertake difficult, controversial work in the future.

ADL was forced to take a delicate path of action when the City Council ordered a ban on further testing. To comply with the ban would mean abandonment of its customer; to fight the ban in the courts, as ADL did, would most likely create a negative image with political leaders and neighbors. The choice had to be made, and ADL did not waffle. The company addressed its customers with detailed information, and, eventually, addressed political leaders and neighbors by creating images, like those associated with President Magee's willingness to locate himself near the testing site.

Other audiences must also be addressed. Important among them are employees and members of the financial community. Union Carbide executives felt an immediate need to address its employees—directly—and President Alec Flamm did so promptly, focusing on the need for compassion regarding the suffering of victims in Bhopal. Subsequent, and regular, communications provided employees with information on the causes of the accident as they became known.

Following the Bhopal disaster, financial markets reflected uneasiness about Union Carbide's ability to survive the expected onslaught of lawsuits. Some observers even speculated on the possibility of bankruptcy. The company was quick in its attempts to reassure stockholders and members of the financial community, stating that it was heavily insured to protect against disasters of this nature, that it hoped to settle all claims out of court and quickly, and that time required of its executives to deal with lawsuits would not detract from the company's requirements for attentive management of day-to-day affairs.

Focus Attention on Shared Objectives.   Each of the companies in this study was involved in work that could have resulted in positive news coverage. For over a

---

[10] *International Herald Tribune*, January 10, 1985, p. 9.

century, Nestlé Corporation had marketed infant weaning formula in order to promote health and save lives of infants. Arthur D. Little was engaged in efforts to prevent nerve gas poisoning, helping to head off almost-inevitable catastrophes. And Union Carbide was manufacturing products that helped Indian farmers grow better fruit, vegetables, and grains, thus helping to alleviate widespread malnutrition in the area.

Few would argue that these were unworthy purposes. However, crises arose as a result of *methods* used by the three companies in pursuing their objectives, and it was the methods—not the objectives—that received most of the attention.

All three companies had knowingly assumed risks in taking on the work that gave rise to their respective crises, and all three had adopted elaborate safety measures to minimize those risks. Their willingness to gamble resources and reputations to do something good is an admirable characteristic. Yet, when crises arose as a result of their endeavors, executives from Nestlé, Arthur D. Little, and Union Carbide found themselves cast in the role of demons. To some degree they played out their roles, almost as if they felt these behaviors were expected. Nestlé took members of the Third World Action Group to court, and won, on a legal technicality—but if the firm had hoped through this action to serve notice that it was doing good things, it lost. Similarly, Arthur D. Little won its initial rounds in court and, as a result, continued testing nerve gases while disillusioned political leaders and neighbors seethed with anger.

For Nestlé and Arthur D. Little the legal contests were, in fact, ''no-win'' situations. While both corporations prevailed in court on technical grounds, they were victimized by a commonly held presumption: that corporations, through superior legal acumen and financial power, always win over the downtrodden and underprivileged.

Corporations facing legal action, public hearings before political bodies, and press conferences should view these situations as opportunities to tell their corporate story in their own behalf. The Third World Action Group used the Nestlé trials as a forum to publicize its worldwide activities, often unrelated to the issues of law being debated; there is no reason why corporations cannot do likewise.

Media representatives are certain to attend controversial court trials, and they all share a common objective: to deliver a good story. Executives who seek to tell their corporate story in a way that produces good stories for journalists can often divert attention away from the confrontation. In so doing they can focus on broader, more worthy, objectives which *they* seek to achieve.

Executives will be comforted to know that most journalists, in seeking a good story, do not care whether they get the story from corporate executives or would-be adversaries. It can also be comforting to know that in their quest for good stories journalists share three major concerns—deadlines, accuracy, and easy access to information. All three can be addressed by anyone, including corporate executives, in a manner consistent with their own objectives.

Use a Wide-Angle Lens.   Photographers and television camerapersons, working with a variety of lenses, can severely narrow the viewers' range of vision, such as when they focus on an individual in a crowd. Viewers who see the picture are usually aware of its larger context, but often forget that the image conveyed may be quite different from what it could be if they could see the entire scene through a wider-angle lens.

So, too, when a crisis occurs there is a tendency to focus on incidents and images—one at a time—and to deal with them as if they represented the entire picture. The result is often a distorted view that can lead to unwise actions.

There were numerous examples of this "narrowed vision" phenomenon in the three cases cited here. Among them were:

- A child's grave in Kenya, with a Nestlé infant formula can in the place of a headstone.

- Delivery of nerve and blister agents to Arthur D. Little, Inc. by a U.S. military convoy.

- The arrest of Union Carbide's Chairman, Warren Anderson, in Bhopal.

Images resulting from these incidents were flashed repeatedly on television screens and appeared in newspapers and magazines.

Sometimes corporate executives themselves even help to narrow the viewers' focus. Typically this happens when they refer to the need for their companies to make sales, control costs, and realize profits. Others in business fully accept these arguments, but members of the nonbusiness community do not necessarily empathize.

For example, Nestlé's senior managers from Switzerland and the United States met with members of various pressure groups in September of 1977 in an effort to resolve what they thought was a poor communication problem by explaining the "facts." Nestlé management argued the company could not compete favorably if it stopped all promotion, as the groups had demanded. Less promotion, argued Nestlé, would mean fewer sales and fewer jobs in developing nations.

Similarly, in an effort to focus attention away from the threat of disaster presented by its nerve gas experiments, Arthur D. Little pointed to the fact that it had spent large sums of money to establish and maintain a testing laboratory, and had committed substantial resources to train personnel for its operation. According to Judith Harris, manager of ADL's research laboratory, the entire effort undertaken by the company had been worth $2.1 million to Arthur D. Little so far and would be worth $10 million or more over 10 years.

Exposed to presentations such as these, it is easy to see why many listeners and viewers concluded that the companies were simply voicing the fact that sales, profits, and jobs were of primary concern, even at the expense of human lives.

This is not to say that companies should shy away from telling a complete story—that they should feel ashamed to talk about their corporate mission or that they should not acknowledge that they are in business to make a profit. However, by demonstrating awareness that others may not share their viewpoints, they often can widen the focus of those who are listening. In the process, the audience begins to develop tolerance and understanding regarding the risks the companies have assumed, the resources they have committed, the sincerity with which they have pursued their objectives, and the concern they feel regarding fears and suffering that have arisen from the crisis at hand.

By focusing narrowly, business executives court the danger that others will seize the opportunity to create controversy. This happened to Nestlé when it focused on the work of their milk nurses. Through the years Nestlé executives came to believe that employment of milk nurses was an unassailable, conscientious effort to educate Third World mothers on proper nutrition practices. Nestlé adversaries, however, viewed the milk nurses as salespeople in disguise who were conveying the message that it was more desirable to feed babies infant formula, manufactured by Nestlé, than mother's milk. As a result, face-to-face controversies occurred over the value of milk nurses. These served mostly to sharpen battle lines, not to achieve understanding of Nestlé's overall aims.

Arthur D. Little's president, John Magee, used a narrow focus when he talked about himself as being among the first to suffer if there was an accident in the testing laboratories. In so doing, he assumed that ADL's adversaries would view the picture in the same way, and would thus come to believe that the work was not hazardous. Many listeners empathized; others, looking at the same picture, expressed the view that if Magee was crazy enough to locate the laboratory near his office, it did not follow logically that the laboratory ought to be located close to their homes. Arguments on this issue were likely to continue as long as the threat of disaster remained.

In a similar vein, some Union Carbide executives focused on the beneficial effects of pesticides, especially Third World countries where the need to provide food to millions of starving people was paramount. Union Carbide opponents, however, argued that pesticides are short-term "fixes" that, in the long term, destroy natural predators. They also charged that over time the pests will develop immunities to the chemicals being used, and that their surviving progeny will be able to inflict far more damage than that which the pesticides were designed to control. Here, too, arguments could go on for years.

On the other hand, Union Carbide's Warren Anderson sought to use a wide-angle lens and encouraged others to view the situation through the same lens. In response to questions from journalists about his arrest in India, Anderson resisted the temptation to deal with the merits of his arrest by directing attention away from himself and expressing concern about the mass suffering and the need for disaster assistance for victims. This helped considerably to defuse a potentially ugly situation. In addition, it helped to cast the company and himself as concerned, compassionate friends, not exploitive, unfeeling villains.

Crises that result in legal action invariably cause viewers to narrow their focus, sometimes without regard to the crisis itself. Lawyers who enter the scene seek to win cases on their clients' behalf, and sometimes resort to legal minutiae in their efforts. This was illustrated when Arthur D. Little's lawyers drew upon the supremacy clause of the U.S. Constitution as justification for the firm's unwillingness to comply with the city's ban on further testing of nerve gas. The tactic, predictably, backfired; citizens, political leaders, and journalists viewed the court decision merely as a legal battle in which the company's lawyers beat the city's lawyers during early court battles on technicalities.

Every business organization needs to have someone who constantly focuses on crisis situations with a wide-angle lens—who alerts executives to the fact that time-honored assumptions about the righteousness of various corporate actions and expressed viewpoints are not necessarily shared. Otherwise stated, the person who uses a wide-angle lens should act as a devil's advocate, constantly focusing upon and communicating worst possible scenarios in order to anticipate and head off unproductive arguments or other unwanted reactions. This is especially important during crises, but it is valuable even in normal times.

CONCLUSION

The Bhopal, India, tragedy of last December emphasized the necessity for business leaders to develop greater competence in crisis negotiations. It is not acceptable for these responsibilities to be delegated. Nor is it possible to rely on facts, figures, and scientific truths to save the day. Rather, executives must develop personal skills to communicate effectively with vast audiences that include political leaders, special interest groups, employees, neighbors, customers, members of the financial community, curious onlookers, and media representatives.

Crises faced by major corporations are often viewed from outside the corporation as opportunities for others to gain attention, to promote special causes, or to derive personal gains. Consequently, adversary relations soon develop, and tempers rise. Corporate leaders who seek to brake the mounting anger must become personally, visibly involved. Even then, if they read long-winded statements, defer to others or utter the phrase "no comment," they will almost certainly complicate rather than alleviate the problem.

Nestlé S.A. of Switzerland, Arthur D. Little, Inc., and Union Carbide Corporation have each provided examples of effective and ineffective management of public crises. In the process, they have also provided meaningful guidance to others who will face crises of their own. It *is* possible to convert a disaster into an opportunity, to build understanding, to convert would-be detractors into supporters, and even to enhance the company's image. But this requires sensitive awareness of, and responses to, the needs of those who would be adversaries.

Get Things Done through Coalitions

Margo Vanover

What do the American Paper Institute, National Coffee Association, Milk Industry Foundation, and American Council on Education have in common?

It may seem unlikely, but the answer is "an interest in sewer user charges."

These four associations and 11 others formed the Coalition for ICR Repeal to protect their members' interests in sewer user charges. Coalition members term industrial cost recovery (ICR) as "an unfair, unnecessary, and costly provision of the 1972 Federal Water Pollution Control Act."

This particular example of a coalition illustrates two very important points that you, a leader of your association, should be aware of. First of all, the coalition was successful. The industrial cost recovery provision was repealed on October 1, 1980, and coalition members frankly admit that they could never have done it alone. It took the efforts and—even more important—the clout of all 14 members to accomplish their goal.

The second point is this: Coalition members seemed like unlikely allies. Who would have thought they had anything in common?

"It's an interesting conglomeration of business groups with one similar interest," acknowledges Sheldon E. Steinbach, general counsel for the American Council on Education, Washington. "We all had one common problem—a proposed increase in sewer user charges.

"I remember the stunned look on the faces of the people at the first coalition meeting," he says with a chuckle. "They found out quickly that my association had the exact concern theirs did."

WHO ARE OUR ALLIES?

Right now, your association is probably a member of a coalition. But do you know what the coalition's purpose is? If you don't, ask your association's chief paid officer. He or she usually represents an association's interests in a coalition effort.

And while you are talking to your chief paid officer, ask what other associations comprise the coalition. You could be surprised. Like the Coalition for ICR Repeal, their names might not suggest a tie-in with your association's cause. In fact, they may be the names of associations that have been adversaries or competitors in the past.

It's not all that unusual, says Mr. Steinbach. "We look for common cause with other groups. We may be allies on one cause and enemies on another. It's happened time after time."

It's important to overlook past differences and concentrate on the present goal of the coalition, agrees Dr. Paul A. Kerschner, associate director for legislation, research, and programs at the National Retired Teachers Association/American Association of Retired Persons, Washington. "Two organizations can be in deep dissent on some issues," he says. "On those issues, we know we disagree. But on the issues where we do agree, it's much more powerful to speak in a unified voice."

Of course, sometimes your association's allies are obvious. Such was the case when the Distributive Services Committee was formed 17 years ago. Eighteen Ohio associations whose members were involved in distributing formed the coalition to reduce property tax on retail inventory. At the time, the tax was 70 percent of the value of the inventory. The coalition has successfully obtained several reductions since its formation, and the coalition's goal of a 35 percent inventory tax will go into effect in two years.

In this case, both the allies and the enemy were obvious. The allies: trade associations with retail merchant members. The enemy: the state legislature.

SO MANY SUCCESS STORIES

Case after case of association coalitions that have been successful in their pursuits can be cited. William T. Robinson, CAE, senior vice president of the American Hospital Association, Chicago, relates one coalition success story.

Several years ago, he says, the annual rate of increase in the level of expenditures for health care was out of control. Predictions were that if health care costs continued at the same rate it would be necessary to spend the entire gross national product on health care alone by the year 2010. In fact, the government's outlay for health care—Medicare and Medicaid—was beginning to compete with the defense budget.

Government officials, concerned, issued a challenge to the health care field to voluntarily control the rate of increase. A coalition called Voluntary Effort was created. It represented the interests of trade associations, commercial insurance companies, and others. Now, three years after the start of the coalition, "the rate of increase has been sufficiently retarded," Mr. Robinson says.

Edie Fraser, president of Fraser/Associates, Washington, has been involved in enough similar success stories to become a firm believer in their power. "Coalitions are the new trend in business relations on policy issues," she says. "I believe they are the most effective means of achieving results."

WHAT'S THEIR PURPOSE?

She explains that the basic purpose of a coalition is "to join forces together behind a mutual interest—generally a policy issue—and work together for common effectiveness and results."

"More and more associations are recognizing the power of coalitions," Ms. Fraser continues, "because they can achieve far more by integrating their resources and dividing the effort behind a common cause."

Paul Korody, director of public affairs for the National Meat Association, Washington, says coalitions are growing in numbers in response to a changing Congress. "Within the past 10 years, we have seen a decentralization of power on Capitol Hill. Today, every congressman is almost as important as another. They all have to be talked to."

That means, he says, that only the really large associations with members in every congressional district can tackle an issue alone. "The rest of us have to pool our memberships to be effective in Congress. Whereas we have a lot of meatpackers in the Northwest and Southwest, there are many congressional districts where we have no members at all. We would be less effective in those states [without a coalition]. By combining resources with a number of associations with different memberships but the same goals, you can cover the country."

He adds that, in most cases, congressional staffs appreciate a coalition's efforts. Why? Because it makes their jobs that much easier. They can get one document or have one conversation with a coalition leader and know who and how many are for or against an issue. That's in lieu of speaking with 50,000—a number that five association executives involved in a coalition can easily represent.

CHOOSING A LEADER

In order for any coalition to be successful, it has to have a leader or coordinator with a commitment to the cause and time to devote to it, says Sheldon Steinbach, American Council on Education. "The effectiveness of the ICR repeal was solely due to the continuous scrutiny and daily monitoring of one person.

"A coalition functions only when one person is given responsibility to make that issue move. Someone must call the shots. A leader must have ample time to spend on the issue, almost to the point of making it his or her primary preoccupation."

Because of the considerable time requirement, choosing a coalition coordinator is often simply a process of elimination. Who has the time to spend on it? Who has the expertise on the issue?

When these questions are answered, only a few eligibles are likely to remain. Usually it's the executive of the association which the outcome of the issue most affects.

Or as Ms. Fraser puts it, "The leader usually represents the one association that has the most to gain . . . or lose."

GUIDELINES FOR EFFECTIVENESS

Obviously, the selection of the leader can either make or break a coalition. But other factors also enter into the outcome of your association's coalition.

Here are just a few elements common to successful coalition efforts:

- A commitment by members to work, not in their own self-interest, but in the interest of the group.
- Expertise on the part of all members on the subject matter and its ramifications.
- Knowledge of how the legislature—either state or federal—works.
- Ability to plan a strategy and allow enough lead time to develop it detail by detail so nothing slips through the cracks and is left undone.
- Communication with members of the coalition—whether it's through meetings, newsletters, memos, or telephone calls.
- Keeping on the offensive, rather than the defensive. "Use facts, data, and public opinion to build on your important points," Ms. Fraser says. "It's not necessary to attack your opposition." She ticks off campaign after campaign that was lost because one side began to react defensively to the opposition.
- Member involvement. "If the issue is important to your members—and it should be or your shouldn't be part of the coalition—get them involved," Ms. Fraser urges. "The grassroots campaign is important. The work should really come from members; your association should serve as the catalyst."
- Latitude from you and your board of directors. "Our board sets broad policy," says John C. Mahaney, Jr., president of the Ohio Council of Retail Merchants in Columbus. "After that, my board leaves me alone. It doesn't tie the staff's hands."

A COMMITMENT TO GO

The last point, the latitude you give to your chief paid executive, can be a crucial item to your association's contribution to the coalition. "The board gives us a broad delegation of authority," Sheldon Steinbach says. "We are paid to exercise good judgment and proceed. If you are hamstrung, it will slow you down, if not completely cripple your coalition."

He explains that if he had to go back to his board of directors every time a decision was made in a coalition, he would lose valuable time—not to mention the confidence of other coalition members.

SURVEY OF MEMBERSHIP

To make sure his board of directors will agree with his decisions, Mr. Steinbach surveys his membership on major issues that concern the association. "If they think it is important, they tell us to go," he says. "But they don't tell us how to go."

Dr. Kerschner explains that the only time he goes back to his board for a coalition decision is when the issue is controversial and the association's stance involves a change in previous policy.

"What do you do with dissent among coalition members?" asks Dr. Kerschner. "How do you handle it? Do you avoid the issue? Do you go with the majority?"

He explains that chief paid officers must answer these questions, and answer them adequately, for a coalition to work. He has found one possible answer for the coalitions he has been involved with: If there is a disagreement on one particular point of an issue, the dissenting party removes his or her name and endorsement from that specific letter but continues to endorse the remainder of the issue.

"Trade-offs are important because one small issue can divide the coalition," he says. "Before you say 'I will not sign that,' look at all sides. You might have to make a compromise. Internal negotiations are necessary to present a united front to those you are dealing with."

GOODWILL A KEY INGREDIENT

William Robinson advises associations to go into a coalition with the idea that there might have to be a trade-off. "Your pet ideas are going to be examined by others," he says. "You might have to accept the fact that the publicity will be given to the coalition and not to your association. A coalition takes goodwill by the participants. Sometimes the goodwill is there in the beginning; sometimes it takes time for it to grow."

Speaking realistically, Edie Fraser says it almost never happens that members of a coalition agree on every item, every detail of a coalition. "That's where the art of negotiation is important. The common end of the allies is more important than the priority of any one association."

SHARING IN THE GLORY

You may wonder why your association's past efforts in coalitions have not been more heavily publicized. . . . why your association didn't take more credit for the outcome.

"A coalition, to be effective, is without limelight or glory for the association involved," says Paul Korody. "The purpose is to get a particular job done. We're there to serve our members, and coalitions are the most effective means of doing that. Any glory is in the fact that we satisfactorily served our members."

Sheldon Steinbach admits that sharing the spotlight is a problem for some associations. Sometimes, they are so greedy for the recognition that they won't participate in a coalition—and risk losing the fight. Other times, they might participate in a coalition, but afterwards they will attempt to garner all of the credit for their association alone.

When William Robinson was working on Voluntary Effort, he says that the businesses and associations involved had no qualms about giving complete credit to the coalition, not to themselves. "It would have been counterproductive to publish under any one member's name," Mr. Robinson says. "We wanted the coalition to become a familiar name. . . to have its own identity."

POTENTIAL PROBLEMS

Powerful though they may be, coalitions are not perfect. Problems arise, and they have to be alleviated before the cause can be won. Here are some snags that can occur. With negotiation, respect, and planning, all can be overcome.

1. One Member Dominates.   Sometimes, when a coalition is composed of one or two large, domineering associations and a variety of small ones, representatives from the smaller associations are not given the chance to express their opinions. Or, if they are given the opportunity, they are not given priority. All members must listen to one another.

2. Jealousy between Members.   This usually occurs at the outset, Ms. Fraser points out, until coalition members realize that "they can achieve far more by integrating their resources and dividing the effort behind a common cause."

3. Conflicting Goals.   "You've got to go for the greatest good for the greatest number," Mr. Steinbach says.

4. Conflicting Strategy.   This occurs most often when two or more coalition members have considerable legislative experience. Because of their backgrounds, each thinks his own plan of attack is best.

5. Minor Disagreements.   Even though the association executives agree on the major issue, they sometimes bicker about a minor part of it. "You can't let a specific point divide and conquer the group," Dr. Kerschner says.

6. Too Formal.   Dr. Kerschner differentiates between organization, which you can never have enough of, and formalization, which you can. He says it's important to remember that each member of the coalition has an association to which he is responsible and that the coalition should not become a substitute for it.

7. Too Many Meetings.   Some coalitions are permanent. Others are temporary—disbanded as soon as their cause is settled. Dr. Kerschner warns that members of permanent coalitions have to be careful not to call a meeting just to be calling a meeting. Unless a crisis has occurred or a new development has come up, he recommends meeting about once a month. Between meetings, he uses the phone for exchanges of information.

8. Lack of Follow-Through.   Sometimes a coalition member will slip up, and the work assigned to him or her will not get done. If that happens, and it is not caught in time, all of the coalition efforts will be wasted.

EVERYONE'S DOING IT

Coalitions are not limited to associations. Business groups, consumer groups— just about any group you can think of is involved in some type of coalition. "On any side of any issue, you can find a coalition that has formed, is being formed, or will be formed," Mr. Korody says.

Whatever type of coalition your association may now be involved in, your chances of victory are better through unity. Mr. Mahaney firmly believes Ohio merchants would not have received inventory tax relief without the Distributive Service Committee. "We could not have done it alone," he states. "It took everyone in the coalition to do it."

Twenty Tips for Making a Coalition Work

If you aren't convinced of the value of coalitions, talk to Edie Fraser, president of Fraser/Associates, Washington, D.C. She's a firm believer in their effectiveness and presents a persuasive argument on their behalf.

She asserts that coalitions are the wave of the future. "On most policy issues, a coalition is the only way to go—if you have a common interest," she says.

In her opinion, more and more association executives are recognizing the potential—and power—of coalitions, but they aren't sure how to proceed. "Carrying out the program is where they often fall down."

Here are her 20 rules for participating in an effective coalition:

1. Clearly define issues and strategy.
2. Determine a timetable and needs.
3. Identify both allies and opposition.
4. Build constituency and recruit allies.
5. Select leadership from within allies.
6. Devise a clear plan of action.
7. Determine resources, budget, and meet those needs.
8. Divide up tasks within the coalition.
9. Establish a working task force or executive committee.
10. Keep coalition members informed and involved.
11. Establish a communication program plan; clearly distribute tasks.
12. Build supportive case materials.
13. Develop an internal communication program with each association involving its members.
14. Enlist experts to support the coalition's case.
15. Explain the issue in economic impact terms when possible; use appropriate public opinion.
16. Utilize all pertinent media for greatest impact.
17. Remember to keep all coalition constituents informed and involved.
18. If it's a legislative issue, review the congressional strategy on a regular basis.
19. Determine if the coalition leadership is serving as a catalyst for communication.
20. Prove the results and communicate them to the member constituencies.

"Sometimes a coalition is the only way to do something," he continues. "Especially now, as the problem becomes more complex. It seems like they are too big for any one—or even two—associations to handle." Paul Korody couldn't agree more. "A smart association executive seeks his peers and works through a coalition. The days of trying to do it all yourself are long gone."

SECTION TEN

Power

In writings about social dynamics, the concept of *power* is one of the most captivating and attention getting. This is also true when focusing on the context of negotiation. Whether one is discussing a "power lunch" with an important business figure, "empowerment" of blue-collar employees or minority groups, or the abuse of power by a public official, power and its use have fascinated students and practitioners of social influence for thousands of years. The writings of Machiavelli, over 450 years ago, continue to stand as a definitive treatise on the effective use of power. More recently, political scientists, psychologists, economists, philosophers, ethicists, and politicians have had much to say about power and influence, its use and misuse.

There are a number of ways to account for the fascination with power. In our society, the possession of power is often coupled with status and affluence. For some people, power itself is an intoxicant—even an addiction. Powerful people get attention, press coverage, and privilege. There is a certain mysticism about power, an elusiveness that makes it hard to define clearly or to explain its dynamics. Yet power must be defined and explained for it to be harnessed—and that is our purpose in this section. We are not going to explore this very broad range of power approaches and dynamics; rather, we will restrict ourselves to those articles that specifically address the types and sources of power commonly available to negotiators and most commonly used in negotiation interaction.

The first article in this section is by a distinguished, eminent social scientist whose name is frequently associated with the systematic study of power and influence—Kenneth Boulding. Boulding begins our discussion of power by cutting through much of the semantic debate in the social sciences about its definition, scope, and parameters. Boulding proposes a simple, straightforward definition: power is the ability to get what we want. As Boulding notes, however, even this simple definition is not so simple, since we quickly get into questions such as, "Who are 'we'?" or "How do 'we' decide what we want?" Boulding considers the nature of power in conflict situations, the problems of measuring power, and the fact that power is unequally distributed in most civilized societies (where a few gather sufficient power to control many). In order to help us understand different sources of power—the ways powerful people derive their power—Boulding proposes a major trichotomy. Power may be distinguished first by its consequences, as destructive, productive, and integrative. Destructive power is the power to destroy things; productive power is the power to create new things; and integrative power is the power to bring things together into more unified wholes. Boulding then associates different characteristic patterns of behavior with each of these categories: threats are likely to lead to destructive power patterns, exchanges (transactions) are likely to lead to productive power patterns, and love or respect (positive affect) is likely to lead to integrative power patterns. Boulding also briefly explores power at the institutional level, examining how political, military, economic, and social power relate to these categories. In summary, the Boulding chapter provides excellent groundwork on which to base our discussion of power; as we have seen in earlier chapters, threats and promises, exchanges, and relationships clearly form the foundation for the use of power and influence in most negotiation contexts.

In its more stereotypic forms, power and its use is associated with the destructive and productive forms. Yet the most effective forms of power use occur in exchange transactions. The prescriptions for the strategy and tactics of power use in exchange are found in the Cohen and Bradford article. After defining the nature of exchange relationships, Cohen and Bradford propose some simple rules for using power in this context: (1) think about the person to be influenced as a potential ally, not an adversary; (2) know the world of our potential allies, the pressures on them, their needs and goals (so you can tailor your influence attempt to those individuals' worlds); (3) be aware of key goals and available resources that may be valued by potential allies; and (4) understand the exchange transaction itself so that win-win outcomes are achieved. The authors also outline a comprehensive list of "currencies," or things that are offered between people in exchange transactions in order to establish a successful deal. These include inspiration-related currencies (visions of the future, commitments to moral principles), task-related currencies (resources, goods, and services), position-related currencies (recognition, reputation, contacts), relationship-related currencies (acceptance and personal support) and personal-related currencies (gratitude, ownership, and involvement, etc.).

While Cohen and Bradford describe the use of power as "currencies" within an exchange transaction, in the next article Keys and Case approach the subject of influence tactics more broadly. In a series of research studies, the authors asked a large number of practicing managers to identify tactics that they used in successful and unsuccessful incidents of interpersonal influence. Tactics were identified that exerted influence upward (toward a boss), laterally (toward peers), and downward (toward subordinates). The results indicate that there are some commonalities in the way managers report their influence attempts upward, downward, and laterally—but also some strong differences. With bosses and peers, the first choice of influence strategy is to present a rational explanation of what they want. (Rational explanations are high among influence attempts with subordinates, but not first.) However, showing support of others, or arguing and persisting in what we want, were also commonly used tactics. Keys and Case also analyze the effectiveness/ineffectiveness of certain tactic profiles; they discover that not all tactics work (nor do they fail) in all circumstances. On the basis of these findings, they suggest five key steps to becoming an influential manager:

- Develop a reputation as a knowledgeable person or expert.
- Balance the time spent in critical relationships based on what the work requires, not on habit or personal preference.

- Develop a network of key resource persons who can be called upon for assistance.

- "Tailor" the combination of influence tactics to the nature of one's objective and to the particular target to be influenced.

- Implement influence tactics with sensitivity, flexibility, and adequate levels of communication.

Specific pointers and examples are offered to implement each of these five key steps.

Finally, the article on networking, courtesy of an American Express campus guide, translates the management of influence in exchanges and relationships into pragmatic skills for the newly minted graduate of a leading college or university. *Networking* is the process of building and maintaining relationships that may be called on, at some point in the future, to get a job done, to help someone out, or to further one's own career. The ability to build and manage networks appears to be tied to both job and career success, and this article offers a number of clear, pragmatic suggestions for how to make it happen.

The Nature of Power

Kenneth Boulding

POWER AS THE ABILITY TO GET WHAT WE WANT

Power, like most important words, has many meanings. Its widest meaning is that of a potential for change. It has a very special meaning in physics: the time rate at which energy is transferred or converted into work. The concept of power is not used very much in the biological sciences, but is of great importance in human and social systems, which is the main subject of this volume. For individual human beings, power is the ability to get what one wants. The term *power* is also used, however, to describe the ability to achieve common ends for families, groups, organizations of all kinds, churches, corporations, political parties, national states, and so on. In this human sense, power is a concept without meaning in the absence of human valuations and human decision. Decision is a choice among a range or set of images of the future that we think are feasible. Power of decision relates to the size of this agenda of potential images of the future. A bedridden person who is dying of cancer has a very small range of possible futures, and a very small agenda of decisions, restricted almost to what the patient is thinking about. A rich person in the prime of life, in good health, has a very wide range of possible futures. As we move up in the hierarchy of organization toward people like Mr. Gorbachev, the pope, or President Bush, the range of agendas of decision includes not only one's personal condition or surroundings but the condition or surroundings of very large numbers of other people; in the extreme case, decisions may affect the condition of the whole planet.

The general concept of power is often confused with the idea of "force," which is a much narrower concept. If an audience is asked to give a symbolic gesture illustrating the concept of "power," many of them will raise their fists, suggesting threat power or the power to do injury. This, however, as we will see later, is only one aspect, and by no means the most important aspect of the general concept of power. Force is linked to the concept of domination, which, indeed, is only a small part of the general nature of power. There is a certain tendency among humans to identify power with the capacity for victory, that is, overcoming some other person, will, or institution. This, again, is a very narrow concept of power and, indeed, by no means the most important aspect of it. In mechanics we have the concept of horsepower, which is what it takes to lift 550 pounds one foot in one second, and reflects the larger concept of

Reprinted from Kenneth Boulding, *Three Faces of Power* (Newbury Park, Calif: Sage Publications, Inc., 1989), pp. 15–33. Reprinted by permission of Sage Publications, Inc.

power in terms of getting something done that we want. It is perhaps significant that there is no concept of "horse force." The unit of force in the centimeter-gram-second system is the dyne, which is the force that applied to one gram will give it an acceleration of one centimeter per second per second. This might almost be described as "grasshopper force." It does have a certain implication of overcoming gravity by hopping. It is interesting that in electronics what overcomes resistance and produces current is called "potential," which is also a form of power. "Power lines" carry electric potential from one place to another.

There is a certain parallel between the concept of power and the economist's concept of a possibility boundary, which divides the total set of future possibilities into those that a person can do and those that a person cannot do. In the next 24 hours I could go to New York by air, I could not go to Antarctica, and I could certainly not go to the moon. This might be called the "ultimate power boundary." This ultimate boundary, however, may not be very significant, because within it there are other boundaries that limit our decisions. One is the "taboo boundary," which divides the ultimate power area into two parts: that part within the taboo boundary, things we can do and do not feel we have to refrain from doing, and that part beyond the taboo boundary, things we can do but refrain from doing. In virtually all societies, with the exception of nudist camps, there is a strong taboo against a lecturer taking all his or her clothes off while lecturing. I have never known this taboo to be broken, although in physical terms there is no obstacle to it at all. Then inside the taboo boundary there are a great many things we can do, but do not want to do. We arrange the various items of the possibility agenda by order of preference and, according to economists at least, we select the one that is highest on our preference order, that is, the thing we want most.

Economists generally assume that what we want most will be on the possibility boundary, implying that what we want most of all is not within our power, that is, it is beyond the boundary. There is no principle of human behavior that says this assumption has to be true. There are many examples of human decisions that let us stay well within the possibility boundary. Monarchs abdicate, rich people set up foundations and give their money away, monks vow "poverty, chastity, and obedience," saints suffer, and martyrs die. It is possible indeed that the freest exercise of the will is the renunciation of power. If we feel we must exercise the power that we have, then we are trapped in an almost deterministic situation. Economists frequently assume that human preferences cannot be analyzed or criticized. This flies in the face of human history and experience. Virtually everyone has experienced changes in their preference structures and their valuations. There is the "sour grapes" principle, that what we cannot get we decide we do not want, which can be very comforting. At the other end of the scale is the addiction principle—that what we cannot get we want all the more. Taboos are not merely what society imposes on us. We set up our own taboos. Some people become teetotalers or vegetarians. Chastity may be rare, but it is not unknown.

The simple definition of human power, the ability to get what we want, turns out to be quite complex, as we have just seen, even when we ask: How do we know what we want? It gets still more complex when we ask: Who are we? All decisions are made by individuals, but nearly always "on behalf" of a larger entity. This is true even of the most personal and individual choice. An individual is not a single mental system but may have a diversity of personalities. It was Bismarck, I think, who said, "I am a committee," and each person possesses a great variety of roles, some of which may conflict. Our decision as a parent, or as an employer, or as a church member, or as a citizen of a national state, or as a president of a national organization, or as a captain of a team, may be different in each role, and this can create internal conflict. Every decision is made on behalf of the committee that is us. As we rise in hierarchies, what we are deciding, and "on behalf of" whom, becomes ever larger and more complex. A decision by a parent to take another job affects the whole family. A decision by an executive officer of a corporation to shut down a factory affects very large numbers of families, communities, and other organizations. A decision on the part of the president of the United States may affect the whole human race. Decisions of the powerful have an agenda that sometimes includes a large part of the total state of the world, or nowadays even of the solar system. Should we leave garbage on the moon?

There is a strong belief that a role transcends and survives the person occupying it. The whole concept of the "national interest" (we might add "corporate interest" or "church interest") implies that no matter who occupies the powerful roles, the agenda of decision making and of the preferences involved do not change very much, although, of course, every occupant of the role changes the role somewhat. The whole concept of a "representative," whether this is a congressman or the president, implies that decisions have to transcend personal interest, for a representative is supposed to make decisions on behalf of his or her constituents. Power may be getting what you want, but this achievement depends on who "you" are and how you know what "you" want. It is clear this is by no means a simple concept.

POWER IN CONFLICT

Another element that complicates the concept of power in social systems is that the various possibility boundaries of one person are where they are because of some decisions and some power exercised by another person, persons, or organizations. Conflict arises when a shift in the possibility boundary between two parties in some sense reduces the power of one and increases the power of the other. Costly and protracted conflict takes place when A pushes the boundary toward B, B pushes it back toward A, A toward B again, and so on. Essential to the resolution of conflict is the establishment of property lines agreed upon by both parties, so that neither attempts to increase his or her power by pushing out the possibility boundary at the expense of the other. Third parties, especially in the form of legal systems and governments, often assist this process by imposing further boundaries in the form of threats on any party who violates the property lines. Law, however, can break down if one or another party attempts to seize the power of government or defy the law, which sometimes happens. This often leads to cultures of violence, like Ulster, Lebanon, or Sri Lanka, with tragic and widespread loss to the whole society.

A significant element in the total structure of power is the way in which individuals evaluate the power and well-being of others. We can first of all distinguish a scale ranging from benevolence, through selfishness as the zero point, to malevolence.[1] A is benevolent toward B if A's perception that B's welfare is increased increases A's own perceived welfare. A is selfish if a perception of an increase in B's welfare does not affect A's perception of A's own welfare. A is malevolent toward B if A's perception of an increase in B's welfare diminishes A's own perceived welfare. Both benevolence and malevolence are exhibited in varying degrees. We may feel very mildly benevolent toward the salesclerk at the store where we are buying something. We pass the time of day and exchange little courtesies. We may feel very highly benevolent toward our own children, other members of our family, close friends, people with whom we cooperate in various tasks and enjoyments. Similarly, we may feel mildly malevolent toward the slowpoke who is in front of us on a narrow road, driving well below the speed limit. We may feel moderately malevolent toward our opponent in an election, and highly malevolent toward our enemies during war. Selfishness, the mere zero point on the scale, is actually rather rare in regard to people with whom we are in actual contact. It is common toward people far away with whom we have no contact, but even there the news of a catastrophe in a faraway land easily induces people to pity. Such news often induces people to make contributions toward ameliorating the disaster. Benevolence seems easier to express than does malevolence. Smiles take fewer muscles than do frowns. It is often harder work to injure somebody than to assist them.

An offshoot, and sometimes a cause, of malevolence is envy and jealousy, a feeling of dissatisfaction with our relative position in the power structure. Envy need only involve two parties, and the envied may be quite unaware of its existence, although envy can be very corrupting to the envious, diverting their attention from increasing their own power toward an often fruitless attempt to diminish the power of the envied. Jealousy involves envy of a relationship between two other people, one of whom the envious person would like to displace. This, again, can be very destructive and can be damaging to all parties, although it is more likely to damage the envious than the envied.[2]

THE MEASUREMENT OF POWER

Another important but very difficult question is whether power can be measured both in regard to its aggregate in the total world system and in regard to its distribution among individuals, groups, and organizations. Because power is a multidimensional concept, it is difficult to quantify and to measure. Perhaps the closest we come to a measure of power is the monetary unit. This only measures certain aspects of power and cannot be used to measure power as a whole. Nevertheless, the concept of the quantity of power is important, even if it is bound to be a little vague and qualitative in character. It would be hard to deny that the power of the human race over its environment, mainly, of course, on earth, but now expanding to the solar system and even

[1]Kenneth E. Boulding, *The Economy of Love and Fear: A Preface to Grants Economics.* Belmont, Calif.: Wadsworth, 1973, p. 94.

[2]Helmut Schoeck, *A Theory of Social Behavior* (from the German), Trans. Michael Glenny and Betsy Ross. New York, Harcourt, Brace & World, 1969.

beyond, has increased pretty steadily and at an accelerating rate over the course of human history. Certainly in the history of the 40,000 years or so of the Paleolithic period, human power was not very great. Probably the earliest acceleration in human power was the discovery of how to use fire, which may even have predated *Homo sapiens*. The use of fire almost certainly expanded the population that used it, but also introduced a new source of forest fires, which could affect the world's ecosystems over wide areas. There is little doubt that humans exterminated the mammoth and other large mammals, especially in North America, perhaps some 10,000 to 15,000 years ago.

With the development of agriculture, the human population expanded substantially, and human impact on the ecosystem and landscape became quite large, as forests and grasslands gave way to fields and farms. This led fairly rapidly to civilization and the rise of cities, coming out of the food surplus of storable foods from agriculture and improvement in the means of transportation, such as the development of wheeled vehicles, boats, and the domestication of horses, donkeys, and camels. Human power over the earth is reflected in the rise of Babylon, Rome, and so on, with dramatic local changes in the ecological pattern of the earth's surface. Human artifacts, which are just as much a part of the world ecosystem as are biological artifacts, have increased in complexity and number almost continuously, with occasional remissions and retreats.

Then comes the rise of modern science, beginning some 500 years ago. In the mid-nineteenth century comes the application of science to technology of many kinds—chemicals, electricity, health and medicine, agriculture, transportation, and so on—producing the "modern world" and an enormous explosion of human population, which has more than doubled in the twentieth century. The world has been mapped and charted, we have been to the highest peaks and the deepest depths, to the poles, and even to the moon. Messengers are going beyond the limits of the solar system. That this process represents an expansion of total human power could hardly be denied.

THE DISTRIBUTION OF POWER

We are also conscious of the fact that human power, especially since the rise of agriculture and civilization, has been very unequally distributed. In hunting-gathering societies there is not much power to distribute, but what there is is distributed fairly equally. The good hunters and the good gatherers do not eat much more than the poorer hunters and the poorer gatherers. There may be shamans and storytellers and leaders who have some power over the others, but all live very much alike. With agriculture and the rise of cities and empires, however, hierarchy develops with the development of organized threat systems, institutions for the collection of taxes, and so on. Then the human race tends to divide into a very small group of the powerful and a large group of the relatively indigent and the powerless—the peasants, the soldiers, the servant class—and a small middle class of artisans, merchants, builders, and so on.

With the development of science-based technology after about 1850 (and even somewhat before this), we begin to get the rise of the middle class to a majority of the society, with political power limited by democracy, and economic power by progressive taxation and fluctuating markets, but still leaving a substantial body of the poor, powerless, and impotent, who cannot fit themselves into the society's expanding sectors.

We now have a situation where science-based technology is fairly widespread in the two temperate zones. Ironically enough, it is the Communist countries, with their ideology of equality, that probably have the greatest inequality of overall power—decision power being extremely concentrated at the top of the hierarchy, without the checks and balances that democratic institutions provide, although even this situation is now being modified. Most of the tropical societies, however, are still impoverished and have very small modern sectors. Hence, the overall distribution of power in the world still seems extremely unequal. Perhaps 25 percent of the human race is still in extreme poverty, frequently threatened by starvation and famine, constantly malnourished, and moving very slowly, if at all, into a better situation.

DESTRUCTIVE POWER

Along with the power to grow crops, build cities, fly airplanes, and have a worldwide communication system, the human race has also expanded its powers of destruction. This goes back a long way to the development of spears and bows and arrows in hunting-gathering societies, swords and catapults in early civilizations, and then gunpowder and the cannon, which really ended the feudal baron and established the national state. Now, of course, we have aerial bombings and the nuclear weapon, which has the potential at least to destroy the whole earth. The power of destruction can be used productively for the human race, as it is in hunting, in the use of explosives in building canals, dams, and so on, although even these structures, while often beneficial, can have disastrous, unexpected ecological and social consequences.

The dark side of the power of destruction is, of course, violence and war. This goes back a long way, as shown in the story of Cain and Abel. Up to now the increase in powers of destruction has not prevented an extraordinary expansion in the overall powers of production. There have been certain times and places where empires, for instance, have collapsed due to the use of the powers of destruction, with a temporary decline in the powers of production as a consequence, for instance, in Mesopotamia, in Europe after the fall of the Roman Empire, and so on. These episodes, however, have seldom lasted very long. In Europe, for instance, techniques of production, which had been fairly stagnant during the Roman Empire, began to improve within a century after its fall, as a result perhaps of the rise of monastic orders and new technologies creeping in from China. Warfare, which figures so prominently in history books, rarely occupies more than 10 percent of human time and energy. The other 90 percent or so goes into plowing, sowing, reaping, weaving, building, and making furniture and implements, utensils, and so on. It is ironic that the increase in the powers of destruction is in a sense a by-product of the strong tendency for the powers of production to increase. Agriculture produces a storable food surplus, which can feed armies; metallurgy produces weapons as well as plows; craftsmen produce chariots as well as carts, and nuclear fission can produce both electric power and bombs.

The future, however, remains in some doubt because of the enormous rise in the destructiveness of weaponry and the diminution in the cost of transport of the means of destruction, represented by the airplane, the missile, and, of course, the nuclear weapon. There have been a few occasions in human history when humans have abandoned some destructive power, as the samurai did in Japan in the sixteenth and seventeenth centuries when they gave up firearms introduced from Europe. One can only hope that the political institutions of the world will change in proportion to the powers of destruction.

THE DIFFERENT KINDS OF POWER: DESTRUCTIVE, PRODUCTIVE, INTEGRATIVE

The structure of power is very complex. The first step to understanding it is to raise the question: How do we identify and categorize different sources of power? One of the greatest obstacles to human knowledge is the difficulty that we have in finding the right categories, that is, the right boxes to classify complex realities. We have to classify in order to be able to use language at all. We cannot talk about each of the 5 billion human beings separately. The same goes for the innumerable individual plants, rocks, clouds, and so on. There is always a danger, however, that when we classify we get the categories—that is, the boxes—wrong. We put unlike things together in one box and separate like things between several boxes. The failure of alchemy and the success of chemistry is a great tribute to the virtue of correct classification. As long as we thought earth, air, fire, and water were the elements, we got nowhere. These are not elements, but very heterogeneous collections of things. It was only when we identified the elements correctly, like hydrogen, oxygen, and carbon, that chemistry became possible. This problem is particularly acute in social systems, with their immense diversity of peoples, cultures, organizations, and structures of all kinds. So we are always putting people who are very diverse in the same box (like "race"), and we scatter things that are similar, like learning ability, among a lot of different boxes. When we move into abstract ideas the classification problem becomes acute. There seems to be no formal theory about it; we can only rely on trial and error to see what works.

Figure 1 illustrates a set of categories of power that will be fundamental to the argument of this volume. None of these categories will be perfectly clear. They are all what the mathematicians call "fuzzy sets," for every example of power is in some sense unique, just as every human being is unique. Nevertheless, these categories are offered as a way of organizing an extremely complex reality in a way that perhaps will make for more realistic appraisals as to what kind of beliefs and actions really create power.

We first divide power into three major categories from the point of view of its consequences: destructive power, productive power, and integrative power. Destructive power is the power to destroy things. It has two very different aspects, reflected in the means of destruction. Some of these are weapons, whether directed toward killing people or destroying valued things. The means of destruction, however, also include such things as bulldozers, plows, furnaces, chain saws, knives, and so on, which are part of the productive process.

Productive power is found in the fertilized egg, in the blueprint, in the idea, in the tools and machines that make things, in the activity of human brains and muscles that sow and reap, weave and build, construct, paint, and sculpt.

Integrative power may be thought of perhaps as an aspect of productive power that involves the capacity to build organizations, to create families and groups, to inspire loyalty, to bind people together, to develop legitimacy. Integrative power has a negative sense, to create enemies, to alienate people; it has a destructive as well as a productive aspect.

FIGURE 1   Categories of
Power: Threat,
Exchange, and Love

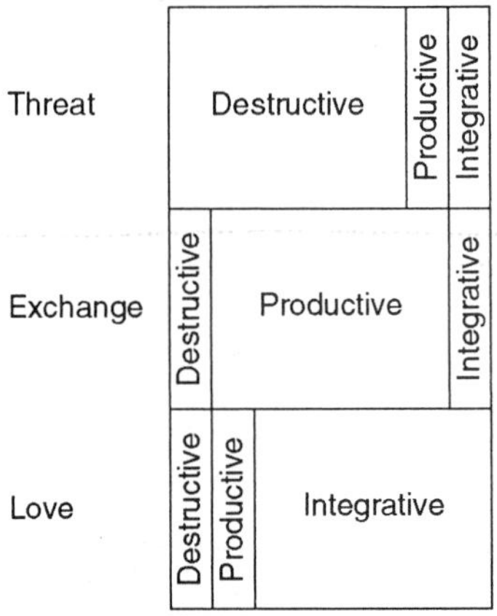

THREAT POWER

The figure shows a rather similar tripartition involving characteristic behavior, roughly, but not exactly, corresponding to the first three categories. Behavior that is particularly associated with destructive power is threat. Threat originates when A says to B, "You do something I want or I will do something you do not want." For the threat to be carried out, of course, A must have control over some destructive power against persons or structures that B values. The dynamics of threat depend very much on how B responds to threat. The threat, of course, may be explicit or implicit, but it always involves some sort of communication. There are a number of possible responses from B. One is submission, that B does what A demands and the threat is not carried out. This is very common. This is why we pay our income taxes, why we stop our vehicle by the side of the road when the traffic cop says "Pull over." It explains in part, although only in part, why children obey parents, and students, teachers. Nations defeated in war submit to their conquerors; colonies submit to imperial powers. Without some element of threat-submission, social life would be very difficult to organize. But there are degrees of willingness to submit, or "grudgingness"; a highly grudged submission may be unstable.

Another possible reaction is defiance. B says to A, "I will not do what you want." This is probably less common than submission, but it is by no means unknown. Then the ball goes back to the threatener, who must then decide whether or not to carry out the threat. Sometimes carrying out a threat is very costly; sometimes the threatener does not have the destructive power that is professed and defiance may succeed, especially if it is widespread, persistent, and the defiers are willing to suffer. This indeed is the secret of success of nonviolent resistance, of which there are numerous examples in human history, Gandhi's being one of the most prominent.

A third reaction to threat may be counterthreat—"You do something nasty to me and I will do something nasty to you." In this case, the threatened party must also have, or convincingly pretend to have, means of destruction. This, again, throws the ball back into the camp of the original threatener, who may either try to carry out the threat or not carry it out, either of which will have a succession of subtle and often unpredictable consequences. Counterthreat leads into a situation of deterrence, the stability of which, as we shall see later, is very questionable, but it is highly characteristic of international systems and is the current justification for much military expenditure.

Another possible reaction to threat is flight, of which there are many examples. Indeed, the spread of the human race around the globe has flight as a very important element. Refugees throughout history, like the Pilgrim Fathers, have had a very profound effect on the geographical distribution of the human race. The success of flight depends on a principle that I have described as "the further, the weaker"—the further we go from the home base of the threatener, the harder it is for the threat to be carried out, simply because the carrying out of threat always has a cost of transport.[3] In the present day, with the enormous reduction in the cost of transport of threat in the form of weaponry, flight becomes very difficult because there may be nowhere to go out of range of the threat. But the very size of the current refugee problem suggests that flight is still with us.

A fifth reaction to threat might be called "disarming behavior." This is the "soft answer that turns away wrath." It involves an ability on the part of the threatened to integrate with the threatener into some sort of community or integrative structure.

Threat power has a productive component in the capacity to produce the means of destruction, like guns, and an integrative factor when the threat is made by a group, such as an army, which must have "morale" in order to function.

EXCHANGE POWER

Another major type of behavior, which like threat involves at least two parties, is exchange, which covers a range of activities, from formal and contractual trade to informal reciprocity. Exchange begins when A says to B, "You do something I want and I will do something you want." If B has a choice of either accepting or refusing the invitation, if B accepts then an exchange takes place. In the simple form of trade, A gives B something and B gives A something. The ratio of exchange—that is, how much one gives per unit of what the other gives—is an important quality of the transaction. Exchange, however, is a wider concept than trade. It involves such things as conversation, reciprocal services, and so on. The dynamics of exchange are much simpler than those of threat. If B accepts, the exchange takes place; if not, the exchange does not take place. There may, however, be more subtle dynamic consequences. If B accepts the exchange but then is not satisfied with what A gives, this may change the terms on which other exchanges may be made in the future. This might be called the "lemon principle."

Another complication is that exchange may or may not involve bargaining. Much exchange is conducted without bargaining under the custom of the fixed price. A the

---

[3]Kenneth E. Boulding, *Conflict and Defense: A General Theory.* New York: Harper, 1962; Reprinted, Lanham, MD: University Press of America, 1988.

seller offers to exchange at a certain price, or ratio of exchange, and B the buyer either accepts the offer or does not. If A is asking too high a price, of course, A will not be able to find people with whom to exchange. A may then lower the asking price. If A asks too low a price, he may be deluged with potential buyers, at which point he is likely to raise the price. Under some circumstances, however, B may offer to bargain— "I will accept the exchange, but at a lower price." A may respond, offering to exchange at a slightly higher price than B asks, and so on, until a bargain either is reached or is not.

Exchange is closely related to productive power simply because unless there is production there is not very much to exchange. Also, as Adam Smith pointed out so well, the development of exchange increases productive power through specialization and the human learning process.

Exchange has an integrative component, simply because without some sort of trust and courtesy exchange is very difficult. Exchange, however, is enough of a positive-sum relationship, in which both parties benefit, that the possibility of exchange may actively create the kind of integrative structure within which it becomes possible. There are old stories of "silent trade," in which two hostile tribes with different resources exchanged without even seeing each other, with one tribe putting out its specialized product in a mutually approved place, and the other coming and picking it up and leaving their own product, which the first tribe then came and took away. It is not quite clear whether this ever really happened, but, if it did, it was clearly a step toward the establishment of a market in which people would meet each other on the basis of mutual trust and courtesy. This is the integrative factor in exchange.

There may also be a little bit of a destructive element underlying exchange in the development of a system of law, organizing punishment for failure to live up to contracts and also punishment for failure to obey the principles of property, that is, for theft. Theft is very destructive of the integrative relationship. Trust is necessary for exchange to flourish. Often there is also a destructive element in producing the goods for exchange, simply because production involves the transformation of less valued things into more valued things, which involves the destruction or alteration of the less valued things, as, for instance, when wheat is ground into flour and flour baked into bread, when quarriers destroy hillsides, when miners extract ores, and so on.

THE POWER OF "LOVE"

Beyond threats and exchange, there are relationships that can be identified by the word *love,* in spite of its many meanings, and using it in the widest possible sense as an aspect of the integrative structure. In the love relationship, essentially, A says to B, "You do something for me because you love me." This may be one spouse to another; a leader talking to a follower; a monarch, especially a constitutional one, talking to his or her subjects; a state, to its citizens; a general, to his soldiers; or a religious leader, to his flock. If the word *love* seems too strong, substitute *respect.* There are degrees of love, as in everything else. Here again, the response and reaction may be important. If A demands too much, B may say, "Well, I do not love you that much." Then A may say, "Look what I do for you," and the situation edges back toward exchange. Love is also closely related to the integrative structures of pride and shame and perhaps guilt. A may say to B, "If you do not do something for me, you will be ashamed of yourself, you will feel guilty." These are subtle, but very important, relationships and they explain a great deal of human behavior. Destructive power—the power to hurt—may also play a small but complex part in the love relationship.

Love, of course, has its negative aspects in hate, and the capacity to create hatred is related to destructive power. A may say to B, "I am going to do this to you because I hate you." This is rather different from threat, although it may have somewhat the same structure of response. The complex dynamics of behavior that underlies the growth of love or of hatred is one of the real puzzles of social systems.

POLITICAL AND MILITARY POWER

A second set of categories of power, shown in Figure 2, relates more to institutions by which power is exercised, here again corresponding fairly closely to the first two sets of categories. We have political and military power, which is based primarily on threat systems and destructive power, although there is an element in it of productive and exchange power, simply because political and military institutions are virtually impossible, at least in any large scale, without something like money, for they have to purchase food, equipment, and buildings, as well as weapons, to feed, clothe, house, and arm their employees and their soldiers. Political institutions need some sort of income accounts, although they do not usually have much in the form of capital accounts. Even though they frequently use threat, for instance, in the form of conscription and the collection of taxes, there nevertheless remains a significant exchange element. There is also an element of love power, as suggested in the figure. Unless a

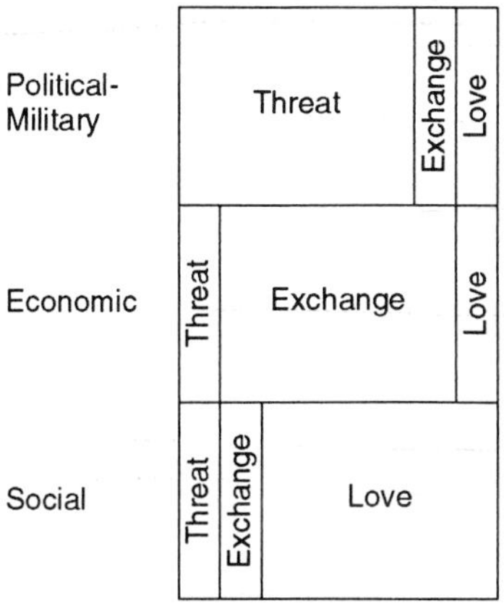

FIGURE 2 Categories of Power: Political-Military, Economic, and Social

ruler or a country is in some sense loved, or at least respected, his (her, or its) power to organize large threat systems will be very much diminished, as the history of revolution and the overthrow of rulers illustrates.

ECONOMIC POWER

Economic power is what the rich have a lot of and the poor, very little of. It has a good deal to do with the distribution of property. It is particularly characteristic of institutions such as the household, the firm, the corporation, the business, and the financial institutions—banks, insurance companies, stock markets, and so on. Its core is the productive and exchange power systems. Productive power and exchange are the basis of income, although the products of productive power do not always accrue to those who have produced them. There is a small element of threat in economic power, particularly noticeable in the institution of slavery. The slave owner in effect says to the slave, "You work for me or I will kill you, or at least make things very unpleasant for you." There is a certain element of threat in all property relations, and there is a good deal of it in the legal and police institutions. The law enforcement system is a public threat to those who privately threaten the existing allocation of property. Economic power also has a certain integrative component. Morale may not be quite so important to a corporation as it is to an army, but it is not insignificant. Unless existing economic institutions are generally accepted as legitimate, they will not be able to function very well.

SOCIAL POWER

It is hard to find a general name for those institutions that are based primarily on integrative power. The family certainly is one of them. Other examples are churches, religious and charitable organizations, the 10,000 or so international nongovernmental organizations, activists and reformist organizations, and so on. In Figure 2 I showed social power as the major characteristic of integrative institutions. Social power is the capacity to make people identify with some organization to which they give loyalty. One mark of such organizations is that they are often supported by grants rather than by exchange, that is, by one-way transfers from the loyal members or affiliates in terms of cash, goods, or labor, what might be called "voluntary grants." There are also involuntary grants that are made under threat, such as taxes or holdups. There may be some threat element in basically integrative organizations. Religious organizations may use the threat of hellfire; secular organizations may use the threat of disapproval, ostracism, and shame.

SOURCES OF POWER

A fourth set of categories of power might be described as the sources of power that underlie all the other forms. There are clearly physical, chemical, and material sources of power. The exercise of power always involves transformations of some kind, and many of these transformations are either physical or chemical, or both. People frequently equate energy with power, and certainly one aspect of energy is that which produces transformations. Energy is a very important condition of both destructive and constructive power. Without energy we cannot blow things up or move them around. Physical and chemical structures impose limits on power. We cannot make compounds out of helium or neon, although we can excite these gases to glow with light. There are only so many chemical compounds that are possible because of the principles of valency in spatial structure. Physical and chemical preconditions impose limits on power. These preconditions, however, should not be identified with human power. The structures and instruments of human power, whether guns, or houses and furniture, or persons or other living creatures, always originate in what might be called a genetic factor, whether this is an idea in the mind of a person or DNA in a fertilized egg. This genetic factor has the potential for power, whether destructive, productive, or integrative. Whether this potential is realized, however, depends on the capacity of the genetic structure to capture energy and to transport and transform appropriate materials into the product, whether a bombed city, an economic commodity, or a church. Energy and materials might be described as limiting factors, to which we might add space and time. The genetic factor fundamentally consists of knowledge, know-how, information, and the capacity for communication. These underlie all forms of power and they are particularly important in integrative power, which is mainly a matter of communication. Communication, of course, requires a physical and chemical medium, which can code the information that is communicated, and the absence of these certainly will limit communication. The physical-chemical structures of the human brain permit an immense amount of information and communication that the physical and chemical structures of a rock do not. Communication, however, may be coded in a great variety of physical and chemical structures—in light waves, sound waves, a printed page, a picture, a gesture or facial expression, and so on. As we move from destructive to productive and integrative systems, the amount of physical and chemical energy substratum probably declines, and knowledge, information, and communication increase.

One condition that underlies all forms of power in a limiting fashion might be described as "vulnerability" in relation to changing environments. Salt crystals are highly vulnerable when put in water; diamonds are not. Some rocks are soft and crumble easily; others are hard and can stand all sorts of environments. Some people are malleable, some are not. Some institutions are malleable, some are not. A suit of armor may render the wearer invulnerable to arrows, but not to cannon balls. Adaptability may lessen vulnerability in all the categories of power. A distinction related to vulnerability is that between defensive power, which is the capacity to prevent unwanted change, and the power to produce wanted change, which might be called "active" power. The general structure of power and the distribution of power often reflect the constantly shifting structures of defensive versus active power. This seems to be particularly important when it comes to threat and military power, but all forms of power are subject to this very fundamental, underlying condition. We even defend ourselves, at times, against being loved. Liquidity in economic organizations is a defense against the unexpected.

Influence without Authority: The Use of Alliances, Reciprocity, and Exchange to Accomplish Work

Allan R. Cohen

David L. Bradford

Bill Heatton is the director of research at a $250 million division of a large West Coast company. The division manufactures exotic telecommunications components and has many technical advancements to its credit. During the past several years, however, the division's performance has been spotty at best; multimillion dollar losses have been experienced in some years despite many efforts to make the division more profitable. Several large contracts have resulted in major financial losses, and in each instance the various parts of the division blamed the others for the problems. Listen to Bill's frustration as he talks about his efforts to influence Ted, a colleague who is marketing director, and Roland, the program manager who reports to Ted.

> Another program is about to come through. Roland is a nice guy, but he knows nothing and never will. He was responsible for our last big loss, and now he's in charge of this one. I've tried to convince Ted, his boss, to get Roland off the program, but I get nowhere. Although Ted doesn't argue that Roland is capable, he doesn't act to find someone else. Instead, he comes to me with worries about my area.
>
> I decided to respond by changing my staffing plan, assigning to Roland's program the people they wanted. I had to override my staff's best judgment about who should be assigned. Yet I'm not getting needed progress reports from Roland, and he's never available for planning. I get little argument from him, but there's no action to correct the problem. That's bad because I'm responding but not getting any response.
>
> There's no way to resolve this. If they disagree, that's it. I could go to a tit-for-tat strategy, saying that if they don't do what I want, we'll get even with them next time. But I don't know how to do that without hurting the organization, which would feel worse than getting even!
>
> Ted, Roland's boss, is so much better than his predecessor that I hate to ask that he be removed. We could go together to our boss, the general manager, but I'm very reluctant to do that. You've failed in a matrix organization if you have to go to your boss. I have to try hard because I'd look bad if I had to throw it in his lap.

Meanwhile, I'm being forceful, but I'm afraid it's in a destructive way. I don't want to wait until the program has failed to be told it was all my fault.

Bill is clearly angry and frustrated, leading him to behave in ways that he does not feel good about. Like other managers who very much want to influence an uncooperative co-worker whom they cannot control, Bill has begun to think of the intransigent employee as the enemy. Bill's anger is narrowing his sense of what is possible; he fantasizes revenge but is too dedicated to the organization to actually harm it. He is genuinely stuck.

Organizational members who want to make things happen often find themselves in this position. Irrespective of whether they are staff or line employees, professionals or managers, they find it increasingly necessary to influence colleagues and superiors. These critical others control needed resources, possess required information, set priorities on important activities, and have to agree and cooperate if plans are to be implemented. They cannot be ordered around because they are under another area's control and can legitimately say no because they have many other valid priorities. They respond only when they choose to. Despite the clear need and appropriateness of what is being asked for (certainly as seen by the person who is making the request), compliance may not be forthcoming.

All of this places a large burden on organizational members, who are expected not only to take initiatives but also to respond intelligently to requests made of them by others. Judgment is needed to sort out the value of the many requests made of anyone who has valuable resources to contribute. As Robert Kaplan argued in his article "Trade Routes: The Manager's Network of Relationships" (*Organizational Dynamics,* Spring 1984), managers must now develop the organizational equivalent of "trade routes" to get things done. Informal networks of mutual influence are needed. In her book *The Change Masters* (Simon & Schuster, 1983), Rosabeth Moss Kanter showed that developing and implementing all kinds of innovations requires coalitions to be built to shape and support new ways of doing business.

A key current problem, then, is finding ways to develop mutual influence without the formal authority to command. A peer cannot "order" a colleague to change priorities, modify an approach, or implement a grand new idea. A staff member cannot "command" his or her supervisor to back a proposal, fight top management for greater resources, or allow more autonomy. Even Bill Heatton, in dealing with Roland (who was a level below him in the hierarchy but in another department), could not dictate that Roland provide the progress reports that Bill so desperately wanted.

EXCHANGE AND THE LAW OF RECIPROCITY

The way influence is acquired without formal authority is through the "law of reciprocity"—the almost universal belief that people should be paid back for what they do, that one good (or bad) deed deserves another. This belief is held by people in primitive and not-so-primitive societies all around the world, and it serves as the grease that allows the organizational wheels to turn smoothly. Because people expect that their actions will be paid back in one form or another, influence is possible.

In the case of Bill Heatton, his inability to get what he wanted from Roland and Ted stemmed from his failure to understand fully how reciprocity works in organizations. He therefore was unable to set up mutually beneficial exchanges. Bill believed that he had gone out of his way to help the marketing department by changing his staffing patterns, and he expected Roland to reciprocate by providing regular progress reports. When Roland failed to provide the reports, Bill believed that Ted was obligated to remove Roland from the project. When Ted did not respond, Bill became angry and wanted to retaliate. Thus Bill recognized the appropriateness of exchange in making organizations work. However, he did not understand how exchange operates.

Before exploring in detail how exchange can work in dealing with colleagues and superiors, it is important to recognize that reciprocity is the basic principle behind all organizational transactions. For example, the basic employment contract is an exchange ("an honest day's work for an honest day's pay"). Even work that is above and beyond what is formally required involves exchange. The person who helps out may not necessarily get (or expect) immediate payment for the extra effort requested, but some eventual compensation is expected.

Think of the likely irritation an employee would feel if his or her boss asked him or her to work through several weekends, never so much as said thanks, and then claimed credit for the extra work. The employee might not say anything the first time this happened, expecting or hoping that the boss would make it up somehow. However, if the effort were never acknowledged in any way, the employee, like most people, would feel that something important had been violated.

The expectation of reciprocal exchanges occurs between an employee and his or her supervisor, among peers, with higher-level managers in other parts of the organization, or all of the above. The exchange can be of tangible goods, such as a budget increase, new equipment, or more personnel; or tangible services, such as a faster response time, more information, or public support; or of sentiments, such as gratitude, admiration, or praise. Whatever form exchanges take, unless they are roughly equivalent over time, hard feelings will result.

Exchanges enable people to handle the give-and-take of working together without strong feelings of injustice arising. They are especially important during periods of rapid change because the number of requests that go far beyond the routine tends to escalate. In those situations, exchanges become less predictable, more free-floating, and spontaneous. Nevertheless, people still expect that somehow or other, sooner or later, they will be (roughly) equally compensated for the acts they do above and beyond those that are covered by the formal exchange agreements in their job. Consequently, some kind of "currency" equivalent needs to be worked out, implicitly if not explicitly, to keep the parties in the exchange feeling fairly treated.

CURRENCIES: THE SOURCE OF INFLUENCE

If the basis of organizational influence depends on mutually satisfactory exchanges, then people are influential only insofar as they can offer something that others need. Thus power comes from the ability to meet others' needs.

A useful way to think of how the process of exchange actually works in organizations is to use the metaphor of "currencies." This metaphor provides a powerful way to conceptualize what is important to the influencer and the person to be influenced. Just as many types of currencies are traded in the world financial market, many types are "traded" in organizational life. Too often people think only of money or promotion and status. Those "currencies," however, usually are available only to a manager in dealing with his or her employees. Peers who want to influence colleagues or employees who want to influence their supervisors often feel helpless. They need to recognize that many types of payments exist, broadening the range of what can be exchanged.

Some major currencies that are commonly valued and traded in organizations are listed in Exhibit 1. Although not exhaustive, the list makes evident that a person does not have to be at the top of an organization or have hands on the formal levers of power to command multiple resources that others may value.

Part of the usefulness of currencies comes from their flexibility. For example, there are many ways to express gratitude and to give assistance. A manager who most values the currency of appreciation could be paid through verbal thanks, praise, a public statement at a meeting, informal comments to his peers, and/or a note to her boss. However, the same note of thanks seen by one person as a sign of appreciation may be seen by another person as an attempt to brownnose or by a third person as a cheap way to try to repay extensive favors and service. Thus currencies have value not in some abstract sense but as defined by the receiver.

Although we have stressed the interactive nature of exchange, "payments" do not always have to be made by the other person. They can be self-generated to fit beliefs about being virtuous, benevolent, or committed to the organization's welfare. Someone may respond to another person's request because it reinforces cherished values, a sense of identity, or feelings of self-worth. The exchange is interpersonally stimulated because the one who wants influence has set up conditions that allow this kind of self-payment to occur by asking for cooperation to accomplish organizational goals. However, the person who responds because "it is the right thing to do" and who feels good about being the "kind of person who does not act out of narrow self-interest" is printing currency (virtue) that is self-satisfying.

Of course, the five categories of currencies listed in Exhibit 1 are not mutually exclusive. When the demand from the other person is high, people are likely to pay in several currencies across several categories. They may, for example, stress the organizational value of their request, promise to return the favor at a later time, imply that it will increase the other's prestige in the organization, and express their appreciation.

ESTABLISHING EXCHANGE RATES

What does it take to pay back in a currency that the other party in an exchange will perceive as equivalent? In impersonal markets, because everything is translated into a common monetary currency, it generally is easy to say what a fair payment is. Does a ton of steel equal a case of golfclubs? By translating both into dollar equivalents, a satisfactory deal can be worked out.

EXHIBIT 1   Commonly Traded Organizational Currencies

Inspiration-Related Currencies	
Vision	Being involved in a task that has larger significance for the unit, organization, customers, or society.
Excellence	Having a chance to do important things really well.
Moral/Ethical Correctness	Doing what is "right" by a higher standard than efficiency.
Task-Related Currencies	
Resources	Lending or giving money, budget increases, personnel, space, and so forth.
Assistance	Helping with existing projects or undertaking unwanted tasks.
Cooperation	Giving task support, providing quicker response time, approving a project, or aiding implementation.
Information	Providing organizational as well as technical knowledge.
Position-Related Currencies	
Advancement	Giving a task or assignment that can aid in promotion.
Recognition	Acknowledging effort, accomplishment, or abilities.
Visibility	Providing chance to be known by higher-ups or significant others in the organization.
Reputation	Enhancing the way a person is seen.
Importance/Insiderness	Offering a sense of importance, of "belonging."
Network/Contacts	Providing opportunities for linking with others.
Relationship-Related Currencies	
Acceptance/Inclusion	Providing closeness and friendship.
Personal Support	Giving personal and emotional backing.
Understanding	Listening to others' concerns and issues.
Personal-Related Currencies	
Self-Concept	Affirming one's values, self-esteem, and identity.
Challenge/Learning	Sharing tasks that increase skills and abilities.
Ownership/Involvement	Letting others have ownership and influence.
Gratitude	Expressing appreciation or indebtedness.

In interpersonal exchanges, however, the process becomes a bit more complicated. Just how does someone repay another person's willingness to help finish a report? Is a simple thank-you enough? Does it also require the recipient to say something nice about the helper to his or her boss? Whose standard of fairness should be used? What if one person's idea of fair repayment is very different from the other's?

Because of the natural differences in the way two parties can interpret the same activity, establishing exchanges that both parties will perceive as equitable can be problematic. Thus it is critical to understand what is important to the person to be influenced. Without a clear understanding of what that person experiences and values, it will be extremely difficult for anyone to thread a path through the minefield of creating mutually satisfactory exchanges.

Fortunately, the calibration of equivalent exchanges in the interpersonal and organizational worlds is facilitated by the fact that approximations will do in most cases. Occasionally, organizational members know exactly what they want in return for favors or help, but more often they will settle for very rough equivalents (providing that there is reasonable goodwill).

THE PROCESS OF EXCHANGE

To make the exchange process effective, the influencer needs to (1) think about the person to be influenced as a potential ally, not an adversary; (2) know the world of the potential ally, including the pressures as well as the person's needs and goals; (3) be aware of key goals and available resources that may be valued by the potential ally; and (4) understand the exchange transaction itself so that win-win outcomes are achieved. Each of these factors is discussed below.

Potential Ally, Not Adversary

A key to influence is thinking of the other person as a potential ally. Just as many contemporary organizations have discovered the importance of creating strategic alliances with suppliers and customers, employees who want influence within the organization need to create internal allies. Even though each party in an alliance continues to have freedom to pursue its own interests, the goal is to find areas of mutual benefit and develop trusting, sustainable relationships. Similarly, each person whose cooperation is needed inside the organization is a potential ally. Each still has self-interests to pursue, but those self-interests do not preclude searching for and building areas of mutual benefit.

Seeing other organizational members as potential allies decreases the chance that adversarial relationships will develop—an all-too-frequent result (as in the case of Bill Heatton) when the eager influencer does not quickly get the assistance or cooperation needed. Assuming that even a difficult person is a potential ally makes it easier to understand that person's world and thereby discover what that person values and needs.

The Potential Ally's World

We have stressed the importance of knowing the world of the potential ally. Without awareness of what the ally needs (what currencies are valued), attempts to influence that person can only be haphazard. Although this conclusion may seem self-evident, it is remarkable how often people attempt to influence without adequate information about what is important to the potential ally. Instead, they are driven by their own definition of "what should be" and "what is right" when they should be seeing the world from the other person's perspective.

For example, Bill Heatton never thought about the costs to Ted of removing Roland from the project. Did Ted believe he could coach Roland to perform better on this project? Did Ted even agree that Roland had done a poor job on the previous project, or did Ted think Roland had been hampered by other departments' shortcomings? Bill just did not know.

Several factors can keep the influencer from seeing the potential ally clearly. As with Bill Heatton, the frustration of meeting resistance from a potential ally can get in the way of really understanding the other person's world. The desire to influence is so strong that only the need for cooperation is visible to the influencer. As a result of not being understood, the potential ally digs in, making the influencer repeat an inappropriate strategy or back off in frustration.

When a potential ally's behavior is not understandable ("Why won't Roland send the needed progress reports?"), the influencer tends to stereotype that person. If early attempts to influence do not work, the influencer is tempted to write the person off as negative, stubborn, selfish, or "just another bean counter/whiz kid/sales-type" or whatever pejorative label is used in that organizational culture to dismiss those organizational members who are different.

Although some stereotypes may have a grain of truth, they generally conceal more than they reveal. The actuary who understands that judgment, not just numbers, is needed to make decisions disappears as an individual when the stereotype of "impersonal, detached number machine" is the filter through which he or she is seen. Once the stereotype is applied, the frustrated influencer is no longer likely to see what currencies that particular potential ally actually values.

Sometimes, the lack of clear understanding about a potential ally stems from the influencer's failure to appreciate the organizational forces acting on the potential ally. To a great extent, a person's behavior is a result of the situation in which that person works (and not just his or her personality). Potential allies are embedded in an organizational culture that shapes their interests and responses. For example, one of the key determinants of anyone's behavior is likely to be the way the person's performance is measured and rewarded. In many instances, what is mistaken for personal orneriness is merely the result of the person's doing something that will be seen as good performance in his or her function.

The salesperson who is furious because the plant manager resists changing priorities for a rush order may not realize that part of the plant manager's bonus depends on holding unit costs down—a task made easier with long production runs. The plant manager's resistance does not necessarily reflect his or her inability to be flexible or lack of concern about pleasing customers or about the company's overall success.

Other organizational forces that can affect the potential ally's behavior include the daily time demands on that person's position; the amount of contact the person has with customers, suppliers, and other outsiders; the organization's information flow (or lack of it); the style of the potential ally's boss; the belief and assumptions held by that person's co-workers; and so forth. Although some of these factors cannot be changed by the influencer, understanding them can be useful in figuring out how to frame and time requests. It also helps the influencer resist the temptation to stereotype the noncooperator.

Self-Awareness of the Influencer

Unfortunately, people desiring influence are not always aware of precisely what they want. Often their requests contain a cluster of needs (a certain product, arranged in a certain way, delivered at a specified time). They fail to think through which aspects are more important and which can be jettisoned if necessary. Did Bill Heatton want Roland removed, or did he want the project effectively managed? Did he want overt concessions from Ted, or did he want better progress reports?

Further, there is a tendency to confuse and intermingle the desired end goal with the means of accomplishing it, leading to too many battles over the wrong things. In *The Change Masters,* Kanter reported that successful influencers in organizations were those who never lost sight of the ultimate objective but were willing to be flexible about means.

Sometimes influencers underestimate the range of currencies available for use. They may assume, for example, that just because they are low in the organization they have nothing that others want. Employees who want to influence their boss are especially likely not to realize all of the supervisor's needs that they can fulfill. They become so caught up with their feelings of powerlessness that they fail to see the many ways they can generate valuable currencies.

In other instances, influencers fail to be aware of their preferred style of interaction and its fit with the potential ally's preferred style. Everyone has a way of relating to others to get work done. However, like the fish who is unaware of the water, many people are oblivious of their own style of interaction or see it as the only way to be. Yet interaction style can cause problems with potential allies who are different.

For example, does the influencer tend to socialize first and work later? If so, that style of interaction will distress a potential ally who likes to dig right in to solve the problem at hand and only afterward chat about sports, family, or office politics. Does the potential ally want to be approached with answers, not problems? If so, a tendency to start influence attempts with open-ended, exploratory problem solving can lead to rejection despite good intentions.

Nature of the Exchange Transaction

Many of the problems that occur in the actual exchange negotiation have their roots in the failure to deal adequately with the first three factors outlined above. Failure to treat other people as potential allies, to understand a potential ally's world, and to be self-aware are all factors that interfere with successful exchange. In addition, some special problems commonly arise when both parties are in the process of working out a mutually satisfactory exchange agreement.

• *Not knowing how to use reciprocity.* Using reciprocity requires stating needs clearly without "crying wolf," being aware of the needs of an ally without being manipulative, and seeking mutual gain rather than playing "winner takes all." One trap that Bill Heatton fell into was not being able to "close on the exchange." That is, he assumed that if he acted in good faith and did his part, others would automatically reciprocate. Part of his failure was not understanding the other party's world; another part was not being able to negotiate cleanly with Ted about what each of them wanted. It is not even clear that Ted realized Bill was altering his organization as per Ted's requests, that Ted got what he wanted, or that Ted knew Bill intended an exchange of responses.

• *Preferring to be right rather than effective*. This problem is especially endemic to professionals of all kinds. Because of their dedication to the "truth" (as their profession defines it), they stubbornly stick to their one right way when trying to line up potential allies instead of thinking about what will work given the audience and conditions. Organizational members with strong technical backgrounds often chorus the equivalent of "I'll be damned if I'm going to sell out and become a phony salesman, trying to get by on a shoe-shine and smile." The failure to accommodate to the potential ally's needs and desires often kills otherwise sound ideas.

• *Overusing what has been successful*. When people find that a certain approach is effective in many situations, they often begin to use it in places where it does not fit. By overusing the approach, they block more appropriate methods. Just as a weight lifter becomes muscle-bound from overdeveloping particular muscles at the expense of others, people who have been reasonably successful at influencing other people can diminish that ability by overusing the same technique.

For example, John Brucker, the human resources director at a medium-size company, often cultivated support for new programs by taking people out to fancy restaurants for an evening of fine food and wine. He genuinely derived pleasure from entertaining, but at the same time he created subtle obligations. One time, a new program he wanted to introduce required the agreement of William Adams, head of engineering. Adams, an old-timer, perceived Brucker's proposal as an unnecessary frill, mainly because he did not perceive the real benefits to the overall organization. Brucker responded to Adams's negative comments as he always did in such cases—by becoming more friendly and insisting that they get together for dinner soon. After several of these invitations, Adams became furious. Insulted by what he considered to be Brucker's attempts to buy him off, he fought even harder to kill the proposal. Not only did the program die, but Brucker lost all possibility of influencing Adams in the future. Adams saw Brucker's attempts at socializing as a sleazy and crude way of trying to soften him up. For his part, Brucker was totally puzzled by Adams's frostiness and assumed that he was against all progress. He never realized that Adams had a deep sense of integrity and a real commitment to the good of the organization. Thus Brucker lost his opportunity to sell a program that, ironically, Adams would have found valuable had it been implemented.

As the case above illustrates, a broad repertoire of influence approaches is needed in modern organizations. Johnny-one-notes soon fall flat.

THE ROLE OF RELATIONSHIPS

All of the preceding discussion needs to be conditioned by one important variable: the nature of the relationship between both parties. The greater the extent to which the influencer has worked with the potential ally and created trust, the easier the exchange process will be. Each party will know the other's desired currencies and situational pressures, and each will have developed a mutually productive interaction style. With trust, less energy will be spent on figuring out the intentions of the ally, and there will be less suspicion about when and how the payback will occur.

A poor relationship (based on previous interactions, on the reputation each party has in the organization, and/or on stereotypes and animosities between the functions or departments that each party represents) will impede an otherwise easy exchange. Distrust of the goodwill, veracity, or reliability of the influencer can lead to the demand for "no credit; cash up front," which constrains the flexibility of both parties.

The nature of the interaction during the influencer process also affects the nature of the relationship between the influencer and the other party. The way that John Brucker attempted to relate to William Adams not only did not work but also irreparably damaged any future exchanges between them.

Few transactions within organizations are one-time deals. (Who knows when the other person may be needed again or even who may be working for him or her in the future?) Thus in most exchange situations two outcomes matter: success in achieving task goals and success in improving the relationship so that the next interaction will be even more productive. Too often, people who want to be influential focus only on the task and act as if there is no tomorrow. Although both task accomplishment and an improved relationship cannot always be realized at the same time, on some occasions the latter can be more important than the former. Winning the battle but losing the war is an expensive outcome.

INCONVERTIBLE CURRENCIES

We have spelled out ways organizational members operate to gain influence for achieving organizational goals. By effectively using exchange, organizational members can achieve their goals and at the same time help others achieve theirs. Exchange permits organizational members to be assertive without being antagonistic by keeping mutual benefit a central outcome.

In many cases, organizational members fail to acquire desired influence because they do not use all of their potential power. However, they sometimes fail because not all situations are amenable to even the best efforts at influencing. Not everything can be translated into compatible currencies. If there are fundamental differences in what is valued by two parties, it may not be possible to find common ground, as illustrated in the example below.

The founder and chairman of a high-technology company and the president he had hired five years previously were constantly displeased with one another. The president was committed to creating maximum shareholder value, the currency he valued most as a result of his M.B.A. training, his position, and his temperament. Accordingly, he had concluded that the company was in a perfect position to cash in by squeezing expenses to maximize profits and going public. He could see that the company's product line of exotic components was within a few years of saturating its market and would require massive, risky investment to move to sophisticated end-user products.

The president could not influence the chairman to adopt this direction, however, because the chairman valued a totally different currency, the fun of technological challenge. An independently wealthy man, the chairman had no interest in realizing the $10 million or so he would get if the company maximized profits by cutting research and selling out. He wanted a place to test his intuitive, creative research hunches, not a source of income.

Thus the president's and chairman's currencies were not convertible into one another at an acceptable exchange rate. After they explored various possibilities but failed to find common ground, they mutually agreed that the president should leave—on good terms and only after a more compatible replacement could be found. Although this example acknowledges that influence through alliance, currency conversion, and exchange is not always possible, it is hard to be certain that any situation is hopeless until the person desiring influence has fully applied all of the diagnostic and interpersonal skills we have described.

Influence is enhanced by using the model of strategic alliances to engage in mutually beneficial exchanges with potential allies. Even though it is not always possible to be successful, the chances of achieving success can be greatly increased. In a period of rapid competitive, technological, regulative, and consumer change, individuals and their organizations need all the help they can get.

How to Become an Influential Manager

Bernard Keys

Thomas Case

A hospital department head attempted in vain to persuade physicians working in a large metropolitan hospital to bring patient medical records up to date. Although doctors consider this an abhorrent chore, hospitals cannot begin the billing process until each record is completed and signed by the physician. After many frustrating attempts, the department head describes how he proved equal to the challenge.

> Every month we served the doctors breakfast and lunch and organized games that would allow them to win prizes. Sometimes we would place balloons on a bulletin board and let them throw darts at the balloons. At other times we would do something ridiculously child-like such as hosting a watermelon seed spitting contest or playing pin the tail on the donkey. The sessions worked beautifully because the doctors knew that when they came in someone would be there to help them and they would even have a little fun. Once when we were really desperate we hired a popular entertainer. The room was full that day and we completed over 1,000 charts.

Influence is simply the process by which people successfully persuade others to follow their advice, suggestion, or order. It can be contrasted with power, which is a personal or positional attribute that enables one to influence others and which can be thought of as "continuing or sustained" influence.[1] A number of popular books have suggested that influence must replace the use of formal authority in relationships with subordinates, peers, outside contacts, and others on whom the job make one dependent.[2] The writers of these books attribute the need for greater influence to the rapidity of change in organizations, the diversity of people, goals, and values, increasing interdependence, and the diminishing acceptability of formal authority.[3] Bennis and Nanus have suggested that leaders must empower themselves by empowering their subordinates. Kouzes and Posner agree with this conclusion, explaining that the more people believe they can influence and control the organization, the greater will be the effectiveness of the organization. Tichy and Devanna extend this thought even further by suggesting that today we need transformational leaders who will allow networks that

Reprinted from *Acadamy of Mangement Executive* 4, no. 4 (1990), pp. 38–49. Used with permission of the authors and publisher.

funnel diverse views upward from the lower level of the organization where a need for change is often first detected. Similarly, John Kotter observes that the increasing diversity and interdependence of organizational role players is creating a "power gap" for managers who often have knowledge and good ideas for organizations but who have inadequate authority to implement their ideas.

For example, effectiveness with subordinates has been found to depend heavily on the ability to develop upward influence with superiors.[4] Influence with the boss often depends on the ability to accomplish things through one's subordinates.[5] Laterally, managers must spend time in group meetings, interorganizational negotiations, and in bids for departmental resources.[6] This is a role replete with power gaps. Most assuredly lateral relationships require the ability to influence without formal authority representatives with unions, customers, and government, or highly autonomous professionals such as the physician in our introductory example.[7]

The concept of "linking groups" seems to drive the middle manager's work while both middle management and executive levels are heavily engaged in "coordinating" independent groups. In this latter role, they must persuade other organizational groups to provide information, products, resources needed, and negotiate working agreements with other groups. Additionally, executive levels of management must frequently maintain relationships with management-level vendors, consultants, and other boundary-spanning agents through outside meetings. Recent research suggests that the "ambassador role" of "representing one's staff" is vitally important to all levels of management. It consists of developing relationships with other work groups and negotiating for information and resources on behalf of the manager's own group.[8]

Building on the previous thoughts and the research of others, we conducted field studies to collect incidents, similar to the one describing the hospital department head, and used these to analyze how managers build and sustain influence. This article explains our research findings and those of related studies for managers who wish to become more influential with subordinates, superiors, peers, and other target groups.

INFLUENCE TACTIC RESEARCH

Only a few writers have identified influence tactics from research investigations. David Kipnis and his colleagues asked evening graduate students to describe an incident in which they actually succeeded in getting either their boss, a co-worker, or a subordinate to do something they wanted. Their analysis revealed that the tactics of ingratiation (making the supervisor feel important) and developing rational plans were the most frequently used methods to influence superiors. When attempting to influence subordinates, respondents most often used formal authority, training, and explanations. Only one tactic, that of requesting help, was frequently associated with influencing co-workers.

Our studies were aimed at strengthening the previous research. Since the studies cited above utilized categories of influence tactics derived from research with MBA students, we developed categories from influence incidents collected from practicing managers. Our three studies used trained students from several universities and structured interview forms to collect a wide geographic dispersion of responses.

Attempts were made to collect one successful incident and one unsuccessful incident from managers in a wide variety of both large and small businesses. One study focused on lateral influence processes, another on upward influence processes, and a third study examined downward influence. The primary question asked of each manager was, "Please think of a time when you successfully/unsuccessfully tried to influence a (superior, peer, or subordinate) toward the attainment of a personal, group, or organizational goal. . . . Please tell exactly what happened."

Exhibit 1 presents the summary of findings from these studies.[10] The numbers to the right of each tactic portray the rank order of the frequency with which influence tactics were reported for each target group.

Influencing Superiors

In influence attempts with superiors and peers, rational explanations were the most frequently used tactic. Often these techniques included the presentation of a complete plan, a comparative or quantitative analysis, or documentation of an idea or plan by way of survey, incidents, or interviews. In a few isolated cases, subordinates challenged their superiors' power, tried to manipulate them, bargained for influence, or

EXHIBIT 1 Rank of Frequency with Which Each Influence Tactic Was Reported by Target Groups

	Boss	Peers	Subordinates
Presenting a rational explanation	1	1	3
Telling, arguing, or talking without support	2	0	0
Presenting a complete plan	3	0	0
Using persistence or repetition	4	0	0
Developing and showing support of others (employees, outsiders, etc.)	5	2	12
Using others as a platform to present ideas	6	0	0
Presenting an example of a parallel situation	7	3	5
Threatening	8	4	10
Offering to trade favors or concessions	9	5	0
Using manipulative techniques	10	6	7
Calling on formal authority and policies	0	8	6
Showing confidence and support	0	0	1
Delegating duties, guidelines, or goals	0	0	2
Listening, counseling, or soliciting ideas	0	0	4
Questioning, reviewing, or evaluating	0	0	9
Rewarding with status or salary	0	0	7
Developing friendship or trust	0	7	11

threatened to quit. When these more assertive techniques were used, the subordinate was successful about 50 percent of the time—not very good odds for the risks which they were taking. In most narratives we found that the subordinate using these methods had discovered a powerless boss, or had developed an unusual position of power themselves by becoming indispensable. In a few cases they had simply become frustrated and thrown caution to the wind.

Upward influence tactics were characterized by numerous supporting tactics such as mustering the support of a variety of other persons (both internal and external to the organization) or by choosing appropriate timing to approach the boss. Only two tactics appeared with significant enough frequency differential to be clearly distinguished as a successful or unsuccessful tactic. Subordinates using the tactic of "talking to or arguing with the boss without support" were more likely to fail. On the other hand, those who continued persistently or repeated an influence attempt continuously were likely to succeed. Caution is in order, however, in interpreting the use of persistence and repetition; this was usually a secondary tactic used in combination with others such as presenting facts and rational plans.

The rational persuasion technique was used by a plant manager to prevent a cutback in his work force when the army phased out one of its tanks.

> First the plant manager sold a new product line to divisional staff who reported to his boss. In the meantime he developed a presentation in the form of a comparative analysis showing the pros and cons of taking on the new product line. Ideas presented included such things as the reduced burden on other products, risk reward factors, and good community relations from the layoff avoided. The presentation was polished, written on viewgraphs, and presented in person. The plant manager made certain that his technical staff would be at the meeting ready to answer any questions that might damage the strength of the presentation.

Not only did the plant manager succeed with this influence attempt, he felt that his boss and peers were easier to convince on subsequent attempts.

Influencing Subordinates

When dealing with subordinates, of course, the manager may simply tell an employee to do something. But our research suggests that managers who rely on formal authority alone are greatly limiting their options. The power gap noted earlier exists with subordinates as well as with other groups. Today more than ever, it must be filled with methods of influence other than authority. The following incident presents an interesting view of a furniture manufacturer trying to persuade his upholstery foreman to accept the position of plant superintendent.

> The manager met with Foreman Z in the foreman's office for short periods to talk about the promotion. Anticipating resistance, he covered small increments of the superintendent's responsibilities and allowed the foreman time to think about each session. The manager made sure that each session ended on a positive note. He pointed out the many tasks and skills required of the superintendent's job were already inherent in the foreman position. He downplayed the more complex responsibilities, relying on his commitment to future training to resolve these. Several such meetings took place in a five-day period. On one occasion the foreman alluded to resentment from fellow foremen. This prompted the

manager to enlist the help of some of the other foremen—several hunting buddies, to talk favorably about Z taking the position. In the last meeting the manager outlined the responsibilities and cited the salary and prestige which accompanied the position.

The senior manager in this incident later commented that he had always had success at using this technique—that is, breaking down a complex influence task into incremental steps and attacking each step separately. While there is some merit to this process, most readers would agree that the major reason for success in this case was the persistence exerted by the senior manager to win in his influence attempt. The mild deception in oversimplifying the open position could merit criticism but must be moderated by the manager's willingness to train and support the foreman. In this case, the influence tactic had positive long-term consequences; the foreman became a very successful plant superintendent and later trained his own successor.

Frequently, subordinates were questioned, reviewed, evaluated, threatened, warned, reprimanded, or embarrassed to change their minds or to solicit compliance with plans of the superior. These more threatening and negative techniques were more frequently associated with failure than success. Occasionally subordinates were transferred or relocated to influence them, but usually with little success. The more assertive tactics were typically used in cases where subordinates were initially reluctant to comply with reasonable requests or had violated policies or procedures.

Influencing Peers

Only one tactic from our lateral influence study was noted significantly more often in successful influence attempts with peers—that of "developing and showing support of others." This tactic was most often used along with others and therefore represented a part of a multiple influence tactic. Often a peer in a staff department or a subordinate is used to support a proposal, as in the influence attempt described by a zone manager with a large tire and rubber company.

> During this time I was managing 25 company-owned stores in which I initiated an effective program to control the handling of detective merchandise. I wanted to see the method utilized by the other store managers throughout the country who were supervised by other zone managers, but I felt that they would consider me to be intruding if I approached them directly. Therefore, I asked my store managers to tell the store managers in other zones about the sizeable savings to be had from the use of the method. The other store managers told their zone managers and soon they came to me for information about my program. The new program saved the company $90,000 per year, which increased our pay in bonuses at the end of the year.

When dealing with peers, managers made extensive use of rational facts or ideas. They often presented an example of another organization using their idea or proposal. Demonstrating that they had the support of others was a frequently used managerial influence tactic. Occasionally they threatened to go to higher level management or called on formal authority or policies to support their case. Assertive and manipulative tactics were used more often when attempting to influence the boss or subordinates, but less frequently with peers.

INFLUENCE TACTIC EFFECTIVENESS

Our research on individual influence attempts somewhat simplifies the area of influence effectiveness. In the first place, the methods listed in Exhibit 1 are the ones that are most frequently used and not necessarily the ones which are most successful. In all three studies we found that techniques that succeed in some instances fail in others. The few exceptions to this finding are noted in Exhibit 1 when the ranks of tactics are underlined. These represent tactics that were reported significantly more often, for either successful or unsuccessful influence attempts. For example, unsuccessful influence attempts with the boss often consisted of simply telling the boss something, arguing, or presenting an idea or suggestion without support. While this technique occasionally succeeded, it was more likely to be associated with unsuccessful episodes. Similarly, the use of persistence or repetition was reported more often in successful influence attempts with the boss than with unsuccessful ones.

Judging from the incidents collected, subordinate influence tactics of "threatening or questioning, reviewing, or evaluating" are significantly more likely to lead to failure than to success. Consider the experience of a plant operations manager attempting to introduce quality circles in an area to improve productivity.

> The operations manager requested the assistance of the manager of organizational development, who warned that such implementation would take time, patience, and the building of trust among his employees. Turnover in the operations area was high and negative attitudes tended to prevail. The operations manager became impatient, viewing QC as a quick fix for morale problems. The OD manager made available several persons who had worked successfully with a QC implementation, but after conversing with them the operations manager elected not to listen. He chose two subordinates to be trained as QC facilitators and immediately upon the completion of their training, began to implement QC. The operations manager and facilitators subtly coerced employees to join the circles and directed them toward the projects that management wanted attacked. After several months employee interest fell sharply and several complaints were filed with employee relations leading to abandonment of the project.

Contrast this occurrence with a less threatening attempt reported by a manufacturing manager in another part of the country:

> The manager first read numerous articles about QC programs and learned the pitfalls to avoid. QC information handouts were given to the supervisors over a period of a couple of months. The supervisors were never pressured and gradually they approached their manager, asking how they could get quality circles started in their departments. The program was then implemented using recognized procedures and is still operating successfully several years later.

The analysis of influence attempts such as the quality circles' incidents demonstrates the need for careful implementation of management processes.

STEPS IN BECOMING AN INFLUENTIAL MANAGER

Power, or sustained influence, may be accumulated and stored by a manager for future use. This allows one to call on existing strength to bolster influence tactics and often affects the future choice of influence tactic. Power may also be provided by the strategic position that one occupies in an organization, but position is often beyond the control of the incumbent. Fortunately, power may also be acquired through the development and exercise of certain skills by the manager within the organization. It is this skill-based power that we discuss throughout the rest of this article.[11]

Our research, and that of other writers reviewed in this article, indicates that there are five key steps to establishing sustained managerial influence.

- Develop a reputation as a knowledgeable person or an expert.
- Balance the time spent in each critical relationship according to the needs of the work rather than on the basis of habit or social preference.
- Develop a network of resource persons who can be called upon for assistance.
- Choose the correct combination of influence tactics for the objective and for the target to be influenced.
- Implement influence tactics with sensitivity, flexibility, and adequate levels of communication.

These steps in developing influence might be compared to the development of a ''web of influence'' (no negative implication intended). Unlike the web of a spider, the manager's web of influence can be mutually advantageous to all who interact within it. The web is anchored by a bridgeline of knowledge and expertise. The structure of the web is extended when invested time is converted into a network of resource persons who may be called upon for information and special assistance or support with an influence attempt. These persons—superiors, peers, subordinates, outside contacts, and others might be thought of as spokes in the web. Establishing the web, however, does not insure influence attempts will be successful. An effective combination of influence tactics must be selected for each influence target and influence objective sought. Finally, the tactics chosen must be communicated well within the sector of the web targeted.

Our research suggests that the web of influence is continually in a state of construction. It is often broken or weakened by an ill-chosen influence attempt requiring patch-up work for a portion of the web. Some webs are constructed poorly, haphazardly, or incompletely like the tangled web of a common house spider, while others are constructed with a beautiful symmetrical pattern like the one of the orb weaver.

Develop a Reputation as an Expert

Of all the influence tactics mentioned by respondents in our interviews, the use of rational facts and explanations was the most commonly reported—although in isolation this method succeeded no more often than it failed. Managers who possess expert knowledge in a field and who continually build that knowledge base are in a position to convert successful attempts into sustained power. In the early stages of a career (or shortly after a move) power from expertise is usually tentative and fragile like the first strands of a web. Hampton and colleagues explain how expertise is extended to become sustained influence with the following example of Bill, a young staff specialist, hired to provide expertise to a number of production managers:

Initially, the only influence process available to the specialist is persuasion—gaining the rational agreement of the managers. To be effective he prepares elaborate, clear presentations (even rehearsing with a colleague to anticipate any questions). By data, logic, and argument, he attempts to gain the agreement of his superiors. After a year of this kind of relationship, he goes one day to talk with Barbara, one of the managers. An hour has been reserved for the presentation. He arrives and begins his pitch. After a couple of minutes, however, the busy manager interrupts: "I'm just too busy to go over this. We'll do whatever you want to do."[12]

But enhancing expert-based power involves publicizing one's expertise as well as acquiring it. For example, Kotter contrasts two 35-year-old vice presidents in a large research and development organization, who are considered equally bright and technically competent.

Close friends and associates claim the reason that Randley is so much more powerful is related to a number of tactics that he has used more than Kline has. Randley has published more scientific papers and managerial articles than Kline. Randley has been more selective in the assignments he has worked on, choosing those that are visible and that require his strong suits. He has given more speeches and presentations on projects that are his own achievements. And in meetings in general, he is allegedly forceful in areas where he has expertise and silent in those where he does not.[13]

Balance Time with Each Critical Relationship

Managers who desire to become influential must strike a reasonable balance in the investment of their time. In another study using a questionnaire, we surveyed managers from the United States, Korea, Hong Kong, and the Philippines to learn how they spent their time. These managers say that they spend about 10 percent of their time interacting with the boss, approximately 30 percent interacting with subordinates, and about 20 percent interacting with peers. As one might expect, the pattern of outside relations varies with the job (i.e., sales, engineering, etc.), but the managers report, on the average, spending from 15–20 percent of their time with external contacts. Time spent alone varies from 15–28 percent.[14] Although we cannot argue that this pattern is descriptive of all managers, it is similar to the pattern of communication distribution discovered from a sample of U. S. managers by Luthans and Larson.[15]

Some popular writers are calling for a heavy rescheduling of time and communications efforts.[16] Peters argues that 75 percent of a middle manager's time must be spent on horizontal relationships to speed up cross-functional communications in the middle of organizations. Johnson and Frostman see this kind of communication as being so critical that it must be mandated by upper level management. Peters emphasizes the argument that upper level managers spend too little time visiting with customers or in face-to-face relationships with subordinates (management by walking around). The bottom line is that time should be spent where influence is most needed to accomplish organizational goals.[17]

During our seminars on influence over the years, managers have often told us that they failed to spend enough time with the boss or with peers, or in simply keeping up with organizational happenings. This may be due to the fact that many managers are uncomfortable spending time with those who have more formal power than they (superiors), or with those with whom they must compete (peers). Sayles believes that managers' uneasiness with peers grows out of the difference in values across departments and work groups, the ambiguities which exist in cross-organizational relationships, and the conflict often generated in lateral relationships.[18] Other things being equal, realigning from a narrow focus on subordinates to a bigger picture which includes lateral and upward relationships can often yield a stronger web of sustained influence and should provide the supporting spokes needed to launch influence tactics.

A strong web of influence may even be quite desirable from the boss's viewpoint. Schilit found that managers who had been working for the same upper manager for a long period of time were quite capable of influencing that manager even on strategic issues facing the company. He concludes that: "(Managers) should be encouraged to be assertive in presenting their strategic thoughts because widespread strategic thinking may have a positive impact on their division or organization."[19]

Develop a Network of Resource Persons

Although managers do not use other people in most influence attempts, the more important attempts invariably involve others. For example, in the incident cited earlier about the furniture manufacturer who wanted a foreman to accept the plant manager's job, the assistance of other foremen (fishing buddies) was solicited. Similarly, in the case of the plant manager who tried to avoid a cutback in his work force after the phaseout of a military contract, the manager sold his idea to division staff and ensured that his own technical staff would be in attendance at the meeting in which he was making a presentation to the boss. The ability to establish and exploit a network is clearly demonstrated by a branch manager of a bank who used the following tactic with his superior, a vice president, when he found his operation in need of additional space.

> My strategy was to convince my immediate superior that the current facilities were too small to not only handle the current volume of business, but too small to allow us to increase our share of the market in a rapidly growing area. First, I persuaded my superior to visit the branch more often, especially at times when the branch was particularly busy. I also solicited accounting's help to provide statistical reports on a regular basis that communicated the amount of overall growth in the area as well as the growth of our competitors. These reports showed that our market share was increasing. I then asked my superior to visit with me as I called on several customers and prospects in the area to let him know the type of potential business in the area. During this period of time, I kept pushing to increase all levels of business at the branch. Finally, I encouraged key customers in the bank to say favorable things about my branch when they visited with my senior managers. Eventually my superior got behind my proposal and we were able to build an addition to the building which allowed me to add several new employees.

Such influence attempts clearly illustrate the fact that many managers do not assume that achievement in traditional areas of management—selling, organizing, promoting customers—will inspire sufficient confidence by others. Rather than waiting for good publicity and resources to come to them, they seek them out through influence approaches built on carefully planned networks and persistent effort. The findings of our influence studies are supported by the observations of Luthans and his colleagues who concluded that managers who are both effective (have satisfied and committed subordinates and high performance in their units) and successful (receive relatively rapid promotions) strike a balanced approach between networking, human resource management, communications, and traditional management activities.[20]

To some extent, networking activities may affect the positional strength of managers. The more contacts a manager has with others and the more independent the position relative to others, the more control the manager has over the flow of information. Positions that involve interaction with more influential managers of the organization or control information on which they rely, will typically be ones of power.[21]

Kaplan compares the strengthening of lateral relationships in the organization to the establishment of trade routes in international trade. According to this writer, managers, unlike countries which trade products, often trade power and the ability to get things done. Their goal is to build strong reciprocal relationships with other departments so that when the manager has immediate needs, sufficient obligation exists to ensure fast cooperation. Often positions on the boundary of an organization can be especially influential. Consider the example referred to by Kaplan when describing a newly appointed manager of corporate employee relations. ''I wanted a base that was different from what the groups reporting to me had and also from what my superiors had, so I established a series of contacts in other American industries until I knew on a first-name basis my counterpart at IBM, TRW, Proctor & Gamble, DuPont, and General Electric, and I could get their input—input which the people in my organization didn't have.''[22] Kaplan suggests that networks of trading partners can be built by rotating jobs frequently, establishing strong friendships (and maintaining them), and seeking commonality with other managers, such as a shared work history.

Choose the Correct Combination of Influence Tactics

Influence tactics are the threads that complete a web, hold the spokes of the webbed network in place, and in turn are supported by the network. They must be chosen carefully on the basis of influence targets chosen and objectives sought.[23] One of the studies by Kipnis and colleagues found, as did we, that considerably more approaches were used to influence subordinates than were used to influence superiors or peers. Incidents in our studies suggested that most first influence attempts by managers involved soft approaches such as requests or reason, but later attempts included stronger tactics when the target of influence was reluctant to comply. This notion was confirmed statistically in the Kipnis study. Both superior and subordinate target groups in the Kipnis sample tended to use reason to sell ideas and friendliness to obtain favors. These authors also emphasize that influence tactics must vary with the target and objective of influence attempts: ''only the most inflexible of managers can be expected to rely rigidly on a single strategy, say assertiveness, to achieve both personal and organizational objectives. It may be appropriate to 'insist' that one's boss pay more attention to cost overruns; it is less appropriate to 'insist' on time off for a game of golf.''[24]

Taking a cue from the fact that few tactics were found to be associated more frequently with success than failure in any of our studies, we began to examine combinations of influence tactics. In each of the three influence studies (upward, downward, and lateral), managers who used a combination of approaches tended more often to be successful than managers who relied on a single tactic.

We noted that in many incidents short-term success seemed to lead to enhanced influence in the long term; therefore, we sought ways to measure sustained influence over time. Consequently, in our downward influence study, we asked managers about the nature of the subordinate-superior relationship that occurred two months following an influence attempt. As we expected, successful influence attempts led the managers to perceive that their relationships had improved and to believe they had expanded their potential for future influence. For example, the bank branch manager, who was able to enlarge his building reported that because of his success with the influence attempt his profile at the bank was raised, that he was given a promotion and a raise, and that he was transferred to the main office.

Although we cannot be certain that the managers experiencing short-term influence success derived power with their boss from these episodes, the fact that managers believed this to be so caused them, in most cases, to plan additional influence attempts. These findings are supported by a study by Kipnis and his colleagues which found that managers who perceive that they have power are more likely to select assertive influence tactics.[26] Failures at influence attempts may cause managers to plan fewer future attempts and to experience a period of weakened relationships with the boss. Frequently when a subordinate attempts to influence upper level management in a manner where his or her intention is clearly for the advantage of the organization, failure is not damaging to future influence. When the purpose of an influence attempt is clearly seen as a personal goal, failure may be more serious. Such a case was reported by a supervisor of security services dealing with a vice president of operations:

> I wanted an assistant so that I could have some help in managing my department and would not have to handle petty problems of my employees. I tried to convince my boss that I was overworked since my staff has almost doubled and I was having a lot of people problems. I failed because I was just trying to make it easier on myself and wanted an assistant to do the job that I was supposed to be doing. I was also asking to increase the payroll of the company with no plans to increase revenue or profits. After my boss turned me down, I pouted for a few weeks and later learned that my boss thought I was immature. I then decided to forget about past disappointments and only worry about the future.

Communicate Influence Tactics Effectively

It is very difficult to separate influence tactic choice with the communications process itself. Cohen and Bradford stress the importance of knowing the world of potential allies—the needs, values, and organizational forces working on them. For example, they suggest that setting the stage for an influence attempt by wining and dining influence targets at a fancy restaurant may work well for a public relations director, but may appear to be a buy-out attempt when directed toward the head of engineering.[27]

Many of our research participants mentioned the importance of their presentation or their manner of approaching the target. Managers who choose rational ideas based on the needs of the target, wrap them with a blanket of humor or anecdotes, and cast them in the language of the person to be influenced, are much more likely to see their influence objective achieved.

Effective communications become interwoven coils of silk in the web of influence that help ensure the success of tactics. Consider for example the combination of influence tactics and communication used by Iacocca in his turn-a-round strategy of Chrysler. Kotter capsules these as follows: "He developed a bold new vision of what Chrysler should be . . . he (then) attracted, held onto, and elicited cooperation and teamwork from a large network. . . labor leaders, a whole new management team, dealers, suppliers, some key government officials and many others. He did so by articulating his agenda in emotionally powerful ways ("Remember, folks, we have a responsibility to save 600,000 jobs"), by using the credibility and relationships he had developed after a long and highly successful career in the automotive business, by communicating the new strategies in an intellectually powerful manner and in still other ways."[28]

Upward and lateral communications require more listening and more appreciation of the ideas and thoughts of others than dictated by subordinate relationships. Laborde suggests that a person who would master the communicator part of influence must see more and hear more than most people and must remain flexible to vary their behavior in response to what they see and hear.[29] Kaplan strongly emphasizes the importance of variation in the arsenal of communications skills—knowing when to meet with a person face-to-face, when to call group meetings, and when to use memos.[30]

Implications of Influence Research for Managers

No research is subtle enough to capture all of the relationships present between managers as they work together as peers, subordinates, and superiors. While incident- or questionnaire-type research may be subject to some self-report bias (if possible managers try to make themselves look rational to the researcher), observers, even if they could remain long enough in an area, could never capture and connect all of the thoughts necessary to precisely determine motives, processes, and outcomes of managers attempting to develop long-term influence relationships. We have attempted to capture some of the pieces, reviewed the best of what other experts have said about the subject, and tried to establish some connections. While recognizing these limitations, our influence research over the past 10 years leads us to the following conclusions.

- Managers are continually in a state of building and extending webs of influence and repairing damaged threads. With every career change new webs must be built. In the early part of a career or after a career move, a manager must establish a web of influence by developing a reputation as an expert, balancing this with key influence targets, networking to establish resources, and selecting and communicating appropriate influence tactics.

- No one influence tactic can be isolated as being superior to others. Tactics must be chosen on the basis of the influence target and objective sought. For more important influence objectives, a combination of influence tactics will be necessary.

- Frequency of reported tactic usage suggests that most contemporary managers initially try positive techniques with targets, but will quickly resort to threats or manipulation if necessary, especially if the target is a subordinate.

- The variety of approaches used to influence subordinates is wider than suggested by the traditional leadership models and wider than the variety used in upward and lateral influence attempts.[31] This appears to be due not only to the additional power bases available when dealing with subordinates, but also to the growing difficulty of obtaining subordinate compliance through traditional means.

- Contrary to traditional views that networking outside the hierarchy is disruptive, today's leaders must recognize the value of reciprocal influence relationships and must encourage them as long as they can be fruitfully directed toward organizational goals. Webs of influence may provide advantages for all involved.

- For these reasons, we are quite convinced that influential managers are ones who have developed and maintained a balanced web of relationships with the boss, subordinates, peers, and other key players; influence in each of these directions is banked for leverage to accomplish goals in the other directions. If knowledge alone and positional authority alone will not accomplish the manager's job, those who would be influential must fill power gaps with webs of influence.

ENDNOTES

The authors appreciate the helpful suggestions to an earlier draft of this manuscript by W. J. Heisler, manager, Management Development and Salaried Employee Training, Newport News Shipbuilding, and Fred Luthans, George Holmes professor of management, University of Nebraska. We especially appreciate the work of the anonymous reviewers who assisted us with the paper. Thanks also to the professors who participated in original research studies Robert Bell, Tennessee Tech University: Lloyd Dosier and Gene Murkinson of Georgia Southern University; Tom Miller and Coy Jones, Memphis State University; Kent Curran, University of North Carolina, Charlotte; and Alfred Edge, University of Hawaii.

1 These definitions allow those of D. R. Hampton, C. E. Summer, and R. A. Webber, Chapter 3, *Organizational Behavior and the Practice of Management* (Glenview, Illinois: Scott, Foresman, 1987), Fifth Edition.

2 See Chapter 1 of A. R. Cohen and D. L. Bradford, *Influence without Authority,* (New York: John Wiley, 1990). For a review of these thoughts, see W. Bennis and B. Nanus, *Leaders: The Strategies for Taking Charge,* (New York: Harper & Row, 1985) and J. M. Kouzes and B. Z. Posner, *The Leadership Challenge,* (San Francisco: Jossey-Bass, 1988). For a book that relates leadership influence to the way in which change is implemented in the American economy, see N. M. Tichy and M. A. Devanna, *The Transformational Leader,* (New York: John Wiley & Sons, 1986). See also, Chapter 2 of J. P. Kotter, *Power and Influence—Beyond Formal Authority,* (New York: The Free Press, 1985).

3 For the review of literature and our conceptualization of an influence model, see J. B. Keys and R. Bell, "The Four Faces of the Fully Functioning Middle Manager," *California Management Review,* 24 (4), Summer 1982, pp. 59–66; a condensed version of this article can be found in *World Executive's Digest,* 4 (7), 1983, pp. 25–31.

4 For the original research on the importance of upward influence to supervisory success, see D. C. Pelz, "Influence: Keys to Effective Leadership in the First Level Supervisor," *Personnel,* 29, 1959, 209–17. For a later discussion with case illustrations, see F. Bartolome' and A. Laurent, "The Manager: Master and Servant of Power," *Harvard Business Review,* 64 (6), Nov/Dec. 1986, pp. 77–81. The ways in which managers, especially middle managers, acquire and sustain upward influence are outlined in D. H. Kreger, "Functions and Problems of Middle Management," *Personnel Journal,* 49 (11), November 1970, p. 935; P. D. Couch, "Learning to Be a Middle Manager," *Business Horizons,* 22 (1), February 1979, pp. 33–41; R. A. Webber, "Career Problems of Young Managers," *California Management Review,* 18 (4), Summer 1976, pp. 19–33; H. E. R. Uyterhoeven, "General Managers in the Middle," *Harvard Business Review,* 50 (2), March–April 1972, pp. 75–85. For an article that has become a best

selling classic on the subject, see J. J. Gabarro and J. P. Kotter, "Managing Your Boss," *Harvard Business Review,* 58 (1), January–February, 1980, pp. 92-100. For a recent article on maintaining loyalty and developing an initial relationship with the boss, see R. Vecchio, "Are You In or Out with the Boss," *Business Horizons,* 29 (6), November–December 1986, pp. 76–78.

5 For the review of the way in which managers create influence downward, see Uyterhoven Endnote 4 and S. H. Ruello, *"Transferring Managerial Concepts and Techniques to Operating Management,"* *Advanced Management Journal,* 38 (3), July 1973, pp. 42–48. For a discussion of the importance of defending and supporting subordinates, see Bartolome' and Laurent Endnote 4.

6 For a discussion of how managers develop political skills, see Ruello, Endnote 5 and Uyterhoeven, Endnote 4. To review the integrative role of middle managers, see J. L. Hall and J. K. Leidecker, "Lateral Relations: The Impact on the Modern Managerial Role," *Industrial Management,* June 1974, p. 3.

7 For a discussion of external relationships, see D. W. Organ, "Linking Pins between Organizations and Environment," *Business Horizons* 14 (6), December 1971, pp. 73-80.

8 A. I. Krautt, P. R. Pedigo, D. D. McKenna, and M. D. Dunnette, "The Role of the Manager: What's Really Important in Different Management Jobs," *The Academy of Management Executive,* 3 (4), pp. 286-293.

9 For other studies on influence tactics see: D. Kipnis, S. M. Schmidt and I. Wilkinson, "Interorganizational Influence Tactics: Explorations in Getting One's Way," *Journal of Applied Psychology,* 65 (4), August 1980, pp. 440–52. This study differed from our field study in that it surveyed evening MBA students and allowed them to describe any successful influence episode in which they had been involved. W. K. Schilit and E. A. Locke, "A Study of Upward Influence in Organizations," *Administrative Science Quarterly,* 1982, 27 (2), pp. 304–16 found that Kipnis and Schmidt's fourteen tactic categories were not sufficient to categorize upward influence incident accounts collected from undergraduate and graduate business students and full-time employees or supervisors. They found evidence supporting the use of 20 types of upward influence tactics. Because these previous investigations relied so heavily on unchallenged global categories derived from a relatively small sample of evening MBA students which might not be representative of managers, we began our studies from scratch and collected narrative accounts of incidents from practicing managers. Each study focused on only one type of target and at least 250 influence tactics were collected. Flanagan's critical incident method was used to develop categories and to content analyze the responses. (J. C. Flanagan, "Defining the Requirements of the Executive's Job," *Personnel,* 28, July, 1951, pp. 28–35.) Our findings for upward influence were more similar to those of Schilit and Locke than to those of Kipnis et al. Over 46 distinct tactics were observed across the three types of targets. Of course, tactics used to influence some targets are rarely, if ever, used to influence other types of targets. The description of managerial influence tactics which emerges from our three studies is much more detailed and therefore more suited to management applications than that provided by the previous investigations. Of equal importance, unlike the previous studies, our investigations also addressed the use of combinations of tactics vis a vis single tactics, and the long term consequences of the influence attempt for the initiator and the organization.

10 For a more complete description of the research methods and statistical findings of the three studies reported here, see J. B. Keys, T. Miller, T. Case, K. Curran, and C. Jones, "Lateral Influence Tactics," *International Journal of Management,* 4 (3), 1987, pp. 425–31; L. Dosier, T. Case, J. B. Keys, G. Murkinson, "Upward Influence Tactics," *Leadership and Organizational Development Journal,* 9 (4), 1988, pp. 25–31; T. Case, J. B. Keys, and L. Dosier, "How Managers Influence Subordinates: A Study of Downward Influence Tactics," *Leadership and Organizational Development Journal,* 9 (5), 1988, pp. 22–28.

11 For an interesting theoretical discussion of these and other power producing factors see D. Mechanic, "Source of Power on Lower Participants in Complex Organizations," *Administrative Science Quarterly,* 7 (3), 1962, pp. 349–64. For an excellent case study of how a middle manager combines expertise, networking and the other techniques noted see D. Izraeli, "The Middle Manager and the Tactics of Power Expansion: A Case Study," *Sloan Management Review,* 16 (2), 1975, pp. 57–69.

12 See Endnote 1, p. 35

13 See Kotter in Endnote 2, p. 35.

14 B. Keys, T. Case, and A. Edge, "A Cross-National Study of Differences Between Leadership Relationships of Managers in Hong Kong with those in the Philippines, Korea, and the United States," *International Journal of Management,* 6 (4), 1989, pp. 390–404.

15 For a look at the pattern of managerial communications and time investment see F. Luthans and J. K. Larson, "How Managers Really Communicate," *Human Relations,* 39 (2), 1986, pp. 161–78.

16 For a discussion of the need for middle managers to spend time in lateral and external relationships, see also T. Peters, *Thriving on Chaos: Handbook for a Management Revolution,* (New York: Harper & Row, 1987), T. Peters and N. Austin, *Passion for Excellence,* (New York: Random House, 1985), and L. Johnson and A. L. Frohman, "Identifying and Closing the Gap in the Middle of Organizations," *The Academy of Management Executive,* 3(2), pp. 107–14.

17 R. E. Kaplan, "Trade Routes: The Manager's Network of Relationships," *Organizational Dynamics,* 12 (4), 1984, pp. 37–52 and J. Kotter, The General Managers, (New York: The Free Press, 1983).

18 For an excellent guide to handling lateral relations complete with case illustrations, see Chapter 5 of L. Sayles, *Leadership: Managing in Real Organizations,* (New York: McGraw Hill), Second Edition.

19 For a discussion of why managers should encourage their subordinates to influence them, see W. K. Schilit, "An Examination of Individual Differences as Moderators of Upward Influence Activity in Strategic Decisions," *Human Relations,* 30 (10), 1986, p. 948. The author's findings from this empirical study lend support to the suggestions about transformational leaders by Tichy and Devana and Kotter in Endnote 2.

20 For a further discussion of the activities of successful and effective managers, see F. Luthans, R. M. Hodgetts, and S. A. Rosenkrantz, *Real Managers,* (Cambridge: Ballenger Publishing Company, 1988).

21 For a review of network theory, see J. Blau and R. Alba, "Empowering Nets of Participation," *Administrative Science Quarterly,* 27, 1982, pp. 363–79. See also Endnote 18.

22 See Kaplan Endnote 17 above.

23 For an excellent treatment of the objectives and targets of influence, see D. Kipnis, S. Schmidt, C. Swaffin-Smith, and I. Wilkinson, "Patterns of Managerial Influence: Shotgun Managers, Tacticians, and By Standers," *Organizational Dynamics,* 12 (3), 1984, pp. 58–67 and Kipnis, et al., 1980, Endnote 9 above. These studies and the Erez, et al study noted below also used a common questionnaire and a similar factor analysis to find broader categories of influence in which individual influence tactics (similar to those in Exhibit 1) fall. The categories derived include: Reason: The use of facts & data to support logical arguments. Manipulation: The use of impression management, flattery, or ingratiation. Coalitions: Obtaining the support of other people in the organization. Bargaining: The use of negotiation and exchange of benefits or favors. Assertiveness: Demanding or acting in a forceful manner. Upward Appeal: Making an appeal to higher levels of management in the organization to back up requests. Sanctions: Threatening to withhold pay, advancement or to impose organizational discipline. M. Erez, R. Rim and I. Keider, "The Two Sides of the Tactics of Influence: Agent vs Target," *Journal of Occupational Psychology,* 59, 1986, pp. 25–39.

24 See D. Kipnis, et al., Endnote 23 above, p. 32.

25 For a discussion of the use of manipulation as an influence, and/or managerial approach, see Erez, Endnote 23 above and A. Zalesnik, "The Leadership Gap," *The Academy of Management Executive,* 4 (1), 1990, pp. 7–22.

26 See D. Kipnis, et al., in Endnote 23, p. 32.

27 A. R. Cohen and D. L. Bradford, "Influence Without Authority: The Use of Alliances, Reciprocity, and Exchange to Accomplish Work," *Organizational Dynamics,* 17 (3), 1989, pp. 5–17.

28 J. P. Kotter, *The Leadership Factor* (New York: The Free Press, 1988), 18.

29 G. Laborde, *Influencing Integrity: Management Skills for Communication and Negotiation* (Palo Alto: Syntony Publishing, 1987).

30 See Endnote 17 above, p. 32.

31 For a discussion of power and influence as a leadership approach, see G. Yukl, "Managerial Leadership: A Review of Theory and Research," *Journal of Management,* 15 (2), 1989, pp. 251–89.

Networking

You are a junior executive for a local restaurant chain and business is down. On a flight home to visit your family you sit next to a young copywriter from a fledgling advertising agency. When the conversation shifts to business, your new acquaintance asks if your firm has ever considered advertising as a means of drumming up new business, and suggests a dynamic campaign that could very well reverse the fortunes of your restaurant chain. When you return to work the following week, you talk to your boss about a campaign based on your in-flight discussion; your copywriting friend, in turn, relates your encounter to his boss. Eventually a deal is struck that is beneficial to both companies, and to the careers of both you and the copywriter. That's networking.

After two years on the job as an electronics engineer, you decide to move on. Through contacts you've made as a dues-paying member of a professional organization—the Young Engineers Society, perhaps—you let the word out that you're looking for a new job. After a few phone calls, a colleague at a competing electronics firm alerts you to an opening with his company that might be right for you. That's networking.

You are a sales assistant for a major publishing house and you notice in a trade publication an article outlining an exciting new way to market a new product line to bookstores. You place a call to the author of the trade publication article—a sales executive at another publishing house—and you tell him you're fascinated by his innovative approach and would love to learn more about it. He's flattered by your interest and more than happy to offer additional insight. When your company introduces a similar product line a few months later, you suggest a marketing strategy based on your inside knowledge of your competitor's methods. That's networking.

"Networking is just another name for making friends," according to author George Mazzei, whose book, *Moving Up: Digging In, Taking Charge, Playing the Power Game and Learning to Like It,* is widely regarded as a valuable guide to a climb up the corporate ladder.

"Networking is contacts building contacts," observes Yippie-turned-Yuppie Jerry Rubin, whose first Networking Salons helped, in theory and practice, to pioneer the term. "Networking is the chance event that will transform your life," he says. "It helps you create your own accidents."

"Networking is getting yourself known and getting to know people who are successful in your field," notes Karen Dowd, director of placement at the University

---

of Virginia's Darden Graduate School of Business. "It's exchanging information, exchanging contacts, exchanging resources."

"Networking is a miserable term," admits Thomas Stanley, professor of marketing at Georgia State University, "because it doesn't really define what it is. It's really influence peddling to a large extent."

Simply put, networking is a fancy term for the aggressive, outgoing, and entrepreneurial spirit that's spreading through today's business world like something of an epidemic. It's getting out from behind your desk and meeting people—from inside your profession and out, from inside your company and out—who can help you perform beyond expectations on your current job or to look discreetly for a second one. It's knowing where to look for advice and career pointers from people who've been where you are and have long since arrived where you want to be. It's establishing a reputation for yourself (what kind of reputation you carry is up to you). It's seeing and being seen, talking and being heard, asking and being told.

Fact: As reported in the last installment of The American Express Real Life Planner, only 15 percent of all available jobs are ever listed in the classified sections of your local newspaper. Nearly 85 percent of all openings, therefore, are filled behind the scenes, by word of mouth. Networking is your key behind the scenes. It's more than likely you'll move on to your second job through contacts made on your first. "Information from third parties and endorsements from third parties *are* in many cases more important than actual performance," notes Georgia State University's Stanley.

Of course, it's important that you put networking and the principles behind it in perspective. Networking won't offer easy answers as you embark on your career path, nor will it serve as any sort of substitute for not doing your job well. What it will do is help keep your professional eyes and ears open to new possibilities, while keeping the senses of your colleagues tuned in to your performance.

"You have to know what's going on in your field, and networking is a great way to do that," claims Mazzei. "It tells you who you are, what you're worth, where you should be, whether you're falling behind. Networking tells you when it's time to go for more money, and if you can't get it from your own company you'll find out where you can get it."

In an age when sophisticated travel and telecommunications technologies have made the world we live in seem smaller than ever before, everyone for the first time is accessible to everyone else. It has been speculated that any two people in this country can be connected to each other by a series of no more than six contacts. An accountant in Phoenix and a nightclub owner in Ft. Lauderdale, for example, might each have a friend who attended the University of Kentucky at the same time. Their friends, perhaps, had a mutual acquaintance at Kentucky and that person stands as the link between the accountant and the nightclub owner, a network made up of only three contacts.

The time has indeed come to expand the old dictum, "It's not what you know, but who you know that counts," in favor of a more modern version: today's yardstick is what you know and who you know—and who will return your phone calls.

"You won't float to the top on merit alone," claims Mazzei. "What it boils down to is people, and networking enables you to get the chemistry going."

As Karen Dowd also points out, "Networking helps you to learn about your field a lot quicker because you actually meet the movers and shakers in your area. The more contacts you generate with people who are successful, and the people who are known, then the better off you are.

"You get to be a part of the profession instead of just someone who happens to pick up a paycheck. It helps you to learn the lingo, to learn what's expected of you. Just by being around people who are successful helps you learn about available resources that you otherwise wouldn't have heard of."

All of this, you'll notice, is nothing really new. "Networking has been around for a long time," agrees Stanley. "Now, some people have commercialized it by writing about it and doing seminars and all, but many of the professions have had networking for ages—doctors, dentists, attorneys, accountants."

The old boys' networks of our parents' generation have given way to a new breed of aggressive and hungry young professionals, determined to call upon all viable resources to help assure success. "When I first started my networking salons a few years ago, I tried to think of what to call them," remembers Rubin. "I thought to myself, 'All I'm doing is introducing my network of friends and contacts to the other people's friends and contacts. That's networking, that's all it is.'"

"Networking diminishes your reliance on luck," claims Mazzei. "A lot of people do luck out, there's no doubt about it. But if you know a lot more people, you know of a lot of opportunities. You know of a lot more right-places-at-the-right-times, and that diminishes the luck aspect and puts it onto your ability to go after it and get it."

"Networking is putting yourself in the right place at the right time," echoes Rubin, and that about says it all. Read on to ensure that when the right times come along in your career, the right places will be right under your feet.

HOW TO NETWORK

There are as many different ways to network as there are college students who graduate, and it's up to you to determine the approach that's right for you. If you're the open and aggressive sort, your methods will probably reflect your personality. You'll be outgoing and initiate contacts faster than you can say, "Hello, my name is . . ." If you tend toward the shy and reserved type, you'll obviously be more passive in your efforts and leave the initiation of contacts to someone else.

"The social skills in networking are important," says the University of Virginia's Dowd, "and they're the same social skills you would use to make a friend."

"In order to be a successful networker," advises Jerry Rubin, "you'll have to show nonstop assertiveness in a classy and charming way." Nonstop assertiveness in a classy and charming way? "I know it sounds like a strange combination," admits Rubin, "but you have to be persistent without appearing pushy. You might turn some people off if you're too aggressive."

This sounds great, but where do you start? Well, the easiest networking tool is right at your fingertips: "The telephone is a wonderful instrument for networking," says George Mazzei. "You can talk to people in Alaska, California, Michigan, Seattle, anywhere, and find out what's going on. And sometimes people in Seattle will know

Networking Dos and Don'ts

Do:

Join a professional association, even if you have to pay for it yourself. (Your membership fees could even be tax-deductible.)

Take people to lunch, even if you have to pay for it yourself.

Carry a set of business cards at all times, even in unlikely places (health clubs, supermarkets); if your company doesn't provide business cards for your position, it's worth the small investment to have some printed up yourself.

Dress for your next job. It's important to fit in at the next level; get to know the people in the jobs you'd like to have one year down the road and start to look like you belong.

Volunteer to help people in your own company, above and beyond your job description, or in your professional association. Offering to help organize an industry symposium or workshop is a great way to meet new people.

Always dress well while traveling, even if you're traveling socially. You never know who you'll meet and you can make such valuable contacts on airplanes.

Don't:

Network for a job with someone you're meeting for the first time. It's always a good idea to get to know somebody—and to let him or her get to know you—before you ask for help in finding a job.

Be in it for yourself. The principle of networking is an exchange of ideas and resources, and if you've got nothing to offer you'll probably get nowhere.

Call someone up and expect he'll offer you his time if he's never met you (or heard of you). Write first, or have someone refer you.

Expect too much time. When arranging for an informational interview, ask for 15 minutes; if he gives you an hour, terrific.

Call someone up and announce you're calling to network. People can be put off if you're too obvious.

Overlook anyone. You never know who'll be in a position to help you.

---

about a job opportunity in your own town that you may not have known about, just because you don't have time to sift through job opportunities when you're working.''

Okay, now put the phone down and try your luck at the art of one-to-one networking. ''There's nothing wrong with someone just starting to network, saying, 'I'm new at this and I want to learn more,' '' suggests Dowd. ''You can start with someone a level up from you at work—and at that point you don't have much to trade, that's true, except a willingness to learn, which can always excite people. It helps the other person feel that he can teach somebody. People love to talk about their jobs, about how they got started, what they learned, and that in itself can be a big help to somebody just starting out.''

Most campuses offer career listings of alumni to soon-to-be graduates, encouraging students to contact alumni in their fields of interest for informational interviews.

"Almost all of our alumni will talk to a student or recent graduate in their field," notes Paula Jones of the University of Texas' Career Placement Office. "We just tell the students to call them up—or write them—and say, 'I just graduated and I'm interested in learning about how another graduate made it.' "

If you adopt the basic principle of networking—that every person you meet becomes a valuable resource to you and that you can become a valuable resource to him or her—you'll quickly see the broad range of opportunities networking provides. The conscientious networker, always on the lookout for new contacts, will never let a networking opportunity pass him by, whether it's on an airplane, at a business conference, or at the family holiday table.

Of course, some are so smitten by the networking bug that their on-the-job performance begins to suffer. Almost every office has at least one employee who spends more time worrying about what's going on outside the office—what jobs are opening up in the industry, the number of names on his/her Rolodex—that the real work just doesn't seem to get done. This is networking gone overboard, also known in some circles as "not-working." Be advised: networking is no answer for "notworking."

In his research, Georgia State University's Stanley has studied the characteristics common among successful businessmen and -women: "It's very important for young workers today to understand that most millionaires—especially self-made millionaires—are extroverted and very personable people," Stanley says. "Unfortunately, much of the college education doesn't reflect that."

Stanley advises recent graduates to get their training, in their profession and in social/networking skills, in a small town environment. "The small town is a marvelous place to train for the real world," he offers. "People there understand, naturally, the importance of networking, of trading favors, because they know each other; they know they need each other to make the system work. Unfortunately, in big cities it's much more impersonal and you don't get sociable enough to be able to network."

"One of the best things to do," coaches Dowd, "is to join a professional association related to your field and volunteer your time. You meet these people not on networking pretenses, but on the pretense of getting to know the field. There's an association for every job under the sun, and those people are the ones from whom you're going to find out how they got started in the field, and how they can be of help to you and how you can be of help to them."

"One of the best ways to get involved in a new community and get to know people," advises Lynette Murphy of the Denver Chamber of Commerce, "is to volunteer in some kind of organization like United Way or Big Brothers or Big Sisters. It's a great way to meet leading members of the community."

Jerry Rubin has gained national attention for his planned New York City networking events, and he has counterparts in other areas of the country who offer serious networkers a structured environment for the padding of Rolodexes. "What I do is provide an arena for networking," Rubin explains. "I lay the groundwork, but it's up to everyone else to do their own part."

According to Bob Paterson of the New York Chamber of Commerce office, most of the country's 1500 Chambers of Commerce offer some form of business card exchange, or "tip party," to allow members to meet other members outside their immediate fields of interest. "Our mission is to help members prosper," he says of the after-hours get-togethers his office sponsors once a month. "We felt one of the best ways was to provide a setting where members can get together comfortably and do business."

The Denver Chamber of Commerce, under Murphy's direction, sponsors a program called "Business After Hours," which she says provides a "nonformal atmosphere to get to know people, a good way for a young worker to meet someone way up the ladder at another company in the same field."

"There have been a lot of success stories," Murphy reports. "At a recent Business After Hours there was an accountant who set up a new relationship with a banker. I came up at the end of their conversation and they were really excited they had met. Most people do come away with a successful contact, if they can get out and mingle and shake a few hands and smile."

Another advocate of Rubin's networking efforts is Harold Rand, vice president/director of marketing at Kaufman-Astoria Studios in Queens, New York: "What networking enabled me to do was to meet some very influential people in a social atmosphere under less formal circumstances, and they were people I might not have ordinarily met during the business day," he says. "I was able to slice through the traditional bureaucracy of brokerage houses and investment banking firms, and meet directly with the people who make the decisions."

Case in Point

Jack Hitt, 28, will have his first book published (in the spring of 1987) by Houghton, Mifflin/American Heritage Books. Four years ago, a graduate of the University of the South in Sewanee, Tennessee, he was a struggling free-lance writer, earning a living with assorted assignments from bases in Oregon and Spain. How he got here from there is a lesson in networking.

First, Hitt enrolled in Columbia University's School of Journalism, and there he met former CBS News President Fred Friendly, a member of the faculty. By the time he earned his master's degree, Hitt found himself working for Friendly's Media and Society organization, producing seminars and television documentaries.

Through his job at Media and Society he met Harvard Law School student Joan Greco, and the two struck a professional friendship. Together they schemed up a proposal for a book on the history of the United States Consitution, aimed to tie in with its 200th anniversary (in 1987).

Though Hitt met his future literary agent at a party, he is quick to point out that his success is not just a case of knowing the right people. "To think that that cocktail party, that handshake, is what produced the book contract is laughably ridiculous," he now says. Instead, he credits meeting his agent as the impetus ("knowing that we had a hangnail of a toe in the door") to pursue the project in earnest.

"To attribute any success singularly to networking is looking at it the wrong way," he now says. "Knowing people is not singularly responsible for getting something accomplished. There's got to be some talent there."

After fine-tuning their proposal, beefing up their outline, and writing a few sample chapters, Hitt and his coauthor called again on their agent acquaintance, who in turn negotiated a sale with Houghton, Mifflin.

"The key to getting something done is not only to throw yourself in the traffic—and that's what networking is—but to make sure what you're throwing in the traffic is worth picking up.

"I think if you're trying to sell something you don't think is worth selling, whether it's you or a book or whatever, you're not going to sell it no matter how many cocktail parties you go to. Really what you're selling is talent and networking is a great way to sell it, but you can't sell air."

Perhaps the most successful—and subtle—key to networking is your own reputation. "There are so many people I've found who are absolutely brilliant but no one's ever heard of them," says Stanley. "The fact is they've never done a successful job of marketing themselves.

On-the-job excellence is only half of the formula you'll need for success in today's work world. "Doing something good on the job isn't worth much," agrees Mazzei. "It isn't marketable if people don't know about it. You don't have to be written up in the papers, but it's important that people in the industry know. It gives you clout."

"There's a marvelous concept called 'The Sleeper Effect,' " reports Stanley, "where people remember the information, but they forget the source. People just say, 'I've heard that name, I've heard that name.' So I think marketing yourself is very significant."

But, of course, you can't promote yourself to the exclusion of all else. "No, networking has to be two-directional," notes Dowd. "By being a resource to other people you can then feel free to call upon them to be a resource to you. I've given lectures before opposing the concept of networking because so many people disregard this principle, and they use it only for their own advancement, just to help out themselves. They don't understand that it's a two-way street."

"A lot of young people today have the attitude of, 'Hey, I don't have to do this,' " notes Stanley. "But the secret of networking and influence peddling is to do things that are perceived as, 'I'm not expecting anything in return.' That has high credibility, and it will pay off. People respect it, they admire it, and you can call in your chips at some point in the future.

"The fact is that most young people today are very shortsighted. They say, 'I want something in return immediately for what I'm doing.' And the fact is that most people in managerial positions are impressed by people who say, 'Look, I'm doing things and at least in the short run there's no visible idea that I'm going to get something immediately in return.' Those kinds of people—with enthusiasm and a willingness to work—are the winners."

HOW TO NETWORK YOUR WAY TO A SECOND JOB

Almost everyone who's ever been in the job market will tell you it's easier to look for a job when you're employed than when you're out of work. "You can't deny that you're in a much better position to find another job if you don't need one," argues author George Mazzei. "If you're already working in a job, you're considered 'in the industry.' People feel much more comfortable about helping somebody who is really

How to Survive a Networking Party or Business Card Exchange: Jerry Rubin's 10 Rules of Networking

1. Always wear a name tag with your name and profession printed in clear view.
2. Start a conversation; go up to someone you don't know and introduce yourself.
3. Hand out (and collect) as many business cards as you can comfortably carry.
4. Avoid too much small talk. Explore with another person how you can support each other's ideas, careers, deals.
5. If a conversation gets stale, end it gracefully.
6. Don't wait for someone to suggest what he/she can do for you; propose how you might help your new contact.
7. Don't talk to one person for too long. If the conversation is productive, make an appointment for drinks or lunch and move on to another person.
8. Don't spend time with people you already know, except to introduce them to your new contacts.
9. Set goals for yourself; during each networking event, try to meet a certain number of new people (aim for 20, to start), and set a target number of follow-up appointments (aim for at least two or three lunch or drink meetings).
10. Keep your contacts up to date. An occasional phone call or a warm greeting at a future networking event will help to solidify your new professional relationship.

not desperate. It's a psychological thing—people don't like to identify with people who are unemployed.''

''When you're working you're viewed as a winner, and when you're unemployed you're viewed as a failure,'' agrees the University of Virginia's Karen Dowd. ''When you're unemployed the first assumption is, whether it's true or not, that there's something wrong with you.''

When using your networking skills and contacts to help facilitate a career move, there are a few rules of the road you should follow:

- Don't start looking for a new job the day you need one; you will need to build a strong and viable network of contacts before you can call on anyone for job tips or recommendations. Start off by helping out as many people as you can (whether by introducing them to new contacts, or by extending yourself on your job to make their jobs easier), and build a network of contacts who ''owe you one.'' Don't call in favors before you've earned them.

- Don't actively look for your next job. The best advertisement for your professional self is a dedicated and loyal track record in your present position. It's usually a good idea to stay on your first job for two years or so before entertaining the notion of moving on.

- Establish a good, solid reputation with your current employer. You'll be surprised at how small certain industries can become, and at how easily a bad rap can follow you around. Be honest and credible in all of your professional dealings.

- Develop good contacts with your cohorts—peers, at your level, at competing firms—and call on them to scout job prospects from their perspective. Many times a job that's not right for them will be perfect for you.

- Never bad-mouth your current job or boss. You don't want to come across as a disgruntled employee; better to say that you see your current job as a stepping stone, or that you feel it's time to move in new directions.

- Try not to take too much credit for a high-profile project you were involved in. You don't want to be too modest—you are, after all, selling yourself—but you don't want to undermine the efforts of your superiors, either. Try to find something positive to say about your boss's contribution to the project—"it was his vision that made it all possible"—while at the same time stressing your instrumental role in its success.

- Use your network to help in assessing whatever job offers you do receive. Often, a firm could have a certain reputation (they don't promote from within; they're trimming back in some areas) you'll want to steer clear of. Ask around and you might turn up some answers that will save you headaches later on.

- Be sure not to burn any bridges; if your boss is sincerely interested in your career growth, alert him/her to your intentions to move on. Chances are your boss will respond so favorably to your honesty that your current work situation will improve dramatically. If you don't have the sort of relationship with your superiors that would make such a disclosure possible, be sure to keep your job-hunting efforts from a third party.

Of course, you can use most of the above guidelines if you're looking to advance internally, within your company. Even if your job keeps you behind your desk all day, keep a visible profile for yourself by joining the company softball team, writing for the company newsletter, or developing an endearing "elevator" personality. Some of your best second- and third-job prospects could be lurking right down the hall.

Case in Point

As a senior at St. Mary's College in Notre Dame, Indiana, Joan Grabowski couldn't decide whether to pursue a career in music (her major) or business (her minor), so she turned to networking to help with her decision and contacted several successful members of the South Bend, Indiana, business and fine arts communities for informational interviews.

One of the people she approached was the manager of the South Bend Symphony: "We had an excellent talk," Grabowski, now 26, remembers. "I said, 'Goodbye, thank you, I enjoyed talking to you, have a good life.' I never planned on seeing her again."

Nevertheless, Grabowski followed up this meeting, as she did most of her networking efforts, by sending a note of thanks, along with a copy of her résumé. Eight months later, just before graduation, the manager called and offered Grabowski the job of assistant manager, overseeing an annual budget of $500,000. She jumped at the chance.

"The fact that I met her the first time under the conditions of an informational interview, that it was kind of networking—I was just trying to figure out what I was

Informational Interviews

As stated elsewhere in these pages, people love to talk about themselves and about their jobs. If you keep that in mind, you'll open up yourself to a wealth of resources in your field. The informational interview, as it has come to be known, is really just a brain-storming (or brain-picking) session that allows you to call on experts in your field for advice and pointers you won't be able to find anywhere else.

Don't be afraid to call up prominent members of your field and ask, professionally, for a moment of their time. Most alumni offices will put you in touch with recent graduates who have expressed interest in meeting other alumni on this basis. Most professional associations provide a similar service. If you're outgoing and aggressive, you'll quickly find that most people will be open to you if you approach them properly.

We can't stress enough the importance of preparation in the job hunting process; the more you know about the company, field, and position you're considering, the better your chances of making a positive impression. The informal, intelligence-gathering meeting with an established practitioner in your field is the surest path to a keen, working knowledge of the job you seek.

Once you've arranged for an informational interview, the rest is up to you. Prepare your questions beforehand; you don't want to take up too much of your host's valuable time.

Some sample questions are listed below:

1. How did you get started in this business?
2. If you had a nephew/niece starting out in the field today, what advice would you give him/her?
3. What kind of hours will I have to put in to start?
4. Are there any particular areas of the field, with better opportunities, that I should be thinking about?
5. Is there anyone else you would suggest I talk to?

Although an informational interview is granted without consideration of any job openings offered by your host, it's a good idea to conduct yourself as though a job is indeed on the line. Some of your best job offers, you'll find, will occur when you're not looking for them directly; if you succeed in impressing your host in an informal, information-gathering setting, who knows what new opportunities will open up to you?

---

going to do with my life—helped me to get the job later,'' assesses Grabowski. ''By coming to her early, and just expressing my interest, she must have sensed that I was interested in making a serious commitment to the field, and not that I was just a recent graduate who wanted a job.

''I am a great advocate of telling people to do just what I did, just to do informational interviews. Be open-minded and try to find out as much information as you can. It's been my experience that when you do that people are very flattered, and they're more than happy to tell you how they got started. People like talking about themselves and you should approach people with that in mind.''

After two years with the South Bend Symphony, Grabowski decided it was time to move on. This time, she called on her job contacts for help in making the move. As an active member of various professional organizations, which she joined at her own expense, Grabowski drew upon her list of professional contacts to restart the informational interview process that had won her first job.

"I was very bold about it," she now remembers. "I called people in high positions, people in major symphony orchestras whom I had met however casually, and just called them up and said, 'Hi, I admire you, you've been an inspiration to me; would you have the time to sit down and talk to me?' And in every case they were just so pleased that I had called them up."

Grabowski's networking efforts soon paid off—she was referred to the manager of the symphony orchestra in Fort Worth, Texas, which led to a job there as executive assistant manager, overseeing a budget this time of close to $3 million.

"I had learned through my first round of networking that music was where I wanted to be," she reflects. "And I learned through my second round that there were lots of opportunities for someone like me, and that I had excellent qualifications and, with time, excellent contacts."

"You have to be sincere, you have to believe in what you're doing, and you have to be assertive. I would relate networking to sales. You really have to sell yourself, and you have to be willing to take risks. No matter how flimsy you think your contacts might be, if you have even the weakest contact with the CEO at your local major industry, call him up. The worst that can happen is that he or she is going to say, 'No, I don't have time to see you, but why don't you try so and so.'"

Individual Differences

Are some people "born negotiators?" Many observers of negotiation have argued that some negotiators, by virtue of their personality, are simply much more capable of winning a negotiation or getting the best outcome. They argue that if we can understand which dimensions of personality contribute to negotiation effectiveness, we would be able to select potentially good negotiators with greater accuracy, or better understand how to train people to adapt their behavior to situations that their personality style does not normally provide.

In spite of these assertions and a great deal of research that has been devoted to identifying the characteristics and personality styles of more and less effective negotiators, the exact role of a negotiator's personality and its impact on outcomes is not well known. Many of these studies have yielded inconclusive results, and others have often yielded contradictory findings. Nonetheless, some facts are known. The articles in this section examine individual differences among negotiators from two perspectives. The first two articles take a behavioral perspective and concentrate on the behavioral skills of successful negotiators. The final two articles in this section take a dispositional perspective and examine the influence of two personality factors on negotiations: gender and Machiavellianism.

In the first article, "The Behavior of Successful Negotiators," Neil Rackham reports the results of a series of studies that identified the behaviors that distinguish between excellent and average negotiators. Rackham found that superior negotiators behaved differently than average negotiators during the planning, bargaining, and reviewing stages of negotiation. While many of the findings of this study echo common sense, there were a few surprises. For instance, Rackham found that superior negotiators used *fewer* arguments to make their point! The article explains clearly how to interpret this and other surprising results, and it is quite easy for the reader to translate the findings into behaviors to add to their own negotiation skills repertoire.

In the article "Six Basic Interpersonal Skills for a Negotiator's Repertoire," Roger Fisher and Wayne Davis describe six fundamental interpersonal skills that every successful negotiator should have. Fisher and Davis discuss three aspects of each of the interpersonal skills examined. First, they describe some of the dysfunctional symptoms that may occur if the negotiator is lacking in the particular interpersonal skill. Second, in their "diagnosis" section they discuss some of the possible reasons why people fail to master each interpersonal skill. Finally, lots of advice about how to master each interpersonal skill is offered in a clear and practical manner.

In the third article in this section, "Our Games, Your Rules: Developing Effective Negotiation Approaches," Leonard Greenhalgh and Roderick Gilkey explore some of the differences between male and female negotiators. Greenhalgh and Gilkey draw their understanding of male-female differences in negotiation from over seven years of studying this topic in classroom, consulting, and laboratory situations. One of their most critical findings is that men and women begin negotiations with very different cognitive frames. Women tend to perceive negotiations as part of a longer-term relationship with the other person where both sides seek a method of reaching the needs of both parties. In contrast, males tend to see negotiations as a single episode where both parties are trying to achieve their own goals. Greenhalgh and Gilkey present a comprehensive picture of the causes and consequences of male-female differences in negotiation and draw numerous implications for negotiators who want to expand their negotiation repertoire.

In the last article in this section, "The Machiavellis among Us," Richard Christie describes a type of individual personality style known as Machiavellianism. Christie began his study of Machiavellianism because of his interest in the effectiveness of certain individuals who were good manipulators. His research lead him to propose that the perfect manipulator was characterized by four attributes. First, the perfect manipulator was not basically concerned with conventional morality. Second, he or she was basically cool and detached with other people. Third, he or she was more concerned with the means than with the ends; that is, how people were conned was more important than what was conned out of them. Lastly, rather than being a psychologically disturbed individual, he or she was very rational—in fact, overrational in dealing with people.

Based on this characterization, Christie then set out to investigate the ways that Machiavellian people manipulate others, and the conditions under which they are most likely to be successful at it. The research findings lead to an important conclusion about the role of personality factors in negotiation, one that we will see repeated again and again: Machiavellians, like other types of personalities who may be more effective in negotiation, are most effective only under certain kinds of conditions. Thus, no personality type is likely to be effective in all situations; rather, different personalities can be more or less effective depending on certain situational factors. These situational factors may include the kind of relationship one can develop with the other person, the nature of the conflict, or the strategic and tactical opportunities available to the negotiator himself.

The Behavior of Successful Negotiators

Neil Rackham

BACKGROUND

Almost all publications about negotiating behavior fall into one of three classes.

1. Anecdotal "here's how I do it" accounts by successful negotiators. These have the advantage of being based on real life but the disadvantage that they frequently describe highly personal modes of behavior which are a risky guide for would-be negotiators to follow.

2. Theoretical models of negotiating which are idealized, complex, and seldom translatable into practical action.

3. Laboratory studies, which tend to be short-term and contain a degree of artificiality.

Very few studies have investigated what actually goes on face-to-face during a negotiation. Two reasons account for this lack of published research. Firstly, real negotiators are understandably reluctant to let a researcher watch them at work. Such research requires the consent of both negotiating parties and constitutes a constraint on a delicate situation. The second reason for the poverty of research in this area is lack of methodology. Until recently there were few techniques available which allowed an observer to collect data on the behavior of negotiators without the use of cumbersome and unacceptable methods such as questionnaires.

Since 1968 a number of studies have been carried out by Neil Rackham of Huthwaite Research Group, using behavior analysis methods. These have allowed direct observation during real negotiations, so that an objective and quantified record can be collected to show how the skilled negotiator behaves.

THE SUCCESSFUL NEGOTIATOR

The basic methodology for studying negotiating behavior is simple—find some successful negotiators and watch them to discover how they do it. But what is the criterion for a successful negotiator? The Rackham studies used three success criteria.

1. *He should be rated as effective by both sides.* This criterion enabled the researchers to identify likely candidates for further study. The condition that both sides should agree on a negotiator's effectiveness was a precaution to prevent picking a sample from a single frame-of-reference.

2. *He should have a track record of significant success.* The central criterion for choosing effective negotiators was track record over a time period. In such a complex field the researchers were anxious for evidence of consistency. They also wished to avoid the common trap of laboratory studies—looking only at the short-term consequences of a negotiator's behavior and, therefore, favoring those using tricks or deceptions.

3. *He should have a low incidence of implementation failures.* The researchers judged that the purpose of a negotiation was not just to reach an agreement but to reach an agreement that would be viable. Therefore, in addition to a track record of agreements, the record of implementation was also studied to ensure that any agreements reached were successfully implemented.

A total of 48 negotiators were picked who met all of these three success criteria. The breakdown of the sample was:

Industrial (Labor) Relations Negotiators	
Union representatives	17
Management representatives	12
Contract negotiators	10
Others	9

Altogether the 48 successful negotiators were studied over a total of 102 separate negotiating sessions. For the remainder of this document these people are called the "skilled" group. In comparison, a group of negotiators who either failed to meet the criteria or about whom no criterion data was available, were also studied. These were called the "average" group. By comparing the behavior of the two groups, it was possible to isolate the crucial behaviors which made the skilled negotiators different.

THE RESEARCH METHOD

The researchers met the negotiator before the negotiation and encouraged her/him to talk about his/her planning and his/her objectives. For 56 sessions with the skilled negotiators and 37 sessions with the average negotiators, this planning session was either tape-recorded or extensive notes were taken.

The negotiator then introduced the researcher into the actual negotiation. The delicacy of this process can be judged from the fact that although most cases had been carefully prehandled, the researchers were not accepted in upward of 20 instances and were asked to withdraw.

During the negotiation the researcher counted the frequency with which certain key behaviors were used by the negotiators, using behavior analysis methods. In all of the 102 sessions interaction data was collected, while in 66 sessions content analysis was also obtained.

HOW THE SKILLED NEGOTIATOR PLANS

Negotiation training emphasizes the importance of planning. How does the skilled negotiator plan?

Amount of Planning Time

No significant difference was found between the total planning time which skilled and average negotiators claimed they spent prior to actual negotiation. This finding must be viewed cautiously because, unlike the other conclusions in this document, it is derived from the negotiators' impressions of themselves, not from their actual observed behavior. Nevertheless, it suggests the conclusion that it is not the amount of planning time which makes for success, but how that time is used.

Exploration of Options

The skilled negotiator considers a wider range of outcomes or options for action than the average negotiator.

	Outcomes/Options Considered during Planning (per negotiable issue)
Skilled negotiator	5.1
Average negotiator	2.6

The skilled negotiator is concerned with the whole spectrum of possibilities, both those which s/he could introduce himself and those which might be introduced by the people s/he negotiates with. In contrast, the average negotiator considers few options. An impression of the researchers, for which, unfortunately, no systematic data was collected, is that the average negotiator is especially less likely to consider options which might be raised by the other party.

Common Ground

Does the skilled negotiator concentrate during his/her planning on the areas which hold most potential for conflict, or does s/he give his/her attention to possible areas of common ground? The research showed that although both groups of negotiators tended to concentrate on the conflict areas, the skilled negotiators gave over three times as much attention to common ground areas as did average negotiators.

Skilled negotiators—38% of comments about areas of anticipated agreement or common ground

Average negotiators—11% of comments about areas of anticipated agreement or common ground

---

This is a significant finding and it can be interpreted in a variety of ways. It may be, for example, that the skilled negotiator has already built a climate of agreement so that undue concentration on conflict is unnecessary. Equally, concentration on the common ground areas may be the key to building a satisfactory climate in the first place. A relatively high concentration on common ground areas is known to be an effective strategy from other Huthwaite Research Group studies of persuasion, notably with "pull" styles of persuasion in selling.

In any event, a potential negotiator wishing to model himself on successful performers would do well to pay special attention to areas of anticipated common ground and not just to areas of conflict.

Long-Term or Short-Term?

It is often suggested that skilled negotiators spend much of their planning time considering the long-term implications of the issues, while unskilled negotiators concentrate on the short term. Is this in practice? The studies found that both groups showed an alarming concentration on the short-term aspects of issues.

	% of Planning Comments about "Long-Term" Considerations of Anticipated Issues
Skilled negotiators	8.5
Average negotiators	4.0

With the average negotiator, approximately one comment in 25 during his/her planning met our criterion of a long-term consideration, namely a comment which involved any factor extending beyond the immediate implementation of the issue under negotiation.

The skilled negotiator, while showing twice as many long-term comments, still only averages 8 ½ percent of his/her total recorded planning comment. These figures must necessarily be approximate, partly because of the research methods (which may have inadvertently encouraged verbalization of short-term issues) and partly because our ignorance of individual circumstances made some comments hard to classify. Even so, they demonstrate how little thought is given by most negotiators to the long-term implications of what they negotiate.

Setting Limits

The researchers asked negotiators about their objectives and recorded whether their replies referred to single-point objectives (e.g., "we aim to settle at 83p") or to a defined range (e.g., "we hope to get 37p but we would settle for a minimum of 34p"). Skilled negotiators were significantly more likely to set upper and lower limits—to plan in terms of a range. Average negotiators, in contrast, were more likely to plan their objectives around a fixed point. Although one possible explanation is that the skilled negotiator has more freedom, which gives him the discretion of upper and lower limits, this seems unlikely from the research. Even where the average negotiator had considerable capacity to vary the terms of an agreement, s/he usually approached the negotiation with a fixed point objective in mind. The conclusion, for would-be negotiators, is that it seems to be preferable to approach a negotiation with objectives specifying a clearly defined range rather than to base planning on an inflexible single-point objective.

Sequence and Issue Planning

The term "planning" frequently refers to a process of sequencing—putting a number of events, points, or potential occurrences into a time sequence. Critical path analysis and other forms of network planning are examples. This concept of planning, called sequence planning, works efficiently with inanimate objects, or in circumstances where the planner has real control which allows him to determine the sequence in which events will occur. The researchers found that average negotiators place very heavy reliance on sequence planning. So, for example, they would frequently verbalize a potential negotiation in terms like "First I'll bring up A, then lead to B, and after that I'll cover C, and finally go on to D." In order to succeed, sequence planning always requires the consent and cooperation of the other negotiating party. In many negotiations this cooperation was not forthcoming. The negotiator would begin at point A and the other party would only be interested in point D. This could put the negotiator in difficulty, requiring him to either mentally change gear and approach the negotiation in a sequence s/he had not planned for, or to carry through his/her original sequence risking disinterest from the other party. In many negotiations, sequences were in themselves negotiable and it was ill-advised for the negotiator to plan on a sequence basis.

Typical Sequence Plan
Used by Average Negotiators

A   then   B   then   C   then   D

in which issues are linked

Typical Issue Plan

Used by Skilled Negotiators

A

B

D

C

in which issues are independent
and not linked by a sequence

They would consider issue C, for example, as if issues A, B, and D didn't exist. Compared with the average negotiators they were careful not to draw sequence links between a series of issues. This was demonstrated by observing the number of occasions during the planning process that each negotiator mentioned sequence of issues.

	Number of Mentions *Implying Sequence in Planning*
Skilled negotiators	2.1 per session
Average negotiators	4.9 per session

The clear advantage of issue planning over sequence planning is flexibility. In planning a negotiation it is important to remember that the sequence of issues itself (unless a preset agenda is agreed) may be subject to negotiation. Even where an agenda exists, within a particular item, sequence planning may involve some loss of flexibility. So it seems useful for negotiators to plan their face-to-face strategy using issue planning and avoiding sequence planning.

FACE-TO-FACE BEHAVIOR

Skilled negotiators show marked differences in their face-to-face behavior, compared with average negotiators. They use certain types of behavior significantly more frequently while other types they tend to avoid.

Irritators

Certain words and phrases which are commonly used during negotiation have negligible value in persuading the other party but do cause irritation. Probably the most frequent example of these is the term "generous offer" used by a negotiator to describe his/her own proposal. Similarly, words such as "fair," "reasonable," and other terms with a high positive value loading, have no persuasive power when used as self-praise, while serving to irritate the other party because of the implication that they are unfair, unreasonable, and so on. Most negotiators avoid the gratuitous use of direct insults or unfavorable value judgments. They know that there is little to gain from saying unfavorable things about the other party during face-to-face exchanges. However, the other side of the coin—saying gratuitously favorable things about themselves—seems harder for them to avoid. The researchers called such words "irritators" and found that although the average negotiator used them fairly regularly, the skilled negotiator tended to avoid them.

	Use of Irritators per Hour Face-to-Face Speaking Time
Skilled negotiators	2.3
Average negotiators	10.8

It is hardly surprising that skilled negotiators use fewer irritators. Any type of verbal behavior which antagonizes without a persuasive effect is unlikely to be productive. More surprising is the heavy use of irritators by average negotiators. The conclusion must be that most people fail to recognize the counterproductive effect of using positive value judgments about themselves and, in doing so, implying negative judgments of the other party.

Counterproposals

During negotiation it frequently happens that one party puts forward a proposal and the other party immediately responds with a counterproposal. The researchers found that skilled negotiators made immediate counterproposals much less frequently than average negotiators.

	Frequency of Counterproposals per Hour of Face-to-Face Speaking Time
Skilled negotiators	1.7
Average negotiators	3.1

This difference suggests that the common strategy of meeting a proposal with a counterproposal may not be particularly effective. The disadvantages of counterproposals are:

- They introduce an additional option, sometimes a whole new issue, which complicates and clouds the clarity of the negotiation.
- They are put forward at a point where the other party has least receptiveness, being concerned with his/her own proposal.
- They are perceived as blocking or disagreeing by the other party, not as proposals. (A study of 87 controlled-pace negotiation exercises by the researchers showed that when one side in a negotiation put forth a proposal there was an 87 percent chance that the other side would perceive it as a proposal. However, if the proposal immediately followed a proposal made by the other side (if in other words it was a counterproposal) the chance of being perceived as a proposal dropped to 61 percent, with a proportionate increase in the chances of being perceived as either disagreeing or blocking).

These reasons probably explain why the skilled negotiator is less likely to use counterproposing as a tactic than is the average negotiator.

Defend/Attack Spirals

Because negotiation frequently involves conflict, negotiators may become heated and use emotional or value-loaded behaviors. When such behavior was used to attack the other party, or to make an emotional defense, the researchers termed it "defending/attacking." Once initiated, this behavior tended to form a spiral of increasing intensity: one negotiator would attack, the other would defend himself, usually in a manner which the first negotiator perceived as an attack. In consequence, the first negotiator attacked more vigorously and the spiral commenced. Defending and attacking were often difficult to distinguish from each other. What one negotiator perceived as a legitimate defense, the other party might see as an unwarranted attack. This was the root cause of most defending/attacking spirals observed during the studies. Average negotiators, in particular, were likely to react defensively, using comments such as "You can't blame us for that" or "It's not our fault that the present difficulty has arisen." Such comments frequently provoked a sharp defensive reaction from the other side of the table.

	% of Negotiators' Comments Classified as Defending/Attacking
Skilled negotiators	1.9
Average negotiators	6.3

The researchers found that average negotiators used more than three times as much defending/attacking behavior as skilled negotiators. Although no quantitative measure exists, the researchers observed that skilled negotiators, if they did decide to attack, gave no warning and attacked hard. Average negotiators, in contrast, usually began their attacking gently, working their way up to more intense attacks slowly and, in doing so, causing the other party to build up its defensive behavior in the characteristic defending/attacking spiral.

Behavior Labeling

The researchers found that skilled negotiators tended to give an advance indication of the class of behavior they were about to use. So, for example, instead of just asking "How many units are there?" they would say, "Can I ask you a question—how many units are there?" giving warning that a question was coming. Instead of just making a proposal they would say, "If I could make a suggestion. . . ." and then follow this advance label with their proposal. With one exception, average negotiators were significantly less likely to label their behavior in this way. The only behavior which the average negotiator was more likely to label in advance was disagreeing.

	% of All Negotiator's Behavior Immediately Preceded by a Behavior Label	
	Disagreeing	*All Behavior Except Disagreeing*
Skilled negotiator	0.4	6.4
Average negotiator	1.5	1.2

This is a slightly unusual finding and it may not be immediately evident why these differences should exist. The researcher's interpretation was that, in general, labeling of behavior gives the negotiator the following advantages.

- It draws the attention of the listeners to the behavior that follows. In this way social pressure can be brought to force a response.
- It slows the negotiation down, giving time for the negotiator using labeling to gather his/her thoughts and for the other party to clear his/her mind from the previous statements.
- It introduces a formality which takes away a little of the cut-and-thrust and, therefore, keeps the negotiation on a rational level.
- It reduces ambiguity and leads to clearer communication.

The skilled negotiator does, however, avoid labeling his or her disagreement. While the average negotiator will characteristically say "I disagree with that because of . . .'' thus labeling that she or he is about to disagree, the skilled negotiator is more likely to begin with the reasons and lead up to the disagreement.

	Skilled Negotiators	
Reason/ explanation	Leading to	Statement of disagreement
	Average Negotiators	
Statement of disagreement	Leading to	Reason/ explanation

If one of the functions of behavior labeling is to make a negotiator's intentions clear, then it is hardly surprising that the skilled negotiator avoids making it clear that s/he intends to disagree. S/he would normally prefer his/her reasons to be considered more neutrally so that acceptance involved minimal loss of face for the other party. But, if labeling disagreement is likely to be counterproductive, why does the average negotiator label disagreeing behavior more than all the other types of behavior put together? Most probably this tendency reflects the order in which we think. We decide that an argument we hear is unacceptable and only then do we assemble reasons to show why. The average negotiator speaks his/her disagreement in the same order as s/he thinks it—disagreement first, reasons afterwards.

Testing Understanding and Summarizing

The researchers found that two behaviors with a similar function, testing understanding and summarizing, were used significantly more by the skilled negotiator. Testing understanding is a behavior which checks to establish whether a previous contribution or statement in the negotiation has been understood. Summarizing is a compact restatement of previous points in the discussion. Both behaviors sort out misunderstandings and reduce misconceptions.

	Percent of All Behavior by Negotiator		
	Testing Understanding	*Summarizing*	*Testing Understanding and Summarizing*
Skilled negotiators	9.7	7.5	17.2
Average negotiators	4.1	4.2	8.3

The higher level of these behaviors by the skilled negotiator reflects his/her concern with clarity and the prevention of misunderstanding. It may also relate to two less obvious factors.

1. *Reflecting*—Some skilled negotiators tended to use testing understanding as a form of reflecting behavior—turning the other party's words back in order to obtain further responses, for example, "So do I understand that you are saying you don't see any merit in this proposal at all?"

2. *Implementation concern*—The average negotiator, in his/her anxiety to obtain an agreement, would often quite deliberately fail to test understanding or to summarize. S/he would prefer to leave ambiguous points to be cleared later. S/he would fear that making things explicit might cause the other party to disagree. In short, his/her predominant objective was to obtain an agreement and s/he would not probe too deeply into any area of potential misunderstanding which might prejudice immediate agreement, even if it was likely to give rise to difficulties at the implementation stage. The skilled negotiator, on the other hand, tended to have a greater concern with the successful implementation (as would be predicted from the success criteria earlier in this document). S/he would, therefore, test and summarize in order to check out any ambiguities at the negotiating stage rather than leave them as potential hazards for implementation.

Asking Questions

The skilled negotiator asked significantly more questions during negotiation than did the average negotiator.

	Questions as a % of All Negotiators' Behavior
Skilled negotiator	21.3
Average negotiator	9.6

This is a very significant difference in behavior. Many negotiators and researchers have suggested that questioning techniques are important to negotiating success. Among the reasons frequently given are:

1. Questions provide data about the other party's thinking and position.
2. Questions give control over the discussion.
3. Questions are more acceptable alternatives to direct disagreement.
4. Questions keep the other party active and reduce his/her thinking time.
5. Questions can give the negotiator a breathing space to allow him/her to marshal his/her own thoughts.

Feelings Commentary

The skilled negotiator is often thought of as a person who plays his/her cards close to the chest, and who keeps his/her feelings to her/himself. The research studies were unable to measure this directly because feelings are, in themselves, unobservable. However, an indirect measure was possible. The researchers counted the number of times that the negotiator made statements about what was going on inside his/her mind. The behavior category of ''Giving Internal Information'' was used to record any reference by the negotiator to his/her internal considerations such as feelings and motives.

	Giving Internal Information As % of All Negotiators' Behavior
Skilled negotiator	12.1
Average negotiator	7.8

The skilled negotiator is more likely to give information about his/her internal events than the average negotiator. This contrasts sharply with the amount of information given about external events, such as facts, clarifications, general expressions of opinion, and so on. Here the average negotiator gives almost twice as much.

The effect of giving internal information is that the negotiator appears to reveal what is going on in his/her mind. This revelation may or may not be genuine, but it gives the other party a feeling of security because such things as motives appear to be explicit and above board. The most characteristic and noticeable form of giving internal information is a *feelings commentary,* where the skilled negotiator talks about his/her feelings and the impression the other party has of him. For example, the average negotiator, hearing a point from the other party which s/he would like to accept but doubts whether it is true, is likely to receive the point in uncomfortable silence. The skilled negotiator is more likely to comment on his/her own feelings saying something like, ''I'm uncertain how to react to what you've just said. If the information you've given me is true, then I would like to accept it; yet I feel some doubts inside me about its accuracy. So part of me feels happy and part feels suspicious. Can you help me resolve this?''

The work of psychologists such as Carl Rogers has shown that the expression of feelings is directly linked to establishing trust in counseling situations. It is probable that the same is true for negotiating.

Argument Dilution

Most people have a model of arguing which looks rather like a balance of a pair of scales. In fact, many of the terms we use about winning arguments reflect this balance model. We speak of ''tipping the argument in our favor,'' of ''the weight of the arguments,'' or how an issue ''hangs in the balance.'' This way of thinking predisposes us to believe that there is some special merit in quantity. If we can find five reasons for doing something, then that should be more persuasive than only being able to think of a single reason. We feel that the more we can put on our scale pan, the more likely we are to tip the balance of an argument in our favor. If this model has any validity, then the skilled negotiator would be likely to use more reasons to back up his/her argument than the average negotiator.

	Average Number of Reasons Given by Negotiator to Back Each Argument/Case S/he Advanced
Skilled negotiator	1.8
Average negotiator	3.0

The researchers found that the opposite was true. The skilled negotiator used fewer reasons to back up each of his/her arguments. Although the balance-pan model may be very commonly believed, the studies suggest that it is a disadvantage to advance a whole series of reasons to back an argument or case. In doing so, the negotiator exposes a flank and gives the other party a choice of which reason to dispute. It seems self-evident that if a negotiator gives five reasons to back his/her case and the third reason is weak, the other party will exploit this third reason in their response. The most appropriate model seems to be one of dilution. The more reasons advanced, the more a case is potentially diluted. The poorest reason is a lowest common denominator: a weak argument generally dilutes a strong.

Unfortunately, many negotiators who had the disadvantage of higher education put a value on being able to ingeniously devise reasons to back their case. They frequently suffered from this dilution effect and had their point rejected, not on the strength of their principal argument, but on the weakness of the incidental supporting points they introduced. The skilled negotiator tended to advance single reasons insistently, only moving to subsidiary reasons if his/her main reason was clearly losing ground. It is probably no coincidence that an unexpectedly high proportion of the skilled negotiators studied, both in labor relations and in contract negotiation, had relatively little formal education. As a consequence, they had not been trained to value the balance-pan model and more easily avoided the trap of advancing a whole flank of reasons to back their cases.

REVIEWING THE NEGOTIATION

The researchers asked negotiators how likely they were to spend time reviewing the negotiation afterward. Over two thirds of the skilled negotiators claimed that they always set aside some time after a negotiation to review it and consider what they had learned. Just under half of average negotiators, in contrast, made the same claim. Because the data is self-reported, it may be inaccurate. Even so, it seems that the old principle that more can be learned after a negotiation than during it may be true. An interesting difference between management and union representatives was observed. Management representatives, with other responsibilities and time pressures, were less likely to review a negotiation than were union representatives. This may, in part, account for the observation made by many writers on labor relations that union negotiators seem to learn negotiating skills from taking part in actual negotiations more quickly than management negotiators.

SUMMARY OF THE SUCCESSFUL NEGOTIATOR'S BEHAVIOR

The successful negotiator:

- Is rated as effective by both sides.
- Has a track record of significant success.
- Has a low incidence of implementation failure.

Forty-eight negotiators meeting these criteria were studied during 102 negotiations.

Planning:

	Negotiators	
	Skilled	*Average*
Overall amount of time spent	No significant difference	
Number of outcomes/options considered per issue	5.1	2.6
% of comments about areas of anticipated common ground	38%	11%
% of comments about long-term considerations of issues	8.5%	4%
Use of sequence during planning (per session)	2.1	4.9

Face-to-Face (Skilled negotiators):

Avoid	*Use*
• Irritators	Behavior labeling (except disagreeing)
• Counterproposals	Testing understanding and summarizing
• Defend/attack spirals	Lots of questions
• Argument dilution	Feelings commentary

Six Basic Interpersonal Skills for a Negotiator's Repertoire

Roger Fisher

Wayne H. Davis

A well-rounded person has a large repertoire of interpersonal skills, and exercises them appropriately depending upon the circumstances. All of us, however, find ourselves stronger in some skills than in others. We naturally tend to use those skills in which we feel more adept and to avoid those in which we feel less comfortable or less competent.

A skilled negotiator not only has a broad repertoire of interpersonal skills, but also uses those most appropriate to the circumstances of a particular situation. He or she recognizes that one's effectiveness within a given negotiation is likely to be enhanced by being able to change pace and approach.

There is an infinite range and variety in interpersonal skills. Many of these skills can be seen as attractive opposites, such as being independent and being cooperative, or being pragmatic and being imaginative, or being controlled and being expressive. We would like to be good at both but tend to be stronger in one than the other.

These desirable qualities can be visualized as lying on the circumference of a circle, so that becoming more skillful is seen as extending our skills in all directions. Improving our skills can then be recognized not as correcting a fault (such as "I am too flexible"), but rather as becoming more skillful at its attractive opposite (e.g., "I want to become better at being firm when that is appropriate.").

To broaden one's repertoire, it may help to think of these qualities as falling into six basic categories of interpersonal skills in which each effective negotiator enjoys some competence and confidence. We have tentatively identified these as follows:

- Expressing strong feelings appropriately.
- Remaining rational in the face of strong feelings.
- Being assertive within a negotiation without damaging the relationship.

Reprinted from Roger Fisher and Wayne H. Davis, "Six Basic Interpersonal Skills for a Negotiator's Repertoire," *Negotiation Journal*, April 1987, pp. 117–22. Used with permission of Plenum Publishing Corporation and the authors.

- Improving a relationship without damage to a particular negotiation.
- Speaking clearly in ways that promote listening.
- Inquiring and listening effectively.

In use, these skills are often closely associated with each other, but in developing the skills and in practicing them it helps to focus on them one at a time. The following checklist can be used as a guide for negotiators who wish to develop a strong, well-balanced repertoire.

Expressing Strong Feelings Appropriately

Disliked Symptoms.   Many negotiations take place as if the only effective mode of influence is the kind of rational dialogue that might take place between two computers. We may suppress or ignore flesh and blood feelings. In other negotiations, we may find our rational arguments overwhelmed by emotions such as anger, fear, insecurity, or hatred.

Possible Diagnoses.   Many of us learn as children that it is naughty to be angry. We may treat feelings as private problems best dealt with by suppressing them, or by denying their existence. Sometimes we may regard feelings as having less merit than reasoned argument—as something to be ashamed of.

At other times, we may contain feelings because we see no way to express them other than by losing our temper—a performance that our rational selves tell us is likely to appear ridiculous, damage our credibility, and at best prove ineffective.

General Prescriptive Approach

- *Recognize feelings.* A negotiator needs to recognize that feelings are a natural human phenomenon. They exist. There is nothing wrong with *having* emotions, although *expressing* them in particular ways may be costly or counterproductive.

- *Be aware.* It is a wise practice to become *aware* of the emotions—both our own and those of the other side—that are involved in any given negotiation. It appears to be true that if we suppress or deny our own feelings, we are likely to be unaware of the feelings of those with whom we are dealing. Before we can safely and appropriately express our feelings, we need to become aware of them, and to acknowledge them consciously.

In general, when some feeling inside seems to be growing larger and out of control, naming or identifying that feeling internally will, by itself, tend to reduce the feeling, make it more life-size, and help bring it under control.

- *Develop a range of expression.* When it comes to communicating feelings to someone else, it is well to recognize that there is a spectrum of ways to do so, ranging from talking rationally about them, through increasing the emotional content of verbal and nonverbal communication, to letting the emotions take charge.

Because of inhibitions, we often err on the side of insufficiently communicating our emotions. It is good to find a safe environment within which to experiment and practice. It is often useful to explore a range of possible expressions of emotion by deliberately overshooting. When we fear going too far, we are unlikely to learn how far we can, in fact, safely go.

• *Relate tone to substance.* Too often we fail to relate the emotional content of a communication to the substantive issue being discussed. It is far easier to be assertive—and certainly more effective—if we have something sensible to assert. Key to an effective communication of feeling is likely to be some well-prepared substantive content that identifies the purpose of the communication, justifies the feeling, and enlists its expression in the furtherance of that purpose.

Remaining Rational in the Face of Strong Feelings

Disliked Symptoms. When others display strong emotions—particularly those hostile to us—we are likely to react and let emotions overwhelm our rationality. The cycle of emotional action and reaction is likely to preclude rational negotiation.

Possible Diagnoses. We get caught up in the fray. We react to the last thing the other side said, and lose sight of the original purposes of talking. We may mistake their expression of strong feelings as a personal attack on us, so we feel obliged to respond in self-defense. If neither side acknowledges the existence or validity of the other's feelings, both may amplify their expression of feelings so that the underlying "message" will be heard. We may try to silence each other's expression of feelings, which compounds the frustration and felt need to be heard.

General Prescriptive Approach. There are several different ways to deal effectively with displays of strong emotion in negotiation. Depending on the circumstances, any one of the following suggestions should prove useful:

• *Acknowledge their feelings.* When others begin to heighten the emotive content of their speech, they may not be fully aware of the feelings growing inside them. If we acknowledge that they *may* (don't attribute!) be feeling a certain way, that will usually help them to become more aware and in control of their feelings, and give us enough distance so that we don't react.

• *Step above the fray.* When the discussion turns so emotional that rational discussion seems pointless, we might withdraw from the discussion long enough for us and others to regain some composure. State frankly our reasons for withdrawing, and couple that with a commitment to return.

• *Step aside; let their emotions hit the problem.* If they're expressing an emotion, encourage them to express it fully and completely—so they can feel that they've "got it all out."

• *Separate the causes of their feelings from the substantive problem, and deal with them in parallel.* Once feelings have been fully expressed and acknowledged, it may be appropriate to analyze what engendered the feelings and take steps to alleviate those causes.

• *Be purposive.* At the outset, consciously consider and decide on the purpose of the negotiation. Then, when emotions run too strong, we can ask the parties to question whether or not the direction of the discussion serves the agreed-upon purposes of the meeting.

Being Assertive without Damaging the Relationship

Disliked Symptoms.   Often in a negotiation, we may refrain from being assertive (we fail to speak with conviction or tenaciously pursue a particular point) for fear that assertiveness will damage either the immediate or the long-term relationship. We may acquiesce when it ill serves our interests to do so.

Possible Diagnoses.   When a relationship seems to be more important than any one substantive issue, some people tend to give in as soon as the other party's preference becomes clear. But giving in does not help the relationship: It may reward bad behavior or be mistaken for a lack of conviction or spinelessness—undesirable qualities for a partner in most relationships.

General Prescriptive Approach.   With or without increasing the emotional content of our expressions, it is possible to be assertive without damage to a relationship. The suggested general strategy is:

• *Disentangle relationship issues from substantive ones and work on them in parallel.* Although substantive disagreements can make a working relationship more difficult, and although a good working relationship can make it easier to reach agreement, the process of dealing with differences is usefully treated as a subject quite distinct and separate from the content and extent of those differences.

• *Be "soft on the people."* Avoid personal judgments. Acknowledge some merit in what the other side has said or done. Be open, polite, courteous, and considerate.

• *Have something to assert.* Know the *purpose* of the session in terms of some product that it is reasonable to expect. Focus on one or two points that we would like to communicate forcefully, such as: the strength of our BATNA (Best Alternative to a Negotiated Agreement); the necessity of meeting some interest of ours; or our adherence to a particular standard of legitimacy unless and until we are convinced that some other standard is at least equally fair.

• *Be firm and open.* Be prepared to remain firm as long as that appears to us to make sense on the substance of the negotiation. At the same time, be open—both in words and thought—to alternative views that are truly persuasive.

Improving a Relationship without Damage to a Particular Negotiation

Disliked Symptoms.   We often hesitate to be open and warm with people on the other side of a negotiation for fear that it will prejudice the outcome. We hesitate to acknowledge merit in what they say for fear that it will undercut what we say.

Possible Diagnoses.   We may operate under a zero-sum assumption about ideas and arguments: To the extent that someone with whom we disagree is right, then we must be wrong. This assumption may stem from childhood fears of being pushed around, from formal high school or college debates, or from the general adversary nature of so much of our society. Some of us may assume that to develop a relationship in a negotiation, we must buy it with substantive concessions.

General Prescriptive Approach

• *Good relations help reach good outcomes*. It is important to recognize that relationship-building moves tend to strengthen rather than weaken our chances for achieving a good agreement.

• *Acknowledge merit in something they have done*. It is almost always possible to find something meritorious that the other side has done—perhaps in an area apart from what is being negotiated. By acknowledging that, we can communicate that we recognize and respect their worth as people.

• *Acknowledge a need on our part*. Relationships tend to be stronger when there is some interdependence: both sides feel and recognize their need or reliance on the other side in order to achieve mutually desired ends.

• *Take steps outside the negotiation to improve the relationship*. We can concentrate our relationship-building actions in temporally discrete segments of the negotiation, or when we are physically away from the table.

Speaking Clearly in Ways that Promote Listening

Disliked Symptoms.   They don't seem to be paying much attention to what we say.

Possible Diagnoses.   We may be including in what we say things that they know or believe to be mistaken. We often do so when we attribute particular intentions or motives to those on the other side. In the course of rejecting what they know to be wrong, they are likely to reject a lot of other ideas that are closely associated with them. Or something we say early in a long statement raises a red flag for them; they then tune out because they're busy thinking of a retort. Or we may be making unwarranted assumptions about what they know, when in fact they lack certain information needed to make our statements comprehensible.

General Prescriptive Approach

• *Speak for yourself.* Phrase statements about their behavior, motives, statements, and so on in first-person terms of our perceptions and feelings. They may deny the accusation, "You're a bigot!" They can't deny the statement, "I'm feeling discriminated against."

• *Avoid attribution and check assumptions.* Recognize when we make assumptions about their thoughts, feelings, motives, and so on, and try to verify those assumptions with the other side before acting on them. Inquire about their understanding of the background issues or information.

• *Use short, clear statements.* The longer any statement we make, the more they will edit it so they can respond. The more important our message is, the more succinct it should be. If the message is complex, break it down into small parts and confirm their understanding of each segment.

• *Ask them to repeat back what we've said.* In effect, encourage them to be active listeners by asking them to confirm in their own words what they've heard us say.

Actively Inquiring and Listening

Disliked Symptoms.   We don't learn as much as we should about the other side's interests and perceptions and the resources they could bring to bear on our joint problem. We may miss options and ideas that could lead to good solutions for us.

Possible Diagnosis.   We are often so concerned with our own interests that we ignore those of the other side. We are often bored or tired. When they say something that surprises or angers us, we may ignore the rest of what they have to say while we ready our response. We may fear that if we understand them, our resolve will weaken; or that if we show we've heard and understood, they will mistake that for acquiescence or agreement.

General Prescriptive Approach

• *Explicitly allocate time to listen and understand the other side.* Set portions of the agenda for them to explain their interests and ideas. That helps to put us into a "listening mode." An added benefit of this practice is that it establishes a precedent for reciprocal treatment of us by them.

• *Separate understanding their arguments from judging and responding to them.* Make sure that their full argument has been stated, and that we understand it before trying to respond.

• *Repeat back their statements in our own words.*

• *Inquire actively about the reasoning behind their statements.* Even if we repeat back what they said, often they haven't said all they were thinking. There will be some implicit reasoning or logic underlying their statements. It's helpful to ask them to make that reasoning explicit, and then to repeat back their explanation.

NOTE

Many of the ideas in this article were developed in collaboration with Richard Chasin, M.D. and Richard Lee, Ph.D.

Our Game, Your Rules: Developing Effective Negotiating Approaches

Leonard Greenhalgh
Roderick W. Gilkey

Consider the following scenario: A female manager is having a discussion with a male counterpart. They are trying to reach agreement on some issue in dispute. The woman takes a flexible, friendly stance; the man is argumentative and holds firmly to his position. When they have made little progress toward agreement after some time, the woman makes concessions, telling the man she will give in on this issue and he can make it up to her next time. Some time after the negotiation is over, she learns that he did not disclose all the information he must have had, and that he even made some claims that subsequently proved to be untrue. But she gave him the benefit of the doubt on both these points; she figured he must have become a little confused while arguing for his position.

A couple of weeks later, they meet again to try to reach agreement on another issue in dispute. The woman politely reminds the man that she was generous on the last issue and therefore it is *his* turn to show some flexibility. He dismisses this reminder out of hand and proceeds to take a firm stand on the current issue. The woman, feeling angry and betrayed, now blames herself for being too unassertive.

The scenario is a familiar one. Assertiveness training, however, is not the answer to this woman's problem. Her poor short-term performance in this negotiation will show little improvement if all she learns are firmer ways of expressing herself. Instead, she needs to understand that there tends to be a fundamental difference in the way men and women view such interactions.

Women in organizations need to understand this difference because the ability to negotiate is a crucial skill in male-dominated organizational life. In theory, business decisions are rational conclusions drawn when problems are considered in the abstract. In practice, however, most significant decisions in organizations emerge from a process of negotiation; that is, reaching the decision involves reconciling the conflicting interests of the people who have some say in the matter. Making an organizational decision that is acceptable and can be implemented may require negotiating with a host of people—peers, subordinates, superiors, people in staff or control roles, customers, suppliers, regulators, news media representatives, perhaps even family members and others who may be indirectly affected by the decision. Most of the time, these people are not conscious of the fact that they are negotiating. Nevertheless, negotiation is such a basic process in organizations that development of people's negotiating skills is as important as any other area of professional development.

During the past seven years of teaching negotiating skills to managers, executives, and MBAs in training for careers in organizations, we sensed a difference in the way men and women approach negotiation. We analyzed videotapes of simulated negotiation and found some of the differences reported in the popular press. For example, we saw that women are more likely to use powerless speech: instead of saying, ''Your price is too high based on what your competitors are charging,'' they tend to say something like, ''I don't suppose you'd consider a slightly lower price.'' Such hesitant, unassuming ways of making a point invite an uncooperative response if the other person is looking for a short-term gain. Women tended to demand less and concede more.

We weren't satisfied, however, that we really understood the nature and full implications of this difference in approach. We studied the relevant literature in social, personality, and developmental psychology, and saw a link between early developmental experiences, adult personality, and the negotiating behavior of young professionals. We then conducted a study to investigate the relationships we expected to find. As a result, we now have a better-informed idea of how to train men and women to reach agreements.

In this chapter, we will talk about what we have learned from our research and how this information is useful in developing women's skills as negotiators.

BACKGROUNDS

One of the most important factors affecting your approach to negotiation is your time perspective. If you view a negotiation as a single event, you will tend to focus on your immediate gain and probably will not make sacrifices in order to preserve and improve your relationship with the other person. This is known as an *episodic orientation:* you see the negotiation as a single episode whereby the history and future of your relationship with the other person are largely irrelevant. The contrasting time perspective is known as a *continuous orientation.* With such a perspective, you pay attention to the long-term relationship between you and the other person. The present negotiation is one event in a stream of interactions. Therefore, the history and future of the relationship are important—perhaps more important than immediate gain. Thus it is natural to expect that differences in time perspective will lead to differences in negotiating behavior. An episodic orientation should be associated with a competitive approach (''I need to come out ahead in this deal, and it's going to be at your expense''), whereas a continuous orientation should be associated with a more cooperative approach (''Let's find a way to meet both our needs'').

Negotiators' different personalities are likely to affect whether they tend to perceive a bargaining situation as more episodic or more continuous. In particular, such differences in time perspective seem to result from a more fundamental difference in men's and women's orientations toward interpersonal relationships. This difference has been noted in a number of studies that have concluded that women tend to be concerned with their need to get along with others, cooperativeness, and fairness to both parties; men, by contrast, are concerned with their own interests, competing, and avoiding being controlled or dominated by others.[1]

One researcher attributes these contrasting orientations to differences in early developmental experiences.[2] Females develop their sex-role identity from an interaction *with* the mother that emphasizes interdependence, whereas males establish their sex-role identity through separation and individuation *from* their mothers. These differing experiences produce fundamental sex differences later in life that lead women to define themselves *in relation* to others and men *in contrast* to others.

A related factor is the difference in the way boys and girls approach games. Boys are brought up to play competitive games, in which the objective is to beat the opponent. It is acceptable to gloat about victory and deride the loser. Girls play games that focus less on winning and losing. In fact, if their games are progressing in such a way that someone is going to feel bad, girls are likely to stop the game or change the rules: girls don't sacrifice relationships in order to win games.

Carol Gilligan, in her now-classic book *In a Different Voice,* examines the consequences of such basic differences when those individuals become older children. She notes that the greater emphasis on interdependence and mutuality in women's development accounts for the difference between the sexes in their perspective on moral dilemmas: women tend to emphasize their long-term responsibilities and men their immediate rights.

Gilligan cites as an example the case of two eleven-year-old children, a boy and a girl, who respond to questions about a moral dilemma. The boy, Jake, uses deductive logic to deal with what he sees as a conflict over rights and principles among three people, and he describes the solution that would quickly resolve the issues. The response of the girl, Amy, seems less clear and more equivocal. It is tempting to view Amy's response as being logically inferior to and less morally mature than Jake's, but on closer examination it becomes clear that she is viewing the conflict in very different terms. For her, the problem is one of trying to resolve a human-relations issue through ongoing personal communication. Jake, by contrast, views it as a conflict over rights that can be resolved through a morally informed legal system (the set of rules by which the "game" is played). Amy's response is actually based on a relatively sophisticated analysis of interpersonal dynamics. Her response calls for an ongoing series of inter-

---

[1] See, for example, the following studies: M. S. Horner, "Toward an Understanding of Achievement-Related Conflicts in Women," *Journal of Social Issues 28* (1972):157–75; N. Chodorow, "Family Structure and Feminine Personality," in M. Z. Rosaldo and L. Lamphere, eds., *Women, Culture and Society* (Stanford: Stanford University Press, 1974); J. B. Miller, *Toward a New Psychology of Women* (Boston: Beacon Press, 1976); C. Gilligan, *In a Different Voice* (Cambridge, Mass.: Harvard University Press, 1982).

[2] See Chodorow, "Family Structure."

actions concerned more with preserving the relationships between conflicting parties than with deciding the parties' rights in the immediate situation.

Support for Gilligan's point of view can be found in studies that investigate the motivation of individuals to determine how they relate to other people. For example, some researchers have found a difference between boys and girls in the kinds of achievement toward which they aspire. Boys primarily strive to achieve success and therefore are more task-oriented; girls strive primarily to achieve praise and therefore are more relationship-oriented. Other studies have shown a tendency for males to be more competitive and women more cooperative in their interpersonal interactions.[3] Still other studies have examined whether males and females want different things from their jobs.[4] Those studies examine the view that women tend to be more concerned with interpersonal relationships in the work environment, whereas men appear to be more concerned with such factors as the opportunity for advancement (winning) and greater responsibility and influence (dominance).

One difficulty in conducting these studies is that women react to the experimental situation itself. A group of studies suggests that females appear to be more sensitive than males to a number of interpersonal cues that can influence their responses to the experiments. Such cues include the sex of the experimenter, whether communication is controlled or free in the experiment, and whether fairness issues are involved in the conflict.[5] These factors tend to affect women more than men and may indeed explain why research findings have been inconsistent.

Thus, some of the traits that tend to characterize women make it difficult for researchers to identify male-female differences accurately.

Taken as a whole, the diverse studies of gender differences show some general tendencies but are inconsistent in their specific conclusions. The inconsistencies are understandable when one takes into account that the behavior of adult negotiators is a function not only of biological sex but also of the effects of developmental experiences. The different childhood socialization experiences of males and females can result in different sex-role orientations, ranging from strongly masculine to strongly feminine. A strongly masculine person is concerned with power and prefers to dominate others rather than be dominated by them; a strongly feminine person is less concerned with dominance and more concerned with nurturance. Masculinity-feminity, however, does not correspond exactly to biological sex. Some boys are raised to have predominantly feminine orientations, and some girls are raised to have predominantly masculine orientations. All people fall on a continuum between these two extremes. Because sex role is expected to have greater effect on negotiating behavior, sex role rather than biological sex is used in the research reported here and in the discussion that follows.

---

[3] See E. E. Maccoby and C. N. Jacklin, *The Psychology of Sex Differences* (Stanford: Stanford University Press, 1974).

[4] See K. M. Bartol and D. A. Butterfield, "Sex Effects in Evaluating Leaders," *Journal of Applied Psychology* 61 (1976):446–54.

[5] See J. Z. Rubin and B. R. Brown, *The Social Psychology of Bargaining and Negotiation* (New York: Academic Press, 1975).

THE STUDY

Having come this far in researching the literature, we were confident that there were masculine-feminine differences in negotiating approaches. As social scientists, however, we realized that our past observations could simply be hunches, that the studies we had read reported some inconsistencies, and that no one had yet directly studied masculine-feminine differences of adult negotiators. The burden of proof was on us to show that such differences really exist.

We decided to study masculine-feminine differences in a controlled, laboratory setting. Instead of observing everyday negotiations, we simulated the situations under controlled conditions and had young professionals role-play the negotiations. There was enough flexibility in the role instructions to allow masculine-feminine differences to emerge as expected. The use of a laboratory study had two advantages over observing naturally occurring negotiations: First, it allowed us to eliminate most extraneous factors that could contaminate the results; second, it would allow other researchers to replicate our study, thereby adding to its scientific value. (A description of the study can be found at the end of this chapter.)

The results of the study proved consistent with what we had hypothesized. Several differences between masculine and feminine negotiators emerged and are summarized in Table 1. The most basic finding was that feminine negotiators tend to visualize the long-term relationship between the people involved when they think about negotiations. Their masculine counterparts tend to visualize a sporting event in which the other person is an opponent who has to be beaten.

Consistent with this basic difference in orientation, feminine negotiators were likely to be more empathic: that is, they had a natural tendency to try to see the situation from the other person's point of view. This put them in a position to meet mutual needs, which is an ideal outcome of negotiations when there is an ongoing

TABLE 1 Summary of the Different Tendencies of Masculine and Feminine Negotiators

Masculine Tendencies	*Feminine Tendencies*
Visualize a one-shot deal	Visualize the present transaction as one event in a long-term relationship.
Seek a sports-type victory	Seek mutual gain
Emphasize rules-of-the-game, precedents, and power positions	Emphasize fairness
Explain logic of their position	Inquire about other's needs and make personal appeals
Conceal or misrepresent their own needs	Be up front about their own needs
Speak in a dominating or controlling manner	Use "powerless" speech
Be intransigent about their position, perhaps trying to conceal their rigid stance	Be willing to compromise
Interrupt and deceive the other party	Avoid tactics that might jeopardize the long-term relationship

relationship. Furthermore, in the absence of an urgency to "win," feminine negotiators sought fairness and were willing to compromise to achieve a fair outcome.

Finally, the feminine negotiators' concern with the long-term relationship seems to lead them to avoid using tactics that might jeopardize that relationship. Thus we found that feminine negotiators were less likely to deceive the other person. Ironically, the stereotypical view of women's and men's relative trustworthiness is just the opposite. When social psychologists ask people whether women or men are more likely to use underhanded tactics, most people choose women as the less trustworthy. Our research shows that, in fact, women are likely to be more trustworthy than men.

IMPLICATIONS FOR NEGOTIATION RESEARCH

The time horizon makes a big difference in how a person approaches a negotiation. If the person visualizes a one-shot deal, any tactic that will produce an advantage is considered because there is no need to worry about future consequences. If, on the other hand, the person's focus is on the longer-term relationship, then immediate gain is less important than maintaining good will.

Two things determine whether a negotiator takes an episodic or a continuous orientation toward a particular transaction. The first is the objective situation: some transactions *are* one-shot deals in which the negotiators have never interacted beforehand and will probably never deal with each other again. Examples of such transactions include buying an item in a bazaar in a foreign country, or selling an automobile through a newspaper advertisement. The second determinant is the negotiator's personality, which may create *tendencies* to perceive the time horizon to be long-term or short-term, regardless of what the objective situation really calls for. We have seen that a person's sex-role orientation, arising from developmental experiences, has such an effect.

The results of this research help explain some of the inconsistencies in the literature on sex differences in interpersonal relations. In many studies, sex is defined in terms of biological gender; but that approach neglects the results of developmental experiences, which vary widely among individuals. If we are confident that sex-role orientation accurately measures the masculine-feminine perspective, it makes more sense to use this dimension rather than biological sex in our research.

This knowledge of masculine-feminine differences in negotiation approaches helps us understand the scenario we presented at the beginning of this chapter. The woman was willing to make concessions in the short term because she visualized a long-term relationship, in which present concessions would be reciprocated in the future. Her male counterpart had no such perspective. He was visualizing a one-shot deal in which the objective was to beat the other party. Because he saw the interaction as a game, any tactics were permissible—including withholding information and outright deception—as long as they did not violate the explicit rules of the game. The future was irrelevant once the game was over, and a victory in a past game did not obligate the man to try less hard in the next. Had the female negotiator realized that the man was approaching the interaction from this perspective, she could have imposed some rules on the game, or convinced the man not to think of it as a game and done a better job of emphasizing the long-term relationship between them.

IMPLICATIONS FOR DEVELOPMENT OF NEGOTIATING SKILL

Differences in socialization are among the many factors that explain personality differences among negotiators. There is no one best way to negotiate that is suitable for all personalities; rather, each person must develop an approach that capitalizes on unique strengths and compensates for weaknesses. Thus the development of individuals' negotiating approaches must be a highly individualized process that ideally begins with personality assessment.

Personality assessment, however, is not a process that can be taken lightly. The adage that "a little knowledge is a dangerous thing" can be particularly true in the case of understanding one's psychological makeup. Thus the personality-assessment phase of our approach to training negotiators is a comprehensive process, involving standardized self-report personality measures, projective tests, psychological histories, observation of negotiating behavior, and an in-depth interview conducted by a clinical psychologist. Only when we have a good understanding of the individual do we feed back the insights thus gained to the person to improve his or her self-understanding. This process also sensitizes the person both to improve his or her self-understanding and to start thinking about how others may be different, so that negotiating tactics can be somewhat tailored to the type of individual being dealt with. This aspect of our program for developing negotiators is very effective, but we caution individuals who may be undertaking their own self-development, as well as those seeking to develop others, to be sure that properly qualified people are involved in the assessment and that the analysis is comprehensive enough so that it does more good than harm.

Our next step is to help people valuate their effectiveness as negotiators, given their uniqueness as individuals. The best way to do this is to help people become good self-critics. They learn to assess the effectiveness of their negotiating approaches by analyzing a videotape of their own negotiation performance. We have found that people tend to downplay their mistakes and overlook important factors in a negotiation such as tone of voice, gestures, and body language. The videotape preserves such evidence for the purpose of constructive feedback.

Videotape feedback supervised by the instructor is extremely time-consuming, however. Therefore, it needs to be supplemented with supervised self-observation. A good way to accomplish this is to have students keep a journal of their negotiations inside and outside the classroom. They are encouraged to experiment with different approaches, and in the journal they analyze what tactics work well or poorly for them. After keeping a journal for a term, our trainees acquire the habit of constantly analyzing and critiquing their own performance in interactions. Finally, we expose them to a wide variety of negotiating situations—buying and selling, dealing with bosses and subordinates, negotiating and implementing a real estate contract, a corporate acquisition, collective bargaining, settling grievances, and various types of negotiations within and between groups.

Tailoring the learning experience to the unique needs of individuals provides the opportunity to address the special needs of women preparing for professional careers in organizations. For instance, the tendency for women to adopt a continuous time perspective can be a considerable asset in some bargaining situations and a liability in others. It is an asset when relationship-oriented, cooperative, and empathic behavior elicits similar behavior from the other party and leads to mutual accommodation. The liability of this time perspective is that it can make the negotiator vulnerable to exploitation by someone who seeks only short-term gain. In short, the woman who is too nice can be ripped off by an unscrupulous opponent.

The need to adapt to different approaches of the other party requires women to develop flexibility in their negotiating approaches. In practice this means that we encourage women to begin with a positive approach but to be ready to fight fire with fire if they encounter an exploitative, unyielding stance. Specifically, we hope to develop the woman's skill at expressing her commitment to a longer-term relationship and persuading the other person of the advantages of this predisposition. If this gentle persuasion doesn't work, she might interrupt the flow of the negotiation to comment on what is going on between the two people. She may approach this by trying to reflect back the position and assumptions of the other person. ("Let me see if I understand where you're coming from. You need to show your boss that you've gotten a good deal, and if you do that, I'm going to look bad to my boss. So why don't we brainstorm some ideas for how we can both look good?") If this positive approach does not work, the woman needs to have a more hard-line approach available, to use as a deterrent to the tactics of a chronically episodic-oriented opponent.

Another example of the ways in which women can constructively adapt their instinctive approaches to negotiation situations is to capitalize on their natural tendency to be empathic—that is, to be able to understand the perspective of the other party. Empathic tendencies give rise to empathy ("I'd like to learn what you would like to achieve by means of this agreement"), which can elicit a wealth of information about the interests of the other party. An empathic appeal is one of the most effective tactics that can be used to exert influence in a negotiation: it involves simply pointing out how settlements that are of benefit to oneself meet the other party's needs ("If we agree to what I suggested earlier, here's how *you'll* benefit").

We realize we may be coming close to suggesting ways to manipulate other people when we explain how to devise empathic appeals. Although it is true that information gained through empathic inquiries *could* be used exploitatively, such information also can be used in a way that ensures that both parties' needs are met and that both people feel good about the deal. Women's tendency to approach interactions from a continuous time perspective makes the manipulative use of information less likely.

The other feature of our development program that is worth mentioning attempts to undo some of the damage done during male socialization. Briefly, our mission is to help stamp out sports metaphors. This mission is as important to males whose thinking is distorted by these metaphors as it is to women who must suffer the effects.

Males become familiar with competitive games at an early age. When they encounter unfamiliar situations later on, they try to understand them in terms of what is familiar. As a result, many types of relationships are described in sports terms, from "making a big hit" in a business presentation to "scoring" on a date. Unfortunately, such metaphors shape the way males think about relationships in unhelpful ways. Sports contests are episodic by nature; they are either won or lost, so meeting mutual needs is inappropriate; any tactics that do not violate explicit rules are permissible; and the other person is defined as an opponent rather than a potential ally in solving a mutual problem.

It is very difficult to stamp out sports metaphors among negotiators. Because they so permeate the vocabulary of both men and women, they become invisible to those who are affected by them. Even some experts on negotiation cannot escape their effects. For example, some describe meeting mutual needs as a *win-win* solution, which stretches the metaphor beyond its logical limits: if there is a winner, someone else must be a loser; *both* people cannot win. Thus win-win imagery at best makes no sense and at worst perpetuates a view of the situation that fosters conflict rather than accommodation.

SUMMARY

Our professional development programs have been considerably enriched by the research we have conducted on masculine-feminine differences in negotiating. Improvement of negotiating skills, properly guided by research findings, is vital as women endeavor to become more influential in settings traditionally dominated by their male counterparts. Negotiation skills also are vital as organizations take new forms, such as matrix management, increasingly complex structures, team-centered work forces, and Japanese-style management. All these innovations emphasize agreement and coordination between people, which in turn call for effective negotiation skills. Thus, individuals should be strongly concerned with this aspect of their professional development, as should their higher-level managers.

A NOTE ON THE STUDY

The specific hypotheses we tested were based on our review of the literature and our experience in observing and training negotiators. We expected that individuals who are primarily feminine in their sex-role orientation would (1) tend to conceptualize interactions as continuous rather than episodic and (2) use negotiating tactics that strengthen the interpersonal relationship between the parties.

Our study used two different simulated business negotiations—an automobile purchase and a television advertising contract negotiation. Both were videotaped. The participants in the study (our experimental subjects) were 64 MBA students, all with previous business experience. Both men and women participated in the study, but the important variable was their sex-role orientation. As mentioned earlier, there is nothing in males' and females' genes or hormones that makes them negotiate differently; masculine-feminine differences arise from childhood socialization.

We measured sex-role orientation by means of a questionnaire.[6] Other personality characteristics were investigated in depth by a clinical psychologist, who used multiple measures to be sure to achieve a comprehensive assessment of each subject. Special instructions in the second simulation (the television advertising contract negotiation)

---

[6] The questionnaire was the Bem Sex-Role Inventory. For details of this measure, see S. L. Bem, "The Measurement of Psychological Androgyny," *Journal of Consulting and Clinical Psychology 42* (1974):155–62.

informed subjects that they were in an episodic *situation*. Specifically, they were instructed that this was truly a one-shot deal; in fact, this was the last time they would be negotiating in this position for the company, and they would not be dealing with the other person again. This situation provided an opportunity to observe which subjects chose to respond to the situation by adopting an episodic *orientation* to their role and which subjects tried to maintain a continuous one.

The videotapes of the subjects' negotiating performance were analyzed by a trained observer, who was kept unaware of our hypotheses so that we could avoid possible biases to the analysis.

One of the clinical psychologist's specific tasks was to assess each subject's characteristic *tendency* to assume an episodic or a continuous orientation. In the one-hour, in-depth interview, he asked the subjects to describe various interactions they were having *outside* the laboratory study. From the patterns in the behavior they described, the psychologist was able to identify *general* tendencies to see situations as one-shot deals or as events within a long-term relationship.

In summary, then, we recruited 64 young professionals to participate in the study. Then we used a questionnaire to determine whether they had acquired a masculine or feminine sex-role orientation during their childhood socialization. Setting this information aside, we then asked the clinical psychologist to determine whether each person had a natural tendency to see negotiations as one-shot deals or as events in a longer-term relationship. Then we asked the participants to role-play two simulated negotiations each with a different (randomly assigned) partner. Videotapes of the negotiations were then analyzed to see what tactics were used. Finally, we put all the data together to see if, as we had hypothesized, the feminine negotiators had different time perspectives and used different tactics than their masculine counterparts.

The Machiavellis among Us

Richard Christie

Because this is to be asserted in general of men, that they are ungrateful, fickle, false, cowardly, covetous, and as long as you succeed they are yours entirely; they will offer you their blood, property, life and children when the need is far distant; but when it approaches they turn against you . . . and men have less scruple in offending one who is beloved than one who is feared, for love is preserved by the link of obligation which, owing to the baseness of men, is broken at every opportunity for their advantage; but fear preserves you by the dread of punishment which never fails.

The Prince (XVII) Niccolò di Bernardo Machiavelli

The use of guile and deceit to influence and control others is a popular theme in myth and folklore throughout history. Political theorists in all ages and countries have been fascinated by the topic, even in cultures as remote as those of ancient China and India. For example, the Arthaśāstra of Kautilya gives rulers very detailed advice on espionage: who should be kept under surveillance, what roles spies should take, how they should be paid, how to verify the accuracy of their reports, how to keep from being stabbed while one is busy in the harem, and so on. He even discussed the use of classmates as spies—more than two millennia before the FBI.

Kautilya's advice to rulers suggests that India in 300 B.C. would have made Machiavelli's Florence in the 1500s look like a kindergarten. Yet it is Machiavelli we remember for his cynical view of man and the way in which man should be manipulated. This may be unfair, and in fact eminent historians are in violent disagreement about Machiavelli's writings. Mattingly Garrett, an American, has argued convincingly that *The Prince* was written as political satire. G. P. Gooch, an Englishman, felt that Machiavelli was unfair to mankind because he saw a limited portion of the vast field of experience. And the German Friedrich Meinecke thought that Machiavelli rose to the highest ethics in advocating that a prince behave unlawfully, cruelly, and shamefully for the sake of the state.

THINKERS

My interest in Machiavellianism began some 15 years ago when I was puzzling over the nature of individuals who are effective in manipulating others. At the time I was at the Center for Advanced Study in the Behavioral Sciences (Stanford) for a year with nothing to do but think great thoughts. To relieve anxiety over this ominous responsibility, my fellow thinkers and I formed work groups on various topics. Some six of us met to discuss the psychology of leaders—manipulators—having discovered that most of the literature was on followers—the manipulated.

Our early conversations led to four hunches about the perfect manipulator:

1. He is not basically concerned with morality in the conventional sense.
2. He is basically cool and detached with other people. Once a person becomes emotionally involved with another person it is difficult to treat him as an object.
3. He is more concerned with means than ends, thus more interested in conning others than in what he is conning them for. Good manipulators, therefore, come in all ideological colors.
4. He is not pathologically disturbed nor would he have clinical symptoms of neurosis or psychosis. The manipulator must be able to function successfully in the real world, and thus must have an undistorted view of reality. If anything, he would be overrational in dealing with others.

SCALE

To get some ideas for a test that could identify this ideal type, we examined the writings of power theorists throughout history. Viewed in this broad perspective, Machiavelli is not unique. He differs from other power theorists in being explicit in the assumptions he made about human nature. Most political theorists or philosophers base their prescriptions on implicit assumptions; namely, that man is basically weak and gullible, and a rational man takes advantage of the foibles of others. Machiavelli's essays in *The Prince* and the *Discourses* each illustrated a particular point.

This explicitness enabled us to construct a scale. Some of the items we chose for it came directly from his essays, with slight updating, such as: *Most men forget more easily the death of their father than the loss of their property.* Some comments we reversed to avoid wholesale agreement or disagreement; for example, his reflection on man's cowardice became *Most men are brave.* Finally, we invented some new statements that we felt Machiavelli would have approved, such as *Barnum was right when he said there's a sucker born every minute.*

CAMOUFLAGE

After pretesting, revising, and eliminating some of our original 71 statements, we ended up with 20 items: 10 worded in a pro-Machiavelli direction and 10 in an anti-Machiavelli direction. This balanced scale, our fourth variation on the theme, was dubbed Mach IV.

However, many persons are reluctant to agree unequivocally with Machiavellian statements, even if they believe in them, because in our culture agreement with Machiavellianism has low social desirability. Thus we constructed another form of the scale (Mach V) to minimize this effect, using the same 20 items.

This done, we began studies that attempted to relate the Mach scales to other pencil-and-paper tests, and to identify the kinds of persons most likely to agree with Machiavelli's precepts. We found:

1. Males are generally more Machiavellian than females.

2. High Machs do *not* do better than Low Machs on measures of intelligence or ability.

3. High Machs, though they are detached from others, are not pathologically so, at least as measured by the Minnesota Multiphasic Personality Inventory psychopath scale or Lykken's sociopath scale.

4. Machiavellianism is not related to authoritarianism, although superficially it seems that it should be. We decided that there is a basic philosophical difference between these two orientations: the moralistic authoritarian says, "People are no damn good *but they should be*"; the Machiavellian says, "People are no damn good, *so why not take advantage of them?*"

5. High Machs are more likely to be in professions that primarily control and manipulate people. Lawyers, psychiatrists, and behavioral scientists, for example (including social psychologists), are more Machiavellian than accountants, surgeons, and natural scientists.

6. Machiavellianism is not related to a respondent's occupational status or education, marital status, birth order, his father's socioeconomic position, or most other demographic characteristics. We base these conclusions on results from a representative national sample of adults, another study of thousands of college students, and findings from a variety of nonstudent samples by other investigators.

7. On a societal level, industrialization and urbanization apparently contribute to the emergence of Machiavellianism. Survey studies have shown that High Machs are likely to come from urban rather than rural backgrounds. In addition, young adults have higher Mach scores than older adults, perhaps because they grew up in a period of transition toward a cosmopolitan society.

GLOBAL

In fact, studies in the United States and in other cultures indicate that increased cosmopolitanism is creating a generation of Machiavellis—worldwide. Armando de Miguel gave a Spanish version of Mach V to 15 groups of Spanish students from nine provinces and found that scores were highly related to the degree of industrialization of the provinces these students were from. Lois Oksenberg translated Mach IV into

Mandarin Chinese and gave it to high school students in Hong Kong. She found that those attending a westernized school, where the language of instruction was English and where the curriculum followed the British system, scored higher on Machiavellianism than students attending a traditional (Confucian) Chinese high school.

A Machiavellianism score, of course, represents only the degree to which a person believes that people in general are manipulable. He does not necessarily claim that *he* would, or does, manipulate. However, we inferred that agreement with such cynical views of human nature might go along with the emotional detachment and amoral attitude necessary for successful deception.

CHEATERS

Ralph Exline and his colleagues constructed a devious experiment that piqued our curiosity. Exline used a confederate—who posed as another subject—to induce individual subjects to cheat on a test. The experimenter then returned for a posttest interview, during which the eye movements of the subjects were recorded. The experimenter first expressed surprise at the subjects' unusually good performances on the test, then became suspicious, and finally accused the subjects of cheating. In this stressful confrontation, subjects who had scored high on Mach IV resisted confessing. They also looked the experimenter in the eye significantly longer while denying that they had cheated than low-scoring subjects did.

MONEY

This defensive maneuver appeared to be consistent with what we might expect from a good manipulator, and it suggested that there were behavioral correlates of Machiavellian attitudes. Would High Machs behave just as predictably when they had the opportunity for aggressive rather than defensive manipulation?

To find out, Florence Geis and I did an experiment we came to call the $10 game. Three subjects–with high, middle, and low scores on the Mach scales–took seats around a table. We placed 10 $1 bills on the table with the following simple instructions: any *two* of the players could divide the money between themselves in any fashion—five and five, six and four, eight and two, etc. The game would end when two of the subjects came to a final decision, with the crucial stipulation that no agreement could be made to cut the third person in after the session. Theoretically this is an endless game: the excluded person can always break any tentative agreements by offering one of the other two a better deal. And on and on the game goes.

When we started we had no notion how long the subjects would sit, dividing and redividing the dollars. It turned out that the game, far from being endless, varied in duration from 15 seconds to 15 minutes. The High Mach was in the winning combination in every group. Overall, High Machs won significantly more money than would be expected by chance. In this case, their winning was due to their persistence and the reluctance of the Low Machs to hassle over money.

A Test: Are You Machiavellian?

	Disagree			Agree	
	A Lot	A Little	Neutral	A Little	A Lot
1. The best way to handle people is to tell them what they want to hear.	1	2	3	4	5
2. When you ask someone to do something for you, it is best to give the real reasons for wanting it rather than giving reasons which might carry more weight.	1	2	3	4	5
3. Anyone who completely trusts anyone else is asking for trouble.	1	2	3	4	5
4. It is hard to get ahead without cutting corners here and there.	1	2	3	4	5
5. It is safest to assume that all people have a vicious streak and it will come out when they are given a chance.	1	2	3	4	5
6. One should take action only when sure it is morally right.	1	2	3	4	5
7. Most people are basically good and kind.	1	2	3	4	5
8. There is no excuse for lying to someone else.	1	2	3	4	5
9. Most men forget more easily the death of their father than the loss of their property.	1	2	3	4	5
10. Generally speaking, men won't work hard unless they're forced to do so.	1	2	3	4	5

Check the point on the scale that most closely represents your attitude. To find your Mach score, add the numbers you have checked on questions 1, 3, 4, 5, 9, and 10. For the other four questions, reverse the numbers you checked—5 becomes 1, 4 is 2, 2 is 4, 1 is 5. Total your 10 numbers. This is your score. The National Opinion Research Center, which used this short form of the scale in a random sample of American adults, found that the national average was 25.

MISS RHEINGOLD

High Machs impressed us as being much more curious about the nature of our experiments than Low Machs did. They asked more questions about the ground rules and in general seemed to case the experimental situation with an eye to taking maximum advantage of it. We began to wonder: were they more attuned to subtle cues in the environment?

Virginia Boehm and I attempted to answer this question in our Miss Rheingold experiment. Perhaps you remember the Miss Rheingold contest. For over 20 years the Liebmann Breweries annually selected six young ladies to vie for the honor of being used in promotional advertising the following year. Before the contest was ended, some 20 million votes per year were being cast.

We decided to use these pictures in our experiment partly on the basis of a grocery clerk's remark that he could always pick the winner. This seemed highly unlikely; the brewery selected fresh-faced, wholesome types who might have been the proverbial girl next door, and it was hard to tell one from another. For this reason, the pictures appeared to be a good way of testing whether High Machs were more perceptive of subtle cues. If so, they should learn more quickly than Low Machs to identify winners.

So we obtained color photographs of the contestants for the preceding 20 years, and made slides of the six girls for each year. We presented the slides in chronological order, and after each exposure, respondents guessed the winner and runner-up. We gave them feedback about the identities of the winners after they made their choices.

To our surprise there was no difference between High Machs and Low Machs in learning to identify the winners. All respondents chose the winner with greater-than-chance accuracy on the first block of 10 trials, and made a much greater number of correct choices on the second block of 10.

PARAMETERS

Why did degree of Machiavellianism make a difference in the $10 game but not in the Miss Rheingold contest? Florence Geis and I have since analyzed some 50 laboratory studies and have found three parameters that determine whether Machiavellianism is salient. High Machs make out better when three crucial conditions are met:

1. When the laboratory interaction is face-to-face with another person.
2. When there is latitude for improvisation; that is, the subject has a chance to respond freely and is not restricted to pushing buttons or taking tests.
3. When the situation permits the arousal of emotions; that is, where the experiment has serious consequences. Playing for money rather than, say, points, is an example.

Of the 50 Machiavelli experiments that we tabulated, High Machs were more likely to "win"—that is, get more money or points, con someone else, or otherwise perform successfully—when all three of these conditions are met. They did not win when the conditions were absent.

	Number of Parameters Present			
	0	*1*	*2*	*3*
High Machs win	0	5	7	13
High Machs don't win	11	8	5	1
Total 50 studies				

It became clear why High Machs won consistently in the $10 game but not the Miss Rheingold contest. In the latter case, there was no face-to-face interaction since all subjects responded to pictures. There was no latitude for improvisation since the choice was limited to one of six pictures per year. There was no competition with other subjects and no reward, except perhaps self-satisfaction for improving one's guesses. And the stimuli were unlikely to arouse much emotional involvement, since the young ladies were characterized by a bland, homogenized wholesomeness. The money game, however, met all three conditions.

COOL

Other experimental studies have shown that the High Machiavellian is extremely resistant to social influence, although he can be persuaded by rational arguments; he appraises a situation logically and cognitively rather than emotionally; and he tends to initiate and control the structure of the situation when possible. The cool syndrome is his trademark.

The Low Machiavellian, by contrast, is the perfect soft touch. He is susceptible to social influence, he empathizes with others, and he tends to accept the existing definitions of the situation. Far from being cool, he is warm and gets caught up in ongoing human interaction.

Geis and I have the impression that the High Machiavellian is an effective manipulator *not* because he reads the other person and takes advantage of his weakness, but because his insensitivity to the other person permits him to bull his way through in pursuit of coolly rational goals. The Low Mach's empathic ability prevents him from being detached enough to take advantage of the other.

Geis and I concluded that Machiavellianism shows up as an interaction between some enduring interpersonal orientation and specified kinds of situations. We then began to wonder about the genesis of such a manipulative style—how soon it appears in children and how it is acquired.

Susan Nachamie ingeniously constructed a Kiddie-Mach scale—modified Mach IV items—for use with elementary-school children, and gave it to a ghetto-school's sixth-graders (mostly of Chinese, black, and Puerto Rican parentage). The children played a dice game that provided immediate payoffs in M&M candies. The game matrix was asymmetric, so that successful bluffing and challenging were rewarded disproportionately. Children with High Mach scores won significantly more M&Ms than those with low scores.

CRACKERS

Dorothea Braginsky administered a modified version of the scale to fifth-grade children in two small Northeastern cities. Those scoring high and low on the test were chosen as subjects, and the middle scorers were used as targets. Braginsky was introduced as a home economist working for a large bakery that was testing a new health cracker—actually a cracker soaked in quinine. After each child had fully savored the bitterness he rated the cracker's flavor on a graphic rating scale and was then given water and chocolate to help kill the taste. (A few children who said they liked the cracker were not used in the rest of the study.)

Braginsky told the children that although they did not like the cracker, it had been found that sometimes if people ate enough crackers they developed a fondness for them. She offered the children a chance to help her by asking each to persuade another student (the Middle-Mach target) to eat as many crackers as possible. For this help, she said, she would give the child one nickel for every cracker he could persuade the target to eat.

Needless to say, the High-Mach children talked the targets into eating over twice as many crackers as the Low Machs did. Interestingly there were no sex differences in scores or persuasive ability.

PARENTS

Machiavellianism apparently does exist in nascent form in preadolescence. Do the children acquire this orientation by modeling themselves after their manipulative parents?

Braginsky obtained Mach-IV and -V scores on the parents of some two thirds of the children. To her surprise, she found that consistently Low-Mach parents had children who were significantly higher on her version of the Kiddie-Mach scale. The children who were more successful in pushing noxious crackers came from Low-Mach parents. This finding seemed to contradict much current research in developmental psychology—and theory that emphasizes the importance of identification with adults (usually parents). How do we account for this?

An infant sends out many signals, from coos to cries, to bring his needs to the attention of a responsible adult, most often the mother. Some of these behaviors are successful, others are not; and those that are rewarded with the mother's attention are more quickly learned. Mothers, of course, vary in their degree of Machiavellianism; some are more manipulable than others. We would therefore predict that the small children of Low-Mach mothers are able to get away with a greater variety of manipulative actions than children of High-Mach mothers.

A preliminary check on these speculations has been started by Dora Dien in Japan. She related Machiavellianism scores of a group of mothers to the amount of cheating done by their nursery-school children. Children of Low-Mach mothers did cheat considerably more when they were alone in the laboratory situation. This study is currently being replicated in the United States.

WRANGLE

It is remarkable to me that the Mach tests seem simple enough and the meaning universal enough to be readily translated into other languages. In 16th-century Italian, modern English, Mandarin Chinese, or Spanish, Machiavelli's concept of human nature still serves to locate individuals along a continuum of agreement to disagreement with his precepts. Whether his advice to rulers was valid or not, I am not qualified to say. I am content to let historians and politicians wrangle about their interpretation of Machiavelli, secure in my appraisal that he was a most astute observer of man.

Conflict Resolution and
Third-Party Intervention

In the earlier sections of this book we focused on the fundamentals of the negotiation process: planning and setting objectives, understanding the fundamental strategic approaches to negotiation, and procedures for developing tactics. We also explored the underlying components and processes of negotiation that lead to particular outcomes—persuasion processes, the use of power, the personality of the negotiator, and so on. These all help in assessing what type of negotiation situation we face, what resources we have to draw upon, how to set objectives and establish a strategy—all things we do to prepare for negotiation.

At the center of any negotiation is conflict. The parties do not agree, and the negotiation that occurs is an effort to resolve that conflict. Even in integrative bargaining, while conflict may be transformed into a more malleable and muted form, it is still there. All parties want to effect and influence the final outcome—and some may want to contribute "more than their fair share." Both parties want to benefit—but can they benefit equally? Tensions become heightened, positions become polarized, parties become deeply committed to their own points of view and no longer trust their opponents. If the parties do not recognize these dynamics as they are occurring, conflicts can grow and threaten to destroy the negotiated agreement they are seeking or even doom the negotiation process itself.

In this section, we examine conflict and the tensions and dynamics that it engenders. The articles here examine various techniques either for resolving disputes more amicably or for allowing third parties to become involved in the resolution of the dispute.

The first article, "Conflict Resolution and Conflict Management" by Jay Folberg and Alison Taylor, provides a detailed overview of conflict. Focusing on the universal nature of conflict, particularly its external or interpersonal aspects, Folberg and Taylor suggest that conflict is, in fact, desirable in many situations. Conflict often helps clarify objectives and establish norms and may force claimants seeking access to limited resources to be more specific, forthright, and reasoned in making their cases. The authors also make the telling point that conflict (and the need to manage it) actually creates relationships, within which negotiations occur to the potential benefit of those in the relationship. The reading then describes and discusses a range of conflict resolution techniques and processes, with special treatment of the value and benefits of mediation, in which parties uninvolved in the substance of the dispute, per se, assist negotiators in the process of managing stalemates or impasses. Finally, Folberg and Taylor examine two important aspects of mediation. First, they explore the difference between conflict *resolution,* which typically relates to closure and outcomes as opposed to conflict *management,* a more mediational, process-focused approach. Second, they speculate on the conciliatory role of mediators by comparing mediation to counseling.

Christopher Moore's reading, "How Mediation Works" (from his 1985 book *The Mediation Process*), does just what it suggests. Moore defines mediation as "essentially negotiation that includes a third party" who is "acceptable, impartial, and neutral" but has no authority to force or control the ultimate resolution of the dispute. This is consistent with the traditional role of the mediator as facilitator or "process mechanic," interested primarily in the procedural aspects of the negotiation as opposed to the substantive. This limited venue, though, does not prevent mediators from using a range of techniques such as process consultation or problem exploration, or from assuming a variety of roles such as agent of reality or even scapegoat. Moore also discusses the uses of mediation, and describes ways in which mediators intervene and act on disputes. The reading also presents a model of the mediation process, involving the development, testing, and evaluation of hypotheses regarding the dispute as the mediator understands it.

In "The Role of the Mediator," Thomas Colosi describes the strategy and tactics that mediators use to help bring the parties to agreement. Colosi suggests that mediators must follow several key steps in order to bring negotiating parties together. First, mediators must win the negotiators' trust through neutrality, listening, and supportiveness. Second, mediators must help disputants transfer that trust to the negotiating process, so that the parties believe that productive negotiations can solve the problem. Finally, the mediator must help disputants transfer the trust a second time, from the negotiation process to the other disputant, to facilitate the building of a relationship that will see them through this (and future) negotiations. Colosi gives several examples of the ways effective mediators work to execute this process.

Colosi also discusses how negotiation and mediation can be an effective solution to problems traditionally resolved in court. In the past, the involvement of lawyers and the courts frequently led to solutions that neither side found acceptable, as well as heavy legal fees that drained what little financial resources were available. Divorce cases, environmental disputes, and even minor civil and criminal cases are areas in which this trend is prevalent and which have been significantly helped by substituting the negotiation-mediation process. While the parties in these situations are not experienced negotiators, and while their hostility levels are usually very high, research has shown that mediation can be a significantly cheaper, quicker, and more satisfactory resolution process for all concerned.

The last reading, "When Negotiations Fail: Causes of Breakdown and Tactics for Breaking the Stalemate" by Bryan Downie, is a case study of "failed" negotiation between Air Canada and the International Association of Machinists (IAM). Expanding on the "principled negotiation" technique proposed by Fisher and Ury in their book *Getting to Yes,* Downie explains that negotiations may bog down due to external factors (that is, factors not controlled by the actual negotiators) but may still be managed past impasse. In this case, management felt bound to then-current industry norms, standards of profitability, and appearance to potential investors. The union, on the other hand, was constrained by the need to represent the desires of local members concerned about the protection of current wages and future pension benefits. The mediator in the Air Canada/IAM case used tactics that helped the negotiating parties frame options in ways more palatable to their constituencies while allowing the negotiators to save face. Drawing lessons from the case, Downie extols the value of mediation, particularly as performed by a proactive, professional mediator.

Conflict Resolution and Conflict Management

Jay Folberg
Alison Taylor

What is the difference between conflict resolution and conflict management? This questions should be answered before we discuss different methods and processes. If conflict is a set of divergent aims, methods, or behavior, then conflict resolution and conflict management are both processes designed to realign those aims, methods, or behavior.

Conflict resolution creates a state of uniformity or convergence of purpose or means; *conflict management* only realigns the divergence enough to render the opposing forces less diametrically opposite or damaging to each other. Conflict management does not demand an identical aim, method, or process, as does conflict resolution, but simply one that is sufficiently aligned to allow unobstructed progress for the separate entities. Using the analogy of the double helix, both conflict resolution and conflict management direct movement from the conflict helix to the convergence helix, the former to a greater degree. In fact, one could say that the term *conflict resolution* is a misnomer since it is named for the condition one is trying to avoid (conflict) rather than its goal. Perhaps it will eventually be known as *convergence promotion*.

Boulding (1962, pp. 308-9) points out that the most commonly used method of conflict resolution is avoidance but the most extreme method is by one side conquering the other, which puts an end to the conflict by coercion or force. If neither method is appropriate or desirable, the third category, procedural resolution, must be used. Our subsequent use of the terms *conflict resolution* and *conflict management* will fall under this category of procedural resolution. To summarize, then, both conflict resolution and conflict management are general terms for specific processes that achieve a balance of power through noncoercive means.

APPROACHES TO CONFLICT RESOLUTION

Table 1 shows the traditional conflict resolution and management models used in our social, business, institutional, legal, and interpersonal relations. Adjudication and arbitration involve the least control by participants. The other approaches offer varying

---

TABLE 1   Conflict Resolution Processes

Process	*Provider (or Decider)*	*Process Sequence*
Adjudication and arbitration	Judge or arbitrator; higher authority	1. Listens to each side's presentation. 2. Decides option based on predetermined criteria (legislation, precedent, fairness, etc.).
Counseling	Counselor or therapist; manager	1. Gains rapport. 2. Assesses the real problems. 3. Applies intervention strategy.
Negotiation[a]	Lawyer or agent; parties themselves	1. Orientation and positioning. 2. Argumentation. 3. Crises. 4. Agreement or final breakdown.
Problem solving[b]	Individual or delegated official of an organization	1. Identifies the problem. 2. Communicates with appropriate people. 3. Develops alternatives. 4. Decides on alternative. 5. Carries out action. 6. Monitors to ensure completion. 7. Evaluates effectiveness.
Mediation	Mediator; selected third-party facilitator	1. Introduces, structures, gains rapport. 2. Finds out facts, isolates issues. 3. Helps create alternatives. 4. Guides negotiation and decision making. 5. Clarifies/writes an agreement or plan. 6. Provides for legal review and processing. 7. Available for follow-up, review, revision.

[a]Williams' (1983) legal negotiation process.
[b]McMaster model (Epstein, Bishop, and Baldwin, 1982).

degrees of participant control depending on the methodology, the setting, and the nature of the conflict.

Adjudication and arbitration are the most rigid and often the least satisfactory methods of conflict resolution for the participants. These processes operate on the following logical principles:

1. Person 1 wants *A*.
2. Person 2 wants *B*.
3. *A* and *B* are mutually exclusive.
4. Either *A* or *B* must be selected.
5. There are no other options.

The conflicting parties tell their viewpoints and present their evidence and the judge or arbitrator makes a decision based on criteria that have been predetermined by the parties themselves or by a higher authority (legislation, case precedent, custom, and practice). Howard (1969) points out that these processes are but one form of conflict resolution. However, litigation has been used so extensively in our society that it has become the norm. The chief justice of the U.S. Supreme Court has urged reform and the development of alternative methods of resolving disputes (Burger, 1977); many others (Curran, 1977; Felstiner and Drew, 1978; Sarat and Grossman, 1975) have pointed to the legal and social problems created by using this form of conflict resolution as a first resort.

Litigation, adjudication, and arbitration have been used successfully where hierarchical systems demand an acceptance of higher authority, but they seem less suited as a first choice for conflict resolution in a society where great value is placed on individual choice and freedom, where structures are more collective and egalitarian, and where few persons or institutions are universally accepted as worthy of having the necessary authority to impose decisions. Moreover, the criteria used to make the decision are often themselves in as much dispute as the ability of the arbitrator or judge to evaluate the information. As Deutsch (1973) points out, if the parties have no faith in the criteria or the arbitrator but are bound by the power vested in them, the issue will resurface in further conflicts and disputes.

Counseling can be used as a conflict management or conflict resolution process primarily for intrapersonal conflicts, although some therapies apply counseling to interpersonal conflicts as well. Counseling has three basic steps: (1) gaining rapport, (2) exploring and assessing the problems, and (3) applying the appropriate intervention. The counselor must gain rapport and project trustworthiness and competence so that the client feels able to divulge painful conflicts and discuss behavior that has become self-defeating, uncomfortable, or socially unacceptable. The counselor must then assess, or help the client assess, the difference between the presenting problem and the real emotional issues. Finally, when the problems have been identified, the counselor applies intervention strategies in order to relieve the client's conflict and help the client change behavior.

This three-step process is valid for all therapies, despite philosophical differences over who should assess problems, what kind of intervention should be applied, and what the goal or outcome should be. Table 2 reduces this often confusing terminology

TABLE 2   Basic Counseling Models

Counseling Model	Current Situation/ Problem	Intervention: Therapy/ Treatment	Goal Outcome Response
Medical	Diagnosis	Treatment	Cure/stabilization
Behavior modification	Behavior to be promoted or stopped	Reinforcement extinction plan	Behavior change
Conflict theories	Conflict	Problem solving	Conflict resolution
(Neo) Freudian	Id control	Psychoanalysis	Ego control
Transactional analysis	Child/parent reaction	Awareness	Adult reaction
Phenomeno-logical	Discontinuity	Environment	Self-actualization
Perceptual	Improper perception	Learning/cues	Proper perception
Social work	Maladjustment	Services	Social order

into a simple formula showing the three-step process inherent in each counseling approach. The following sentence plots the course: "The (current situation/problem), when given appropriate (intervention/therapy/treatment), leads to the desired (goal/ outcome/response)."

Counseling is traditionally used when the presenting problems have their origin in intrapersonal conflict. Adaptations of the counseling model for use with interpersonal conflict have, however, been introduced to the profession in such works as *Conjoint Family Therapy* (Satir, 1967). Conjoint family therapy is now commonly employed to address problems that originate primarily between people. Whether it is used for conflict management or for conflict resolution depends on the counselor's orientation and goal.

Many books on business management, personnel development, and administration use essentially this same model for preventing, eliminating, or managing interpersonal conflict in the work setting. Managers "counsel" their subordinates by implementing the three-stage process (rapport, assessment, and application). In that context, counseling is seen as a better management tool than imposed decisions, because it directly involves the conflicting parties in seeking understanding of their problems.

Negotiation is the most pervasive and diverse approach to dispute resolution. Negotiation of disputes need not follow an established framework, although some have systematically studied the process (Williams, 1983). It is often pursued through the use of designated representatives such as attorneys. Most writers equate negotiation with bargaining—that is, the exchange of one thing for another (Bellow and Moulton, 1981).

Williams (1983) has observed that negotiations between legal representatives predictably follow the four-stage pattern set forth in Table 1. Above all, negotiation involves the formulation of opposing positions, and fulfilling one negotiator's position necessarily defeats fulfillment of the other's. Negotiating to achieve one position at the expense of another is a function of perceived power, bargaining tactics, and a crisis orientation. Viewing negotiation as a competitive, adversarial zero-sum game, which requires considerable game playing and manipulative skills, has been the hallmark of professional texts (Illich, 1973) as well as popular "Me Decade" books telling how to get what you want by bullying your way through any conflict in life.

More recently, both popular and professional books on negotiation have emphasized the cooperative model that seeks mutual gain through constructive settlement of disputes. These books echo Deutsch's win/win analysis. The most helpful and concise of the new works on win/win negotiating flows from the experience of the Harvard Negotiation Project. Roger Fisher and William Ury, in their national bestseller, *Getting to Yes* (1983), urge negotiators not to bargain over positions. The method they offer for successful negotiation provides a four-part approach based on these simple statements:

- Separate the people from the problem.
- Focus on interests, not positions.
- Invent options for mutual gain.
- Insist on objective criteria.

Stating these four maxims is, of course, easier than implementing them in a dispute. One role of a mediator is to help the parties avoid positional bargaining and guide negotiations toward a resolution of mutual gain for which power alone is not the criterion. In the next chapter we shall have more to say about the use of win/win negotiation methods as a phase of the mediation process.

Problem solving is a process that can be used alone or with other conflict resolution methods. The McMaster model of family functioning (Epstein, Bishop, and Baldwin, 1982) explains how families can engage in group problem solving to keep functioning. The McMaster model defines two categories of problems and formulates a sequence for solving them. This sequence is not limited to family functioning; it applies to all problem-solving situations. *Instrumental* problems are related to "mechanical" issues involving provision of necessary materials such as food, money, time, and the like. *Affective* problems deal with feelings. Effective problem solving is seen as a sequence of seven steps that can be applied to both categories of problems (Epstein, Bishop, and Baldwin, 1982, pp. 119-22):

1. Identifying the problem.
2. Communicating with appropriate people about the problem.
3. Developing a set of alternative solutions.
4. Deciding on one of the alternatives.
5. Carrying out the action.
6. Monitoring to ensure that the action is carried out.
7. Evaluating the effectiveness of the problem-solving process.

This model is similar to the mediation process, but it can be used by individuals or groups to solve problems without outside facilitators or helpers. Not every person or group is able to use the problem-solving process outlined above, however.

Mediation incorporates many of the same stages, but it has the advantage of being facilitated by a neutral third party who is not a member of the group and thus can direct the entire process.

Hayes (1981) has further analyzed the problem-solving process and found that it contains four general methods: (1) trial and error methods, (2) proximity methods, (3) fractionalization methods, and (4) knowledge-based methods. *Trial and error* methods can be either blind or systematic, but both approaches are unsatisfactory for some problems. *Proximity* methods are based on the question, "What step can I take that will bring me closer to the goal?" Hayes describes two proximity methods, *hill-climbing* and *means-end* analysis, both of which lend themselves to computer programs or subroutines for problem solving.

Fractionalization methods involve subgoals to guide the problem solver around detours. This tactic can often be used by mediators to facilitate problem solving with their participants. The idea is to take a complex situation, such as an environmental dispute or a divorce, and break it down into subgoals that lead the participants closer to the overall goal. Thus if a couple's overall goal is to part amicably and fairly, each issue of child custody, visitation, division of property, and financial planning can be related to the "fair and friendly" criterion. If the overall goal is to preserve the splendor of an area such as the Columbia River Gorge, decisions about each issue—fishing rights, tourism, housing developments and zoning, recreational use, navigational rights—should all be tied to the original criterion: preservation of a unique scenic area. *Knowledge-based* methods of problem solving have been further classified into four areas: learning, searching for related problems, pattern matching, and search algorithms (routine procedures leading to correct solutions—long division, for example).

The final process discussed here, *mediation,* is approached in this book as a seven-stage conflict resolution process:

1. Introduction—creating trust and structure.
2. Fact finding and isolation of issues.
3. Creation of options and alternatives.
4. Negotiation and decision making.
5. Clarification and writing a plan.
6. Legal review and processing.
7. Implementation, review, and revision.

Our seven-stage model is intended as a "megaprocess" that can form the basis of mediation in all situations. Each stage is composed of separate tasks, but not all stages will be completed in every case. Other authors portray a similar mediation process but divide the stages differently or use different labels. In the next chapter we illustrate our seven-stage process and suggest specific techniques and roles for the mediator. Other conflict resolution processes—such as avoidance, legislation, marketplace supply and demand, boycotts, violence, coercion, dictatorial fiat, civil disobedience, and peace-winning or peace-keeping strategies—are tangential and important but beyond the scope of this book.

COMPARING THE ALTERNATIVES

It will be helpful here to compare the seven-stage mediation process we have outlined with the counseling/therapy process and the process of adjudication. . . . Mediation does not have the same goal as counseling and therapy. The primary goal of mediation is to create a set of agreements that will guide future actions and consequences between the participants. Its other goal is to reduce the negative effects of the conflict by improving communication and enhancing negotiation skills. The goal of counseling and therapy is to change certain behavior or perceptions. While some counseling approaches may involve "behavioral contracting," it is usually not a written contract and certainly is not legally binding upon the client, as a signed agreement or mediated plan may be.

Sheila Kessler (1979) has suggested that counselors are becoming mediators, yet many counselors are unaware of the mediation process and how it differs from counseling. Many counselors and therapists do not work with interpersonal problems but see their role as dealing only with the "cause" of the problems: the underlying intrapersonal conflicts. Although the majority of counselors do not work with clients simultaneously, whereas mediation requires at least two participants, counselors can use mediation as the second of their three-step process if they are trained in mediation techniques.

The basic assumption of counseling could be stated as follows: *If* the counselor and client have developed a sufficient relationship of trust, and *if* the counselor has accurately assessed the real problem, and *if* the client's problems match the style of the counselor, and *if* the counselor applies the intervention correctly, the client's problems can be resolved. These assumptions put the responsibility for success or failure primarily on the counselor; in the mediation process, by way of contrast, success or failure rests primarily with the participants.

Mediation furthers the policy of minimum state intervention in interpersonal conflicts. The argument for minimum state intervention is founded not only on economic considerations but also on the value placed on personal autonomy. If litigation or other adversarial proceedings can be avoided, the savings to the public and the parties can be considerable. Mediation is most often conducted in private so that private matters may be freely discussed without concern that the discussion is part of a public record, as in adjudication. Mediation is also usually speedier than adjudication. The principal advantage of mediation compared to adjudication is not economy or speed, however. The primary benefit is self-determination.

Disputants should be presumed to have the capacity, authority, and responsibility to determine consensually what is best for themselves through the process of mediation. People are encouraged in mediation to assess and meet their own needs and resolve their conflicts responsibly without professional paternalism or state interference.

One of the most noble functions of law is to serve as a model of what is expected. Adjudicatory procedures, instead of providing models, are too often used coercively to supplant self-determination with no evidence that the disputants have been encouraged and helped to resolve their differences. The law should be premised on the expectation that people will not abdicate to a lawyer or a judge the responsibility of deciding what is fair. Using mediation to facilitate conflict resolution and encourage self-determination thus strengthens democratic values and enhances the dignity of those in conflict.

The legal system is not able to supervise the fragile and complex interpersonal relationships between family members, parents and teachers, landlord and tenants, neighbors and others that may continue after their immediate dispute is resolved. Once lawyers and judges intrude into the decision-making role between those in conflict, the disputants are less likely to function independently in the future—thus promoting further professional involvement and individual noncooperation with imposed orders. By definition, a consensual agreement, whether reached through mediation or negotiation, reflects the parties' own preferences and will be more acceptable and durable than one imposed by a court. Since the participants in mediation formulate their own agreement and invest emotionally in its success, they are more likely to adhere to its terms than one negotiated or ordered by others. Mediation is particularly advantageous for conflicts between those who must have continued contact together, such as people involved in family disputes and divorce. Continuing contact on unresolved conflicts may produce postdivorce skirmishes in court that exceed the intensity of the initial dispute.

Mediators can facilitate private ordering, or negotiated outcomes, between disputants by helping them get information on applicable legal norms and principles, as well as the probable outcome in court if the case is litigated. Mnookin and Kornhauser (1979), in developing the theme of private ordering, pointed out that a rational client will want an accurate assessment of the costs of alternative modes of dispute settlement. A mutual assessment of the alternatives during the mediation process helps assure a fair and rational outcome. Mediation can also educate the participants about each other's needs and provide a personalized model for dispute resolution both now and in the future. In such situations, mediation can teach the participants to work together, isolate the crucial issues, and realize that cooperation can be to their mutual advantage.

How Mediation Works

Christopher Moore

Although mediation is widely practiced in interpersonal, organizational, community, and international disputes, and techniques have been documented in particular applications or cases, there has been little systematic study or description of specific strategies and tactics used by mediators. What analysis and description have been conducted either have been presented on the most general level or are so specific as to limit their broad application.

*   *   *   *   *

A DEFINITION OF MEDIATION

When a mediator from the United Nations enters an international dispute, a labor mediator is engaged in negotiations prior to a strike, or a family mediator assists a couple in reaching a divorce settlement, what activities are they performing? What is their relationship to the parties? What are the objectives of the mediators?

Mediation is the intervention into a dispute or negotiation by an acceptable, impartial, and neutral third party who has no authoritative decision-making power to assist disputing parties in voluntarily reaching their own mutually acceptable settlement of issues in dispute. I will examine several components of the definition.

For mediation to occur, the parties must begin negotiating. Labor and management must be willing to hold a bargaining session, governments and public interest groups must create forums for dialogue, and families must be willing to come together for mediation to begin. *Mediation is essentially negotiation* that includes a third party who is knowledgeable in effective negotiation procedures, and can help people in conflict to coordinate their activities and to be more effective in their bargaining. Mediation is an extension of the negotiation process in that it involves extending the bargaining into a new format and using a mediator who contributes new variables and dynamics to the interaction of the disputants. Without negotiation, however, there can be no mediation.

Intervention means "to enter into an ongoing system of relationships, to come between or among persons, groups, or objects for the purpose of helping them. There

Reprinted from Moore, C. W. *The Mediation Process: Practical Strategies for Resolving Conflict*, 1986, pp. 13–43. © Jossey-Bass and Christopher W. Moore. Used with permission.

is an important implicit assumption in the definition that should be made explicit: the system exists independently of the intervenor'' (Argyris, 1970, p. 15). The assumption behind an outsider's intervention is that a third party will be able to alter the power and social dynamics of the conflict relationship by influencing the beliefs or behaviors of individual parties, by providing knowledge or information, or by using a more effective negotiation process and thereby helping the participants to settle contested issues. Rubin and Brown (1975) have argued that the mere presence of a party who is independent of the disputants may be a highly significant factor in the resolution of a dispute.

The third aspect of this definition is *acceptability,* the willingness of disputants to allow a third party to enter a dispute and assist them in reaching a resolution. Acceptability does not mean that disputants necessarily welcome a mediator and are willing to do exactly as he or she says. It does mean that the parties approve of the mediator's presence and are willing to listen to and seriously consider the intervenor's suggestions.

Impartiality and neutrality are critical to the process of mediation (Young, 1972). *Impartiality* refers to the attitude of the intervenor and is an unbiased opinion or lack of preference in favor of one or more negotiators. *Neutrality,* on the other hand, refers to the behavior or relationship between the intervenor and the disputants. Mediators often either have not had a previous relationship with disputing parties or have not had a relationship in which they have directly influenced the rewards or benefits for one of the parties to the detriment of the other. Neutrality also means that the mediator does not expect to directly gain benefits or special payments from one of the parties as compensation for favors in conducting the mediation.

People seek a mediator's assistance because they want procedural help in negotiations. They do not want an intervenor who is biased or who will initiate actions that are detrimental to their interests.

The need for impartiality and neutrality does not mean that a mediator may not have personal opinions about a dispute's outcome. No one can be entirely impartial. What impartiality and neutrality do signify is that the mediator can separate his or her opinions about the outcome of the dispute from the desires of the disputants and focus on ways to help the parties make their own decisions without unduly favoring one of them. The final test of the impartiality and neutrality of the mediator ultimately rests with the parties. They must perceive that the intervenor is not overtly partial or unneutral in order to accept his or her assistance.

Kraybill (1979) and Wheeler (1982) address the tensions between impartiality and neutrality and the personal biases of mediators by distinguishing between the substantive and procedural interests. Wheeler argues that mediators generally distance themselves from commitments to specific substantive outcomes—the amount of money in a settlement, the exact time of performance, and so forth—but have commitments to such procedural standards as open communication, equity and fair exchange, durability of a settlement over time, and enforceability. Mediators are advocates for a fair process and not for a particular settlement.

Conflicts involve struggles between two or more people over values, or competition for status power and scarce resources (Coser, 1967). Mediators enter a variety of levels of conflicts—latent, emerging, and manifest—according to their degree of organization and intensity. Latent conflicts are characterized by underlying tensions that have not fully developed and have not escalated into a highly polarized conflict. Often, one or more parties may not even be aware that a conflict or the potential for one even exists (Curle, 1971). Changes in personal relationships in which one party is not aware of how serious a breach has occurred, future staff cutbacks, unannounced plans for the siting of a potentially controversial facility such as a mine or waste disposal site, or potential unpopular changes in public policy are examples of latent conflicts.

Mediators (or facilitators) working with people involved in the resolution of latent disputes help participants to identify people who will be affected by a change or those who may be concerned about the future problem, assist them in developing a mutual education process about the issues and interests involved, and work with participants to design and possibly implement a problem-solving process.

Emerging conflicts are disputes in which the parties are identified, they acknowledge that there is a dispute, and most issues are clear, but no workable negotiation or problem-solving process has developed. Emerging conflicts have a potential for escalation if a resolution procedure is not implemented. Many disputes between coworkers, businesses, and governments illustrate this type of conflict. Both parties recognize that there is a dispute, and there may have been a harsh verbal exchange, but neither knows how to handle the problem. In this case the mediator helps establish the negotiation process and helps the parties begin to communicate and bargain.

Manifest conflicts are those in which parties are engaged in an ongoing dispute, may have started to negotiate, and may have reached an impasse. Mediator involvement in manifest conflicts often involves changing the negotiation procedure or intervention to break a specific deadlock. Labor mediators who intervene in negotiations before a strike deadline are working to resolve manifest conflicts. Child custody and divorce mediators also usually intervene in fully manifest disputes.

A mediator has *no authoritative decision-making power*. This characteristic distinguishes the mediator from the judge or arbiter, who is designated by law or contract to make a decision for the parties based on societal norms, laws, or contracts rather than the specific interests or personal concepts of justice held by the parties. The goal of the judicial decision is not reconciliation but a decision concerning which of the parties is right.

The judge examines the past and evaluates "agreements that the parties have entered into, violations which one has inflicted on the other," and "the norms concerning acquisition of rights, responsibilities, etc. which are connected with these events. When he has taken his standpoint on this basis, his task is finished" (Eckhoff, 1966–67, p. 161).

The mediator, on the other hand, works to reconcile the competing interests of the two parties. The mediator's goal is to assist the parties in examining the future and their interests or needs, and negotiating an exchange of promises and relationships that will be mutually satisfactory and meet their standards of fairness. The mediator does not have decision-making authority, and parties in dispute therefore often seek the services of a mediator because they can retain ultimate decision-making power.

If the mediator does not have authority to decide, does he or she have any influence at all? The mediator's authority, such as it is, resides in his or her ability to appeal to the parties to reach an agreement based on their own interests or the past performance or reputation of the mediator as a useful resource. Authority, or recognition of a right to influence the outcome of the dispute, is granted by the parties themselves rather than by an external law, contract, or agency.

So far I have identified that a mediator is a third party who is impartial in attitude and neutral in relationship toward disputing parties. I will now describe the mediator's functions. The definition states that a mediator *assists* disputing parties. Assistance can refer to very general or to highly specific activities. I will examine here some of the more general roles and functions of the mediator, and will discuss specifics later when analyzing intervention moves made during particular phases of negotiation.

The mediator may assume a variety of roles and functions to assist parties in resolving disputes (American Arbitration Association, n.d.):

- *The opener of communications channels* who initiates communication or facilitates better communication if the parties are already talking.
- *The legitimizer* who helps all parties recognize the right of others to be involved in negotiations.
- *The process facilitator* who provides a procedure and often formally chairs the negotiation session.
- *The trainer* who educates novice, unskilled, or unprepared negotiators in the bargaining process.
- *The resource expander* who provides procedural assistance to the parties and links them to outside experts and resources, such as lawyers, technical experts, decision makers, or additional goods for exchange, that may enable them to enlarge acceptable settlement options.
- *The problem explorer* who enables people in dispute to examine a problem from a variety of viewpoints, assists in defining basic issues and interests, and looks for mutually satisfactory options.
- *The agent of reality* who helps build a reasonable and implementable settlement and questions and challenges parties who have extreme and unrealistic goals.
- *The scapegoat* who may take some of the responsibility or blame for an unpopular decision that the parties are nevertheless willing to accept. This enables them to maintain their integrity and, when appropriate, gain the support of their constituents.
- *The leader* who takes the initiative to move the negotiations forward by procedural, or on occasion, substantive suggestions.

The last component of the definition refers to mediation as a voluntary process. *Voluntary* refers to freely chosen participation and freely chosen settlement. Parties are not forced to negotiate, mediate, or settle by either an internal or external party to a dispute. Stulberg (1981b, pp. 88–89) notes that "there is no legal liability to any party refusing to participate in a mediation process. . . . Since a mediator has no authority unilaterally to impose a decision on the parties, he cannot threaten the recalcitrant party with a judgment."

Voluntary participation does not, however, mean that there may not be pressure to try mediation. Other disputants or external forces, such as judges or constituents, may put significant pressure on a party to try negotiation and mediation. Some courts in family and civil cases have even gone so far as to order that parties try mediation as a means of resolving their dispute before the court hears the case. Attempting mediation does not, however, mean that the participants are forced to settle.

ARENAS OF MEDIATION

Mediation has a long history. The Bible refers to Jesus as a mediator between God and man: ''For there is one God, and one mediator between God and man, the man Christ Jesus; who gave himself as ransom for all, to be testified in due time'' (I Timothy 2:5–6). Churches and clergy have often been mediators between their members or other disputants. Until the Renaissance, the Catholic church in Western Europe was probably the central mediation and conflict management organization in Western society. Clergy mediated family disputes, criminal cases, and diplomatic disputes among the nobility. Bianchi (1978), in describing one mediated case in the Middle Ages, details how the church and the clergy provided the sanctuary where the offender stayed during dispute resolution and served as intermediary between two families in a case involving rape. The families agreed to settle with monetary restitution to the woman's family and promises to help her find a husband.

Jewish rabbinical courts and rabbis in Europe were vital in mediating or adjudicating disputes among members of that faith. These courts were crucial to the protection of cultural identity and ensured that Jews had a formalized means of dispute resolution. In many locales they were barred from other means of dispute settlement because of their religion.

With the rise of nation-states, mediators took on new roles as formal secular diplomatic intermediaries. Diplomats such as ambassadors and envoys acted to ''raise and clarify social issues and problems, to modify conflicting interests, and to transmit information of mutual concern to parties'' (Werner, 1974, p. 95).

The practice of mediation is not confined to Western culture. In fact, mediation has probably been more widely practiced in China and Japan, where religion and philosophy place a strong emphasis on social consensus, moral persuasion, and striking a balance or harmony in human relations (Brown, 1982). Mediation is currently widely practiced in the People's Republic of China through People's Conciliation Committees (Ginsberg, 1978; Li, 1978).

Latin America and other Hispanic cultures also have a history of mediated dispute settlement. Nader (1969) reports on the dispute resolution process in the Mexican village of Ralu'a, where a judge assists the parties in making consensual decisions. Lederach (1984) describes other mediation models in Hispanic culture such as the *Tribunal de las Aguas* (water courts) in Spain.

Mediation is also utilized in Africa, where the *moot court* is a common means for neighbors to resolve disputes (Gulliver, 1971). Mediated settlement is also practiced in some Arab villages in Jordan (Antoun, 1972).

In Melanesia, the Tolai villages in New Britain each have a counselor and committee that meet regularly to hear disputes (Epstein, 1971). The role of the counselor and committee is to ''maintain conditions for orderly debate and freedom of argument by the disputants and anyone else who wishes to express opinion'' (Gulliver, 1979,

p. 27). The process is both a "mode of adjudication" and a "settlement by consensus" of the parties (Epstein, 1971, p. 168).

Mediation also has a long history in the American colonies and the United States. Auerbach's *Justice Without Law* (1983) is an excellent history that describes the dispute resolution mechanisms of the Puritans, Quakers, and other religious sects; procedures of Chinese and Jewish ethnic groups; and informal alternative dispute resolution efforts.

For the most part, mediation historically and in other cultures has been performed by people with informal training, and the intervenor's role has usually occurred within the context of other functions or duties. Only since the turn of the twentieth century has mediation become formally institutionalized and developed into a recognized profession.

The first arena in which mediation was formally institutionalized in the United States was in labor-management relations (Simkin, 1971). In 1913 the U.S. Department of Labor was established, and a panel, the "commissioners of conciliation," was appointed to handle conflicts between labor and management. This panel subsequently became the United States Conciliation Service, and in 1947 was reconstituted as the Federal Mediation and Conciliation Service. The rationale for initiating mediation procedures in the industrial sector was to promote a "sound and stable industrial peace" and "the settlement of issues between employer and employees through collective bargaining" (Labor-Management Relations Act, 1947). It was expected that mediated settlements would prevent costly strikes or lockouts for workers and employers alike and that the safety, welfare, and wealth of Americans would be improved.

Federal use of mediation in labor disputes has provided a model for many states. Numerous states have passed laws, developed regulations, and trained a cadre of mediators to handle intrastate labor conflicts. The private sector has also initiated labor-management and commercial relations mediation. The American Arbitration Association was founded in 1926 to encourage the use of arbitration and other techniques of voluntary dispute settlement.

Mediation sponsored by government agencies has not been confined to labor-management issues. The U.S. Congress passed the Civil Rights Act of 1964 and created the Community Relations Service (CRS) of the U.S. Department of Justice. This agency was mandated to help "communities and persons therein in resolving disputes, disagreements, or difficulties relating to discriminatory practices based on race, color, or national origin" (Title X, Civil Rights Act, 1964). The agency assists people in resolving disputes through negotiation and mediation rather than having them utilize the streets or the judicial system. CRS works throughout the country on such issues as school desegregation and public-accommodation cases. In 1978, a team from CRS mediated the dispute that erupted when a neo-Nazi political group announced its intention to demonstrate in Skokie, a predominantly Jewish suburb of Chicago (Salem, 1984).

Diverse state agencies, civil rights commissions, and private agencies also use mediation to handle charges of sex, race, and ethnic discrimination conflicts (Chalmers and Cormick, 1971; Kwartler, 1980; "Municipal Human Relations Commissions . . . ," 1966).

Since the mid-1960s, mediation has grown significantly as a formal and widely practiced approach to dispute resolution. In the community sector, the federal government funds Neighborhood Justice Centers (NJCs) that provide free or low-cost mediation services to the public to resolve disputes efficiently, inexpensively, and informally. Many of these NJCs are institutionalized and have become part of city, court, or district attorney programs for alternative dispute resolution. Some community programs are independent of governmental agencies and offer a grass roots independent dispute resolution service in which community members sit on mediation or conciliation panels and help neighbors resolve their disputes (Shonholtz, 1984).

Mediation is also practiced in schools and institutions of higher education. In this setting, disputes are mediated among students, such as the potentially violent interracial conflict handled by Lincoln (1976); between students and faculty; between faculty members; or between faculty and administration (McCarthy, 1980; McCarthy and others, 1984).

The criminal justice system also utilizes mediation to resolve criminal complaints (Felsteiner and Williams, 1978) and disputes in correctional facilities (Reynolds and Tonry, 1981). Mediation in the latter arena takes the form of both crisis intervention in case of prison riots or hostage negotiations and institutionalized grievance procedures.

Perhaps the fastest-growing arena in which mediation is practiced is in family disputes. Court systems and private practitioners provide mediation to families in child custody and divorce proceedings (Coogler, 1978; Haynes, 1981; Irving, 1980; Saposnek, 1983; Moore, forthcoming); disputes between parents and children (Shaw, 1982; Wixted, 1982), conflicts involving adoption and the termination of parental rights (Mayer, 1985), and spousal disputes in which there is domestic violence (Bethel and Singer, 1982; Orenstein, 1982; Wildau, 1984). In family disputes, mediated and consensual settlements are often more appropriate and satisfying than litigated or imposed outcomes. Models of practice in this area include mandatory court-connected programs in which disputants must try mediation before a judge will hear the case; voluntary court programs; and forms of private practice such as sole practitioners, partnerships, and private nonprofit agencies.

Mediation is also used within and between organizations to handle interpersonal and institutional disputes. The scope of mediation application ranges from mediating one-on-one personnel disputes, managing problems between partners (such as in law or medical practices), interdepartmental conflicts, and altercations between companies (Biddle and others, 1982; Blake and Mouton, 1984; Brett and Goldberg, 1983; Brown, 1983).

Mediation is also applied to a variety of larger disputes over environmental and public policy issues (Talbot, 1983; Bingham, 1984; Carpenter and Kennedy, 1977; Cormick, 1976; Lake, 1980; and Mernitz, 1980). Disputes over power plant siting, dam construction, and land use have all been successfully mediated. Government agencies are experimenting with negotiated rule making in public policy issues (Bingham, 1981; Harter, 1984). The Negotiated Investment Strategy, a mediated procedure initiated by the Kettering Foundation, enables local, state, and federal agencies to coordinate their decisions on program funding (Shanahan and others, 1982).

Mediation is also being applied in landlord-tenant conflicts (Cook, Rochl, and Shepard, 1980), personal injury cases ("AAA Designs . . .," 1984), police work (Folberg and Taylor, 1984), disputes between elderly residents and nursing home owners, and consumer disputes (Ray and Smolover, 1983). The arenas in which mediation is being applied are very broad. If trends continue, the process will be used to resolve a variety of disputes in arenas not conceived of today.

MEDIATION ACTIVITIES: MOVES AND INTERVENTIONS

Negotiation is composed of a series of complex activities or "moves" people initiate to resolve their differences and bring the conflict to termination (Goffman, 1969, p. 90). Each move or action a negotiator conducts involves rational decision making in which outcomes of alternative actions are assessed according to their relationships to the following factors: the moves of the other parties, their standards of behavior, their styles, their perceptiveness and skill, their needs and preferences, their determination, how much information the negotiator has about the conflict, his or her personal attributes, and resources available.

Mediators, like negotiators, also initiate moves. A *move* for a mediator is a specific act of intervention or "influence technique" focused on the people in the dispute that encourages the selection of positive actions and inhibits the selection of negative actions relative to the issues in conflict (Galtung, 1975b). The mediator, a specialized negotiator, does not *directly* effect changes in the disputants by initiating moves; he or she is more of a catalyst. Changes are the result of a combination of the intervenor's moves with the moves of the negotiators (Bonner, 1959).

In negotiations, people in conflict are faced with a variety of procedural or psychological problems or "critical situations" (Cohen and Smith, 1972) that they must solve or overcome if they are to reach a settlement. All problem-solving groups face these situations, which can be categorized according to size, type, time, and frequency. The largest categories and most frequent problems are hereafter referred to as *stages* because they constitute major steps that parties must take to reach agreement. There are stages for both negotiation and mediation, which, for the most part, directly correspond to each other.

Mediators make two types of interventions in response to critical situations: *general* or *noncontingent* and *specific* or *contingent* moves (Kochan and Jick, 1978).

Noncontingent moves are general interventions that a mediator initiates in all disputes. These moves are responses to the broadest categories of critical situations and correspond to the stages of mediation. They are linked to the overall pattern of conflict development and resolution. Noncontingent moves enable the mediator to

1. Gain entry to the dispute,
2. Assist the parties in selecting the appropriate conflict resolution approach and arena,
3. Collect data and analyze the conflict,
4. Design a mediation plan,
5. Practice conciliation,
6. Assist the parties in beginning productive negotiations,
7. Identify important issues and build an agenda,

8. Identify interests,

9. Aid the parties in developing settlement options,

10. Assist in assessing the options,

11. Promote final bargaining, and

12. Aid in developing an implementation and monitoring plan.

I will examine these moves and stages in more detail later in this chapter.

Smaller noncontingent moves are initiated by mediators within each stage. Examples of this level of moves include activities to build credibility for the process, promote rapport between the parties and the mediator, and frame issues into a more manageable form, as well as develop procedures to conduct cost-benefit evaluations on settlement options.

Contingent moves are responses to special or idiosyncratic problems that occur in some negotiations. Interventions to manage intense anger, bluffing, bargaining in bad faith, mistrust, or miscommunication are all in this category of specific interventions. While some contingent moves, such as the caucus—private meetings between the parties and the mediators—are quite common, they are still in the contingent category because they do not happen in all negotiations.

HYPOTHESIS BUILDING AND MEDIATION INTERVENTIONS

For a mediator to be effective, he or she needs to be able to analyze and assess critical situations and design effective interventions to counteract the causes of the conflict. Conflicts, however, do not come in neat packages with their causes and component parts labeled so that the parties, or the intervenor, know how to creatively respond to them. The causes are often obscured and clouded by the dynamics of the interaction.

To work effectively on conflicts, the intervenor needs a conceptual road map or "conflict map" of the dispute (Wehr, 1979) that should detail why a conflict is occurring, should identify barriers to settlement, and should indicate procedures to manage or resolve the dispute.

Most conflicts have multiple causes; usually it is a combination of problems in the relations of the disputants that leads to a dispute. The principal tasks of the mediator and the parties are to identify central causes of the conflict and take action to alleviate them. The mediator and participants in a dispute accomplish this by trial-and-error experimentation in which they generate and test hypotheses about the conflict.

First, the parties and the mediator observe the aspects of the dispute. They examine attitudinal or behavioral problems in the interactions of the disputants, disagreements over "facts," compatible and competing interests, interaction dynamics, power relations, and value similarities and differences. From the observations, the mediator tries to identify the central critical situations or causes of the dispute. He or she often uses a framework of explanatory causes and suggested interventions such as those identified in Figure 1. Once the mediator believes that a central cause has been identified, he or she builds a hypothesis.

FIGURE 1 Sphere of Conflict—Causes and Interventions

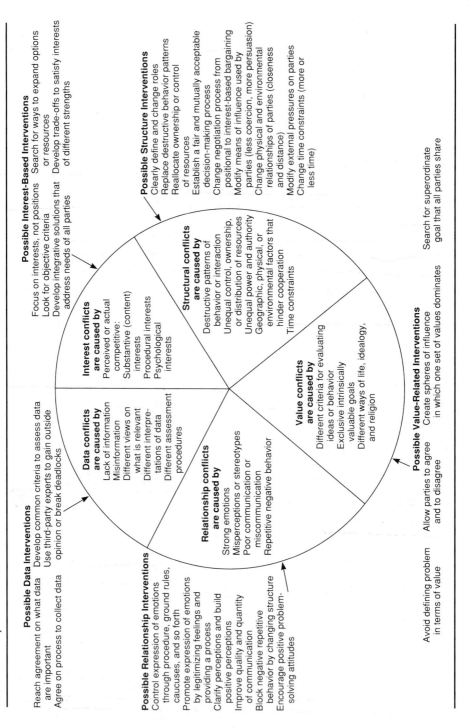

"This conflict is caused by *a,* and if *b* is changed, the parties will be able to move toward agreement." The hypothesis must then be tested.

Testing hypotheses about conflicts involves designing interventions that challenge or modify the attitudes, behaviors, or structural relationship of the disputants. These interventions are often grounded in a theory that identifies a particular cause for the conflict and suggests prescriptive actions. For example, one theory about the cause of conflict has communication as its base. Most communication theories propose that conflict is the result of poor communication in either quality, quantity, or form. The theory postulates that if the *quality* of the information exchanged can be improved, the right *quantity* of communication can be attained, and if these data are put into the *correct form,* the causes of the dispute will be addressed and the participants will move toward resolution.

A mediator following the communications theory of conflict might begin by observing disputants communicating very poorly: One can hardly speak without the other interrupting, they have difficulty focusing on present issues and constantly digress to arguments over past wrongs that tend to escalate the conflict, and the dispute develops into a shouting match. The mediator observes the interaction, hypothesizes that one cause of the dispute is the inability of the disputants to talk with each other in a constructive and restrained manner, and proceeds to experiment with modifications of their communication patterns (quality, quantity, and form) to see if he or she can change the conflict dynamics. The mediator may suggest that they discuss one topic at a time, may obtain their permission to monitor them, may establish ground rules about insults, or may even separate them so that they can communicate only through the mediator.

Each intervention is a test of the theory and a hypothesis that part of the dispute is caused by communication problems, and that if these difficulties can be lessened or eliminated, the parties will have a better chance of reaching settlement. If the desired effect is not achieved, the intervenor may reject the specific move as ineffective and try another. If several interventions based on one theory do not work, the intervenor may shift to another theory and begin trial-and-error testing again. The cycle of hypothesis building and testing is the basic process of intervention and conflict resolution (see Figure 2).

THE STAGES OF MEDIATION

One of the broadest spheres of mediator hypothesis building occurs in the process of conceptualizing the stages of mediation and designing appropriate interventions based on the stage of development that a particular dispute has reached.

The stages of mediation are often difficult to identify. Mediator and negotiator moves seem to blend together into an undifferentiated continuum of interaction. Only through careful observation of negotiations and mediated interventions can distinct stages composed of general moves be identified and hypotheses generated about the critical situations that the disputants will experience.

The stages of mediator intervention fall into roughly two broad categories: work that the mediator performs before joining the parties in joint session, and moves made

FIGURE 2   Mediator Process of Building and Testing a Hypothesis

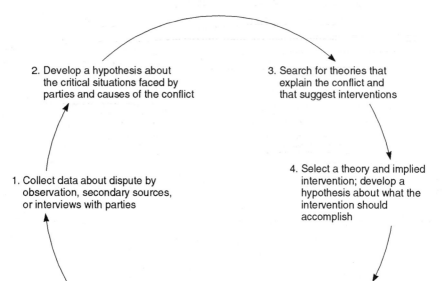

once the mediator has entered into formal negotiations. Five stages occur in the prenegotiation work of the mediator, and seven stages occur after the mediator begins to work jointly with the disputants (see Figure 3).

In each of the twelve stages the mediator will design hypotheses and appropriate strategies and will execute specific moves. These moves are both sequential and developmental and are designed to assist disputing parties in accomplishing specific tasks at particular times in the negotiation process. If a task has not been completed either by the negotiators alone or with the assistance of a mediator, the parties generally encounter great difficulties in moving on to the next stage of negotiation.

Regardless of when a mediator enters negotiations—at the beginning, middle, or end—he or she will usually perform all the general or noncontingent moves. Naturally, the amount of time spent in each stage and the emphasis on each set of moves will vary considerably according to variables that will be discussed in the remaining section of this chapter—level of conflict development, timing of entry, productive conflict resolution capabilities of the disputants, power and influence relations of the parties, negotiation procedures being used, complexity of the issues, and definition of the mediator's task.

VARIABLES THAT INFLUENCE MEDIATION STRATEGIES AND MOVES

Although mediators make a variety of interventions to help parties move through the negotiation and mediation stages, their moves are not perfectly identical from case to case. While there are general patterns of moves, each mediator will have to modify his or her activities according to variables present in the case. The most critical variables that influence interventions are

1. The level of conflict development and the timing of a mediator's entry.
2. The capability of negotiators to resolve their own dispute.
3. The power equality of the disputants and the mediator's role as a power balancer and agent of empowerment.
4. The negotiation procedures used by the parties.
5. The complexity of the issues negotiated.
6. The role and tasks of the mediator as mutually defined by the parties and the intervenor.

I will examine each of these variables and how they affect the role of the mediator and his or her application of general and specific strategies.

Conflict Development and Timing of Entry.   The stage of conflict development and the degree of emotional intensity of the parties influence the tasks that negotiators have to perform. If a mediator enters a dispute in its early stages before extreme issue polarization or the development of intense emotions, he or she will use a different strategy and set of moves to assist the parties than if he or she arrives at a later stage when the parties have been negotiating and have reached a substantive impasse. In viewing mediation as a general process, however, the change in strategy and moves is primarily one of emphasis rather than a specific change in the type of move. Conciliation, for example, generally must occur more at the beginning of negotiations rather than later. If, however, a mediator enters in the later phases of a negotiation, after impasse, for example, he or she will probably still have to conciliate. The mediator will generally have to complete this phase prior to pursuing developmental moves more appropriate to the stage in which the parties have reached impasse.

Capability of Disputants to Resolve Their Own Disputes.   Whether the disputants are capable of resolving their own dispute also strongly affects the mediator's intervention strategies. Parties who are able to negotiate rationally, who are aware of problem-solving procedures, and who appear to be progressing toward a settlement will require little assistance from a mediator. In this situation, the mediator may lend support to the work of the parties merely by his or her presence or by minimal support of the principal negotiators (Perez, 1959; Kolb, 1983). On the other hand, if parties are in the grip of intense emotions, do not have skills or expertise in negotiations or problem-solving procedures, or have reached an impasse on substantive issues, the mediator will probably be more active and more visible in the negotiations. He or she may assist the parties in productively venting strong emotions, narrowing the bargain-

FIGURE 3   Twelve Stages of Mediator Moves and Critical Situations to Be Handled

Stage 1: Initial Contacts with the Disputing Parties
- Making initial contacts with the parties
- Building credibility
- Promoting rapport
- Educating the parties about the process
- Increasing commitment to the procedure

Stage 2: Selecting a Strategy to Guide Mediation
- Assisting the parties to assess various approaches to conflict management and resolution
- Assisting the parties to select an approach
- Coordinating the approaches of the parties

Stage 3: Collecting and Analyzing Background Information
- Collecting and analyzing relevant data about the people, dynamics, and substance of a conflict
- Verifying accuracy of data
- Minimizing the impact of inaccurate or unavailable data

Stage 4: Designing a Detailed Plan for Mediation
- Identifying strategies and consequent noncontingent moves that will enable the parties to move toward agreement
- Identifying contingent moves to respond to situations peculiar to the specific conflict

Stage 5: Building Trust and Cooperation
- Preparing disputants psychologically to participate in negotiations on substantive issues
- Handling strong emotions
- Checking perceptions and minimizing effects of stereotypes
- Building recognition of the legitimacy of the parties and issues
- Building trust
- Clarifying communications

Stage 6: Beginning the Mediation Session
- Opening negotiation between the parties
- Establishing an open and positive tone
- Establishing ground rules and behavioral guidelines
- Assisting the parties in venting emotions
- Delimiting topic areas and issues for discussion
- Assisting the parties in exploring commitments, salience, and influence

FIGURE 3   *(concluded)*

Stage 7: Defining Issues and Setting an Agenda
- Identifying broad topic areas of concern to the parties
- Obtaining agreement on the issues to be discussed
- Determining the sequence for handling the issues

Stage 8: Uncovering Hidden Interests of the Disputing Parties
- Identifying the substantive, procedural, and psychological interests of the parties
- Educating the parties about each other's interests

Stage 9: Generating Options for Settlement
- Developing an awareness among the parties of the need for options
- Lowering commitment to positions or sole alternatives
- Generating options using either positional or interest-based bargaining

Stage 10: Assessing Options for Settlement
- Reviewing the interests of the parties
- Assessing how interests can be met by available options
- Assessing the costs and benefits of selecting options

Stage 11: Final Bargaining
- Reaching agreement through either incremental convergence of positions, final leaps to package settlements, development of a consensual formula, or establishment of a procedural means to reach a substantive agreement

Stage 12: Achieving Formal Settlement
- Identifying procedural steps to operationalize the agreement
- Establishing an evaluation and monitoring procedure
- Formalizing the settlement and creating an enforcement and commitment mechanism

ing range, creating agendas, generating and assessing options, and initiating a variety of other procedures or moves that assist the parties in reaching a settlement.

Power Equality between Disputants.   In order to derive mutually satisfactory and acceptable decisions from negotiations, all parties must have some means of influence, either positive or negative, on other disputants at the table. This is a prerequisite for a settlement that recognizes mutual needs (Lovell, 1952). If the power or influence potentials of the parties are well developed, fairly equal in strength, and recognized by all disputants, the mediator's job will be to assist parties in using their influence effectively while producing mutually satisfactory results. If, however, influence on each other is not equal and one party has the ability to impose an unsatisfactory settlement on another, an agreement that will not hold over time, or a resolution that will result in renewed conflict later, the mediator will have to decide whether and how to assist the weaker party.

Assistance or possible empowerment of the weaker party by the mediator requires very specific intervention moves—activities that shift the mediator's function dangerously close to advocacy. This problem in mediation has been debated among mediators (Bernard, Folger, Weingarten, and Zumeta, 1984). One argument states that a mediator has an obligation to create just settlements and must therefore help empower the underdog to reach equitable and fair agreements (Laue and Cormick, 1978; Suskind, 1981; Haynes, 1981). Another school argues that mediators should not do anything to influence the power relations of disputing parties because it taints the intervenor's impartiality (Bellman, 1982; Stulberg, 1981b).

In examining this question and how it affects the mediator's choice of intervention moves, it is important to distinguish between a mediator assisting in recognizing, organizing, and marshaling existing power of a disputant and a mediator becoming an advocate and assisting in generating new power and influence. The latter strategy clearly shifts the mediator out of his or her impartial position, while the former keeps the mediator within the power boundaries established by the parties. There is no easy answer to this strategic and ethical problem, but it does have an important impact on the types of moves a mediator initiates.

Negotiation Procedures.   Negotiation is a form of joint problem solving. The topical problems that negotiators focus on are often called *issues.* An issue exists because the parties do not agree on a particular topic and because they have perceived or actual exclusive needs or interests.

* * * * *

Parties to a conflict select one of two major negotiation procedures to handle issues in dispute: *positional bargaining* or *interest-based bargaining* (Fisher and Ury, 1981). Positional bargaining usually occurs when a negotiator perceives that contested resources are limited and a distributive solution, one that allocates shares of gains and losses to each party, is the only possible outcome (Walton and McKersie, 1965). Interest-based bargaining, on the other hand, occurs when negotiators seek integrative solutions that meet as many of the needs of both parties as possible (Walton and McKersie, 1965). Generally, interest-based bargaining occurs when parties do not see resources as limited and solutions can be found in which all parties can have at least some of their needs met.

Positional bargaining derives its name from the practice of selecting a series of positions—particular settlement options that meet a party's interests—and presenting these to an opponent as the solution to the issue in question. A party's position may or may not be responsive to the needs or interests of other negotiators. Positions are generally ordered sequentially so that the first position is a large demand and represents a negotiator's maximum expectation of gain should his or her opponent acquiesce. Each subsequent position demands less of an opponent and results in fewer benefits for the initiating party. Characteristically, positional bargaining often commits parties early in negotiations to very specific solutions to issues in dispute and often reduces flexibility to generate other equally acceptable options.

*   *   *   *   *

Disputants often adopt positional bargaining when

- The stakes for winning are high.
- The resources (time, money, psychological benefits, and so forth) are perceived to be limited.
- A win for one side will mean a loss for another.
- Interests of the parties are not interdependent or are contradictory.
- Future relationships have a lower priority than immediate substantive gain.
- All major parties have enough power to damage the others if an impasse in the negotiations occurs (Moore, 1982b).

Interest-based bargaining, in contrast to positional bargaining, is based on different assumptions about the substantive issues to be negotiated, the contents of an acceptable solution, and the process by which an agreement is to be reached.

In interest-based bargaining, the negotiators do not necessarily assume that the substantive resource in question—money, time, behavior, and so forth—is necessarily limited. They do not assume that the resource must be divided into shares in which one bargainer is a winner and the other a loser. The attitude of the interest-based bargainer is that of a problem solver. The goal of negotiation is to find a solution that is mutually satisfactory and results in a win-win outcome.

Interest-based bargainers believe that settlements in negotiations are reached because a party has succeeded in having his or her interests satisfied. *Interests* are specific conditions (or gains) that a party must obtain for an acceptable settlement to occur. Interests are of three broad types: substantive, procedural, and psychological. *Substantive interests* refer to the needs that an individual has for particular tangible objects such as money and time. Substantive interests are usually the central needs on which negotiations focus.

Procedural interests refer to the preferences that a negotiator has for the *way* that the parties discuss their differences and the *manner* in which the bargaining outcome is implemented. Possible procedural interests may be that each person have the opportunity to speak his or her mind, that negotiations occur in an orderly and timely manner, that the parties avoid derogatory verbal attacks, that the plan for implementing the agreement be worked out in detail prior to final settlement, and that a written document or contract should result from bargaining.

Psychological interests refer to the emotional and relationship needs that a negotiator has both during and as a result of negotiations. Negotiators want to have high self-esteem, want to be respected by their opponent, and do not want to be degraded in negotiations. If the relationship is to be ongoing, the negotiators may want to have ongoing positive regard from the other party for their openness to future communication.

* * * * *

Interest-based bargaining begins with an understanding of each of the interests of the two parties, not statements of positions. Often the parties identify their interests and those of other disputants in private and then hold a joint meeting to share their results. Parties discuss and modify their interests based on these early discussions. Once the interests have been revealed, explored, and accepted at least in principle, the parties can begin a mutual search for solutions that will meet their needs. Reaching an agreement requires negotiators to develop settlement options that meet at least some of the combination of substantive, procedural, and psychological needs of all parties.

Interest-based bargaining focuses on the satisfaction of particular interests rather than advocacy of a particular position that may or may not meet the needs of the individuals, as is the case in positional bargaining. The procedure in interest-based bargaining is one of mutual problem solving, similar to the process involved in putting together a puzzle. The parties sit side by side and attempt to develop a mutually acceptable settlement.

Mediators can help parties conduct either positional or interest-based bargaining more efficiently and effectively. Since the goal of mediation is to help parties reach a mutually acceptable settlement, mediators generally have a bias toward interest-based and integrative solutions. Often parties are engaged in a positional process that is destructive to their relationships, is not generating creative options, and is not resulting in wise decisions. One of the mediator's major contributions to the dispute resolution process is assisting the negotiators in making the transition from positional to interest-based bargaining.

Complexity of the Case and Issues Negotiated.   Disputes come in a variety of levels of complexity. The simple-issue landlord-tenant case in which two parties argue over a security deposit is very different from the complexity of a child custody and divorce dispute that involves multiple issues and very complex psychodynamics between the disputants. The latter case may in its own right be very uncomplicated when compared to a multiparty case that involves American Telephone and Telegraph, a local Bell company, multiple independent phone companies, the Public Utilities Commission, and numerous consumer or public interest groups and that centers around multiple and complex technical issues.

Mediators entering disputes must design intervention strategies that respond to the complexity of a specific dispute. In one case, detailed data collection procedures may be required to understand the causes and dynamics of the conflict, while in another case a simple intake interview at the first joint session with the parties is sufficient. In some cases the mediator must break a particularly difficult impasse, and, when successful, may withdraw and return the parties to negotiations on their own. In other cases, the mediator may play an active role throughout negotiations and provide the major procedural framework for negotiations. In exploring the stages of mediation in later chapters, it is important to consider the complexity of the dispute to determine the amount of detail required in the intervention.

Definition of the Mediator's Role and Types of Interventions. The final variable that affects the noncontingent and contingent moves of a mediator is the definition of the tasks and role that the mediator is to perform in the negotiations. Mediators differ significantly when deciding their role and involvement in promoting successful negotiations. The division usually occurs when determining how much the mediator should focus on process and substance.

One school argues that mediators should focus primarily on the process of negotiations and leave decisions about the substantive content as the exclusive domain of the parties (Stulberg, 1981b). Procedurally oriented mediators define their role this way for a variety of reasons. First, mediators often believe that the parties are better informed about the substantive issues in dispute than any third party could ever be. These intervenors believe that the best quality decision is that determined by the parties. Second, mediators from this school believe that what the parties need is procedural help, not a substantive suggestion or decision. Third, these intervenors believe that the parties' commitment to implement and adhere to a settlement will be enhanced if they make the substantive decisions themselves, as opposed to having the deal decided or forged by the intervenor. Finally, the mediators of this school believe that a focus on the process and an impartial stance toward substance builds trust between the intervenor and disputants, decreases the risk to the parties of involving another party in the dispute, and makes them more open to procedural assistance.

Many labor-management mediators, especially intervenors from the Federal Mediation and Conciliation Service, subscribe to this role for the mediator (Kolb, 1983). They see themselves as "orchestrators" of a process that enables the parties to make their own substantive decisions.

Some environmental mediators also follow this procedurally oriented definition of the mediator's role. Bellman (1982) generally does not try to influence the substantive outcome of a dispute even if he ethically disagrees with the outcome, considers the settlement environmentally unsound, or believes that it is based on inaccurate or inadequate information. He sees himself purely as a process consultant.

Some family mediators also adhere to the procedurally oriented approach to intervention. They argue that in a divorce, for example, the parents generally know what is best for both the children and the family system as a whole (Phear, 1984; Saposnek, 1985). The parents do not need a substantive expert to tell them what to do. What they need is procedural help to assist them in problem solving.

The other school of thought argues that although the mediator is impartial and neutral, this does not mean that he or she should not work with the parties directly on substantive matters to develop a fair and just decision according to the intervenor's values. Suskind (1981, pp. 46–47), an environmental mediator, argues that intervenors should be involved in substantive decisions when (1) "the impacts of negotiated agreement [will affect] underrepresented or unrepresented groups," (2) there is "the possibility that joint net gains have not been maximized,'' (3) the parties are not aware of the "long-term spill-over effects of the settlements," and (4) the precedents that they set "may be detrimental to the parties or the broader public." Suskind further notes that "although such intervention may make it difficult to retain the appearance of neutrality and the trust of the active parties, environmental mediators cannot fulfill their responsibilities to the community-at-large if they remain passive" (p. 47). Some labor-management mediators also belong to this school. These "deal-makers" intervene substantively when the parties are uninformed, ill-prepared to negotiate, or unaware of mutually acceptable substantive settlements (Kolb, 1983).

Child custody and divorce mediators also have advocates in the second school. Saposnek (1983) argues that the mediator should advocate the unrepresented interests of the children in negotiations between the parents and believes that the mediator should intervene and influence the substantive outcome if those interests are violated and not taken into consideration. Coogler (1978) also urges the mediator to engage in substantive negotiations and advocates that the intervenor write a letter of nonconcurrence that is sent to the court if the mediator seriously disagrees with the settlement.

Haynes (1981), another family mediator, believes that the intervenor should be active in power balancing help to define the terms of the substantive decision. Haynes, Coogler, and Saposnek directly disregard the concept of substantive impartiality as a critical component of the mediator's role.

There is a spectrum along which mediators place themselves in defining their degree of involvement in the procedure and substance of negotiations. On one side are those who advocate mostly procedural interventions; on the other side are advocates of substantive involvement by the mediator that may include actually forging the decision. Between them are mediators who pursue a role with mixed involvement in process and substance.

I lean strongly toward the process end of the spectrum because I believe that the parties should have the primary responsibility for self-determination. On rare occasions, however, the mediator has an ethical responsibility to raise critical questions about substantive options under consideration by the parties. These situations include cases where the agreement appears to be extremely inequitable to one or more of the parties, does not look as if it will hold over time, seems likely to result in renewed conflict at a later date, or where the terms of settlement are so loose (or confining) that implementation is not feasible. I believe the mediator should also intervene in cases involving the potential for violence or actual violence to one or more parties, either primary or secondary.

Depending on the role that the mediator or the mediator and the parties assign the intervenor, he or she will have to decide which types of interventions he or she will perform. In defining interventions, the mediator must decide on (1) the level of intervention, (2) the target of intervention, (3) the focus of intervention, and (4) the intensity of intervention.

The *level of intervention* refers to how much the mediator concentrates on helping negotiators move through the general critical situation, for example, the stages of bargaining, versus a focus on particular idiosyncratic problems that are pushing the parties toward impasse. In some disputes the parties may need assistance to break a particular deadlock, while others will need mediator assistance throughout the bargaining process.

The *target of intervention* refers to the person or people to whom the mediator directs his or her moves. Should moves be directed to all parties, to a relationship within the group such as a subgroup or team, or to a particular person? In a postmarital dispute, for example, should the mediator focus on changing the ex-wife's move, the ex-husband's, or both, or should he or she focus on the entire family system, including children, ex-spouses, stepparents, and grandparents? In a community dispute, should the mediator focus on the spokespeople, specific team members, the team as a whole, or the constituents of the parties?

The *focus of intervention* refers to the particular critical situations at which the mediator directs his or her moves. The mediator may focus his or her energies on changing the *psychological relationship* of parties to each other. This is often referred to as a conciliation. He or she may aim at creating the psychological conditions that are necessary for productive negotiations. The mediator may also focus on changing the *negotiation process* or the procedure that is being used by one or more people to solve the dispute. The focus may be on the process for moving through the stages of solving a specific problem, such as how to help a party make a proposal that will be acceptable to the other side.

The focus may also be on changing the *substance* or *content* of the dispute. The mediator may look for ways to explore data, to expand the number of acceptable options on the negotiation table, to narrow the choices when the parties are overwhelmed with possibilities, or to integrate proposals made by the disputants.

Finally, the intervenor may focus on changing the relationship *structure* among the parties. This may mean influencing their personal or interactive relationship in regard to such factors as power, communication patterns, face-to-face versus private negotiations, team structure, or a party's relationship to its constituents.

*   *   *   *   *

The Role of the Mediator

Thomas Colosi

Because the essence of negotiations is to provide an opportunity for parties or disputants to exchange promises and thus resolve their differences, some measure of trust between the parties is critical. While some students of negotiation contend that trust is irrelevant to negotiations, it is hard to see how a serious exchange of promises can occur without trust. Each side must have some confidence that the other will keep its word once a promise is given (whether the promises involve benefits or threats). Trust need not be blind, of course. It may be supported by information that is uncovered and processed in the course of negotiation; it may rest on relationships that have strengthened in the course of negotiation; ultimately it may emerge even from the shared experience of coming to understand the negotiation process.

Parties can reach an impasse in negotiations, where no further discussion is possible because either their trust has run out or there was too little trust in the first place. Indeed, in the absence of trust, negotiations might never even begin. Parties with no trust between them can be said to be in a trust vacuum. This underlies their fears of each other. Moreover, it interferes with the very communication that might dispel such fears. Without open lines of productive communication, very little education can take place.

The necessary trust between the parties may be developed in three steps. First, a mediator must work to win the trust of the parties. Next, the mediator educates the parties about the negotiation process (not the mediation process) and works to encourage them to transfer their trust from him to it. Finally, the mediator persuades the parties to begin trusting each other, again using the negotiation process as a vehicle to demonstrate that trust.

THE EVOLUTION OF TRUST

Trust in the Outside Third-Party Mediator

The mediator wins the trust of the parties principally by demonstrating that he or she is truly neutral. The capacity of a mediator to win trust may be at its highest if intervention occurs when the situation is particularly polarized and trust between the parties is at its lowest.

From "Negotiation in the Public and Private Sectors," in *American Behavioral Scientist* (Newbury Park, Calif.: Sage Publications, Inc., 1983), pp. 237-47. Reprinted by permission of Sage Publications, Inc.

Others contend that a mediator should intervene before the parties are frozen into positions, but the particular mediator (and mediation in general) may very well be rejected early in the dispute. At best, the mediator may be underutilized or "bargained with" by parties, both of which make it difficult for him to determine their true objectives.

Just as nature abhors a vacuum, the negotiation process abhors the absence of trust. When parties are polarized, they also have a better idea of what they want the mediator to do. The issues and alternatives are better defined and, as a result, the disputants will be more likely to understand that it is they (and not the mediator) who must assume responsibility for the outcome of negotiations. This is, after all, a fundamental objective of the mediator. In addition, the more time the mediator is involved in the dispute, the less he or she will appear neutral to everyone involved. This perception, of course, can sabotage the mediator's effectiveness.

Mediators may use a number of techniques to demonstrate their neutrality and win the parties' trust. Mediators must learn, for example, how to listen and not say much; likewise, they cannot reveal their emotions and attitudes. Taking care to express only positive or neutral opinions of the groups involved in the dispute is one important approach. Mediators should listen to people's ideas with an open mind, not only to obtain a comprehensive view of the problem but to set an example by showing that there is little risk in entertaining other points of view. Mediators should emphasize that they are only there to help the parties, and have absolutely no decision-making authority regarding the substance or the issues. Mediators must also assure the parties that all conversations will be held in strict confidence. Additionally, a hard-won reputation for helping people in other cases obviously provides a solid foundation for winning the parties' trust.

A mediator may also be able to use other processes for gaining trust. For example, parties who shy away from mediation nevertheless may be willing to engage in fact-finding. Viewed narrowly, fact-finding is a process of gathering information, understanding and organizing the issues in a dispute, and giving advice about a possible settlement; the parties are not bound by the fact-finder's recommendations. Sophisticated mediators, however, see broader potential in fact-finding: It can serve as a first step in negotiations, the mechanism by which the mediator gets to meet with all the parties and begins to win their trust.

The process of enhancing trust in the mediator is not without risk. Inexperienced mediators frequently feel empowered by the confidence and acceptance that the disputants may quickly show toward them. Mediators must keep in mind, however, that their perception of power comes from the parties' need to fill the trust vacuum. Furthermore, their perceived power is only an early stage in a developmental process that ideally should lead to the empowering of the negotiators themselves through the help of the mediator.

Trust in the Process

Having obtained the parties' trust, the mediator must next work to transfer it from himself to the negotiation process. The parties must be shown that the negotiation process is the way through their problem. They must become comfortable with the negotiation process, experiment with it, and use it to achieve success. In the early stages of a dispute, the best kind of intervenor often will avoid substantive issues and concentrate instead on procedural matters in order to educate the parties about negotiation and mediation. The parties should know that mediation is available if they want it, but they should not move into mediation until they really need it.

Because negotiating skills are not taught in our society to any great extent, there is very poor understanding about how the negotiation process works. People tend to concentrate on whether or not another *party* should be trusted, rather than on trusting the process itself. Learning to trust negotiations is a useful interim step between no trust and trust in another party. Disputants who do not take the interim step usually end up using alternative dispute resolution processes. In some cases, the alternative may be litigation; in others, a strike or a riot. The role of the mediator is to call attention to the need for establishing an understanding of, and confidence in, the negotiation process before trust in the other parties is sought.

Trust among the Parties

Once the interim steps have been taken and trust in both the mediator and in the negotiation process is established, the professional mediator must work hard to transfer that trust to the parties themselves. This can occur in two ways. First, the mediator acts as a role model: demonstrating good listening skills; showing respect for other people's opinions and constraints; and creating an atmosphere of trust by encouraging the negotiators to develop a statement of common goals. Second, trust is established among the parties though practice. The preliminary stages of negotiation involve some cooperation among the parties in relatively simple process decisions. These may involve minor procedural matters—"housekeeping issues" if you will—yet over time they provide a shared experience that allows the parties slowly to develop a more trusting relationship, one that is essential when more fundamental, high-stakes issues are tackled.

The case that follows illustrates how these trust-building steps are implemented in practice.

Building Trust: An Example in Community Multilateral Negotiations

In 1973 a riot in a Rochester, New York, high school sent 16 students and teachers (8 blacks and 8 whites) to the hospital. I was one of two intervenors from the American Arbitration Association's National Center for Dispute Resolution in Washington, D.C., who entered the dispute as fact-finders. In truth, we borrowed from the public sector labor-management model to characterize our roles, using the Newman model of "mediators wearing fact-finders' hats." The particular intervenors were teamed because one is white and the other black.

About 18 different organizations, representing students, specific racial and ethnic groups, teachers, parents, and local citizens, were identified by the school board and one another as interested parties. They were invited by the American Arbitration Association to meet each other and the fact-finders. The purpose of the meeting was to determine what had caused the riot and to try to set up a process for avoiding future disruption. Once this group was assembled, one of the first questions that had to be answered was whether still other parties and organizations should be involved. Some groups already present voiced objections about inviting certain others, contending that they would ruin the process. Nevertheless, as mediator/fact-finders, we encouraged those who were involved to invite the threatening groups to participate on the ground that any outsiders who had enough power to stymie the process would likely be important to implementing any agreement. Ultimately, the original participants did decide who would be at the table and added several parties. In effect, the negotiators defined themselves.

Once the group's composition was established, the parties had to determine how decisions would be made. Two competing models of decision making were offered: majority vote and full consensus. Some conservative groups supported the majority vote, while the minority organizations felt better protected by full consensus; indeed, they threatened to leave the table over this issue. The intervenors kept the parties together by observing that an effective solution to the high school problem would be possible only if all the groups present were involved in the negotiations. The intervenors pointed out that a settlement unanimously endorsed by a group as broadly based as those convened would carry a great deal of clout with the school board and the public. The parties remained at the table because they had begun to believe that some common goals and solutions were possible, even though these had yet to take concrete form.

Each group's attitudes on the decision-making issue was affected, in part, by its own internal structure and experience. Some groups that were accustomed to operating under an authoritarian model assumed that the mediator/fact-finders would make the decisions. Others thought that committees would be formed to discuss the issues and be given delegated powers. Majority rule, with and without minority opinion reports, were other suggestions. Before long, participants came to see how differently they all made decisions, and began to educate one another about the relative merits of each process.

The intervenors had to conduct side-bar meetings (caucuses with groups in isolation from other groups) because of one minority group's flat refusal to participate under any process except full consensus. The mediator/fact-finders created doubts in the conservative camp as to the viability of the majority rule process by asking its members if they realized how much power was available to them through the full consensus process. The intervenors pointed out that a simple veto could be exercised by any group to prevent proposals and directions that were perceived to be inappropriate or undesirable from being adopted. After many internal discussions with the conservative group, full consensus decision making was accepted.

Continuing the process discussions, we next suggested to the group that they begin their negotiations by agreeing upon a common goal. The initial proposals were sweeping and often contradictory. Some said that the goal should be to stop busing. Others said that desegregation should be eliminated. One proposal was to abolish the school board. Even amendments to the U.S. Constitution were put forth. It was clear that the parties were still a long way from reaching a mutually acceptable goal.

We worked patiently in a variety of process configurations and settings to try to close the many gaps. Talks took place chiefly in informal meetings. Internal discussions took place within some of the parties; there was also direct talk between the parties, both with and without the mediators. In the course of these discussions, the mediators came to realize that despite the parties' obvious differences, they shared a common attitude: fear. They feared each other, but beyond that they feared what might happen in the schools and in the community if accommodation could not be achieved. Still, they were not ready to trust each other to be reasonable or to deliver on promises.

The parties met over a six-month period with the mediators and a local coordinator. A church basement was used as the formal meeting area. There was near-perfect attendance at all the weekly and biweekly meetings; no group pulled out of the process. Ultimately, the groups agreed on a common goal: to have *safe schools*. In retrospect, the goal may seem obvious, yet the fact that it eluded the parties for so long shows that polarization and lack of trust can keep disputants from recognizing their shared interests that, under other circumstances, might be easily perceived. Once the common goal was articulated, the parties tried to formulate an overall strategy for achieving it. Their initial strategy was to continue negotiations. Trust in the negotiation process and in each other was beginning to be established, and as the parties assumed greater responsibility for tasks, the mediators of course did less.

The outside neutrals entered this polarized situation as fact-finders, worked to establish trust—first in themselves and then in the negotiation process—by showing the parties how mediation could help them. By encouraging the parties to work together on small, seemingly procedural issues, the intervenors demonstrated how people with different priorities and outlooks could work cooperatively.

Once trust is established in the negotiation process and in each other, the negotiators will find that they no longer need a mediator. When this happens, the mediator should begin to leave the dispute, as his job may essentially be over. The mediator may make himself available for other process-management tasks, of course, or to resume mediation if the trust relationship breaks down for any reason.

THE MEDIATOR'S CAPACITY TO RAISE AND MAINTAIN DOUBTS

Effective mediators create and maintain doubts by raising questions about alternatives and implications that the negotiators may not have considered or fully appreciated. Like any good negotiator, the mediator avoids flat statements. If, for instance, a mediator wants a negotiator to think about the reaction of the negotiator's superiors to a certain proposal, the mediator is better off asking, "What would your boss say?" rather than declaring, "Your boss may not support you on that." The same axiom would apply in a situation in which a mediator and a negotiator are discussing a negotiator's decision to leave the bargaining table. Assuming that the negotiators are using full consensus in their decision-making process, the mediator might privately say to the reluctant negotiator, "The other parties might come to some decision in your absence. Have you considered the implications of your not being present to veto decisions that would hurt your side?" The use of questions rather than statements gives negotiators more room to respond and more freedom to consider what the mediator is saying. It also allows the mediator to play a more neutral, laissez-faire role as declarations tend to be more leading and value-loaded than questions. The negotiators are thus subtly encouraged to take maximum responsibility in the negotiation process.

As noted earlier, most important negotiating takes place in the internal team caucuses. As a consequence, this usually is where the mediator is most active as well. Private meetings are normally the best forum for the mediator to raise doubts.

During horizontal (across-the-table) negotiations, each team tries to educate the other about its position. The negotiators try to raise new doubts in the minds of their counterparts. As a result, a new set of assumptions and proposals may become plausible, and new issues and problems may arise as well. In this phase of negotiation, the stabilizers and nonstabilizers tend to open up to each other in the caucuses when these new concerns are discussed. If the quasi mediator is unable to create doubts in the nonstabilizer's mind, an outside, neutral mediator may be enlisted before the team resorts to autocratic decision making or internal disciplinary measures to bring the dissenter along. Committed to stability, the mediator concentrates on internal team bargaining and similarly tries to raise doubts about the viability of nonsettlement in the mind of the nonstabilizer. Sometimes the emphasis is less on outcomes and more on process. If the nonstabilizer does not trust the negotiation process because of preconceived notions, the mediator must raise doubts about the competing process alternatives. By contrast, of course, effective mediators would not work to create doubt in the minds of the stabilizers, since this group wants settlement.

Parties Who Will Not Settle

The mediator's function is thus to create and maintain doubts in the minds of individual negotiators who oppose settlement. What can a mediator do if an entire team is composed of nonstabilizers?

Some negotiators enter the process quite committed to talking but not to settling. For them negotiation may only be a device to stall for time. They may be waiting for the other side to exhaust its strike fund or other resources. They may have calculated that in time public opinion will shift in their favor. Time may be needed to prepare a lawsuit, launch a media campaign, or use some other external pressure on the other side. It may simply be that these "negotiators" prefer the status quo to any foreseeable alternative.

When one team is negotiating just to buy time, the situation between the contending parties is similar in many respects to the internal process that occurs within a team between stabilizers and nonstabilizers. The nonstabilizers are the ones who must be convinced by the quasi mediator (and the stabilizers) to remain at the table, to listen to the other teams, to consider their arguments, and, ideally, to revise their positions to enable their negotiating team to offer deliverable proposals. The quasi mediator first tries to raise doubts in the mind of the uncooperative teammates about the consequences of nonsettlement. (What losses would have to be incurred: a strike, litigation, violence; can the group afford such losses?)

A team dedicated to nonsettlement occupies the same position in horizontal negotiations as does the nonstabilizer within his team. It, too, is uninterested in settlement. In this instance, however, it is the mediator rather than the quasi mediator who steps in. Although the person is different, the role is much the same. The mediator relies on the same basic technique of raising doubts about the team's decision to stall, probing to see if all the implications of nonsettlement have been evaluated.

In any case when it becomes obvious that a party has carefully considered its position and has determined that settlement is not in its interest, then, after appropriate probing, the mediator ultimately must accept the party's own judgment. When a party believes that it is better to stall than to settle, the mediator might reasonably continue with the process if the other party accedes.

NEGOTIATION AND LITIGATION

Deadlines are important monitors of the parties' success at reaching an agreement. Timing is a critical factor in a mediator's assessment of a party's willingness to settle. When there is no court-imposed or other "natural" deadline (for example, the expiration of a labor contract), the mediator can help the parties set the clock. He can warn the parties that if settlement is not reached by a certain time, then the parties may have to proceed without him. Mediators have to take care in using this tactic. The deadline should not be artificial; disputes are not poker games for bluffing. Instead, the mediator should use his general experience, combined with his knowledge of the specific dispute, to determine at what future point a failure to agree would show that his time was spent inefficiently.

The difficulty a mediator may have in getting negotiators to settle within a time limit gives much support to arguments that favor the deadlines imposed by the litigation process. In litigation, deadlines are perceived to be firmer and more believable. Disputes therefore can be settled within a set period of time. Although some proponents of negotiation extoll it as an alternative to the courts, nothing settles a dispute better than the combined force of the strong arm of the court (or an arbitrator) and active negotiation.

Negotiation is often called an "alternative" dispute resolution process, a characterization that implicitly regards the judicial system as dominant. This view also seems predicated on a belief that negotiation and litigation represent entirely divergent paths, yet practice often reveals that the two can be inextricably bound.

This point is illustrated by a heated land use dispute in New York State in which negotiation and litigation occurred in tandem. A group of Mohawk Indians occupied some open land, and town officials moved to have them evicted. Before the state police were deployed, however, help was sought from the National Center for Dispute Settlement. The center (a division of the American Arbitration Association) was contacted to serve as "Rumor Control Experts." (This term was carefully chosen to help the intervenors win the trust of all the parties, as rumors were potentially harmful to everyone.) Under that authority, representatives of the center began the delicate process of building trust. In time, the process came to be directed explicitly at negotiation. Prosecutorial actions were held in abeyance. Nevertheless, the specter of a court-imposed resolution kept the process on track. The mediators assured the parties that no action would be taken by the court so long as the negotiation process was reported as being fruitful. Neither side was confident what the judge would order if negotiation broke down.

In disputes that erupt spontaneously (such as the one just described), parties often find themselves simultaneously involved in lawsuits and negotiations. Usually their lawyers are likewise involved in both processes. But is a lawyer the best representative for a party in a negotiation process? Certainly, lawyers are assumed to be good negotiators. Yet the parties themselves may be just as good if they are educated properly about the process. Moreover, many lawyers are biased in favor of the judicial process and act with little enthusiasm for negotiation. Sophisticated clients could become knowledgeable about the negotiation process (using the mediator as a mentor, if necessary) and employ lawyers for advice on how the negotiations could influence the simultaneous litigation. In such a case, the lawyers should not take over the negotiation process, though their advice could be useful. The mediator, in turn, could help the negotiator and the lawyers coordinate their respective responsibilities. In a sense, this is just another example of building team cohesion: It is similar to the work a mediator does to produce greater harmony among the stabilizers and nonstabilizers.

*   *   *   *   *

When Negotiations Fail:
Causes of Breakdown and Tactics
for Breaking the Stalemate

Bryan M. Downie

There have been a number of articles in *Negotiation Journal* that provide counsel to negotiating parties on how they might improve their negotiations, particularly in cases where talks have failed or threaten to do so (for example, see Bazerman and Sondak, 1988; Chen and Underwood, 1988; Fisher, 1985; McCreary, 1989). The assumption underlying this literature is that the parties could preempt a breakdown in their negotiations by utilizing the tactics of "principled negotiation"—that is, by avoiding positions, exploring interests, separating people from the problem, utilizing a one-text procedure, or following other integrative techniques. This view flows, at least in part, from the approach proposed in *Getting to Yes* (Fisher and Ury, 1981).

Fisher and Ury (1981): 10–11) define principled negotiation as follows:

> At the Harvard Negotiation Project we have been developing an alternative to positional bargaining: a method of negotiation explicitly designed to produce wise outcomes efficiently and amicably. This method, called principled negotiation or negotiation on the merits, can be boiled down to four basic points.
>
> These four points define a straightforward method of negotiation that can be used under any circumstance. Each point deals with a basic element of negotiation, and suggests what you should do about it.
>
> People: Separate the people from the problem.
> Interests: Focus on interests, not positions.
> Options: Generate a variety of possibilities before deciding what to do.
> Criteria: Insist that the result be based on some objective standard.

There is a great deal of merit in "principled negotiation" and in utilizing other similar tactics. This article is not intended to denigrate or dismiss the literature that embraces those concepts. However, some negotiations are certain to be protracted and doomed to failure or breakdown because of factors outside the control of the involved

---

Reprinted from Bryan M. Downie, "When Negotiations Fail: Causes of Breakdown and Tactics for Breaking the Stalemate," *Negotiation Journal*, April 1991, pp. 175–86. Used with permission of the author and Plenum Publishing Corporation.

parties. The problem-solving and principled negotiation literature needs to be expanded to offer suggestions to the parties for dealing with those types of situations.[1]

For example, McKersie (1989) has commented on the Eastern Airlines-IAM (International Association of Machinists) strike and has attributed the failure of negotiations in that case to personalities. This may be true in that particular case. But it is equally true that in other cases failure, or breakdown, is due not to the actions of the actors at the table but to extraneous causes. In this article, I will illustrate the innate intractability of some negotiations by describing a 1987 case involving the same union (the IAM) in negotiations with a different company (Air Canada), and then exploring the implications of this for conflict resolution and principled negotiation.

Specifically, the purposes of this article are as follows: (1) to present a case based on field research that illustrates the type of external factors that often lead to negotiation breakdown and stalemate; (2) to illustrate that the choices the parties can exercise in negotiations, and the substantive outcomes they can accept, are often greatly constrained by factors external to the table; (3) to itemize the tactics actually used by the negotiating parties in the case, and the third party assigned to the dispute, to break the stalemate; and (4) to draw some lessons for future research in order to extend and strengthen principled negotiation and conflict resolution techniques. I will be arguing that there is a need to conceive of principled negotiation not only as a process between the major actors sitting at the table but also as a structure that must embrace and satisfy wider interests and concerns.

THE SITUATION

In late 1987, negotiations between Air Canada and the International Association of Machinists broke down and this was followed by a rotating strike (members walked off the job at a different location each day), then a full strike, and finally, a shutdown of the entire operation by the company. The airline was shut down for 19 days before a settlement was negotiated with the assistance of one of Canada's top labor mediators. Moreover, several weeks *prior* to the rotating strike and shutdown, the union introduced what became known as a "phantom strike" when union leaders announced their unequivocal intention of calling a strike at the airline. This announcement led to a dramatic decline in business and revenue for Air Canada as the public ceased to consider the company a reliable carrier and shifted their reservations to the company's main rival. The ensuing strike and shutdown, of course, also resulted in a large loss of revenue and market share (in the short run) for the company. The shutdown also imposed economic loss on IAM members and on members of the other bargaining units at the company.

My analysis is based on extensive field research with the major actors in the dispute. I spent several months examining company documents related to the negotiations (including the minutes of the negotiations). Extensive interviews were conducted with the corporate executives who were directly and indirectly involved in the negotiations, with all of the union officials directly and indirectly involved in the negotiations and in day-to-day labor relations, and with the labor mediator who helped the parties resolve their dispute.[2]

THE NEGOTIATIONS

For the purpose of analysis, the negotiations can be divided into two parts. Stage 1 encompasses the period from 14 April 1987, when the negotiations began, to 14 October 1987, when a first settlement (which was reached on 15 September 1987) was *not* ratified by the membership. Stage 2 encompasses the negotiations and activities from the ratification vote (October 14) to December 15, when a second agreement, which was subsequently ratified, was reached. The key dates are presented in Figure 1.

Both parties felt, up until September, that a strike was highly probable. Indeed, little progress was made towards settlement throughout the summer months. This led to the appointment of a third-party neutral in September. Under federal labor law in Canada, before a union can strike, the parties must be assisted by a conciliation commissioner who has the authority to mediate and, if mediation fails to bring about a settlement, to issue a fact-finding report with or without recommendations. The report is released to the parties and to the public.

The commissioner who was appointed to the Air Canada/IAM dispute is one of Canada's most effective mediators and, in current dispute resolution parlance, an "activist" third party, viz., strong and forceful. To the surprise of both parties, after intensive around-the-clock negotiations in a Montreal hotel in mid-September, a settlement was reached. Significantly (as things turned out), the ratification vote was not scheduled for a month.

During the period between the tentative settlement and the ratification vote, a highly publicized agreement was reached between Chrysler Canada and the Canadian Auto Workers. This settlement had a very notable impact at Air Canada. The agreement included a breakthrough on a cutting-edge issue in Canadian industrial relations, the indexation of pensions against increases in the Consumer Price Index. Indexation had been an issue in the earlier negotiations at Air Canada, and in mid-October (at least in part because of the Chrysler settlement), the IAM membership at the company

FIGURE 1   Key Dates in the 1987 Air Canada/IAM Negotiations

Stage 1
14 April 1987—negotiations begin.
15 September 1987—tentative agreement reached.

Stage 2
14 October 1987—negative ratification vote.
21 October 1987—negotiations reconvene with conciliation commissioner.
27 October 1987—release of conciliation commissioner's report.
3 November 1987—negotiations resume between the parties.
14 November 1987—union indicates it will strike ("phantom strike").
25 November 1987—rotating strikes begin.
27 November 1987—full strike begins/Air Canada shuts down.
13 December 1987—mediator-assisted talks begin.
15 December 1987—settlement reached.

rejected the tentative agreement. Negotiations would have to start up again and the "playing field" had clearly changed in the dispute.

The unratified September settlement at Air Canada had been a two-year agreement that provided a 4 percent increase in the first year and a 4 percent in the second year. The agreement also included a pension improvement—a reduction from 60 months to 48 months for calculating final average earnings for pension benefits. Following rejection of this settlement by the IAM membership, the negotiations quickly became deadlocked.

It is true that the parties began to escalate their dispute at this time, but the conflict was not the result of escalation followed by rigidity and suspicion. Pruitt and Rubin (1986, p. 265) note, quite correctly, that disputes can become a "pit" that the parties "jointly engineer." In the case at hand, however, Air Canada and the IAM found themselves in a quagmire that included *real* differences and complexity. Stalemate occurred because of the nature of issues; the external pressures on the corporation; union preferences, politics, and internal structure; and externally imposed differences and dilemmas with respect to concession making. Each of these will be discussed.

THE NATURE OF THE ISSUES

The parties returned to the bargaining table on October 21 (a week after the first settlement had been rejected) with the same conciliation commissioner who had mediated the settlement in September. He was unable to make any progress toward a second settlement through mediation and released a two-page report to the Minister of Labor the following day which included the following:

> The Union's position is that without a 7.2 percent increase in wages for one year *and* a plan to index pensions for both current and future retirees, no settlement is possible. To achieve these goals they claim to be prepared to strike. (commissioner's emphasis).

The commissioner's report criticized the union's position on wages. The IAM's position, he argued, ignored two key facts: (1) the rejected settlement of four percent in the first year and four percent in the second year was higher than those of any other group bargaining with Air Canada; and (2) the union had recently reached a tentative agreement with Air Canada's main competitor (CAIL) for 4 percent in the first year, 4 percent in the second year, and 5 percent in the third year.

On the issue of indexed pensions, the union's position at this point was that the funds for indexing would come out of the company's pension fund "surplus." Therefore, the union argued, the demand was a noncost item. The company's position at this point in the negotiations was that no other Air Canada bargaining unit and no other company in the industry had indexed pensions. The company estimated the cost of the union demand at $21 million per year. Perhaps more importantly, the indexing issue was a symbolic one and had far-reaching significance in Canadian industrial relations at that time. Labor and management across the country, as well as the general public, were following the negotiations with great interest to see if there would be a breakthrough on indexed pensions at a major Canadian corporation. Therefore, both parties had broader constituencies watching their negotiations to see if either side would bend on the issue.

Neither the wage nor the pension issue on its own would be easy to resolve. Both were "either-or" issues; that is, the issues per se had no middle ground. Air Canada knew that a settlement that included *any* movement on *either* issue would have important repercussions for future collective bargaining with the IAM and its other unions. For example, as the conciliation commissioner noted, the company had settled with its other unions for the same terms as the first agreement with the IAM. Any improvement on either issue would have a ripple effect throughout the company. On the other hand, in light of the ratification vote and feedback from its membership, the union had to negotiate some improvement on *both* issues.

EXTERNAL PRESSURES ON THE CORPORATION

The dispute, then, was a two-issue dispute—wages and indexed pensions—with no middle ground within each issue and with no trade-off point between the two issues. The company was also concerned with two other factors. First, for competitive reasons, Air Canada had little or no negotiating room following rejection of the September settlement. As noted, the first settlement was essentially identical to the one negotiated by the same union with Air Canada's major competitor in the product market. Air Canada was in a major battle with that competitor for market share, and the competitor already had an advantage in terms of labor costs.

Secondly, if the company agreed to indexed pensions, Air Canada's costs would be out of line with its principal competitor (and this would be the perception of outsiders) at a time when Air Canada was going to be privatized. The company at that time was a Crown corporation owned by the Canadian government. The federal government, however, was on the verge of approving plans for privatization, and a public stock offering was to take place in a few months. Top executives at Air Canada were in favor of privatization and wanted the company's stock to sell at the highest possible price because it had very large capital requirements. Those in the marketplace believed that an aberrant settlement would have a negative effect on the stock offering. Further, decision makers at the company were concerned that the federal government would not push forward to privatize if it appeared that labor relations at Air Canada were being mismanaged.

UNION PREFERENCES, POLITICS, AND STRUCTURE

The union had consistently opposed privatization of the corporation. It was of the view that there would be greater pressure for union concessions from a private (rather than a Crown) corporation. Because the likelihood of privatization had been very great at the time, union negotiators had been under pressure to gain an exceptional settlement in what would probably be the last round of negotiations with a government-owned corporation. When the first settlement was rejected, the union leadership was under renewed pressure from the membership to gain breakthroughs in both wages and indexed pensions. The membership apparently saw this round as its last opportunity to make significant gains.[3] A breakthrough on the second issue was particularly important to the membership because of the highly publicized Chrysler Canada agreement on indexed pensions. But this pressure was most intense from the Montreal membership. On the other hand, because of rapidly escalating consumer prices in Toronto, the membership in that city wanted emphasis placed on wages and had voted to reject the first settlement because they felt the package did not include enough "up-front" money.

The same team for the union that had negotiated the first agreement came to the table for the new round of talks and reflected the above developments. The union team was not only split into militants and moderates, but also there were different preferences between various members on the two outstanding issues. For example, the highest preference of those from Montreal was a breakthrough on pensions while those from Toronto had a higher preference for a breakthrough with regard to "up-front" money.

The union negotiating team, then, lacked cohesion, and the IAM's structure (under its constitution) added additional complexity to the negotiations. Those who were elected to negotiate for the membership were engaged only during negotiations. The individuals who would administer the collective agreement were *not* among those elected to negotiate. This arrangement obviously reduced the accountability of those negotiating. Furthermore, there had been a struggle for power, and a shift in power, between the Toronto and Montreal executives (the two largest locals). In recent years, power had shifted to the Toronto executive. This split, too, made the negotiations more difficult, because it further reduced the cohesiveness of the union table team.

Finally, the union membership had decided to strike long before they actually introduced economic sanctions. In his report, the conciliation commissioner did not make any recommendations on the two outstanding issues. Instead, in discussing the union's attitudes, he concluded (four weeks before the rotating strike) that "recommendations based on rational analysis of relevant collective bargaining considerations will not impact a party who . . . has decided to flex its economic muscles."

ISSUE MANAGEMENT AND DILEMMAS IN CONCESSION MAKING

Because of membership pressures and preferences, the union refused to negotiate on the basis of anything other than one item at a time. It refused to give management a new position on wages (or for that matter, even to discuss the issue). It insisted, instead, that the pension issue be resolved first and in isolation from the wage issue. The union was concerned that if it considered the issues together as a package it might get one item but not the other, and for political purposes, it felt it was necessary to negotiate the pension issue first.

The company initially refused to make a new offer (on wages or pension indexing) and, instead, pressed the union to indicate its specific position on the two issues. In response, the union indicated that the company must first agree to the principle of indexed pensions. The company ultimately did indicate a willingness to discuss indexed pensions, but only within the context of a total package. For economic and market reasons, the company believed it had to consider the cost of the entire package and that it could not cost significantly more than the first agreement.

Therefore, the parties found themselves in classic negotiation stances which occur in many negotiations. For political and economic reasons, they would have had great difficulty negotiating on any other basis, even privately. The membership expected the union team to pursue the two issues one at a time and the different preferences of the members of the union team reinforced that attitude. At the same time, the company had to take into account the total cost of the settlement, and from its perspective, as well as that of outsiders, any settlement could not be seen as aberrant.

The company ultimately offered a new position through a mediator (17 days into the strike/shutdown, 32 days since the ''phantom strike'' was called, and only at the point in time beyond which both parties would have suffered huge losses). The union representatives reluctantly accepted this, and the new agreement was ratified by the membership. Why didn't the company simply table its deal making proposal earlier and resolve the dispute short of a strike and a shutdown, or at an earlier point once the sanction began? Unfortunately, given the nature of the conflict, the company faced a dilemma with respect to its concession-making strategy:

If Air Canada granted indexed pensions *prior* to the rotating strike, the union would have taken that as a negotiating base and would still have exercised its strike mandate to extract further concessions on indexing. The union was asking for a far more generous form of indexing than the company ultimately did settle for after the shutdown.

However, even if the union found the company's proposal on indexed pensions acceptable (assuming it had been made prior to the rotating strike), the union then would have used the strike to extract a higher wage package.

In either case, from its perspective, the company would have had the worst of all possible worlds. It would have had a higher economic package and possibly one outside corporate parameters (determined by competitive factors and the upcoming privatization of the corporation), certainly a further erosion of its labor cost position, and/or rotating strikes and a shutdown with no further concessions to give the union to resolve the dispute.

There is no question that the union was after two things—a wage increase above the market norms (at that time) and indexed pensions. The former was just as important to the union as the latter. A solution on indexed pensions alone in prestrike negotiations would not have satisfied the union. This was confirmed in an interview with the general chairman of the IAM. In the opinion of the mediator who ultimately mediated the final settlement, if the company had tabled its proposals on indexed pensions earlier, this would not have resulted in an agreement. Moreover, he is of the view that if the position had been put on the table prior to his entry, he would have had much more difficulty resolving the dispute.

The union faced a dilemma of its own if it decided to concede and negotiate on a package basis. It would be an admission that it would have to make choices and, in the result, force it to abandon the wage demand in order to get indexed pensions. Prior to (and in the early stages of) the shutdown, the union could not trade off one issue for the other. The membership (or at least a large enough segment of it to get the attention of the negotiating committee) would not have accepted that compromise.

LESSONS

If we are to find principles and tactics to reach settlements in these types of situations (and/or reach them more efficiently and quickly and with minimal damage to the parties and the public), we need to broaden the framework of principled negotiation and conflict resolution. We must start in our analysis by confronting, and dealing with, the realities that often challenge the parties. The reality is that numerous negotiations reach impasse or stalemate through no fault of the parties at the table but because of constituent and other pressures and dilemmas. The external pressures and factors significantly constrain the actors at the table in terms of negotiating behavior and acceptable outcomes.

These types of situations have been analyzed, although rarely, in the negotiation and conflict management literature. For example, useful analyses of stalemate exist (Kaufman and Duncan, 1990; Pruitt and Rubin, 1986; Stevens, 1967; Stevens, 1976), but much more conceptual and empirical support is necessary. Stevens (1976, pp. 183–84), in particular, urges practitioners to contribute their insights:

> The first step would be to develop a number of straightforward, nontechnical accounts of cases comprising an etiology of impasses . . . The cases should be accompanied by some institutional illustrative material . . . The next step would be to identify negotiators who would be willing to be serious participants in the research program.

Put another way, a starting point in positing pragmatic conflict resolution techniques is to consider the tactics actually used by the negotiating parties (and third parties) in successfully concluding cases of stalemate. The tactics drawn from the Air Canada/IAM dispute are not new, but they do highlight a set of tactics that serve as a useful point of departure for future work on principled negotiation and conflict resolution.

Introducing a Mediator.   A mediator was used to end the dispute, and he fashioned the settlement by utilizing the tactics discussed below. Each of the tactics played a role in resolving the dispute. They did so because they helped the parties deal with constituent and other pressures. Their major contribution can be summed up in one adjective—face-saving. In the end, face-saving provisions and gestures became of paramount importance—on the union side, masking the real level of achievement and clearly messaging constituents that all concessions had been extracted; and, on the company side, messaging outside stakeholders and future stockholders that the company had a greater amount of stability under the new (as against its old) settlement and that its labor cost situation had not deteriorated. The mediator's entry itself was a face-saving mechanism and introduced a change in process that allowed the parties to communicate their commitments without each concession being interpreted as a sign of weakness. This, of course, is not new, but we should not underestimate the function of process. Mediators are aware of the importance of both substance and process in their interventions, and the Air Canada/IAM case underscores the vital role that process can play in dispute resolution.

The Design of the Final Package.   The final settlement contained a provision for indexed pensions that was a major achievement for the union. But the victory was, to a large extent, more *perceptual and symbolic* than real. First, the pension plan was indexed to only 50 percent of future increases in the CPI, and the maximum increase in CPI was capped at 8 percent. That is, the company's maximum, and worst case, commitment was a future adjustment of 4 percent. Secondly, the pension change included in the first agreement was dropped from the package. It had been an important and costly concession. Thirdly, while under the terms of the agreement, indexed pensions must be funded out of the operating budget, in the past the pension plan fund had been increased regularly by the company each year in any case. This had been done to adjust for about 40 percent of the increase in CPI. Air Canada had been prepared to put a variation of this practice into the collective agreement prior to the involvement of the mediator.[4] Finally, the costs were not at all close to those associated with the union's demand on the matter. Nevertheless, the final package allowed the union to announce to its constituents that it had achieved an important victory; and it had. The company was able to argue that its labor cost position had not deteriorated. Importantly, once indexing was a part of the package, the mediator was able to isolate and pressure those on the union committee who were pushing for an extraordinary wage increase.

Changing the Players at the Table.   The company's concession on indexed pensions was important to the union. Also, the *appearance* of concession making was important. On December 10, the company sent its senior director of labor relations to the table for the first time, and on December 13, the company's CEO went to Ottawa to join the talks (not at the table but in the company's caucus room). These events did not change the substance of the talks but constituted a clear change in the process. This development, too, allowed the union to indicate to constituents that it had achieved concessions from the very top of the organization. The message was clear—they had extracted all the concessions from the company that were possible under the circumstances. The mediator had insisted that the CEO be on site although not present at the table. The mediator felt that this would be an important signal to the union that the time had come to settle. The CEO never did meet face-to-face with the union negotiators, but his presence in Ottawa was an important symbol that, in essence, the mediator had stage-managed.

Dealing with Extraneous Issues.   After the membership rejected the first agreement, the company introduced the issue of utilizing part-time workers in some job categories. This would lower labor costs, and the company representatives suggested a trade-off of this item for indexed pensions. A concession on this issue, however, was neither acceptable nor of interest to the union. But, the company's demand concerning part-time employees gave the mediator an issue to work with to resolve the dispute. This was an issue that the mediator was able to get the company to withdraw. The demand was ultimately withdrawn at the request of the mediator which then made his job of selling the final package to the union team somewhat easier. In other words the withdrawal was an important symbol to the union and enhanced the mediator's credibility with the union committee.

Changing the Time Horizon of the Agreement.   The addition of a third year to the collective agreement with a wage increase of 5 percent was a positive feature from the company's perspective. This gave Air Canada a longer period of labor peace at a time when that had become important to the company. The extension of the contract by a year with an increase at the same level as the company's main rival was not only a positive aspect but also a *face-saving* feature for the company. Increasing the length of the agreement was a concession, not to the union, but to the company. In light of the plan to privatize, the company very much wanted a period of stability in labor relations. A three-year term, while not essential, was helpful to the corporation in that regard.

The Use of Pressure and Persuasion.   The parties agreed to a solution because of pressure, and out of expediency and necessity. When the parties settled, they had experienced very high costs of disagreement, and the strain on them was considerable. The pressures were particularly severe because the company sells a service. There is no opportunity to stockpile before a strike or make up for lost activity once the strike is over. Furthermore, while the phantom strike had begun at a relatively slow period for the company (November), by mid-December the company would have been entering it peak period, including the Christmas travel rush. By January, however, both parties knew travel activity would slow down dramatically.

This timing had obvious implications for the company. But it also had repercussions for the union. For example, premium and overtime pay (a normal occurrence during the peak season) would be permanently lost. As well, not surprisingly, both parties were under pressure from the public to end their dispute. The situation was affecting the travel plans of thousands of individuals. There was a great deal of cajoling, too, from federal politicians who, among other things, wanted to fly home from Ottawa for the holiday break.

In this light, it is significant that the mediator refused to become involved until pressure had built on the two sides. He was assigned to the dispute in November but did not become actively engaged until December 13. When he pushed for settlement by bringing the CEO into the negotiations, he used information (that only he had access to) to change the parties' *perceptions*. For example, he had confidential information that the government would pass back-to-work legislation to end the strike within days. He used this particular information to put pressure on the company. Company officials opposed back-to-work legislation because it would include a provision for compulsory binding arbitration to resolve the dispute. He talked pointedly, too, about "the Grinch who stole Christmas"—an obvious reference to the parties and the views held by important politicians and the public. This tension and pressure pushed the parties to look for a way out.

All of this gives credence to a framework recently developed by Kaufman and Duncan (1989 and 1990) on mediation. They argue that effective mediators change *how* a dispute is perceived rather than changing the factual characteristics of the dispute. They argue that through persuasive tactics, including manipulation through the application of pressure, mediators alter the parties' perceptions and beliefs about preferences for outcomes and the probabilities regarding the consequences of various courses of action.[5]

The role of pressure in the Air Canada/IAM dispute was pivotal, and in this light, it is worth noting that the value of pressure in negotiations seems to be underplayed in the current literature. We need to approach the issue of power and pressure in a more positive and constructive light. For example, what, if anything, can be done by a mediator to change the assumptions and thought of the parties short of their actually experiencing the costs of disagreement? What can be done by third parties to apply pressure so that the parties do not miscalculate their bargaining or power positions? What can be done to persuade the parties to make concessions and trade-offs earlier in the process? In short, how can we increase the parties' motivation and, more importantly, the motivation of their constituents to settle earlier than they otherwise would? Finding answers to these questions is an important challenge facing those who are interested in principled negotiation and the peaceful resolution of differences.

CONCLUSIONS

Studying the actions of mediators is not only important for the theory and practice of mediation but also for possible conflict resolution prescriptions for those who are interested in breaking a stalemate. While the settlement in this case was worked out with the assistance of a third party, the tactics are not indigenous to mediation. The tactics, in other words, are instructive for parties who face deadlock and for those who are interested in extending the use of principled negotiation to highly complex disputes. We should not lose sight of the fact that nebulous mechanisms are sometimes all that can be utilized to find a "way out." The Air Canada/IAM case documents that timing, process, symbols, information, and face-saving are as important, if not more so, than substance. When there is an impasse, they seem to be at the crux of the settlement process. So, too, is the issue of pressure. How (from the perspective of bringing about settlement) should the parties exercise their power and exert pressure on the other party? This is rarely addressed in the literature. Recently, Fisher and Brown (1988, pp. 132–48) have done so, but more elaboration, theory building and research concerning this very important topic are necessary.

Finally, students of conflict resolution owe it to the parties to provide prescriptions for those situations that are the most challenging for practitioners. We need much more understanding of complex negotiations and how the ideas contained in *Getting to Yes* can be applied to those types of situations. In this regard, it is important to note that Fisher (1989) has recognized the problem of constituents and the importance of intraorganizational bargaining. The Air Canada/IAM case suggests that much more analysis of that subprocess and how it interacts with, or restricts, principled negotiation is needed. A lesson would seem to be that we need to learn how to build parallel structures and processes that encompass and involve constituents; and/or we need to devise tactics to message constituents that their interests are being thoroughly considered. Whatever the approach, our emphasis should shift significantly to beyond those sitting at the table. As noted earlier, the case described is not an isolated or unusual example. There are numerous cases where constituent and other pressures (not necessarily the lack of skill by the parties) result in deadlock and seem to inhibit problem solving. The Meech Lake talks in Canada (which ultimately collapsed in June 1990) were an archetype in this regard. But that is another story.

NOTES

1. I am not the first to suggest changes to *Getting to Yes*. McCarthy (1985), for example, was an early critic. I also realize that more recently the original framework has been broadened to embrace relationship building in *Getting Together* (Fisher and Brown, 1988).
2. In this regard, I would like to thank the following individuals for their assistance: George Smith, Senior Director-Labor Relations, Air Canada; Vince Blais, President and General

Chairman, District Lodge 148, IAMAW; and William Kelly, Deputy Minister of Labor, Ottawa (now retired), who mediated the final settlement between the parties.

3. Events since privatization suggest that this view was correct. Privatization has been followed by branch closings, subcontracting, downsizing, and concession bargaining.

4. Whether tabled early or late, however, a formalization of the ad hoc arrangements would not have come close to settling the dispute. The minutes of the negotiations of November 3 reveal that such a solution was totally unacceptable to the union. It continued to be so throughout the November and December meetings.

5. There is, of course, a developing literature on third-party intervention. Part of that literature is concerned with the use of content versus process interventions. Content interventions involve such things as mediator suggestions and mediator ideas on the reasonableness of demands, while process interventions concern such aspects as the management of caucusing and improving communication. Jones (1989, p. 221) has noted that ''content interventions are preferred when the major barrier to resolution is disagreement about substantive issues in dispute; and process interventions are preferred when the barrier is the interpersonal relationship of the conflicting parties.'' The Air Canada/IAM case, however, illustrates that process also may be used to influence the parties' preferences and subjective probabilities regarding substantive outcomes.

REFERENCES

Bazerman, M., and Sondak, H. (1988). ''Judgmental limitations in diplomatic negotiations.'' *Negotiation Journal* 4: 303–17).

Chen, K., and Underwood, S. (1988). ''Integrative analytical assessment: A hybrid method for facilitating negotiation. *Negotiation Journal* 4: 183–97.

Fisher, R. (1985). ''A code of negotiation practices for lawyers.'' *Negotiation Journal* 1: 105–10.

———— (1989). ''Negotiating inside out: What are the best ways to relate internal negotiations with external ones?'' *Negotiation Journal* 5: 33–41.

———— and Brown, S. (1988). *Getting Together: Building a relationship that gets to YES.* Boston: Houghton Mifflin.

———— and Ury, W. (1981). *Getting to YES: Negotiating agreement without giving in.* Boston: Houghton Mifflin.

Jones, T. (1989). ''A taxonomy of effective mediator strategies and tactics for nonlabor-management mediation.'' In *Managing conflict: An interdisciplinary approach,* edited by M. Rahim. New York: Praeger.

Kaufman, S., and Duncan, G. (1989). ''Third party intervention: A theoretical framework.'' In *Managing conflict: An interdisciplinary approach,* edited by M. Rahim. New York: Praeger.

———— (1990). ''Preparing the ground for mediation: Foothills revisited.'' *The International Journal of Conflict Management* 1: 191–211.

McCarthy, W. (1985). ''The role of power and principle in *Getting to YES.*'' *Negotiation Journal* 1: 59–66.

McCreary, D. M. (1989). ''The NFL players dispute: Leave the hard hitting on the gridiron, bring cooperative techniques to the negotiation.'' *Negotiation Journal* 5: 289–300.

McKersie, R. B. (1989). ''The Eastern Airlines saga: Grounded by a contest of wills.'' *Negotiation Journal* 5: 213–18.

Pruitt, D., and Rubin, J. (1986). *Social conflict: Escalation, stalemate, and settlement.* New York: Random House.

Stevens, C. M. (1967). "Mediation and the role of the neutral." In *Frontiers of collective bargaining* edited by J. K. Dunlop and N. W. Chamberlain. New York: Harper & Row.

——— (1976). "Negotiation theory and dispute management." Paper presented at the Fourth Annual Meeting of the Society of Professionals in Dispute Resolution. Toronto, Canada, October 1976.

Ethics

In this section we turn our attention to the role played by personal values and ethics in the negotiation process. We do not place it near the end of the book because we believe it has low importance; in fact, the reverse is true. If you (the reader) have been participating in role plays and simulations as part of a negotiation course, questions of ethics have no doubt already come up in discussion. Someone may have bluffed or even lied in a role play, and won "unfairly" as a consequence. Someone else may have gained access to the other side's confidential briefing information and used it to (unfair) advantage. People may have been outraged, not because they lost, but because they lost as a result of tactics that were somehow determined to be "out of bounds." Your reactions to these events—whether you saw them as acceptable or unacceptable, fair or unfair, moral or immoral—are largely guided by your own personal ethics and values, and by the appropriate values and ethics that you believe should govern negotiation settings. The articles in this section focus on the ways we make these judgments.

Until recently the area of ethics in negotiation has received almost no formal attention from ethicists or researchers. Fortunately, several new articles have appeared in recent years. Perhaps this work has been spurred by what most social observers believe to be a significant "moral decline" in our society, and an increased frequency of ethical violations by businesspeople, politicians, and public figures. The nightly news regularly features stories on fraud, corruption, and violations of ethics and public trust. It may occur in the world of sports (violation of recruiting or eligibility rules, bribe taking), religion (televangelists misspending their funds), business (fraudulent practices in the stock market and savings and loan industry or environmental abuse), or politics (political favoritism, misuse of campaign funds, or simply making campaign promises one doesn't keep). Similarly, in the academic world, incidents of cheating on examinations, falsifying research studies, or falsifying personal backgrounds and credentials on a résumé have been frequent occurrences. It thus seems very appropriate to define the ethical issues likely to arise in negotiation, and the boundaries (if they exist) that commonly delineate ethical from unethical conduct.

In the first article, Lax and Sebenius define some common reasons why people want to be ethical in negotiation. Some do it for reasons of intrinsic motivation—that is, they determine that conducting oneself ethically has some personal value in and of itself, because it "feels good" or it's "the right thing to do." Other people do it for instrumental reasons—that is, it pays to be ethical; ethical behavior has some direct payoff, it can be traded for a good reputation or credibility. Regardless of which of these approaches one espouses, the authors argue that ethics apply to three general areas of negotiation: the selection of negotiation tactics, the process of deciding on a "fair" distribution of outcomes as a result of a negotiation, and externalities, or the consequences of making decisions during negotiations about the fate of those who are not represented in the negotiation process. Clearly, the first issue—tactics—has received the most attention. Lax and Sebenius offer a number of helpful "decision rules" or tests to determine which tactics might be appropriate in a negotiation. For example, are the "rules" (category of appropriate and inappropriate tactics) known and accepted by both sides? Can the situation be freely entered and left by all parties, so that those who do not want to play in this game have other alternatives? Similar rules and standards are offered to help us think more broadly about the fairness of rules used to divide up a negotiated outcome and the way that outsiders, whose fates are tied to a negotiation, should be represented in those deliberations.

In the second article, "The Ethics and Profitability of Bluffing in Business," Wokutch and Carson focus specifically on a tactic that is ethically very controversial in negotiation: bluffing. A bluff is common in negotiation, particularly in distributive bargaining. A negotiator, asking $1,300 for a used car, argues that $1,000 would never be acceptable; yet after 20 minutes of hard bargaining with a neighbor, the negotiator walks away with $1,000 in cash. The authors point out that on the one hand, a bluff is a lie—a false statement, an untruth—and is thus prima facie wrong. Thus, to engage in it, we need some special justification or reason to commit this "immoral action." The authors then explore (and rebut) the common "excuses" that people use to justify bluffing, lying, and deception. First, some lying and deception are necessary to be economically profitable; for example, if the negotiator "told the truth" and only asked for $1,000 for the car, and then engaged in the give-and-take of negotiation over the car's price, he or she would most likely wind up settling for less than $1,000! Second, some lying and deception may be necessary in "extreme" situations, where personal or corporate survival is at stake, such as avoiding bankruptcy or financial ruin. Third, some lying and deception may help the party being lied to; thus, advertising that inflates the advantages of a new drug might result in people being more convinced that the drug "works," and this strengthened faith in the product itself will make the drug more successful. Finally, some lying and deception in negotiation is necessary because the other side has no "right" to know our true bargaining position, or because it is "common practice" and most people are already using these tactics. In evaluating these common arguments and justifications, Wokutch and Carson evolve a set of clear-cut principles for determining when bluffing and deception are appropriate behaviors in business conduct.

While Wokutch and Carson attempt to define the ethical boundaries of bluffing and deception, the next article, by Richard Shell, draws the legal boundaries around lying. Many negotiators may not be as concerned about ethics as they should be, but are quite concerned about legality. It is certainly easier to rationalize and justify unethical conduct than it is to rationalize and justify illegal behavior. In a technically written but nevertheless important article, Shell frames his arguments around several basic legal definitions: the definitions of "good faith," or fraud, of the conditions under which one "knowingly" commits an action, of the conditions under which actions may be legally defined as "misrepresentation." He then turns to consider the conditions under which bluffing, misrepresentation, or "puffery" in negotiated business transactions may be considered as fraudulent or "bad faith" under the law. These constraints not only apply to bluffs or puffery about your walkaway price (statements of "objective fact"); they may also apply to stated intentions to do something, or stated opinions about something's worth or value. Shell ends with a good piece of advice; the advice was originally offered by the noted financier H. Ross Perot to Michael Milken, the "junk bond king" who was convicted of securities fraud: "Don't govern your life by what's legal or illegal; govern it by what's right or wrong." As Shell notes, this is not only good legal advice, it's good business (and negotiating) advice!

In the final article, Harry Stein discusses the ethics of a common motivation: revenge. Stein shows that revenge is a common tendency in competitive interaction, but that it is also common to ignore the costs or consequences of pursuing a revenge strategy. While parties who have been "wronged" by their opponent frequently seek revenge as a way to "settle the score" or "get even," retribution for its own sake is hardly a rational or cost-effective approach to achieving a successful negotiation. Moreover, as Stein points out, there are a number of moral and ethical dilemmas in vengeance that are seldom experienced until after the deed is done.

Three Ethical Issues in Negotiation

David A. Lax

James K. Sebenius

The agent for a small grain seller reported the following telephone conversation, concerning a disagreement over grain contracted to be sold to General Mills:

> We're General Mills; and if you don't deliver this grain to us, why we'll have a battery of lawyers in there tomorrow morning to visit you, and then we are going to the North Dakota Public Service [Commission]; we're going to the Minneapolis Grain Exchange and we're going to the people in Montana and there will be no more Muschler Grain Company. We're going to take your license.[1]

Tactics mainly intended to permit one party claim value at another's expense inescapably raise hard ethical issues. How should one evaluate moves that stake out positions, threaten another with walkout or worse, misrepresent values or beliefs, hold another person's wants hostage to claim value at that person's expense, or offer an "elegant" solution of undeniable joint benefit but constructed so that one side will get the lion's share?

    One approach to these questions is denial, to believe, pretend, or wish that conflict and questions of dividing the pie have no part in negotiation and hence such tactical choices are falsely posed: "If one really understood that the whole process was effective communication and joint problem solving, one could dispense with any unpleasant-seeming tactics, except to think about responding to their use by nasty opponents." However, denying that conflict over process and results is an essential part of negotiation is badly flawed conceptually.[2] Or, one can admit that there are hard ethical questions but deny they are relevant, as suggested by the following advice (Beckman, 1977) from a handbook on business negotiation:

> Many negotiators fail to understand the nature of negotiation and so find themselves attempting to reconcile conflicts between the requirements of negotiation and their own senses of personal integrity. An individual who confuses private ethics with business morality does not make an effective negotiator. A negotiator must learn to be objective in his negotiations and to subordinate his own personal sense of ethics to the prime purpose of securing the best deal possible for his principals.

Reprinted from David A. Lax and James K. Sebenius, "Three Ethical Issues in Negotiation," *Negotiation Journal,* October 1986, pp. 363–70. Used with permission of the authors and Plenum Publishing Corporation.

Just as we are uncomfortable denying the reality of conflict in bargaining in order to evade ethical issues, it is scarcely more satisfying to admit that ethical issues exist but, following the author of the above remark, simply to assert that they are irrelevant. Instead, we find at least two kinds of reasons to be concerned with ethical issues in negotiation.[3]

Many people want to be "ethical" for *intrinsic* reasons—apart from the effect of such choices on future encounters. Why? Variously, because it simply feels better, because one ascribes an independent value to acting "ethically," because it may be psychologically healthier, because certain principles of good behavior are taken as moral or religious absolutes, or for other reasons.[4] Yet it is often hard in negotiation to decide what actions fit these criteria, especially when values or principles appear to conflict.

Ethical behavior may also have *instrumental* value. One hears that "it pays to be ethical" or "sound ethics is good business," meaning that if a negotiator calculates correctly, taking into account the current and long-run costs of overly shrewd behavior, profits and benefits will be higher. The eighteenth century diplomat Francois de Callières (1716) made a more expansive version of this point:

> It is a capital error, which prevails widely, that a clever negotiator must be a master of the art of deceit . . . . No doubt the art of lying has been practiced with success in diplomacy; but unlike that honesty which here as elsewhere is the best policy, a lie always leaves a drop of poison behind, and even the most dazzling diplomatic success gained by dishonesty stands on an insecure foundation, for it awakes in the defeated party a sense of aggravation, a desire for vengeance, and a hatred which must always be a menace to his foe . . . the negotiator will perhaps bear in mind that he will be engaged throughout life upon affairs of diplomacy and that it is therefore his interest to establish a reputation for plain and fair dealing . . . [which] will give him a great advantage in other enterprises on which he embarks in the future.

Of course, such justifications of ethics in terms of *prudence* rely on the calculation of its benefits turning out the right way: "Cast they bread upon the waters," the Bible says, "and it shall return to thee after many days." The harder case, however, is when ethical behavior does *not* seem to pay—even after correctly factoring in the long-term costs of reputation, credibility, how others may react, and any ill social effects. Then one is back to intrinsic justifications.

Assuming, however, that ethical issues *are* relevant to bargaining, for whatever reasons, three characteristic areas strike us as especially useful to discuss: the appropriateness of certain tactics, the distribution among the bargainers of value created by agreement, and the possible effects of negotiation on those not at the table (externalities).[5] Without elaborating the philosophical frameworks within which such questions can be more fully addressed, we offer some thoughts on making these kinds of inescapable ethical choices.[6]

TACTICAL CHOICE

The essence of much bargaining involves changing another's perceptions of where in fact one would settle. Several kinds of tactics can lead to impressions that are at variance with the truth about one's actual position: persuasive rationales, commitments, references to other no-agreement alternatives, calculated patterns of concessions, failures to correct misperceptions, and the like. These tactics are tempting for obvious reasons: one side may claim value by causing the other to misperceive the range of potentially acceptable agreements. And both sides are generally in the same boat.

Such misrepresentations about each side's real interests and the set of possible bargaining outcomes should be distinguished from misrepresentations about certain aspects of the substance of the negotiation (e.g., whether the car has known difficulties that will require repair, whether the firm being acquired has important undiscussed liabilities, and so on). This latter category of tactics, which we might dub "malign persuasion," more frequently fails tests of ethical appropriateness. Consider two such tests.

Are the "Rules" Known and Accepted by All Sides?

Some people take the symmetry of the bargaining situation to ease the difficulty of ethical choice. The British statesman, Henry Taylor, is reported to have said that "falsehood ceases to be falsehood when it is understood on all sides that the truth is not expected to be spoken." In other words, if these tactics are mutually accepted as within the "rules of the game," there is no problem. A good analogy can be found in a game of poker: Bluffing is expected and thus permissible, while drawing a gun or kicking over the table are not. Yet often, the line is harder to draw.

For instance, a foreigner in Hong Kong may be aware that at least some tailors bargain routinely, but still be unsure whether a particular one—who insists he has fixed prices—is "just bargaining." Yet that tailor may reap considerable advantage if in fact he bargains but is persuasive that he does not. It is often self-servingly easy for the deceiver to assume that others know and accept the rules. And a worse problem is posed if many situations are often not even recognized as negotiation, when in fact they exhibit its essential characteristics (interdependence, some perceived conflict, opportunistic potential, the possibility of explicit or tacit agreement on joint action).[7] When, as is often the case in organizational life, such less acknowledged negotiation occurs, then how can any "rules" of the game meet the mutual "awareness and acceptance of the rules" test?

Can the Situation Be Freely Entered and Left?

Ethicist Sissela Bok (1978, pp. 137–40) adds another criterion: For lying to be appropriate, not only must the rules be well-understood, but the participants must be able freely to enter *and* leave the situation. Thus to the extent that mutually expected, ritual flattery or a work of fiction involve "lying," there is little problem. To make an analogy between deception and violence: though a boxing match, which can involve rough moves, meets this criterion, a duel, from which exit may be impossible, does not.

Yet this standard may be too high. Bargaining situations—formal and informal, tacit and explicit—are far more widespread than many people realize. In fact, a good case can be made that bargaining pervades life inside and outside of organizations, making continual free entry and exit impractical. So if bargaining will go on and people will necessarily be involved in it, something else is required.

Other Helpful Questions

When it is unclear whether a particular tactic is ethically appropriate, we find that a number of other questions—beyond whether others know and accept it or may leave—can illuminate the choice. Consider several such questions:

Self-Image. Peter Drucker (1981) asks a basic question: When you look at yourself in the mirror the next morning, will you like the person you see? And there are many such useful queries about self-image, which are intended to clarify the appropriateness of the choice itself and not to ask about the possible consequences (firing, ostracism, etc.) to you of different parties being aware of your actions: Would you be comfortable if your co-workers, colleagues, and friends were aware that you had used a particular tactic? Your spouse, children, or parents? If it came out on the front page of the *New York Times* or *The Wall Street Journal?* If it became known in 10 years? Twenty? In the history books?

Reciprocity. Does it accord with the Golden Rule? How would you feel if someone did it to you? To a younger colleague? A respected mentor? A member of your family? (Of course, saying that you would mind very much if it were done to another need not imply that the tactic is unethical; that person may not be in your situation or have your experience—but figuring out the reason you would be bothered can give a clue to the ethics of the choice.)

Advising Others. Would you be comfortable advising another to use this tactic? Instructing your agent to use it? How about if such advice became known?

Designing the System. Imagine that you were completely outside the setting in which the tactic might be used, but that you were responsible for designing the situation itself: the number of people present, their stakes, the conventions governing their encounters, the range of permissible actions, and so on. The wrinkle is that you would be assigned a role in that setting, *but* you would not know in advance the identity of the person whose role you would assume. Would you build in the possibility for the kind of tactics you are now trying to evaluate?[8] A simpler version of this test is to ask how you would rule on this tactic if you were an arbitrator, or perhaps an elder, in a small society.

Social Result. What if everybody bargained this way? Would the resulting society be desirable? These questions may not have obvious answers. For example, hard, individual competition may seem dehumanizing. Yet many argue that, precisely because competition is encouraged, standards of living rise in free-market societies and some forms of excellence flourish.[9]

Alternative Tactics.   Are there alternative tactics available that have fewer ethical ambiguities or costs? Can the whole issue be avoided by following a different tack, even at a small cost elsewhere?

Taking a Broader View.   In agonizing over a tactic—for instance, whether to shade values—it is often worth stepping back to take a broader perspective.

First, there is a powerful tendency for people to focus on conflict, see a "zero sum" world, and primarily aim to enlarge their individual shares. Such an emphasis on "claiming" is common yet it can stunt creativity and often cause significant joint gains to go unrealized. In such cases, does the real problem lie in the ethical judgment call about a tactic intended to claim value, or is it a disproportionate focus on claiming itself? If it is the latter, the more fruitful question may be how to make the other face of negotiation—moves jointly to "create value"—more salient.

Second, does the type of situation itself generate powerful tendencies toward the questionable tactics involved? Is it an industry in which "favors" to public officials are an "expected" means for winning good contracts? If so, evaluating the acceptability of a given move may be less important than deciding (1) whether to leave the situation that inherently poses such choices, or (2) which actions could alter, even slightly, the prevalence of the questionable practices.

DISTRIBUTIONAL FAIRNESS

One reason that a tactical choice can be uncomfortable is its potential effect on the distribution of value created by agreement. If a "shrewd" move allows a large firm to squeeze a small merchant unmercifully or an experienced negotiator to walk away with all the profit in dealings with a novice, something may seem wrong. Even when the nature of the tactics is not in question, the "fairness" of the outcome may be.

This difficulty is inherent in negotiation: Since there is a bargaining set of many potential agreements that are better for each person than his or her respective alternatives to agreement, the value created by agreement must necessarily be apportioned. Ultimately, when all joint gains have been discovered and common value created, more value for one party means less for another. But just where should the value split be? This, of course, is the age-old problem of "distributive justice," of what a just distribution of rewards and risks in a society should be. In the same way that this is a thorny, unresolved problem at the social level, so it is for individual negotiators—even when less well-recognized.[10] And this is why the problem is so hard, and does not admit easy answers.

A classic problem among game theorists involves trying to develop fair criteria to arbitrate the division of $200 between two people.[11] An obvious norm involves an even split, $100 for each. But what if one is rich and the other poor? More for the poor man, right? "Not at all!" protests the rich woman, "you must look at *after-tax* revenue, even if you want a little more to end up going to the poor man. Moreover, you should really try to equalize the amount of good done for each of us—in which case $20 to him will improve his life much more than $180 will mine. Or look at it the other way:

Ask who can better afford to *lose* what amounts—and he can afford to lose $5 about as much as I can $195. Besides, he is a wino and completely on his own. I will sign this pledge to give the money to Mother Teresa, who will use it to help dozens of poor people in India. After all, that poor man *was* rich just two weeks ago, when he was convicted of fraud and had all his money confiscated to pay back his victims.''

Who ''should'' get what in a negotiated agreement? The preceding tongue-in-cheek discussion should not obscure the importance of distributional questions; certainly negotiators argue for this solution or that on the basis of ''fairness'' all the time. But the rich woman's objections should underscore how fragile and divisive conceptions of equity may be. One person's fairness may be another's outrage.

And fairness not only applies to the process of bargaining but also to its underlying structure. Think of the wage ''bargaining'' between an illegal alien and her work supervisor who can have her deported at a moment's notice. Is such a situation so loaded against one of the participants that the results are virtually certain to be ''unfairly'' distributed?

Many times, by contrast, we will be comfortable answering that we do *not* care about the actual result, only that the process was within normal bounds, that the participants were intelligent and well-informed enough, and that no one outside the negotiation was harmed by the accord.

EXTERNALITIES

A third broad question involving others who are not at the bargaining table deserves some mention. If the Teamsters Union, major trucking firms, and a ''captive'' Interstate Commerce Commission informally bargained and agreed on higher rates, what about the interests of the unrepresented public? How do the childrens' interests figure into a divorce settlement hammered out by two adversarial lawyers who only know that each parent wants custody? Or, suppose that a commission negotiates and decides to raise *current* Social Security benefits dramatically but pay for them by issuing very long-term bonds, the bulk of whose burden will fall on the *next* two generations?

It is often easy to ''solve'' the negotiation problem for those in the room at the expense of those who are not. If such parties cannot take part directly, one way to ''internalize'' this ''externality'' is to keep their interests in mind or to invite the participation or observation of those who can represent their interests, if only indirectly.[12] Deciding that the process could be improved this way may not be too hard, though the mechanics of representation can be trickier. Yet, even with ''proper'' representation, what about the actual outcome? We are back to questions akin to those in the last section on distribution.

There is another, more subtle, external effect of the way in which ethical questions in bargaining are resolved. It involves the spillover of the way one person bargains into the pattern of dealings of others. Over time, each of us comes to hold assumptions about what is likely and appropriate in bargaining interactions. Each tactical choice shapes these expectations and reverberates throughout the circles we inhabit. And many people lament that the state of dealings in business and government is such that behavior we might prefer to avoid becomes almost irresistible, since others are doing it and overly idealistic actions could be very costly.

CONCLUSION

The overall choice of how to negotiate, whether to emphasize moves that create value or claim it, has implications beyond single encounters. The dynamic that leads individual bargainers to poor agreements, impasses, and conflict spirals also has a larger social counterpart. Without choices that keep creative actions from being driven out, this larger social game tends toward an equilibrium in which everyone claims, engages constantly in behavior that distorts information, and worse.

Most people are willing to sacrifice something to avoid such outcomes, and to improve the way people relate to each other in negotiation and beyond. The wider echos of ethical choices made in negotiation can be forces for positive change. Each person must decide if individual risks are worth general improvement, even if such improvement seems small, uncertain, and not likely to be visible. Yet a widespread choice to disregard ethics in negotiation would mark a long step down the road to a more cynical, Hobbesian world.

NOTES

This article is adapted from a section in the authors' book, *The Manager as Negotiator* (New York: Free Press, 1986). The authors are particularly indebted to Howard Raiffa and to the discussion of ethics in his book, *The Art and Science of Negotiation* (Cambridge, Mass.: Harvard University Press, 1982).

1. *Jamestown Farmers Elevator, Inc.* v. *General Mills.* 552 F.2d 1285, 1289 (8th Cir. 1977).

2. In Chapters 2, 6, and 7 of our book, *The Manager as Negotiator* (1986), we elaborate this point.

3. For an insightful, common sense discussion of the reasons for being "moral," see Hospers (1961).

4. If certain precepts are taken as Kantian categorical imperatives or as otherwise correct in an absolute sense, regardless of the consequences (the strong deonto-logical position), the decision problem may be easy—unless more than one such principle appears to conflict.

5. Of course, there are many ethical issues involved in bargaining beyond those treated here (e.g., How should an attorney bargain on behalf of a client that she believes is guilty? Should a bargaining agent be solely guided by his principal's conception of her own interests? Even where the agent thinks he "knows better" or is more "expert"? Where one party psychologically "dominates" the other? How can one party "properly" represent a constituent group, especially where the interests of the group members diverge? And so on.)

6. For a good informal discussion of these questions, especially the first, see Raiffa (1982, pp. 344–55).

7. For an extended discussion, see Chapter 1 of *The Manager as Negotiator*.

8. This discussion draws from John Rawls (1971).

9. But, the welfare theorems of economics—that prove that competitive equilibria are Pareto-optimal and that Pareto-optimal allocations of goods and services are

competitive equilibria—assume that bargaining is Pareto-efficient. The thrust of our argument about the "Negotiator's Dilemma" (see Lax and Sebenius, 1986) and the work on bargaining with incomplete information (see, for example, Chatterjee, 1982; Rubinstein, 1983; Cramton, 1983, 1984A and 1984B; and Myerson, 1985) is that bargained outcomes will tend to be inefficient since bargainers act on the temptation to misrepresent.

10. In fact, bargaining is a time-honored way of resolving this dilemma, just as pure markets, legislative action, and judicial ruling are in other spheres where distributive issues must be settled. See Lindblom (1977).

11. For a very clear look at how analysts have approached this kind of problem, see Raiffa (1982, pp. 235–55).

12. For a discussion of this problem in the context of public disputes, see Susskind and Ozawa (1985).

REFERENCES

Beckman, N. *Negotiations.* Lexington, Mass.: Lexington Books, 1977.

Bok, S. *Lying: Moral Choice in Public and Private Life.* New York: Vintage Books. 1978.

Chatterjee, K. "Incentive Compatibility in Bargaining Under Uncertainty." *Quarterly Journal of Economics* 82 (1982): 1 26.

Cramton, P. C. "Bargaining with Incomplete Information: An Infinite Horizon-Model with Continuous Uncertainty." Stanford Graduate School of Business Research Paper No. 680, 1983.

———. "Bargaining with Incomplete Information: A Two-Period Model with Continuous Uncertainty." *Review of Economic Studies* 51 (1984A).

———. "The Role of Time and Information in Bargaining." Stanford Graduate School of Business Research Paper No. 29, 1984B.

deCallières, F. *On the Manner of Negotiating with Princes,* trans. A. F. Whyte. Boston: Houghton Mifflin. 1919: originally published, Paris: Michel Brunet, 1716.

Hospers, J. *Human Conduct.* New York: Harcourt, Brace & World, 1961.

Lax, D. A. and Sebenius, J. K. *The Manager as Negotiator.* New York: The Free Press, 1986.

Lindblom, C. E. *Politics and Markets.* New York: Basic Books, 1977.

Myerson, R. "Analysis of Two Bargaining Problems with Incomplete Information." In *Game Theoretic Models of Bargaining.* ed. Alvin Roth., Cambridge: Cambridge University Press, 1985.

Raiffa, H. *The Art and Science of Negotiation.* Cambridge, Mass.: Harvard University Press, 1982.

Rawls, J. *A Theory of Justice,* Cambridge, Mass.: Harvard University Press. 1971.

Rubinstein, A. "A Bargaining Model with Incomplete Information." Unpublished. Department of Economics, Hebrew University, Jerusalem, 1983.

Susskind, L. and Ozawa, C. "Mediated Negotiation in the Public Sector." *American Behavioral Scientist.* 2 (1983): 255–79.

The Ethics and Profitability of Bluffing in Business

Richard E. Wokutch

Thomas L. Carson

Consider a standard case of bluffing in an economic transaction. I am selling a used car and say that $1,500 is my final offer, even though I know that I would accept considerably less. Or, suppose that I am a union representative in a labor negotiation. Although I have been instructed to accept $10 an hour if that is the highest offer I receive, I say that we will not accept a wage of $10 an hour under any circumstances. This sort of bluffing is widely practiced and almost universally condoned. It is thought to be morally acceptable. It is our contention, however, that bluffing raises serious ethical questions. For bluffing is clearly an act of deception; the bluffer's intent is to deceive the other parties about the nature of his bargaining position. Furthermore, bluffing often involves lying. The two examples of bluffing presented here both fit the standard definition of lying: they are deliberate false statements made with the intent of deceiving others.[1]

Common sense holds that lying and deception are prima facie wrong. One could also put this by saying that there is a presumption against lying and deception: that they require some special justification in order to be permissible.[2] Almost no one would agree with Kant's view that it is wrong to lie even if doing so is necessary to protect the lives of innocent people. According to Kant it would be wrong to lie to a potential murderer concerning the whereabouts of his intended victim.[3]

Assuming the correctness of the view that there is a moral presumption against lying and deception, and assuming that we are correct in saying that bluffing often involves lying, it follows that bluffing and other deceptive business practices require some sort of special justification in order to be considered permissible. Business people frequently defend bluffing and other deceptive practices on the grounds that they are profitable or economically necessary. Such acts are also defended on the grounds that they are standard practice in economic transactions. We will argue that these standard justifications of bluffing are unacceptable. Then we will propose an alternative justification for lying and deception about one's bargaining position.

Reprinted from the *Westminster Institute Review*, May 1981, pp. 77-83. Used with permission of the authors.

There are those who hold that lying and deception are never profitable or economically necessary. In their view, honesty is always the best policy. One incentive for telling the truth is the law, but here we are referring to lying or bluffing which is not illegal, or for which the penalty or risk of being caught is not great enough to discourage the action.

Those who hold that honesty is always in one's economic self-interest argue that economic transactions are built on trust and that a violation of that trust discourages an individual or organization from entering into further transactions with the lying party for fear of being lied to again. Thus, some mutually beneficial transactions may be foregone for lack of trust. Moreover, word of deceitful practices spreads through the marketplace and others also avoid doing business with the liar. Thus, while some short-run profit might accrue from lying, in the long run it is unprofitable. If this argument were sound, we would have a nonissue. Lying, like inefficiency, would be a question of bad management that would be in one's own best interest to eliminate.

Unfortunately, there are some anomalies in the marketplace which prevent the system from operating in a perfectly smooth manner. The very existence of bluffing and lying in the first place suggests that the economists' assumption of perfect (or near perfect) market information is incorrect. Some transactions, such as buying or selling a house, are one-shot deals with little or no chance of repeat business. Thus, there is no experience on which to base an assessment of the seller's honesty, and no incentive to build trust for future transactions. Even when a business is involved in an ongoing operation, information flows are such that a large number of people can be duped before others hear about it (e.g., selling Florida swampland or Arizona desertland sight unseen). Other bluffs and lies are difficult or even impossible to prove. If a union negotiator wins a concession from management on the grounds that the union would not ratify the contract without it—even though he has reason to believe that this is untrue—it would be extremely difficult for management to prove later that ratification could have been achieved without the provision. By the same token, some product claims, such as the salesman's contention that "this is the best X on the market," are inherently subjective. When the competing products are of similar quality, it is difficult to prove such statements untrue, even if the person making the statement believes them to be untrue. Another exception to the assumption of perfect information flows is the confusion brought on by the increasing technological complexity of goods and services. In fact, a product information industry in the form of publications like *Consumer Reports, Canadian Consumer, Consumer Union Reports, Money,* and *Changing Times* has arisen to provide, for a price, the kind of product information that economic theory assumes consumers have to begin with.

These arguments suggest not only that the commonly cited disincentives to bluffing and lying are often ineffective, but that there are some distinct financial incentives for these activities. If you can convince consumers that your product is better than it really is, you will have a better chance of selling them that product and you may be able to charge them a higher price than they would otherwise be willing to pay. It is also obvious that in a negotiating setting there are financial rewards for successful lies and bluffs. If you can conceal your actual minimal acceptable position, you may be able to achieve a more desirable settlement. By the same token, learning your negotiating opponent's true position will enable you to press toward his minimal acceptable position. This is, of course, why such intrigues as hiding microphones in the opposing negotiating team's private quarters or hiring informants are undertaken in negotiations—they produce valuable information.

An individual cannot, however, justify lying simply on the grounds that it is in his own self-interest to lie, for it is not always morally permissible to do what is in one's own self-interest. I would not be justified in killing you or falsely accusing you of a crime in order to get your job, even if doing so would be to my advantage. Similarly, a businessman cannot justify lying and deception simply on the grounds that they are advantageous, that is, profitable, to his company. This point can be strengthened if we remember that any advantages that one gains as a result of bluffing are usually counterbalanced by corresponding disadvantages on the part of others. If I succeed in getting a higher price by bluffing when I sell my house, there must be someone else who is paying more than he would have otherwise.

Economic necessity is a stronger justification for lying than mere profitability. Suppose that it is necessary for a businessman to engage in lying or deception in order to insure the survival of his firm. Many would not object to a person stealing food to prevent himself or his children from starving to death. Perhaps lying in an extreme situation to get money to buy food or to continue employing workers so that *they* can buy food would be equally justifiable. This case would best be described as a conflict of duties—a conflict between the duty to be honest and the duty to promote the welfare of those for/to whom one is responsible (one's children, one's employees, or the stockholders whose money one manages). However, it is extremely unlikely that bankruptcy would result in the death or starvation of anyone in a society which has unemployment compensation, welfare payments, food stamps, charitable organizations, and even opportunities for begging. The consequences of refraining from lying in transactions might still be very unfavorable indeed, involving, for example, the bankruptcy of a firm, loss of investment, unemployment, and the personal suffering associated with this. But a firm which needs to practice lying or deception in order to continue in existence is of doubtful value to society. Perhaps the labor, capital, and raw materials which it uses could be put to better use elsewhere. At least in a free-market situation, the interests of economic efficiency would be best served if such firms were to go out of business. An apparent exception to this argument about economic efficiency would be a situation in which a firm was pushed to the edge of bankruptcy by the lies of competitors or others. It seems probable that the long-term consequences of the bankruptcy of a firm which needs to lie in order to continue in existence would be better, or no worse, than those of its continuing to exist.

Suppose, however, that the immediate bad consequences of bankruptcy would not be offset by any long-term benefits. In that case it is not clear that it would be wrong for a company to resort to lying and deception out of economic necessity. One can, after all, be justified in lying or deceiving to save individuals from harms far less serious than death. I can be justified in lying about the gender of my friend's roommate to a nosy relative or boss in order to protect him from embarrassment or from being fired. If the degree of harm prevented by lying or deception were the only relevant factor, and if bankruptcy would not have any significant long-term benefits, then it would seem that a businessman could easily justify lying and deceiving in order to protect those associated with his business from the harm which would result from the bankruptcy of the firm. There is, however, another relevant factor which clouds the issue. In the case of lying about the private affairs of one's friends, one is lying to others about matters about which they have no right to know. Our present analogy warrants lying and deception for the sake of economic survival only in cases in which the persons being lied to or deceived have no right to the information in question. Among other things, this rules out deceiving customers about dangerous defects in one's products, because customers have a right to this information; but it does not rule out lying to someone or deceiving them about one's minimal bargaining position.

We have argued that personal or corporate profit is no justification for lying in business transactions, and that lying for reasons of economic necessity is also morally objectionable in many cases. But what about lying in order to benefit the party being lied to? There are certainly many self-serving claims to this effect. Some have argued that individuals derive greater satisfaction from a product or service if they can be convinced that it is better than is actually the case. On the other hand, an advertising executive made the argument in the recent Federal Trade Commission hearings on children's advertising that the disappointment children experience when a product fails to meet their commercial-inflated expectations is beneficial because it helps them develop a healthy skepticism. These arguments are not convincing. In fact, they appear to be smoke screens for actions taken out of self-interest. It is conceivable that consumers might benefit from it. For example, deceptive advertising claims may cause one to purchase a product which is of genuine benefit. While lying and deception can sometimes be justified by reference to the interests of those being lied to or deceived, such cases are very atypical in business situations. As was argued earlier, successful bluffing almost always harms the other party in business negotiations. The net effect of a successful bluff is paying more or receiving less than would otherwise have been the case.

A further ground on which lying or deception in bargaining situations is sometimes held to be justifiable is the claim that the other parties do not have a right to know one's true bargaining position. It is true that the other parties do not have a right to know one's position, that is, it would not be wrong to refuse to reveal it to them. But this is not to say that it is permissible to lie or deceive them. You have no right to know where I was born, but it would be prima facie wrong for me to lie to you about the place of my birth. So, lying and deception in bargaining situations cannot be justified simply on the grounds that the other parties have no right to know one's true position. However, other things being equal, it is much worse to lie or deceive about a matter concerning which the other parties have a right to know than one about which they have no right to know.

But what of the justification that lying and deception are standard practice in economic transactions? Certainly, lying and deception are very common, if not generally accepted or condoned. Bluffing and other deceptive practices are especially common in economic negotiations, and bluffing, at least, is generally thought to be an acceptable practice.[4] Does this fact in any way justify bluffing? We think not. The mere fact that something is standard practice or generally accepted is not enough to justify it. Standard practice and popular opinion can be in error. Such things as slavery were once standard practice and generally accepted. But they are and were morally wrong. Bluffing cannot be justified simply *because* it is a common and generally accepted practice. However, we shall now use the prevalence of bluffing involving lying and deception as a premise of an argument to show that there is a presumption for thinking that bluffing of this sort is morally permissible. If one is involved in a negotiation, it is very probable that the other parties with whom one is dealing are themselves bluffing. The presumption against lying and deception does not hold when the other parties with whom one is dealing are themselves lying to or otherwise attempting to deceive one. Given this, there is no presumption against lying or deceiving others about one's bargaining position in the course of an ordinary business negotiation, since the parties with whom one is dealing may be presumed to be doing the same themselves.

It is prima facie wrong to use violence against another person, but when one is a victim of violence oneself, it is permissible to use violence if doing so is necessary in order to prevent or limit harm to oneself. One is not morally required to refrain from self-defense. Similarly, other things being equal, if X is being harmed by the lies or deception of Y and if X can avoid or mitigate that harm only by lying to or deceiving Y, then it is permissible for X to lie to or deceive Y. These intuitions are captured by the following principle:

> (P) Other things being equal, it is permissible for X to do *a* to Y, even if *a* is a prima facie wrong, provided that X's doing *a* to Y is necessary in order to prevent or mitigate harm to X caused by Y's doing *a* to X.[5]

In business negotiations an individual can typically gain some benefit (balanced by corresponding harm to the other party) if he is willing to lie or deceive the other person about his own negotiating position. The other party can avoid or mitigate this harm only by being willing to do the same. In our society most people routinely practice this sort of lying and/or deception in business negotiations. Given this, (P) implies that one may presume that one is justified in bluffing (by means of lying and deception about one's negotiating position) in ordinary circumstances, unless either: (i) one has special reasons to suppose that the other party will not do the same (e.g., one might know that the individual with whom one is dealing is unusually scrupulous or naive), or (ii) one has special reasons for thinking that one will not be harmed by the bluffing of the other party, even if one does not bluff oneself.

Space does not permit an extended discussion or defense of (P). We would, however, like to forestall two possible objections. (i) (P) does not constitute a blanket endorsement of retaliation or the policy of "an eye for an eye and a tooth for a tooth." (P) would not justify my killing your child in retaliation for your having killed mine. (P) would justify my killing another person X only if my killing X is necessary in order to prevent X from killing me. (ii) It is standard practice for people involved in negotiations to misrepresent the terms they are willing to accept. In ordinary circumstances (P) will justify such actions. However, there are types of lying and deception which are not generally practiced in negotiations. For example, while meeting with a prospective buyer a person selling a house might have a friend pretend to make an offer to buy the house in order to pressure the prospective buyer. (P) does not imply that there is any presumption for thinking that such a ruse would be morally permissible.

NOTES

We are indebted to Thomas Beauchamp for comments on a previous version of this paper. Earlier versions of this paper were presented to a conference on Business and Professional Ethics at Kalamazoo College and Western Michigan University, November 1979, and to the Philosophy Department at Denison University.

1. For a much more thorough defense of the claim that bluffing involves lying, with an appeal to a somewhat different definition of lying, see our paper "The Moral Status of Bluffing and Deception in Business" in *Business and Professional Ethics,* ed., Wade L. Robison and Michael S. Pritchard (New York: Humana Press). Also see our paper "Bluffing in Labor Negotiations: Legal and Ethical Issues," with Kent F. Mursmann, *Journal of Business Ethics,* vol. 1, no. 1, January 1982.

2. The classic statement of this view is included in Chapter II of Sir David Ross' *The Right and the Good* (Oxford: Oxford University Press, 1930).

3. Immanual Kant, "On the Supposed Right to Tell Lies from Benevolent Motives," (1797), in *Moral Rules and Particular Circumstances,* ed. Baruch Brody (Englewood Cliffs, N.J.: Prentice Hall, 1970), pp. 32 and 33.

4. In a well-known defense of bluffing, Albert Carr claims that it is permissible to make false statements in the course of business negotiations because doing so is "normal business practice," and part of what is involved in "playing the business game." See "Is Business Bluffing Ethical?." *Harvard Business Review,* January–February 1968.

5. It seems plausible to say that it would be permissible to do an act that is prima facie wrong to another person (X) if doing so were necessary in order to prevent X from harming a third party by doing the same act. For example, one would be justified in killing another person if doing so were necessary in order to prevent him from killing a third party. We accept the following stronger version of P:

> P'   Other things being equal, it is permissible for X to do *a* to Y, even if *a* is prima facie wrong, provided that X's doing *a* to Y is necessary in order to prevent or mitigate harm to *someone* caused by Y's doing *a* to that person.

The weaker principle (P) is sufficient for the purposes of our argument.

When Is It Legal to Lie
in Negotiations?

G. Richard Shell

Commercial negotiations seem to require a talent for deception. In simple, distributive bargaining, when someone asks, "What is your bottom line?" few negotiators tell the truth. They dodge, they change the subject, or they lie.[1] In more complex, multi-issue negotiations, even relatively cooperative bargainers often inject straw issues or exaggerate the importance of minor problems in order to gain concessions on what *really* matters.[2] In nearly all bargaining encounters, a key skill is the ability to communicate that you are relatively firm on positions when you are, in fact, flexible—in short, to bluff about your intentions.

The apparent necessity for misleading conduct in a process based on cooperation and coordination makes bargaining deception a prime target for ethical theorizing and empirical investigation. Given the high degree of academic interest, one would think that the investigation of deception would have included by now a detailed look at what one of our most powerful social institutions—the law—has to say on the subject. Curiously, academic students of negotiation have essentially ignored the law. Ethical discussions of deception either overlook it completely or assume that it proscribes only the most clear-cut types of fraud, leaving moralists to distinguish, and in some instances justify, the finer points of deceptive conduct.[3] Behavioral studies of bargaining deception, meanwhile, usually take place in academic laboratories where the problems are not subject, as are actual transactions, to legal limits or consequences.[4]

This article fills the existing gap in the bargaining literature. As the recent legal cases discussed here will demonstrate, what moralists would often consider merely "unethical" behavior in negotiations turns out to be precisely what the courts consider *illegal* behavior.[5] In light of the rather broad legal standards that are beginning to govern bargaining, behavioral investigators should consider research on how legal incentives affect negotiator conduct. Business negotiators and teachers of negotiation skills in business schools and executive training programs need to be aware of the legal consequences of deceptive bargaining tactics.

LEGAL FRAUD: THE BASICS

American law disclaims any general duty of "good faith" in the negotiation of commercial agreements.[6] As the United States Court of Appeals for the Seventh Circuit recently stated:

> In a business transaction both sides presumably try to get the best deal. That is the essence of bargaining and the free market. . . . [N]o legal rule bounds the run of business interest. So one cannot characterize self-interest as bad faith. No particular demand in negotiations could be termed dishonest, even if it seemed outrageous to the other party. The proper recourse is to walk away from the bargaining table, not sue for "bad faith" in negotiations.[7]

This general rule assumes, however, that no one has committed fraud. As we shall see, fraud law reaches deep into the complexities of negotiation behavior.

The elements of common law fraud are deceptively simple. A statement is fraudulent when the speaker makes a knowing misrepresentation of a material fact on which the victim reasonably relies and which causes damages.[8] A car dealer commits fraud when he resets an odometer and sells one of his "company" cars as brand new. The dealer knows the car is not new; he misrepresents its condition to the buyer; the condition of the car is a fact that is important, or "material," to the transaction; the buyer is acting reasonably in relying on the dealer's assertions that the car is new; and damages result. Similarly, a person selling her business commits fraud when she lies about the number and kind of debts owed by the business.

Lies about important facts are not unknown in business negotiations, but most negotiators know to avoid them. The interesting questions about lying come up on the margins of fraud law. What if the dealer says you had better buy the car today because he has another buyer ready to snatch it away tomorrow? That is a statement of fact. Is it fraudulent if it is a lie? What if the person selling her business says that a large account debt might be renegotiated if you buy the business? That is not really a statement of fact; it is an opinion. Could it nevertheless be deemed so misleading as to be fraudulent when she knows that the creditor would not consider renegotiation? Below, I address these and other questions by exploring in depth each element in the legal definition of fraud with reference to recent cases that have extended the boundaries of the law.

Knowing

The common law definition of fraud requires that the speaker have a particular state of mind with respect to the fact he misrepresents: the statement must be made "knowingly." This generally means that the speaker knows what he says is false. One way of getting around fraud, therefore, might be for the speaker to avoid contact with information that would lead to a "knowing" state of mind. For example, a company president might suspect that his company is in poor financial health, but he does not yet "know" it because he has not seen the latest quarterly reports. When his advisers ask to set up a meeting to discuss these reports, he tells them to hold off. He is about to go into negotiations with an important supplier and would like to be able to say, honestly, that so far as he knows the company is paying its bills. Does this get the president off the hook? No. The courts have stretched the definition of "knowing" to include statements that are "reckless," that is, those made with a conscious disregard for their truth. Thus, when the information that will give the speaker the truth is close at hand and he deliberately turns away in order to maintain a convenient state of ignorance, the law will treat him as if he spoke with full knowledge that his statements were false. A recent case applied this concept, complete with a punitive damage award, against a company that negotiated a sale of computer and other equipment based on reckless assertions of performance capability.[9]

Nor is reckless disregard for truth the limit of the law. Victims of misstatements that were made *negligently* or even innocently may obtain relief in the proper circumstances. These kinds of misstatements are not deemed fraudulent, however. Rather, they are a way of recognizing that a deal was based on a mistake. If someone sells land relying, either carelessly or without any fault whatsoever, on a deed that contains incorrect notations of the land's proper boundaries, the buyer may be able to have the sale rescinded or the boundaries reformed. But if the seller knows that the deed is incorrect and does not tell the buyer, she has committed fraud.

Misrepresentation

In general, the law requires the speaker to make a positive misstatement before it will attach liability for fraud. Thus, a basic rule for commercial negotiators is to "be silent and be safe." As a practical matter, of course, silence is difficult to maintain if one's bargaining opponent is an astute questioner. In the face of inconvenient questions, negotiators are often forced to resort to verbal feints and dodges such as, "I don't know about that," or, when pressed, "That is not a subject I am at liberty to discuss."

There are circumstances when such dodges will not do, and it may be fraudulent to keep your peace about an issue. When does a negotiator have a duty to frankly disclose matters that may hurt his bargaining position? Under recent cases, the law imposes affirmative disclosure duties in the following four circumstances:

1. *When the nondisclosing party makes a partial disclosure that is or becomes misleading in light of all the facts.* If you say your company is profitable, you may have a duty to disclose whether you used questionable accounting techniques to arrive at that statement. If you show a loss in the next quarter and negotiations are still ongoing, you may be required to disclose the loss. One way to avoid this is to make no statements on delicate subjects in the first place. Then you have no duty to correct or update yourself.

2. *When the parties stand in a fiduciary relationship to one another.* In negotiations involving trustees and beneficiaries, parties must be completely frank and cannot rely on the "be silent and be safe" rubric. Note, however, that courts have recently broadened the notion of a "fiduciary" to include banks, franchisors, and other commercial players who deal with business partners on a somewhat-less-than-arm's-length basis. In short, it is becoming increasingly risky to withhold important information in negotiations with parties who depend on you for their commercial well-being.

3. *When the nondisclosing party has "superior information" vital to the transaction that is not accessible to the other side.* This is a slippery exception, but the best test is one of conscience. Indeed, courts often state that the legal test of disclosure is whether "equity or good conscience" requires that the fact be revealed.[10] Would you feel cheated if the other side didn't tell you about the hidden fact? Or would you secretly kick yourself for not having found it out yourself? If the former, you should consult an attorney. A recent case applying this exception held that an employer owed a duty to a prospective employee to disclose contingency plans for shutting down the project for which the employee was hired.[11] In general, sellers have a greater duty than buyers to disclose things they know about their own property. Thus, a home seller must disclose termite infestation in her home.[12] But an oil company need not disclose the existence of oil on a farmer's land when negotiating a purchase.[13]

4. *When special transactions are at issue,* such as insurance contracts. Insurers must fully disclose the scope of coverage, and insureds must fully disclose their insurance risk. If you apply for a life insurance policy and do not disclose your heart condition, you have committed fraud.

If none of these four exceptions applies, you are not likely to be found liable for common law fraud based on a nondisclosure. Beware of special statutory modifications of the common law rules, however. For example, if the sale of your company involves a purchase or sale of securities, state and federal antifraud rules may impose a stiffer duty of disclosure than may apply under the common law. Companies repurchasing stock from employee-shareholders in anticipation of a lucrative merger, for example, have been held liable for failing to disclose the existence of the merger negotiations to their employees.[14] And companies selling their securities are required to disclose important adverse facts about their business to prospective buyers.

Material

Most people lie about something during negotiations. Often they seek to deceive others by making initial demands that far exceed their true needs or desires. Sometimes they mislead others about their reservation price or "bottom line." Of course, demands and reservation prices may not be "facts." One may have only a vague idea of what one really wants or is willing to pay for something. Hence, a statement that an asking price is too high may not be true misrepresentation as much as a statement of preference. Suppose, however, that a negotiator has been given authority by a seller to peddle an item for any price greater than $10,000. Is it fraud for the negotiator to reject an offer of $12,000 and state that the deal cannot be closed at that price? In fact, the deal could be closed for that price so there has been a knowing misrepresentation of fact. The question is whether this fact is material in a legal sense. It is not.

Lies about reservation price are so prevalent in bargaining that many professional negotiators do not consider such misstatements to be lies.[15] Indeed, some social science researchers, noticing that exaggerated demands and misstatements about reservation price seem to be the norm across cultures, have hypothesized that they serve a ritual function in negotiation. Lies about initial demands enable the parties to assert the legitimacy of their preferences and set the boundaries of the bargaining range without risk of loss.[16] Misleading statements about reservation prices enable parties to test the other side's commitment to their expressed preferences.

The U.S. legal profession has gone so far as to enshrine this practice in its Model Rules of Professional Conduct. These rules provide that "estimates of price or value placed on the subject of a transaction and a party's intention as to an acceptable settlement of a claim" are not material facts for purposes of the rule prohibiting lawyers from making false statements to a third person.[17]

There are thus no legal problems with lying about how much you might be willing to pay or which of several issues in a negotiation you value more highly. Demands and reservation prices are not, as a matter of law, material to a deal.

Some experienced negotiators may be surprised to learn, however, that there are legal problems when negotiators try to embellish their refusals to accept a particular price with supporting lies. Lies about "other offers" are classic problem cases of this sort. For example, take the following relatively older but still leading case from Massachusetts.[18] A commercial landlord bought a building and proceeded to negotiate a new lease with a toy shop tenant when the tenant's lease expired. The proprietor of the toy shop bargained hard and refused to pay the landlord's demand for a $10,000 increase in rent. The landlord then told the shop owner that he had another tenant willing to pay the amount and threatened the current tenant with immediate eviction if he did not promptly agree to the new rate. The tenant paid, but learned several years later that the threat had been a bluff; there was no other tenant. The tenant sued successfully for fraud.

In a more recent case, this time from Oklahoma, a real estate agent was held liable for fraud, including *punitive* damages, when she pressured a buyer into closing on a home with a story that a rival buyer (the contractor who built the house) was willing to pay the asking price and would do so later that same day.[19] In these cases, the made-up offer was a lie; it concerned an objective fact (either someone had made an offer or they had not), and the courts ruled that the lie could be material given all the circumstances. Note that such lies are not *always* illegal. Rather, the law is content to leave the ultimate question of liability to a jury, with all the expense and risk of a full trial. Of course, victims of such conduct may decide that litigation is not worth the trouble.

Fact

On the surface of the legal doctrine, it appears that only misstatements of objective fact are illegal. Negotiators seeking to walk close to the legal line are therefore careful to couch their "sales talk" in negotiation as opinions, predictions, and statements of intention, not statements of fact. Moreover, the law views a good deal of exaggeration or "puffing" about product attributes and likely performance as "part of the game." Buyers and sellers cannot take everything said to them at face value.

The surface of the law can be misleading, however. Courts have found occasions to punish statements of intention and opinion as fraudulent when faced with particularly egregious cases. The touchstone of fraud law is not whether the statement at issue was one of pure fact, but whether the statement was designed to conceal a set of facts detrimental to the negotiator's position.

Is it fraud if you misstate an intention—state that you are going to spend a loan on new equipment if you are really going to pay off an old debt? Yes. In the memorable words of a famous English judge, "The state of a man's mind is as much a fact as the state of his digestion."[20] Lies regarding intention even have a special name in the law: promissory fraud. All but a handful of states judicially recognize the tort of promissory fraud.[21] The key element in such a case is proof that the speaker knew he would not live up to his promise *at the time the promise was made,* that is, that he made the promise with his fingers crossed behind his back. Strict proof requirements would make this claim a legal rarity, because subjective intent can rarely, if ever, be conclusively proven. But the courts have not been uniformly strict in the proof required to show an intent not to keep a promise. Fraudulent intent cannot be inferred solely from nonperformance of the promise,[22] but circumstantial evidence such as "sharp" dealing throughout the transaction[23] or a refusal to acknowledge that a contract was made[24] is enough to get to the jury.

A particularly vivid example of this sort of conduct was litigated in *Markov* v. *ABC Transfer & Storage Co.*[25] A commercial tenant entered into negotiations to renew its lease on a warehouse and railroad yard. The warehouse was vital to the tenant's continued business relationship with its main client, the Scott Paper Company, because Scott used the warehouse as a regional product distribution facility. At a meeting during contract renewal negotiations, the landlord assured all parties, including Scott, that the tenant's lease would be renewed for a three-year term.

Unbeknownst to the tenant, the landlord was secretly negotiating to sell the property to the Boeing Company at the same time it was negotiating the lease renewal. The sale went through, and the landlord notified the tenant that it would have to vacate within 20 days. As a result, the tenant lost the Scott Paper contract and incurred extraordinary relocation expenses. The court found that the landlord's promise regarding the lease renewal was fraudulent, essentially made to string the tenant along in case the sale did not go through. It awarded damages for the tenant's lost profits from the Scott Paper contract and required the defendant to pay the tenant's extra moving expenses.

What about statements of opinion? Self-serving statements about the value of your goods or the qualifications of your product or company are standard fare at the negotiating table. However, when negotiators offer opinions that are flatly contradicted by facts known to them about the subject of the transaction, they may be liable for fraud. In one recent New York case, for example, the seller of a machine shop business opined to a prospective buyer that the buyer would have no trouble securing work from his largest customer.[26] In fact, the seller was in debt to his customer, intended to pay off the debt from the sale's proceeds, and had virtually no work there due to his reputation for poor workmanship. The buyer was able to prove that the sale was induced by the seller's fraudulent statement of opinion.

In summary, the seemingly strict requirement that fraud be based on statements of fact is, in reality, a flexible concept informed by a notion that parties must take responsibility for the impression they create by the words they use. What is important is not whether some verifiable object exists that corresponds to the speaker's statement. What matters is whether a statement so conceals the true nature of the negotiation proposal that a bargaining opponent cannot accurately assess an appropriate range of values or risks to price the transaction.

Reliance and Causation

Negotiators who lie sometimes defend themselves by saying, in effect, "Only a fool could have believed what I said. He had no business relying on me to tell him the truth!" The standard elements of fraud give some support to such defenses. The burden of proof is on the fraud victim and, among other things, the victim is supposed to prove she relied on the misstatement that caused damages. Surprisingly, however, most courts do not inquire too deeply into the reasonableness of the victim's reliance when the defendant is shown to have made a positive misrepresentation of fact. Courts have trouble swallowing the idea that overt fraud should go unpunished just because victims are lazy or fools. Where statements of opinion or mere nondisclosures are concerned, however, courts are more sympathetic to defendants. When the facts were obvious or the truth was accessible to the complaining party, courts will reject their claims of fraud.

Finally, in cases of promissory fraud, victims of false promises have particular trouble proving reasonable reliance when the speaker can show that the final written contract language flatly contradicts his earlier statements. So long as the contract document accurately corrects the representation alleged to be fraudulent, negotiators may escape liability.[27] If the misstatements are quite specific, however, and the contract terms negating them are only general, vague disclaimers, the negotiator may be in trouble. Two examples will help illustrate the legal limits on fraud in these circumstances. A seller named Turner negotiated the sale of his company's principal asset, an electronic thermometer, to Johnson & Johnson. The detailed contract included, as part of the purchase price, a promise of future royalties from the thermometer sales.[28] During the negotiations, Johnson & Johnson assured Turner that it would aggressively market the thermometer. The contract as signed, however, specifically stated that Johnson & Johnson had the legal right to shelve the product if it wished. Johnson & Johnson elected to stop marketing the product soon after the sale in favor of another thermometer it had acquired, and Turner sued for fraud. The court held that, even if Johnson & Johnson made its promise without intent to keep it, the plaintiffs were not entitled to rely on it after seeing that the final written contract negated the promise. "[I]f a jury is allowed to ignore contract provisions directly at odds with oral representations allegedly made during negotiations," the court said, "the language of a contract simply would not matter anymore. . . . And the give and take of negotiations would become meaningless if, after making concessions in order to obtain other contractual protections, a knowledgeable party is later able to reclaim what it had given away by alleging that it had, in fact, relied not on the writing but on the prior oral statements."[29]

By contrast, when the contract says only that the subject of the transaction is being sold "as is," such language does not provide ironclad protection to a seller for exaggerated or false negotiation claims about the condition of the property.[30] As one federal appeals court explained, "When a contract contains an 'as is' clause or other ambiguous language, the agreement is to some extent left undefined, and the plaintiff's understanding of the agreement logically may be colored by the defendant's prior statements, fraudulent or otherwise. Moreover, there is nothing on the face of the contract to trigger alarm."[31] Courts have similarly held that fraud victims may sue even if the contract contains language integrating all precontract representations into the final written document.[32]

The lessons of these cases are twofold. First, *read contracts carefully before you sign* and do not accept assurances that changed contract language is "just a technicality" or is "required by the lawyers." Second, if you have made some bold assurances in negotiations that you cannot live up to, *make sure the final contract document negates them specifically.* A general disclaimer may not protect you from fraud liability.

THE BOUNDARIES OF BAD FAITH: IMPLIED FRAUD

Although U.S. law disclaims a general duty of good faith in negotiations, it will nevertheless stretch to punish clear instances of bad faith. In such cases, even though the strict legal elements of fraud are missing, the courts will "imply" a promise or misrepresentation and will bend the usual rules to achieve a desired result.

For example, buyers usually have no duty to disclose the value of the object a seller is selling. Misrepresentations of value are considered nothing to get excited about because they are neither facts nor material to the seller's estimate of what the transaction is worth. However, if an elderly widow is selling an old painting that is, unknown to her, a museum piece, and a professional art dealer assures her that he is buying the work "primarily for the frame," he may run afoul of fraud law.[33] Misrepresentations of value may conceal an important fact to a relatively helpless seller, and the law is flexible enough to respond to such abuses in extreme cases.

Occasionally, negotiators use the bargaining process itself to get what they want, then walk away from the table. The law has a variety of ways of penalizing such bad faith conduct. In *Skycom Corp.* v. *Telstar Corp.*, for example, a company negotiating a sale of all its assets agreed, as part of preliminary negotiations, to let the prospective buyer take over ongoing negotiations with a third party for a valuable license.[34] The prospective buyer succeeded in getting the license but ultimately refused to go forward with the asset purchase. The disappointed seller sued. The court held that the parties' "letter of intent" left too many issues open to be construed as a completed contract, but it let the seller sue for the value of the lost license. The court said the buyer "may have induced [the seller] to turn over the negotiations and that [the seller] may have relied in a commercially reasonable way on representations made to him."

Courts have similarly ruled in favor of inventors and others who have disclosed trade secrets in the course of negotiations to sell their discoveries.[35] The prospective buyers in these cases have, in effect, attempted to use the negotiation process to get something for nothing, and the law is not sympathetic to such breaches of common good faith and trust. In essence, the courts have held that the buyer assumes an implied duty of confidentiality when it undertakes to review ideas or inventions. It can be fraudulent to breach this duty by trying to misappropriate the inventor's property during negotiations.

CONCLUSION: BUSINESS ETHICS AND THE LAW

When business theorists ask if lying in business negotiations is "ethical," they assume that deceptive conduct is often legal and argue that ethical sensibilities should govern one's negotiating behavior. As it turns out, this perspective on law and ethics is distorted. As this review of cases has shown, business negotiation law is infused with the norms of ethical business conduct. Indeed, the leading legal treatise writers on fraud candidly admit that "a new standard of business ethics" has resulted in complete shifts of legal doctrine in the past 50 years.[36] Unethical bargaining practices are, as often as not, illegal or become so after they are brought to light. The law simply expands to include them, definitions notwithstanding. However, when ethically acceptable conduct such as lying about reservation price appears to run foul of legal definitions, the law adjusts and refuses to penalize it. Thus, an ethical sensibility, far from being a "luxury" in business negotiations, may be a negotiator's best counselor.

In commenting on Michael Milken's recent guilty plea to securities law violations, financier H. Ross Perot gave this advice to young businesspeople: "Don't govern your life by what's legal or illegal, govern it by what's right or wrong." It turns out this is good legal as well as business advice, at least insofar as negotiation is concerned. In negotiation, people who rely on the letter of legal rules as a strategy for plotting unethical conduct are very likely to get into deep trouble. But people who rely on a cultivated sense of right and wrong to guide them in legal matters are likely to do well.

REFERENCES

Research for this paper was funded by the Reginald H. Jones Center for Management Policy, Strategy, and Organization.

1. Professor Robert H. Frank summed this up best when he wrote, "The art of bargaining, as most of us eventually learn, is in large part the art of sending misleading messages about [reservation prices]." See R. H. Frank, *Passions within Reason* (New York: Norton, 1988), p. 165.
2. Bargaining situations are often characterized as either distributive (zero-sum negotiations) or integrative (non-zero-sum negotiations). Distributive negotiations typically involve a single, divisible issue such as money. Integrative bargaining involves many issues that differ in importance to the parties, making possible mutual gains from trade across issues. See R. E. Walton and R. B. McKersie, *A Behavioral Theory of Labor Negotiations* (New York: McGraw-Hill, 1965).

   Both distributive and integrative bargaining situations, however, are "mixed motive" in character and contain within them incentives to lie or at least mislead. See D. A. Lax and J. K. Sebenius, *The Manager as Negotiator* (New York: The Free Press, 1986), pp. 30–35.
3. The most famous recent treatment of the ethics of lying is Sissela Bok's book *Lying: Moral Choice in Public and Private Life* (New York: Vintage, 1978).

   Other influential articles include:

   A. Z. Carr, "Is Business Bluffing Ethical?" *Harvard Business Review,* January-February 1968, pp. 143–50; and R. E. Wokutch and T. L. Carson, "The Ethics and Profitability of Bluffing in Business," in *Ethical Issues in Business,* 3rd ed., eds. T. Donaldson and P. H. Werhane (Englewood Cliffs, N.J.: Prentice Hall, 1988), pp. 77–83. None of these works focuses on legality of lying and some, such as Carr's piece, explicitly assume that the law's reach extends only to the most blatant forms of fraud.

4. I have conducted an extensive search of the social scientific literature on bargaining deception and have found none that examines the effects of legal rules on bargaining behavior.
5. This trend extends to other areas of law as well. See G. R. Shell, "Substituting Ethical Standards for Common Law Rules in Commercial Cases: An Emerging Statutory Trend," *Northwestern University Law Review* 82 (1988): 1198–1254.
6. The Uniform Commercial Code states that the UCC's general duty of good faith applies only to the performance and enforcement of agreements, not their negotiation. *Uniform Commercial Code* 1–203. See also *Restatement (Second) of Contracts* 205 (1981) comment c ("Bad faith in negotiation" is not "within the scope of this Section.") *Id.*205 comment c.
7. *Feldman* v. *Allegheny International, Inc.*, 850F.2d 1217, 1223 (7th Cir. 1988).
8. W. P. Keeton, D. B. Dobbs, R. E. Keeton, and D. G. Owen, *Prosser and Keeton on the Law of Torts* (St. Paul, Minnesota: West, 1984), p. 728.
9. *Computer Systems Engineering, Inc.* v. *Qantel Corp.*, 740 F.2d 59 (1st Cir. 1984).
10. *Eckley* v. *Colorado Real Estate Commission*, 752 P.2d 68 (Colo. 1988).
11. See *Berger* v. *Security Pacific Information Systems, Inc.*, No. 88CA0822 (Colo. App. April 5, 1990); and "Companies Must Disclose Shaky Finances to Some Applicants, a Colorado Court Rules," *The Wall Street Journal*, 20 April 1990, p. B12. Award of $250,000 in actual and punitive damages against employer.
12. *Miles* v. *McSwegin*, 388 N.E.2d 1367 (Ohio 1979).
13. *Zaschak* v. *Traverse Corp.*, 333 N.W.2d 191 (Mich. App. 1983).
14. *Jordon* v. *Duff & Phelps, Inc.*, 815 F.2d 429 (7th Cir. 1987).
15. Rather, they refer to them as "puffery" or "feints." See P. Freund, *The Acquisition Mating Dance* (Clifton, New Jersey: Prentice Hall, 1987), p. 164; and G. Nierenberg, *Fundamentals of Negotiating* (New York: Hawthorn/Dutton, 1973), p. 159.
16. See J. G. Cross, *The Economics of Bargaining* (New York: Basic Books, 1969), pp. 166–179; and P. H. Gulliver, *Disputes and Negotiation: A Cross-Cultural Perspective* (New York: Academic Press, 1979), pp. 135–141.
17. American Bar Association, *Model Rules of Professional Conduct* Rule 4.1(a) official comment (1983).
18. *Kabatchnick* v. *Hanover-Elm Building Corp.*, 103 N.E.2d 692 (Mass. 1952).
19. *Beavers* v. *Lamplighters Realty, Inc.*, 556 P.2d 1328 (Okla. App. 1976).
20. *Edgington* v. *Fitzmaurice, L. R.* 29 Ch. Div. 359 (1885).
21. Indiana courts have rejected the doctrine. Illinois courts require that the plaintiff prove a "scheme" to defraud in addition to other promissory fraud elements. Tennessee courts have explicitly reserved judgment on the existence of the tort. States such as New York, California, and Texas approve the doctrine.
22. *Britt* v. *Britt*, 359 S.E.2d 467, 471 (N.C. 1987); and *Hodges* v. *Pittman*, 530 So.2d 817, 818 (Ala. 1988).
23. *Hanover Modular Homes* v. *Scottish Inns*, 443 F. Supp. 888, 891–92 (W.D. La. 1978); and *Brier* v. *Koncen Meat Co.*, 762 S.W.2d 499, 500 (Mo. App. 1988).
24. *New Process Steel Corp.* v. *Steel Corp.*, 703 S.W.2d 209, 214 (Tex. App. 1985).
25. 457 P.2d 535 (Wash. 1969). See also *Gibraltar Savings* v. *I. D. Brinkman Corp.*, 860 F.2d 1275 (5th Cir. 1988). Debtor promised creditor to keep holding company solvent when plans were under way to dissolve holding company. This was deemed fraudulent, resulting in a $6 million verdict.
26. *Alio* v. *Saponaro*, 520 N.Y.S.2d 245 (A.D. 1987).
27. The statement in the text does not extend to "consumer" cases. See, for example: *Boykin* v. *Hermitage Realty*, 360 S.E.2d 177 (Va. 1987). Condominium owners claimed fraud

based on assurances by a realtor that the lot behind their units would remain undeveloped even though readily available public records showed that it was the site of a future playground.

28. *Turner* v. *Johnson & Johnson,* 809 F.2d 90 (1st Cir. 1986).
29. *Turner* v. *Johnson & Johnson,* 809 F.2d 96.
30. See *V.H.S. Realty, Inc.* v. *Texaco, Inc.,* 757 F.2d 411, 418 (1st Cir. 1985).
31. *Turner* v. *Johnson & Johnson,* 809 F.2d at 96.
32. *Turner* v. *Johnson & Johnson,* 809 F.2d at 95 (citing cases). But see *Grumman Allied Industries, Inc.* v. *Rohr Industries, Inc.,* 748 F.2d 729 (2d Cir. 1984). Contractual language stipulating that a buyer of company assets has not relied on any warranties or representations regarding design of new bus precludes claim based on failure to disclose poor ''stress test'' results on bus prototype.
33. *Zimpel* v. *Trawick,* 679 F.Supp. 1502 (W.D. Ark. 1988). An elderly, sick widow was defrauded when a professional land speculator bought her land without telling her that oil and gas had been discovered on it.
34. 813 F.2d 810 (7th Cir. 1987).
35. See *Smith* v. *Snap-On Tools Corp.,* 833 F.2d 578 (5th Cir. 1988). No liability was found when the inventor made a gift of invention to the company. See also *Smith* v. *Dravo Corp.,* 203 F.2d 369 (7th Cir. 1953). Liability was found when the inventor intended negotiations to lead to sale of a trade secret.
36. Keeton et al. (1984), pp. 739, 751–52. In the past half-century, nondisclosure law has evolved to a ''standard requiring conformity to what the ordinary ethical person would have disclosed,'' and the ''new standard of business ethics'' has ''led to an almost complete shift'' in law regarding reasonable reliance.

Ah, Sweet Vengeance!

Harry Stein

Martha had a plan. In circumstances like these, Martha always had a plan. Her friend Jake, a minor executive at the New York office of a film studio, had been maneuvered out of a promotion by an ambition-consumed rival, and Martha damn well wasn't about to take it sitting down.

"Here's what we do," she said, leaning forward conspiratorially although the restaurant was empty except for the five of us at the table. "We're gonna make a total fool out of the guy. We're gonna make him the laughingstock of the industry."

Jake grinned. "I could go for that," he said.

"How?" I asked.

Martha drummed her fingers on the table. "It's complicated," she said. "We're going to need some help out on the Coast, but I think I know where to get it." And then she presented the plan, a caper rivaling that of *The Sting* in its scope. A few days hence, the rival would receive a call from an actor friend of Martha's posing as an important executive at Twentieth Century-Fox in California. The friend would hint at a job offer and urge him to drop everything in New York and come to California the next day. This important executive would add, casually, that the rival should fly out first class, register at the Beverly Hills Hotel, and drop the receipts off with the executive's secretary when he arrived for the meeting. Then—this was the beauty part—another pal of Martha's, who worked as a secretary at the studio, would make sure there was a pass in the rival's name waiting at the gate. He would actually make his way up to the executive's office—to face the humiliation of learning that no one there had the slightest idea who he was.

"Who knows?" concluded Martha triumphantly. "With luck, his current boss will find out about it. He might even get fired!"

There followed such an eruption of good cheer around the table that a waitress was drawn over to inquire whether we might be interested in a bottle of champagne. Only one of us—Jake's wife, Susan—remained aloof from the bonhomie.

"I'd just like to ask one thing," she ventured finally. "What is all of this going to accomplish?"

The rest of us looked at her in bald astonishment. "What will it accomplish?" repeated Martha. "It will accomplish *revenge*."

In the end, thanks to Susan's considerable powers of dissuasion, Jake refused to give the plan his go-ahead, and Martha was left more than a little disappointed. But I

From Harry Stein, "Ah, Sweet Vengeance," *Esquire*, May 1981, pp. 14-16. Reprinted by permission.

don't mean to convey the wrong impression about Martha. She is, in general, a very decent woman—thoughtful, courteous, and as loyal as anyone I have ever known. Indeed, that is why she lashes out with such energy at those who cross her or hers, why she will arrange to screw those who are needlessly vicious in their professional dealings.

That impulse is understandable because it is so terribly human. Most of us have felt surges of hostility so violent, so compelling, that we have literally fantasized murder. There was a period five or six years ago—it lasted a month—when I used to lie awake at night wondering how I might do away (inconspicuously yet very, very painfully) with a particularly loathsome agent who had double-crossed me. I still have to swallow hard when I think about the creep.

Indeed, imagining any act of violence seems far more comprehensible than maintaining utter calm in the face of terrible provocation. That "don't get mad, get even" mentality has been embraced not only by the efficiency experts who direct organized crime but by legions of political leaders and chamber of commerce types as well. It is a major reason that the machinations of *Dallas's* J. R. ring true to so many millions of us, and it has something to do with the unhappy state of our society.

However, as Jake's wife pointed out, retribution for its own sake is hardly a reasonable alternative. Almost all of Martha's acts of revenge appear to have been justly motivated, and some of them have even worked, but not one has succeeded in righting the initial wrong. Nor, for that matter, has one served to make Martha or her friends feel better for more than a few minutes. For, of course, none has ever touched the source of the pain.

With depressing frequency, the traveler along the low road actually ends up feeling a lot worse. For starters, we *look* so irredeemably small when we're caught being vindictive. I shudder to imagine how Jake would have reacted if the California scheme had gone through and his rival or—Jesus!—his boss had chanced upon its origin.

But detection is almost beside the point. The fact is, vindictive behavior and meanness of spirit finally make us as small as those we despise. Even when we do manage to hurt others as we have been hurt, we succeed, in a real sense, only in further victimizing ourselves. Obviously, that is not an easy thing for one fixated on vengeance to recognize. The vengeful impulse tends to obscure our better instincts and to stymie logic as well.

Vindictive behavior is not only self-destructive; it can also wound people who had nothing to do with the initial dispute. A friend of mine told of arriving at her office one morning to find her boss, a prominent magazine editor, in tears. "She'd recently been dumped by her husband," said my friend, "and she was absolutely shattered. But suddenly she stopped crying. 'I'm going to get even,' she announced. 'I'm going to tell our daughter how her father screwed around when I was pregnant.' And I swear to God, she meant it!"

Relatively few people would be quite that candid about their vindictive intentions, but it is a pretty good bet that the editor would not be the first on her block to have adopted such a tactic.

"I tried to get her to calm down," continued my friend. "I explained to her how sorry she'd be later.

" 'Okay, she replied, 'then what do you suggest I do to him?'

" 'Nothing. Just go along as best you can, and eventually you'll get past this. The best way to get back at him is to show him how well you can do without him.' "

My friend, as you might surmise, is a soul of staggering sweetness, and she continued to express dismay at her boss's reaction. The editor ordered her from the room forthwith. Like most of us, my friend's boss was so used to operating the other way—to getting even—that she was incapable of recognizing the elementary truth of that famous maxim: Living well *is* the best revenge.

At this juncture another, more recent, adage springs to mind: What goes around comes around. It is, all in all, a terrific sentiment, and I know a lot of people who would turn handsprings if only they could be assured it was true.

Well, I'm here to do some assuring. The fact is, the editor's husband (if he is as vicious a bastard as she maintains) will almost certainly get his, and so will Jake's rival and all of Martha's many wrongdoers. They might be successful professionally—might even, conceivably, seem to lead placid domestic lives—but it is almost a sure thing that all of those people are in knots inside. People at peace with themselves simply don't act cruelly toward others. When the rest of us finally accept that law of human behavior, we'll be a hell of a lot better off ourselves.

I am all too well aware that such wisdom about the way of the world is easier to set down on paper than to apply to one's own experience. Just a couple of weeks ago, I laid aside the beginnings of this piece to thumb through a local magazine of some repute, and there, to my astonishment, I found a vicious attack on the character of a very close friend of mine, whose much-acclaimed first novel had recently been published. Now, I care immensely about this fellow and am familiar with the fragility of his ego, and I found myself irate on his behalf. Not only had the attack—by a supposedly reputable journalist—been needlessly vituperative, it was also, I knew, completely without foundation. When I called my friend, I discovered that he had moved from deep depression to rage and was now ready to sling a little mud himself. "What do you think," he asked, "of my getting a friend in the press to blast the son of a bitch? Or would it be better just to call his editor myself? *I want the bastard to pay.*"

So, as it happened, did I, but for the moment we decided to do nothing more dramatic than discuss it over dinner. As I was leaving for this rendezvous I got a call from another old friend, a guy just back from a long business trip, and I suggested that he join us.

This other fellow made it to the restaurant just as the novelist and I were warming to the unpleasant subject at hand. When he'd gotten an earful, he broke into a broad grin.

"What's so funny?" I demanded. "Did you read what that guy wrote?"

"Yeah, I read it."

"So what's so funny?" I asked.

He laughed. "That you two are taking it so seriously." He turned to our friend. "Don't you know about that guy?" he asked. "For years he's been trying to get someone to pay attention to his own fiction. He's the most bitter guy in town."

This last, I understood, was hyperbole—the town in question was, after all, New York—but the revelation was more than enough to restore our friend's good mood. After eliciting a few more details about his adversary's ugly disposition, he settled back to enjoy his meal.

And enjoy it he did. By dessert he was in better spirits than I'd seen him in for months.

"No more plotting?" I inquired.

He laughed. "His private demons seem to be handling him just fine."

International Negotiations

More and more businesses conduct business overseas. Be it a joint venture in China, technology transfer in Europe, outsourcing in the Far East, or new ventures in the former Eastern Bloc, American business is looking beyond its own borders more than ever before. Negotiating across national and cultural boundaries complicates the negotiation process. Obvious challenges such as logistics and language are just the tip of the iceberg of the special circumstances of international negotiations. More subtle issues such as the meaning of time, how concessions are made, who should be members of the bargaining team, and so on, abound in international negotiations. To make this even more complex, our most basic assumptions about what negotiation is, how it works, why it is done, and where it is appropriate may or may not be shared by the other party with whom we are negotiating.

The literature on international negotiations has grown rapidly in the last 10 years. Both practitioners and academics have been studying international negotiations, and the size and complexity of the topic ensures that this research will continue well into the future. While a great deal has been written about international negotiations, much of it is fragmented and impressionistic. Recent work has been more holistic, but it is a large challenge to understand the complexity of even one culture in addition to our own. The first two articles in this section integrate and summarize a great deal of recent research on international negotiation; the first discusses special constraints involved in international negotiations, and the second explores how culture and negotiation are linked. The third article investigates in detail the Japanese negotiation style. The section concludes with an article that discusses the American negotiation style from the European perspective.

In the first article in this section, "Making Deals in Strange Places," Jeswald Salacuse argues that international negotiating is a complicated process that is much more than merely "making deals in strange places." Salacuse discusses six factors that act to constrain international negotiations: political and legal pluralism, international monetary problems, foreign governments and bureaucracies, instability and sudden change, ideology, and cultural differences. He discusses each of the constraints in detail and uses examples of international negotiations from around the world throughout the article. For Salacuse, the six constraints act to increase the risk of conducting international business negotiations, and the superior negotiator works to recognize and understand their effects.

In the article "Rethinking the Culture – Negotiation Link," Robert Janosik discusses the links between culture and negotiation. Janosik reviews the vast literature on cross-cultural negotiation and identifies four ways that academics and practitioners have examined the link between culture and negotiation: culture as learned behavior, culture as shared value, culture as dialectic, and culture in context. Each of these approaches is discussed in detail, and Janosik provides numerous examples of cross-cultural negotiations throughout. Janosik suggests that each perspective contains elements that are necessary for obtaining a comprehensive understanding of international negotiation.

In their reading "The Japanese Negotiation Style," John Graham and Yoshihiro Sano present a detailed discussion of the Japanese style of negotiation. Few cultures have intrigued North Americans as much as the Japanese, and Japanese business practices have captured the interest of Westerners for the last two decades. A central aspect of conducting business in Japan, as in the West, is negotiating. Graham and Sano discuss the cultural and environmental roots of the Japanese negotiation style and present the key aspects that are unique to Japanese business negotiations. They discuss how buyers and sellers are treated differently in Japan, and how this translates into the negotiation process. The article contains a discussion of special problems that occur when American sellers negotiate with Japanese buyers, and concludes with a point-by-point comparison between American and Japanese negotiation styles.

In the final article in this section, "John Wayne Goes to Brussels," Samfrits Le Poole offers a European perspective on negotiating with Americans. Le Poole cautions the reader from treating all Europeans as identical negotiators before noting that there are many similarities among European negotiators that distinguish them from American negotiators. He discusses some of the cultural differences between Europeans and Americans before discussing six key differences in the negotiation process between Europe and the United States.

Making Deals in Strange Places:
A Beginner's Guide to
International Business Negotiations

Jeswald W. Salacuse

The decline in U.S. business competitiveness abroad has led policymakers and scholars to point to many causes: protectionism in foreign markets, unfair trade practices by other nations, failures in international economic cooperation, and inadequacies in our own educational system. While these institutional and policy factors certainly influence global trade and capital flows, and therefore deserve careful study, discussions about competitiveness have generally neglected the basic molecule of those flows—the international business deal.

Most economic commentators take international deal making for granted, apparently on the assumption that if the right policies and structures are in place, business among nations will automatically follow. Experience clearly shows, however, that negotiating an international business transaction is a difficult, painstaking process that can fail even in the presence of the most favorable policies and institutions.

A second unstated assumption underlies much of the current talk about competitiveness and the need to "go international" as a solution to U.S. economic problems—that American corporations, so skillful at what they do domestically, only have to do the same things outside our borders to succeed internationally. For many government officials and corporate leaders, international business is really just an extension of domestic business. They seem to believe that the attitudes, skills, and knowledge that have served American companies in Akron and Kansas City will, with some adjustment to the local climate, almost certainly work just as well in Accra and Kuala Lumpur. After all, business is business, products are products and, when you come right down to it, international business is really nothing more than making deals in strange places.

Both of those assumptions are false, and both are damaging to U.S. international competitiveness. First, success in international business will require U.S. executives to

Reprinted from Jeswald W. Salacuse, "Making Deals in Strange Places: A Beginner's Guide to International Business Negotiations," *Negotiation Journal*, January 1988, pp. 5–13. Used with permission of the author and Plenum Publishing Corporation.

know much more about and to become more expert in negotiating international trans-actions, regardless of the policies and institutions that emerge to foster global trade and investment. Second, negotiating international business transactions must be seen as fundamentally different from making domestic deals, and not merely an extension of domestic activity.

Indeed, international business may be as much an extension of international relations as it is of domestic business. With only slight exaggeration, one might say that domestic business dealings probably have about the same relationship to international business as domestic politics do to international diplomacy. Just as we have come to realize that the craft of the diplomat is different from that of the politician, we must also recognize that the knowledge, skills, and attitudes necessary for international business negotiation are not those ordinarily found in the average U.S. executive whose work is essentially local.

To become more competitive internationally, the United States must develop international negotiation as a distinct body of knowledge and expertise that can be taught in our schools, discussed in our management seminars, and analyzed in our journals. Certainly, the literature on the subject of negotiation is vast, but much of it is anecdotal, unsystematic, and limited to a specific country or region. It may tell us when to cross our legs in Saudi Arabia or how to drink our tea in Singapore, but it does not often provide a basic approach to international negotiations as a fundamental task in international business. My purpose in this brief chapter is to offer one such general approach—a beginner's guide, if you will—to thinking about international deal making.

SIX COMMMON FACTORS IN INTERNATIONAL DEALS

International business transactions are extremely diverse. At first glance, it is difficult to see many similarities among a Eurodollar loan by a group of London banks, a manufacturing joint venture with a rural commune in China, a technology licensing agreement with a Japanese multinational, and a barter deal with a state trading organization in the Soviet Union. Nonetheless, the basic argument of this article is: (1) that international business transactions, *as a group*, are shaped by certain basic common factors that are not present in the ordinary domestic business deal; and (2) that these factors both give international transactions, of whatever type, a conceptual unity, while at the same time differentiating them sharply from ordinary U.S. domestic dealings. Equally important, these factors fundamentally shape the process of negotiating international business deals of all sorts, and they must therefore be studied and mastered.

In general terms, international business negotiations are conditioned by six fundamental constraints: (1) political and legal pluralism; (2) international monetary factors; (3) the role of governments and bureaucracies; (4) instability and sudden change; (5) ideological diversity; and (6) cultural differences. Together these six factors constitute a framework for analyzing the negotiation of international business transactions and perhaps eventually for building a general theory of international deal making.

1. Political and Legal Pluralism

By engaging in international business, a company enters into an arena of intense legal and political pluralism. An export sale, a direct foreign investment, or a technology transfer brings at least one of the parties to the deal into contact with the laws and political authority of more than one country. As a result, a transaction may be taxed by two or more governments, a contract may be subject to two or more legal systems, and a dispute may be decided by two or more courts.

A notorious example of the kind of political and legal pluralism that a business deal may face is the construction of the Trans-Siberian pipeline in the early 1980s. American companies and their European subsidiaries were caught between the law and political power of the United States and the law and political authority of our European allies. In that case, the U.S. government ordered the European subsidiaries of American companies not to supply equipment and technology for the Trans-Siberian pipeline, while the European governments demanded that they respect their supply contracts. Only diplomacy at the highest level finally resolved the problem.

Although the Soviet pipeline case attracted considerable attention, it is certainly not a unique example of legal and political pluralism in international business. The practice of negotiating international business transactions is always a matter of complying with or avoiding a multiplicity of different national rules, laws, and policies—of weaving between overlapping legislation and political decisions of numerous governments.

Although this problem is hardly ever a consideration in a domestic deal, it is constantly present in any international business negotiation, and clearly conditions the thinking of international business negotiators. As a result, international business transactions always include special measures, including provisions for international commercial arbitration, specific choice of the governing law, and the use of tax havens.

2. International Monetary Factors

Monetary problems are a second set of special contraints to be faced in international business negotiations. Unlike purely domestic deals, international business transactions take place in a world of many currencies and monetary systems. Transactions cross monetary as well as political boundaries and there is no single world currency for making payment. The existence of so many different monetary systems creates two fundamental problems in negotiating any international business transaction.

First, the relative values of the world's currencies constantly fluctuate, and that factor creates special risks for the party who is to be paid in a currency that is not its own. Between the time an agreement is signed and the time that payment is actually received, the value of the payment currency may either increase or decrease, thereby creating an unexpected loss for one side and an undeserved gain for the other.

The rapid rise in the value of the yen in recent months, for example, has certainly affected Japanese negotiators in structuring new transactions. To cope with this problem, negotiators may seek to use various complicated devices whose function is basically to reallocate currency risk between the two sides or to shift it to a third party such as a bank.

The second major monetary problem that conditions international business negotiations derives from the fact that most governments try to control the entry to, possession in, and exit from their territories of both foreign and local currencies. These regulations, known as exchange controls, may be imposed virtually without warning, and they can seriously affect the profitability of a transaction.

In many countries, a company's ability to pay for imported raw materials, to service foreign loans, or to repatriate profits depends on the ability and the willingness of the host government to make convertible foreign currency available. In structuring direct foreign investments and joint ventures, one of the principal preoccupations of the negotiator is to find means to avoid or blunt the effect of these controls.

In purely domestic transactions, currency questions are hardly ever of concern; however, they are pervasive in negotiating any international business transaction. In long-term contracts, the parties often have to devise complicated mechanisms to protect themselves from currency fluctuations. Special arrangements and guarantees may have to be negotiated with local governments to assure the availability of foreign exchange. The lack of convertible currency has led to the growth of sophisticated types of barter transactions known as "countertrade," in which payment is made in goods, rather than cash. The possibility of countertrade is always present in business negotiation with many nations, including China and the Soviet Union.

3. The Role of Foreign Governments and Bureaucracies

Americans are often unprepared for the extensive—indeed pervasive—role played by foreign governments in international business. Governments not only regulate economic activities and organize public utilities, as is fairly common in the United States, but they are also active as participants through governmental ministries, corporations, and agencies in all sorts of business activities from trading and insurance to manufacturing and agriculture.

In many nations, government corporations have an exclusive monopoly over all imports entering the country and all exports leaving it. Indeed for American corporations seeking major customers or joint-venture partners in many parts of the world, governmental entities are the only realistic possibilities. As a result, transactions that in the United States are conducted between private parties are accomplished abroad with governments.

Does that fact make a difference in negotiating international transactions? Absolutely. Negotiations with government corporations and enterprises involve a host of different considerations from those with private firms. For example, freedom of negotiation may be limited. State corporations, like those in the Soviet Union, may be required to use standard form contracts that include mandatory clauses on payment terms, insurance, and guarantees, to mention just a few. They may also be tied by the rigid rules and regulations controlling government departments. The attitudes, work habits, and styles of operation of their officials often resemble those of a government bureaucracy, rather than of private enterprise, and their goals may conflict with those of a private company.

And, since they are subsidized by the state treasury, the principal goal of these state entities may not be the maximization of profit, but rather social and political ends.

For example, if a manufacturing joint venture between a U.S. company and a state-owned foreign corporation were to be faced by a decline in product demand, the reaction of the U.S. partner might be to lay off workers while the foreign government corporation, despite reduced profitability, might reject that solution so as not to increase unemployment.

Foreign government officials often bring to the negotiating table bureaucratic attitudes and approaches that introduce rigidity into the negotiating process. Moreover, negotiations with foreign state enterprises raise special legal problems including sovereign immunity and their authority to act without specific government approval.

4. Instability and Sudden Change

Change, of course, is a fact of life, and change in circumstances is to be found in both domestic and international business. Nevertheless, the nature and magnitude of the risk of change in the international arena appear to be far greater than in a purely domestic setting. The outbreak of war and revolution, the closing of international trade routes, the devaluation of currencies, coups d'états, and sudden shifts in government policies are just a few examples of events that have severe and widespread consequences for any international transaction. Within the past few years, we need only give such examples as the closing of the Suez Canal as a result of the Arab-Israeli conflict, the fall of the Shah of Iran, and most recently the Iran/Iraq War as examples of sudden changes that have affected international business transactions in the Middle East alone.

To cope with these risks, business negotiators use a variety of mechanisms and strategies that they would not ordinarily employ in purely domestic transactions, including political risk analysis, *force majeure* clauses that allow cancellation of the contract upon the happening of specified events, the purchase of foreign investment insurance, and the provision of international arbitration in a neutral third country.

The risk of instability places strong pressure on international business negotiators to anticipate change, and in this sense, negotiating an international deal is very much a predictive process. How does a negotiator anticipate change? How does he or she plan for it? Predictions, of course, are always difficult; they are especially difficult, it has been said, when they concern the future.

But surely the wise negotiator must begin with a thorough knowledge of the country and the region concerned, and of the political, economic, and social forces at work. Consequently, these factors require the international business negotiator to have a breadth of knowledge and social insight that would not ordinarily be necessary in negotiating a U.S. business arrangement.

5. Problems of Ideology

Whether they are Republicans or Democrats, American business negotiators generally share a common ideology, but in the international arena business negotiators normally encounter—and must be prepared to deal with—ideologies vastly different from their own. Three areas of ideological difference often faced by U.S. negotiators are private investment, profit, and individual rights.

Americans tend to view private investment as a positive good, a force to create wealth, jobs, useful products, and income; however, many foreign countries look at it more circumspectly. For them, foreign investment has its benefits and its costs, and they seek to maximize the benefits and minimize the costs through governmental regulation. The subject of profit is also viewed differently. For Americans, profit results from growth and is good because it can be reinvested to yield further benefits; however, in some countries the profit one party gains is seen as value taken away from someone else. Similarly, Americans tend to stress the rights of the individual, but other nations emphasize the rights of the group.

The existence of a conflict in ideologies often requires the negotiator to find ways of wrapping proposals in ideological packages that are acceptable to the other party, and to find neutral means of communicating with negotiators on the other side.

6. Cultural Differences

International business transactions not only cross political and ideological boundaries, they also cross cultures. As a powerful factor shaping thought, communication, and behavior, culture conditions the negotiating process in some very fundamental ways. Negotiators from different cultures may have quite distinct approaches to negotiations, and their styles of negotiating may be markedly different. Numerous books and articles have stressed the differences in negotiating styles of such diverse cultural groups as the Japanese (e.g., Tung, 1984); the Soviets (e.g., Vlachoutsicos, 1986); the Chinese (e.g., Pye, 1982); and the Americans (e.g., Graham and Herberger, 1983). While this literature is useful, some works are overly anecdotal and tend to create cultural stereotypes.

Persons of different cultures often speak different languages, a factor that certainly complicates the negotiating process, requiring interpreters and translators or forcing one side to negotiate in a foreign language. But communicating with another culture is not just a matter of learning the other side's vocabulary; it also requires an understanding of its values, perceptions, and philosophies. Different cultures operate on the basis of different unspoken assumptions, and each may interpret the same phenomenon in very different ways.

For example, it is possible for negotiators from different cultures to interpret the very purpose of their negotiation differently. For most Americans, the purpose of negotiations, first and foremost, is to arrive at a signed contract between the parties. Americans view a signed contract as a definitive set of rights and obligations that strictly binds the two sides, an attitude succinctly summed up in the declaration that "a deal is a deal."

Japanese and Chinese, on the other hand, view the signed contract in a very different light. For them, the "deal" being negotiated is not the contract, but the relationship between the parties. Although the written contract expresses that relationship, the essence of the deal is the relationship, and it is understood that the relationship may be subject to reasonable changes over time. For the American, signing a contract is "closing a deal"; for the Japanese, signing the contract might more appropriately be called "opening a relationship."

Since the Japanese and the American view the end product of negotiations differently, perhaps one can say that, from an intercultural perspective, "a deal is not always a deal." The consequences of this difference in perception are important. For example, if a Japanese joint-venture partner seeks to modify the terms of the contract because of a change in business conditions, the American participant may view these efforts as an outrageous attempt to renege on a deal. The Japanese participants, on the other hand, may consider the American reaction to be unreasonable rigidity and a refusal to allow the contract to conform to the underlying relationship.

A reflection of this dichotomy is also found in differing approaches to writing a contract. Generally, Americans prefer very detailed contracts that attempt to foresee and anticipate all possible circumstances, no matter how unlikely. Why? Because the "deal" is the contract itself, and one must go to the contract to determine how to handle a new circumstance that may arise.

Other cultures, such as China, prefer a contract in the form of general principles, rather than detailed rules. Why? Because the essence of the deal is the relationship of trust that exists between the parties. If unexpected circumstances arise, the parties should look to their relationship, not the written contract, to solve the problem.

So in some cases, the American drive at the negotiating table to foresee all possible contingencies may be seen by another culture as evidence of mistrust in the stability of the underlying relationship.

Related to this issue is the question of whether negotiating a business deal is an *inductive* or a *deductive* process. Does it start from agreement on general principles and then proceed to specific items, or does it begin with agreements on specifics (e.g., price, delivery date, product quality), the sum total of which becomes the contract?

One observer (Pye, 1982, p. 95) believes that the Chinese prefer to begin with agreement on general principles, while Americans seek first to agree on specifics. For Americans, negotiating a deal is basically making a whole series of compromises and trade-offs on a long list of particulars. For Chinese, the essence is to agree on basic general principles which will guide and indeed determine the negotiation process afterward.

A further difference in negotiating style is the dichotomy between the "building-down approach," where the negotiator begins by presenting the maximum deal if the other side accepts all the stated conditions, and the "building-up approach," where one side starts by proposing a minimal deal that can be broadened and increased as the other party accepts further conditions. According to many observers, Americans tend to favor the building-down approach, while the Japanese prefer the building-up style of negotiating a contract.

The purpose of any negotiation is not merely to reach an agreement, but to reach an agreement that will regulate the parties' behavior. For the Westerner, this necessary element raises the question of contract enforcement, of creating mechanisms to impose the agreement on one of the parties who at some later time may refuse to respect its provisions.

For Westerners, enforcement means the use of the courts, compulsory arbitration, and, ultimately, state power in some form. Many countries in Asia resist this tendency. China, for example, has opposed the use of Western courts and even international arbitration, preferring instead to resort to friendly negotiations, conciliation, and mediation in the event of a dispute.

As many authors have pointed out, culture also influences the organization of the negotiators. Here, the American approach to organization is sometimes characterized as "John Wayne" style of negotiations: one person has all the authority and plunges ahead to do the job, and to do the job as quickly as possible (Graham and Herberger, 1983, p.162). Other cultures, notably the Japanese and the Soviets, stress team negotiations and collective decision making. Indeed, it may not be fully apparent who has the authority to bind the side.

In East-West deals, the American style of one-person management often collides with the collective decision-making approach found in the Soviet Union. In negotiating with the Soviets, decision-making authority may not always rest with the most visible member of the negotiating team and one must not overlook the power of lesser officials on the negotiating team. (Vlachoutsicos, 1986, p. 83) In any international business negotiation, it is therefore important for each side to determine how the other side is organized, who has the authority, and how decisions on each side are made.

The various methods of organization, the varying degrees of authority given to the negotiators, and the differing needs to foster mutual trust and to build relationships all may significantly affect the pace of the negotiation process. Americans are often accused of wanting to go too fast in negotiations, of pushing to close the deal in the quickest time possible. On the other hand, one of the commonest complaints from American negotiators about any given international business negotiation—with virtually any foreign enterprise—is that the negotiations are proceeding too slowly. Rarely does one hear an American complain that negotiations are going too quickly.

Whether a negotiation is proceeding too quickly or too slowly may be less a function of some objective universal criteria than of the cultural perspective of the individual negotiators. Nonetheless, the pace of negotiations is an important factor and the party who is able to control the pace generally has an advantage, particularly in international transactions where one side is required to negotiate at a great distance (and therefore usually at great expense) from its home base.

Although cultural differences may create difficulties in international business negotiations, they are not insuperable obstacles. Through experience, negotiators begin to understand each other's perspectives and develop effective ways of cross-cultural communication.

Contrary to what some of the literature on international negotiations would lead us to believe, all negotiators from a particular culture are not cut from a uniform mold and do not represent a single stereotype. China, Japan, the United States, and the Soviet Union each are blessed with experienced negotiators capable of dealing effectively with foreigners, and they also have numerous parochial novices for whom cultural and other negotiating constraints may be nearly insurmountable.

This phenomenon would seem to argue for specialized formal training in international business negotiation. Such education would develop business negotiators in a systematic way rather than leave the process to costly, on-the-job training, which all too often assumes that international business negotiation is merely making deals in strange places.

CONCLUSION

Any business negotiation, whether domestic or international, must treat a host of difficult commercial issues—price, product quality, size of capital contribution, delivery dates—depending on the nature of the transaction in question.

In failing to discuss these issues in this chapter, I do not mean to suggest that they are unimportant or are somehow easy to solve in the international setting. On the contrary, they go to the essence of the transaction, and are always subject to hard bargaining.

But in addition to the strictly commercial issues, an international business negotiation is profoundly influenced by the six special factors outlined in this chapter. The primary effect of these factors is that they increase the risks of the negotiation process—the risk that the parties will not reach agreement, the risk that their agreement may prove to be more apparent than real, the risk that any agreement reached will not in fact regulate their future behavior. The challenge for international negotiators is to find ways to reduce these risks. Certainly, the first step in this direction is to recognize the existence of these six constraints and to understand their implications.

REFERENCES

Graham, J. and Herberger, R. (1983). "Negotiators Abroad—Don't Shoot from the Hip." *Harvard Business Review* 61 (July-August): pp. 160–83.

Pye, L. (1982). *Chinese Negotiating Style*. Cambridge, Mass.: Oelgeschlager, Gunn & Hain.

Tung, R. (1984). *Business Negotiations with the Japanese*. Lexington, Mass.: Lexington Books.

Vlachoutsicos, C.A. (1986). "Where the Ruble Stops in Soviet Trade." *Harvard Business Review* 64 (September-October) pp. 82–86.

Rethinking the Culture-Negotiation Link

Robert J. Janosik

Practicing negotiators have tended to rely on the concept "culture," or on related notions like national style, to explain behavior encountered at the international bargaining table. Scholars, too, have on occasion investigated the relationship of culture to negotiation, but with less vigor, perhaps because of the methodological problems inherent in such studies.[1]

Since the notion of culture as an explanatory tool holds such allure for negotiation analysts, this paper will examine the treatment of "culture" in the anecdotal and scholarly literature. It will soon become apparent that the concept has been used in a number of ways. Perhaps such an examination can sharpen the clarity of the discussion, since many analysts seem to agree that culture does have an impact on behavior, at least to some extent. But without a general working understanding of the various approaches to culture currently in use, practitioners and academics may use the concept in different ways without sufficient analysis of the possibilities and limits of these various approaches to culture and its impact upon negotiating behavior.

I have identified four distinct approaches in the negotiation literature which imply a connection between culture and behavior: culture as learned behavior; culture as shared value; culture as dialectic; and culture-in-context. Each approach differs from the others conceptually in significant ways with important consequences for the understanding of the culture-negotiation connection. Illustrations, drawn primarily from writings about Japanese, Russian, Chinese, and American negotiating practices, will serve to illustrate the four approaches since the investigation of these four national groups has drawn the bulk of the attention given to this question.

CULTURE AS LEARNED BEHAVIOR

The variety of human experience has daunted even the most persistent analyst. This variety has led observers to search for organizing principles that allow for valid generalizations which hold true despite "incidental" variations from overall patterns.

Reprinted from Robert J. Janosik, "Rethinking the Culture-Negotiation Link," *Negotiation Journal*, October 1987, pp. 385–95. Used with permission of the author and Plenum Publishing Corporation.
[1]Rubin and Brown (1975) suggest this hypothesis to explain the scarcity of such studies.

The notion of culture has proven to be one such basis for generalization. Much of the literature on diplomacy resorts to generalizations based on the observed typical characteristics and behaviors of the inhabitants of a particular geographic entity.

The focus of the literature produced by such writers is often primarily on what negotiators *do*, rather than what they *think*. It is quintessentially pragmatic. There is little felt need for detailed analysis of when, why, and how a pattern of behavior occurs; rather, the primary consideration has to do with the reliability and sensitivity of the observer. For the practitioner in the audience, little more is thought to be necessary than an accurate and comprehensive catalog of what to expect. It makes little difference why negotiators from a particular culture resist negotiations over dinner; what is important is that one can always expect such behavior.

As early as 1716, de Callieres devoted sections of his classic, *On the Manner of Negotiating With Princes*, to the question of national "styles." At several points in the essay, he attributed certain favorable negotiating traits to the diplomats of specific nations, and hypothesized that there is a direct relationship between negotiating behavior and place of birth (De Callieres, 1963, p. 36):

> . . . patience is one of the advantages which the Spanish nation has over our own; for we are naturally lively, and have hardly embarked on one affair before we desire the end in order to embark on another . . . . Whereas it has been remarked that a Spanish diplomatist never acts with haste, that he never thinks of bringing a negotiation to an end simply from *ennui*, but to finish it with advantage. . .

Another classic, Harold Nicholson's *Diplomacy* (1963, p. 68) also suggests that the style of the diplomats of a nation is a function of that society's norms and values:

> . . . there are marked differences in the theory and practice of the several Great Powers. These differences are caused by variation in national character, traditions, and requirements. . .

The long line of diplomatic diarists who have represented the United States and Great Britain in Japan since the first modern contacts in the 19th century similarly reflect an assumption about birthplace and negotiation. Townsend Harris, America's first Consul General to Japan, though unusually sympathetic to the Japanese he encountered, nonetheless commented on certain unsavory attributes of the Japanese style of dealing with foreign envoys to their nation. As his dealings in Japan dragged on, frustration increased, and he remarked (Harris, 1930, p. 366):

> They (the Japanese) do not regard the promise they gave me last August as worth the breath it cost them to utter it. However, to *lie* is, for a Japanese, simply to speak.

It should be noted that this approach can include observations about various levels of the process of negotiation. Learned behaviors may touch upon notions of reciprocity and justice, attitudes about acceptable outcomes, or concepts about the appropriate timing for certain bargaining behaviors. However, it is my sense that most of the observations derived from this approach involve comments on negotiating "etiquette"—on matters dealing with proper social customs and usages that surface in the typical bargaining encounter.

Many of the "how to" manuals about negotiating abroad focus on negotiating etiquette. Howard F. Van Zandt's much read "How to Negotiate in Japan" (1970) is a good example. In that article he notes 13 "distinctive behavioral characteristics" which are commonly encountered by Americans in talks with the Japanese, including the "avoidance of no," the "reluctance to enter into arguments" and gift-giving. Although admittedly important to good relations, such customs do not really go to the heart of the matter: whether participants have fundamentally different perspectives on the process of negotiation.

A second example can be located in Flora Lewis's astute observations in a brief analysis of U.S.-Saudi Arabian relations that appeared in the February 27, 1979 edition of the *New York Times:*

> . . . As a sign of politeness and hospitality, the Arabs tend to listen and nod when high-level Americans talk with them. But this does not mean that they agree.

This approach to negotiation analysis, which involves the search patterns for patterns of behavior in groups of individuals, is akin to early 20th century "culture studies" in psychology, anthropology, and sociology. It is often typical of the writing of practicing negotiators who, not surprisingly, base their observations on experience at the negotiating table, and who view their task primarily in terms of making it possible for others in the same position to successfully manage for others in the same or similar situations in the future. Such experientially based advice is, of course, invaluable to those facing comparable situations; however, the approach carries important limitations, as I hope to demonstrate.

CULTURE AS SHARED VALUE

A second commonly employed approach shifts the focus of investigation in an important way. Using this approach, the analyst begins with a description of a controlling concept or value assumed to be embedded in the culture and derives from that observation a series of predictions about how a participant in that culture will behave in negotiation. The assumption, simply put, is that thinking precedes doing, and that one's thinking patterns derive from one's cultural context.

For the purposes of comparison across cultures or groups, the analyst will search for a *central* cultural value or norm that distinguishes each of the groups being compared. From the practitioner's point of view, this approach—culture as shared value— like the first approach—culture as learned behavior—is appealing because it suggests an almost inevitable, and therefore entirely predictable, pattern of negotiating behavior.

Mushakoji Kinhide, for example, uses this approach to contrast American and Japanese understandings of the process of negotiation. Mushakoji (1976, p. 40) proposes that the Japanese negotiator represents an *awase* culture, while the United States is an *erabi* culture. The American *erabi* view implies "a behavioral sequence whereby a person sets his objective, develops a plan designed to reach that objective, and then acts to change the environment in accordance with that plan." Environments are perceived as offering dischotomies for choice. By contrast, the Japanese *awasi* view assumes that the environment must be adjusted to, not changed, and "the environment consists of a constantly changing continuum of fine gradations."

According to Mushakoji, these cultural differences have profound implications for the American and Japanese perspectives on the process. Americans, for example, present a clear statement of their position and expect the same of others. The Japanese, on the other hand, would rather infer the other's position and avoid early commitment to stated objectives. Other, comparable cultural typologies are legion.[2]

There are several common variants of the "culture as shared value" approach to negotiation. One example, also drawn from the literature concerning the Japanese approach to negotiation, can be found in *Smart Bargaining: Doing Business with the Japanese*. After summarizing relevant factors in Japanese history and geography, Graham and Sano (1984) trace the "typical" Japanese bargaining style to a *cluster* of values implicit in Japanese culture that are said to generate the observed Japanese style. Like Mushakoji, Graham and Sano derive a predicted set of behaviors from certain postulated values in Japanese culture. Graham and Sano differ, however, in that they do not attempt to isolate one key aspect of culture; rather, they point to a set of cultural norms and values that contribute to the Japanese style. For example, Graham and Sano point to "amae," which they translate as "indulgent dependency," "wa" (the maintenance of harmony), and "shinyo" (gut feeling), as some of the components of the Japanese value set. As regards "shinyo," the authors argue that this value encourages Japanese negotiators to spend a great deal of time at activities not directly related to the negotiation, including gift-giving.

The same authors sketch an American style of bargaining which they refer to as the "John Wayne Style." Pointing to the American frontier experience, Graham and Sano note a tendency on the part of American negotiators to prefer short, informal negotiations that emphasize the equality of the participants.

Yet another variant of this approach to the question of the nexus between culture and negotiation attributes aspects of a nation's negotiation style to ideology rather than culture. Political scientists define ideology as a tight-knit system of ideas which constitutes a full world view. Three modern systems—Liberalism, Fascism, and Communism—are typically cited as examples of ideologies. Although no extended study linking negotiation behavior to Fascism or Liberalism has, to my knowledge, been attempted, Kenneth T. Young's *Negotiating with the Chinese Communists* (1968) does just that as regards Communism. Young examines the history of American-Chinese negotiating encounters for the period between 1953 and 1967 for patterns in Chinese behavior. Chinese behavior in these negotiations featured a high degree of antagonism toward American counterparts and a casualness about reaching agreement which contrasted to the American desire to come to agreement quickly. Young attributes these patterns to the fact that "A Chinese Communist negotiator is an ideologist more than anything else." The result, he argues, is that:

> . . . the United States Government and the American negotiators are dealing with a closed mind in which conceptual thinking and logical analysis have not developed or matured for over a generation. The world has changed but Maoist ideology has enclosed China within a new ideological wall. (Young, 1968, p. 364)

---

[2]See, for example, Okabe (1983), which contains an extensive list of such dualities.

534 Section Fourteen   International Negotiations

Chinese negotiating behavior during this period, then, followed certain predictable patterns:

> Tactically, this kind of negotiator tried to outflank his opponent, demoralize and weaken him by every conceivable means at every possible point, take over his strategic position, separate him from allies, leave him no exit, and give him no quarter. (Young, 1968, p. 363)

Studies of Soviet negotiating patterns have also been done. An early example of the genre can be found in the essays contained in Dennett and Johnson's *Negotiating with the Russians* (1951). More recent examples are summarized by Louis J. Samelson (1976), who finds that Western observers typically ascribe deception, dissimulation, rigidity, nonaccommodation, hostility, and harassment to both Soviet and Chinese Communist diplomatic representatives.

Despite the variants, all proponents of this approach assume that either a single shared value, a commonly held cluster of values, or an ideology produce a typical bargaining style. Here, the attempt is to create a cultural explanation for behavior rather than a mere description of a pattern of negotiating behavior. This viewpoint represents a higher level of abstraction than the first approach—culture as learned behavior—since implicit in it is a causal relationship between the values of a cultural group and bargaining behavior.

It should also be noted that the "shared value" approach appears to minimize the role of individual choice for the bargaining actor. In other words, because a negotiator belongs to a culture or adheres to an ideology, he or she necessarily behaves in particular ways. As with the first approach, there seems to be a suggestion that culture largely predetermines negotiating behavior.

CULTURE AS DIALECTIC

Analysts who favor the "shared value" approach typically assume a homogenity in the culture's dominant value or value set. Graham and Sano, for example, appear to be suggesting that though a "bundle" of Japanese and American and cultural norms guide the negotiating behavior of those groups respectively, there is nothing inconsistent in the units that comprise the bundle of cultural norms. "Amae" and "shinyo" are presented as different but mutually reinforcing norms which lead to regularized Japanese negotiating patterns.

A quite different model of the make-up of culture is also available. Erik H. Erikson in *Childhood and Society* proposed a model of personal identity which is based on sets of opposites, or "polarities":

> . . . the functioning American, as the heir of a history of extreme contrasts and abrupt changes, bases his final ego identity on some tentative combination of dynamic polarities such as migratory and sedentary, individualistic and standardized, competitive and cooperative, pious and freethinking, responsible and cynical, etc. (Erikson, 1963, p. 286)

Erikson was interested in explaining child development; a similar model of culture, explicitly derived from Erikson, was used by Michael Kammen (1972) to interpret the American historical experience. Kammen asserts that sets of "biformities," values which are in dialectic tension, pervade the American national experience: "Collective individualism,'' ''conservative liberalism,'' ''pragmatic idealism,'' and ''godly materialism'' are a few examples of such pairs.

Proponents of this approach to culture suggest, at least implicitly, a criticism of the single value or ''homogenous bundle'' notion of culture discussed above. A culture, for an analyst of this approach, is defined by the tensions, the dialectics, which exist among values embedded in a particular culture. Tension, not consistency, typifies the component parts of any given culture.

Analysts of the culture-as-shared-value approach may find it difficult to come to grips with two problems: the problem of individual variations in a culture and changes over periods of time. If a culture is entirely homogenous, it is difficult to explain discrepancies from the modal pattern when they occur since all participants in the culture are thought to subscribe to the dominant value or value bundle. Similarly, change over time can only be explained by the complete rejection of whatever the dominant value or value bundle is in a particular culture under certain historical circumstances. The ''culture as shared value'' approach is static; it does not comfortably allow for the analysis of change or variation. By contrast, the third approach—culture as dialectic—can easily accommodate the study of both individual variation and changes over time.

An interesting use of the culture-as-dialectic approach can be found in Michael Blaker's *Japanese International Negotiating Style*. Blaker posits a dialectic in Japanese culture which parallels, but does not duplicate, the dualities Kammen and Erickson noted in the American case. Blaker notes two quite different ''domestic ideals of conflict resolution,'' which he calls ''harmonious cooperation'' and ''the warrior ethic.'' (Baker, 1977, p. 4) The first, which often seems to take prominence in western commentaries on Japanese negotiation, involves an extended effort to avoid discord at all costs within the elaborately constructed social matrix that has characterized Japan historically. Such conflict is avoided through narrowly defined obligations which are understood to operate between Japanese at different levels of society. The ''warrior ethic,'' by contrast, encourages risktaking in dogged pursuit of a cause, even at the cost of social turmoil. Obviously, these two ideals are in some real sense incompatible. But the point Blaker underscores is that *both* ideals have a strong grounding in Japanese history and tradition; both are seen to be legitimate in certain circumstances.

From these general conflict resolution ideals in Japanese culture, Blaker derives five ''norms of Japanese bargaining action'': overcoming domestic opposition; dispelling western resistance; secrecy; careful deliberations; and situational adaptation. He also derives three ''norms relating to Japanese negotiating tactics'' (Blaker, 1977, p. 23): optimism; fatalism; and nonmoral pragmatism. Given this understanding of Japanese culture, Blaker then examines Japanese behavior in a variety of international negotiations in the latter part of the 19th century and the early 20th century; and in light of Japan's ongoing sense of itself as a beleaguered country. Through his analysis of these cultural premises, then, Blaker finds a distinctive Japanese negotiation style, which in another context (Blaker, 1977a), he dubbed the Japanese ''probe/push/panic'' tactical style of negotiation.

The ''culture as dialectic'' approach does not present the intellectual difficulties regarding change and choice that were noted in connection with ''culture as shared value.'' Indeed, since both value sets within a culture are seen as legitimate, a negotiator must somehow reconcile them in light of the individual's perceptions of the demands of a situation. Reconciliation of two or more competing values sets is a continuing task for each culture-participant in all situations, including negotiation. This tension between competing "cultural commands" can lead the individual partic- ipant to paralysis since the choice may seem difficult; or, one or the other of these values may be chosen; or, finally, the tension may encourage the participant to attempt some synthesis of the competing values. Indeed, the latter possibility is precisely the kind of fusion Blaker seems to be suggesting in the Japanese case. "Optimism" and "fatalism" seem hardly coherent to the outside observer; but to the Japanese negotiator faced with competing cultural demands, both attitudes may somehow "make sense."

This third model becomes increasingly interesting to the academic observer of the process of negotiation since it allows for the resolution of several persistent questions concerning the observed lack of uniformity in the negotiating behavior among the participants of a particular culture. On the other hand, to the practitioner who must know how to prepare for and react to negotiating strategies and tactics from foreign actors, this model may appear problematic. Since the "culture as dialectic" approach is not deterministic in the same sense as the first two approaches (because, theoreti- cally, one could equally expect quite contrary behaviors from participants in such a dialectic culture), practitioners may wonder about the utility of the third approach for their purposes.

CULTURE–IN–CONTEXT

A fourth approach to the question of the impact of culture on negotiating behavior is even more complex than the approach just discussed. It reflects the dominant current understanding of the relationship between behavior and ideas among social scientists, and takes its cue from Max Weber, Talcott Parsons, Gabriel Almond, and other modern scholars.

In attempting to understand the relationship between ideas and action, Parsons (1936) elaborated a complex model of human behavior. For Parsons, the notion of culture was critical to the endeavor. He understood culture in terms of its ability to generate certain values which, in turn, predispose individuals to prefer certain goals or choices (interest). A culture, in other words, generates values or human wants which individuals then act to fulfill. But Parsons and others went further—well beyond a single factor understanding of the sources of human behavior. This group of social scientists, often referred to as "systems theorists," suggests that an understanding of human behavior cannot rest on single-cause explanations. Several interdependent sources must be accounted for prior to achieving a relatively complete understanding of human behavior. Though a complete exegesis of these ideas would go well beyond the confines of this essay, the basic insight is that analysis must encompass many factors, must be multicausal.

More specifically, the individual's personality, cultural values, and the social context in which the individual operates are three of the primary components which account for human behavior. Such a multicausal approach, in short, suggests that any attempt to understand negotiation behavior as a genre of human action which attends only to the culturally defined values of the negotiator will, ultimately, be inadequate. The constraints of the social context or situation and the role of the individual personality must also be taken into account.

Such complex, multicausal models of negotiating behavior are typical of many academic analyses of negotiating behavior. Sawyer and Guetzkow's early monograph (1965) on negotiation is a notable and still useful effort in this direction. They create a "social-psychological model" of the process of negotiation in which situation-specific goals, conditions which structure the specific negotiation (including the negotiation's setting, and the number of parties), and a series of "background factors" (including "cultural variation," the negotiator's personality, status, and background) have an impact upon the events which unfold in a particular negotiation and its outcome.

The efforts of many scholars at negotiation model building are deeply indebted to this multicausal mode of thinking about the nature of negotiation. Though some analysts give more prominence to the culture factor than others, it seems clear from the evidence in the textbooks being written on the subject[3] that the multicausal approach is now greatly favored by academic analysts. All of these writers hold in common the assumption that though culture is important, it is not the only contributor to an individual's negotiating behavior. Rather, culture is interdependent, interactive.

A few examples of the application of this approach will serve to illustrate the distinctive features of it. A monograph by Druckman et al. (1976) examined the bargaining behavior of children from India, Argentina, and the United States. The authors collected and compared data concerning the subject-negotiator (age, gender, and nationality) and the negotiating context (the existence or absence of an audience). While the investigators found evidence to support the proposition that culture matters in determining behavior (Indian bargainers were more competitive than Argentinians and Americans), the study also underscores the important contributory efforts that *all* of these factors have in determining bargaining behavior. For example, the Druckman investigators noted male bargainers were more competitive than females in the United States and India, while the opposite was the case in terms of Argentinian subjects. In other words, nationality/culture does have an important role to play, but any generalizations about the nationality/culture nexus might require modification to account for age, gender, and the negotiating environment.

In another study, Mushakoji (1972), whose thoughts in another context were noted earlier, compared Japanese and American negotiators using a negotiation game and found that any comparisons between the two groups had to be qualified by an analysis of the specific negotiating conditions faced by the subject in the simulation. Similarly, Janosik (1983) observed that though cultural differences could be observed when Americans and Japanese were asked to perform the same negotiating tasks, the occupations of the negotiators as well as the bargaining situation (the "toughness" of the simulated negotiating adversary) made absolute cross-cultural comparisons difficult. For example, Americans initially tended to make more counterresponses to an

---

[3]See, for example, Wall (1985). Wall includes "cultural norms" as one of a number of "environmental factors" which can affect the negotiation process.

opponent than Japanese negotiators did under all conditions of opponent toughness; however, this phenomenon became less noticeable as the negotiating opponent became tougher, more unyielding.

Each of these examples of multicausal modeling attempts to put the cultural factor into perspective with other factors that are thought to be operative in negotiation. Particularly important are the factors which define the individual negotiator (age, gender, religion, and personality, for example) as well as those factors which define the context of the negotiation. These latter situational factors can encompass the presence or absence of an audience, the nature of the bureaucratic controls on a negotiator, and the observed patterns of an opponent's conduct, to name a few.

But as the complexity of the model increases, its utility for the practitioner seems to decrease. And there's the rub. The beauty of the first two approaches to culture and negotiation discussed here is that they yield readily usable lists of dos and don'ts, of straightforward characterizations of the bargaining styles of individuals from other cultures. The third and fourth approaches, by contrast, involve increasing degrees of indeterminancy. The insights gained from laboratory experiments rather than on-site observations come laden with qualifiers that make them difficult to utilize efficiently at the bargaining table.

OBSERVATIONS

The question of the relationship of culture to negotiating style is an important one since it points to a view of negotiation which differs considerably from that advanced by early negotiation theorists. These early students of negotiation theory were frequently economists who developed process models that considered various concession patterns and optimal solutions for various negotiating problems. Oran Young's anthology (1975) brings together many of these early essays. Often the authors assume a ''rational'' actor/negotiator who was engaged in maximizing his or her own outcome in a negotiating encounter. Such ''rational'' calculations were directed to the subject matter being negotiated. However, these models left little room for unconscious factors in the process of negotiation.

Although I do not wish to understate the importance of the rational actor model of the negotiation process, since it has yielded important insights about the nature of the phenomenon, I do feel that an alternative (rather, complementary) view must also be elaborated before our understanding of negotiation truly matures. This second perspective on negotiation, represented by the scholars whose work has been briefly described in this article, attempts to account for situational and individual factors, including culture, in the process of negotiation.

These two views—one based in economics, the other in social psychology—have created one divide in the literature about negotiation. Another gap exists between practitioners and academics, but for different reasons. Since the goals of the scholar and the participant-observer of negotiation differ somewhat, there has at times been a tendency to dismiss or downplay the problems of definition and conceptualization in the examination of the various ''contributory'' factors to the phenomenon of negotiation, including the question of the impact of culture on the process. Yet, since the consideration of national styles and cultural differences appears to be essential to the practitioner's interest in behavior at the international bargaining table, the failure to establish a fruitful dialogue on the subject may have inhibited the development of a truly comparative perspective.

This survey of discussions of culture and negotiation indicates that practitioners prefer to employ the "culture as learned behavior" or the "culture as shared value" approaches; the academics more frequently use the "culture as dialectic" or "culture in context" approaches. The reason seems clear. The first two approaches allow a high degree of predictability concerning the negotiating behavior of the culture group being analyzed. The third and fourth approaches are rather less deterministic. The "culture as dialectic" and "culture in context" approaches make prediction a more complex and risky enterprise.

The insights garnered from all are important. But it should be remembered that observations tied to the first and second approaches are likely to yield a particular type of prediction—one that has more to do with what has been called negotiating "etiquette" than with descriptions of what Zartman and Berman (1982, p. 229) have called the "deeper 'causes'" of negotiating behavior.

A real dialogue between academics and pracititioners would consider matters of negotiating "etiquette"—whether business may be discussed over dinner, whether business cards should be exchanged, how to use interpreters, and the like. Clearly, the failure to observe good manners in negotiation can reduce the likelihood of agreement. But such a dialogue must ultimately move on to more complex matters, matters that lie at the heart of the question of whether there is some transnational, transcultural understanding of the fundamental nature of negotiation itself.

A sophisticated understanding of the "culture" concept in the negotiation process may present difficult methodological problems. Nevertheless, grappling with these problems can lead, in the end, to more reliable diagnoses of negotiation and a product that is useful to the practitioner and satisfying to the scholar.

REFERENCES

Blaker, M. (1977). *Japanese international negotiating style*. New York: Columbia University Press.

_____ (1977a). "Probe, push, and panic: The Japanese tactical style in international negotiations." In *The foreign policy of modern Japan*, ed. R. A. Scalapino. Berkeley: University of California Press.

De Callieres, F. (1716) *On the manner of negotiating with princes*, trans. A. F. Whyte. Notre Dame, Ind.: University of Notre Dame Press, 1963.

Dennett, R. and Johnson, J. E., eds. (1951). *Negotiating with the Russians*. New York: World Peace Foundation.

Druckman, D., et al. (1976). "Cultural differences in bargaining behavior: India, Argentina, and the U.S." *Journal of Conflict Resolution*. 20: pp. 413-52.

Erikson, E. H. (1963). *Childhood and society*, 2nd ed. New York: W.W. Norton & Co.

Graham, J. L. and Sano, Y. (1984). *Smart bargaining: Doing business with the Japanese*. Cambridge, Mass.: Ballinger.

Harris, T. (1930). *The complete journal of Townsend Harris, first American consul general and minister to Japan*. Garden City, N.Y: Doubleday, Doran & Co.

Janosik, R. (1983). "Negotiation theory: Considering the cultural variable in the Japanese and American cases." Ph. D. dissertation. New York University.

Kammen, M. (1973). *People of paradox: An inquiry concerning the origins of American civilization*. New York: Vintage Books.

Mushakoji, K. (1972). "The strategies of negotiation: An American-Japanese comparison." *In Experimentation and simulation in political science*. ed. J. A. Laponce and P. Smoker. Toronto: University of Toronto Press.

——, (1976). "The cultural premises of Japanese diplomacy." In *The silent power: Japan's identity and world role*, ed. Japan Center for International Exchange. Tokyo: The Simul Press.

Nicholson, H. (1939). *Diplomacy*, 3rd ed. Oxford: Oxford University Press, 1963.

Okabe, R. (1983). "Cultural assumptions of East and West: Japan and the United States." In *Intercultural communication theory; Current perspectives*, ed. W. B. Gudykunst. Beverly Hills, Calif.: Sage Publications.

Parsons, T. (1937). *The structure of social action*. New York: Free Press.

Rubin, J. Z. and Brown, B. R. (1975). *The social psychology of bargaining and negotiation*. New York: Academic Press.

Samelson, L. J. (1976). *Soviet and Chinese negotiating behavior: The Western view*. Sage Professional Paper in International Studies. no. 02-048. Beverly Hills, Calif.: Sage Publications.

Sawyer, J. and Guetzkow, H. (1965). "Bargaining and negotiation in international relations. In *International behavior*, ed. H. Kelman, New York: Holt, Rinehart and Winston.

Van Zandt, H. F. (1970). "How to negotiate in Japan." *Harvard Business Review* 48: pp. 45-56.

Wall, J. A. Jr. (1985). *Negotiation: Theory and practice*. Glenview, Ill.: Scott, Foresman and Co.

Young, K. T. (1968). *Negotiating with the Chinese Communists*. New York: McGraw-Hill.

Young, O., ed. (1975). *Bargaining: Formal theories of negotiation*. Urbana, Ill.: University of Illinois Press.

Zartman, I. W. and Berman, M. R. (1982). *The practical negotiator*. New Haven: Yale University Press.

The Japanese Negotiation Style

John Graham

Yoshihiro Sano

The Japanese negotiation style is perhaps the most distinctive in the world. Moreover, contrary to what one might expect, the Japanese style is far different from negotiation styles in Taiwan and Korea, Japan's closest neighbors. Compared to the aggressive haggling more typical of Korean and Chinese businesspeople, the subtle, low-key bargaining of Japanese executives appears foreign indeed.

The historical and cultural roots of the Japanese negotiation style run far deeper than those of the American style. Their history is much longer and relatively uninfluenced from the outside. Another characteristic that sets the Japanese style apart from all others is the suitability of the Japanese style for international use. An important aspect of the Japanese style of business negotiations includes adapting bargaining behaviors to those of the host country or firm. For now, let's consider the historical and cultural foundations of the Japanese negotiation style.

THE ROOTS OF THE JAPANESE STYLE OF BUSINESS NEGOTIATION

The natural environment of Japan has had a pervasive influence on the character of social systems, personal relationships, and, yes, even the process of business negotiations. Three environmental factors are salient: (1) the insular and mountainous geography, (2) the dense population, and (3) the importance of rice as the basic food crop.

Throughout its history Japan has been an isolated country. Until the 15th century the surrounding seas formed a substantial barrier preventing invasions and limiting influence from the Asian continent. Even with the dramatic changes throughout the rest of the world brought about by Western European maritime power in the 16th century, the political policies of the Tokugawa Shogunate kept foreigners out of the country. Indeed, Japan was the country least influenced by Western European culture through the mid-19th century. And not only did the maritime barriers keep foreigners out, but they also kept Japanese from leaving. Thus, social systems and personal relationships developed in a concentrated environment where geography dictated that cooperation was essential. Ethnicity, cultural values, and behavioral norms are therefore uniquely consistent and homogeneous.

The mountains in Japan have always made travel within the country difficult, adding further to the isolation of social groups. Because of the mountains, only about 10 percent of the land can be cultivated. Japan is the most densely populated of all countries in the world with respect to people per square mile of arable land. This crowding has fostered a tightly organized society that highly values obedience and cooperation. Crowding does not permit the aggressive independence and equality so characteristic in the United States.

The final environmental factor influencing values and behaviors in Japan is the historical importance of rice cultivation. Until 100 years ago, five sixths of the population of Japan was employed in rice cultivation. Rice production requires community effort and cooperation. Irrigation, planting, and harvesting are most efficiently accomplished with the participation of groups of families. Thus, the small group has evolved as the salient social unit in Japan. Individual needs and desires are de-emphasized in favor of one's social unit. In the historical agrarian society the family and village were key. Now in Japan, one's family and one's work group are central. Loyalty and consensus decision making are key elements that bind such groups together.

Because of this unique combination of environmental influences, a social system has evolved in Japan that avoids conflict and promotes harmony. And as in America, classroom behavior is influenced by and tends to reinforce these cultural values and behavioral norms. Lively case discussions are not part of the educational experience in Japan. Rather, professors present lectures with no questions and feedback from students. Listening skills and obedience, rather than debating skills and independent thinking, are rewarded in the Japanese educational system. It should be understood that the Japanese negotiation style characterized in the paragraphs to follow is deeply influenced by and reflects these salient environmental factors and the values and social structures associated with them.

Tate Shakai (Living and Working in a Vertical Society)

Perhaps the most important difference between the Japanese negotiation style and others, particularly the American, concerns status relationships. At the interpersonal level the bases for the status distinction might be age, sex, education, or occupation. The power position in business relationships has more to do with size and prestige of the company, industry structure (e.g., number of competitors), and very often, which company is the buyer. There are cases when sellers are more powerful—large manufacturers versus small retailers—but most often Japanese buyers expect and receive deference from Japanese sellers. Indeed, in Japan the buyer is said to be "kinger." Note the following excerpt from a pamphlet provided by the Manufactured Imports Promotion Organization of Japan:

> In Japan, as in other countries, the "buyer is king," only here he or she is "kinger." Here, the seller, beyond meeting pricing, delivery, special specifications, and other usual conditions, must do as much as possible to meet a buyer's wishes. . . . Many companies

doing business in Japan make it a practice to deliver more than called for under the terms of their contracts.[1]

The key point here is that the roles of the buyer and seller are very different in Japan. Status relations dictate what is said and what bargaining strategies may be used during Japanese business negotiations. The norms of behavior for the seller are very different from those for the buyer.

In America the way in which status distinctions affect how we behave is almost the opposite of that in Japan. In Japan people at all levels feel uncomfortable if status distinctions do not exist or are not understood. But in our egalitarian American society, we often go out of our way to establish an interpersonal equality. There is little distinction between roles and relatively few rules for adjusting behavior.

Americans expect to, and do, affect business outcomes at the negotiation table. For Japanese, negotiation is more of a ritual, with actions predetermined and prespecified by status relations.

Amae (Indulgent Dependency)

Hierarchical personal and business relationships are difficult for Americans to understand. "Doesn't the lower status seller get taken advantage of? That's what would happen in the United States." However, understanding an additional aspect of Japanese hierarchical relationships is essential for full appreciation of the Japanese business system. It is true that Japanese buyers have the freedom to choose the deal they want. They will get little argument from the Japanese sellers. But along with this freedom goes an implicit responsibility to consider the needs of the sellers. Japanese sellers can trust the buyers not to take advantage of them. This theme of *amae* is woven into every aspect of Japanese society. Consider, for example, the relationship between management and labor. Management has much more control over labor in Japan than in the United States. But with that control comes a large measure of responsibility for the welfare of the labor force, exceeding that in America.

In Japan buyers take care of sellers. Buyers consider the needs of sellers before making demands that sellers defer to. In America, conversely, we all take care of ourselves. If buyers make unreasonable demands, they will most likely hear an argument.

Nagai Tsukiai (Long-Term Relationships)

Another aspect of business relationships in Japan that influences negotiation behavior regards the importance and expectation of long-term relationships. The fact that Japanese managers are more predisposed than American managers to take a long view of business affairs has been given much attention. The importance of establishing long-term relations is grounded in the cultural heritage of being isolated and having no

---

[1]Manufactured Imports Promotion Organization, *Penetrating the Japanese Market* (Tokyo, 1980), p. 16.

other place to go. Personal and group relationships are for life and therefore entered into slowly, carefully, and in a socially prescribed way. The same is true for business relationships.

This aspect of Japanese values has two important implications for business negotiations with Japanese clients or partners. First, the Japanese side will want to spend more time getting to know prospective American associates. They will be more willing to invest time and money in negotiation preliminaries and rituals. The second and perhaps the more important implication regards the structure and presentation of the business deal itself. Japanese bargainers will be looking for long-term commitments. Short-run profits are important, but secondary to a long-run business association benefiting both sides.

Shinyo (Gut Feeling)

In the previous chapter we mentioned four stages of the negotiation process: nontask sounding, task-related information exchange, persuasion, and concessions and agreement. We also pointed out that, from the American point of view, the persuasion stage is the heart of the matter. It is different in Japan. Compared to Americans, Japanese spend a considerable amount of time in nontask sounding activities. The Japanese view the time and money spent in the initial stages of bargaining as an important investment.

The typical Japanese negotiation involves a series of nontask interactions and even ceremonial gift giving. The *aisatsu* described earlier is prescribed behavior in Japan. Moreover, witness the recent attention given to the very large *kosai-hi* (literally, entertainment expenses) typical of business dealings in Japan. "While the Japanese defense budget is 0.9 percent of the country's GNP, corporate wining and dining accounts for 1.5 percent of the total national output."[2] To the American critic this may seem extravagant. However, the Japanese place great importance on establishing a harmonious relationship. This helps them avoid expensive litigation if things go wrong, which seems more and more common in the United States.

Naniwabushi (A Seller's Approach)

In Japan, information exchange during the second stage of negotiations is generally unidirectional. Sellers describe in great detail what they need, and buyers consider this information and make a decision. Sellers don't object to or question the decision because they can trust the buyers to take care of them. Thus, the information flows principally from sellers to buyers.

Robert March, at Aoyama Gakin University in Tokyo, explains that the seller's agenda is often ordered like a Japanese narrative chant going back to the 15th century. A *naniwabushi* (both the chant and the negotiation approach) consists of three phases: "The opening, which is called *kikkake*, gives the general background of the story and tells what the people involved are thinking or feeling. Following this is the *seme*, an account of critical events. Finally, there is the *urei*, which expresses pathos

---

[2]"Long Workdays," *Time*, January 12, 1981, p. 56.

and sorrow at what has happened or what is being requested."[3] The request comes last, after long explanation of the reasons why it is being made.

Alternatively, the American style of information exchange we have observed starts with the request (without the sorrow), and the explanation is provided only if necessary. American persuasive appeals are couched in terms of "you should . . ." rather than the Japanese, "my company needs. . . ." To the American mind the *naniwabushi* seems melodramatic and a waste of time. However, this is the kind of behavior higher status buyers expect from lower status sellers. It is the kind of behavior that makes Japanese negotiators feel comfortable.

We have seen many examples of this approach to business negotiation. One case stands out. Safeway Stores, Inc. and Allied Import Company (AIC is a consortium of four of Japan's major retailers: JUSCO, UNY, Izumiya, and Chujitsuya) were discussing an agreement for the distribution of Safeway products in Japan. The Japanese presentation followed the *naniwabushi* approach. All aspects of the partnership had been agreed upon except for the exclusivity provisions. That is, the AIC representatives wanted to be the sole distributor of Safeway products in Japan. The presidents of the four Japanese companies had flown into San Francisco International Airport in preparation for signing ceremonies scheduled for that day. Yet no agreement had been reached regarding the exclusivity provision. Finally, at the last minute the head Japanese negotiator resorted to *urei* and "cried on the shoulder" of an executive vice president of Safeway, using an emotion-drenched personal appeal. Thus, the time pressure and the *urei* broke the impasse; the deal was consummated that day with the Japanese receiving the exclusive rights of distribution.

Banana No Tataki Uri (The Banana Sale Approach)

In the days of street vendors in Japan banana salesmen were notorious for asking outrageous prices and quickly lowering the prices when faced with buyers' objections. The term *banana no tataki uri* is now used in Japan to describe a similar approach often taken by Japanese businesspeople. But instead of bananas, factories, distribution chains, even banks are sometimes bargained for using the "banana sale" approach. Japanese executives are more likely to use such a tactic during international negotiations because they don't know what to expect from foreign buyers and they feel that it's safer to leave room to maneuver.

Wa (Maintaining Harmony)

Western negotiators universally complain about the difficulties of getting feedback from Japanese negotiators. There are three explanations for this complaint. First, the Japanese value interpersonal harmony, or *wa*, over frankness. Second, the Japanese perhaps have not come to a consensus regarding the offer or counteroffer. Third, Westerners tend to miss the subtle but clear signals given by the Japanese.

---

[3]Robert March, "Melodrama in Japanese Negotiations," *Winds* (Japan Airlines Publication Group, April 1982) p. 23.

Wa, like *amae,* is one of the central values of the Japanese culture. Negative responses to negotiation proposals are principally nonexistent, and when they are given, they are given very subtly. We've all heard the classic story about the Japanese response of, "We'll think it over," to an American's request. A simple response like this usually means no in American terms, for if the Japanese really wanted to think it over he would explain the details of the decision-making process and the reason for the delay. A Japanese negotiator would be loathe, however, to use the word "no." Indeed, one Japanese scholar, Keiko Ueda, has described 16 ways to avoid saying no in Japan (see Table 1). Moreover, we have found that Japanese negotiators tend to use the word "no" less than two times per half-hour in bargaining simulations, while Americans use "no" five times per half-hour, Koreans seven times, and Brazilian executives forty-two times. And we must add a couple of other options to Ueda-san's table: (17) changing the topic, and (18) letting lower level negotiators say "no" in informal settings.

Regarding the ambiguous responses (see items 13 and 14 in Table 1), Japanese negotiators follow the cultural double standard of *tatemae* and *honne. Tatemae* can be translated as "truthful" (or "official stance") and *honne* as "true mind" (or "real intentions"). It is important for Japanese to be polite and to communicate the *tatemae* while reserving the possibly offending, but also informative, *honne.* Additionally, this difference in the Japanese value system manifests itself in statements by Japanese negotiators in retrospective interviews. The Japanese often describe Americans as honest and frank, but to the point of discomfort for the Japanese. Finally, eye contact is much

TABLE 1   Sixteen Ways the Japanese Avoid Saying No

1. Vague "no"
2. Vague and ambiguous "yes" or "no"
3. Silence
4. Counterquestion
5. Tangential responses
6. Exiting (leaving)
7. Lying (equivocation or making an excuse—sickness, previous obligation, etc.)
8. Criticizing the question itself
9. Refusing the question
10. Conditional "no"
11. "Yes, but . . ."
12. Delaying answers (e.g., "We will write you a letter.")
13. Internally "yes," externally "no"
14. Internally "no," externally "yes"
15. Apology
16. The equivalent of the English "no"—primarily used in filling out forms, *not* in conversation

source: Keiko Ueda, "Sixteen Ways to Avoid Saying No in Japan," in J.C. Condon and M. Saito, eds., *Intercultural Encounters with Japan* (Tokyo: Simul Press, 1974), pp. 185–92.

less frequent during Japanese negotiations (13 percent of the time in negotiations between Japanese, 33 percent for both Americans and Koreans, and 52 percent in negotiations between Brazilian executives). Thus, in Japan leakage of potentially offending feelings is limited and the *honne* is kept intact. To the American point of view this distinction between *tatemae* and *honne* seems hypocritical. However, the discrepancy is borne by the Japanese in good conscience and in the interest of the all-important *wa*.

Ringi Kessai (Decision Making by Consensus)

Because of the importance of *wa* it is very difficult to get a "no" from a Japanese client. But because of group decision making by consensus, it may also be difficult to get a "yes." Often, the Japanese side simply hasn't made up its mind.

In the voluminous comparative management literature, much has been made of the bottom-up approach to decision making typical in Japanese organizations. It has the disadvantage of slowing down the decision making, but the advantage of quick and orchestrated implementation. Moreover, this approach to decision making has proved very successful in coordinating group efforts in modern companies as well as in the traditional rice-growing agricultural communities. However, it has also been a substantial stumbling block and source of frustration for executives of American companies dealing with Japanese firms.

In business schools in the United States we teach the importance of identifying the key decision makers in an organization. In marketing terms, we look for the key buying influences. Generally, these key executives are located higher up in the organization. Once the key decision makers have been identified, special persuasive efforts are directed toward them. We try to determine the special interests (commercial and personal) of these key individuals, and communications are tailored accordingly.

Such an approach isn't likely to work in Japan. The decision-making power isn't centralized in key or high positions. Rather, the decision-making power is spread throughout the organization, and all executives involved in or influenced by the deal are important. All of them will have to be convinced that your proposal is the best before anything happens. The key buying influence in Japan is the executive who says no. Thus, the typical business negotiation in Japan will include talking to more people and will require repetition of the same information and persuasive appeals—much to the frustration of impatient Americans.

For American bargainers perhaps the greatest source of frustration associated with the consensus style of decision making has to do with the difficulty of getting feedback. American bargainers asking, "What do you think of our proposal, or our counteroffer?" often receive no answer. The Japanese are not being cagey, or coy, or dishonest; more often than not, a consensus has not been reached and Japanese negotiators (even senior people) are simply unwilling and unable to speak for the group.

Ishin-Denshin (Communication without Words)

The third reason foreigners complain about little feedback from Japanese negotiators has to do with the importance of nonverbal communication and subtlety in Japanese history, society, and business talk. Japan's ethnic homogeneity, isolation, and tradition of lifetime personal relationships with daily contact all permit the use of very subtle forms of communications. Subtlety is not only possible in such a fixed social system but is also required from the standpoint of *wa*.

America's tradition as a melting pot and the general transience of our personal relations make explicit communication necessary. Words are considered to be the most important vehicle of communication. In Japan much more is communicated nonverbally—through tone of voice, eye contact, silence, body movements, and the like. It's difficult for Americans to appreciate this difference in communication style and the importance of nonverbal channels in Japan. Takeo Doi, at the University of Tokyo, explains that in Japan the most important information, the content of the communication, is transmitted via nonverbal channels.[4] The verbal communication provides a context for the central information. The opposite is true in the United States, where communications researchers think of nonverbal signals as providing a context for the words spoken, the content of communication.

From the American point of view this Japanese mode of communication is incomprehensible. We know that nonverbal communication is very important, but how can a delivery date or a purchase price be communicated nonverbally? The explanation goes back to the concept of *shinyo* (gut feeling). To the Japanese, the key information in a negotiation concerns the qualities of the long-term, personal relationships that exist in the context of the business deal. The long discussion of minute details so prevalent in Japanese negotiations provides a context for development of comfortable personal relationships and a positive *shinyo*. And this *shinyo* is what makes the business deal go or not. Information about *shinyo* is communicated nonverbally and subtly. Delivery dates and purchase prices, which must be communicated verbally, are important; but these details are not the critical information in a Japanese business deal. So, Americans bargaining with Japanese are not only looking for the less important information but are also focusing on the wrong channel of communication. Thus, we have another explanation for the difficulty Americans have in getting feedback from Japanese clients and partners.

Kazuma Uyeno further explains the importance of nonverbal communication in his definition of *hara-gei:*

> Anatomically, *hara* is the abdomen or stomach. Used in figures of speech, the word can mean the heart or the mind of a man but not of a woman. *Hara* appears in a large number of expressions.
>
> The author who devoted a whole book to *hara-gei* (stomach art) would probably say that it is presumptuous to try to explain in just a few lines this Japanese problem-solving technique. *Hara-gei* may be explained as a technique for solving a problem through negotiation between two individuals without the use of direct words. You don't reveal to the other party what is in your *hara* but you unmistakably and effectively communicate your purpose, desire, demand, intention, advice or whatever through *hara-gei*.
>
> To do this, you bring into play psychology, intuition and your knowledge of the other party's personality, background, ambitions, personal connections, etc. and also what the

---

[4]Takeo Doi, ''Some Psychological Themes in Japanese Human Relationships,'' in J.C. Condon and M. Saito, eds., *Intercultural Encounters in Japan* (Tokyo: Simul Press, 1974), pp. 17–26.

other party knows about you. Only people with plenty of experience and cool nerves can make it succeed, but a lot of communication between Japanese in high positions is through *hara-gei.*[5]

Nemawashi (Preparing the Roots)

"Care to prepare the roots and the tree grows tall and strong," is an old Japanese saying. Its traditional wisdom holds critical importance for Americans bargaining with Japanese executives. The idea is that in Japan what goes on at the negotiation table is really a ritual approval of what has already been decided before, through numerous individual conversations in restaurants, bath houses, and offices. In Japan the negotiation table is not a place for changing minds. Persuasive appeals are not appropriate or effectual. If an impasse is reached, typical Japanese responses are silence, a change of subject, a request to consult the home office, or any of the several options for avoiding saying no. All members of the group must be consulted before new concessions or commitments are made.

As mentioned in the last chapter, the John Wayne approach to business negotiations is almost the opposite. Americans *do* expect minds to change at the negotiation table. Why else have the meeting? When an impasse arises we use our best arguments and persuasive appeals to change the other side's point of view. Although the *nemawashi* approach is often used in the United States—we sometimes call it lobbying—and it may often be the smart strategy, it is not the norm.

Shokai-Sha (Introducer), Chukai-Sha (Mediator)

In his book, *The Japanese Way of Doing Business,* Boye DeMente mentions the importance of friendly and neutral third parties in establishing relationships and settling disputes between Japanese firms.[6] This is not a new idea in the West, but in Japan the functions of *shokai-sha* and *chukai-sha* are institutionalized.

Generally, business relationships in Japan are established only through the proper connections and associated introductions. "Cold calls" are simply not made. Instead, a third party (often a bank or trading company executive) familiar with both parties arranges and attends the initial meeting. This third party is called *shokai-sha* in Japan. At later stages in the negotiation, if things go wrong, another outside party or *chukai-sha* may be asked to mediate the conflicts. The *shokai-sha* will usually act in both capacities. Only in rare instances will the *shokai-sha* feel it necessary to call in another person to act as *chukai-sha.*

In the recent General Motors-Toyota joint venture, an executive vice president of a major Japanese trading company called on executives in GM's Product Planning Department prior to the negotiations. He had worked previously with GM executives and was partially responsible for the American company's recent investment in Isuzu

---

[5]Kazuma Uyeno, *Japanese Business Glossary* (Tokyo: Mitsubishi Corporation, Toyo-keizai-Shiyosha, 1983), pp. 58–60.

[6]Boye DeMente, *The Japanese Way of Doing Business* (Englewood Cliffs, N.J.: Prentice Hall, 1981).

Motors. His trading company had worked with Toyota frequently in the past. He also participated in the initial discussion between the two firms. Because of his connections with both companies, this particular executive was the ideal *shokai-sha*.

THE SPECIAL PROBLEM FOR AMERICAN SELLERS

A special point of conflict exists when American sellers call on Japanese buyers. Given the horizontal relationship between American negotiators and the vertical relationship between Japanese negotiators, what happens in cross-cultural negotiations? It is our belief that a Japanese seller and an American buyer will get along fine, while the American seller and Japanese buyer will have great problems. Moreover, we believe this consideration to be a key factor in our trade difficulties with Japan. Our observations in the field and in the management laboratory (summarized in Table 2) provide strong evidence for such a proposition.

When Japanese sellers come to America to market their products, they naturally assume the lower status position, act accordingly (showing great deference for the American buyer), and a sale is made. Initially, Japanese sellers are taken advantage of. After all, they expect American buyers to respect their needs. But in any case, a relationship is established between firms. The door is open and the Japanese sellers have the opportunity to learn the American way, to adjust their behavior, and to establish a more viable long-term relationship.

Such a conception of the Japanese experience in America is supported by both field interviews and experiences and by our laboratory observations. Universally, Japanese executives in the United States report that their companies "took a beating" when entering the American market. But they also report adjusting their business and negotiation practices to fit the American system. Moreover, in the management laboratory the Japanese were more likely to adjust their behavior. In cross-cultural interactions, Japanese executives dramatically increased eye contact, increased the number of smiles, and decreased the number of aggressive persuasive tactics. The Americans were found to make a few analogous adjustments. Also, there were fewer silent periods in cross-cultural negotiations. But this is apparently not due to Japanese adjustments as much as to Americans filling potential silent periods with new arguments.

There is an important implication underlying this apparent adjustment made by the Japanese but not by the American negotiators. Anthropologists tell us that power relations usually determine who adapts their behavior in a cross-cultural setting. Japanese executives in an American business setting are likely to be the ones to modify their behavior. Moreover, in American negotiations status relations are less defined and less important. Japanese sellers can apparently fit into such a situation without offending American buyers.

However, if American sellers take their normative set of bargaining behaviors to Japan, negotiations are apt to end abruptly. American sellers expect to be treated as equals and act accordingly. Japanese buyers are likely to view this rather brash behavior in lower status sellers as inappropriate and disrespectful. Japanese buyers are made to feel uncomfortable and thus, without explanation, politely shut the door to trade. American sellers do not make the first sale, and hence do not learn the Japanese system.

TABLE 2 Key Points of Conflict between American and Japanese Business Negotiation Styles

Category	American	Japanese
Basic cultural values	Individual competition	Individual cooperation
	Individual decision making and action	Group decision making and action
	Horizontal business relations	Vertical business relations
	Independence	*Amae*
Negotiation process		
1. Nontask sounding	Short	Long, expensive
	Informal	Formal
2. Task-related exchange of information	"Fair" first offers	"Banana sale" first offers include room to maneuver
	Full authority	Limited authority
	"Cards on the table"	*Tatemae* and *honne*
	Immediate reciprocity	Long-term reciprocity
	Explicit communication	Implicit communication
3. Persuasion	Aggressive, persuasive tactics (threats, promises, arguments, and logic)	*Nemawashi* and *chukai-sha*
	"You need this"	*Naniwabushi*
4. Concessions and agreements	Sequential	Holistic
	Goal = "good deal"	Goal = long-term relationship

Edward T. Hall is the seminal thinker when it comes to international business negotiations. With Mildred Reed Hall, he has written one of the best books on the topic, *Hidden Differences: Doing Business with the Japanese*. The three basic premises of the book are important.

First, cultural differences are crucial. The Halls state: "Despite popular beliefs to the contrary, the single greatest barrier to business success is the one erected by culture."[7] Second, most cultural differences are hidden, affecting our behavior and attitudes below our level of awareness—thus the title of the book. And third, it would

[7]Edward T. Hall and Mildred Reed Hall, *Hidden Differences: Doing Business with the Japanese* (Garden City, N.Y.: Anchor Press/Doubleday, 1987), p. xvii.

be difficult to find two cultures that are more different than the Japanese and the American, and therefore more susceptible to business disharmony. (The Halls' long experience in studying many cultures around the world qualifies them to make this last statement, and we couldn't agree more.)

Indeed, given these several and substantial points of conflict in negotiation styles it seems truly remarkable that American and Japanese businesspeople ever agree on anything. It is our belief that two things have made business deals between the two largest economic powers possible. The first is the powerful reality of commercial interdependence. American and Japanese companies can, and do, achieve substantial economic benefits from cooperation. Second, businesspeople on both sides of the Pacific have learned to manage these differences in negotiation styles. The Japanese have been better at making adjustments.

*   *   *   *   *

John Wayne Goes to Brussels

Samfrits Le Poole

Any discussion about Americans and Europeans will be replete with unfair stereotypes and generalizations. Just take the terms "Americans" and "Europeans." Are we talking about Boston Brahmins? Iowa farmers? Texas oilmen? California beachcombers? Frenchmen? Austrians? Spaniards?

Europeans have mixed feelings about Americans: admiration and dislike, envy and condescension, affinity and bafflement. Most of these feelings are very subjective and arbitrary, but Americans *do* tend to be ignorant about the world beyond their borders. They suffer from what former Senator Fullbright termed "cultural myopia," and they are not at their best when they are abroad because international business is not their forte.

This is very understandable. Most Americans simply do not have much experience in being abroad or dealing with foreigners. America is such a vast country and marketplace that one can be very successful in the United States without ever leaving it—except perhaps for an occasional quick visit to Canada or the Caribbean. Not so for Europeans, not at all. Internationalism varies from country to country. It may be less important in France and England than in smaller countries like Denmark, Belgium, or Holland, but overall, from the day he or she is born, every European lives in a world that is larger than just his or her own country.

They spend their vacations abroad. At school they learn foreign languages (of necessity, because how many people in the world speak Danish, Dutch, or German?). A majority of what they read in the newspapers happened abroad. Most of the books they read were written by foreigners. Almost all movies they go to are foreign-made. Watching television, they will learn more about foreign countries than about their own.

And no business can survive without crossing borders. From day one, almost every businessperson in Europe exports; deals with foreign customers, suppliers, and partners; receives payments in foreign currency; communicates in foreign languages; and has to cope with foreigners and foreign business practices.

Reprinted from "Negotiating with Clint Eastwood in Brussels," *Management Review,* October 1989, pp. 58–60. Samfrits Le Poole is president of the International Negotiation and Mediation Institute of Amsterdam, Holland. He is the author of *Never Take No for an Answer,* Kogan Page Ltd., 1991, second edition.

ARROGANT IGNORANCE

Americans have neither the tradition nor the necessity of living internationally. Their ignorance about foreign countries, cultures and customs, their lack of linguistic abilities, and their inability to always respect foreign sensitivities are entirely understandable by most Europeans.

But Europeans sometimes take offense when, in their eyes, American ignorance goes arm-in-arm with American arrogance. Americans do not know the world at large very well and all too often not at all, but nevertheless many assume—and tend to proclaim loudly—that their country is the richest, bravest, the most powerful, generous, fair, and compassionate in the world. Anything, for sure, but the most modest!

Europeans wonder how Americans can be so certain of their country's superiority. Europeans readily grant that America is the richest nation and probably the most powerful. But is it also so brave, so generous, so compassionate, so fair? There seems to be some room for improvement in those areas, as is the case everywhere else. And do Americans really have sufficient knowledge of a sufficient number of countries to be able to compare? Why do they feel that need to compare in the first place?

I sometimes think there are two kinds of Americans: The American at home and the American abroad—and the latter misses many of the admirable qualities that shine in the former. Americans abroad all too often forget or ignore that they are abroad. Or perhaps they think that, in essence, the entire world is one big America.

Irritating incidents occur at all levels. American politicians are notorious for behaving in Madrid, Salzburg, or Brussels as if they are in Fort Worth or Casper, Wyoming. Very few American lawyers seem to grasp that the city ordinances of Tampa, Florida, are not applicable in Stuttgart, Germany. Many American businessmen take it as a personal affront if their check in U.S. dollars drawn on a local bank in Jackson, Mississippi, is not accepted in Davos, Switzerland, and are even more amazed when Europeans mistake Rome for Rome, Italy, and not Rome, New York. Of course, these incidents are an exception, but it is nevertheless true that instances are known of Americans who knew that they were staying in the Hilton hotel, but were not quite sure whether that particular Hilton was in Lisbon or Brussels.

All these differences affect negotiations between Americans and Europeans—and let's not forget that each and every business transaction is preceded in one form or another by negotiations.

   • *Time is not always money.* A pivotal difference between Americans and Europeans is their concept of time, although this difference is even more apparent between Americans and Japanese. To Europeans, Americans always seem to be in a hurry. Time is money. There is always another deal waiting, another flight to catch, another buck to be chased.

It cannot be overemphasized how much of a handicap it is for a negotiator to be in a rush and impatient, and how much power can be derived from patience and allowing time to be on your side. Negotiating in a rush generally means negotiating without sufficient information. Fact-finding is an essential part of preparing for negotiations. People who don't make much time available for negotiations are usually prone to prepare in a rush or skip preparations altogether.

- *Small talk may make a big difference.* Even if well-prepared, the facts are never all in hand before the negotiations begin. There will always be missing information and information that is soft, based on assumptions or opinions—even rumors and gossip. Therefore, it is extremely important to use the negotiations themselves to obtain additional information and to double-check the information one already has.

Especially during the first phase of negotiations—the orientation phase—one can casually, without alerting the other party, raise questions to gather and verify information. This orientation phase is also an ideal time to get a better feel for the other party. Ask yourself: What kind of person am I dealing with, how should I approach him or her, what kinds of arguments and other means of persuasion should I use? Americans often skip that orientation phase altogether. They consider the small talk at the beginning as something that is done for politeness' sake, not something truly useful.

Americans frequently come in, introduce themselves, crack a joke or two, make a few kind remarks about the country they are visiting and then, feeling that by now enough time has been wasted, they say "Okay, let's talk business now." They don't realize that the small talk was also business in the sense that it is part of the negotiation process. For Europeans—and even much more so for the Japanese—engaging in small talk, talking about every subject under the sun except for the strict business at the hand, is not a waste of time. They were busy sizing up their competitor while the American wasn't paying attention because he or she thought that nothing important was going on.

- *Concessions—Better never than late, better late than now.* Impatience, the strong urge not to spend more time on anything than absolutely necessary, puts Americans at a disadvantage in another important respect. Americans tend to make concessions much too early in the game. They build some "fat" into their starting position, which is a good habit. Then they stick to their opening position for a while, but as soon as they feel that they will have to make concessions, they make them quickly and in large jumps, often in one big move. Americans forget that any concession that could be made now could also be made 10 minutes from now or this afternoon or next week. They also overlook the fact that everything that comes easily tends to be taken for granted and not really appreciated. The longer and more intensely the other party has to fight for concessions, the more they are appreciated and the more he or she will be inclined to reciprocate.

Concessions should be made slowly and reluctantly. The Soviets are masters at that!

Not allowing sufficient time for negotiations has a direct impact on their outcome. How many international negotiations have ended with one of the parties—usually the Americans—having just one overwhelming desire: to bring the whole thing to an end? In negotiations, as in wars, the quickest way to end the session is to lose. It is simple to end negotiations quickly. Just give in, say "yes," sign the paperwork and go home. But you will not have won.

- *Taking time to take the time.* Americans worship efficiency, and negotiating is not an efficient process at all. In negotiations, the quickest route between two points is hardly ever a straight line. Negotiators often must be willing to waste time in order not to waste opportunities. Europeans are well aware of the American tendency to consider many negotiation ploys a waste of time, and you can be sure they will capitalize on it—at your expense.

The American unwillingness to take sufficient time to negotiate has a direct bearing on their cultural myopia, because in international negotiations, a pivotal part of fact-finding consists of getting information about the country you are going to or your visitor is coming from.

I do not advocate that when you are in Rome, you should do as the Romans do (you should not and you could not); but you should know what the Romans do, you should acquaint yourself thoroughly with local customs, traditions, habits, dos and don'ts, and sensitivities. This is more than a matter of courtesy; it is a matter of practicality to avoid misunderstandings, to enhance your understanding of and feel for the person you want to do business with, and to increase the chances that the negotiations will succeed.

- *Know thy opponent.* The last thing Americans should do is to imitate the European negotiation style. But they should be aware that there is a European negotiating style. They should know that the European way of doing business is utterly different from the American way. They should not be surprised when their Belgian counterpart spends lots and lots of time on pleasantries and social chit-chat and never seems to get down to business. In fact, the Belgian may see the American more as a future business partner than as a business adversary and, for a fruitful partnership to develop, knowing one another well is quite essential.

American negotiators should not consider British counterparts cool and distant just because they do not use their first names. In England, people who have shared the same office for 30 years often still call each other "Sir." An American would be wrong to think that a foreign businessman is slippery or has something to hide just because he does not look you in the eye. Constant eye-contact is considered impolite in many cultures.

- *Never take yes for an answer.* In many cultures—particularly Latin and Oriental cultures—it's not polite to say "no." As a consequence, the word "yes" has many meanings. It might mean "no." It might mean "maybe." It might even mean "yes." All depends on context, tone, and nonverbal factors. And nobody should have any illusion when Spaniards say they will try their best. In what he or she considers a rather blunt, unambiguous way the Spaniard has told you to take a walk. I know of instances in which an American businessman assumed, just because his Spanish opponent used the word "yes," that the deal was concluded and immediately left for the airport. The American learned later that the Spaniard was amazed by his abrupt departure in the middle of negotiations.

WINNING THE BATTLE, LOSING THE WAR

Americans are very competitive, Europeans much less so. In Europe, gentlemen do not win. Nice guys finish last in America. That American competitive streak greatly affects their approach to negotiations. It comes naturally to Americans to negotiate in a win/lose spirit. They want to win and they want their business competitor to lose. They emphasize confrontation and areas of disagreement.

Europeans like to take a win/win approach. Europeans prefer to emphasize cooperation and common ground. They are not out to outsmart their opponent. They want the agreement to be good not only for themselves but also for their opponent. This is not because they are noble or generous, but because they understand that if the agreement is good for the business partner it very often is good for themselves as well. They also realize that they may depend on the business partner for an uncomplicated, timely implementation of the agreement. By forcing the business partner to accept a lousy agreement, it only enhances the risk that as soon as the partner has a chance to walk away from the deal or to cut corners, he or she will do so.

Americans take a very legalistic approach to negotiations, and attorneys are often present. Americans assume the negotiations will lead to long, written contracts. And they always consider litigation a viable option if the opponent does not live up to the agreement.

Europeans also litigate, but only as a very last resort. Trust and a shared perception of common interest should govern the relationship, not lengthy, detailed contracts, they believe. "What's the sense of doing business with him if you need a written contract?" they wonder. They consider attorneys undesirable in negotiations. And they are also very much aware that, particularly in international transactions, litigation is often not a realistic proposition.

What do all these differences add up to? Are Europeans by and large more effective negotiators than Americans? Maybe, and by European standards probably. But that is not the point. In negotiations it is very important to know yourself and to know your competitor.

An understanding of how your opponent views you helps in this respect. It teaches you about yourself and also about him or her. It provides both a mirror and a guide that, if used wisely, will facilitate the negotiations and improve the relationship.

Exercises

The Disarmament Exercise

INTRODUCTION

The purpose of this exercise is to engage you in working together in a small group, making decisions about the nature of your relationship with another group. Your group will be paired with another group. Each group will have the opportunity to make a decision about a series of "moves." The outcome of those moves (in terms of the amount of money that your team wins or loses) will be determined by the choice that your group makes, *and* the choice that the other group makes. Your group cannot independently determine its outcomes in this situation. The nature of your group's choices, and how well it performs in this exercise, will be determined by: (1) your group's behavior toward the other group, (2) the other group's behavior toward your group, and (3) the communication between groups when this is permitted.

ADVANCE PREPARATION

None.

PROCEDURE

Step 1: 5 Minutes

Divide the class into three to six persons per group (your group leader will tell you how to do this). Pair off the groups so that all groups are paired. If there is more than one pair, the group leader will assign a referee to monitor each pair of teams. Designate specific rooms for each team.

Step 2: 15 Minutes

Read the following instructions—Rules for the Disarmament Exercise—carefully. When you have finished reading the instructions, the group leader will answer any questions that you have. You will then be given time to discuss the rules with your teammates, and plan the strategy you will use.

Adapted by Roy J. Lewicki from an exercise developed by Norman Berkowitz and Harvey Hornstein. Reprinted from *Experiences in Management and Organizational Behavior*, by Douglas T. Hall, Donald Bowen, Roy J. Lewicki, and Francine Hall (Chicago: St. Clair Press, 1975). Used with permission.

RULES FOR THE DISARMAMENT EXERCISE

The Objective

You and your team are going to engage in a disarmament exercise in which you can win or lose money. You may think of each team as a country with weapons—some of them are armed and others are not. There are three rounds in the exercise, and each round has seven moves. In this exercise your objective as a team is to win as much money as you can. The team opposing yours has the identical objective.

The Task

1. Each team is given 20 cards. These are your weapons; each card represents one weapon. Each card has one side marked X and an unmarked side. When the marked side of the card is displayed, this indicates that the weapon is armed; conversely, when the blank side of the card is displayed this shows the weapon to be unarmed. Each team also has an A (Attack) card; this will be explained later.

2. At the beginning of the exercise, each team places 10 of its 20 weapons (cards) in the armed position with the marked side up, and the remaining 10 in the unarmed position with the marked side down. All weapons will remain in your possession throughout the exercise; they must be placed so that the referee (group leader) can see them, and out of the sight of the other team.

3. During this exercise there are three rounds with up to seven moves each. Payoffs are calculated after each round (*not* after each move), and are cumulative.

    a. A move consists of a team turning two, one, or none of its weapons from armed (X) to unarmed (blank) status, or vice versa.

    b. Each team has three minutes to decide on its move and to make that move. There are 30-second periods between moves. At the end of three minutes, a team must have turned two, one, or none of its weapons from armed to unarmed status, or from unarmed to armed status. Failing to decide on a move in the allotted time means that no change can then be made in weapon status until the next move. In other words, failure to make a move by the deadline counts as a move of 0 weapons.

    c. The length of the three-minute period is fixed and unalterable.

    d. The referee (instructor) will verify each move for both teams after it has been made.

4. Each new round of the exercise begins with all weapons returned to their original positions, 10 armed and 10 unarmed.

The Finances

If your referee chooses to use real money in this exercise, money will be distributed as described. If you use imaginary money, assume that each team member has made an imaginary contribution of $2.00, and that the money is also distributed as described.

1. Each member will contribute to the treasury. The money you have contributed will be allocated in the following manner:

   a. 60 percent will be returned to your group to be used in the task. Your group may diminish or supplement this money depending on the outcomes during the exercise. At the end of the exercise your group's treasury will be divided among the members.

   b. 40 percent will be donated to the World Bank, which is to be managed by the referee. This money will *not* be returned at the end of the exercise, and should be considered as no longer yours.

   c. The opposing team's money will be allocated in the same way.

The Payoffs

1. If there is an attack during a round:

   a. Each team may announce an attack on the other team (by notifying the referee) during the 30 seconds following any three-minute period used to decide upon a move (including the seventh, or final, decision period in any round). To attack, you must display your A (attack) card to the referee. You may not attack without a card. The moves of both teams during the decision period immediately before an attack *count*. An attack may not be made during negotiations (see below).

   b. If there is an attack (by one or both teams) the round ends.

   c. The team with the greater number of armed weapons wins 5 cents per member for each armed weapon it has over and above the number of armed weapons of the other team. These funds are paid directly from the treasury of the losing team to the treasury of the winning team. If both teams have the same number of armed weapons, the team that attacked pays 2 cents per member for each armed weapon to the World Bank, and the team that was attacked pays 1 cent per member for each armed weapon to the World Bank. If both teams attacked, both pay the 2-cent rate.

2. If there is no attack by the end of a round:

   a. At the end of each round (seven moves), when there has been no attack, each team's treasury receives from the World Bank 2 cents per member for each of its weapons that is at that point unarmed, and each team's treasury pays to the World Bank 2 cents per member for each of its weapons remaining armed.

   b. When a team wins funds, they are awarded by the World Bank. When a team loses funds, they are paid to the World Bank.

3. Teams may run a deficit with the World Bank.

The Negotiations

1. Between moves each team has the opportunity to communicate with the other team through negotiators chosen by the team members for this purpose. You may not communicate with the other team before the first move.

2. Either team may call for negotiations (by notifying the referee) during any of the 30-second periods between decisions. A team is free to accept or reject any invitation from the other team.

3. Negotiators from both teams are *required* to meet after the third and sixth moves.

4. Negotiations can last no longer than five minutes. When the two negotiators return to their teams, the three-minute decison period for the next move begins.

5. Negotiators are bound only by: (*a*) the five-minute time limit for negotiations, and (*b*) required appearance after the third and sixth moves. They are otherwise free to say whatever they choose, and to make an agreement which is necessary to benefit themselves or their teams. They are not required to tell the truth. Each team is similarly not bound by any agreements made by their negotiators, even when those agreements were made in good faith by the negotiators.

Reminders

1. Each move can consist of turning over two, one, or zero of your weapons to the unarmed side—*or* the armed side.

2. You have three minutes to decide which of the above moves you will choose.

3. If there is *no* attack, at the end of the round (seven moves) your team receives 2 cents per member for each unarmed weapon and loses 2 cents per member for each armed weapon.

4. If there *is* an attack, the team with the greater number of armed weapons wins 5 cents per member for each armed weapon it has *over* the number the other team has.

5. A team may call for negotiations after any move. Mandatory meetings of negotiators occur after moves three and six.

Step 3: 15 Minutes

1. Once you have clarified and understood the rules, each team has 15 minutes to organize itself and to plan team strategy.

   a. You must select people to fill the following roles (the persons can be changed at any time by a decision of the team): (1) A negotiator—activities as stated under ''The Negotiations''; (2) a team spokesperson to communicate decisions to the referee about team moves, attacks, initiations or acceptances of negotiations, etc. The referee will only listen to the team spokesperson, and the spokesperson cannot also be the negotiator; (3) a team recorder to record moves of the team, and to keep running accounts of the team's treasury.

   b. You should discuss with your team members the way that you want to play, what the other team might do and how that affects your strategy, the first move that you will make for the first round, whether or not you desire negotiations, and what you might say to the other team if you or they initiate them.

Step 4: 10–20 Minutes

Round 1:

1. The referee will signal that the first round begins.
2. Your team has three minutes to decide on its first move, and then to actually move one, two, or no cards.
3. When the referee returns, show him or her your move. You may also attack at this point, and/or you may call for negotiations.
4. If neither team attacks or calls for negotiations, the referee will proceed to the second move.
5. Remember that there will be mandatory negotiations after moves three and six. Also remember that the game will proceed for seven moves, unless there is an attack.
6. When the round ends, the referee will state how many missiles each team had armed, and whether either team attacked. Each team will calculate its financial status. Money (if used) will be transferred from one team's treasury to the other, or to/from the World Bank.
7. After accounts are settled, return the cards to their "opening" position (10 X-side up and 10 X-side down).

Step 5: 5 Minutes (at the Referee's Discretion)

Answer the questions for round 1 on the Disarmament Exercise Questionnaire.

Step 6: 5 Minutes

Evaluate your team's strategy and outcomes in round 1. Use your reactions to the Disarmament Exercise Questionnaire as a guide, then discuss the strategy you wish to pursue in round 2.

Step 7: 5–20 Minutes

Round 2.   Proceed as in round 1 (Step 3).

Step 8: 5 Minutes (at the Referee's Discretion)

Complete the questions for round 2 on the questionnaire.

Step 9: 5–20 Minutes

Additional rounds may be played at the discretion of the referee.

Disarmament Exercise Questionnaire

For round 1, circle the appropriate number on each scale which best represents your feelings. (For subsequent rounds, uses boxes or triangles or colored pencils to indicate appropriate number.)

1. To what extent are you satisfied with your team's current strategy?

| highly satisfied | 1 | 2 | 3 | 4 | 5 | 6 | 7 | highly dissatisfied |

2. To what extent do you believe the other team is now trustworthy?

| highly trustworthy | 1 | 2 | 3 | 4 | 5 | 6 | 7 | highly untrustworthy |

3. To what extent are you now satisfied with the performance of your negotiator?

| highly dissatisfied | 7 | 6 | 5 | 4 | 3 | 2 | 1 | highly satisfied |

4. To what extent is there now a consensus in your team regarding its moves?

| great deal | 1 | 2 | 3 | 4 | 5 | 6 | 7 | very little consensus |

5. To what extent are you now willing to trust the other people on your team?

| more than before | 1 | 2 | 3 | 4 | 5 | 6 | 7 | less than before |

6. Select one word to describe how you feel about your team :

7. Select one word to describe how you feel about the *other* team :

Negotiators Only: Please respond to the following question.

How did you see the other team's negotiator?

| phoney and insincere | 1 | 2 | 3 | 4 | 5 | 6 | 7 | authentic and sincere |

DISCUSSION QUESTIONS

1. How effectively did your team work together?

   a. How did your team make decisions? (Did one or two persons make the decision for the whole team? A minority make decisions for the whole team? Always a democratic vote? Majority kept overriding the minority?)

   b. Did your team make maximum use of information available? Did the team members really listen to each other? Why not? Were the opinions of the less vocal members sought? Why not? Did the team really try to obtain every piece of information from the negotiators, which was the team's only direct source of information about the other team?

2. Did your team have a viable strategy?

   a. Did your team have a *consistent* plan or was it "pushed around" by other teams?

   b. Was your team's plan *naive?* If so, why?

Disarmament Exercise Team Record Sheet

	Round 1		Round 2		Round 3		Round 4	
	Armed	*Unarmed*	*Armed*	*Unarmed*	*Armed*	*Unarmed*	*Armed*	*Unarmed*
Start:	10	10	10	10	10	10	10	10
Move 1								
Move 2								
Move 3								
Negotiation								
Move 4								
Move 5								
Move 6								
Negotiation								
Move 7								

Financial status prior to first move:
    Funds in team treasury
    Funds of other team
    Funds in World Bank

At end of each round:
    Funds in team treasury
    Funds of other team
    Funds in World Bank (include penalties)

    c. To what extent was your team trying to "win a lot," but not risking anything to do that?

3. How did your team react to cooperation and competition?

    a. Why is cooperation so difficult to achieve?

    b. What are the barriers that stand in the way of developing trust?

    c. What assumptions did your team have about the other team which may have prevented trust and cooperation?

    d. What happened to your team's morale and decision-making structure when it won? When it lost?

4. How did the negotiator get chosen? Delegated? Volunteered? Discussion of "qualifications"?

    a. How committed were you to your negotiator? Where you willing to stand by him or her through thick and thin, or did you abandon trust in your negotiator at some point?

    b. Did some of the negotiators lie? If they are not basically dishonest people, why did they? If they lied, how did they feel about this afterward?

Pemberton's Dilemma

INTRODUCTION

This exercise creates a situation in which you and the other person(s) will be making separate decisions about how to manage your firm. In this situation the outcomes (profits and losses) are determined not only by what you do, but also by a number of other factors, such as the goals and motives that you and the other party have, and the communication that takes place between you and the other party.

ADVANCE PREPARATION

None.

PROCEDURE

Step 1: 5 Minutes

The class will be broken into six-person groups; three will play the management team of Country Market, three will play the management team of Corner Store. The teams should sit far enough from each other to allow private meetings.

Step 2: 10 Minutes

Read the background information for Pemberton's Dilemma below. If you have any questions, clarify them with your instructor at this time.

In this exercise, you will represent your store in discussions with the other store about the hours that each store should open on Sundays. You and the other store will be making decisions simultaneously, and your profits will be directly affected by these decisions. How well you perform will depend in part on your goals, the other store's goals, and the communication between you.

Written by Gregory Leck under the supervision of the authors.

BACKGROUND INFORMATION

Pemberton is a quaint little town located in the heartland of our great country. Although it is only a 30-minute drive to a major metropolitan center, most of the townfolk prefer to do their shopping at one of the two general stores located in Pemberton. At these stores, one can buy a variety of goods, ranging from groceries to hardware equipment. Both establishments boast a soda fountain, which is quite popular among the younger generation as well.

Like most small towns, Pemberton is proud of the fact that it has been able to preserve its many traditions, some of which date back to the 1890s. One of these grand traditions, which became official in 1923 when the town hall passed a resolution to this effect, is the cessation of all commercial activity on Sunday. Times have changed, however, and "Sunday shoppers" are becoming more and more prevalent. In fact, every Sunday there is a mass exodus to the nearby metropolitan center where Sunday shopping has been permitted for years.

You are a member of the management team from one of the two general stores in Pemberton. Both Country Market and Corner Store have been consistently losing potential profit as Sunday shopping becomes more popular. Your management team, as well as the team from the competing general store, has recently contemplated opening the store on Sunday, in spite of the municipal resolution that prohibits this.

The ramifications of such decisions are important since the profitability of such an action will depend upon the decision made by the competing store. For instance, if neither store decides to open on Sunday, it will be business as usual, and both stores will make a profit of $20,000 for the week in question.

If only one store decides to open on Sunday, that particular store would enjoy the patronage of all those Sunday shoppers and would manage to make a $40,000 profit for the week. Unfortunately, the store that decided to remain closed on that Sunday would actually incur a loss of $40,000 that week. This would be due to various reasons, most notably the preference of customers to continue to do their shopping throughout the week at the store that remained open on Sunday.

If both stores decided to stay open on the Sunday of a particular week, adverse consequences would be faced by both establishments. Although town hall may be able to turn a blind eye to one store violating the municipal resolution, two stores would be looked upon as a conspiracy against the traditionalists of Pemberton. Eukariah Hampton, Pemberton's mayor and direct descendant of one the town's founders, would no doubt pressure town hall into levying the highest possible fine allowable by law. In this case, the penalty would be so excessive that both stores would incur losses of $20,000 each for the week. While your lawyers have suggested that the municipal resolutions prohibiting Sunday shopping in Pemberton might be overturned in a court case, this too would be a costly option. In either case, if both stores open on Sunday, they will each incur losses of $20,000 for the week.

Keeping the above information in mind, your team is to decide each week, for the next 12 weeks, whether your store is to remain open on the Sunday of that week. The decision made for the first week must be made without prior consultation with the management team of the competing store. Subsequent decisions may be made after consulting with your competitors. Both teams shall reveal their decisions simultaneously. Remember, the goal is to maximize profits over the next 12-week period.

| | Country Market | | | |
		Close Sunday		Open Sunday
Corner Store Close Sunday	Corner:	$20,000	Corner:	− $40,000
	Country:	$20,000	Country:	$40,000
Open Sunday	Corner:	$40,000	Corner:	− $20,000
	Country:	− $40,000	Country:	− $20,000

Step 3: 10 Minutes

Review the details of the situation and understand how you can make or lose money. Familiarize yourself with the profit chart above. Members of each management team should now plan their strategy. There may not be any communication between the teams before the first round.

There will be 12 one-minute rounds where the stores will either open or close. Each round represents one Sunday, and every fourth Sunday is part of a long weekend. A three-minute planning session separates each Sunday. There may not be any communication between the stores during the planning sessions.

Step 4: 30–45 Minutes

The exercise begins when representatives from the stores (one from each) meet and indicate with a card if their store will open or close on the first Sunday. There may be no communication between the stores before this decision is registered. After each Sunday, representatives from the stores *may* meet and negotiate for five minutes before each three-minute planning session. Negotiations are optional, except after moves four and eight when they are required. If negotiations occur, they will be followed by a three-minute planning period. If there are no negotiations, the three-minute planning period will follow the sharing of the previous decision to open or close. Profits and losses are calculated after each Sunday and are cumulative for the 12 weeks.

Each team will record the outcome of each Sunday on their profit chart. The time periods between each Sunday are fixed, and may not be altered. Each team will complete a total of 12 moves.

Step 5: 30 Minutes

The instructor will record the total profit for each team in each negotiating group. Differences in performance will be noted and possible reasons explored. Participants should describe what happened, particularly in regard to their perceptions of and reactions to the other party. Some suggested questions and issues for discussion are given below.

DISCUSSION QUESTIONS

1. What were your basic objectives and strategy when you started the exercise? Did they change? What outcomes did you achieve as a result of these plans?
2. What did you talk about after the first round of negotiation?
3. Did the content of your negotiating discussion change? Why?
4. What were the most important things that lead to the outcome of the exercise?

Profit Chart

	Corner Store's Choice	Country Market's Choice	Profit	
			Corner Store	Country Market
15-Minute Planning Period				
1.				
2.				
3.				
4. Double profit				
5-Minute Required Negotiation Period				
5.				
6.				
7.				
8. Triple profit				
5-Minute Required Negotiation Period				
9.				
10.				
11.				
12. Quadruple profit				

The Used Car

INTRODUCTION

The scenario for this role-play involves a single issue: the price of a used car that is for sale. While there is a great deal of other information that may be used to construct supporting arguments or to build in demands and requests in addition to the price, the sale price will ultimately be the indicator used to determine how well you do in comparison to other role-play groups.

ADVANCE PREPARATION

1. The instructor is likely to assign preparation for this exercise in advance. If so, read and review the Background Information section on the used car, and the buyer or seller position information that you have been assigned. Read only your own position, as described in the information provided by the instructor.

2. If you are working with others as a team, meet with the team and prepare a negotiation strategy. If you are working alone, plan your individual strategy for your position.

3. Whether working in a small group or alone, make sure that you complete the section at the bottom of your confidential information sheet.

PROCEDURE

Step 1: 5 Minutes

The instructor will determine whether this exercise is to be conducted individually or in small groups. If it is individual, pairs of individuals will be assigned buyer and seller roles. Alternatively, groups of two or three persons will be assigned buyer and seller roles.

Revised version of an original role-play that was developed by Professor Leonard Greenhalgh, Dartmouth College. Used with permission.

Step 2: 30 Minutes

Read and prepare your negotiating position, if this assignment was not done as part of the advanced preparation.

Step 3: 30 Minutes or as Recommended by Instructor

Meet with the opposite side to negotiate a price for the used car. During this time, you may observe the following procedures:

1. Use any plan or strategy that will help you achieve your objectives.
2. Call a caucus at any time to evaluate your strategy or the opponent's strategy.
3. Reach an agreement by the end of the specified time period, or conclude that you are not able to agree and that buyer and seller will explore other alternatives.
4. Complete the Statement of Agreement form and submit it to the instructor. Be sure to write down any additional terms or conditions that were agreed to.

Step 4: 30 Minutes

Be prepared to discuss your settlement with the opposite side, and with other groups in the role-play.

BACKGROUND INFORMATION

You are about to negotiate the purchase/sale of an automobile. The seller advertised the car in the local newspaper. (Note: Both role-players should interpret "local" as the town in which the role-play is occurring.) Before advertising it, the seller took the car to the local Volkswagen dealer, who has provided the following information:

1988 VW Scirocco diesel, standard shift.

White with red upholstery, tinted glass.

AM/FM radio.

30,450 miles; steel-belted radial tires expected to last another 30,000 miles.

45 miles per gallon on diesel fuel at current prices; this is about 10 percent less than regular gasoline.

No rust; dent on passenger door barely noticeable.

Mechanically perfect except exhaust system, which may or may not last another 10,000 miles (costs $300 to replace).

"Blue book" retail value, $5,000; wholesale, $4,400 (local 1992 prices).

Car has spent its entire life in the local area; it is the only used diesel Scirocco within a 60-mile radius.

Statement of Agreement for Purchase of the Automobile

Price: _____

Manner of Payment: _____

Special Terms and Conditions: _____

_____

_____

_____

_____

_____   _____
          Seller   Buyer

DISCUSSION QUESTIONS

1. Did you reach an agreement in this negotiation? If so, how satisfied are you with the price? If not, are you satisfied that you did not agree? Why?
2. If you reached a settlement, how does the settlement price compare to your target price, to the buyer's opening offer, and to the lowest (highest) price that you were willing to accept? Who ''won'' in this exercise?

Knight Engines/Excalibur Engine Parts

INTRODUCTION

Negotiation can be described as a process that combines economic transactions with verbal persuasion. A great deal of what transpires in negotiation is the verbal persuasion—people arguing for and supporting their own preferred position, and resisting similar arguments from the other party. At the same time, underlying this layer of persuasive messages is a set of economic transactions—bids and counterbids—that are at the economic core of the negotiation process.

The purpose of this exercise is to give you some experience with combining the economic transactions and the persuasive messages to support your preferred economic outcome.

ADVANCE PREPARATION

If assigned by the instructor, read the role-play briefing information (provided by the instructor) in advance.

PROCEDURE

Step 1: 20 Minutes

If your instructor has not already done so, you will be assigned the role of Knight Engines or Excalibur Engine Parts for this exercise. You will be told how to locate the appropriate information for your side. Read this information. You will also be assigned a partner (other party) for this exercise.

Step 2: 30–40 Minutes

Meet with the opposite side to negotiate a settlement to the issues in this scenario. Your objective is to negotiate a deal that is most advantageous to you and your company. During this negotiation, you may observe the following guidelines:

Written by Gregory Leck under the supervision of the authors.

1. Use any plan or strategy that will help you achieve your objectives.
2. Call a caucus at any time to evaluate your strategy or the other party's strategy.
3. Reach an agreement by the end of the specified time period, or conclude that you are not able to agree.

Step 4: 30–60 Minutes

Be prepared to discuss your settlement with the other party, and with other groups in the large group setting.

DISCUSSION QUESTIONS

1. What did you set for your goal to be achieved in this negotiation? Your opening bid? Your bottom line?
2. Did you have a "Best Alternative" or "Option" if a deal was not struck? How good was this option? How did it affect your negotiations?
3. Did you reach an agreement in the negotiation? If yes, how satisfied were you with your agreement after you reached it? If not, were you convinced that it was a good idea not to agree?
4. How satisfied were you with your agreement after you heard other groups report in the general session? What was the impact of hearing others' solutions on your own level of satisfaction?
5. In addition to a price for the pistons, what were the other elements of the deal that you agreed to? Did these factors help to make the negotiation more or less competitive?
6. What strategy and tactics did you use to help you achieve your objectives in this negotiation? Did your strategy and tactics "work"?
7. What strategy and tactics did the other party use? Did these tactics "work"? Why or why not?
8. As a result of these negotiations, what is the current state of your relationship with the other negotiator? Would you be more or less likely to do business with this opponent in the future? Why?
9. What did you learn from this exercise that you feel you will want to continue (or change) in future negotiations?

Universal Computer Company

INTRODUCTION

In this exercise you will play the role of a plant manager who has to negotiate some arrangements with another plant manager. You will be in a potentially competitive situation where cooperation is clearly desirable. Your task is to find some way to cooperate, when to do so might seem to put you at a disadvantage.

ADVANCE PREPARATION

Prior to class, read the Universal Computer Company Background Information section and the role information that the instructor has provided. Do not discuss your role with other class members. Plan how you will handle the forthcoming meeting with the other plant manager. Record your initial proposal on the Initial Settlement Proposal form. Do not show this to the other party you are negotiating with until after the negotiations are completed.

PROCEDURE

Step 1: 5 Minutes

The class will be divided into teams of two, one person in the dyad representing the Crawley plant and the other representing the Phillips plant.

Step 2: 20–45 Minutes

Each dyad of plant managers conducts its meeting, trying to reach a solution to its problems. When an agreement is reached, both parties record the outcome on the Final Settlement Agreement form.

Step 3: 10–20 Minutes

With your partner in the dyad, review the Initial Settlement Proposals you each prepared. What bargaining range did you have? What actions by either party lead to the particular outcome you reached and recorded on the Final Settlement Agreement form?

Step 4: 15–20 Minutes

The instructor will poll each dyad on the Initial Settlement Proposals of the parties and the final agreement reached. The instructor will also ask any groups who have not been able to reach an agreement where they were at the time negotiations were halted, and what might have been standing in the way of their reaching an agreement.

BACKGROUND INFORMATION

Universal Computer Company is one of the major producers of computers. Plants in the company tend to specialize in producing a single line of products or, at the most, a limited range of products. The company has considerable vertical integration. Parts made at one plant are assembled into components at another which in turn are assembled into final products at still another plant. Each plant operates on a profit center basis.

The Crawley plant produces modules, cable harnesses, and terminal boards which in turn are shipped to other company plants. It makes more than 40 different modules for the Phillips plant. The two plants are about five miles apart.

The Quality Problem

Production at the Phillips plant has been plagued by poor quality. Upon examination it has been found that a considerable portion of this problem can be traced to the quality of the modules received from the Crawley plant.

The Crawley plant maintains a final inspection operation. There has been considerable dispute between the two plants as to whether the Crawley plant was to maintain a 95-percent acceptance level for all modules shipped to the Phillips plant, or to maintain that standard for each of the 42 modules shipped. The Phillips plant manager has insisted that the standard had to be maintained for each of the 42 individual modules produced. The Crawley plant manager maintains that the requirements mean that the 95-percent level has to be maintained for the sum of modules produced. Experience at the Phillips plant shows that while some module types were consistently well above the 95-percent acceptance level, 12 types of modules had erratic quality and would often fall far below the 95-percent level. As a result, while individual types of modules might fall below standard, the quality level for all modules was at or above the 95-percent level.

This raised serious problems at the Phillips plant since the quality of its products is controlled by the quality of the poorest module.

The Interplant Dispute

The management of the Phillips plant felt that the quality problem of the modules received from the Crawley plant was causing them great difficulty. It caused problems with the customers, who complained of the improper operation of the products that contained the Crawley modules. As a result, the Phillips plant operation had earlier added secondary final inspection of its completed products. More recently it had added

Initial Settlement Proposals

_____ Plant

How do you propose that the following expenses and repairs should be handled?

Expense of repairing all faulty modules _____

_____

Expense of repairing faulty modules other than the 12 types that fall below 95 percent

level _____

_____

Expense of repairing the faulty modules of the 12 types that fall below the 95 percent

level _____

_____

How to handle the repair of the faulty modules of the 12 types that fall below the 95 percent

level _____

_____

How to handle the repair of the modules other than the 12 types that fall below the 95

percent level _____

_____

an incoming inspection of 12 poor quality modules received from the Crawley plant. There were times when the number of modules rejected was large enough to slow or even temporarily stop production. At those times, to maintain production schedules, the Phillips plant had to work overtime. In addition, the Phillips plant had the expense of correcting all the faulty units received from the Crawley plant.

Ideally the management of the Phillips plant would like to receive all modules free of defects. While this was recognized as impossible, they felt that the Crawley plant

Final Settlement Agreement

How, exactly, did you agree that the following expenses and repairs would be handled?

Expense of repairing all faulty modules _____

_____

Expense of repairing faulty modules other than the 12 types that fall below 95 percent

level _____

_____

Expense of repairing the faulty modules of the 12 types that fall below the 95 percent

level _____

_____

How to handle the repair of the faulty modules of the 12 types that fall below the 95 percent

level _____

_____

How to handle the repair of the modules other than the 12 types that fall below the 95

percent level _____

_____

_____   _____
Representative, Phillips Plant   Representative, Crawley Plant

should at least accept the expense of repairs, extra inspections, and overtime required by the poor quality of the parts.

Since installing incoming inspection procedures on the 12 modules, the Phillips plant had been rejecting about $8,000 of modules a week. For the most part these had been put into storage pending settlement of the dispute as to which plant should handle repairing them. Occasionally, when the supply of good modules had been depleted, repairs were made on some of the rejected units to keep production going. The Phillips plant had continued to make repairs on the remaining 30 types of modules as the need for repairs was discovered in assembly or final inspection.

From its perspective, the Crawley plant management felt that it was living up to its obligation by maintaining a 95 percent or better quality level on all its modules shipped to the Phillips plant. Further, they pointed out that using sampling methods on inspection meant that some below-standard units were bound to get through, and that the expense of dealing with these was a normal business expense which the Phillips plant would have to accept as would any other plant. They pointed out that when buying parts from outside suppliers it was common practice in the company to absorb the expenses from handling the normal level of faulty parts.

The Phillips plant management argued that the Crawley plant management was ignoring its responsibility to the company by forcing the cost of repairs on to their plant where only repairs could be made—rather than to have the costs borne by the Crawley plant where corrections of faulty processes could be made.

DISCUSSION QUESTIONS

1. What differences in strategy and tactics were followed in groups that completed negotiations versus those that did not? Were relationships competitive or cooperative, conflictful, or problem solving?

2. What factors did the various dyads find that contributed most to the outcome they reached?

3. Did the members of dyads change their feelings about the settlement after they learned how well they did relative to their initial goals for the negotiation? Why? What does this say about how we evaluate "good" and "bad" actions in negotiation?

EXERCISE 6

Twin Lakes Mining Company

INTRODUCTION

In this role-play, you will have the opportunity to negotiate a serious problem—a conflict between a mining company and the government of a small town regarding an environmental cleanup. While the issues in this scenario have been simplified somewhat for the purpose of this role-play, such conflicts between industry and governmental groups are typical throughout the country. Try to introduce as much realism into this situation as you can, based on your own personal experiences.

ADVANCE PREPARATION

The nature of advanced preparation will be determined by your instructor. You may be required to read these materials and/or to meet with your other team members in advance of the class session in which this problem will be actually negotiated.

PROCEDURE

1. You will be assigned to a small group to represent either the Twin Lakes Mining Company or the Tamarack Town Council in this negotiation.
2. Before meeting with your group, you should read the common Background Information statement, and your own individual briefing sheet for either the company or the council. This information will be provided by your instructor.
3. When you meet with your group, review the issues and determine a strategy that you intend to pursue. Also assign group members realistic roles that might actually be represented if this were a real-life negotiation. These roles are described in your individual briefing sheets.
4. Negotiate for as long as you need to arrive at a solution, or follow the time limits set by your instructor.
5. When you arrive at an agreement, make sure that you write down exactly what was agreed to. Have a representative of each side sign this document and either submit it to your instructor or bring it to class as instructed.

BACKGROUND INFORMATION

The Twin Lakes Mining Company is located in Tamarack, Minnesota, in the northern part of the state. It was established there in 1941. The town of Tamarack has a year-round population of approximately 12,000. Although there is a growing revenue that accrues to the town as a result of heavy summer tourism (summer homes, fishing, etc.) and several "cottage industries," Tamarack is basically a one-industry town. Two thousand five hundred people, 60 percent of whom live within town limits, work for the Twin Lakes Mining Company; 33 percent of the town's real estate tax base consists of Twin Lakes property and operations. Both in terms of direct tax revenue and indirect contribution to the economic stability of the local population, Tamarack is strongly dependent on the continued success of the Twin Lakes Mining Company.

The Twin Lakes Mining Company is an open-pit, iron ore mine. Open-pit mining consists of stripping the top soil from the ore deposit with the use of power shovels. Train rails are then laid, and most of the ore is loaded into railroad cars for transportation to a central collecting point for rail or water shipment. As mining operations progress, rails are relaid or roads constructed to haul ore by truck. The ore is transported to a "benefication plant" located on the outskirts of Tamarack. Benefication of ore involves crushing, washing, concentrating, blending, and agglomerating the ore. In the early days of ore production, such treatment was unnecessary; however, benefication is necessary today for several reasons. First, transportation costs of rejected material (gangue) are minimized. The crude ore may lose as much as one third its weight in grading, and, in addition, impurities are removed at a much lower cost than if removed during smelting. Second, ores of various physical and chemical properties can be purified and blended during this process. Finally, fine ore materials, which previously may have been rejected as a result of smelting problems, can now be briquetted and pelletized to increase their value. After the ore proceeds through this process of cleaning and agglomerating into larger lumps or pellets, it is shipped by railroad car to steel mills throughout the Midwest. Rejected materials are returned to "consumed" parts of the mine, and the land restored.

Twin Lakes' benefication plant is located approximately five miles outside of Tamarack. As a result of the expansion of the residential areas of the town, summer home development, and various Twin Lakes operations, the plant has become a major problem for local citizens. For years, the Tamarack Town Council has been pressing the company to clean up the most problematic operations.

While most of these discussions have been amicable, Twin Lakes has done little or nothing to remedy the major concerns. Now, as a result of more stringent environmental laws and regulations, Twin Lakes has come under pressure from both the state of Minnesota and the federal government for environmental cleanup. Both the state and the Federal Environmental Protection Agency have informed Twin Lakes that they are in major violation of water and air pollution quality standards, and that immediate action must be taken. Twin Lakes' estimates indicate that total compliance with the cleanup regulations will cost the company over $18 million. Because Twin Lakes is now mining reasonably low-grade ore and because foreign competition in the steel market has significantly eroded the demand for ore, environmental compliance will put the company out of business. Many local citizens, as individuals and through the local chapter of the United Mineworkers Union, are putting significant pressure on the Town Council to help the Twin Lakes Company in its environmental cleanup operations.

The imposition of the environmental controls on Twin Lakes, and the resulting pressure from all segments of the community, has led to renewed discussions between company officials and the Town Council. As a result of these discussions, the following environmental issues have emerged:

1. Water Quality. The Twin Lakes plant requires large amounts of water to wash the crushed ore. In addition, much of the highest quality ore is reduced to an almost powderlike texture after washing, and is being lost in the washing operation. As a result, the company has built a series of settlement recovery ponds alongside Beaver Brook near the plant. Water that has been used for washing ore is allowed to stand in these ponds; they are then periodically drained and the ore recovered. Nevertheless, granules of iron ore and other impurities continue to wash downstream from the plant.

The environmental agents have insisted that the effluent from the plant and the ponds be cleaned up. Estimates for the cost of a filtration plant are $10 million. Twin Lakes claims that it cannot afford to build the plant with its own revenue. Since Tamarack has periodically talked about Beaver Brook as a secondary water source for the town (and residential development makes this a more pressing concern in two-three years) the Twin Lakes officials hope that they might interest Tamarack in a joint venture.

2. Air Quality. The entire process of mining, transporting, and crushing ore generates large amounts of dust. This has significantly increased the levels of particulates in the air. In addition, during the dry summer months, the operation of many large trucks along dirt roads intensifies the problem considerably.

Twin Lakes believes that it can control a great deal of the dust generated immediately around the plant at a cost of approximately $4 million. The most significant debate with the town has been over a series of roads around the outskirts of town. Approximately half of the roads are town-owned; the rest have been specially constructed for the transportation of ore and material. Estimates for paving all the roads are $2.4 million with a yearly maintenance cost of $300,000; periodic oil spraying of the roads, to keep down the dust, would run approximately $400,000 annually, but an agreement to do this as a short-term measure may not satisfy the environmental agencies.

3. Taxation of Company Land. The land for the mine itself is outside of town limits. However, the plant lies within township boundaries, and current taxes on the town land are $400,000 annually. The company has always felt that this taxation rate is excessive.

In addition, several of the railroad spurs used to move ore into the plant, and out to the major railway line, cross town land. The town has continued to charge a flat rate of $200,000 annually for right-of-way use. It has occasionally offered it for sale to the company at rates varying from $1.1 million to $1.2 million. Again, the company has felt that this rate is excessive.

Both the company and the town believe that if some resolution could be obtained on these three major issues, the remaining problems could be easily resolved, and Twin Lakes would agree to keep the mine open.

DISCUSSION QUESTIONS

1. How did you go about preparing for this role-play? What type of strategy did you decide to employ?

2. Did you set goals or targets that you wanted to achieve on each issue or the total package, and did you set "bottom lines" or resistance points? How did having these (or not having these) affect your own negotiation effectiveness?

3. What roles did group members decide to play? How did this affect your own team and the way that it worked with the other group?

4. How satisfied are you with the final agreement (if you reached one)? What factors in your negotiation make you feel satisfied or dissatisfied with this outcome?

5. What did you personally learn from this situation that you feel you will want to continue (or try to change) in future negotiation situations?

Salary Negotiations

INTRODUCTION

In this simulation you will play the role of either a manager or subordinate in a negotiation over salary. Both in securing employment as well as promotions, we frequently are in a position to negotiate with our superiors over salary; and, once we achieve managerial rank, we do the same with subordinates. This is one of the most common and, at the same time, most personal forms of negotiation; for many people, it is also the most difficult. Since salary can be a means of satisfying many needs — economic, recognition, status, or competitive success measure — it leads to complex negotiations.

PROCEDURE

Step 1: 5 Minutes

The class will be divided into groups of three; two will be assigned the roles of manager and subordinate, the other as an observer. Role-players will be assigned either an "A" or a "B" role in one of the Salary Simulations; your instructor will provide this information. Assemble with your trio in the place specified by the instructor.

Step 2: 5 Minutes

Read your assigned role and prepare a strategy. If you are an observer, review the Observer Reporting Sheet and make sure you understand what to look for.

Step 3: 10 Minutes

Carry out your discussion with your counterpart. If you finish before the allotted time is up, review the sequence of events with the other party and tell the other what he or she did that was productive or unproductive to the negotiations.

Developed from examples used by John Tarrant, *How to Negotiate a Raise,* Van Nostrand Reinhold, 1976.

If you are an observer, make brief notes during the role-play on your Observer Reporting Sheet. When the role-play is over, review the sheet and add further details where necessary.

Step 4: 10 Minutes

Discuss the outcome of the negotiation in your trio. The observer should report what he or she saw each party doing. Review what steps or positions seemed most and least useful.

At the end of the time for step 4, the observer should hand the Observer Reporting Sheet to the instructor.

Step 5: 5 Minutes

In your trio, change role assignments so that the person filling an A role now fills a B role, the person filling the B role now becomes observer, and the previous observer now fills an A role.

Step 6: 5 Minutes

Repeat step 2.

Step 7: 10 Minutes

Repeat step 3.

Step 8: 10 Minutes

Repeat step 4.

Steps 9, 10, 11, 12: 30 Minutes

Repeat steps 5, 6, 7, 8.

Step 13: 30 Minutes

The instructor will post the results from the three sets of role-plays. Examine the different outcomes and explore reasons why they occurred and their consequences

DISCUSSION QUESTIONS

1. Were there any differences in the way negotiations were handled when:

   a. Both parties in a role-play were satisfied?

   b. One was satisfied?

   c. Both were dissatisfied?

Observer Reporting Sheet

Round _____

How did A open the meeting? _____

_____

_____

How did B respond to the way A opened the meeting? _____

_____

_____

Was an agreement reached? Yes _____ No _____

What was the salary agreed to, if there was an agreement? _____

Were there any other added features in the settlement achieved? _____

_____

Will future relations between A and B be better ($+$), worse ($-$), or the same ($=$) as a result of this meeting? List the opinions of A, B, and the observer.

A _____ B _____ Observer _____

2. Were some people playing the same role dissatisfied with an outcome that others in the same role found satisfying? Why? How do you account for this?

3. Poll quickly those who were satisfied with the outcome. Ask why they were satisfied.

4. Poll quickly those who were dissatisfied with the outcome. Ask why they were dissatisfied.

5. What was the effect of observing another's negotiation on how you negotiated? Did what you see as an observer affect how satisfied you felt with your own outcome?

Newtown School Dispute

INTRODUCTION

In this simulation, you will play a member of either a school board or teachers' association bargaining team. You and the other members of your team, and the members of the other team, are negotiators representing constituencies. You will deal with a complex mix of bargaining issues which have differing preference functions for each side, and you will be subject to a variety of pressures during the negotiations.

ADVANCE PREPARATION

Prior to class, read the Background Material on the Newtown School Dispute. You have been assigned to either the Board of Education or the Teachers' Association. Read the appropriate position paper the instructor has given you.

Prior to class, meet with the members of your bargaining team, determine your objectives and strategy, and prepare your initial offer. Record this offer on the Initial Offer Form.

PROCEDURE

Step 1: 5 Minutes

The instructor will announce the team assignments and time schedules, and designate locations for negotiations and caucuses.

Step 2: 60–90 Minutes

Teams negotiate. Teams may negotiate as a whole or through spokespersons. Who makes the first offer, how time is used for caucus, and so on, are all controlled by the negotiators themselves. At the end, record your settlement on the Final Settlement Form and hand it to the instructor. If there has not been a complete settlement, note which items have been agreed upon.

Revised version of material originally developed by Frank W. Masters. Used with permission.

Step 3: 30–60 Minutes

The instructor will post the initial offers and the final settlements.

BACKGROUND INFORMATION

It is now September 10, the opening day of the school year in Newtown. The contract between Newtown School District and the Newtown Teachers' Association expired on June 30. Since then the Board of Education and representatives of the Teachers' Association have met on several occasions in an attempt to finalize a contract, but these attempts have not been successful.

Prior to June 30 and during the summer months, there was increasing talk among the membership of the Teachers' Association of the desirability of calling a strike if the contract was not finalized by opening day. However, the leadership of the Teachers' Association agreed, for the benefit of the community, to resume normal operations throughout the system (without a contract) on opening day *on a day-to-day basis*. This is in response to parent pressures to resume normal operations. Parents have been placing pressure on both teachers and the board to keep the schools operating, but have twice defeated referendums for increased taxes to cover budgetary increases over and above those of the previous year. Due to decreases in enrollments, income from local taxes and state and federal aid, as well as increased costs, maintenance of the school budget at par with the previous year would produce a 4.08 percent budgetary shortfall, which the board feels would begin to exhaust budgetary categories beginning in April of the present school year. Therefore, the board feels that programs and personnel must be cut while, at the same time, productivity (work load) of teachers must be increased if the system is to function effectively within its budgetary constraints to the end of the current fiscal year (June 30). In this regard, the district must provide 190 instructional days, as mandated by state law.

The Board of Education is caught between the Teachers' Association and community pressure groups. The board believes that it must satisfy these pressure groups, while at the same time keeping the teachers on the job with a contract that is acceptable to the bargaining unit's membership. The board is concerned that if it fails to respond appropriately to community pressures for cost reductions, it may be removed. The board's primary objective, therefore, is to cut costs while retaining as many programs as possible. It hopes to do so through cutbacks in teaching personnel and increases in teacher productivity (work load). The board also wishes to eliminate certain existing agreements in order to increase productivity. In this connection, the board wants to negotiate a three-year contract that will "stabilize" the situation by creating orderly and predictable budgetary needs that will be less likely to be seen as excessive by various community groups. In contrast, the Teachers' Association wants to obtain a one-year contract to maintain flexibility.

The Teachers' Association also feels caught between community pressure groups, who want to avert a strike, and the board's apparent unwillingness to fight for increased budget allocations to run the system. The teachers feel the board has not faced up to the community's unwillingness to accept increased taxation to pay for education, and that the board is simply responding to community unwillingness by passing the burden along to teachers.

Newtown is a relatively settled and stable upper middle-income community, with a strong interest in quality education, but is disinclined to increase its already burden-

Newtown School District Teachers' Salary Schedule

Step	Amount	Last Year's Number of Teachers	Cost	Current Year's Number of Teachers	Cost
Entry	$22,500	20	$ 450,000	0	0
1	23,000	20	460,000	20	$ 460,000
2	24,000	28	672,000	20	480,000
3	25,000	31	775,000	26	650,000
4	26,000	30	780,000	28	728,000
5	27,500	23	632,500	26	715,000
6	28,500	24	684,000	23	655,500
7	29,500	15	442,500	22	649,000
8	31,000	16	496,000	15	465,000
9	32,000	13	416,000	16	512,000
10	33,000	180	5,940,000	179	5,907,000
Totals		400	$11,748,000	375	$11,221,500

some tax rate. The Newtown School District consists of 12 schools; 9 elementary schools (K–8) and 3 senior high schools. The student population is 12,000, with 8,000 elementary and 4,000 high school students. The bargaining unit, representing 95 percent of all teachers, consists of 250 elementary teachers in all categories and 125 high school teachers in all categories.

Both sides wish to conclude an agreement to avert a strike. However, the Teacher's Association bargaining team is adamantly committed to improving the lot of its membership, and the board is just as committed to keeping its costs as low as possible. Nevertheless, each side feels it has some room to move on certain issues.

DISCUSSION QUESTIONS

1. The different sides in the negotiations should describe their initial strategies and positions, how well they worked together, and how their positions and strategies changed during negotiation.

2. The different sides should identify changes they made in their objectives during negotiations, what they saw to be the strengths and weaknesses of their own position, and of the opposing team's position.

3. Was there any discussion at the beginning of the negotiation about how the discussions were to be handled? If so, did they have any effect? If not, would some discussion have had an effect? How?

Current School Year
July 1–June 30
Projected Budget

1. Income
   1.1 Local tax (same rate as last year will continue,
       $4.86 per $1,000. No significant increase in
       values expected.) $18,424,100
   1.2 State (formula yield per pupil will remain the
       same. Legislature may meet and possibly raise
       formula for next year.)   7,455,360
   1.3 Federal   1,137,200
       Total $27,016,660

   Note: This is a decrease of $576,882 ($-2.09$%) from the previous year's income.

2. Expenditures
   2.1 Administration
       2.1.1 Professional salaries $ 1,724,750
       2.1.2 Clerical/secretaries   426,500
       2.1.3 Other   379,000
             Total   2,530,250
   2.2 Instruction
       2.2.1 Teachers
             Salaries $11,221,500[a]
             Fringes   2,210,000
       2.2.2 Aides   1,800,700
       2.2.3 Materials/supplies   1,481,350[b]
             Total   16,713,550
   2.3 Plant operation/maintenance
       2.3.1 Salaries $ 1,920,000
       2.3.2 Utilities   1,475,000[c]
       2.3.3 Other   395,650[d]
             Total   3,790,650
   2.4 Fixed charges
       2.4.1 Retirement $ 1,784,000[e]
       2.4.2 Other   649,850[f]
             Total   2,433,850
   2.5 Debt service $1,555,650[g]

   2.6 Transportation
       2.6.1 Salaries   607,000
       2.6.2 Other   598,450[h]
             Total $ 1,205,450
             Grand Total $28,229,400

Notes   Total number of pupils   = 12,000
        Total number of teachers = 375
        Per pupil expenditure   = $2,352

	Percent of Last Year's Total Expenditure
a. Twenty-five teachers did not return to the system either due to retirement or other reasons.	−1.91%
b. Costs of materials and supplies will be up 16 percent over last year's cost based upon currently known price increases.	+.74%
c. Cost of utilities is expected to increase by approximately 20 percent for the current year.	+.88%
d. Cost projections indicate a 16 percent increase in this category.	+.20%
e. Teacher retirement is up 5 percent due to increases mandated by the legislature to pay for new benefits. This was partially offset by attrition.	+.31%
f. Other fixed charges are up 32 percent for this current year.	+.57%
g. Debt service is up 14 percent due to increased difficulty in floating bonds.	+.69%
h. Other transportation costs are up 31 percent due to increases in operating and maintenance costs.	+.51%
Total cost adjustments	+1.99%
Summary: Change in costs including income decrease	+4.08%

4. What was the bargaining range that existed at the beginning of negotiation?

5. Who made the opening offer? What effect did it have on the conduct of negotiations?

6. Were there attempts to use constituencies and/or bystanders? To what effect?

7. Who made the final offer? How was it structured?

Last School Year
July 1–June 30
Actual Audit

1. INCOME

   1.1 Local tax ($4.86 per $1,000 worth assessed real
       property. Assessment is at full value.) $18,505,138

   1.2 State (based on an equilization formula, improved
       during the last legislative session. Yielded
       $621.28 per pupil in administration last year.)   7,952,354

   1.3 Federal   1,136,050

      Total   27,593,542

2. EXPENDITURES

   2.1 Administration

2.1.1 Professional salaries	$ 1,724,367	
2.1.2 Clerical/secretarial	426,171	
2.1.3 Other	395,940	
Total		2,546,478

   2.2 Instruction

2.2.1 Teachers		
Salaries	$11,748,000	
Fringes	2,114,644	
2.2.2 Aides	1,794,155	
2.2.3 Materials/supplies	1,277,653	
Total		16,934,452

   2.3 Plant operations/maintenance

2.3.1 Salaries	$ 1,919,967	
2.3.2 Utilities	1,231,611	
2.3.3 Other	341,460	
Total		3,493,038

   2.4 Fixed changes

2.4.1 Retirement	$ 1,698,863	
2.4.2 Other	492,441	
Total		2,191,304

   2.5 Debt service $ 1,365,030

   2.6 Transportation

2.6.1 Salaries	$ 606,046	
2.6.2 Other	457,194	
Total		$ 1,063,240
Grand Total		27,593,542

Notes

  Total number of pupils = 12,800
  Total number of teachers = 400
  Per pupil expenditure = $2,156
  Last year, the year of the audit on this page, there were 12,800 students in the public school system.
  The current year's projected enrollment is 12,000.

Initial Offer Form

Board of Education _____   Teachers' Association _____

Item	"Bottom Line" Position	Desired Settlement	Opening Offer
Salary	_____	_____	_____
Reduction in staff	_____	_____	_____
Work load	_____	_____	_____
Evaluation of teachers	_____	_____	_____
Binding arbitration	_____	_____	_____
Benefits	_____	_____	_____

Final Settlement Form

Board of Education _____   Teachers' Association _____

Item	Settlement
Salary	_____
Reduction in staff	_____
Work load	_____
Evaluation of teachers	_____
Binding arbitration	_____
Benefits	_____

Bestbooks/Paige Turner

INTRODUCTION

This situation involves a negotiation between two representatives: one for an author and the other for a publishing company. This is clearly a competitive situation, but some cooperation is also required. Your challenge is to get the best contract possible for your side.

ADVANCE PREPARATION

None.

PROCEDURE

Step 1: 15 Minutes

The class will be broken into teams of two, one person representing Paige Turner and the other representing Bestbooks. Read the private material that your instructor has provided, and prepare your strategy for the negotiations.

Step 2: 20–30 Minutes

Each dyad of representatives will conduct its meeting trying to reach a new contract between Paige Turner and Bestbooks. When an agreement is reached, write down the settlement on the final settlement agreement form. Agreement must be reached on all eight issues in order for a final agreement to be struck. If you and your partner finish the negotiation early, review your strategies and the process of negotiations. What bargaining range did you have? What actions by either party led to the particular outcome reached?

Written by Gregory Leck under the supervision of the authors.

Final Settlement Agreement Form

Issue	*Settlement Point*
Royalties	_____
Signing bonus	_____
Weeks in publication	_____
Weeks of promotion	_____
Duration of contract	_____
Contract renewals	_____
Countries distributed	_____
Book clubs	_____
(Signed) _____	(Signed) _____
Bestbooks Representative	Paige Turner Representative

Step 3: 15–20 Minutes

The instructor will gather the agreements reached by each dyad. Any groups who have not reached an agreement by the end of the negotiating period will be asked to record their final offers.

DISCUSSION QUESTIONS

1. What tactics and strategies did the teams use to reach an agreement? Was there a difference in the approaches taken by those reaching agreement and those who did not settle?

2. Which team in the class reached the best settlement? What are the criteria for the best settlement in this exercise?

3. How where the issues structured in this exercise? What assumptions did people make about the structure of the issues? How did these assumptions influence the negotiation process? Outcome?

Elmwood Hospital Dispute

INTRODUCTION

In this exercise you will be dealing with a very complex negotiation situation. In contrast to earlier exercises where there may have been a single opponent and one or two clearly defined issues, this simulation creates a negotiation between larger groups with less clearly defined issues. The key roles played by mediators are also introduced in this simulation.

ADVANCE PREPARATION

Read the Background Information section for the Elmwood Hospital Dispute in this exercise; then read the role information the instructor has provided. Prepare to play this role. Familiarize yourself with the facts and be prepared to act as you think you would act if you were a person in the situation described in this case.

PROCEDURE

Step 1: 30 Minutes

Participants assigned to the same role, that is, board members and administrators, members of the Community Coalition, and the mediators will meet separately to plan how they will handle the upcoming meeting. If there are several sets of roles, that is, the class is so large that there are several Elmwood City hospitals, the role teams for each hospital will meet separately to plan strategy.

Step 2: 60 Minutes

The mediator(s) will call the parties together for the meeting. Discussion begins on the purpose of the meeting.

Adapted from an activity developed for the Institute of Mediation and Conflict Resolution, 1972.

BACKGROUND INFORMATION

The situation described below is a composite, with some data drawn from a number of similar disputes, and other information constructed specifically for this training exercise. The scenario is not to be interpreted as an account of any actual dispute. This simulation is one of several developed and tested by the Institute for Mediation and Conflict Resolution in New York, and adapted with permission by the Community Conflict Resolution Program.

* * * * *

Elmwood is a medium-sized, 450-bed private hospital in a southwestern city of approximately 600,000. It is well equipped for inpatient care, and has an open-heart surgery team which is a matter of special pride to the board of trustees and the hospital's director. None of the trustees live in the hospital's immediate neighborhood, though some of their parents once did. Most of them are professionals or businesspeople, and one of their main functions as trustees is to help in fund raising for the hospital.

Until 10 years ago, Elmwood was in the middle of a white, middle-class community. Now, however, it is on the eastern edge of an expanding low-income neighborhood, which has moved across the nearby expressway and is continuing to grow eastward. A good part of the low-income community is served by West Point Hospital, back on the western side of the expressway. People on the east, however, are turning to Elmwood. There are very few private physicians left in the Elmwood area, and the hospital, through its outpatient clinic, is the main source of medical care for the newer residents.

These newer residents, who now make up approximately 65 percent of the service area, are a mix of relatively recent newcomers to the city, some from other parts of the United States and others from various foreign countries. Most are in low-paying service jobs. Many are on public assistance. Infant mortality is three times as high as the rest of the city. Malnutrition is a problem, as are tuberculosis, lead poisoning, and other diseases associated with a slum environment. Most of these new residents cannot afford to be admitted to the hospital when sick, and rely instead on outpatient treatment in what is now an overburdened facility at Elmwood.

Like most hospitals, Elmwood is in a financial squeeze. In addition, it has become increasingly difficult to attract new interns and residents and harder to retain present professionals. Although the hospital director is somewhat sympathetic to the medical care problems of the community, he sees his first priority as building the hospital's institutional strength by such measures as increasing intern- and resident-oriented research opportunities and adding facilities which would induce the staff to stay on rather than go elsewhere. He has apparently given some thought to sponsoring a neighborhood health center, but it has been put off by location problems. He has also heard about some heated conflicts over control of services at other hospitals in the state that took state and federal health grants. Right now, the director apparently intends to put these matters on the "back burner" until he gets the other things going.

Residents of the low-income community have organized a Concerned Community Coalition (CCC). The community has been asking the hospital to increase its almost nonexistent efforts in preventative medical care, improve and expand outpatient facilities, establish a satellite health center with day-care facilities, and train a roving paraprofessional health team to administer diagnostic tests throughout the community. Elmwood is their neighborhood hospital and, to them, this is what a neighborhood hospital should be doing for the residents.

Two weeks ago, the CCC sent a letter to the director asking that the hospital initiate these efforts and requesting that he meet with them to discuss how the community and the hospital could work together. Although the community is deeply concerned about its medical problems and resents the fact that a city institution has not acted before this of its own volition, the letter was not unfriendly.

To date, the letter has not been answered.

Three days ago, the director and the chairman of the board announced the acquisition of a site about 15 blocks from the hospital on which it said it would build a heart research facility, a six-story nurses residence, and a staff parking lot, with shuttle bus service to the hospital grounds.

On learning of the plans, the leaders and members of the CCC were incensed. They decided to sit in at the director's office until the hospital met their needs.

The day before yesterday, about 50 CCC adherents took over the director's office, vowing not to leave until the hospital agreed to meet the following demands:

1. Replacement of the board of trustees with a community-controlled board.
2. A 100 percent increase in outpatient facilities.
3. Establishment of a neighborhood health center and a day-care facility on the newly acquired site.
4. Establishment of a preventative diagnostic mobile health team, consisting of neighborhood residents chosen by CCC.
5. Replacement of the director by one chosen by the community.

While the hospital director indicated that he would be glad to meet with the group's leader to discuss the matters raised in its letter, he also stated quite forcefully that he considered the new demands arrogant and destructive and that, in any event, he would not meet under duress (i.e., as long as the sit-in continued).

The CCC said it would not leave until a meeting took place and the demands were accepted.

The sit-in began two days ago. This morning the hospital's lawyers moved to get an injunction against the sit-in. The CCC, aided by a Legal Services attorney, resisted.

The judge reserved decision, stating that to grant an injunction might only make the situation worse. He noted that both the hospital and the CCC would have to learn to live together for their own joint best interest. He therefore instructed the parties to meet to try to work out the problems between them, and has appointed a mediator to assist them. The mediator is a staff member of the city's Human Rights Commission, a unit of the municipal government.

At the judge's suggestion, the sides have agreed to meet with the mediator in the hospital library. The meeting has been scheduled for later today.

Step 3: 15–30 Minutes

At the end of the meeting, meet with your own team members and answer the following questions.

a. Review your original plans. Did you follow them? Meet your objectives? Why? Why not?

b. For those playing a board member or CCC member: Did having a mediator help or hinder you? How? For those filling the role of mediator: What strategy did you try to employ? What things did the other parties do that helped or hindered you in your work as mediator?

c. If you were in this position again, what would you do differently?

d. What things did you notice or think about that would have helped people in the other roles be more effective in dealing with you in your role?

e. For members of CCC: What power tactics did you employ? How effective were they? For board members and mediators, what power tactics did the CCC employ? How did you react to these tactics?

f. What characteristics did this bargaining situation have that were different from those of other bargaining situations you have been in?

Step 4: 30–60 Minutes

Next, join the rest of the class and report what you have concluded for (a) through (f).

The Power Game

INTRODUCTION

The concept of "power" is a complex, elusive, and almost paradoxical one. It is complex because there is a wide variety of definitions of what constitutes power, and how it is effectively accumulated and used. It is elusive because there seems to be very little consensus about the definitions, or the best way to describe power and talk about it in action. Finally, power is paradoxical because it doesn't always work the way it is "expected" to; sometimes those who seem to have the most power really have the least, while those who may appear to have the least power are most in control.

This simulation offers an opportunity to experience power in a wide variety of forms and styles. During the activity, you will become aware of your own power, and the power of others. Your objective will be to determine who has power, how power is being used, and how to use your own power in order for you to achieve your goals. This type of analysis is essential to effective negotiations when power relationships have not been well defined.

ADVANCE PREPARATION

Your instructor will probably ask you to make a monetary contribution for this activity. Otherwise, no advance preparation is necessary.

PROCEDURE

Step 1

Your instructor will ask you for your monetary contribution. This money is to be given to the instructor. The instructor will then announce what will be done with the money.

Adapted from an exercise developed by Lee Bolman and Terrence Deal, Harvard Graduate School of Education, and published in *Exchange: The Organizational Behavior Teaching Journal*. Used with permission.

Step 2

Your instructor will assign you to a group. You will become acquainted with the group that you are assigned to, and that others are assigned to. You will be given a place to meet.

Step 3

Your instructor will give you descriptions of the duties and responsibilities of the group that you are assigned to. Please read this information closely.

Step 4

You will have exactly one hour to conduct the exercise, unless your instructor gives you different instructions.

DISCUSSION QUESTIONS

1. What did you learn about power from this experience?
2. Did this experience remind you of events you have experienced in other organizations? If so, what were the similarities?
3. What did you learn about yourself personally, and the way that you react to power and its use?
4. What power events occurred in your own subgroup? Did you feel satisfied with the amount of power you had? With the way you used it? Why?
5. What did you or your group do to exercise power, or to gain more power? How did it work out?

Jordan Electronics Company

INTRODUCTION

In this simulation, you will play the role of a committee member on the New Products Committee of Jordan Electronics Company. The committee oversees the development of all new products. In particular, it approves the research and design of all new products and authorizes the release from R&D to begin the manufacturing process. At the moment, the committee is faced with a decision: whether or not to authorize the manufacture of a new model of the Jordan Auto Correlator Model 36, known as the JAC 36.

As a member of the committee working on this problem, you will face some of the complex and tense deliberations that often confront senior management. You will have several levels of concern on the committee: your own job and the problems you may have in getting it done, representing the members of your unit whom you supervise, and worrying about the welfare of Jordan Electronics as a whole.

ADVANCE PREPARATION

Prior to class, read the Background Information section of the Jordan Electronics Company. Also read the information on the role that has been provided by your instructor. Plan what you are going to do in the forthcoming meeting.

BACKGROUND INFORMATION

Jordan Electronics is a manufacturing company that produces two major lines of scientific measuring instruments: instruments for use in scientific laboratories (laboratory products) and industrial instruments for use in manufacturing processes (industrial products). The management of Jordan Electronics is currently confronted with a problem in authorizing the manufacture of a redesigned model of the Jordan Auto Correlator Model 36 (JAC 36).

The original measuring instrument was designed over 20 years ago by Norman Bass (now president of the company, but, at that time, a professor at the state university). Bass had teamed up with two others to found Jordan Electronics: Kenneth Lawson (now director of research and development but at the time also a state university professor) and Beth Shonberg (now senior engineer but then an independent electronics engineer specializing in computers).

The original mission of the company was to manufacture the auto correlator and other scientific instruments. (An auto correlator is a device used to monitor flow processes by measuring data at different points in the process. It might measure the rate of flow of chemicals through a pipeline as well as changes in temperature of the chemical at two different points along a pipeline and then correlate that information.) At the time, the instrument revolutionized the market. The JAC 36 (so-called because it was launched on Bass's 36th birthday) permitted a researcher to make correlations simultaneously on 256, 512, or 1024 channels (monitoring levels). This device was initially picked up by physicists doing research in diffraction and gradually was adopted by scientists from other fields and by manufacturing firms using complex chemical processes. The JAC 36 became the market leader in its field and maintained that position for over 15 years.

The past few years have brought changes. First, new, faster, and more-powerful microprocessors are now in existence. The use of a 16-bit microprocessor chip has been made obsolete by superior 32-bit microprocessor chips. A leading Japanese microprocessor manufacturing company has just introduced a new 64-bit chip that would certainly overshadow the speed and capacity of its predecessors. Using these components would reduce the size and weight of the completed machine and would permit greater portability. The existence of flat LCD screens would enable the manufacturing of a portable JAC 36 unit that would resemble the very popular "lap-top" computers. Although the hardware aspect was technically quite feasible, such a unit would be successful only if a special type of software was developed that would enable the smaller units to emulate the functions of the larger ones. Changeover to this manufacturing process is costly, but once the "bugs" are worked out, manufacturing cost per unit could be cut significantly.

Second, although the JAC 36 holds a strong share of the market, Jordan's competitors have been nibbling away at that market share by adding a variety of new features to their instruments. One addition has been to provide voice-activated command entry which enables one to control the auto correlator using verbal commands. This frees the user to perform other manual functions during the verbal command process. A second feature was the implementation of optical coupling. Although optical devices did not enhance the capacity or speed of the units, they did reduce the amount of heat that was emitted by the auto correlator. This aspect was appreciated by those who had to use the units in strict laboratory conditions. Although it was not perceived to be a widespread problem, the erratic behavior of some microprocessors was sometimes attributed to the excess heat generated by units that did not use optical coupling. Competing products with these features sell for $3,000 to $5,000 more than the present JAC 36. Finally, as mentioned above, some competitors are rumored to be working on a "lap-top" design that would enhance the portability of such units. While the JAC 36 typically is used as a laboratory instrument, scientists now seem to want the flexibility of a lighter machine for field experiments and mobile laboratories. Lightness and ease of movement are even more attractive in industrial applications. Although use of the new technologies requires some change in the basic circuit design, it requires extensive change in the physical design of the instrument and in the manufacturing methods.

Six months ago, Sales Vice President Joe Little made a very strong pitch to management to encourage the production of a JAC 36 that incorporated reduced size, voice-activated control, and optical-coupling features. He pointed out that Jordan's sales representatives were becoming increasingly embarrassed by customer complaints about the outdated nature of the JAC 36 and their requests for a newer version similar to the competition. Little also said that he would like to see two versions of the JAC sometime in the future, a portable machine and a stationary one, but that the portable unit was clearly second priority because strong demand was not anticipated for several years.

In response to this request, President Norm Bass requested an intensive study of the market for an updated JAC 36 and an estimate for the manufacturing costs. The market study, conducted by an independent marketing research firm, reported that there was still a very strong market for the current JAC 36. In fact, many of the companies that had purchased auto correlators from competitors—machines that included the voice-activated command features—reported that they rarely used these features. In other words, many of the newer machines on the market were "overdesigned" for their customers' actual use. Market research on the portable versus nonportable units was inconclusive: Some purchasers clearly wanted it, but the overall demand for portability was not strong.

Cost estimates for an updated JAC 36 were developed by Beth Shonberg (senior electrical engineer), Peter O'Malley (vice president of manufacturing), and Ted Slocum (an electronics designer in the R&D department). They calculated that there would be a very high cost in changeover to the more advanced microprocessors as well as the associated costs in adapting the software used on the present JACs. Adding the voice-activated control mechanism to the present manual controls was the most simple and least costly change. Manufacturing the units with optical couplers would involve considerable redesign of the cabinet and manufacturing methods and would cost considerably more than the voice-activated control feature but considerably less than if the new machine was adapted to the new microprocessors. Moreover, there were a few nagging technical problems in the electronic design of a portable unit; the longer it took to work these problems out, the higher the R&D costs would go and the longer it would take to put the portable JAC 36 on the market.

Bass reviewed all of this information. He decided that in spite of these reports, Jordan needed to come out with a new JAC 36 model, if only to satisfy the need to be competitive with other machines. Since the old standard JAC 36 units were holding their market share and since the development of the portable model was plagued with problems, Bass decided to proceed with a redesign of the old JAC 36 unit that would include both the voice-activated command and optical coupling features. At the meeting announcing the decision, Bass stated that he wanted the new model to maintain Jordan's reputation for providing flexible, high-quality equipment. Joe Little commented that the new JAC 36 should be offered at about the same price as the present model. Since the revised model was not designed to be portable, weight was not a problem for the new machine. Shonberg and Slocum, after reviewing the design specifications, said they could probably have the development work done in three to four months.

Shonberg and Slocum finished the development work in early January. Production was sent the information it needed to set production methods and to estimate costs. After talking it over with his factory superintendent, Peter O'Malley described the production methods and costs in detail in a memorandum to Norman Bass. O'Malley's

estimates were considerably higher than anticipated. The current JAC 36 sold for
$16,000, but O'Malley estimated that it would be impossible to sell the new model for
less than $20,000. Bass and Little were very upset by this memorandum. They asked
O'Malley to review all of the figures and distribute them to all members of the New
Products Committee, who would then make the decision whether to start manufacturing the revised JAC 36.

It is now early March, and the meeting of the New Products Committee is about
to occur. O'Malley's revised figures were not substantially different from his original
estimates. The basic costs are presented in Exhibit 1.

The committee has a real problem on its hands. In addition, Bass, who normally
chairs the meeting, will not be present because he is scheduled to undergo minor
surgery; he asked Maria D'Moro, vice president for finance, to chair the meeting in his
place. The purpose of this meeting is to determine if the JAC 36 should be put into
production and, if so, at what price it should be marketed. In attendance will be:

Maria D'Moro, vice president, finance (chairman)

Ken Lawson, director of R&D

Joe Little, vice president, sales

Pete O'Malley, vice president, manufacturing

Beth Shonberg, senior electrical engineer

EXHIBIT 1   Jordan Electronics Company Cost Structures

	Present Cost Structure JAC 36	*Estimated Cost Structure Revised JAC 36*
Factory price	$16,000	$20,000
Costs:		
Direct labor	1,650	2,300
Raw materials	6,700	8,500
Factory overhead	3,700	5,200
Margin	3,950	4,000
	Variance Report Last Year JAC 36	
Labor:		
Metal shop	−2%	
Electronics components	+8%	
Other components	—	
Assembly	+5%	
Test	+10%	
Materials:		
Metal	−3%	
Electronics	+10%	
Overhead	−11%	

PROCEDURE

Step 1: 5 Minutes

If this has not already been done, you will be assigned a role on the New Products Committee.

Step 2: 45 Minutes

The New Products Committee will meet and work towards settling the major issues.

Step 3: 15 Minutes

If you have not reached an agreement, stop the discussion at this point. Each member of the group should state the goals he or she was trying to achieve, the least-preferred solution that he or she would still accept for a settlement, and any other issues that must be included in a minimally acceptable deal. Then each member should state what factors in the group's decision blocked achieving a settlement within the time limits.

If a settlement was reached, each member of the group should report what his or her minimally acceptable terms were and what factors helped the group reach a solution.

Step 4: 30 Minutes

The instructor will gather information from each New Products Committee on their outcome and the information assembled by each group in step 3. The exercise will then be reviewed and evaluated.

DISCUSSION QUESTIONS

1. What were the most frequently cited obstacles to reaching an agreement?
2. What was or could be done to overcome these obstacles?
3. Were there any common features to the groups that did successfully achieve an agreement? That did not achieve an agreement?
4. Should this type of issue be handled by a committee in organizations? What are the pros and cons of this approach?

EXERCISE 13

Third-Party Conflict Resolution

INTRODUCTION

In addition to being involved in their own conflicts, managers are often called upon to intervene and to settle conflicts between other people. The two activities in this section are designed to explore how third parties may enter conflicts for the purpose of resolving them, and to practice one very effective approach to intervention. In the first activity, you will read about a manager who has a problem deciding how to intervene in a dispute, and you will discuss this case in class. Part 2 of this exercise contains a Mediation Guide, which will be useful in completing the role-playing activity in Part 3, in which some of you will attempt to resolve a managerial dispute.

ADVANCE PREPARATION

The instructor will specify whether the case (Seatcor Manufacturing Co.) or the Mediation Guide should be read in advance. Role playing materials (The Summer Interns) may also be provided in advance.

PART 1

PROCEDURE

Step 1: 5 Minutes

Read The Seatcor Manufacturing Company case.

THE SEATCOR MANUFACTURING COMPANY

You are senior vice president of operations and chief operating officer of Seatcor, a major producer of office furniture. Joe Gibbons, your subordinate, is vice president and general manager of your largest desk assembly plant. Joe has been with Seatcor for 38 years and is two years away from retirement. He worked his way up through the

Developed by Roy J. Lewicki. The Mediation Guide developed by Larry Ray, American Bar Association, and Robert Helm, Oklahoma State University. "The Seatcor Manufacturing Company" and "The Summer Interns" developed by Blair Sheppard, Fuqua School of Business, Duke University. Used with permission.

ranks to his present position and has successfully operated his division for five years with a marginally competent staff. You are a long-standing personal friend of Joe's and respect him a great deal. However, you have always had an uneasy feeling that Joe has surrounded himself with minimally competent people by his own choice. In some ways, you think he is threatened by talented assistants.

Last week you were having lunch with Charles Stewart, assistant vice president and Joe's second in command. Upon your questioning, it became clear that he and Joe were engaged in a debilitating feud. Charles was hired last year, largely at your insistence. You had been concerned for some time about who was going to replace Joe when he retired, especially given the lack of really capable managerial talent on Joe's staff. Thus, you prodded Joe to hire your preferred candidate—Charles Stewart. Charles is relatively young, 39, extremely tenacious and bright, and a well-trained business school graduate. From all reports he is doing a good job in his new position.

Your concern centers around a topic that arose at the end of your lunch. Charles indicated Joe Gibbons is in the process of completing a five-year plan for his plant. This plan is to serve as the basis for several major plant reinvestment and reorganization decisions that would be proposed to senior management. According to Charles, Joe Gibbons has not included Charles in the planning process at all. You had to leave lunch quickly and were unable to get much more information from Charles. However, he did admit that he was extremely disturbed by this exclusion and that his distress was influencing his work and probably his relationship with Joe.

You consider this a very serious problem. Charles will probably have to live with the results of any major decisions about the plant. More important, Joe's support is essential if Charles is to properly grow into his present and/or future job. Joe, on the other hand, runs a good ship and you do not want to upset him or undermine his authority. Moreover, you know Joe has good judgment; thus, he may have a good reason for what he is doing.

How would you proceed to handle this issue?

Step 2: 5 Minutes

Before discussing this case with anyone else, answer the following two questions:

1. Assume you were the senior vice president of operations. Exactly what would you do in this situation regarding the conflict between Joe and Charles?
2. Why would you take this action—that is, what are your primary objectives by intervening in this way?

Step 3: 20–30 Minutes

The instructor will discuss this case with the entire class.

Step 4: 10–15 Minutes

The instructor will summarize the case discussion and present a framework for understanding how participants analyzed the case and decided to intervene.

DISCUSSION QUESTIONS

1. How much agreement was there within the class about the way that the senior vice president should approach the problem? How did this compare with your own preferred strategy?
2. Which style of conflict intervention do you use most frequently? Which one do you use least frequently? Are there other styles that are commonly used which are not listed here?
3. Which one of the four criteria (efficiency, effectiveness, participant satisfaction, and fairness) are typically most important to you when you intervene in someone else's dispute? Which one is most important when someone intervenes to settle a dispute you are having? If these are different, what are the implications of these differences for training managers in dispute resolution?
4. Do you use different styles in different situations? If so, what kind of situational factors affect which styles you use?

GENERALIZATIONS AND CONCLUSION

Compare your answers to the questions in step 2 with the ways that others approached the problem. To practice your own comprehension of third-party dynamics, answer the following questions:

1. What are four different criteria that managers can have when they intervene in disputes?
2. What are the various styles that managers use to intervene in disputes?
3. Which of these styles is most effective given each of the four criteria?

PART 2: THE MEDIATION GUIDE

Step 1: Stabilize the Setting

Parties often bring some strong feelings of anger and frustration into mediation. These feelings can prevent them from talking productively about their dispute. You, as mediator, will try to gain their trust for you and for the mediation process. Stabilize the setting by being polite; show that you are in control and that you are neutral. This step helps the parties feel comfortable, so they can speak freely about their complaints, and safe, so they can air their feelings.

1. _____ Greet the parties.
2. _____ Indicate where each of them is to sit.
3. _____ Identify yourself and each party, by name.
4. _____ Offer water, paper and pencil, and patience.
5. _____ State the purpose of mediation.
6. _____ Confirm your neutrality.

7. _____ Get their commitment to proceed.

8. _____ Get their commitment that only one party at a time will speak.

9. _____ Get their commitment to speak directly to you.

10. _____ Use calming techniques as needed.

Step 2: Help the Parties Communicate

Once the setting is stable and the parties seem to trust you and the mediation process, you can begin to carefully build trust between them. Both must make statements about what has happened. Each will use these statements to air negative feelings. They may express anger, make accusations, and show frustration in other ways. But, with your help, this mutual ventilation lets them hear each other's side of the story, perhaps for the first time. It can help calm their emotions, and can build a basis for trust between them.

1. _____ Explain the rationale for who speaks first.

2. _____ Reassure them that both will speak without interruption, for as long as is needed.

3. _____ Ask the first speaker to tell what has happened.

    a. _____ Take notes.

    b. _____ Respond actively; restate and echo what is said.

    c. _____ Calm the parties as needed.

    d. _____ Clarify, with open or closed questions, or with restatements.

    e. _____ Focus the narration on the issues in the dispute.

    f. _____ Summarize, eliminating all disparaging references.

    g. _____ Check to see that you understand the story.

    h. _____ Thank this party for speaking, the other for listening quietly.

4. _____ Ask the second speaker to tell what has happened.

    a. _____ Take notes.

    b. _____ Respond actively, restate and echo what is said.

    c. _____ Calm the parties as needed.

    d. _____ Clarify, with open or closed questions, or with restatements.

    e. _____ Focus the narration on the issues in the dispute.

    f. _____ Summarize, eliminating all disparaging references.

    g. _____ Check to see that you understand the story.

    h. _____ Thank this party for speaking, the other for listening quietly.

5. _____ Ask each party, in turn, to help clarify the major issues to be resolved.

6. _____ Inquire into basic issues, probing to see if something instead may be at the root of the complaints.

7. _____ Define the problem by restating and summarizing.

8. _____ Conduct private meetings, if needed (explain what will happen during and after the private meetings).

9. _____ Summarize areas of agreement and disagreement.

10. _____ Help the parties set priorities on the issues and demands.

Step 3: Help the Parties Negotiate

Cooperativeness is needed for negotiations that lead to agreement. Cooperation requires a stable setting, to control disruptions, and exchanges of information, to develop mutual trust. With these conditions, the parties may be willing to cooperate, but still feel driven to compete. You can press for cooperative initiatives by patiently helping them to explore alternative solutions, and by directing attention to their progress.

1. _____ Ask each party to list alternative possibilities for a settlement.

2. _____ Restate and summarize each alternative.

3. _____ Check with each party on the workability of each alternative.

4. _____ Restate whether the alternative is workable.

5. _____ In an impasse, suggest the general form of other alternatives.

6. _____ Note the amount of progress already made, to show that success is likely.

7. _____ If the impasse continues, suggest a break or a second mediation session.

8. _____ Encourage them to select the alternative that appears to be workable.

9. _____ Increase their understanding by rephrasing the alternative.

10. _____ Help them plan a course of action to implement the alternative.

Step 4: Clarify Their Agreement

Mediation should change each party's attitude toward the other. When both have shown their commitment, through a joint declaration of agreement, each will support the agreement more strongly. For a settlement that lasts, each component of the attitudes toward each other—their thinking, feeling, and acting—will have changed. Not only will they now *act* differently toward each other, they are likely to *feel* differently, more positively, about each other, and *think* of their relationship in new ways.

1. _____ Summarize the agreement terms.

2. _____ Recheck with each party his or her understanding of the agreement.

3. _____ Ask whether other issues need to be discussed.

4. _____ Help them specify the terms of their agreement.

5. _____ State each person's role in the agreement.

6. _____ Recheck with each party *when* he or she is to do certain things, *where*, and *how*.

7. _____ Explain the process of follow-up.

8. _____ Establish a time for follow-up with each party.

9. _____ Emphasize that the agreement is theirs, not yours.

10. _____ Congratulate the parties on their reasonableness and on the workability of their resolution.

EXHIBIT 1

Steps in a Mediation Process

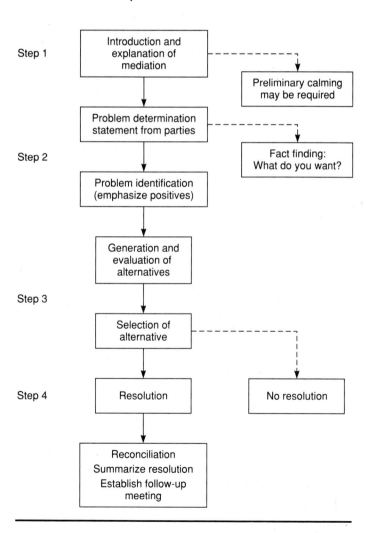

PART 3

PROCEDURE

Step 1: 15 Minutes

Read "The Mediation Guide" in Part 2, if it has not been previously assigned as advanced preparation.

Step 2: 5 Minutes

The instructor will divide the class into subgroups of three or four (the latter if an observer is to be used). One person should play the role of Samantha (Sam) Pinder, who will mediate the dispute. The other two parties will play the roles of Brenda Bennett (director of personnel) and Harold Stokes (vice president, engineering), who are having a dispute over the hiring of summer interns. The instructor will provide this information.

Step 3: 10 Minutes

Each party should read his or her role information and prepare to play the role. Remember to:

1. Empathize with the role. Try to see the world as your assigned character sees it, and behave accordingly.
2. Do not add facts that are not in the case.
3. Stay in your role. Do not jump out of the role to comment on the process.
4. Try to make it realistic.

The person playing the third party will try to defuse the conflict and seek a resolution. Do not make it unnecessarily difficult for this person; "play along" to observe how third-party dispute resolution can work. On the other hand, you are not required to settle if you believe that your character's needs are truly not being met by the proposed agreement.

Step 4: 20–30 Minutes

Sam Pinder will "lead" each small group in an effort to resolve the summer interns problem. When you have achieved a resolution, write it down so you can report it to the class later.

Step 5: 10–20 Minutes (optional)

Discuss how the mediation session went in each of the small groups. Use the Mediation Guide. If you had an observer assigned, the observer can comment on the strengths and weaknesses of the mediator's efforts.

Step 6: 20–30 Minutes

Be prepared to report to the class on the outcome of the mediation session, and particular problems that may have occurred with the mediation session in your small group.

DISCUSSION QUESTIONS

1. What were some of the different settlements arrived at by different groups?
2. How did your group's specific settlement emerge? How much influence did Pinder have in shaping the final settlement? How much influence did Stokes and Bennett have?
3. Was the mediation process fair? Was the achieved outcome fair? What made them fair or unfair?
4. What tactics did the mediator use that were most effective? Least effective?
5. When would it be most useful to use mediation in an organization? When would it be least useful to use mediation?
6. What are some of the major problems and obstacles to using mediation as a manager?

Connecticut Valley School

INTRODUCTION

In this situation you must allocate a limited capital budget among six or seven competing projects. Three parties are involved in the negotiation: the headmaster, the faculty budget committee, and the board of trustees. While the issues in this exercise appear straightforward, the parties do not necessarily perceive the budget process in the same manner.

ADVANCE PREPARATION

Read the Background Information section for the Connecticut Valley School in this exercise; then read the role information that the instructor has provided for you. Prepare to play this role. Familiarize yourself with the facts, and prepare to meet with your team and the other side.

Step 1: 30–45 Minutes

Participants who have been assigned to the same team (faculty budget committee, board of trustees, headmaster) will meet separately to decide how to manage the upcoming meeting. Each group should prepare a ranking and rating of the capital projects to be discussed.

Step 2: 45–60 Minutes

The different parties will meet together to negotiate an agreement about the capital projects that will be funded. The chairperson of the board of trustees will chair this meeting. Participants will leave this meeting with an agreement about the priority of the capital spending projects. If no agreement is reached, then each team should have a record of their final rankings and where they are willing to make further concessions.

Written by Peter Nye, Northeastern University. Used with permission.

BACKGROUND INFORMATION

The Connecticut Valley School (CVS) is a private boarding school in Massachusetts. Headmaster John Loring has just submitted his annual recommendations for capital spending to the board of trustees. Capital spending will be funded from two sources, new debt and the accumulated interest on the school's endowment. Since the school is approaching its debt capacity and the trustees are committed not to draw on the principal of the endowment, the school can afford to spend only $450,000 to $500,000 on capital improvements over the next year. The six major projects under consideration are described briefly below.

1. *Swimming Pool*
   Cost $320,000   Expected life: 15 years

   Currently the school rents a local facility for $30,000 per year. In addition, the school pays $5,000 per year to bus students to the facility. If the school owned its own pool, it could rent out pool time to local organizations for $15,000 per year. The headmaster feels that more students would use the pool if it were located on campus.

2. *Buses*
   Cost: $135,000 (3 buses)   Expected life: 6 years
   Salvage value: Nil

   CVS owns two campuses several miles apart. A private bus company transports students between campuses at a cost of $90,000 per year. If the school owns and operates its own buses, it will incur $35,000 in operating expenses in the first year and $40,000 each year thereafter.

3. *New Roof for Hockey Rink*
   Cost: $30,000

   A new roof is essential to prevent further damage to the rink and to the arena's infrastructure. The project could be delayed one year; but due to the additional damage that would result, total repair costs would jump to $60,000.

4. *Wood Chip Heating System*
   Cost : $400,000   Expected life: 15 years

   Cold New England winters and the high cost of fuel oil have been draining the school's operating funds. This new heating system would save the school at least $80,000 per year over the next 15 years.

5. *Renovation of Fine Arts Building*
   Cost: $100,000

   The faculty and trustees agree that an improved fine arts program is critical to the school's "liberal arts mission." The renovated fine arts building would include a photography lab, a pottery shop, and art studios, as well as a small gallery. The building would not generate any incremental revenues or cost savings. However, a wealthy benefactor (after whom the building would be named) has offered to contribute $50,000 to subsidize the project. In addition, the facility would provide some "marketing benefits," as a strong arts program attracts quality students.

6. *Renovations to Women's Locker Room*
Cost: $20,000

The women's locker room has not been renovated since it was built 33 years ago for visiting men's teams. Many of the women have complained that the facility is dirty, depressing, and overcrowded. Some women refuse to use the facility. The headmaster insists that these complaints are "unfounded." The renovations would generate no incremental revenues or cost savings.

Since not all of these projects can be undertaken, they must be prioritized. In his report to the trustees, Headmaster Loring ranked the six projects as follows:

1. Swimming pool $320,000
2. Hockey rink roof $ 30,000
3. Buses $135,000
4. Heating system $400,000
5. Fine arts building $ 50,000
6. Women's locker room $ 20,000

He recommended that this year's capital funds be spent on the construction of a swimming pool, repairs to the roof of the hockey rink, and the purchase of three buses. These projects would require a total expenditure of $485,000. Loring's rankings were based on his subjective evaluation of cost/benefit trade-offs.

While the trustees must make the final decision, they have solicited advice from the faculty. The faculty is in touch with the day-to-day operations of the school and with the needs of the students. In addition, many faculty members feel that they were closed out of the decision process last year and that the ultimate allocation of funds was inconsistent with the school's objectives. In an attempt to improve the decision process, the trustees appointed a faculty budget committee to advise them on capital spending priorities. A meeting of the trustees, the budget committee and the headmaster has been scheduled. The purpose of this meeting is to prioritize capital spending projects. It is expected to be a lively and productive session.

Step 3: 30 Minutes

All groups will bring their final agreements (or within-team rankings) back to class. The instructor will share the final agreements with the rest of the class. The exercise will then be discussed and evaluated.

DISCUSSION QUESTIONS

1. Did the teams agree on appropriate decision criteria before debating the merits of the specific projects? Which party's decision criteria best promoted an integrative decision? A distributive decision?

2. What strategies and tactics were used to reach a solution? How were they similar and different from the strategies and tactics used during the within-team discussions?

3. Which group had the greatest power? How did the distribution of power across the groups influence the process of negotiations? The outcome?

4. Was this an integrative or distributive situation? Why? Was the outcome integrative or distributive? Why?

Towers Market

INTRODUCTION

In this situation you must make a number of decisions about the management of an upscale marketplace. You will play the role of one of the merchants in Towers Market. Each merchant has his or her own store, but also shares common interests and areas with the other merchants. Merchants may have similar or different preferences for how to resolve these common issues.

ADVANCE PREPARATION

Read the Background Information section for Towers Market in this exercise; then read the role information that the instructor has provided. Prepare to play this role. Familiarize yourself with the facts, and prepare to meet with the other merchants in the market.

Step 1: 15–20 Minutes

Participants will read the common background information and the private role information assigned by the instructor.

Step 2: 60 Minutes

The different parties will meet together to negotiate an agreement about the common management issues at Towers Market. Participants will leave this meeting with an agreement about the five management issues to be discussed. If no agreement is reached, then each person should have a record of his or her final rankings and where he or she is willing to make further concessions.

This exercise was developed by Rebecca Beggs, Jeanne Brett, and Laurie Weingart, Kellogg Graduate School of Management, Northwestern University. Used with permission.

BACKGROUND INFORMATION

Parducci's Grocery, a successful East Side establishment, has proposed developing a Market consisting of a number of shops all catering to a similar upscale clientele. Parducci's idea is to have each shop owned and managed by specialists, other retailers who have successfully created a niche for themselves by providing quality products to a similar consumer group.

The Market will have an open plan with a common decor. The food and other products would be arranged in "departments," where customers will be able to purchase imported beer and wines, deli sandwiches, and fresh pastries by crossing aisles instead of crossing streets. There will also be a common area with tables where customers may sit down and sample some of the items sold in the stores. Also, because several stores will share the same location, shopping will be more convenient for customers and they will be likely to make purchases from more than one of the merchants. Member stores will gain from the arrangement not only by gaining access to a larger group of customers, but also by sharing maintenance and upkeep costs of the building.

The Market plans to lease two floors of a primarily residential building, one level for the Market and the other for storage, offices, preparation areas, and so on. The Market would be located on the upper West Side, an area which is currently being settled by young urban professionals—the potential customer pool.

A suitable building has been located, the 88th Street Towers. The owner is quite excited about leasing the retail space of his building to one group, since this will reduce his searching for new tenants and he will be able to negotiate only one contract. He also feels that the quality of the Market's products will attract a desirable group of customers, who might be interested in renting an apartment in his building as well. Since he has much to gain from this union, he is willing to reduce the standard rent he receives for individual units in his building as well as to aid in remodeling the first floor.

The merchants interested in joining the Market are Parducci's Grocery, Jardin Florist, Jacqui's Bakery, and Donovan's Liquors. Parducci's is a successful gourmet grocery currently located on the East Side. They carry a wide range of high-quality grocery items ranging from Russian caviar to English tea biscuits to organically grown products.

Jardin Florist has built a reputation for their artistic styling of bouquets reminiscent of French and English country gardens. Their past business catered mostly to special orders, and they are interested in using the Market to demonstrate their unique style and to expand their production to include made-to-order, while-you-wait arrangements that will still incorporate their elegant styling.

Jacqui's Bakery is a traditional French bakery currently located on the East Side. They offer a wide selection of French breads, croissants, brioches, and pizzas, as well as delectable pastries and desserts. In previous discussions with the other partners, they agreed to sell coffee, espresso, and tea.

Donovan's Liquors is proud of its claim that they stock over 300 international beers as well as many prized wines. Customers are drawn by their fine selection of

Scotches and other liquors as well. In spite of declining per capita alcohol consumption, Donovan's sales continue to rise.

The potential partners, while seriously interested in the idea of the Market, nevertheless are concerned about several issues that are not yet resolved. They have agreed to meet to try to resolve these issues so that they can make preparations to open the market. The issues they are to resolve include:

Temperature. Since the merchants will be sharing common space, they must decide as a group what temperature to maintain. Some of the merchants feel that the temperature of their department as well as the common area might affect the demand for their products.

a. 77 degrees

b. 74 degrees

c. 71 degrees

d. 68 degrees

e. 65 degrees

Advertising. Some of the interested merchants feel that the Market should be promoted as a unit, while others would prefer to do their own advertising in the manner that they have found to be most successful. Some suggested options are:

a. Combined campaign, advertising for market as a whole, costs to be divided equally among the Market merchants.

b. Combined campaign, advertising for market as a whole, to be paid according to percentage of the market's gross profits contributed by the merchant.

c. Combined campaign, advertising the stores as individual units but on the same flyers, with each member given (and paying for) one fourth of ad.

d. Separate campaign for each member, 6 percent of expected gross profits to be spent on advertising.

e. Separate campaign for each member, amount spent up to individual merchant.

Clerks. The major issue here seems to be whether the Market should continue to offer the extremely personalized service that the participating merchants offered in their original stores, or whether they should economize and share costs of hiring and training. The options are:

a. Hire by group, train by group, distribute equally, paid for by group.

b. Hire by group, train by group, distribute according to floor space, paid for by group.

c. Hire by group, train individually, distribute according to demand for service, paid for by group.

d. Hire individually, train individually, distribute according to demand for service, each merchant to pay from individual profits.

e. Hire individually, train individually, each merchant to decide how many clerks, each merchant to pay from individual profits.

Maintenance.   One of the benefits of this venture is the reduction in maintenance costs for each merchant's retail space. However, there is a disagreement on how those costs should be distributed and whose responsibility maintenance of the common areas should be. Options are:

a. Shared, each responsible for one fourth of total costs.

b. Shared, each responsible for percentage according to floor space occupied.

c. Shared, each responsible for percentage according to floor space occupied, but with the bakery paying double its percentage because of the nature of its carryout business.

d. Separate, each responsible for own floor space, plus common area maintenance cost as a function of floor space occupied.

e. Separate, each responsible for own floor space plus equal contributions for common area maintenance.

Position of Departments.   The first floor of the building must somehow be divided up among the participating merchants. The owner of the building is willing to remodel the available space, but the merchants must first decide what the layout of the Market will be. Options to be discussed include:

a. "Spontaneous purchases" near entrance way.

b. Smaller departments near entrance way.

c. Common area near entrance way.

d. Convenient location for department with highest volume of sales.

e. Merchants stocking heavier products should be located near entrance-exits.

Step 3: 30 Minutes

All groups will bring their final agreements (or individual rankings) back to class. The instructor will share the final agreements with the rest of the class. The exercise will then be discussed and evaluated.

DISCUSSION QUESTIONS

1. How did you discover the other parties' interests?

2. Why did some groups not reach an agreement? Why did groups not reaching optimal solutions settle for an inefficient agreement when all negotiators could have done as well as or better than they did?

3. Where any discussions dominated by coalitions? Did any negotiators try to form coalitions? Did it work? Was your coalition helpful in meeting your needs?

4. Did cooperative groups or competitive groups attain better outcomes in this exercise?

Alpha–Beta

INTRODUCTION

In this situation you will negotiate a possible robot manufacturing and marketing agreement with another company. You will be a member of a team that represents either an electrical company in the nation of Alpha, or a manufacturer of electrical machinery in the nation of Beta.

ADVANCE PREPARATION

Read the Background Information section for Alpha–Beta in this exercise; then read the role information that the instructor has provided. Prepare to play this role. Familiarize yourself with the facts, and prepare to meet with the other members of your team to develop a strategy to negotiate with the other organization.

Step 1: 10–15 Minutes

Participants will read the common background information and the private role information assigned by the instructor.

Step 2: 25 Minutes

Participants will meet with other members of their team and develop a strategy for negotiating with the other organization.

Step 3: 20 Minutes

Representatives of the two organizations will meet and negotiate the remaining issues in the Alpha–Beta contract. Participants will leave this meeting with an agreement about all of the issues to be discussed. If no agreement is reached, then each team should have a record of their final offers and where they are willing to make further concessions.

This exercise was first developed by Thomas N. Gladwin in 1984, and is copyrighted 1990–1991 by Thomas N. Gladwin, Stephen E. Weiss, and Allen J. Zerkin. Used with permission.

BACKGROUND INFORMATION

Alpha

Alpha Inc. is a large, broadly diversified electrical company based in the nation of Alpha. The company is one of the leading makers of numerical control equipment and plans to become a leader in equipping the "factory of the future." It has recently spent hundreds of millions of dollars putting together a collection of factory automation capabilities ranging from robotics to computer-aided design and manufacturing. Alpha Inc. has been acquiring companies, investing heavily in new plants, and spending considerable sums on product development. Innovative robots, some equipped with vision, are being developed, but they have been a bit slow in making their way out of the company's R&D labs. To meet its objective of quickly becoming a major world-wide, full-service supplier of automation systems, Alpha Inc. has found it necessary to tie up, in various ways, with foreign firms that are further down the robotics learning curve.

Robotics in the Nation of Alpha.   There are 30 robot manufacturers in Alpha, and big computer and auto firms have recently been entering the business. During 1980, use and production of robots in Alpha was only about 33 percent of what it was in the nation of Beta. One survey reported 4,370 robots in use in Alpha in 1980, mainly in the auto and foundry-type industries, and 1,269 produced. Robot sales in 1980 were estimated at $92 million, with a significant share accounted for by imports. The industrial automation market as a whole is growing at well over 20 percent a year, and the robotics portion of it is expected to become a $2 billion a year domestic market by 1990.

Beta

Beta Inc. is the leading manufacturer of integrated electrical machinery in the nation of Beta. Run by scientists since its founding, the company is Beta's most research-oriented corporation: it employs over 9,000 researchers, and its R&D spending equals 5.9 percent of corporate sales. Beta Inc. started producing robots only in 1979 but plans within a few years to become the world's largest robot producer. To do so, it must double its manufacturing capacity and strongly push exports (to date, nearly all of its output has been sold at home). The company's deep commitment to robotics is reflected in the recent formation of a 500-man technical task force to develop a universal assembly robot with both visual and tactile sensors. Beta Inc. expects to be using the new robots for some 60 percent of its in-house assembly operations within three years.

Robotics in the Nation of Beta.   Beta Inc. is only 1 of 150 companies making or selling robots in Beta, a nation with "robot fever" and a government that has declared automation a national goal. An estimated 12,000 to 14,000 programmable robots are already on the job in the nation, representing 59 percent of those in use worldwide. In 1980, Betan firms churned out nearly $400 million worth of robots (approximately 3,200 units or 50 percent of world production). The nation exported only 2.5 percent of its production and imported less than 5 percent of its robots. Industry analysts see robot production in Beta rising to $2 billion in 1985 and to $5 billion in 1990.

Over the past five months, Alpha Inc. and Beta Inc. have held preliminary negotiations over a possible robot manufacturing and marketing tie-up. The two companies have reached the following tentative agreement:

1. The tie-up over 7 years will proceed in two phases: (*a*) in years 1–4, Beta will supply Alpha with fully assembled Beta Inc. robots for sale under Alpha's brand name; (*b*) in years 5–7, Alpha will begin producing these robots themselves in Alpha, using Beta technology and key components.
2. The tie-up will focus on the robots that Beta Inc. currently has on the market.
3. The agreement will be nonexclusive; that is, Beta Inc. will be allowed to enter the Alphan market directly at any time and allowed to tie up with other Alphan firms.

The two companies' negotiation teams are now scheduled to meet for discussion of remaining issues. They include the following:

1. The number of different models involved.
2. The quantity of Beta Inc. units to be imported and/or produced under license by Alpha during each year.
3. The unit price to be paid to Beta.
4. Access to Alpha's vision technology.
5. The royalty rate to be paid to Beta.

Step 4: 30 Minutes

All groups will bring their final agreements (or final offers) back to class. The instructor will share the final agreements with the rest of the class. The exercise will then be discussed and evaluated.

DISCUSSION QUESTIONS

1. How did these negotiations feel? What did they feel like during the negotiations? How do they feel now?
2. What was it like negotiating with the other organization? How was their negotiating style similar to your own? Different?
3. How much did you adapt your negotiating style to match the other side's style? How much did you want to do this?

EXERCISE 17

The New House Negotiation

INTRODUCTION

Many negotiations involve only two parties—a "buyer" and a "seller." However, there are many other negotiations in which the parties are represented by "agents." An agent is a person who is paid to negotiate on behalf of the buyer or seller and usually collects some fee or commission based on these services.

The purpose of this negotiation is to gain experience by negotiating through agents. The negotiation simulates the sale and purchase of a piece of real estate, a transaction which is normally conducted through agents. Some of you will play the role of agents; others will play the role of buyers and sellers. This experience should provide a simple but rich context in which to observe the ways that negotiation can very quickly become highly complex.

ADVANCE PREPARATION

None, unless your instructor assigns you to read and prepare your role in advance.

PROCEDURE

Step 1: 20 minutes

Parties will be assigned one of four roles: seller of house, buyer of house, seller's agent, and buyer's agent. Observers may also be assigned to watch each "foursome" as they negotiate.

Each group of negotiators—parties, their agents, and an observer—will have a separate negotiation "territory" and operate on their own. Several groups may be operating in the classroom simultaneously.

If prior preparation has not occurred, each party should take 20 minutes to read and prepare roles. Your instructor will provide this information. Also study the following information which is available to all sides:

This simulation was developed by Conrad Jackson, College of Administrative Science, The University of Alabama at Huntsville. Used with permission.

The House.   The house is a 3 bedroom, 2½ bath one-story. It was listed in *Multilist* two weeks ago at $87,000. The house has the following features:

- 2,100 sq. ft.
- 6 years old (one owner prior to current owner).
- 2-car garage.
- Contemporary styling (back wall of house is basically all glass, with sliding draperies).
- ⅓ acre lot (no flooding problems).
- Brick exterior.
- Built-in range, dishwasher, garbage disposal, and microwave.
- Electric cooling and gas heat.
- Fireplace and ceiling fan in the family room.
- No fence.
- Assumable FHA loan.

EXHIBIT 1

N

| Bedroom 1 | Bedroom 2 | Living | Garage |
| Master Suite | Family Room | Dining | Kitchen |

Step 2: 10 minutes

Seller talks to seller's agent. Buyer talks to buyer's agent.

Step 3: 10 minutes

Seller's agent and buyer's agent negotiate. Sellers and buyers may observe but not talk to agent.

Step 4: 5 minutes

Seller confers with seller's agent; buyer confers with buyer's agent.

Step 5: 5 minutes

Agents negotiate. Parties may observe.

Steps 6 and 7: 15 minutes

Parties may confer with agents, and agents negotiate, until either a deal is struck or the agents agree that no deal is possible.

If a deal is reached, record exactly what was agreed to in the negotiation. Be prepared to report this to the instructor during class discussion.

DISCUSSION QUESTIONS

1. What goals (target price, opening bid, bottom line, etc.) did the seller(s) and buyer(s) set for themselves in the negotiation? Did they reveal these goals to their agent?
2. How did the meeting with the agents reshape or redefine any of these goals?
3. What did the agents tell each other about their clients' goals?
4. What new strategy and tactics were introduced into the negotiation as a result of using agents?
5. Did the instructor give either side additional information during the role-play? What effect did this additional information have?
6. Did the agents reach agreement? How easy was it to achieve this agreement?
7. If the agents reached agreement, did their client support the agreement? Why or why not?
8. What are the advantages and disadvantages of negotiating through an agent, rather than dealing with the opponent directly? Overall, does having an agent make the negotiation easier or more difficult? Why?

EXERCISE 18

Detection Technologies, Inc.

INTRODUCTION

This role-play brings two additional new features to your negotiating experience. First, the context of this negotiation is *inside* an organization. In this scenario, you will be asked to represent one of two groups: a management team or a group of scientists who are protesting against a major management decision. Second, this simulation is considerably less "structured" than others, in that there is a great deal more flexibility and opportunity for creative solutions. We hope you find this simulation an interesting negotiating opportunity.

ADVANCE PREPARATION

Follow the instructor's requirements. You may be required to read the common background information published in this book. You may also be required to read your own group's role information, which will be given to you by your instructor.

PROCEDURE

Step 1: 10 minutes

This is a group negotiation. Your instructor will divide you into teams of two or three per side. Each team will be assigned to one of two roles: the management team of DTI, or the scientist group.

If you have not already done so, you should read the common background information that begins on the next page. You should then read the confidential information for either management or scientists, as assigned by your instructor.

This case and role-play was prepared by Roy J. Lewicki and Robert E. Reinheimer. The case and role-play have been prepared as a basis for class discussion, rather than to illustrate either effective or ineffective handling of an administrative situation.

DETECTION TECHNOLOGIES, INC.— GENERAL INFORMATION

Detection Technologies, Inc. (DTI) is a San Francisco-area firm that employs about 900 people. It is a high-technology division of Mentor, whose corporate offices are in New York City. DTI's primary product is an elaborate bio-electronic detection system developed and manufactured under contract with the U.S. government. This system is used for detecting various types of life forms through radar-like procedures. Because of the highly classified nature of the manufacturing process and the need for manufacturing to occur in a relatively pollution-free environment, DTI has chosen to separate its manufacturing facilities from its main offices.

The manufacturing facilities are located in a remote area near San Ramone, California, approximately 40 miles from downtown San Francisco. DTI has purchased several hundred acres of land that provide the adequate security and air quality for manufacturing and full-scale test operations. While it is a picturesque area far away from the congestion of the Bay area, it is not without its faults. Access to the plant requires travel over 10 miles of poor county-owned road; manufacturing employees constantly complain of worn brakes, tire wear, and strain on their cars. The road is often rain-slicked, muddy, and treacherous in the winter. Most of the 630 workers (450 hourly, 150 staff, and 30 R&D personnel) employed in this plant commute from a 30–40 mile radius over this road into the plant; traffic congestion, particularly around the times of shift changes, makes travel and access a highly undesirable aspect of working for this plant. Employees have nicknamed the facility "San Remote".

The manufacturing facility itself is not air conditioned and, hence, frequently hot in the summer and stuffy in the winter. The closest town, San Ramone, is 10 miles away. The San Ramone plant has a cafeteria, but the food is cooked elsewhere and reheated at the plant. The menu is limited and expensive.

There are two groups of support personnel at San Ramone. One group (approximately 110 employees) is directly connected with the manufacturing operations as supervisors, shipping and receiving, plant operation and maintenance, stock and inventory, clerical, and so on. The remainder (40 employees) are professional engineers who are responsible for providing technical support and quality maintenance for manufacturing. Facilities for this support staff are somewhat better than for hourly employees; office space and lighting are adequate and the building is air conditioned. There is no separate cafeteria, and no place to "entertain" visitors; staff alternate between bringing their lunches, occasionally purchasing the cafeteria food and taking it back to their offices to eat, or car-pooling for the 20-minute drive down to San Ramone. Dissatisfaction and low morale among the professional staff is rampant.

The Downtown Location

The executive staff offices, the U.S. Government Liaison Offices, and the research and development laboratory are located in suburban San Francisco, just north of Palo Alto, California. Also there are test facilities on a one-tenth scale for ongoing research and development programs. All administrative services are conducted from here: employment, payroll, security, data processing and system analysis, and research engineering and design. The buildings are spacious, clean, air conditioned, and boast two cafeterias: one for hourly workers and one for research personnel and executive officers. Employees can also go out for lunch, and many good restaurants are nearby. Working hours are more flexible, and the environment more relaxed with less visible pressure. While normal starting time is 8:00 A.M., professional staff drift in as late as 9:30 and often leave early in the afternoon; working at home is frequent. On the other hand, when deadlines or schedules have to be met, it is not unusual to find them working 60 hours a week. The work environment is more informal and displays a casualness similar to a university setting.

As the majority of the San Francisco-based employees are professional people, they consider themselves a "cut above" the manufacturing and technical service employees at San Ramone. While they will acknowledge the value of the revenue generated by San Ramone, they are convinced that it is really the Bay area group that "carries" the company. Without their high-level technical advances, DTI would not have the outside reputation it has for premium-quality products. Inside DTI, however, the rivalries between various engineering and scientific personnel had led to the creation of "domains" or "kingdoms." The primary split is between San Ramone and San Francisco, and over the years it has fostered extensive duplication of efforts. Each group (testing, maintenance, etc.) has been able to procure tools and equipment for itself that normally would be shared if the two locations were closer. The San Francisco Technical divisions have even subcontracted certain testing and development operations to suppliers who are competitors of DTI, due to their basic lack of respect for in-house capabilities at San Ramone and due to the red tape and expense of having to work through their own planning and scheduling staffs. Additionally, the San Francisco R&D group has taken consulting contracts from other firms and has consistently failed to involve any San Ramone personnel in those projects.

The Contract Bidding History

In recent years, DTI has put out numerous competitive bids for civilian and military contracts, but few projects have been forthcoming. Analysis of failures revealed that rejections have been due to excessive cost estimates rather than weak technical capabilities. DTI is considered to be one of the top 10 "quality-based" manufacturing firms of its kind in the country. However, their overhead costs are prohibitive. The cost of operating two sites, duplication of effort, overstaffing, and a blurring of goals for corporate growth and expansion have caused the overhead rate to be three times higher than that of competitors. For example, the Air Force had recently issued a request for bids on the development of a new bio-electronic system, similar to DTI's current product. The "development contract" alone was worth $15 million, and production of these units would be worth $90 million. DTI was positive they would get the contract. When the government evaluated the bids from five different companies, however, DTI came in first in the technical aspect of the bidding and fifth in the cost aspect; they did not get the contract.

The Alternatives

Top management's reaction to this setback was to propose a 20 percent cost reduction plan. Many high-salaried, technical and engineering personnel were destined to be laid off. The house-cleaning was overdue; some "deadwood" and duplication of effort was eliminated. But after six months, it became a hard, cold fact that further reductions in overhead costs would be necessary in order to continue to be competitive.

DTI owned the Bay area facility, and top management believed the most obvious way to achieve this reduction was to close it, move all of the Bay area employees to the San Ramone facility, and to lease out the vacated buildings. The leases would be excellent tax shelters and an additional source of revenue. This consolidation was expected to reduce much of the duplication of effort, as well as provide better coordination on existing and future projects.

In thinking through how the proposed move might be accomplished, they considered features designed to make it as palatable as possible. First, they proposed to spread the relocations over one full year. Each employee could either accept the move or reject it and accept termination from the company. DTI would go as far as possible with those employees who rejected the relocation. They would offer a liberal "time off" policy to those involved so the employee could seek other employment, would provide a special bonus of one month's salary for relocation expenses, would notify other companies in the Bay area of the names and résumés of terminating employees, and set up employment interviews with these companies. They also would notify all placement agencies in the area and pay all placement agency fees.

It was clear to management that even with the generous plan they had outlined, the move would be hugely painful for the organization and would represent some very real costs in terms of overall effectiveness. Yet, they saw no alternative but to proceed with studying the proposed consolidation.

When the details of the proposal leaked, the plan was met with a massive reaction of hostility and despair. Almost all the Bay area professional employees felt that a transfer to San Ramone would mean a sharp decline in status with their peers in similar industries. Most had their homes close to San Francisco, and the drive to San Ramone would increase their commuting time and cause wear and tear on their automobiles. The company thus knew that a certain percentage of employees would terminate because of the relocation. It estimated that a "safe level" of termination was 22 percent; if it reached 35 percent in any occupational group, it could be considered a critical problem. Management informally surveyed employees and found that among the administrative staff, the termination rate was likely to be near 25 percent.

The strongest reaction came from the company's research and development staff. They had grown used to having their laboratory and test facilities in the Bay area and drew heavily on informal relationships with faculty at the area's most prestigious universities for ideas and information. Their view was that being forced to move to San

Ramone, in addition to being undesirable, would cripple their ability to function effectively because of their loss of contact with other professionals. Of the 11 members of the research and development staff, only two expressed a willingness to consider the move to San Ramone. The others claimed they would avail themselves of the many other employment opportunities their specialties commanded. They formally expressed their resistance in a letter to the company president (Exhibit A).

The letter was written by a committee of R&D personnel formed to represent the group's interests regarding the proposed move. In the letter, they outlined their concerns and volunteered to take 20 percent salary cuts to contribute to the reduction of overhead costs. This reduction would total approximately $150,000.

EXHIBIT A

P. Jensen, President
Detection Technologies, Inc.
300 Commonwealth Ave.
Mountain View, CA

Dear P.:

Our committee, representing your research and development personnel, wishes to express its serious concern about the recent events which have affected our company. We believe that DTI's survival depends on our retaining our technical excellence and we are dismayed that you and your management team seem to be contemplating actions which would cripple that capability.

We have all been shocked by our recent loss of contracts. However, it is critical for you to note that we have never been faulted for our technical expertise. It is our cost structure that prevents us from winning these bids. But an action which addresses the cost problem while destroying our ability to compete technically simply trades one problem for a more disastrous one. Closing the San Francisco facility and consolidating operations at San Ramone creates just such a trade, and that is unacceptable.

Although no formal announcement of management's response to the current situation has been provided, it is clear that consolidation is in the wind. We believe that forcing R&D to move to the San Ramone location will ruin the professional network that is our (and the company's) treasured asset. Some alternative must be found and, if it is not, the members of our department will seek individual solutions to their personal dilemmas.

It is time that management emerges from behind closed doors and asks vital members of the company team to become involved in this decision. If management intends to launch this consolidation effort, we believe it will have disastrous results and that it is unlikely that research and development personnel will remain with the company.

Our interest is in the company's survival. If it is necessary, the members of the committee would be willing to agree to a 20 percent salary reduction in return for being able to remain in the Bay area network. We request an opportunity to speak with management about this vital decision which massively effects all of us.

Sincerely,
(signed by all members of the committee)

The committee members consisted of the following six employees:

- J. O'Hara, age 52. Oldest member of the group, but only one year at DTI. Previously worked with several environmental engineering firms in the Bay area. Moved to DTI because of the quality of the other people in the research group and because of interest in the projects that were being considered.
- H. Loew, age 49. Most senior member of the DTI group (24 years), and a likely candidate to be the next vice president of research and development. Loew always lived in Palo Alto, and currently lives a block away from P. Jensen, the president.
- L. Berkowitz, age 42. Fifteen years with DTI, and the most "professionally aggressive" of the group. Most active in research with high professional visibility.
- A. Sharfstein, age 47. Twenty-two years with DTI. Also very professionally active, second to Berkowitz. Sharfstein has spent a number of years developing professional contacts in the Bay area, and has been the most articulate in defending the richness of the professional stimulation to be derived from the area.
- F. Jones, age 36. Five years with DTI. Worked for two years at San Ramone before being assigned to the San Francisco group. A definite "up and comer" in this group.
- T. Black, age 32. Four years with DTI. Strong research orientation, a close collaborator with Berkowitz on several professional papers. Berkowitz also served as a "mentor" to Black while Black was completing a Ph.D. at Stanford.

After reading the statement sent by the committee, the president of DTI, P. Jensen, conferred with the vice president for research and development (and the immediate superior of the scientists), and the vice president for human resources. The three discussed the statement that they had received, and agreed that the situation was serious. It was clear that the San Ramone move created unforseen legitimate problems for the vital R & D personnel and that management had erred in not seeking wider input in considering their cost reduction alternatives.

The management team debated the alternatives. They understood the frustrations of the research and development staff but were faced with having to cut almost $6 million from annual costs in order for DTI to remain competitive. Consolidation still seemed the obvious answer but the problems were mounting with this employee disclosure.

Jensen wrote a letter to the committee acknowledging their concerns and inviting the members of that group to come to a meeting with the president, the vice president of research and development, the vice president of human resources, and other senior company officials. Jensen was careful to make no commitments or promises in the letter; simply, the scientists were invited to come to a meeting (Exhibit B).

Step 2 (optional, may be done in advance): 45–60 minutes

If you have been assigned an individual role within your group, read your individual role information. Each management or scientist team should meet and plan their negotiation strategy.

EXHIBIT B

(addressed to all committee members)
Research and Development
Detection Technologies, Inc.
300 Commonwealth Ave.
Mountain View, CA

Dear (names):

I have given my most serious consideration to the points you raised in your recent letter. We share your interest in doing what is best for DTI and welcome your interest in contributing to that goal.

It is clear that our technical expertise is one of our greatest assets and that your work in research and development is a vital contributor to that expertise. We have no wish to reduce our technical competitiveness. Nevertheless, our failure to produce cost competitive contract bids is a problem which requires a painful solution and we have only eighteen months to produce an effective response.

We acknowledge that we have begun to examine the consolidation of our operations at the San Ramone facility. Such a consolidation would reduce duplication of facilities, equipment, and personnel and these reductions would contribute significantly to an overall cost saving. Page two of this letter is an exhibit of the cost savings we believe would result from such a move.

At the same time, we believe that this action would be unwise if it truly has the crippling effect on your effectiveness that you forecast. Our dilemma, as the management team for DTI, is to address the need for major, fast cost reduction while providing for the continuation of our technical excellence. We also believe that any proposal must be fair to the many employees who are a part of the Detection Technologies family.

In response to your letter, I have ordered that further evaluation of the San Ramone alternative be halted for the time being. I ask that your committee send some of its members to a meeting with myself and members of the management team to discuss the situation as it has evolved. We share an interest in DTI's survival if we can develop a plan that is mutually acceptable in achieving that goal. I look forward to meeting with you.

Sincerely,

(Signed, P. Jensen)

Detection Technologies Expense Statement and Projections

		Current Expenses		Expenses Projected After Consolidation
	San Ramone	San Francisco	Current Combined Total	New Projected Total
1. Overhead	12,130,000	———		12,130,000
Manufacturing	3,267,000	6,633,000		7,425,000
Administration	592,000	5,328,000		5,560,000
R & D	15,989,000	11,961,000	27,950,000	25,115,000
2. R & D Operations				
Utilities	100,000	250,000		300,000
Computer lease	———	1,205,000		1,205,000
Misc. supplies	261,250	550,740		603,000
Consulting fees		929,000		929,000
	361,250	2,934,740	3,295,990	3,037,000
3. Personnel (assumes likely attrition rates)				
Prof. salaries	312,000	468,000		610,000
Prof. benefits	64,272	96,408		125,660
Staff salaries	19,650	111,350		116,050
Staff benefits	4,047	22,938		23,906
Hourly wages	1,338,050	26,890		1,378,300
Hrly. benefits	208,735	4,194		215,014
	1,946,754	729,780	2,676,534	2,468,930
4. Facilities				
Debt svc.	1,000,000	2,000,000		1,000,000
Ops and ins.	500,000	700,000		500,000
	1,500,000	2,700,000	4,200,000	1,500,000
Totals	**19,797,004**	**18,325,520**	**38,122,524**	**32,120,930**

Savings $6,001,594 annually. Lease revenue San Francisco facility $2,000,000 annually.

Step 3: 90–120 minutes

Teams meet to negotiate. Either team may call a caucus as necessary. If a deal is reached, record exactly what was agreed to in the negotiation. Be prepared to report this to the instructor during class discussion.

Step 4: Debriefing 60 minutes (more if you have more than 4–5 groups.)

DISCUSSION QUESTIONS:

1. What goals did management or the scientists set for themselves in the negotiation? What goals were actually achieved?

2. Did group members play individual roles—that is, did particular managers or scientists also try to play an individual character or pursue a individualistic strategy? Did this make the negotiation simpler or more difficult to resolve? Why?

3. What were the interests of each side? How could these interests be met in a joint solution?

4. What creative options were explored? Which ones were finally accepted?

5. How good was your solution to the problem? Is it practical? Easy to implement? Costly? Will it really help the company in reducing its overhead rates?

6. What would be the consequences if one or both sides pursued a distributive strategy in this negotiation?

7. After your negotiation, how would you describe the quality of the relationship between management and the scientists? Will you be able to work together effectively in the future? Why or why not?

Cases

Capital Mortgage Insurance Corporation (A)

Frank Randall hung up the telephone, leaned across his desk, and fixed a cold stare at Jim Dolan.

> OK, Jim. They've agreed to a meeting. We've got three days to resolve this thing. The question is, what approach should we take? How do we get them to accept our offer?

Randall, president of Capital Mortgage Insurance Corporation (CMI), had called Dolan, his senior vice president and treasurer, into his office to help him plan their strategy for completing the acquisition of Corporate Transfer Services (CTS). The two men had begun informal discussions with the principal stockholders of the small employee relocation services company some four months earlier. Now, in late May 1979, they were developing the terms of a formal purchase offer and plotting their strategy for the final negotiations.

The acquisition, if consummated, would be the first in CMI's history. Furthermore, it represented a significant departure from the company's present business. Randall and Dolan knew that the acquisition could have major implications, both for themselves and for the company they had revitalized over the past several years.

Jim Dolan ignored Frank Randall's intense look and gazed out the eighth-floor window overlooking Philadelphia's Independence Square.

> That's not an easy question, Frank. We know they're still looking for a lot more money than we're thinking about. But beyond that, the four partners have their own differences, and we need to think through just what they're expecting. So I guess we'd better talk this one through pretty carefully.

Capital Mortgage Insurance Company (A)-(F) 9-480-057-062.

Copyright © 1980 by the President and Fellows of Harvard College.

This case was prepared by James P. Ware as a basis for class discussion rather than to illustrate either effective or ineffective handling of an administrative situation. Reprinted by permission of the Harvard Business School.

COMPANY AND INDUSTRY BACKGROUND

CMI was a wholly owned subsidiary of Northwest Equipment Corporation, a major freight transporter and lessor of railcars, commercial aircraft, and other industrial equipment. Northwest had acquired CMI in 1978, two years after CMI's original parent company, an investment management corporation, had gone into Chapter 11 bankruptcy proceedings.

CMI had been created to sell mortgage guaranty insurance policies to residential mortgage lenders throughout the United States. Mortgage insurance provided banks, savings and loans, mortgage bankers, and other mortgage lenders with protection against financial losses when homeowners defaulted on their mortgage loans.

Lending institutions normally protected their property loan investments by offering loans of only 70 percent to 80 percent of the appraised value of the property; the remaining 20 percent to 30 percent constituted the homeowner's down payment. However, mortgage loan insurance made it possible for lenders to offer so-called high-ratio loans of up to 95 percent of a home's appraised value. High-ratio loans were permitted only when the lender insured the loan; although the policy protected the lender, the premiums were paid by the borrower, as an addition to monthly principal and interest charges.

The principal attraction of mortgage insurance was that it made purchasing a home possible for many more individuals. It was much easier to produce a 5 percent down payment than to save up the 20 percent to 30 percent that had traditionally been required.

CMI had had a mixed record of success within the private mortgage insurance industry. Frank Randall, the company's first and only president, had gotten the organization off to an aggressive beginning, attaining a 14.8 percent market share by 1972. By 1979, however, that share had fallen to just over 10 percent even though revenues had grown from $18 million in 1972 to over $30 million in 1979. Randall attributed the loss of market share primarily to the difficulties created by the bankruptcy of CMI's original parent. Thus, he had been quite relieved when Northwest Equipment had acquired CMI in January 1978. Northwest provided CMI with a level of management and financial support it had never before enjoyed. Furthermore, Northwest's corporate management had made it clear to Frank Randall that he was expected to build CMI into a much larger, diversified financial services company.

Northwest's growth expectations were highly consistent with Frank Randall's own ambitions. The stability created by the acquisition, in combination with the increasing solidity of CMI's reputation with mortgage lenders, made it possible for Randall to turn his attention more and more toward external acquisitions of his own. During 1978 Randall, with Jim Dolan's help, had investigated several acquisition opportunities in related insurance industries, with the hope of broadening CMI's financial base. After several unsuccessful investigations the two men had come to believe that their knowledge and competence was focused less on insurance per se than it was on residential real estate and related financial transactions. These experiences had led to a recognition that, in Frank Randall's words, "we are a residential real estate financial services company."

THE RESIDENTIAL REAL ESTATE INDUSTRY

Frank Randall and Jim Dolan knew from personal experience that real estate brokers, who played an obvious and important role in property transactions, usually had close ties with local banks and savings and loans. When mortgage funds were plentiful, brokers often "steered" prospective home buyers to particular lending institutions. When funds were scarce, the lenders would then favor prospective borrowers referred by their "favorite" brokers. Randall believed that these informal relationships meant that realtors could have a significant impact on the mortgage loan decision and, thus, on a mortgage insurance decision as well.

For this reason, CMI had for many years directed a small portion of its marketing effort toward real estate brokers. CMI's activities had consisted of offering educational programs for realtors, property developers, and potential home buyers. The company derived no direct revenues from these programs, but offered them in the interest of stimulating home sales and, more particularly, of informing both realtors and home buyers of how mortgage insurance made it possible to purchase a home with a relatively low down payment.

Because he felt that real estate brokers could be powerful allies in encouraging lenders to use mortgage insurance, Randall had been tracking developments in the real estate industry for many years. Historically a highly fragmented collection of local, independent entrepreneurs, the industry in 1979 appeared to be on the verge of a major restructuring and consolidation. For the past several years many of the smaller brokers had been joining national franchise organizations in an effort to gain a "brand image" and to acquire improved management and sales skills.

More significantly, in 1979, several large national corporations were beginning to acquire prominent real estate agencies in major urban areas. The most aggressive of these appeared to be Merrill Lynch and Company, the well-known Wall Street securities trading firm. Merrill Lynch's interest in real estate brokers stemmed from several sources; perhaps most important were the rapidly rising prices on property and homes. Realtors' commissions averaged slightly over 6 percent of the sales price; *Fortune* magazine estimated that real estate brokers had been involved in home sales totaling approximately $190 billion in 1978, netting commissions in excess of $11 billion (in comparison, stockbrokers' commissions on all securities transactions in 1978 were estimated at $3.7 billion).[1] With property values growing 10–20 percent per year, commissions would only get larger; where 6 percent of a $30,000 home netted only $1,800, 6 percent of a $90,000 sale resulted in a commission well in excess of $5,000—for basically the same work.

There were also clear signs that the volume of real estate transactions would continue to increase. Although voluntary intercity moves appeared to be declining slightly, corporate transfers of employees were still rising. One of Merrill Lynch's earliest moves toward the real estate market had been to acquire an employee relocation company several years earlier. Working on a contract basis with corporate clients, Merrill Lynch Relocation Management (MLRM) collaborated with independent real

---

[1]"Why Merrill Lynch Wants to Sell You a House," *Fortune*, January 29, 1979.

estate brokers to arrange home sales and purchases for transferred employees. Like other relocation companies, MLRM would purchase the home at a fair market value and then handle all the legal and financial details of reselling the home on the open market. MLRM also provided relocation counseling and home search assistance for transferred employees; its income was derived primarily from service fees paid by corporate clients (and augmented somewhat by referral fees from real estate brokers, who paid MLRM a portion of the commissions they earned on home sales generated by the transferred employees).

Later, in September 1978, Merrill Lynch had formally announced its intention to acquire at least 40 real estate brokerage firms within three to four years. Merrill Lynch's interest in the industry stemmed not only from the profit opportunities it saw, but also from a corporate desire to become a "financial services supermarket," providing individual customers with a wide range of investment and brokerage services. In 1978 Merrill Lynch had acquired United First Mortgage Corporation (UFM), a mortgage banker. And in early 1979 Merrill Lynch was in the midst of acquiring AMIC Corporation, a small mortgage insurance company in direct competition with CMI. As *Fortune* reported:

> In combination, these diverse activities hold some striking possibilities. Merrill Lynch already packages and markets mortgages through its registered representatives. . . . If all goes according to plan, the company could later this year be vertically integrated in a unique way. Assuming the AMIC acquisition goes through, Merrill Lynch will be able to guarantee mortgages. It could then originate mortgages through its realty brokerages, process and service them through UFM, insure them with AMIC, package them as pass-through or unit trusts, and market them through its army of registered representatives. (January 29,,1979, p. 89.)

It was this vision of an integrated financial services organization that also excited Frank Randall. As he and Jim Dolan reviewed their position in early 1979, they were confident that they were in a unique position to build CMI into a much bigger and more diversified company. The mortgage insurance business gave them a solid financial base with regional offices throughout the country. Northwest Equipment stood ready to provide the capital they would need for significant growth. They already had relationships with important lending institutions across the United States, and their marketing efforts had given them a solid reputation with important real estate brokers as well.

Thus, Randall, in particular, felt that at least he had most of the ingredients to begin building that diversified "residential real estate financial services company" he had been dreaming about for so long. Furthermore, Randall's reading of the banking, thrift, and real estate industries suggested that the time was ripe. In his view, the uncertainties in the financial and housing industries created rich opportunities for taking aggressive action, and the vision of Merrill Lynch "bulling" its way into the business was scaring realtors just enough for CMI to present a comforting and familiar alternative.

THE METROPOLITAN REALTY NETWORK

Frank Randall spent most of the fall of 1978 actively searching for acquisition opportunities. As part of his effort, he contacted David Osgood, who was the executive director of The Metropolitan Realty Network, a national association of independent real estate brokers. The association, commonly known as "MetroNet," had been formed primarily as a communication vehicle so its members could refer home buyers moving from one city to another to a qualified broker in the new location.

Randall discovered that Osgood was somewhat concerned about MetroNet's long-term health and viability. Though MetroNet included over 13,000 real estate agencies, it was losing some members to national franchise chains, and Osgood was feeling increasing pressures to strengthen the association by providing more services to member firms. Yet the entrepreneurial independence of MetroNet's members made Osgood's task particularly difficult: He had found it almost impossible to get them to agree on what they wanted him to do.

One service that the MetroNet brokers *were* agreed on developing was the employee relocation business. Corporate contracts to handle transferred employees were especially attractive to the brokers, because the contracts virtually guaranteed repeat business in the local area, and they also led to intercity referrals that almost always resulted in a home sale.

MetroNet brokers were also resentful of how Merrill Lynch Relocation Management and other relocation services companies were getting a larger and larger share of "their" referral fees. Osgood told Randall that he had already set up a committee of MetroNet brokers to look into how the association could develop a corporate relocation and third-party equity[2] capability of its own. Osgood mentioned that their only effort to date was an independent firm in Chicago named Corporate Transfer Services, Inc. (CTS), that had been started by Elliott Burr, a prominent Chicago broker and a MetroNet director. CTS had been formed with the intention of working with MetroNet brokers, but so far it had remained relatively small and had not met MetroNet's expectations.

As Randall explained to Osgood the kinds of activities that CMI engaged in to help lenders and increase the volume of home sales, Osgood suddenly exclaimed, "That's exactly what *we're* trying to do!" The two men ended their initial meeting convinced that some kind of working relationship between CMI and MetroNet could have major benefits for both organizations. Osgood invited Randall to attend the next meeting of MetroNet's Third-Party Equity Committee, scheduled for March 1. "Let's explore what we can do for each other," said Osgood. "You're on," concluded Randall.

THE THIRD-PARTY EQUITY BUSINESS

Randall's discussion with David Osgood had opened his eyes to the third-party equity business, and he and Jim Dolan spent most of their time in preparation for the March 1 committee meeting steeped in industry studies and pro forma income statements.

They quickly discovered that the employee relocation services industry was highly competitive, though its future looked bright. Corporate transfers of key employees appeared to be an ingrained practice that showed no signs of letting up in the foreseeable future. Merrill Lynch Relocation Management was one of the two largest

---

[2]The term *third-party equity capability* derived from the fact that a relocation services company actually purchased an employee's home, freeing up the owner's equity and making it available for investment in a new home. Within the industry the terms *third-party equity company* and *employee relocation services company* were generally used interchangeably.

EXHIBIT 1 Major Employee Relocation Services Companies

Relocation Company	Parent Organization	Estimated 1978 Home Purchases	Estimated Value of Homes Purchased*	Estimated Gross Fee Income†
Merrill Lynch Relocation	Merrill Lynch	13,000	$975,000,000	$26,800,000
Homequity	Peterson, Howell, & Heather	12,000	900,000,000	24,750,000
Equitable Relocation	Equitable Life Insurance	5,000	375,000,000	10,300,000
Employee Transfer	Chicago Title and Trust	5,000	375,000,000	10,300,000
Relocation Realty Corporation	Control Data Corporation	3,000	225,000,000	6,200,000
Executrans	Sears/Coldwell Banker	3,000	225,000,000	6,200,000
Transamerica Relocation	Transamerica, Inc.	3,000	225,000,000	6,200,000

*Assumes average home values of $75,000.
†Assumes fee averaging 2.75 percent of value of homes purchased.

firms in the industry; most of the prominent relocation companies were well-funded subsidiaries of large, well-known corporations. Exhibit 1 contains Jim Dolan's tabulation of the seven major relocation firms, along with his estimates of each company's 1978 volume of home purchases.

Dolan also developed a pro forma income and expense statement for a hypothetical firm handling 2,000 home purchases annually (see Exhibit 2). His calculations showed a potential 13.1 percent return on equity. Dolan then discovered that some companies achieved a much higher ROE by using a Home Purchase Trust, a legal arrangement that made it possible to obtain enough bank financing to leverage a company's equity base by as much as 10 to 1.

Randall and Dolan were increasingly certain that they wanted to get CMI into the employee relocation services business. They saw it as a natural tie-in with CMI's mort-

EXHIBIT 2

HYPOTHETICAL EMPLOYEE RELOCATION COMPANY
PRO FORMA INCOME STATEMENT

Key assumptions:
1. Annual purchase volume of 2,000 homes.
2. Assume average holding period of 120 days. Inventory turns over three times annually, for an average of 667 units in inventory at any point in time.
3. Average home value of $75,000.
4. Existing mortgages on homes average 50 percent of property value. Additional required capital will be 40 percent equity, 60 percent long-term debt.
5. Fee income from corporate clients will average 2.75 percent of value of properties purchased (based on historical industry data).
6. Operating expenses (marketing, sales, office administration) will average 1 percent of value of properties purchased (all costs associated with purchases, including debt service, are billed back to corporate clients).

Calculations	
Total value of purchases (2,000 units at $75,000)	$150,000,000
Average inventory value	50,000,000
Capital required:	
Existing mortgages	25,000,000
New long-term debt	15,000,000
Equity	10,000,000
Fee income at 2.75%	4,125,000
Operating expenses at 1%	1,500,000
Net income	$ 2,625,000
Tax at 50%	(1,312,500)
Profit after tax	$ 1,312,500
Return on equity	13.1%

gage insurance operations—one that could exploit the same set of relationships that CMI already had with banks, realtors, savings and loans, and other companies involved in the development, construction, sale, and financing of residential real estate. The two men felt that real estate brokers had a critically important role in the process. Brokers were not only involved in the actual property transactions, but in addition they almost always had local contacts with corporations that could lead to the signing of employee relocation contracts. Equally important, from Randall's and Dolan's perspective, was their belief that a close relationship between CMI and the MetroNet brokers would also lead to significant sales of CMI's mortgage insurance policies.

The March 1 meeting with MetroNet's Third-Party Equity Committee turned into an exploration of how CMI and MetroNet might help each other by stimulating both home sales and high ratio mortgage loans. After several hours of discussion, Frank Randall proposed specifically that CMI build an operating company to handle the corporate relocation business jointly with the MetroNet brokers. As a quid pro quo, Randall suggested that the brokers could market CMI mortgage insurance to both potential home buyers and lending institutions.

The committee's response to this idea was initially skeptical. Finally, however, they agreed to consider a more formal proposal at a later date. MetroNet's board of directors was scheduled to meet on April 10; the Third-Party Equity Committee could review the proposal on April 9 and, if they approved, present it to the full board on the 10th.

As the committee meeting broke up Randall and Dolan began talking with Elliott Burr and Thomas Winder, two of the four owners of Corporate Transfer Services, Inc. (CTS). Though Burr had been the principal founder of CTS, his primary business was a large real estate brokerage firm in north suburban Chicago that he operated in partnership with William Lehman, who was also a CTS stockholder.

The four men sat back down at the meeting table, and Randall mentioned that his primary interest was to learn more about how an employee relocation business operated. Burr offered to send him copies of contracts with corporate clients, sample financial statements, and so on. At one point during their discussion Burr mentioned the possibility of an acquisition. Randall asked, somewhat rhetorically, "How do you put a value on a company like this?" Burr responded almost immediately, "Funny you should ask. We've talked to an attorney and have put together this proposal." Burr reached into his briefcase and pulled out a two-page document. He then proceeded to describe a complex set of terms involving the sale of an 80 percent interest in CTS, subject to guarantees concerning capitalization, lines of credit, data processing support, future distribution of profits and dividends, and more.

Randall backed off immediately, explaining that he needed to learn more about the nature of the business before he would seriously consider an acquisition. As Jim Dolan later recalled:

> I think they were expecting an offer right then and there. But it was very hard to understand what they really wanted; it was nothing we could actually work from. Besides that, the numbers they were thinking about were ridiculously high—over $5 million. We put the letter away and told them we didn't want to get specific until after the April 10 meeting. And that's the way we left it.

Preparation for the April 10 Meeting

During the next six weeks Randall and Dolan continued their investigations of the employee relocation industry and studied CTS much more closely.

One of their major questions was how much additional mortgage insurance the MetroNet brokers might be able to generate. Frank Randall had CMI's marketing staff conduct a telephone survey of about 25 key MetroNet brokers. The survey suggested that most brokers were aware of mortgage insurance, although few of them were actively pushing it. All of those questioned expressed an interest in using CMI's marketing programs, and were eager to learn more about CMI insurance.

By early May a fairly clear picture of CTS was emerging. The company had been founded in 1975; it had barely achieved a break-even profit level. Annual home purchases and sales had reached a level of almost 500 properties, and CTS has worked with about 65 MetroNet brokers and 35 corporate clients. Tom Winder was the general manager; he supervised a staff of about 25 customer representatives and clerical support staff. Conversations with David Osgood and several MetroNet brokers who had worked with CTS suggested that the company had made promises to MetroNet about developing a nationwide, well-financed, fully competitive organization. To date, however, those promises were largely unfulfilled. Osgood believed that CTS' shortage of equity and, therefore, borrowing capacity, had severely limited its growth potential.

Jim Dolan obtained a copy of CTS' December 1978 balance sheet that, in his mind, confirmed Osgood's feelings (see Exhibit 3). The company had a net worth of only $420,000. Three of the four stockholders (Elliott Burr, William Lehman, and Michael Kupchak) had invested an additional $2 million in the company—$1.3 million in short-term notes and $700,000 in bank loans that they had personally guaranteed. While CTS owned homes valued at $13.4 million, it also had additional bank loans and assumed mortgages totaling $9.8 million. Furthermore, the company had a highly uncertain earnings stream; Frank Randall believed the current business could tail off to almost nothing within six months.

During late March both Randall and Dolan had a number of telephone conversations with Burr and Winder. Their discussions were wide-ranging and quite open; the CTS partners struck Randall as being unusually candid. They seemed more than willing to share everything they knew about the business and their own company. On one occasion, Burr asked how much of CTS Randall wanted to buy, and how Randall would feel about the present owners retaining a minority interest. Burr's question led Randall and Dolan to conclude that in fact they wanted full ownership. They planned to build up the company's equity base considerably, and wanted to gain all the benefits of a larger, more profitable operation for CMI.

In early April, Randall developed the formal proposal that he intended to present to MetroNet's board of directors (see Exhibit 4). The proposal committed CMI to enter negotiations to acquire CTS and to use CTS as a base for building a third-party equity company with a capitalization sufficient to support an annual home purchase capability of at least 2,000 units. In return, the proposal asked MetroNet to begin a program of actively supporting the use of CMI's insurance on high-ratio loans.

EXHIBIT 3

CORPORATE TRANSFER SERVICES, INC.
Unaudited Balance Sheet
December 1978

	($ 000)
Assets:	
Cash	$ 190
Homes owned	13,366
Accounts and acquisition fees receivable	665
Other (mainly escrow deposits)	143
	$14,364
Liabilities:	
Client prepayments	$ 1,602
Notes payable to banks	4,161
Assumed mortgages payable	5,670
Loan from stockholders	700
Advance from MetroNet	300
Other liabilities	211
	$12,644
Capital:	
Subordinated debenture due stockholder (April 1981)	1,300
Common stock	450
Deficit	(30)
	$14,364

Randall and Dolan met again with the Third-Party Equity Committee in New York on April 9 to preview the CMI proposal. The committee reacted favorably, and the next day MetroNet's board of directors unanimously accepted the proposal after discussing it for less than 15 minutes.

FORMAL NEGOTIATIONS WITH CORPORATE TRANSFER SERVICES

On the afternoon of April 10, following the MetroNet board meeting, Randall and Dolan met again with Elliott Burr and Tom Winder. Now that CMI was formally committed to acquisition negotiations, Burr and Winder were eager to get specific and talk numbers. However, Randall and Dolan remained very cautious. When Burr expressed an interest in discussing a price, Randall replied, "We don't know what you're worth. But we'll entertain any reasonable argument you want to make for why we should pay more than your net worth." The meeting ended with a general agreement to firm things up by April 25.

EXHIBIT 4

Board of Directors
The Metropolitan Realty Network
New York, NY

April 9, 1979

Gentlemen:

It is our intention to enter negotiations with the principals of Corporate Transfer Services, Inc., for the acquisition of the equity ownership of this Company by Capital Mortgage Insurance Corporation.

In the event Capital Mortgage Insurance Corporation is successful in the acquisition of Corporate Transfer Services, Inc., it is our intention to capitalize this Company to the extent required for the development of a complete bank line of credit. The initial capital and bank line of credit would provide the MetroNet association members an annual equity procurement of 1,500–2,000 units. In addition, we would be prepared to expand beyond this initial capacity if the MetroNet Association volume and profitability of business dictate.

We are prepared to develop an organizational structure and support system that can provide a competitive and professional marketing and administrative approach to the corporate transfer market.

Our intentions to enter negotiations with Corporate Transfer Services, Inc., are subject to the following:

1. The endorsement of this action by you, the board of directors of MetroNet, for Capital Mortgage Insurance Corporation to acquire this organization.
2. The assurance of the MetroNet Association for the continuation of their support and use of CTS. Upon the completion of the acquisition, the MetroNet Association would agree to sign a Letter of Agreement with the new owners of Corporate Transfer Services.
3. The assurance of the MetroNet Association to cooperate in the development of a close working relationship with CMI for the influence and control they may provide when seeking high-ratio conventional mortgage loans using mortgage insurance.

Capital Mortgage Insurance will need the support of expanded business by the MetroNet Association, due to the heavy capital commitment we will be required to make to CTS to make this acquisition feasible. In this regard, CMI is prepared to offer the MetroNet nationwide members a range of marketing programs and mortgage financing packages that will help earn and deserve the mortgage insurance business and expand the listings, sales and profitability of the MetroNet members.

Upon receiving the endorsement and support outlined in this letter from the board of directors of MetroNet, we will proceed immediately with the negotiations with Corporate Transfer Services, Inc. It would be our intention to have the acquisition completed and the company fully operational by the time of the MetroNet national convention in San Francisco in July 1979.

Sincerely,

Franklin T. Randall
President and Chief Executive Officer

Later, reflecting on this session, Jim Dolan commented:

Our letter of agreement committed us to having an operating company by July 12, so the clock was running on us. However, we knew that after the April 10 board meeting they would be hard pressed not to be bought, and besides they were obviously pretty eager. But at that point in time we had not even met the other two stockholders; we suspected the high numbers were coming from them.

Further Assessment of CTS

Even though the April 10 meeting had ended with an agreement to move ahead by April 25, it quickly became evident that a complete assessment of CTS and preparation of a formal offer would take more than two weeks. Other operating responsibilities prevented both Randall and Dolan from devoting as much time as they had intended to the acquisition, and the analysis process itself required more time than they had expected.

During the first week of May, Jim Dolan made a "reconnaissance" trip to Chicago. His stated purpose was to examine CTS' books and talk with the company's local bankers. He also scrutinized the office facilities, met and talked with several office employees, observed Tom Winder interacting with customers and subordinates, and generally assessed the company's operations. Dolan spent most of his time with Winder, but he also had an opportunity to have dinner with William Lehman, another of CTS' stockholders. Dolan returned to Philadelphia with a generally favorable set of impressions about the company's operations, and a much more concrete understanding of its financial situation. He reported to Randall, "They're running a responsible organization in a basically sensible manner." At the same time, however, Dolan also reported that CTS was under increasing pressure from its bankers to improve its financial performance.

Dolan's trip also provided him with a much richer understanding of the four men who owned CTS: Elliott Burr, William Lehman (Burr's real estate partner), Michael Kupchak (a private investor), and Tom Winder. Of these four, only Winder was actively involved in the day-to-day management of the company, although Elliott Burr stayed in very close touch with Winder and was significantly more involved than either Lehman or Kupchak. From their meetings and telephone conversations. Randall and Dolan pieced together the following pictures of the four men:

Elliott Burr, in his middle 50s, had been the driving force behind Corporate Transfer Services. He was a "classic" real estate salesman—a warm, straightforward, friendly man who enthusiastically believed in what he was doing. An eternal optimist, he had been an early advocate of MetroNet's getting into the employee relocation business. Burr knew the relocation business extremely well; he personally called on many of the large Chicago corporations to sell CTS' services.

Burr appeared to be very well off financially. Burr and Lehman Real Estate was one of the largest realty firms on Chicago's North Shore, and Burr was held in high regard by local bankers. One banker had told Dolan, "Burr's word is his bond."

William Lehman, Burr's real estate partner, was in his mid-60s. He appeared to be much more of a financial adviser and investor than an operating manager. Lenman personally owned the shopping center where Burr and Lehman Real Estate was located, as well as the office building where CTS was leasing space.

Dolan characterized Lehman as an "elder statesman—a true gentleman." Dolan recalled that when he had dinner with Lehman during his visit to Chicago, Lehman had kept the conversation on a personal level, repeatedly expressing concern about Dolan's plane reservations, hotel accommodations, and so on. He had hardly mentioned CTS during the entire dinner.

Michael Kupchak was the third principal stockholder. Kupchak, who was about 50, had been a mortgage banker in Chicago for a number of years. Recently, however, he had left the bank to manage his own investments on a full-time basis.

Dolan met Kupchak briefly during his Chicago visit, and characterized him as a "bulldog"—an aggressive, ambitious man much more interested in financial transactions than in the nature of the business. He had apparently thought Dolan was coming to Chicago to make a firm offer, and had been irritated that one had not been forthcoming.

Frank Randall had not yet met Kupchak face to face, although they had talked once by telephone.

Thomas Winder, 44, had spent most of his career in real estate-related businesses. At one time he had worked for a construction company, and then he had joined the mortgage bank where Michael Kupchak worked.

Kupchak had actually brought Winder into CTS as its general manager, and the three original partners had offered him 25 percent ownership in the company as part of his compensation package.

Winder was not only CTS' general manager, but its lead salesperson as well. He called on prospective corporate clients all over the country, and he worked closely with MetroNet as well. That activity primarily involved appearing at association-sponsored seminars to inform member brokers about CTS and its services.

It was obvious to Jim Dolan that CTS had become an important source of real estate sales commissions for the Burr and Lehman partnership. Most of CTS' clients were in the Chicago area, and a large portion of the real estate transactions generated by CTS were being handled by Burr and Lehman Real Estate.

Dolan also inferred that the three senior partners—Burr, Lehman, and Kupchak— were close friends socially as well as professionally. The men clearly respected each other and valued each other's opinions. On one occasion Burr had told Dolan, "It's because of Bill Lehman that I have what I do today. I can always trust his word." Tom Winder was also woven into the relationship, but he was apparently not as closely involved as the other three. Randall and Dolan both sensed that Elliott Burr was the unofficial spokesman of the group: "I have the impression he can speak for all of them," commented Dolan.

In late April, Randall obtained a copy of a consultant's report on the employee relocation industry that had been commissioned by MetroNet's Third-Party Equity Committee. The report estimated that there were more than 500,000 homeowner/employees transferred annually, generating over 1 million home purchases and sales. However, fewer than 55,000 of these transfers were currently being handled by relocation services companies. Dolan's own analysis had projected a 10 percent–15 percent annual growth rate in the use of relocation companies, leading to industry volume estimates of 60,000 in 1979, 67,000 in 1980, and 75,000 by 1981.

The consultant's report stressed that success in the relocation business depended upon a company's ability to provide services to its corporate clients at lower cost than the clients could do it themselves. In addition, profitability depended on a company's ability to turn over its inventory of homes quickly and at reasonable prices.

Dolan's own financial projections showed a potential return on equity of over 30 percent by 1983, assuming only an 8 percent share of the market. And that return did not include any incremental profits resulting from new sales of CMI mortgage insurance policies generated by MetroNet brokers. Randall in particular was confident that the close ties between CMI and MetroNet would result in at least 5,000 new mortgage insurance policies annually—a volume that could add over $400,000 in after-tax profits to CMI's basic business.

On May 10, Randall and Dolan attended a Northwest Equipment Corporation financial review meeting in Minneapolis. Prior to their trip west Randall had prepared a detailed analysis of the CTS acquisition and the employee relocation industry. The analysis, in the form of a proposal, served as documentation for a formal request to Northwest for a capital expenditure of $9 million. Randall had decided that he was willing to pay up to $600,000 more than the $420,000 book value of CTS' net worth; the remaining $8 million would constitute the initial equity base required to build CTS into a viable company.

The financial review meeting evolved into a lengthy critique of the acquisition proposal. Northwest's corporate staff was initially quite skeptical of the financial projections, but Randall and Dolan argued that the risks were relatively low (the homes could always be sold) and the potential payoffs, both economic and strategic, were enormous. Finally, after an extended debate, the request was approved.

FORMAL NEGOTIATIONS WITH CTS

When Randall and Dolan returned from Minneapolis, they felt it was finally time to proceed in earnest with the acquisition negotiations. Randall sensed that at present CTS was limping along to no one's satisfaction—including Elliott Burr's. The company was sucking up much more of Burr's time and energy than he wanted to give it, and its inability to fulfill MetroNet's expectations was beginning to be an embarrassment for Burr personally.

In spite of these problems, Randall remained interested in completing the acquisition. Buying CTS would get CMI into the relocation business quickly, would provide them with immediate licensing and other legal documentation in 38 states, and would get them an experienced operations manager in Tom Winder. More importantly, Randall knew that Elliott Burr was an important and respected MetroNet broker, and buying CTS would provide an effective, influential entry into the MetroNet "old boy" network. Though he couldn't put a number on the value of that network, Randall believed it was almost more important than the acquisition of CTS itself. Randall was convinced that the connection with the MetroNet brokers would enable him to run CTS at far lower cost than the established relocation companies, and he also expected to realize a significant increase in CMI's mortgage insurance business.

May 21, 1979

Now, as Randall and Dolan sat in Randall's office on May 21, they discussed the draft of a formal purchase offer that Dolan had prepared that morning (see Exhibit 5

EXHIBIT 5   Excerpts from Draft of Purchase Letter

The Board of Directors and Stockholders
Corporate Transfer Services, Inc.
Chicago, IL

May 24, 1979

Gentlemen:

Capital Mortgage Insurance Corporation (the "Purchaser") hereby agrees to purchase from you (the "Stockholders") and you, the Stockholders, hereby jointly and severally agree to sell to us, the Purchaser, 100 percent of the issued and outstanding shares of capital stock of Corporate Transfer Services (the "Company") on the following terms and conditions.

Purchase Price. Subject to any adjustment under the following paragraph, the Purchase Price of the Stock shall be the sum of $400,000.00 (four hundred thousand dollars even) and an amount equal to the Company's net worth as reflected in its audited financial statements on the closing date (the "Closing Date Net Worth").

Adjustment of Purchase Price. The Purchase Price shall be reduced or increased, as the case may be, dollar-for-dollar by the amount, if any, by which the net amount realized on the sale of homes owned as of the Closing Date is exceeded by, or exceeds, the net value attributed to such homes in the Closing Date Net Worth.

Continuation of Employment. Immediately upon consummation of the transaction, the Purchaser will enter into discussion with Mr. Thomas Winder with the intent that he continue employment in a management capacity at a mutually agreeable rate of pay. Mr. Winder will relocate to Philadelphia, Pennsylvania, and will be responsible for the sale of all homes owned by the Company at the Closing Date.

Covenant-Not-to-Compete. At the closing, each Stockholder will execute and deliver a covenant-not-to-compete agreeing that he will not engage in any capacity in the business conducted by the Company for a period of two years.

If the foregoing correctly states our agreement as to this transaction, please sign below.

Very truly yours,

CAPITAL MORTGAGE INSURANCE
CORPORATION

By_____
President

The foregoing is agreed to and accepted.

---

for relevant excerpts). The two men had decided to make an initial offer of $400,000 more than the $420,000 book value of CTS' net worth, subject to a formal audit and adjustments depending on the final sales prices of all homes owned by CTS as of the formal purchase date. This opening bid was $200,000 below Randall's ceiling price of $600,000 for the firm's goodwill. The offer was for 100 percent of the ownership of the company. The $2 million in outstanding notes would pass through to the new company owned by Randall and Dolan. The offer also included a statement of intent to retain Tom Winder as CTS' general manager, and to move the company to CMI's home office in Philadelphia.

As Randall and Dolan reviewed their plans, it was clear that they were more concerned about how to conduct the face-to-face negotiations than with the formal terms themselves. In the telephone call he had just completed, Randall had told Elliott Burr only that they wanted to meet the other stockholders and review their current thinking. At one point during the conversation Jim Dolan commented:

> I really wonder how they'll react to this offer. We've been putting them off for so long now that I'm not sure how they feel about us anymore. And our offer is so much less than they're looking for . . .

Randall replied:

> I know that—but I have my ceiling. It seems to me the real question now is what kind of bargaining stance we should take, and how to carry it out. What do you think *they* are expecting?

DISCUSSION QUESTIONS

1. Prepare, and be ready to discuss, a negotiation strategy for Randall and Dolan.
2. What should CMI be expecting from CTS?

CASE STUDY 2

Pacific Oil Company (A)

For the session on Pacific Oil Company, please prepare the following:

1. As background information, read: "Petrochemical Supply Contracts: A Technical Note."

2. After reading Pacific Oil Company (A), prepare the following questions for class discussion:

   a. Describe the "problem" that faced Pacific Oil Company as it reopened negotiations with Reliant Chemical Company in early 1985.

   b. Evaluate the styles and effectiveness of Messrs. Fontaine, Gaudin, Hauptmann, and Zinnser as negotiators in this case.

   c. What should Frank Kelsey recommend to Jean Fontaine at the end of the case? Why?

THE PACIFIC OIL COMPANY

"Look, you asked for my advice, and I gave it to you," Frank Kelsey said.

"If I were you, I wouldn't make any more concessions! I really don't think you ought to agree to their last demand! But you're the only one who has to live with the contract, not me!"

Static on the transatlantic telephone connection obscured Jean Fontaine's reply. Kelsey asked him to repeat what he had said.

"OK, OK, calm down, Jean. I can see your point of view. I appreciate the pressures you're under. But I sure don't like the looks of it from this end. Keep in touch—I'll talk to you early next week. In the meantime, I will see what others at the office think about this turn of events."

Frank Kelsey hung up the phone. He sat pensively, staring out at the rain pounding on the window. "Poor Fontaine," he muttered to himself. "He's so anxious to please the customer, he'd feel compelled to give them the whole pie without getting his fair share of the dessert!"

Kelsey cleaned and lit his pipe as he mentally reviewed the history of the negotiations. "My word," he thought to himself, "we are getting eaten in little bites in this Reliant deal! And I can't make Fontaine see it!"

This case was prepared by Roy J. Lewicki for use in executive seminars.

BACKGROUND

Pacific Oil Company was founded in 1902 as the Sweetwater Oil Company of Oklahoma City, Oklahoma. The founder of Sweetwater Oil, E. M. Hutchinson, pioneered a major oil strike in north central Oklahoma that touched off the Oklahoma "black gold" rush of the early 1900s. Through growth and acquisition in the 1920s and 30s, Hutchinson expanded the company rapidly, and renamed it Pacific Oil in 1932. After a period of consolidation in the 1940s and 50s, Pacific expanded again. It developed extensive oil holdings in North Africa and the Middle East, as well as significant coal beds in the western United States. Much of Pacific's oil production is sold under its own name as gasoline through service stations in the United States and Europe, but also it is distributed through several chains of "independent" gasoline stations. In addition, Pacific is also one of the largest and best known worldwide producers of industrial petrochemicals.

One of Pacific's major industrial chemical lines is the production of vinyl chloride monomer (VCM). The basic components of VCM are ethylene and chlorine. Ethylene is a colorless, flammable, gaseous hydrocarbon with a disagreeable odor; it is generally obtained from natural or coal gas, or by "cracking" petroleum into smaller molecular components. As a further step in the petroleum "cracking" process, ethylene is combined with chlorine to produce vinyl chloride monomer, also a colorless gas.

VCM is the primary component of a family of plastics known as the vinyl chlorides. VCM is subjected to the process of polymerization, in which smaller molecules of vinyl chloride are chemically bonded together to form larger molecular chains and networks. As the bonding occurs, polyvinyl chloride (PVC) is produced; coloring pigments may be added, as well as "plasticizer" compounds that determine the relative flexibility or hardness of the finished material. Through various forms of calendering (pressing between heavy rollers), extruding and injection molding, the plasticized polyvinyl chloride is converted to an enormous array of consumer and industrial applications: flooring, wire insulation, electrical transformers, home furnishings, piping, toys, bottles and containers, rainwear, light roofing and a variety of protective coatings. (See Exhibit 1 for a breakdown of common PVC-based products.)

In 1979, Pacific Oil established the first major contract with The Reliant Corporation for the purchase of vinyl chloride monomer. The Reliant Corporation was a major industrial manufacturer of wood and petrochemical products for the construction industry. Reliant was expanding its manufacturing operations in the production of plastic pipe and pipe fittings, particularly in Europe. The use of plastic as a substitute for iron or copper pipe was gaining rapid acceptance in the construction trades, and the European markets were significantly more progressive in adopting the plastic pipe. Reliant already had developed a small polyvinyl chloride production facility at Abbeville, France, and Pacific constructed a pipeline from its petrochemical plant at Antwerp to Abbeville.

The 1979 contract between Pacific Oil and Reliant was a fairly standard one for the industry, and due to expire in December of 1982. The contract was negotiated by Reliant's purchasing managers in Europe, headquartered in Brussels, and the senior marketing managers of Pacific Oil's European offices, located in Paris. Each of these individuals reported to the vice presidents in charge of their company's European offices, who in turn reported back to their respective corporate headquarters in the States. (See Exhibits 2 and 3 for partial organization charts.)

EXHIBIT 1 Polyvinyl Chloride Major Markets, 1982 (units represented in MM pounds)

Market	MM Pounds	Percent of Market Share
Apparel		
Baby pants	22	0.6
Footwear	128	3.2
Misc.	60	1.5
	210	5.3
Building and Construction		
Extruded foam moldings	46	1.2
Flooring	428	10.8
Lighting	10	0.3
Panels and siding	64	1.6
Pipe and conduit	720	18.5
Pipe fittings	78	2.0
Rainwater systems	28	0.7
Swimming pool liners	40	1.0
Weather stripping	36	0.9
Misc.	50	1.2
	1,500	38.2
Electrical		
Wire and cable	390	9.9
Home Furnishings		
Appliances	32	0.8
Misc.	286	9.8
Wall coverings	418	10.6
Housewares	94	2.4
Packaging		
Blow molded bottles	64	1.6
Closure liners and gaskets	16	0.4
Coatings	16	0.4
Film	124	3.2
Misc.	80	2.0
	300	7.6
Recreation		
Records	136	3.4
Sporting goods	46	1.2
Misc.	68	1.7
	250	6.3
Transportation		
Auto mats	36	0.9
Auto tops	32	0.8
Misc.	164	4.2
	232	5.9

EXHIBIT 1   *(concluded)*

Market	MM Pounds	Percent of Market Share
Miscellaneous		
Agriculture (including pipe)	106	2.6
Credit cards	24	0.4
Garden hose	40	1.0
Laminates	44	1.1
Medical tubing	42	1.1
Novelties	12	0.3
Stationery supplies	32	0.8
Misc.	12	0.3
	312	7.6
Export	146	3.7
Misc.	98	2.5
Total	3,960	100.0

THE 1982 CONTRACT RENEWAL

In February 1982, negotiations began to extend the four-year contract beyond the December 31, 1982 expiration date. Jean Fontaine, Pacific Oil's marketing vice president for Europe, discussed the Reliant account with his VCM marketing manager, Paul Gaudin. Fontaine had been promoted to the European vice presidency approximately 16 months earlier after having served as Pacific's ethylene marketing manager. Fontaine had been with Pacific Oil for 11 years, and had a reputation as a strong "up and comer" in Pacific's European operations. Gaudin had been appointed as VCM marketing manager eight months earlier; this was his first job with Pacific Oil, although he had five years of previous experience in European computer sales with a large American computer manufacturing company. Fontaine and Gaudin had worked well in their short time together, establishing a strong professional and personal relationship. Fontaine and Gaudin agreed that the Reliant account had been an extremely profitable and beneficial one for Pacific, and believed that Reliant had, overall, been satisfied with the quality and service under the agreement as well. They clearly wanted to work hard to obtain a favorable renegotiation of the existing agreement. Fontaine and Gaudin also reviewed the latest projections of worldwide VCM supply which they had just received from corporate headquarters. (See Exhibit 4.) The data confirmed what they already knew—that there was a worldwide shortage of VCM and that demand was continuing to rise. Pacific envisioned that the current demand-supply situation would remain this way for a number of years. As a result, Pacific believed that it could justify a high favorable formula price for VCM.

Fontaine and Gaudin decided that they would approach Reliant with an offer to renegotiate the current agreement. Their basic strategy would be to ask Reliant for their five-year demand projections on VCM and polyvinyl chloride products. Once these projections were received, Fontaine and Gaudin would frame the basic formula price that they would offer. (It would be expected that there would be no significant changes or variations in other elements of the contract, such as delivery and contract language.) In their negotiations, their strategy would be as follows:

EXHIBIT 2 Partial Organization Chart—Pacific Oil Company

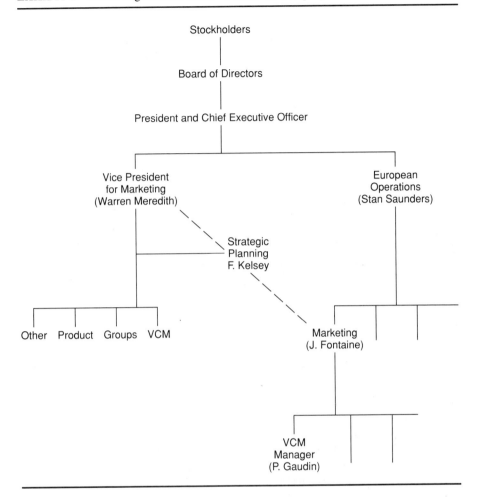

a. To dwell on the successful long-term relationship that had already been built between Reliant and Pacific Oil, and to emphasize the value of that relationship for the success of both companies.

b. To emphasize all of the projections that predicted the worldwide shortage of VCM, and the desirability for Reliant to ensure that they would have a guaranteed supplier.

c. To point out all of the ways that Pacific had "gone out of its way" in the past to ensure delivery and service.

d. To use both the past and future quality of the relationship to justify what might appear to be a high formula price.

e. To point out the ways that Pacific's competitors could not offer the same kind of service.

EXHIBIT 3   Partial Organization Chart—Reliant Chemical Company

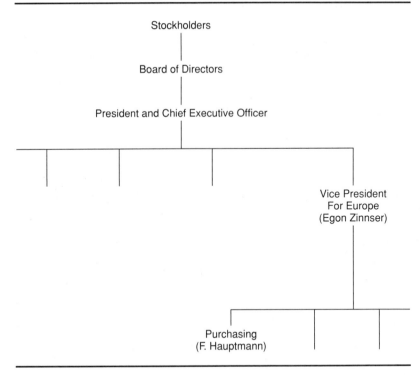

Over the next six months, Gaudin and Fontaine, independently and together, made a number of trips to Brussels to visit Reliant executives. In addition, several members of Pacific's senior management visited Brussels and paid courtesy calls on Reliant management. The net result was a very favorable contract for Pacific Oil, signed by both parties on October 24, 1982. The basic contract, to extend from January 1983 to December 1987 , is represented as Exhibit 5 on pages 666 through 669.

A CHANGED PERSPECTIVE

In December of 1984, Fontaine and Gaudin sat down to their traditional end-of-year review of all existing chemical contracts. As a matter of course, the Reliant VCM contract came under review. Although everything had been proceeding very smoothly, the prospects for the near and long-term future were obviously less clear, for the following reasons:

1. Both men reviewed the data that they had been receiving from corporate headquarters, as well as published projections of the supply situation for various chemicals over the next 10 years. It was clear that the basic supply-demand situation on VCM was changing. (Exhibit 6.) While the market was currently "tight"—the favorable supply situation that had existed for Pacific when the

EXHIBIT 4

MEMORANDUM

TO: All VCM Marketing Managers
FROM: F. Kelsey, Strategic Planning Division
RE: Worldwide VCM Supply/Demand Projections
DATE: January 17, 1982

CONFIDENTIAL—FOR YOUR EYES ONLY

Here are the data from 1980 and 1981, and the five-year projections that I promised you at our last meeting. As you can see, the market is tight, and is projected to get tighter. I hope you will find this useful in your marketing efforts—let me know if I can supply more detailed information.

Year	Demand Total Projected Demand (in MM Pounds)	Supply Plant Capacities	Operating Rates to Meet Demand (percent)
1980	4,040	5,390	75%
1981	4,336	5,390	80
1982	5,100	6,600	77
1983	5,350	6,600	81
1984	5,550	6,600	83
1985	5,650	7,300	75
1986	5,750	7,300	78

Reliant contract was first negotiated—the supply of VCM was expected to expand rapidly over the next few years. Several of Pacific's competitors had announced plans for the construction of VCM manufacturing facilities that were expected to come on line in 20–30 months.

2. Fontaine and Gaudin knew that Reliant was probably aware of this situation as well. As a result, they would probably anticipate the change in the supply-demand situation as an opportunity to pursue a more favorable price, with the possible threat that they would be willing to change suppliers if the terms were not favorable enough. (Although rebuilding a pipeline is no simple matter, it clearly could be done, and had been, when the terms were sufficiently favorable to justify it.)

3. Fontaine was aware that in a situation where the market turned from one of high demand to excess supply, it was necessary to make extra efforts to maintain and "re-sign" all major current customers. A few large customers (100 million pounds a year and over) dominated the marketplace, and a single customer defection in an oversupplied market could cause major headaches for marketing and sales. It would simply be impossible to find another customer with demands of that magnitude; a number of smaller customers would have to be found, while Pacific would also have to compete with spot market prices that would cut profits to the bone.

EXHIBIT 5 Agreement of Sale

This Agreement, entered into this <u>24th</u> day of <u>October</u>, <u>1982</u>, between <u>Pacific Oil Company</u>, hereinafter called Seller, and <u>Reliant Chemical Company of Europe</u>, hereinafter called Buyer.

WITNESSETH:

Seller agrees to sell and deliver and Buyer agrees to purchase and receive commodity (hereinafter called "product") under the terms and conditions set forth below.

1. Product: Vinyl Chloride Monomer

2. Quality: ASTM requirements for polymer-grade product

3. Quantity: 1983: 150 million pounds
             1984: 160 million pounds
             1985: 170 million pounds
             1986: 185 million pounds
             1987: 200 million pounds

4. Period: Contract shall extend from January 1, 1983 and extent until December 31, 1987, and evergreen thereafter, unless terminated within 180 days prior notification at the end of each calendar year, but not before December 31, 1987.

5. Price: See Contract formula price.

6. Payment Terms:
    a. Net <u>30 days</u>.
    b. All payments shall be made in United States dollars without discount or deduction, unless otherwise noted, by wire transfer at Seller's option, to a bank account designated by Seller. Invoices not paid on due date will be subject to a delinquency finance charge of 1 percent per month.
    c. If at any time the financial responsibility of Buyer shall become impaired or unsatisfactory to Seller, cash payment on delivery or satisfactory security may be required. A failure to pay any amount may, at the option of the Seller, terminate this contract as to further deliveries. No forebearance, course of dealing, or prior payment shall affect this right of Seller.

7. Price Change:

   The price specified in this Agreement may be changed by Seller on the first day of any calendar *half-year* by written notice sent to the Buyer not less than thirty (30) days prior to the effective date of change. Buyer gives Seller written notice of objection to such change at least ten (10) days prior to the effective date of change. Buyer's failure to serve Seller with written notice of objection thereto prior to the effective date thereof shall be considered acceptance of such change. If Buyer gives such notice of objection and Buyer and Seller fail to agree on such change prior to the effective date thereof, this Agreement and the obligations of Seller and Buyer hereunder shall terminate with respect to the unshipped portion of the Product governed by it. Seller has the option immediately to cancel this contract upon written notice to Buyer, to continue to sell hereunder at the same price and terms which were in effect at the time Seller gave notice of change, or to suspend performance under this contract while pricing is being resolved. If Seller desires to revise the price, freight allowance or terms of payment pursuant to this agreement, but is restricted to any extent against doing so by reason of any law, governmental decree, order or regulation, or if the price, freight allowance or terms of payment then in effect under this contract are nullified or reduced by reason of any law, governmental decree, order or regulation, Seller shall have the right to cancel this contract upon fifteen (15) days written notice to purchaser.

EXHIBIT 5   *(continued)*

8. Measurements:

Seller's determinations, unless proven to be erroneous, shall be accepted as conclusive evidence of the quantity of Product delivered hereunder. Credit will not be allowed for shortages of ½ of 1 percent or less of the quantity and overages of ½ of 1 percent or less of the quantity will be waived. The total amount of shortages or overages will be credited or billed when quantities are greater and such differences are substantiated. Measurements of weight and volume shall be according to procedures and criteria standard for such determinations.

9. Shipments and Delivery:

Buyer shall give Seller annual or quarterly forecasts of its expected requirements as Seller may from time to time request. Buyer shall give Seller reasonably advanced notice for each shipment which shall include date of delivery and shipping instructions. Buyer shall agree to take deliveries in approximately equal monthly quantities, except as may be otherwise provided herein. In the event that Buyer fails to take the quantity specified or the pro rata quantity in any month, Seller may, at its option, in addition to other rights and remedies, cancel such shipments or parts thereof.

10. Purchase Requirements:

   a. If during any consecutive three-month period, Buyer for any reason (but not for reasons of force majeure as set forth in Section 13) takes less than 90 percent of the average monthly quantity specified, or the prorated minimum monthly quantity then applicable to such period under Section 13, Seller may elect to charge Buyer a penalty charge for failure to take the average monthly quantity or prorated minimum monthly quantity.

   b. If, during any consecutive three-month period, Buyer, for any reason (but not, however, for reasons of force majeure as set forth in Section 13) takes Product in quantities less than that equal to at least one half of the average monthly quantity specified or the prorated minimum monthly quantity originally applicable to such period under Section 13, Seller may elect to terminate this agreement.

   c. It is the Seller's intent not to unreasonably exercise its right under *(a)* or *(b)* in the event of adverse economic and business conditions in general.

   d. Notice of election by Seller under *(a)* or *(b)* shall be given within 30 days after the end of the applicable three-month period, and the effective date of termination shall be 30 days after the date of said notice.

11. Detention Policy:

Seller may, from time to time, specify free unloading time allowances for its transportation equipment. Buyer shall be liable to the Transportation Company for all demurrage charges made by the Transportation Company, for railcars, trucks, tanks, or barges held by Buyer beyond the free unloading time.

12. Force Majeure:

Neither party shall be liable to the other for failure or delay in performance hereunder to the extent that such failure or delay is due to war, fire, flood, strike, lockout, or other labor trouble, accident, breakdown of equipment or machinery, riot, act, request, or suggestion of governmental authority, act of God, or other contingencies beyond the control of the affected party which interfere with the production or transportation of the material covered by this Agreement or with the supply of any raw material (whether or not the source of supply was in existence or contemplated at the time of this Agreement) or energy source used in

EXHIBIT 5   *(continued)*

connection therewith, or interfere with Buyer's consumption of such material, provided that in no event shall Buyer be relieved of the obligation to pay in full for material delivered hereunder. Without limitation on the foregoing, neither party shall be required to remove any cause listed above or replace the affected source of supply or facility if it shall involve additional expense or departure from its normal practices. If any of the events specified in this paragraph shall have occurred, Seller shall have the right to allocate in a fair and reasonable manner among its customers and Seller's own requirements any supplies of material Seller has available for delivery at the time or for the duration of the event.

13. Materials and Energy Supply:

If, for reasons beyond reasonable commercial control, Seller's supply of product to be delivered hereunder shall be limited due to continued availability of necessary raw materials and energy supplies, Seller shall have the right (without liability) to allocate to the Buyer a portion of such product on such basis as Seller deems equitable. Such allocation shall normally be that percent of Seller's total internal and external commitments which are committed to Buyer as related to the total quantity available from Seller's manufacturing facilities.

14. Disclaimer:

Seller makes no warranty, express or implied, concerning the product furnished hereunder other than it shall be of the quality and specifications stated herein. Any implied warranty of FITNESS is expressly excluded and to the extent that it is contrary to the foregoing sentence; any implied warranty of MERCHANTABILITY is expressly excluded. Any recommendations made by Seller makes no warranty of results to be obtained. Buyer assumes all responsibility and liability for loss or damage resulting from the handling or use of said product. In no event shall Seller be liable for any special, indirect or consequential damages, irrespective of whether caused or allegedly caused by negligence.

15. Taxes:

Any tax, excise fee, or other charge or increase thereof upon the production, storage, withdrawal, sale, or transportation of the product sold hereunder, or entering into the cost of such product, imposed by any proper authority becoming effective after the date hereof, shall be added to the price herein provised and shall be paid by the Buyer.

16. Assignment and Resale:

This contract is not transferable or assignable by Buyer without the written consent of Seller. The product described hereunder, in the form and manner provided by the Seller, may not be assigned or resold without prior written consent of the Seller.

17. Acceptance:

Acceptance hereof must be without qualification and Seller will not be bound by any different terms and conditions contained in any other communication.

18. Waiver of Breach:

No waiver by Seller or Buyer of any breach of any of the terms and conditions contained in this Agreement shall be construed as a waiver or any subsequent breach of the same or any other term or condition.

19. Termination:

If any provision of this agreement is or becomes violate of any law, or any rule, order or regulation issued thereunder, Seller shall have the right upon notice to Buyer, to terminate the Agreement in its entirety.

EXHIBIT 5   *(concluded)*

20. Governing Law:

The construction of this Agreement and the rights and obligations of the parties hereunder shall be governed by the laws of the State of New York.

21. Special Provisions:

BUYER: SELLER:

_____   PACIFIC OIL CORPORATION
             (firm)

By:_____   By:_____

Title: Senior Purchasing Manager   Title: Marketing Vice President

Date:_____   Date:_____

4. In a national product development meeting back in the States several weeks prior, Fontaine had learned of plans by Pacific to expand and diversify its own product line into VCM derivatives. There was serious talk of Pacific manufacturing its own PVC for distribution under the Pacific name, as well as the manufacture and distribution of various PVC products. Should Pacific decide to enter these businesses, not only would they require a significant amount of the VCM now being sold on the external market, but Pacific would probably decide that as a matter of principle, it would not want to be in the position of supplying a product competitor with the raw materials to manufacture his product line, unless the formula price were extremely favorable.

As they reviewed these factors, Gaudin and Fontaine realized that they needed to take action. They pondered the alternatives.

A NEW CONTRACT IS PROPOSED

As a result of their evaluation of the situation in December of 1984, Fontaine and Gaudin decided to proceed on two fronts. First, they would approach Reliant with the intent of reopening negotiation on the current VCM contract. They would propose to renegotiate the current agreement, with an interest toward extending the contract five years from the point of agreement on contract terms. Second, they would contact those people at corporate headquarters in New York who were evaluating Pacific's alternatives for new product development, and inform them of the nature of the situation. The sooner a determination could be made on the product development strategies, the sooner the Pacific office would know how to proceed on the Reliant contract.

EXHIBIT 6

MEMORANDUM

TO: All VCM Marketing Managers
FROM: F. Kelsey, Strategic Planning Division
RE: Worldwide VCM/Supply/Demand Projections
DATE: December 9, 1984

CONFIDENTIAL—FOR YOUR EYES ONLY

This will confirm and summarize data that we discussed at the national marketing meeting last month in Atlanta. At that time, I indicated to you that the market projections we made several years ago have changed drastically. In early 1983, a number of our competitors announced their intentions to enter the VCM business over the next five years. Several facilities are now under construction, and are expected to come on line in late 1986 and early 1987. As a result, we expect a fairly significant shift in the supply/demand relationship over the next few years.

I hope you will give this appropriate consideration in your long range planning effort. Please contact me if I can be helpful.

Year	Demand Total Projected Demand (in MM pounds)	Supply Plant Capacities	Operating Rates to Meet Demand (percent)
1982	5,127 (actual)	6,600	78%
1983	5,321 (actual)	6,600	81
1984	5,572 (rev. 11/84)	6,600	84
1985	5,700	7,300	78
1986	5,900	8,450	70
1987	6,200	9,250	64
1988	6,500	9,650	67
1989	7,000	11,000	63

Gaudin contacted Frederich Hauptmann, the senior purchasing manager for Reliant Chemicals in Europe. Hauptmann had assumed the position as purchasing manager approximately four weeks earlier, after having served in a purchasing capacity for a large German steel company. Gaudin arranged a meeting for early January in Hauptmann's office. After getting acquainted over lunch, Gaudin briefed Hauptmann on the history of Reliant's contractual relationships with Pacific Oil. Gaudin made clear that Pacific had been very pleased with the relationship that had been maintained. He said that Pacific was concerned about the future, and about maintaining the relationship with Reliant for a long time to come. Hauptmann stated that he understood that the relationship had been a very productive one, too, and also hoped that the two companies could continue to work together in the future. Bouyed by Hauptmann's apparent enthusiasm and relative pleasure with the current agreement, Gaudin said that he and Jean Fontaine, his boss, had recently been reviewing all contracts. Even though the existing Pacific-Reliant VCM agreement had three years to run, Pacific felt that it was never too soon to begin thinking about the long-term future. In order to ensure that Reliant would be assured of a continued supply of VCM, under the favorable terms and working relationship that was already well established, Pacific hoped that Reliant might be willing to begin talks now for contract extension past December 31, 1987. Hauptmann said that he would be willing to consider it, but needed to consult other people in the Brussels office, as well as senior executives at Corporate headquarters in Chicago. Hauptmann promised to contact Gaudin when he had the answer.

By mid-February, Hauptmann cabled Gaudin that Reliant was indeed willing to begin renegotiation of the current agreement, with interest in extending it for the future. He suggested that Gaudin and Fontaine come to Brussels for a preliminary meeting in early March. Hauptmann also planned to invite Egon Zinnser, the regional vice president of Reliant's European operations and Hauptmann's immediate superior.

MARCH 10

Light snow drifted onto the runway of the Brussels airport as the plane landed. Fontaine and Gaudin had talked about the Reliant contract, and the upcoming negotiations, for most of the trip. They had decided that while they did not expect the negotiations to be a complete "pushover," they expected no significant problems or stumbling points in the deliberations. They thought Reliant negotiators would routinely question some of the coefficients that were used to compute the formula price as well as to renegotiate some of the minimum quantity commitments. They felt that the other elements of the contract would be routinely discussed, but that no dramatic changes should be expected.

After a pleasant lunch with Hauptmann and Zinnser, the four men sat down to review the current VCM contract. They reviewed and restated much of what Gaudin and Hauptmann had done at their January meeting. Fontaine stated that Pacific Oil was looking toward the future, and hoping that it could maintain Reliant as a customer. Zinnser responded that Reliant had indeed been pleased by the contract as well, but that it was also concerned about the future. They felt that Pacific's basic formula price on VCM, while fair, might not remain competitive in the long-run future. Zinnser said that he had already had discussions with two other major chemical firms who were planning new VCM manufacturing facilities, and that one or both of these firms were due to come on line in the next 24–30 months. Zinnser wanted to make sure that Pacific could remain competitive with other firms in the marketplace. Fontaine responded that it was Pacific's full intention to remain completely competitive, whether it be in market price or in the formula price.

Zinnser said he was pleased by this reply, and took this as an indication that Pacific would be willing to evaluate and perhaps adjust some of the factors that were now being used to determine the VCM formula price. He then presented a rather elaborate proposal for adjusting the respective coefficients of these factors. The net result of these adjustments would be to reduce the effective price of VCM by approximately 2 cents per pound. It did not take long for Fontaine and Gaudin to calculate that this would be a net reduction of approximately $4 million per year. Fontaine stated that they would have to take the proposal back to Paris for intensive study and analysis. The men shook hands, and Fontaine and Gaudin headed back to the airport.

Throughout the spring, Gaudin and Hauptmann exchanged several letters and telephone calls. They met once at the Paris airport when Hauptmann stopped over on a trip to the States, and once in Zurich when both men discovered that they were going to be there on business the same day. By May 15, they had agreed on a revision of the formula price that would adjust the price downward by almost one cent per pound. Gaudin, relieved that the price had finally been established, reported back to Fontaine that significant progress was being made. Gaudin expected that the remaining issues could be closed up in a few weeks, and a new contract signed.

MAY 27

Hauptmann contacted Gaudin to tell him that Reliant was now willing to talk about the remaining issues in the contract. The two men met in early June. Gaudin opened the discussion by saying that now that the formula price had been agreed upon, he hoped that Reliant would be willing to agree to extend the contract five years from the point of signing. Hauptmann replied that Reliant had serious reservations about committing the company to a five-year contract extension. He cited the rapid fluctuations in the demand, pricing structure, and competition of Reliant's various product lines, particularly in the construction industry, as well as what appeared to be a changing perspective in the overall supply of VCM. Quite frankly, Hauptmann said, Reliant didn't want to be caught in a long-term commitment to Pacific if the market price of VCM was likely to drop in the foreseeable future. As a result, Reliant only wanted to make a commitment for a two-year contract renewal.

Gaudin tried to give Hauptmann a number of assurances about the continued integrity of the market. He also said that if changing market prices were a concern for Reliant, Pacific Oil would be happy to attempt to make adjustments in other parts of the contract to ensure protection against dramatic changes in either the market price or the demand for Reliant's product lines. But Hauptmann was adamant. Gaudin said he would have to talk to Fontaine and others in Paris before he could agree to only a two-year contract.

The two men talked several times on the telephone over the next two months and met once in Paris to discuss contract length. On August 17, in a quick 45-minute meeting in Orly Airport, Gaudin and Hauptmann agreed to a three-year contract renewal. They also agreed to meet in early September to discuss remaining contract issues.

SEPTEMBER 10

Hauptmann met Gaudin and Fontaine in Pacific's Paris office. Hauptmann stressed that he and Zinnser were very pleased by the formula price and three-year contract duration that had been agreed to thus far. Fontaine echoed a similar satisfaction on behalf of Pacific, and stated that they expected a long and productive relationship with Reliant. Fontaine stressed, however, that Pacific felt it was most important to them to complete the contract negotiations as quickly as possible, in order to adequately plan for product and market development in the future. Hauptmann agreed, saying that this was in Reliant's best interest as well. He felt that there were only a few minor issues that remained to be discussed before the contract could be signed.

Fontaine inquired as to what those issues were. Hauptmann said that the most important one to Reliant was the minimum quantity requirements, stipulating the minimum amount that Reliant had to purchase each year. Gaudin said that based on the projections for the growth of the PVC and fabricated PVC products over the next few years, and patterns established by past contracts, it was Pacific's assumption that Reliant would want to increase their quantity commitments by a minimum of 10 percent each year. Based on current minimums stipulated in the current contract, Gaudin expected that Reliant would want to purchase at least 220 million pounds in year 1,240 million pounds in year 2, and 265 million pounds in year 3.

Hauptmann responded that Reliant's projections were very different. The same kind of uncertainty that had led to Reliant's concern about the term of the contract also contributed to a caution about significantly overextending themselves on a minimum quantity commitment. In fact, Reliant's own predictions were that they were likely to take less than the minimum in the current year ("underlifting," in the parlance of the industry), and that if they did so, they would incur almost a $1 million debt to Pacific. Conservative projections for the following year (1987) projected a similar deficit, but Reliant hoped that business would pick up and that the minimum quantities would be lifted. As a result, Hauptmann and Zinnser felt that it would be in Reliant's best interest to freeze minimum quantity requirements for the next two years—at 200 million pounds—and increase the minimum to 210 million pounds for the third year. Of course, Reliant *expected* that, and most likely, they would be continuing to purchase much more than the specified minimums. But given the uncertainty of the future, Reliant did not want to get caught if the economy and the market truly turned sour.

Fontaine and Gaudin were astonished at the conservative projections Hauptmann was making. They tried, in numerous ways, to convince Hauptmann that his minimums were ridiculously low, and that the PVC products were bound to prosper far more than Hauptmann seemed willing to admit. But Hauptmann was adamant, and left Paris saying he needed to consult Zinnser and others in Brussels and the States before he could revise his minimum quantity estimates upward. Due to the pressure of other activities and vacation schedules, Gaudin and Hauptmann did not talk again until late October. Finally, on November 19, the two men agreed to a minimum quantity purchase schedule of 205 million pounds in the first year of the contract, 210 million pounds in the second year, and 220 million pounds in the third year. Moreover, Pacific agreed to waive any previous underlifting charges that may be incurred under the current contract when the new contract was signed.

OCTOBER 24

Jean Fontaine returned to Paris from meetings in New York and a major market development meeting held by senior Pacific executives at Hilton Head. After a number of delays due to conflicting market research, changes in senior management, as well as the general uncertainty in the petroleum and chemical markets, Pacific had decided not to develop its own product lines for either PVC or fabricated products. The decision was largely based on the conclusion—more "gut feel" than hard fact—that entry into these new markets was unwise at a time when much greater problems faced Pacific and the petrochemicals industry in general. Fontaine had argued strenuously that the VCM market was rapidly going soft, and that failure to create its own products lines would leave Pacific Oil in an extremely poor position to market one of its basic products. Fontaine was told that his position was appreciated, but that he and other chemical marketing people would simply have to develop new markets and customers for the product. Privately, Fontaine churned on the fact that it had taken senior executives almost a year to make the decision, while valuable time was being lost in developing the markets; but he wisely decided to bite his tongue and vent his frustration on 36 holes of golf. On the return flight to Paris, he read about Pacific's decision in the October 23rd issue of *The Wall Street Journal,* and ordered a double martini to soothe his nerves.

DECEMBER 14

Fontaine and Gaudin went to Brussels to meet with Hauptmann and Zinnser. The Pacific executives stressed that it was of the utmost importance for Pacific Oil to try to wrap up the contract as quickly as possible—almost a year had passed in deliberations, and although Pacific was not trying to place the "blame" on anyone, it was most concerned that the negotiations be settled as soon as possible.

Zinnser emphasized that he, too, was concerned about completing the negotiations quickly. Both he and Hauptmann were extremely pleased by the agreements that had been reached so far, and felt that there was no question that a final contract signing was imminent. The major issues of price, minimum quantities and contract duration had been solved. In their minds, what remained were only a few minor technical items in contract language. Some minor discussion of each of these should wrap things up in a few weeks.

Fontaine asked what the issues were. Zinnser began by stating that Reliant had become concerned by the way that the delivery pipeline was being metered. As currently set up, the pipeline fed from Pacific's production facility in Antwerp, Belgium, to Reliant's refinery. Pacific had built the line, and was in charge of maintaining it. Meters had been installed at the exit flange of the pipeline, and Reliant was paying the metered amount to Pacific. Zinnser said that some spot-checking by Reliant at the manufacturing facility seemed to indicate that they may not be receiving all they were being billed for. They were not questioning the integrity of the meters or the meter readers, but felt that since the pipe was a number of years old, it may have developed leaks. Zinnser felt that it was inappropriate for Reliant to absorb the cost of VCM that was not reaching its facility. They, therefore, proposed that Pacific install meters directly outside of the entry flange of Reliant's manufacturing facility, and that Reliant only be required to pay the meter directly outside the plant.

Fontaine was astonished. In the first place, he said, this was the first time he had heard any complaint about the pipeline or the need to recalibrate the meters. Second, if the pipeline was leaking, Pacific would want to repair it, but that it would be impossible to do so until spring. Finally, while the meters themselves were not prohibitively expensive, moving them would mean some interruption of service and definitely be costly to Pacific. Fontaine said he wanted to check with the maintenance personnel at Antwerp to find out whether they could corroborate such leaks.

Fontaine was unable to contact the operating manager at Antwerp, or anyone else who could confirm that leaks may have been detected. Routine inspection of the pipeline had been subcontracted to a firm which had sophisticated equipment for monitoring such things, and executives of the firm could not be reached for several days. Fontaine tried to raise other contract issues with Zinnser, but Zinnser said that this was his most important concern, and this issue needed to be resolved before the others could be finalized. Fontaine agreed to find out more about the situation, and bring the information to the next meeting. With the Christmas and New Year holidays approaching, the four men could not schedule another meeting until January 9.

JANUARY MEETINGS

The January 9 meeting was postponed until January 20, due to the death of Mr. Hauptmann's mother. The meeting was rescheduled for a time when Hauptmann needed to be in Geneva, and Gaudin agreed to meet him there.

Gaudin stated that the investigation of the pipeline had discovered no evidence of significant discharge. There were traces of *minor* leaks in the line, but they did not appear to be serious, and it was currently impossible to determine what percentage of the product may be escaping. The most generous estimate given to Gaudin had been 0.1 percent of the daily consumption. Hauptmann stated that their own spot monitoring showed it was considerably more, and that Reliant would feel infinitely more comfortable if the new metering system could be installed.

Gaudin had obtained estimates for the cost of remetering before he left Paris. It was estimated that the new meters could be installed for approximately $20,000. Tracing and fixing the leaks (if they existed) could not be done until April or May, and may run as much as $50,000 if leaks turned out to be located at some extremely difficult access points. After four hours of debating with Hauptmann in a small conference room off the lobby of the Geneva Hilton, Gaudin agreed that Pacific would remeter the pipeline.

Hauptmann said that as far as he was concerned, all of his issues had been settled, however, he thought Zinnser might have one or two other issues to raise. Hauptmann said that he would report back to Zinnser, and contact Gaudin as soon as possible if another meeting was necessary. Gaudin, believing that Pacific was finally beginning to see the light at the end of the tunnel, left for Paris.

JANUARY 23

Hauptmann called Gaudin and said that he and Zinnser had thoroughly reviewed the contract, and that there were a few small issues of contract language which Zinnser wanted to clarify. He said that he would prefer not to discuss them over the telephone, and suggested that since he was going to be in Paris on February 3, they meet at the Pacific offices. Gaudin agreed.

Fontaine and Gaudin met Hauptmann on February 3. Hauptmann informed them that he felt Reliant had been an outstanding customer for Pacific in the past, and that it probably was one of Pacific's biggest customers for VCM. Fontaine and Gaudin agreed, affirming the important role that Reliant was playing in Pacific's VCM market. Hauptmann said that he and Zinnser had been reviewing the contract, and were concerned that the changing nature of the VCM market might significantly affect Reliant's overall position in the marketplace as a purchaser. More specifically, Reliant was concerned that the decline in market and price for VCM in the future might endanger its own position in the market, since Pacific might sign contracts with other purchasers for lower formula prices than were currently being awarded to Reliant. Since Reliant was such an outstanding customer of Pacific—and Fontaine and Gaudin had agreed to that—it seemed to Reliant that Pacific Oil had an "obligation" to write two additional clauses into the contract that would protect Reliant in the event of further slippage in the VCM market. The first was a "favored nations" clause, stipulating that if Pacific negotiated with another purchaser a more favorable price for VCM than Reliant was receiving now, Pacific would guarantee that Reliant would receive that price as well. The second was a "meet competition" clause, guaranteeing that Pacific would willingly meet any lower price on VCM offered by a competitor, in order to maintain the Reliant relationship. Hauptmann argued that the "favored nations" clause was protection for Reliant, since it stipulated that Pacific valued the relationship enough to offer the best possible terms to Reliant. The "meet competition" clause, he argued, was clearly advantageous for Pacific since it ensured that Reliant would have no incentive to shift suppliers as the market changed.

Fontaine and Gaudin debated the terms at length with Hauptmann, stressing the potential costliness of these agreements for Pacific. Hauptmann responded by referring to the costliness that the absence of the terms could have for Reliant, and suggesting that perhaps the Pacific people were truly *not* as interested in a successful long-term relationship as they had been advocating. Fontaine said that he needed to get clearance from senior management in New York before he could agree to these terms, and said that he would get back to Hauptmann within a few days when the information was available.

FRANK KELSEY'S VIEW

Frank Kelsey was strategic planning manager, a staff role in the New York offices of the Pacific Oil Corporation. Kelsey had performed a number of roles for the company in his 12 years of work experience. Using the chemistry background he had achieved in college, Kelsey worked for six years in the research and development department of Pacific's Chemical Division, before deciding to enter the management ranks. He transferred to the marketing area, spent three years in chemical marketing, and then assumed responsibilities in marketing planning and development. He moved to the strategic planning department four years ago.

In late 1985, Kelsey was working in a staff capacity as an adviser to the executive product vice president of the Pacific Oil Company. Pacific had developed a matrix organization. Reporting relationships were determined by business areas and by regional operating divisions within Pacific Oil. Warren Meredith, the executive vice president, had responsibility for monitoring the worldwide sale and distribution of VCM. Jean Fontaine reported to Meredith on all issues regarding the overall sale and marketing of VCM, and reported to the president of Pacific Oil in Europe, Stan

Saunders, on major issues regarding the management of the regional chemicals business in Europe. In general, Fontaine's primary working relationship was with Meredith; Saunders only became involved in day-to-day decisions as an arbiter of disputes or interpreter of major policy decisions.

As the negotiations with Reliant evolved, Meredith became distressed by the apparent turn that they were taking. He called in Frank Kelsey to review the situation. Kelsey knew that the VCM marketing effort for Pacific was going to face significant problems following the company's decision to stay out of the PVC/fabrication business. Moreover, his dominant experience with Pacific in recent years had been in the purchasing and marketing operations, and knew how difficult it would be for the company to maintain a strong negotiation position in VCM contracts.

Meredith asked Kelsey to meet with Fontaine and Gaudin in Paris, and review the current status of negotiations on the Reliant contract. While Kelsey could only act in an advisory capacity—Fontaine and Gaudin were free to accept or reject any advice that was offered, since they were the ones that had to "live with" the contract—Meredith told Kelsey to offer whatever services the men would accept.

Kelsey flew to Paris shortly after New Year's Day 1986. He met with Fontaine and Gaudin, and they reviewed in detail what had happened in the Reliant contract negotiations over the past year. Kelsey listened, asked a lot of questions, and didn't say much. He felt that offering "advice" to the men was premature, and perhaps even unwise; Fontaine and Gaudin seemed very anxious about the negotiations, and felt that the new contract would be sealed within a month. Moreover, they seemed to resent Kelsey's visit, and clearly didn't want to share more than the minimum amount of information. Kelsey returned to New York, and briefed Meredith on the state of affairs.

When Fontaine called Meredith for "clearance" to give Reliant both "favored nations" and "meet competition" clauses in the new contract, Meredith immediately called Kelsey. The two of them went back through the history of events in the negotiation, and realized the major advantages that Reliant had gained by its negotiation tactics.

Meredith called Fontaine back and advised against granting the clauses in the contract. Fontaine said that Hauptmann was adamant, and that he was afraid the entire negotiation was going to collapse over a minor point in contract language. Meredith said he still thought it was a bad idea to make the concession. Fontaine said he thought he needed to consult Saunders, the European president of Pacific Oil, just to make sure.

Two days later, Saunders called Meredith and said that he had complete faith in Fontaine, and Fontaine's ability to determine what was necessary to make a contract work. If Fontaine felt that "favored nations" and "meet competition" clauses were necessary, he trusted Fontaine's judgment that the clauses could not cause significant adverse harm to Pacific Oil over the next few years. As a result, he had given Fontaine the go-ahead to agree to these clauses in the new contract.

MARCH 11

It was a dark and stormy night, March 11, 1986. Frank Kelsey was about to go to bed when the telephone rang. It was Jean Fontaine. Kelsey had not heard from Fontaine since their meeting in Paris. Meredith had told Kelsey about the discussion with Saunders, and he had assumed that Fontaine had gone ahead and conceded on the two contract clauses that had been discussed. He thought the contract was about to be wrapped up, but he hadn't heard for sure.

The violent rainstorm outside disrupted the telephone transmission, and Kelsey had trouble hearing Fontaine. Fontaine said that he had appreciated Kelsey's visit in January. Fontaine was calling to ask Kelsey's advice. They had just come from a meeting with Hauptmann. Hauptmann and Zinnser had reported that recent news from Reliant's corporate headquarters in Chicago projected significant downturns in the sale of a number of Reliant's PVC products in the European market. While Reliant thought it could ride out the downturn, they were very concerned about their future obligations under the Pacific contract. Since Reliant and Pacific had already settled on minimum quantity amounts, Reliant wanted the contractual right to resell the product if it could not use the minimum amount.

Kelsey tried to control his emotions as he thought about this negative turn of events in the Reliant negotiations. He strongly advised against agreeing to the clause, saying that it could put Pacific in an extremely poor position. Fontaine debated the point, saying he really thought Reliant might default on the whole contract if they didn't get resale rights. "I can't see where agreeing to the right to resale is a big thing, Frank, particularly given the size of this contract and its value to me and Pacific."

Kelsey:

"Look, you asked for my advice, and I gave it to you. If I were you, I wouldn't make any more concessions. Agreeing to a resale clause could create a whole lot of unforeseen problems. At this point I think it's also the principle of the thing!"

Fontaine:

"Who cares about principles at a time like this! It's my neck that's on the line if this Reliant contract goes under! I'll have over 200 million pounds of VCM a year to eat in an oversupplied market! It's my neck that's on the line, not yours! How in the world can you talk to me about "principle" at this point?"

Kelsey:

"Calm down, Jean! I can see your point of view! I appreciate the pressures on you, but I really don't like the looks of it from this end. Keep in touch—let me ask others down at the office what they think, and I'll call you next week."

Kelsey hung up the telephone, and stared out of the window at the rain. He could certainly empathize with Fontaine's position—the man's neck was on the block. As he mentally reviewed the two-year history of the Reliant negotiations, Kelsey wondered how they had gotten to this point, and whether anyone could have done things differently. He also wondered what to do about the resale clause, which appeared to be the final sticking point in the deliberations. Would acquiescing to a resale clause for Reliant be a problem to Pacific Oil? Kelsey knew he had to take action soon.

CASE STUDY 3

Petrochemical Supply Contracts: A Technical Note

Supply contracts between chemical manufacturing/refining companies and purchasing companies are fairly standard in the industry trade. They are negotiated between supplier and purchaser in order to protect both parties against major fluctuations in supply and demand. Any purchaser wishing to obtain a limited amount of a particular product could always approach any one of a number of chemical manufacturing firms and obtain the product at "market price." The market price is controlled by the competitive supply and demand for the particular product on any given day. But purchasers want to be assured of a long-term supply and do not want to be subject to the vagaries of price fluctuation; similarly, manufacturers want to be assured of product outlets in order to adequately plan manufacturing schedules. Long-term contracts protect both parties against these fluctuations.

A supply contract is usually a relatively standard document, often condensed to one page. The major "negotiable" elements of the contract, on the "front side" of the document, include the price, quantity, product quality, contract duration, delivery point, and credit terms (see Exhibit 1 for a sample blank contract). The remainder ("back side") of the contract is filled with traditionally fixed legal terminology that govern the conditions under which the contract will be maintained. While the items are seldom changed, they may be altered or waived as part of the negotiated agreement.

The primary component of a long-term contract is the price. In the early years of the petrochemical industry, the raw product was metered by the supplier (either in liquid or gaseous form) and sold to the purchaser. As the industry became more competitive, as prices rose rapidly, and as the products developed from petrochemical supplies (called "feedstocks") became more sophisticated, pricing became a significantly more complex process. Most contemporary contract prices are determined by an elaborate calculation called a "formula price," composed of several elements:

> *1.* Feedstock Characteristics. Petrochemical feedstock supplies differ in the chemical composition and molecular structure of the crude oil. Differences in feedstocks will significantly affect the refining procedures and operating efficiency of the refinery that manufactures a product, as well as their relative usefulness to particular purchasers. While some chemical products may be drawn

---

This note was prepared by Roy J. Lewicki for use in executive seminars.

EXHIBIT 1   Agreement of Sale

This Agreement, entered into this _____ day of _____ , _____ , between <u>Pacific Oil Company</u>, hereinafter called Seller, and _____ , hereinafter called Buyer.

WITNESSETH:

Seller agrees to sell and deliver and Buyer agrees to purchase and receive commodity (hereinafter called "product") under the terms and conditions set forth below.

1. PRODUCT:

2. QUALITY:

3. QUANTITY:

4. PERIOD:

5. PRICE:

6. PAYMENT TERMS:

   (a) Net_____.

   (b) All payments shall be made in United States dollars without discount or deduction, unless otherwise noted, by wire transfer at Seller's option, to a bank account designated by Seller. Invoices not paid on due date will be subject to a delinquency finance charge of 1% per month.

   (c) If at any time the financial responsibility of Buyer shall become impaired or unsatisfactory to Seller, cash payment on delivery or satisfactory security may be required. A failure to pay any amount may, at the option of the Seller, terminate this contract as to further deliveries. No forebearance, course of dealing, or prior payment shall affect this right of Seller.

7. PRICE CHANGE:

   The price specified in this Agreement may be changed by Seller on the first day of any calendar _____ by written notice sent to the Buyer not less than thirty (30) days prior to the effective date of change. Buyer gives Seller written notice of objection to such change at least ten (10) days prior to the effective date of change. Buyer's failure to serve Seller with written notice of objection thereto prior to the effective date thereof shall be considered acceptance of such change. If Buyer gives such notice of objection and Buyer and Seller fail to agree on such change prior to the effective date thereof, this Agreement and the obligations of Seller and Buyer hereunder shall terminate with respect to the unshipped portion of the Product governed by it. Seller has the option immediately to cancel this contract upon written notice to Buyer, to continue to sell hereunder at the same price and terms which were in effect at the time Seller gave notice of change, or to suspend performance under this contract while pricing is being resolved. If Seller desires to revise the price, freight allowance or terms of payment pursuant to this agreement, but is restricted to any extent against doing so by reason of any law, governmental decree, order or regulation, or if the price, freight allowance or terms of payment then in effect under this contract are

EXHIBIT 1 *(continued)*

nullified or reduced by reason of any law, governmental decree, order or regulation, Seller shall have the right to cancel this contract upon fifteen (15) days written notice to purchaser.

8. MEASUREMENTS:

Seller's determinations, unless proven to be erroneous, shall be accepted as conclusive evidence of the quantity of Product delivered hereunder. Credit will not be allowed for shortages of ½ of 1% or less of the quantity and overages of ½ of 1% or less of the quantity will be waived. The total amount of shortages or overages will be credited or billed when quantities are greater and such differences are substantiated. Measurements of weight and volume shall be according to procedures and criteria standard for such determinations.

9. SHIPMENTS AND DELIVERY:

Buyer shall give Seller annual or quarterly forecasts of its expected requirements as Seller may from time to time request. Buyer shall give Seller reasonably advanced notice for each shipment which shall include date of delivery and shipping instructions. Buyer shall agree to take deliveries in approximately equal monthly quantities, except as may be otherwise provided herein. In the event that Buyer fails to take the quantity specified or the pro rata quantity in any month, Seller may, at its option, in addition to other rights and remedies, cancel such shipments or parts thereof.

10. PURCHASE REQUIREMENTS:

(a) If during any consecutive three month period, Buyer for any reason (but not for reasons of force majeure as set forth in Section 13) takes less than 90 percent of the average monthly quantity specified, or the prorated minimum monthly quantity then applicable to such period under Section 13, Seller may elect to charge Buyer a penalty charge for failure to take the average monthly quantity or prorated minimum monthly quantity.

(b) If, during any consecutive three month period, Buyer, for any reason (but not, however, for reasons of force majeure as set forth in Section 13) takes Product in quantities less than that equal to at least one half of the average monthly quantity specified or the prorated minimum monthly quantity originally applicable to such period under Section 13, Seller may elect to terminate this agreement.

(c) It is the Seller's intent not to unreasonably exercise its rights under (a) or (b) in the event of adverse economic and business conditions in general.

(d) Notice of election by Seller under (a) or (b) shall be given within 30 days after the end of the applicable three month period, and the effective date of termination shall be 30 days after the date of said notice.

11. DETENTION POLICY:

Seller may, from time to time, specify free unloading time allowances for its transportation equipment. Buyer shall be liable to the Transportation Company for all demurrage charges made by the Transportation Company, for railcars, trucks, tanks or barges held by Buyer beyond the free unloading time.

12. FORCE MAJEURE:

Neither party shall be liable to the other for failure or delay in performance hereunder to the extent that such failure or delay is due to war, fire, flood, strike, lockout, or other labor trouble, accident, breakdown of equipment or machinery, riot, act, request, or suggestion of governmental authority, act of God, or other contingencies beyond the control of the affected

EXHIBIT 1 *(continued)*

party which interfere with the production or transportation of the material covered by this Agreement or with the supply of any raw material (whether or not the source of supply was in existence or contemplated at the time of this Agreement) or energy source used in connection therewith, or interfere with Buyer's consumption of such material, provided that in no event shall Buyer be relieved of the obligation to pay in full for material delivered hereunder. Without limitation on the foregoing, neither party shall be required to remove any cause listed above or replace the affected source of supply or facility if it shall involve additional expense or departure from its normal practices. If any of the events specified in this paragraph shall have occurred, Seller shall have the right to allocate in a fair and reasonable manner among its customers and Seller's own requirements any supplies of material Seller has available for delivery at the time or for the duration of the event.

13. MATERIALS AND ENERGY SUPPLY:

If, for reasons beyond reasonable commercial control, Seller's supply of product to be delivered hereunder shall be limited due to continued availability of necessary allocate to the Buyer a portion of such product on such basis as Seller deems equitable. Such allocation shall normally be that percent of Seller's total internal and external commitments which are committed to Buyer as related to the total quantity available from Seller's manufacturing facilities.

14. DISCLAIMER:

Seller makes no warranty, express or implied, concerning the product furnished hereunder other than it shall be of the quality and specification stated herein. Any implied warranty of FITNESS is expressly excluded and to the extent that it is contrary to the foregoing sentence; any implied warranty of MERCHANTABILITY is expressly excluded. Any recommendations made by Seller makes no warranty of results to be obtained. Buyer assumes all responsibility and liability for loss or damage resulting from the handling or use of said product. In no event shall Seller be liable for any special, indirect or consequential damages, irrespective of whether caused or allegedly caused by negligence.

15. TAXES:

Any tax, excise fee or other charge or increase thereof upon the production, storage, withdrawal, sale or transportation of the product sold hereunder, or entering into the cost of such product, imposed by any proper authority becoming effective after the date hereof, shall be added to the price herein provided and shall be paid by the Buyer.

16. ASSIGNMENT AND RESALE:

This contract is not transferable or assignable by Buyer without the written consent of Seller. The product described hereunder, in the form and manner provided by the Seller, may not be assigned or resold without prior written consent of the Seller.

17. ACCEPTANCE:

Acceptance hereof must be without qualification and Seller will not be bound by any different terms and conditions contained in any other communication.

18. WAIVER OF BREACH:

No waiver by Seller or Buyer of any breach of any of the terms and conditions contained in this Agreement shall be construed as a waiver or any subsequent breach of the same or any other term or condition.

EXHIBIT 1   *(concluded)*

19. TERMINATION:

If any provision of this agreement is or becomes violate of any law, or any rule, order or regulation issued thereunder, Seller shall have the right upon notice to Buyer, to terminate the Agreement in its entirety.

20. GOVERNING LAW:

The construction of this Agreement and the rights and obligations of the parties hereunder shall be governed by the laws of the State of New York.

21. SPECIAL PROVISIONS:

BUYER: SELLER:
_____   PACIFIC OIL CORPORATION
            (firm)

By:_____   By:_____

Title:_____   Title:_____

Date:_____   Date:_____

from a single feedstock, large-volume orders may necessitate the blending of several feedstocks with different structural characteristics.

2. Fuel Costs. Fuel costs include the price and amount of energy that the manufacturing company must assume in cracking, refining, and producing a particular chemical stream.

3. Labor costs. Labor costs include the salaries of employees to operate the manufacturing facility for the purpose of producing a fixed unit amount of a particular product.

4. Commodity costs. Commodity costs include the value of the basic petrochemical base on the open marketplace. As the supply and demand for the basic commodity fluctuate on the open market, this factor is entered into the formula price.

A formula price may therefore be represented as a function of the following elements:

$$\text{Formula price} = \text{Feedstock cost} + \text{Energy cost} + \text{Labor cost} + \text{Commodity cost (per unit)}$$

If only one feedstock were used, the chemical composition of the feedstock would determine its basic cost, and the energy, labor, and commodity costs of producing it. If several feedstocks were used, the formula price would be a composite of separate calculations for each particular feedstock, or a weighted average of the feedstock components, multiplied by the cost of production of each one.

Each of the elements in the formula price is also multiplied by a weighting factor (coefficient) that specifies how much each cost will contribute to the determination of the overall formula price. The supplier generally sets a "ceiling price," guaranteeing that the formula price will not exceed this amount. Below the ceiling price, however, the supplier endeavors to maximize profits while clearly specifying the costs of production to the purchaser, while the purchaser attempts to obtain the most favorable formula price for himself. Since basic cost data and cost fluctuations are well known, negotiations typically focus on the magnitude of the coefficients that are applied to each element in the formula. Hence, the actual formula computation may be represented as:

$$
\begin{aligned}
\text{Formula price} = \ &(\text{Weighting coefficient} \times \text{Feedstock cost}) \\
&+ (\text{Weighting coefficient} \times \text{Commodity cost}) \\
&+ (\text{Weighting coefficient} \times \text{Labor cost}) \\
&+ (\text{Weighting coefficient} \times \text{Commodity cost})
\end{aligned}
$$

A fairly typical ratio of the weighting coefficients in this formula would be 70 percent (0.7) for feedstock cost, 20 percent (0.2) for energy costs, 5 percent (0.05) for labor costs, and 5 percent (0.05) for commodity costs. Multiple feedstocks supplied in a particular contract would be composed of a different set of costs and weighting elements for each feedstock in the supply.

The computation of a formula price, as opposed to the determination of a market price, has a number of advantages and disadvantages. Clearly, it enables the supplier to pass costs along to the purchaser, which minimizes the risk for both parties in the event of rapid changes in cost during the duration of the contract. The purchaser can project directly how cost changes will affect his supply costs; the supplier is protected by being able to pass cost increases along to the purchaser. However, when the market demand for the product is very high, the formula price constrains the seller in the ceiling price he can charge, hence curtailing potential profit for the product compared to its value on the open marketplace. Conversely, when market demand is very low, the contract may guarantee a large market to the supplier, but at a price for the product that could be unprofitable compared to production costs.

QUANTITY

Formula prices are typically computed with major attention given to quantity. Costs will fluctuate considerably based on the efficiency with which the production plant is operated, number of labor shifts required, and so on. Hence, in order to adequately forecast demand, attain particular "economics of scale" in the manufacturing process, and plan production schedules, suppliers must be able to determine the quantities that a particular customer will want to acquire. (Because of the volumes involved, no significant inventory is produced.) Quantities will be specified in common units of weight (pounds, tons, and so forth) or volume (gallons, and so on).

Quantity specifications are typically treated as minimum purchase amounts. If a purchaser desires significantly more than the minimum amount ("overlifting") in a given time period (e.g., a year), the amount would be sold contingent on availability, and delivered at the formula price. Conceivably, "discount" prices or adjustments in the formula price could be negotiated for significant purchases over minimum quantity. Conversely, underpurchase of the minimum amount ("underlifting") by a significant degree typically results in penalty costs to the purchaser. These are typically referred to as "liquidated damages" in the industry, and may be negotiated at rates anywhere from a token fine of several thousand dollars to as much as 30 percent of the formula price for each unit underlifted. Faced with the possibility of underlifting (due to market or product demand changes that require less raw material in a given time period), purchasers typically handle underlifting in one of several ways:

a. Pay the underlifting charges ("liquidated damages") to the supplier, either as stated or according to some renegotiated rate.

b. Not pay the liquidated damages, under the assumption that the supplier will not want to press legal charges against the purchaser at the expense of endangering the entire supply contract.

c. Resell the commodity to another purchaser who may be in need of supply, perhaps at a discounted price. Such action by the purchaser could cause major instability in the market price and in supply contracts held at the original manufacturer or other manufacturers. For this reason, sellers typically preclude the right of the purchaser to resell the product as part of the "standard contract language."

QUALITY

The quality of the product is related to the particular feedstock from which it is drawn, as well as the type and degree of refining that is employed by the supplier. Standard descriptions for gradations of quality are common parlance for each major chemical product.

DELIVERY

Most contracts specify the method of delivery, point of delivery, and way that the quantity amounts will be measured as the product is delivered. Gases are typically metered and delivered by direct pipeline from the manufacturer to the purchaser; liquids and liquified gases may be sold by pipeline, or shipped via tank truck, railroad tank car, tank barges, and tank ships.

CONTRACT DURATION

Most typical supply contracts extend for a period from one to five years; significantly longer or shorter ones would probably only be negotiated under extreme circumstances. Negotiations for contract renewal are typically begun several months prior to contract expiration.

PAYMENT TERMS

Payment terms are determined by the credit ratings and cash flow demands of both parties. Typical contracts specify payment within 30 days of delivery, although this time period may be shortened to payment on delivery, or lengthened to a period of three months between delivery and payment.

CONTRACT LANGUAGE

As can be determined from Exhibit 1, there are a number of elements in the contract that delineate the conditions under which the parties agree to bind themselves to the contract, or to deviate from it. Terminology and agreements were typically standard, unless altered by negotiation prior to contract signing. These elements include:

1. *Measurements.* A mechanism for specifying how quantity amounts will be determined, and how disputes over differences in delivered quantity will be resolved.

2. *Meet Competition.* The seller agrees to meet competitive market prices for the product if they become substantially lower than the current negotiated formula price.

3. *Favored Nations.* The supplier agrees that if he offers a better price on the product to any of the purchaser's competitors, he will offer the same price to this buyer.

4. *Purchase Requirements.* These govern the conditions and terms under which liquidated damages may be invoked.

5. *Force Majeure.* This clause exempts the parties from contract default in the event of major natural disasters, strikes, fires, explosions, or other events that could preclude the seller's ability to deliver the product or the buyer's ability to purchase.

6. *Disclaimers.* These protect both buyer and seller against unreasonable claims about the product or its quality.

7. *Assignability.* This clause limits the right of either party to assign the contract to another purchaser or supplier if they so desire.

8. *Notifications.* This is the lead time specified during which one or both parties must notify the other party of any change in the contract or its renewal.

9. *Other Clauses.* These include conditions under which the product may be assured delivery, application of taxes, provisions for resale, definitions of contract breach and termination, the legal framework used to enforce the contract (in the event of cross-state or cross-national agreements), and methods of notification of one party to the other.

CONTRACT MANAGEMENT AND MAINTENANCE

While a supply contract is a legally binding document that attempts to articulate the way two companies will work together, it more commonly stands as the cornerstone of a complex long-term social relationship between buyer and seller. This relationship requires constant monitoring, evaluation, and discussion by representatives of both organizations. Thus, while similar supply contracts may exist between a particular manufacturer and three different buyers, there may be major differences in the day-to-day interactions and quality of relationships between the manufacturer and each buyer. Experienced sales representatives have defined a ''good'' seller-buyer relationship as meeting the following criteria:

The purchaser can be counted on to live up to the terms and conditions of the contract as negotiated. The purchaser accepts a fair formula price in price negotiations, and does not attempt to push the supplier into an artificially low price. The purchaser lifts as much of the product per time period as he agreed to lift under the contract. The purchaser is trustworthy, and follows a course of action based on sound business ethics.

The purchaser does not attempt to take advantage of fluctuations or abberations in the spot market price to gain advantage. He accepts the fact that a formula price has been negotiated, and that both parties agree to live up to this price for the duration of the contract. He does not seek contract price changes as the market price may drop for some time period.

When there is a mutual problem between seller and purchaser, it can be openly discussed and resolved between the two parties. Problems resulting from the continued inability of the supplier to provide the product, and/or the continued inability of the buyer to consume the product, can be openly addressed and resolved. Problems in the quality of the product, labor difficulties resulting in problems in manufacturing, loading, shipping, unloading, cleanliness of the shipping equipment, and so on, can be promptly explored and resolved to mutual satisfaction. Finally, changes in the business projections of one or both parties can be shared, so that difficulties anticipated by the supplier in providing all of the product, or difficulties anticipated by the purchaser in consuming all of the product, can lead to amicable and satisfactory resolutions for both parties. Ability to resolve these problems requires mutual trust, honesty, open lines of communication, and an approach to problem solving that seeks the best solution for both sides.

Olympic Television Rights (A)
A Contract with the Kremlin

William Oscar Johnson

They want us to be like three scorpions fighting in a bottle. When it's over, two will be dead and the winner will be exhausted.

Thus spoke Roone Arledge, president of ABC Sports, of the way it was when the three major American television networks joined in bitter battle with the government of the Soviet Union over the U.S. rights to televise the 1980 Summer Olympic Games. It was a Cold War confrontation with an absolutely classic—if also a somewhat comic—cast of adversaries. On one side stood the network executives, representing all that is richest, sleekest, most glamorous about the free-enterprise system. They came from stately Manhattan skyscrapers, quick-witted, supersophisticated salesmen given to Gucci shoes and manicured hands. If they were not the cream of U.S. business, the network men were certainly from the tip of the vast capitalist iceberg.

On the other side stood a battery of grim Russian bureaucrats—burly, pallid fellows, some former peasants with hands still hard from years of labor in the fields of Mother Russia. They were canny technocrats and politicians from the cold corridors of the Kremlin: some were in their 70s, and their longevity alone made it clear that they were among the wiliest of men in this land of purges. It also is worth noting that the network representatives were not entirely without this instinct for survival, being no less vulnerable than Soviet politicians to swift turns of fortune that could send them to the Siberias of American business.

So they joined the conflict well matched—the minions of Red Square, Moscow versus the moguls of Sixth Avenue, New York. It would be nice to report that the result was a hard, clean, clear-cut battle between two ideological juggernauts, that two gleaming machines performed in a way that displayed the best of both systems. This did not happen. The big Olympic TV deal became bogged down in misunderstanding, misjudgment, and mistakes.

In fact, during the critical closing phase of negotiations that concluded three weeks ago with an astonished National Broadcasting Company being presented with the Olympic rights for $85 million, the only real link between the two adversaries was

The following article is reprinted courtesy of *SPORTS ILLUSTRATED* from the February 21, 1977, issue. Copyright © 1977, Time, Inc. ''A Contract with the Kremlin'' by William Oscar Johnson. All Rights Reserved.

a garrulous little German named Lothar Bock. He is a small-time "impresario" (the term he uses to describe himself) who had more experience as a booking agent for Georgian saber dancers and Mongolian tumblers than as the indispensable middleman between a bunch of cold-eyed Soviets and high-rolling TV executives. It is true that one network man described Bock as being "a bit of a klutz," but it was Bock—and Bock alone—who plodded between Moscow and Manhattan to forge the final bond that gave the Olympics to NBC. In the bargain, he earned himself a million bucks and made his name a household word from the bar at P. J. Clarke's to the boardroom at the A. C. Nielsen Company.

This bizarre situation officially began in Vienna in October 1974, when the International Olympic Committee awarded the Soviet Union the 1980 Summer Olympics. All three networks were there just to shake hands with their new adversaries. No one was selling, no one was buying. Only one network—ABC—was absolutely certain that it would bid for the Moscow Games. Under the masterful guidance of Arledge, ABC had won the rights to six of the last eight Olympics, and it covered each with increasing excellence. But except for sport, the network had been No. 3 in the ratings for many years. That changed in the 1976–77 TV season when ABC burst to the fore, partially because of its hugely successful telecasting of the Montreal Games.

CBS had televised the Rome Olympics of 1960. That was in TV's dark ages, when rights could be purchased for $550,000. Since then, CBS had never bid successfully—or even seriously—for an Olympics. The network had been rated No. 1 for so long that it seemed to be living on its own Mount Olympus, showing a godlike disdain for the Games of mere mortals. However, in mid-1974, Robert F. Wussler became CBS's vice-president in charge of sports, and he was very interested in the Moscow Games.

As for NBC, it had televised the 1972 Winter Olympics from Sapporo—an esthetic disaster and a financial disappointment. Top management was at best neutral toward the Moscow Olympics. Carl Lindemann Jr., NBC's vice president for sports, made a couple of trips to the Soviet capital in the early going but says, "I was essentially there to wave the flag. Higher network management was ambivalent. I wanted the Games in the worst way. We had lost the Munich Olympics because of a lousy $1 million." (ABC paid $13.5 million for the rights.)

During 1974 and 1975 the American network executives—Arledge, Wussler, Lindemann, and an ever-growing cast of presidents, board chairmen, lawyers, diplomats, politicians, and public-relations men—launched into a lumbering courtship that was intended to win the hearts and minds of the Soviet Olympic hierarchy. In the end, none of it seems to have made any difference in the selection of NBC. Yet the courtship was fervent, relentless—and sometimes quite public.

For example, in the fall of 1975, ABC's faltering morning show, *A.M. America,* woke up the nation to a week of reports on life in the Soviet Union that were so uncritical an embarrassed ABC man said, "We made Moscow look like Cypress Gardens without the water skiers." In 1976 CBS aired a prime-time bomb that featured a shivering Mary Tyler Moore standing on a wintry Moscow street corner, hosting a show about the Bolshoi Ballet. When Wussler was asked if this was part of his Olympic campaign, he replied, "No question about it."

As the time approached for the Montreal Games, there was a constant shuttling of network people to Moscow to wine and dine with Soviet Olympic officials. East and West became palsy-walsy, even kidding each other about whether it was the KGB or the CIA that was bugging their conversations. Mostly it was social, but in Montreal the plot at last thickened.

The U.S.S.R.'s Olympic Organizing Committee glittered with Kremlin stars. The leader was a hulking, dark-haired Ignati Novikov, 70. He had started his career as a laborer in the Ukraine, rising through the ranks until he became one of the top half dozen men in the U.S.S.R., the deputy premier in charge of all power construction projects. Second in command was Sergei Lapin, 64, a stern and polished diplomat who had been Ambassador to Austria and China and general director of Tass. Now, as Minister of the State Committee for Television and Radio, Lapin became the Soviet Union's head propagandist. They were invariably accompanied by a battery of deputy chairmen, vice commissars, translators, and stenographers. The Americans quickly noted a difference between two factions: Novikov, an old Kremlin hand, came on in the intransigent shoe-rapping manner of Nikita Khrushchev, while Lapin and others on the TV-radio committee seemed more subtle.

On a Saturday afternoon in Montreal, the Soviets gave a lavish party on the good ship *Alexander Pushkin,* which was moored in the St. Lawrence. The decks were awash with gallons of Stolichnaya vodka and Armenian cognac. The tables groaned beneath platters of cracked lobster, sliced sturgeon, caviar. The event was purely social, even jolly. But Novikov & Co. were in town to do some serious shoe rapping. They contacted the networks one by one and made their demand: they wanted $210 million. In cash. The networks laughed. An NBC man said to a Russian, "210 million dollars? We were thinking of 210 million *pennies.*" The Soviet representative stalked off in anger, but one of his comrades confided to a CBS representative that no one in Moscow expected more than $65 million.

In fact, none of the numbers meant much of anything. NBC's Lindemann says, "We all knew the price would be between $70 and $100 million. I think all three of us would have gone to $100 million." Perhaps so. But the real numbers would come later. The most troubling aspect of the Russian demands in Montreal had to do with the sensitive issue of just how much selling of the Soviet Union a U.S. network would have to do to buy into the Olympics. The fine line between propaganda and news seemed particularly fuzzy to Novikov. Wussler recalls, "He made it clear to us he expected some kind of favorable political coverage. We said we could *not* compromise CBS News. We might do something like the Mary Tyler Moore show, ice shows, circuses, sports."

Arledge says, "I wanted a clause in the contract that said ABC would have total control over our telecast of the Olympics. Novikov had said to me earlier in the year, 'If you show things we don't like, we will pull the plug.' I doubt they would do that, but the problem of even *seeming* like a propaganda arm for the Russians is delicate. For example, if you show the subways of Moscow—and they are superb—some people in the United States are going to see it as a selling job for the Soviets just because it isn't something negative."

The Soviets did not demand specific schedules of pro-U.S.S.R. programming, but the prospect of having to do such shows hung heavy over the networks throughout the negotiations.

As the Montreal Games ended, the Soviets said they would like to see some preliminary money bids in Moscow that fall. They would be secret, of course. NBC was particularly careful about security. It wrote a two-sentence bid on a page of company stationery, sealed it in a film can, sent it by courier to New York's Kennedy Airport where it was given to an airline pilot, who carried it in the cockpit to Moscow. There he gave it to the driver for NBC News, who took it straight to the committee. An hour later in New York Wussler knew NBC's bid.

The early bids received by the Soviets were: NBC $70 million, CBS $71 million, and ABC a surprising $33.3 million for nonexclusive rights, meaning that it was already thinking of the possibility of pool coverage in which all three networks would participate. Arledge later bid $73 million for exclusive rights.

The autumn of 1976 arrived in New York, but in Moscow it suddenly seemed to be the season of CBS. Almost two years earlier Wussler had gotten enthusiastic encouragement in his Olympic quest from William Paley, the venerable CBS board chairman. Paley said, "I'm delighted you boys want to go after this, just delighted!" Thus blessed, Wussler and Arthur Taylor, then president of the network's parent company (CBS Inc.), had begun a series of trips between Manhattan and Moscow where they established warm friendships with important committee members. However, nothing they did was as important as the signing of Bock to be CBS's representative in Moscow.

Wussler had first met Bock, 38, in the spring of '75 as the result of a phone call from film producer Bud Greenspan. "Bob, if CBS is really serious about the Olympics, the man to get them for you is sitting here in my office," Greenspan said. Wussler met Bock and invited him to dinner. Later Taylor met Bock in Moscow, and a consulting contract was arranged for him.

Who is Bock? And how did this energetic little fellow with a real-estate salesman's smile ingratiate himself with a pathologically suspicious crowd of Kremlin politicians? The answers are not clear. Was it because Bock arranged a few years ago to have a memorial plaque placed on the house in Munich where Lenin did some of his most important writing? This impressed the Soviets. Beyond that, Wussler says, "The Russians trust him at least partly because in 1968 Lothar imported a troupe of Russian singers for a tour of West Germany. They were there at the same time the Russians invaded Czechoslovakia to crush the uprising. That week the West Germans wouldn't touch anything Russian with a 10-foot pole. Lothar had to eat about a $75,000 loss. And he did. The Russians never forgot that. They thought Lothar showed class. They trusted him."

There are stories around Munich that contradict this theory. Some people say they cannot understand why the Soviets even let Bock into the U.S.S.R. because he allegedly once left a troupe of Georgian saber dancers flat broke in Hamburg until the Soviet government sent money to pay their bills. On another occasion, Bock reportedly marooned 60 Mongolian tumblers in a Bavarian country inn, forcing Moscow to come to the rescue again.

Whatever else he may be, Bock is a loquacious chap who is seemingly quite open about himself. Sitting in his office, which is located in the basement of a green bungalow on an unpaved street in a Munich suburb, he explained last week how his prosperous Soviet connection came to be: "In 1965 I happened to see the Osipov

Balalaika Orchestra, and I thought I would bring it to Germany. I wrote to Moscow and got a letter back in Russian. I hardly even speak the language now, and I certainly didn't understand it then. But instead of having it translated, I took the next flight to Moscow. They translated it for me there. It said: 'Dear Mr. Bock. We are not interested in your offer.' But I was insistent, I continued talking to them. After a while, they saw my point, and I have been dealing with them ever since. We are fair and square with each other."

Pressed further for his formula for gaining friends in the most remote recesses of the Kremlin, Bock said, "I always tell them I am a capitalist, making no attempt to hide that I am working for profit. They accept it. They love it."

That seems all too simple. But whatever the reasons, the Soviets trust Bock. As one Russian told Wussler, "All U.S. networks are bad, but you are less bad, because you know Lothar Bock." By October 1976, with Bock running interference, Wussler and Taylor felt they were on the brink of closing a deal. "We had contracts all drawn up between CBS and the organizing committee," says Wussler. They came triumphantly back to New York to tell the network the Olympics were wrapped up, and arranged a big party for the Russians at the IOC meetings that were scheduled in Barcelona a day later. Wussler was packing to go to Spain when he got the stunning news: Taylor had been fired by Paley.

If there is one thing the Soviets understand with razor-sharp clarity, it is the sudden purge of high-level personnel. And it makes them nervous. "They were shook, I mean *shook!*" says Wussler, who six months before had moved up from head of CBS sports to the presidency of the network. "I tried to assure them it had nothing to do with the Olympics, but it was hard for them to believe." Even the sprightly Bock was numb—for a while. Then he phoned Wussler and said, "I think if Mr. Paley would come to Moscow himself, we could put the deal together again." Wussler doubted whether Paley would agree, but when he asked him to go, Paley's only question was "How soon do we leave?" Early in November, the patriarch of American television and a leading patrician of world capitalism was welcomed with almost adoration by the old Ukrainian laborer, Novikov. They toasted each other warmly during a lavish dinner of chicken Kiev fit for a czar. Then, after two long days of meetings, the two old lions had a *tête à tête* in a small room. They toasted each other. They shook hands. Wussler recalls, "Mr. Paley and I left Moscow with the definite feeling that the deal was firm."

Oddly, nothing further was heard from Moscow until Dec. 8. Then the networks received a communication outlining the framework under which the final bidding for the rights would take place. It was an amazing document. Only ABC's men had heard anything like it mentioned in Montreal, and nothing resembling it had come up in CBS's private talks. No one was quite sure what it meant.

Nevertheless, all three networks went to Moscow to find out. NBC was planning to seriously enter the fray now. Robert Howard, president of the network, went to Moscow along with Lindemann and nine other executives and technicians. "Most of our guys had never been to Moscow," says Lindemann. "I had been there only four times. I was surprised when Wussler said he had been there 11 or 12 times."

When the Americans arrived for the showdown on Dec. 15, two of the networks—CBS and ABC—were dead certain they had been chosen. Only NBC figured it was an underdog, and it was correct. NBC was about as far under as a dog could be. Novikov could never remember the network's call letters; even during the final signing, he twice referred to it as ABC.

Nevertheless, the Soviets treated the three networks exactly the same—like dirt. One by one, they were informed of the new conditions for bidding—which were outrageous. For one thing, the U.S.S.R. demanded $50 million for equipment and facilities, to be paid in staggering increments of $20 million in 1977 and $30 million in 1978.

All along one of the Russians' most irrational demands had been for huge sums of cash to be paid two or three years before the Games. Recent Olympics have taken place in such a politically charged atmosphere that it was not unreasonable to fear that an international incident might cancel the Moscow Games, leaving the Soviets with the loot and TV with no programs. But the network executives were less afraid of losing money because of political disruption—after all, in a tightly controlled country like the U.S.S.R., the chances of disruption are slim—than because of an old-fashioned business reason.

Though the networks would have no problem raising the money, an enormous amount of interest would be lost if millions of dollars were tied up over such a long period. Arledge figured that if the $50 million for facilities was paid on the timetable the Soviets demanded, $17.5 million in interest would be forfeited.

Along with the ruinous pay schedule for the equipment, the Soviets had decided to hold an auction to sell the actual rights to the Games. In effect, the $50 million was merely an admission ticket to the final round of bidding. Arledge recalls, "Their plans involved an unending series of bids that went on as long as two guys were able to stand. There was a new sealed bid every 24 hours. The winner would be announced, then the losers could up the ante by a minimum of 5 percent. That's when I made the remark about scorpions in a bottle."

Wussler was most shocked by the U.S.S.R. proposal. He had a letter with him from Paley reminding Novikov of their deal, and he asked for an audience with the chairman. They talked for 45 minutes. Novikov was stony. He told Wussler, "We are here to get the most money possible. That is our sole purpose. We need it for the Games." Wussler asked him about the agreement with Paley. Novikov replied. "It is a pity."

Wussler was appalled. He hurried to his hotel room. It was 4:00 P.M. Moscow time, 7:00 A.M. in the eastern United States. He phoned Jack Schneider, president of CBS Broadcasting, at home in Greenwich, Connecticut, and told him that CBS'S deal had collapsed. He suggested that Schneider contact the other networks and arrange a pool. Within two hours, CBS, NBC, and ABC had agreed to file a brief with the Justice Department, asking it to waive the antitrust laws so the three networks could negotiate as a unified front.

Now it was 7 P.M. in Moscow, and the Soviets had decided to throw one last lavish supper before they put the three scorpions into the bottle. It was held in an elegant banquet room of the Hotel Sovietskaya. The party was a mistake. It was the first time that the three networks had been brought together in the same room in Moscow, and they were seething. At this point, no one but Wussler knew that a pool was in the works. The others were shouting angrily about the crude and insulting tactics of the Soviets. Almost immediately there was talk of walking out en masse. The hosts stood against the wall, aghast at the uproar among the Americans. Lindemann says, "They had figured there was no limit to the manic competitive zeal of the networks. That was insulting, of course. But what bothered me even more was the fact that this wasn't just another ball game, this wasn't a spat with Bowie Kuhn or Pete Rozelle. This was the United States against the Soviet Union—and we just couldn't let this happen.''

The next day, taking a page from the Soviet book on diplomacy, the Americans walked out. At a meeting attended by Arledge, Wussler, and Howard, Novikov was impassive. He told them, "If any of you leave Soviet soil on this day, you will never, *never* be allowed to return." The three said they had no choice. After leaving Novikov's office, they promised to leave the U.S.S.R. and they showed each other their airline tickets as a display of good faith.

Arledge had earlier made an appointment for a private session with Novikov. He decided to keep the date. "I was bound not to negotiate," says Arledge, "but I didn't think Novikov understood. He said he would make a deal with me right there on the spot. He said the Olympics were mine. I told him I couldn't take the Olympics at that point if he gave them to me for five million."

A few days after the networks left, the Soviets announced that the rights now belonged to a mysterious fourth party, an American trading and manufacturing company called SATRA, which does a lot of business with the U.S.S.R. This move was—and still is—seen by most network men as both a threat and a face-saving move by the Soviets. But SATRA apparently took it seriously and has filed a $275 million suit against NBC for interfering with its agreement with the Soviets.

Back in Manhattan, each network pledged to have no contact of any kind with the Soviets while the Justice Department considered the pool waiver request. However, Bock was still loose in Moscow. When the networks departed, he was shaken. Technically he was not a network employee, but he still had his contract with CBS. Soon Bock got word to Wussler that Novikov was sorry, that the Soviets wanted CBS to please come back. Then Novikov wired Paley, saying, in effect, that the U.S.S.R.-CBS deal was still on. Meanwhile, Bock continued to negotiate.

Was this a breach of the agreement between the networks? Wussler claims Bock was working on his own. "I told him specifically and in person when we left Moscow that he was not to continue any talks with the Russians on our behalf." Wussler says.

Arledge got disturbing news from Moscow in late December. "I heard that Lothar was negotiating for CBS," he says. "I kept hearing it. Then in mid-January I got word of the terms of a new contract. And I said. 'This has gone too far.' ''

Arledge contacted Wussler and told him, "The Russians believe Bock is speaking in your behalf." Wussler said no, he is not. Arledge said that CBS could verify that by sending the Moscow Olympic Committee a wire stating that Bock had no authorization to bargain for CBS. Later, ABC indicated it would be satisfied if CBS sent a letter to Bock telling him he could not act in its behalf or sent a letter to ABC saying the same thing. CBS pondered this move for several days, then out of the blue it announced it was not only dropping out of the pool but also, because of various "imponderables." would have nothing further to do with the 1980 Olympics.

The shocking decision had been made after a series of CBS senior staff meetings, the last a 24-hour marathon. Bock had indeed brought a letter from Moscow that gave the Olympics to CBS for $81 million; he also brought assurances that a reasonable payment schedule could be worked out. It was a very good deal. Why did CBS quit with the battle at last won? Wussler says, "We saw nothing but trouble ahead. We couldn't see living with their deviousness. Their refusal to stick to the deal they made with Mr. Paley was the most telling point. I figured if they'd go back on a deal with him, how could I ever trust them with anything?''

Some people thought this explanation less than complete—especially after CBS had undertaken such an intense, well-organized two-year campaign to land the Games. It was suggested that perhaps a more compelling reason was that Bock's unauthorized work in Moscow on CBS's behalf would be embarrassing if it got cut. As one network man says, ''They got caught with their hand in the cooky jar.''

Bock was stricken. He pleaded his case with Wussler, then took a Lear jet to the Bahamas to plead with Paley. The answer was no, although the network arranged for Bock to be paid a little extra cash for his trouble. Bock asked to be released from his CBS contract so he could contact NBC. It was done.

With the CBS pullout, the attempts to form a pool had disintegrated, and both NBC and ABC were free to operate unilaterally. Bock and Lindemann met for breakfast at the Edwardian Room of Manhattan's Plaza Hotel. Lindemann recalls, ''The conversation was remarkably low key, considering its substance. Lothar started telling me his deal. We ordered something to eat. He kept talking. We drank our orange juice, then it dawned on me what he was saying. He was delivering the Olympics to us. We left without eating.'' Within hours, NBC signed a contract with Bock to pay him $1 million, to buy 15 programs he would produce, to retain him as a special consultant for four years. It was a dazzling package. Bock then delivered his part. A series of phone calls to Moscow clinched the deal that night. A day later Lindemann, Howard, and an NBC lawyer were on their way to Moscow for the final negotiating and the formal signing.

NBC had hoped to complete the entire contract in Moscow before ABC learned it was there. It could not be done, even though the Soviets sent a wire telling Arledge not to come to Moscow. ABC was not dissuaded. Arledge says, ''I knew the Russians were panicky. Novikov made a terrible mistake in December. Even his peers were accusing him of having bungled the deal with CBS. He was faced with the prospect of no American network at all. And by that time, he figured all Americans were crazy anyway, so when Bock said he had NBC, Novikov jumped at it. NBC was never in the Russian plans until CBS quit.

''And Novikov never understood what we were doing about the pool and why I had never contacted him after we walked out. When I finally saw him, he said, 'You never phoned, you never wrote. I waited and waited, and you never called.' I suppose if I had it to do over, maybe I'd do things differently. But I really felt relieved when it was over. I hated to lose the Games, but I had been wondering way back last summer whether I really wanted to have them.''

ABC's presence at the last minute in Moscow did boost the price some. Lord Killanin, president of the previously somnolent IOC (which shares the rights fees with the host country), had heard ABC would go higher, and he had wired the Soviets to be certain they were getting top dollar. The deal wound up at $85 million—but there was no demand this time for the kind of pro-Soviet propaganda old Ignati Novikov had once seemed so determined to have.

Now the question is: Who won this confrontation between the U.S.S.R. and the networks? No one knows. This was just the first skirmish in the conflict. Only late in the summer of 1980, when the Games are over and the NBC cameras and crews have gone home, will we know exactly who sold what, who bought what, and who got the better of whom.

Creating the GM-Toyota Joint Venture: A Case in Complex Negotiation

Stephen E. Weiss

During the last four years, the joint venture between General Motors and Toyota Motor to assemble subcompact cars has become a symbol of international cooperation within the auto industry and beyond. Academics, managers, and government officials have all emphasized the parent companies' reputations and the joint venture's achievements in labor relations, production efficiencies, and product quality. Yet, as deserved as this attention to operations and performance may be, an important aspect of the venture has been neglected—its birth.

Creating an international joint venture is neither an easy nor certain process. Like other negotiations, joint venture negotiations may at worst fail completely. Undertaking negotiations in an international context, moreover, adds obstacles as well as opportunities. Before its talks with GM, for example, Toyota negotiated with Ford (unsuccessfully as it turned out) for 13 months. Even the GM-Toyota talks were in participants' words, "long," "hard," and "frustrating."[1] So the agreement leading to the establishment of the joint venture now known as New United Motor Manufacturing, Inc. (NUMMI) represents an important accomplishment.

The story of the GM-Toyota negotiations is also significant as an illustration of the complexity common to international business negotiations. They entail complicated issues, parties that are large organizations, and multiple, dynamic, and differing environments—all of which are given little attention in existing management research on negotiation.[2] This case study may stimulate future work. At the same time, it invokes concepts from existing literature on negotiation that further understanding of the GM-Toyota discussions. Finally, this article draws out strategic implications and guidelines for automakers and other firms considering international collaboration.

Stephen E. Weiss, a specialist in negotiation and conflict management, is currently Associate Professor of Policy and International Business, York University Faculty of Administrative Studies (Toronto).

The assistance of the Faculty Editor, Susan Douglas, Thomas Gladwin, Stephen Kobrin, and especially the participants in the negotiations interviewed by the author is gratefully acknowledged.

AN ANALYTIC APPROACH

News and other reports on the GM-Toyota negotiations have focused only on the two companies and their actions, but a number of factors describe and explain the negotiations. Other organizations, groups, and individuals took significant steps; their relationships as well as distinct actions deserve attention, as do the particular conditions and contexts in which those actions took place. In short, this study endeavors to enrich the understanding of the two companies' efforts by assuming an approach sensitive to most of these factors.[3]

With respect to the actors involved, the analysis that follows treats GM and Toyota as the two primary organizations. In addition to their intercompany (primary) talks they met in critical ancillary negotiations with the United Auto Workers (UAW) and with the Federal Trade Commission (FTC). Chart 1, which guides this discussion, places the foursome at the center of activity as the most deeply involved organizational actors (Ring 1a).

Other actors also influenced and were affected by the negotiations. Chart 1 identifies and classifies several organizations by their degree of involvement (Rings 1a-4a). The chart also recognizes three levels of analysis for behavior: organizational wholes (a), groups such as negotiating teams (b), and individuals (c). The activities of each organization listed, which shaped conditions for the negotiations, could be analyzed at the two other levels. For clarity and brevity, only the groups and individuals representing the four major organizations appear in the chart (Box 1b, c).

The following account concentrates on the four main parties in Chart 1 and addresses their actions, relationships, and contexts. First, GM's and Toyota's motivations for a joint venture are considered. Then the discussion traces in detail the primary negotiations between GM and Toyota and the ancillary talks with the UAW and with the FTC. Each of the three negotiations is described according to the issues stemming from the parties' (organizations') relationship, the individual players involved, relevant conditions, the negotiation process (sessions held, proposals made), and the outcome.

MOTIVATING FACTORS

From late 1979 to late 1981, the General Motors Corporation and the Toyota Motor Company (as it was then called) were the largest car producers in their respective home countries and the first and third largest producers worldwide. They each saw the rise of several corporate needs, especially in the predominant U.S. market. Some of the needs, or interests, were straightforward and typical of firms that eventually seek the cooperation of another firm,[4] while other interests drawing less public attention also existed. All of these interests set the stage for the negotiations that followed.

The U.S. Market

February 1979 brought the second oil shock in six years to American consumers, and they reacted by postponing purchases and shifting preferences to small, fuel-efficient cars. During 1980, domestic subcompact and compact cars captured 36.37 percent of the U.S. car market. The subcompacts alone doubled their 1971 share of

CHART 1

Actors and Audiences in the GM-Toyota Negotiations*

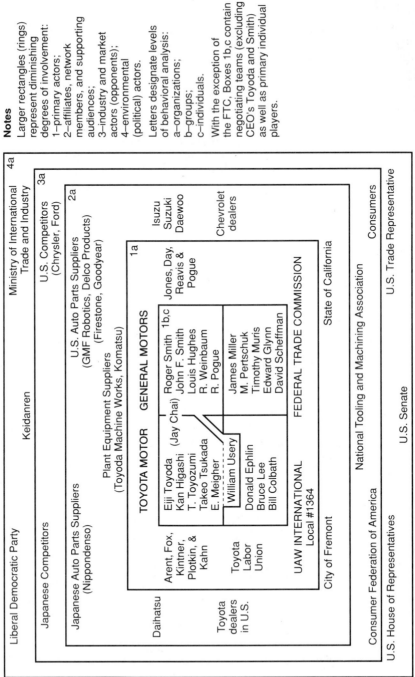

This structure was suggested by Ian Wise.

7.42 percent.[5] In this segment of the market GM, like the rest of the U.S.'s Big Three, was confronted with highly competitive Japanese imports. In January of 1980, Japanese car imports jumped 86.5 percent over those of the previous January.[6] The U.S.'s Motor Vehicle Manufacturers Association reported 1,991,502 Japanese car imports in 1980, which translated into a 22.2 percent share of the market and a 23 percent increase over the 1979 total.[7]

General Motors' Performance

General Motors' position during this period was dramatically reflected in its net income for 1980 — minus $763 million. The loss was the company's first since 1921. From 1979 to 1980, total sales dropped 20 percent, U.S. car (unit) sales dropped 17 percent, and U.S. car production fell 20 percent. (See Table 1.)

Toyota's Performance

Toyota did well. Ironically, the company earned almost as much as GM lost in 1980. From the 1979 to 1980 fiscal years, net sales increased 18 percent, and car production went up 9 percent. In fiscal year 1980, overseas (unit) sales of all motor vehicles as a percentage of world sales was 54.4 percent, and about 25 percent of total car production went to the United States. From 1979-1980, Toyota's car (unit) sales in the United States increased 15 percent for a 6.5% share of the market.

Environmental Forces

As early as November 1979, however, environmental forces began to darken this picture for Toyota and other Japanese automakers. Politicians and other opinion leaders in the United States blamed the poor sales of domestic cars and layoffs not as much on the oil crisis, economic recession, and U.S. automakers' strategies as they did on Japanese industrial policy and export levels. The salience of the U.S. "road transportation" industry itself, which accounted for 1 out of 5 nonagricultural jobs and 18% of GNP in 1978 sustained attention on these problems; so did the U.S. deficit in trade with Japan. Forty-five percent of Japan's total exports to the United States were auto exports. Complaints culminated in demands for the production of Japanese autos within the United States, cutbacks of exports, liberalization of the Japanese market for autos and auto parts, and domestic content legislation in the United States.

In early 1980, Japan's Ministry of International Trade and Industry (MITI) pressured Toyota and other Japanese automakers to invest in the United States. Toyota, a conservative company historically reluctant to expand overseas, resisted. By early April, though, Honda and Nissan had each announced plans for U.S. production. These responses apparently failed to satisfy the U.S. government. Formal, intergovernmental negotiations commenced April 7th and continued until an agreement to restrict Japanese auto exports was reached 13 months later.[8]

Thus, during this 1979–1981 period both Toyota and GM faced significant threats. For GM there were changes in consumer preferences, a lingering inability to

TABLE 1   Financial and Competitive Profiles, 1979–1983

	General Motors		Toyota Motor		U.S. Total
Net Sales/					
Net Income[1]					
(U.S.$ mn.)					
1979	66,311.2	2,892.7	12,911.6	470.2	—
1980	53,173.0	(762.5)	15,212.2	659.8	—
1981	62,698.5	333.0	15,528.8	587.8	—
1982*	60,025.6	962.7	15,063.8	554.1	—
1983	74,581.6	3,730.2	20,450.0	841.7	—
Car Sales in U.S. (retail)[2]					
(units, % share)					
1979	4,931,726[a]	46.2	507,816	4.8	10,673,435
1980	4,116,482	45.8	582,195	6.5	8,979,194
1981	3,796,696	44.5	576,491	6.8	8,536,039
1982*	3,515,660	44.1	530,246	6.6	7,981,673
1983	4,053,561	44.2	555,766	6.1	9,182,067
Car Production in U.S.[3]					
(units, % change)					
1979	5,091,908	−3.6	0[b]	0	8,433,662[c]
1980	4,064,556	−20.2	0	0	6,375,506
1981	3,904,083	−4.0	0	0	6,253,138
1982*	3,173,145	−18.7	0	0	5,073,496
1983	3,975,291	25.3	0	0	6,781,184
Car Production in World[4]					
Overseas Car Sales[5]					**World Total**
(units, % of world [unit] sales)					
1979	—[d]	23.2[e]	2,174,202[f]	38.7[g]	30,774,627
1980	5,728,769	24.7	2,370,124	—	28,577,518
1981	5,497,052	25.2	2,337,471	50.8	27,457,792
1982*	4,869,672	28.9	2,347,293	46.6	26,626,660
1983	6,098,880	28.5	2,480,033	45.9	29,680,193

Sources
[1, 5]GM, Toyota Motor annual reports. For GM: consolidated figures, year end Dec. 31. For Toyota: unconsolidated, year end June 30, converted from yen by exchange rate in Tokyo on June 30 of each year.
[2, 3, 4]Motor Vehicle Manufacturers Association, U.S. For Toyota world production, Japan Automobile Manufacturers Association, Inc.
Notes
[a]Column figures include GM imports. In 1980, 514,396 from Canada.
[b]During the 1979–83 period, Toyota's only production in the U.S. was small-scale truck assembly (Toyota Long Beach Fabricators, California.)
[c]For 1979–82, column figures include GM, Ford, Chrysler, AMC, VW of America (84,246 in 1982) and Checker Motor (2,000 in 1982.) The 1983 figure drops Checker but includes Honda of America.
[d]Approximate figure for 1979 (based on factory sales) is 7,000,000.
[e]Retail sales. Canada excluded from calculations.
[f]Column figures include knock-down (KD) sets.
[g]Based on FY domestic sales and export statistics. KD sets excluded. For 1982, total motor vehicle KD sets: 297,282.
*Indicates main year of negotiation between GM and Toyota.

produce high-quality, low-cost subcompact and compact cars in the United States, and stiff competition in those segments of the market. Toyota had an increasingly hostile political environment to contend with, among other factors.

Toyota's Interests

More specifically, for Toyota, one can identify several strategic interests:

- Placating the U.S. and Japanese governments.
- Responding to U.S. and Japanese competition.
- Determining the feasibility of U.S. car production.
- Developing an internal consensus regarding U.S. plans.

And if go-ahead plans were made for production in the United States:

- Minimizing financial costs and risk.
- Building or obtaining a satisfactory plant.
- Locating a good labor pool.
- Finding suppliers for high-quality, cost-effective parts.

Placating the governments was probably the foremost of these interests, especially during the period preceding May 1981, when there was still the hope of avoiding export restraints. After this, however, other protectionist measures loomed, and pressure for responses specifically from Toyota, Japan's leading automaker, persisted. At the same time, Toyota officials considered subcompact demand in the U.S. market "explosive" and predicted in February 1980, that the "subcompact contest" would climax in 1983.[9] The company obviously wanted to be a major player. Setting up an assembly plant for annual production of 240,000 cars (the usual number for a profitable operation in the United States) was estimated to cost $800–$1,000 million overall and to take 3–4 years to reach startup.

General Motor's Interests

GM also had a number of specific interests during this period. They included:

- A replacement for the aging subcompact Chevette.
- Responding to Japanese and U.S. subcompact competition.
- Responding to union complaints about layoffs.
- Meeting fuel standards to protect profitable large cars.

And if a go-ahead decision was made for production of a new car:

- Minimizing development costs and time.
- Developing a broad, organizational commitment to the project.
- Lowering the $1500–$2000 per car Japanese cost advantage (innovating in production and in the workplace).
- Attracting customers back to GM products.

In 1981, the Chevette had been on the U.S. market six years, and it was selling poorly even at a $800 per car loss.[10] GM wanted to replace the car and to attract new, young buyers to Chevrolet products. Development and production of a new car would take up to six years and a heavy investment. The Chevette, borrowed from overseas operations in 1973, cost $1.5 billion; Ford's newer Escort, which debuted in 1980, ran $3.0 billion. GM also had to respond to federal regulations on corporate average fuel economy (CAFE) and in the long run, to the competitiveness of Japanese automakers. This last concern went beyond mere replacement of the Chevette. It had the potential to call for new methods of production and management.

General Motors' Strategic Options

From a strategic perspective, GM and Toyota each had several possible courses of action. For GM, there was:

- "Going it alone."
- Joining up with one of several competitive subcompact automakers (e.g., Nissan, Volkswagen).
- Given the size of the company (i.e., the use of "bigness" as a competitive tool), some well-defined combination of the first two.

In fact, in 1979, GM had begun a $40 billion, seven-year investment in new technology, new plants, and new cars. In compacts, the company reportedly moved two years ahead of domestic competitors with the introduction of its X-cars. For subcompacts, GM's existing "Asian strategy" called for captive imports. The company had acquired 34.2 percent of Isuzu in 1971 (later increased to 38–40 percent) and on August 12, 1981, bought 5.3 percent of Suzuki.[11]

Toyota's Strategic Options

Toyota seems to have had options as well. The company could have:

- Continued producing from its massive plant-and-supplier complex in Toyota City, Japan.
- Undertaken a wholly owned investment in the United States.
- Joined a U.S. automaker for production in the United States.
- Implemented some combination of the above.

Toyota had just built new plants in Toyota City in 1979–1980. It could have exploited its superior productivity there, partly countering export restraints on units by shipping high value-added models to the United States, and sending knock-down sets to overseas points for assembly and export to the United States. Restraints in other markets (e.g., Australia, Mexico, EEC) were compelling Toyota to build and expand foreign production facilities (its foreign plants in 1980–1981 merely assembled kits) but it may have been able to postpone investment in the United States. On the other hand, the U.S. market (the world's largest) was growing rapidly for subcompacts, and

Toyota had ample reserves to finance a wholly owned venture. Considering these options further would digress from the negotiation case study, but they offer clues as to Toyota's bargaining position, approach, and power.

In June 1980, Toyota ostensibly decided to pursue the joint venture route by contacting Ford Motor Company. Talks went on until July 1981, when they broke down completely.[12] In light of Chrysler's alliance with Mitsubishi Heavy Industries and AMC's with Renault, Toyota's only remaining prospective American partner was GM.

The Joint Venture Option—Bases for Collaboration

GM's decision to enter joint venture negotiations, like Toyota's, appears to follow naturally from the two companies' interests and complementary resources and skills. Through collaboration GM could learn production and management techniques from a company renowned for them, and Toyota could gain low-cost entry to the U.S. auto industry with the assistance of the industry leader. Other concerns and motivations are also worth noting.

On the skeptical side, one could speculate that each company could gain merely from the act of negotiating, regardless of the result. During the Toyota-Ford talks, after all, several American observers opined that Toyota was simply trying to demonstrate responsiveness to MITI and the U.S. government without intending to reach an agreement.[13] The same motivation coupled with gathering information about GM is conceivable here. GM too could benefit from "side-effects" such as learning more about its competitor and delaying Toyota's move to produce and to sell without restraints in the United States. The delays, expressed "worries,"[14] and actions that came up during the negotiations are consistent with these possibilities.

One GM participant who was interviewed mentioned that the possibility of Toyota's simply "buying time" did occur to the GM team and concerned them enough to ask Toyota about it. Toyota responded that they were negotiating in good faith and would go into the joint venture with an "open mind." GM itself had no desire to learn just from negotiating, according to another GM interviewee.

Other twists on the companies' motives include a UAW interviewee's assertion that GM simply wanted a replacement for the Chevette, not innovative techniques. One American news article reported that GM Chairman and CEO Roger Smith called the joint venture a "stalling tactic,"[15] or otherwise put, a bridge between GM's product offerings. At one point during the negotiations, Vice Chairman Shigenobu Yamamoto of Toyota also cited his company's desire to *help* GM and the U.S. auto industry, likening this to the traditional Japanese idea of "offering salt to our enemy."[16] While these comments should be evaluated with regard to their sources and intended audiences, they do suggest additional factors for the negotiations.

In the main, however, the participants interviewed by the author and reporters felt that the companies' motivation for pursuing a joint venture was a shared interest in exploring the feasibility of profitable subcompact car production in the United States. GM stood to gain working experience with Japanese techniques that neither licensing alone nor companies other than Toyota might effectively provide.[17] The prospective advantages included the demonstration to American labor that they could work in plants managed by Japanese techniques (a so-called "labor demonstration effect.") On the other hand Toyota could respond to political forces, enter the United States at low risk, and move more quickly up "the learning curve." These and other interests listed above were all reasons for the companies to try to reach an agreement.

In November 1981, Jay Chai, an executive vice president of C. Itoh and Company (America) and the Adviser to the Chairman (of GM) on Japanese Affairs, broached with Toyota executives in Tokyo the possibility of a joint venture with GM. Then on December 21, 1981, Seishi Kato, Chairman of Toyota Motor Sales, met with Roger Smith in Detroit. Language barriers made the visit "bewildering" in Smith's words,[18] but it got the ball rolling.

ISSUES

GM and Toyota faced a wide range of issues. The product, production site, financing, and target market segment had to be selected. The international context brought up issues such as foreign exchange rate fluctuations. And there were issues common to joint venture negotiations: ownership, organizational structure, and operational control (shared, dominant/passive).[19]

Some of the remaining issues were less typical. A car generally comprises 15,000–20,000 parts, so the companies faced a tremendous number of decisions about suppliers. Unionization of the work force, which typified GM's but not Japanese automakers' (Honda, Nissan) U.S. plants, was on the agenda. Lastly, a strategy would have to be formulated to meet any concerns about competition raised by the U.S. Federal Trade Commission.

PRENEGOTIATION PREPARATIONS

Toyota

Like many Japanese organizations, Toyota undoubtedly prepared assiduously for the negotiations.[20] In April 1980, as the U.S. and Japanese governments began auto export restraint negotiations, Toyota contracted one Japanese consulting firm, Nomura Research Institute, and two American firms, SRI International and Arthur D. Little, to study the feasibility of manufacturing in the United States. The intended effect then was probably to assuage government officials. After their completion in the spring of 1981, the studies probably also abetted preparations for the talks with Ford and with GM, although Nomura's study advised against a move to the United States while the two American studies supported it.

There was also dissent within Toyota on a move to the United States. According to one Toyota interviewee, those against it were concerned about UAW strikes and product quality. Eiji Toyoda, the President of Toyota Motor Company, and others supporting the move thus had to negotiate internally as well as externally before and during the joint venture negotiations.

Shortly after the first formal intercompany contact in March 1982 (see below), Eiji Toyoda assembled a five-person project team consisting of representatives from production technology, finance, legal affairs, and overseas projects. Toshio Morita, Executive Vice President of Production Technology, led the team. One American insider who was interviewed revealed that Toyota's planning concentrated on the general relationship with GM; details were set aside. Plans were developed verbally and with little documentation in "numerous" meetings. One document, a draft memorandum of understanding for the joint venture, served as the centerpiece for those and subsequent internal efforts.[21]

In the legal realm, Toyota hired three American law firms. Their advice and "compatibility" with the company were assessed over several months. Toyota then narrowed its choice to Arent, Fox, Kintner, Plotkin, and Kahn, a prominent firm in Washington, D.C., among whose partners was a former FTC chairman.

General Motors

GM's preparations were also "very thorough" and "well-organized" in the words of non-GM observers. In January 1981, John F. Smith, Director of Worldwide Product Planning and a close associate of Roger Smith, went to Japan with Jay Chai to research Toyota's projects intensively. After his return GM concentrated on Toyota's Corolla, and the two Smiths, with some ideas perhaps from reports of the Toyota-Ford experience, outlined a proposal for joint production in the United States.[22]

Early in the process, a marketing group was put together to study the demand for a joint venture car. A design group looked into ways to differentiate a joint venture car from the common Corolla. A cost study for the venture was also undertaken.

Within the company a number of mid-level managers, operations people, and even executives resisted this plan. Perhaps they viewed it as an admission that GM could, or had to, learn from Toyota. That compelled Roger Smith, like Eiji Toyoda at Toyota, to devote a lot of energy during the negotiations to supporting the project and building organizational commitment to it.

Finally, GM continued to consult Chai on strategic and cultural matters since he knew the industry, the ways of Japanese business, and the Japanese language. For antitrust concerns, GM employed an outside law firm, Jones, Day, Reavis, and Pogue in Cleveland, Ohio, and an outside economist along with several antitrust lawyers within the company. The company also arranged to monitor carefully all negotiations with Toyota to ensure that parties avoided areas sensitive to the FTC.

THE PRIMARY NEGOTIATIONS

One approach to negotiations commonly taken in government and in business has been labeled "framework/detail."[23] The first phase entails the parties' development of a formula, or framework, of broad objectives and principles. In the second phase, the formula guides discussion toward a detailed agreement.

Although no interviewee cited explicit use of this approach, it provides a useful structure for a description of the negotiations between GM and Toyota. A memorandum of understanding signed on February 17, 1983, delineates two phases. Alternatively, one could refer to the company heads' agreement in principle in March 1982, not the memorandum, as the "framework." The memorandum was probably a more meaningful framework given the complexity of the overall agenda. Thus, the discussion below treats Phase One as March 1, 1982, to February 17, 1983; Phase Two extends beyond that, through the drafting of the joint venture contract to the incorporation of the joint venture on February 21, 1984.

Actions during the two phases are outlined in Table 2. As a comprehensive timeline of significant points during the primary and ancillary negotiations, the table serves as a reference for the detailed accounts that follow. Bear in mind that Chart 1 identifies the main actors.

Phase One: Developing a Framework

The first formal intercompany negotiation concerning a joint venture occurred on March 1, 1982, in New York City, between Eiji Toyoda, President of Toyota Motor Company, and Roger Smith, Chairman and CEO of GM. A GM source indicated that they discussed only the overall concept of a joint venture, not initial proposals. By the end of the month, he continued, the two company heads had agreed in principle to undertake a feasibility study for a joint venture. Interestingly, a Toyota interviewee read from an official company history of the talks that Smith had made a "very specific" proposal during March, namely a joint venture with equal capital contributions, use of an idle GM plant in California, production of a Corolla-class car beginning Fall 1984, and an output of 200,000–400,000 cars.

Issues.   Whatever the actual circumstances, the issues for subsequent negotiation between the companies constituted a rather full agenda (see Issues above.)

Players.   Responsibility for the day-to-day talks was given to John Smith, GM's Director of Worldwide Product Planning, and Kan Higashi, Toyota's General Manager of Overseas Operations. The balance of both negotiating teams (Chart 1) was made up of representatives from finance (Hughes, Toyozumi) and legal affairs (Weinbaum and staff, Tsukada). Flavio Cella, an assistant to Hughes responsible for special projects, also participated. Each team included outside counsel (Pogue, Meigher), and interpreters were present. Louis Hughes, an assistant treasurer with responsibility for GM's overseas group, and Toyota's Higashi would become chief spokesmen.

Jay Chai officially participated as a member of the GM team but took a facilitating, intermediary role once talks got underway. At several points, he acted as an interpreter. More critically, at impasses Chai would carry and explain to Toyota representatives proposals written by Roger Smith and others.

In addition to this core negotiating group, there were several auxiliary "working groups" that communicated with counterparts across company lines and fed information to their companies' main negotiators.

Conditions.   During the months of negotiation that ensued in 1982, several noteworthy events took place beyond the talks. During March, the same month of the E. Toyoda–R. Smith meeting, GM joined with Fujitsu Fanuc to establish GMF Robotics. In July, Toyota Motor Company and Toyota Motor Sales merged to become the Toyota Motor Corporation. On August 6, the U.S. Internal Revenue Service began an investigation of Toyota for underreporting taxable income. During the first week of February 1983, the Department of Justice actually sued Toyota for data on production costs, sales, and management.

Year-end statistics also reveal part of the broader picture during 1982. All of GM's production and sales figures dropped from 1981 totals, although net income improved (Table 1.) Toyota's performance was mixed. Net sales in Japanese yen increased about 10 percent from 1981 (cf. dollar amounts in Table 1) but U.S. car (unit) sales declined. As a whole, Japanese imports increased their percentage share of the market in 1982 because overall U.S. demand was down. The value of imports also increased, notwithstanding the weaker yen in 1982, since Japanese automakers shipped more expensive models. No doubt one consequence was the passing in the U.S. House of Representatives of domestic content legislation, the "Fair Practices in Automotive Product Act (HR 5133)," on December 15, 1982. This was the context of the negotiations during Phase One.

The Negotiation Process.   In April 1982, talks at the operational level began. (See Table 2.) The negotiating teams divided up the agenda and assigned pieces to working groups. The facility planning group, for example, comprised 3–4 engineers from Toyota and 2 from GM. Other groups were formed for costing, logistics planning, and labor. A schedule was charted; the target date for agreement was set for September 1982.

According to two reports,[24] GM initially proposed a large venture involving two plants and production of some 400,000 subcompact cars. Toyota sought a limited venture based on one abandoned plant with a capacity of 200,000. GM also may have become concerned about the antitrust ramifications of the larger venture, for the limited plan prevailed.

GM sought the Corolla, Toyota's best selling car worldwide, as the product for the joint venture. Toyota offered instead the Sprinter, a sporty subcompact that had been produced since 1968 solely for domestic sale in Japan. One GM participant stated that GM was "very happy" with this offer because it obviated the investment needed to differentiate a Corolla-based joint venture car from the common Corolla.

Formal and informal negotiation sessions took place over several months, moving from discussion of the joint venture concept to feasibility studies to costing studies. (See Table 2.) By late summer 1982, news articles reported agreement on production volume, plant location, and sales channels as well as the type of product.

Sourcing of components had also been decided. Toyota would supply the engine and transmission, and all other parts would be procured through competitive bids. Most of the parts would be Japanese, and Toyota provided the list of bids from Japanese companies. They included affiliates (e.g., Nippondenso) and nonaffiliates (see Chart 1). GM provided the bids from its affiliates (e.g., Delco Products) and other American companies who would primarily supply parts such as radiators, glass, seats, and tires. Since just-in-time (*kanban*) inventory was integral to its production system, Toyota sought explicit assurances from GM that supply decisions would be based on product quality and vendor reliability as well as cost.

The issues were more complicated and the discussion more arduous than either party had anticipated. Citing the number of parts to a car, one GM official reportedly stated, "dozens of decisions have to be made with practically every part . . . . If any

TABLE 2 Chronology of GM-Toyota Negotiations

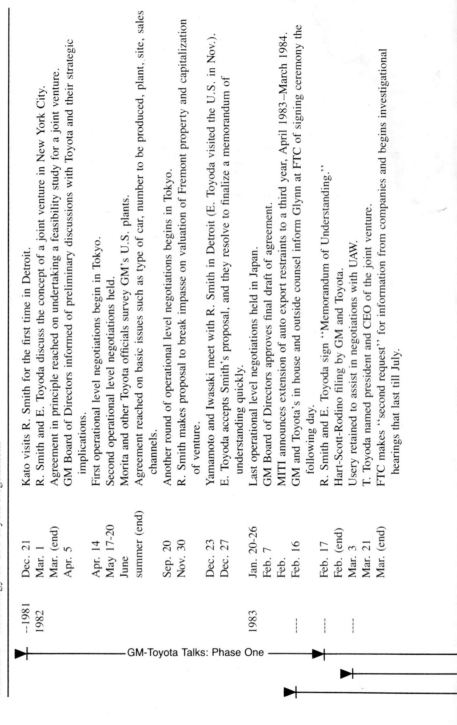

–1981	Dec. 21	Kato visits R. Smith for the first time in Detroit.
1982	Mar. 1	R. Smith and E. Toyoda discuss the concept of a joint venture in New York City.
	Mar. (end)	Agreement in principle reached on undertaking a feasibility study for a joint venture.
	Apr. 5	GM Board of Directors informed of preliminary discussions with Toyota and their strategic implications.
	Apr. 14	First operational level negotiations begin in Tokyo.
	May 17–20	Second operational level negotiations held.
	June	Morita and other Toyota officials survey GM's U.S. plants.
	summer (end)	Agreement reached on basic issues such as type of car, number to be produced, plant, site, sales channels.
	Sep. 20	Another round of operational level negotiations begins in Tokyo.
	Nov. 30	R. Smith makes proposal to break impasse on valuation of Fremont property and capitalization of venture.
	Dec. 23	Yamamoto and Iwasaki meet with R. Smith in Detroit (E. Toyoda visited the U.S. in Nov.).
	Dec. 27	E. Toyoda accepts Smith's proposal, and they resolve to finalize a memorandum of understanding quickly.
1983	Jan. 20–26	Last operational level negotiations held in Japan.
	Feb. 7	GM Board of Directors approves final draft of agreement.
	Feb.	MITI announces extension of auto export restraints to a third year, April 1983–March 1984.
	Feb. 16	GM and Toyota's in house and outside counsel inform Glynn at FTC of signing ceremony the following day.
	Feb. 17	R. Smith and E. Toyoda sign "Memorandum of Understanding."
	Feb. (end)	Hart-Scott-Rodino filing by GM and Toyota.
	Mar. 3	Usery retained to assist in negotiations with UAW.
	Mar. 21	T. Toyoda named president and CEO of the joint venture.
	Mar. (end)	FTC makes "second request" for information from companies and begins investigational hearings that last till July.

GM-Toyota Talks: Phase One

Apr.	First negotiations between Toyota's counsel and FTC staff concerning release of requested information.
May 18	Bieber succeeds Fraser as president of the UAW.
May 25	Formal Toyota-UAW negotiations begin.
June	Toyota provides FTC with a number of company documents.
June 20	First deadline (120 days) for labor agreement stipulated in Memorandum of Understanding; extension granted.
Aug.	Toyota's counsel informs FTC that firm cannot release cost and profit data; Miller publicly demands the data.
Sep. 2	UAW Local #1364 (former GM Fremont workers) sue GM and UAW International for negotiating without them.
Sep. 22	UAW International reaches agreement in principle with GM and Toyota ["letter of intent"].
Nov. 16	New FTC Commissioner Calvani begins term.
Nov. 24–27	FTC staff has access to depository of Toyota documents at offices of outside counsel, breaking two-month impasse.
Dec. 22	GM and Toyota sign consent accord with FTC.
Feb. 21	Joint venture shareholders agreement executed, by-laws accepted, company established in California as New United Motor Manufacturing, Inc.
Apr. 11	FTC grants final approval to joint venture in 3–2 vote.
May	NUMMI begins hiring workers.
Dec. 10	Dedication of first NUMMI Nova (CL Sedan) off the line.

GM-Toyota Talks: Phase Two ➤

UAW "Intent" Talks ➤

FTC Talks ➤ (FTC) ➤

-1984

project ever required patience, this is it."[25] Participants interviewed by the author echoed that assessment for additional reasons.

Communication was difficult due to culturally based factors. For example, Japanese negotiators for Toyota addressed issues in ways that appeared "oblique" to the GM team. Some silences and affirmations at the negotiating table were mistaken for agreement. Translation also slowed the negotiation process considerably.

Negotiating and decision-making styles also contrasted. According to the participants interviewed, the Japanese tended to start talks with statements of general principles and usually did not respond to proposals before checking with their headquarters. The Americans preferred specific proposals and responses at the table. In fact, the GM team received so few proposals from Toyota initially that they wondered where they stood. Further, Toyota was struck by GM negotiators' ability to source information quickly from particular individuals within their organization; GM saw the Toyota team's ability as less clear-cut. In the end, the September 1982 target date for agreement passed, and the date was moved to December.

During the fall of 1982, unresolved issues included the licensing fee to Toyota for its car design, management of operations, prices of the cars (destined for GM), and exchange rate fluctuations.

A major impasse developed on capitalization of the venture and the evaluation of the idle GM plant in Fremont, California, that the companies had selected. GM had reportedly renovated the plant at a cost of $280 million in the months before its closing in March 1982. Toyota, according to its written history of the talks, considered the equipment too old to be effective in increasing production. Toyota also must have figured that GM could at least write off much of that amount. On November 30, 1982, Roger Smith personally wrote to Eiji Toyoda softening GM's stand.[26] Toyoda accepted Smith's proposal on December 27.

A final set of negotiations was held in January 1983 in Tokyo. Early in the month, Shoichiro Toyoda, President of Toyota said, "It is too early to predict the possibility of reaching a final agreement between our companies by the end of January."[27] Among other issues, the pricing of the joint venture car, which had been repeatedly set aside, remained unsettled. Even at the end of the month as *The Wall Street Journal* reported the plan, a Toyota spokesman denied that the companies had an agreement.[28] By February 7, GM's Board of Directors had already twice authorized Roger Smith to sign an agreement. GM awaited Toyota.

The Outcome. On February 14, 1983, only days after MITI notified the U.S. government that it would extend auto export restraints to a third year, GM and Toyota formally announced their agreement on a joint venture. Signed on the 17th, the 15-page "Memorandum of Understanding"[29] stipulated:

- Limited production of a car derived from Toyota's "new frontwheel Sprinter" for sale directly to GM.

- Equal shares of capital from the parent companies (as it turned out, $100 million cash from Toyota; from GM, $11 million cash and the Fremont plant ($89 million); another $250 million was later raised.

- Equal ownership by the parents.

- Design of the Fremont manufacturing layout by Toyota.
- Construction of a stamping plant.
- A "reasonable" royalty to Toyota for the license to manufacture the car.
- Technical assistance from GM and Toyota on a cost-plus basis.
- Nominal annual production capacity of 200,000 cars.
- Pricing joint venture cars on a market-basket standard.[30]
- Startup for the 1985 model year.

Toyota would designate the president (who would serve as chief executive and operating officer) of the joint venture.

Several other clauses bear particular mention. One stipulated that an "acceptable labor relations structure" be established within 120 days. Both governments were also to review the agreement, and until the U.S. government approved it, either party could withdraw. The agreement did not prevent GM from establishing similar relationships with other companies and gave Toyota the opportunity to produce vehicles for itself at the new plant. Lastly, the companies agreed to negotiate remaining issues in "good faith" and to use "best efforts" to complete details by May 15, 1983.

How well this joint venture agreement would serve GM and Toyota's individual interests could only be partly assessed at that point. GM found a replacement for the Chevette, made an idle plant valuable without additional investment, created jobs for its laid-off workers, and gained access to a working model of the Toyota production system. Toyota eased government pressure (except for domestic content legislation in the United States), established a foothold from which to compete with Nissan and Honda (its Japanese forerunners in the U.S. auto industry) at a 50 percent savings, and gained access to the most extensive auto parts supplier network in the United States.

Some American observers complained in the American press that Toyota outnegotiated GM.[31] Toyota did gain operational control of the venture, although that could have been seen by GM as necessary for creating an accurate and didactic model of Toyota's system. Most of the components were to be Japanese. Toyota also had a built-in client and royalties and other fees that considerably lowered its risk. Toyota clearly gained a great deal. But the achievement of each company's primary goal, learning from the other, depended on yet to be designed mechanisms and on experiences of the joint venture well after startup.

Phase Two: Completing the Details

From the February 1983 signing of the Memorandum to the May 15th target for a contract, and even up to the February 1984 incorporation of the joint venture, a number of additional issues required negotiation. Many concerned the United Auto Workers and the Federal Trade Commission, whose negotiations with the two companies will be discussed in the next section. There also remained detailed items for intercompany negotiations.

Issues. The companies had previously agreed to establish the joint venture as a corporation, and that called for certain discussions and legal documentation. The names of the corporation and of the product were open. Furthermore, management structure and selection (except for the president) had to be decided and formulated, as did agreements on vehicle supply, component supply, service parts, technical assistance and license, realty, and "product responsibility" (liability).

Players.   For this phase Eiji Toyoda and Roger Smith assumed very limited roles. Some of the working groups (e.g., costing) had also largely completed their tasks. The core group of negotiators (Chart 1) stayed in place to work out the fine points.

Conditions.   The environment for the negotiations in 1983, like conditions throughout the joint venture talks, is again noteworthy. Commerce Secretary Malcolm Baldridge, among others, applauded the companies' February accord as "a significant development for the auto industry in the U.S. and in the world." Before that, however, opposition came from Ford, Chrysler, Toyota dealers in the United States and others, and it continued throughout the year (Chart 1). Toyota itself continued to be pursued by the IRS. On March 14, a U.S. District Court ordered the company to explain why it could not provide the IRS with cost and profit information.

In July, MITI hinted at ending the auto export restraints but relented, in October, to an extension. After bargaining with the U.S. Trade Representative to get a 10 percent increase, MITI announced a fourth year of restraints (April 1984–March 1985) on November 1. Two days later, the U.S. House of Representatives passed another bill on domestic content of autos (HR 1234).

The companies' activities beyond their joint talks in 1983 included Toyota's talks with the government of Taiwan for a joint venture in autos. The talks broke down in the fall. During the year, Isuzu and Suzuki built new plants to increase their export capacity, and on October 6th, GM (who opposed Japanese auto export restraints) announced plans to import 200,000 subcompacts from Isuzu and 100,000 minicars from Suzuki. In November, GM also announced the establishment of the Saturn Project, an internal attempt to produce domestically a competitive small car. By year's end, GM's fortunes, and those of the U.S. auto industry, had clearly improved: Net sales and net income topped all four previous years. Toyota's net income rose 52 percent in dollars[32] (Table 1).

The Negotiation Process and Outcome.   Negotiations between the two companies during Phase Two entered particularly sensitive areas, so information about meetings and proposals is scarce. A Japanese newspaper reported that the agreed licensing fee to Toyota was about 2.5 percent of factory shipments with no down payment.[33] A delivery system for American parts was also developed. Since California did not have a developed auto parts industry, nothing close to the hundreds of suppliers in Toyota City, the logistic planning group looked to the Midwest's infrastructure. They set up a central supply point in Chicago and arranged for daily rail shipments to Fremont. Japanese supplies could be shipped right into the Port of Oakland.

During this period Toyota also moved ahead on its own. On March 21, 1983, Tatsuro Toyoda, a nephew of Eiji Toyoda, was informally named CEO of the yet to be approved joint venture (Table 2). Having gained the right to lay out the plant and coordinate acquisition and installation of equipment, Toyota also requested bids from a number of suppliers and builders. By the summer of 1983, Toyoda Machine Works (a Toyoda Group member) and Komatsu, among others, had been selected as equipment suppliers for the new stamping plant. (Japanese suppliers provided most of the plant equipment for the venture, which all told ran about $450 million.)

When GM and Toyota began drafting the final joint venture contract, GM offered a version that, like many American companies' legal documents, covered numerous contingencies. Toyota's thinner initial draft came closer in size and form to the final contract. The joint venture was to be called New United Motor Manufacturing, Inc., and its product would be sold as the Chevrolet Nova. NUMMI was incorporated in California on February 21, 1984.

ANCILLARY NEGOTIATIONS

To create their joint venture, GM Toyota had to go beyond their intercompany negotiations. Talks were undertaken with suppliers, the State of California, which provided $2 million in training funds, the City of Fremont, and many other organizations, so that the overall process was generally complicated by having to negotiate several agendas with several parties in different arenas. Still, the talks with the United Auto Workers and the Federal Trade Commission, which went on largely during Phase Two of the intercompany negotiations, were vital for the joint venture.

Negotiations with the UAW

In late 1979 and in 1980, a year that saw layoffs of 300,000 auto workers and twice that number in related industries, UAW President Douglas Fraser galvanized the American public to push for remedies. U.S. car production was still dropping in 1982. In this atmosphere, a venture that represented up to 3,000 direct jobs drew a lot of union attention.

Issues.   For the UAW, the primary issue to resolve with GM and Toyota was the rehiring of workers laid off when GM closed the Fremont plant in March 1982. (At its peak in 1978, the plant had employed 6,000.) Other issues included recognition of the UAW at the new plant, the hiring selection process, job classifications, and seniority. Toyota's concerns about production standards and compulsory overtime, among other points, would also come up in the talks.

A number of factors augmented the seriousness of these issues. The UAW had represented the Fremont work force, as it did the rest of the GM system. At the same time, Toyota had very serious reservations about labor relations, cost, and quality in the United States. The reputation of GM-Fremont workers did not alleviate these concerns. In early 1982, there was absenteeism of 20 percent and a backlog of 1,000 grievances, while production costs and product quality were GM's worst.

Players.   Toyota took sole responsibility for working out a labor agreement for the new venture. The company could thereby pursue its concerns fully; the decision also set the venture somewhat apart from GM's existing bargaining agreement with the

UAW. Takeo Tsukada, effectively Toyota's general counsel, led the negotiators' working group on labor.

On March 3, 1983, Toyota hired former U.S. Secretary of Labor William Usery as labor relations consultant to the still fetal joint venture[34] (Chart 1). He led the team that negotiated directly with the UAW. The team included one of his associates and an attorney hired by Toyota.

On the UAW side, Douglas Fraser played a supportive role in the early stages when he was president. The major union negotiators, however, were Donald Ephlin, a vice president of the UAW International and Director of the GM Department; Bruce Lee, a regional representative of the International in California; and Bill Colbath, a personal representative of Fraser's successor, Owen Bieber.

Conditions.   At least three conditions for the talks, conditions beyond the GM-Fremont community and the improving fortunes of the U.S. auto industry, deserve mention. First, the UAW International changed leadership on May 18, 1983, at its triennial conference. The new president, Bieber, was less enthusiastic than Fraser about the joint venture. He appointed Ephlin, who took on the primary role at the talks, but he sent Colbath as well. During the summer the International revoked the charter of the GM-Fremont local (#1364). Although it was ultimately unsuccessful, the local sued GM, Toyota, and the UAW International for depriving it of a voice in the negotiations.

During this period, GM was making Guaranteed Income Stream payments to some 828 former GM-Fremont workers. The 1982 national GM-UAW contract provided that workers with 10 years seniority who were laid off because of a permanent plant closing would receive 50 percent of their wages until retirement. News reports suggested that as Fremont workers depleted other benefits, up to 2,100 workers might receive the GIS payments.

The third and most interesting condition was the UAW's legal position. The organization could not bargain or sign a contract because it had not been certified, and it could not be certified before the joint venture had a work force. Thus, the negotiators had to consider and work toward an alternative form of agreement.

The Negotiation Process.   Beginning in March 1983, Usery met several times with Toyota executives in Japan and in the United States. He also met with Fraser and Bieber before the UAW election (Table 2). At a press conference on May 12, Usery announced his role and the willingness of Toyota to use former GM employees as the "primary source" for recruitment. Different interpretations of that statement and other issues underscored the need for negotiations.

Full-fledged talks began May 25. In addition to meetings between the Usery and UAW teams, there were several one-on-one sessions between Usery and Ephlin, among others. The talks went into mid-September, past the June 20th deadline set in the Memorandum and past even a second deadline.

One participant called these negotiations "very, very difficult." He cited conceptual and linguistic hurdles in conversations between Usery and the Japanese. With the UAW, the scope of the rehiring commitment was, as expected, a major issue. Job classifications also caused difficulty since the UAW had 100 different classifications at some GM plants, whereas Toyota had only a few classifications and rotated workers.

The Outcome.   On September 22, 1983, Usery announced an agreement between the joint venture and the UAW. The resulting ''binding letter of intent'' set forth general principles such as ''undertaking this new proposed relationship with the full intention of fostering an innovative labor relations structure, minimizing traditional adversarial roles and emphasizing mutual trust and good faith.''[35] Specific points included:

- Recognition of the UAW as the bargaining agent for workers once hiring began.
- Using laid-off GM workers as the primary source of new hires.
- Not preserving seniority rights from GM-Fremont.
- Pegging wages at going industry rates.
- Willingness of the UAW to be flexible on work rules.
- Negotiating a contract with the UAW by June 1985.

This then, provided the joint venture with an ''understanding'' with the UAW and a hiring pool of skilled workers.[36]

Negotiations with the FTC

The second critical ancillary arena for negotiation involved the Federal Trade Commission.

Issues.   The primary concern here was GM's and Toyota's compliance with antitrust regulations. From the FTC's viewpoint, the joint venture agreement potentially violated Section 5 of the Federal Trade Commission Act, which alludes to unfair methods of competition. If the agreement were consumated, the joint venture could violate Section 7 of the Clayton Act, which prohibits joint ventures that may substantially lessen competition. These were the bases for a complaint drafted by the FTC staff during the summer of 1983. A more immediate issue, however, was the type and amount of company information that GM and Toyota would provide for the FTC's deliberations.

Players.   The ultimate decision makers in this arena were the five FTC Commissioners. James Miller, a Reagan appointee, chaired the Commission. The other members were Michael Pertschuk (a Carter appointee), Patricia Bailey (Carter), George Douglas (Reagan), and until his replacement in the fall of 1983, David Clanton (Ford).

For the GM-Toyota-FTC negotiations per se though, other individuals were more involved; Eugene Meigher and Dennis Cuneo from Toyota's outside law firm, and Richard Pogue, from GM's outside law firm, participated actively along with their clients' in-house counsel (Chart 1). At the FTC, Edward Glynn, Assistant Director of International Antitrust in the Bureau of Competition, and David Scheffman, Deputy Director of the Bureau of Economics, led day-to-day activities. In the late stages, Timothy Muris, Director of the Bureau of Competition, drafted the final FTC staff position.

Conditions.   Within the FTC at that time, Chairman Miller and Commissioner Pertschuk, a former chairman, often led opposing viewpoints, and during this case, their differences again emerged. One of Pertschuk's allies, Commissioner Clanton, was scheduled to leave office on September 25, 1983. GM and Toyota thus faced the possibility that the swing vote in the final decision by the commission would be a new commissioner, a Reagan appointee.

The companies also had to contend with overt outside opposition to their plans. On February 21, 1983, days after the Memorandum was signed, Lee Iacocca, Chairman of Chrysler Corp., stated, "I don't like it. I don't think the two biggest [auto companies] should make an assault on the U.S. market and carve it up."[37] For the next 14 months Chrysler maintained a "full court press" in the media, at the FTC, in Congress, and in the courts. On January 16, 1984, the company sued GM and Toyota in U.S. District Court, charging violation of antitrust laws and asking for compensation. Other opponents of the joint venture included Ford, Toyota dealers in the United States, the National Tooling and Machining Association, and the Consumer Federation of America (Chart 1). With this backdrop, GM and Toyota's efforts with the FTC staff must have been especially trying. The joint venture rested in the balance.

The Negotiation Process.   The companies concentrated on two steps: a favorable staff position, and the commissioners' ruling. The effort involved both companies. Because of the information available to the author, however, the account below highlights Toyota.

On February 16, 1983, the day before the signing of the Memorandum of Understanding, the companies' in-house and outside counsel met with Glynn at the FTC and informed him of the scheduled signing[38] (Table 2). Within the next two weeks, they made a Hart-Scott-Rodino filing, which basically entails notifying the FTC of certain merger or acquisition activities. A month later the FTC staff sent the companies a "Second Request" for company documents. The FTC also began investigational hearings that called in all the major auto companies. They would go on for four months.

It was over the "Second Request" that the major negotiations occurred. In its first talks with a large FTC team in April, Toyota's outside counsel stated that Toyota would never fully comply with Hart-Scott-Rodino guidelines. Concerned about the confidentiality of cost and profit data, the company sent documents excluding that information to the FTC in June. Late in August, Chairman Miller publicly demanded the cost and profit data. Toyota reiterated its position, and negotiations came to a halt.

Some American observers felt Toyota awaited the departure of Commissioner Clanton who allegedly opposed the joint venture. Others cited Toyota's interest in preventing company information from ultimately reaching the IRS, and still others speculated with little foundation that Toyota had lost interest in the venture because the improving U.S. auto industry had quieted protectionist voices.

In any event, Roger Smith said in October that GM was "anxious for Toyota to get their data in to get the so-called clock running."[39] The FTC's Muris wrote to Toyota, giving the company "one last chance."

The FTC staff and Toyota representatives resolved their two-month impasse over documents rather creatively. Documents on cost and profit were set aside in a depository at the company's outside law firm. Over the Thanksgiving weekend, a week after Terry Calvani replaced Clanton as the new FTC commissioner, FTC staff studied the documents in place. (GM also set up a depository for its documents.)

Throughout these negotiations, complications beyond the substantive issues arose. Ironically, FTC staff found that Toyota's documents, like those of many Japanese companies, were in a brief one-page format that offered them insufficient detail. Interviews became a more important source of information. Glynn took a staff team to Japan in September to take depositions from Toyota's negotiators, but only after the FTC had worked through the issue of extraterritoriality. Toyota's general expectations concerning legal matters also struck American observers as unusual, at least for American firms. For example, Toyota underestimated the amount of information needed by American attorneys before offering advice. Such were the international dimensions of legal and governmental affairs.

In mid-December, the FTC staff proposed that GM and Toyota sign a consent order, that is, that they agree to undertake certain obligations and limitations on their future conduct. From the FTC staff's point of view the deal had been satisfactorily structured. Its main concern was that the companies follow through with the agreement as planned.

The Outcome.   On December 22, 1983, the companies signed the order, and a 60-day period for public comment began.

The consent order contains nine sections. The most significant features are prohibitions against exchanging nonpublic information about cars, parts, costs, marketing plans, sales forecasts, and model changes, and a requirement to maintain files on all communications. The FTC also limited the duration of the joint venture to 12 years after the start of production, but not beyond December 31, 1997.

The order went into effect on April 11, 1984, when the commissioners approved the venture by a 3–2 vote. On that day, GM and Toyota surmounted the last major hurdle in the creation of their joint venture.

STRATEGIC IMPLICATIONS

From the initial Kato-Smith meeting to the consent agreement with the FTC, a 24-month period, GM and Toyota engaged in a complex process of negotiation. As Chart 1 illustrated, they each dealt with a number of actors in varied arenas: the intercompany talks, critical ancillary negotiations, interorganizational networks, the market and industry, and the political environment. Each party brought an agenda of issues. Furthermore, several negotiations went on concurrently (recall Table 2), on more than one level of activity, in an environment that continually changed.

The two companies succeeded in reaching agreements that created, facilitated, and allowed a joint venture. An assessment of the contents of the intercompany agreement in particular is a subject for another study. This study delved into the process of negotiation, and from it one can draw five strategic implications for complex (specifically international joint venture) negotiations.

(1) Preparation and Monitoring

In light of the information and activity required in complex negotiations, careful planning seems especially important. Interests and options should be identified and evaluated for one's own company as well as the prospective partner(s). Assessment must continue through the negotiations. Moreover, the activities of a counterpart beyond the negotiating table and other forces in the dynamic multifaceted environment (recall Chart 1) may call for reevaluations of anticipated benefits and costs.

The timing of a venture and the expected duration of negotiations also deserve consideration. Restraints on Japanese auto exports are still in place today six years after the Kato-Smith meeting, but now products from even lower cost sources (Korea, Taiwan, Brazil, Mexico) have entered the U.S. market. Moreover, in July 1985, Toyota announced plans for its own assembly plants in the United States and in Canada, and in September 1986, began producing cars at NUMMI under its own nameplate. In late 1984, GM arranged to source from Korea's Daewoo, and in August 1986, set up a joint venture with Suzuki in Canada. Such factors must be monitored and anticipated without injuring the budding joint venture relationship.

(2) Top-Level Support

The GM-Toyota negotiations also illustrate the impact of top-level support on one's own organization and negotiators and on the counterpart. Both sides look for signals of commitment. At the same time, if too active, CEOs run the risk of diminishing the perceived authority of their more involved negotiators. Executive intervention may be most effective if used sparingly, for example, at major impasses.[40]

Leadership among the most involved negotiators also seems important given the diffusion of activity—the multiple negotiating arenas, internal and external negotiations—and dependence of resolution of issues in one arena on resolutions in other arenas. (See also (5) below). It was because of the "highly motivated" core group of negotiators, according to one participant, that the GM-Toyota talks succeeded.

(3) Intermediaries and Other Outside Experts

For negotiations involving a number of disparate issues and parties having different negotiating styles, outside experts may be especially helpful. The GM-Toyota talks entailed labor and antitrust as well as auto parts issues. Further, the two companies' predominantly domestic outlooks, ethnic differences and unknowns, and corporate cultures and attitudes based on being "Number One" complicated the talks. GM employed Chai for strategic and cultural affairs, Toyota hired Usery for labor concerns, and both companies hired outside counsel for the antitrust issues. Intermediaries and other outside experts have facilitated other international auto negotiations as well (e.g., AMC and Beijing Automotive Works).[41]

(4) "Fractionating"[42] the Agenda and the Format

One way to handle very large agendas is to break them into manageable issue clusters. GM and Toyota, for example, formed working groups such as logistics planning to "feed" the main negotiating teams. Moreover, formal, full team-on-team formats should probably not be the only venue for talks. Individuals can also accomplish a great deal in formal and informal one-on-one meetings.

(5) Referring to the "Big Picture"

For several reasons (the complexity and detail of the agenda, the various arenas of activity, the months of effort involved (recall Table 2), and strong partisan positions), key players should refer regularly to the basic relationship being sought and to the potential benefits of the companies' cooperation. (See (2) above.) Internally, Toyota seems to have done so by concentrating on a single draft memorandum of understanding. In joint sessions, the negotiators can also reframe in order to stimulate and sustain momentum as needed. (This also counterbalances some of the drawbacks of (4) above.) This tack is effective as long as the companies see more benefits than costs in the joint venture relationship.

Joint Ventures and Negotiation

By now, in 1987, each of the Big Three is allied with a Japanese automaker. Other international joint ventures and tie-ups are readily apparent elsewhere: AMC and Beijing Automotive Works, Ford and VW's formation of Autolatina, and Toyota and Kuozui Motors (Taiwan). Others have been attempted, but the negotiations failed: Saab and Volvo, GM and Leyland-Land Rover, and Ford and Fiat. And some are in progress: Ford and Nissan, Toyota and VW.

The reputations of GM and Toyota made their joint venture negotiations prominent. But aspects of the process will be similar for others. As alliances continue to be sought in the auto industry, their creation will entail a number of the challenges encountered by General Motors and Toyota Motor in the early 1980s.

NOTES

1. Those interviewed in structured and open-ended formats include 11 individuals from C. Itoh and Company, the Federal Trade Commission, General Motors, GM's outside counsel, NUMMI management, Toyota Motor, Toyota's outside counsel, and the UAW. Unless stated otherwise in the text, however, the views herein are the responsibility of the author.
2. See M. Bazerman and R. Lewicki, eds., *Negotiating in Organizations,* Sage, 1983, and J. Wall, *Negotiation: Theory and Practice,* Scott Foresman and Co., 1985. Cf. G. R. Winham, "Complexity in International Negotiation" in *Negotiations: Social Psychological Perspectives,* ed. by D. Druckman, Sage, 1977.
3. For an elaboration of this approach, see S. E. Weiss, "Forests and Trees in International Business Negotiations: An Integrative Framework of Analysis," mimeo, New York University, 1987. [See now "Analysis of Complex Organizations in International Business: The RBC Perspective," *Organization Science,* 1993.]
4. K. R. Harrigan, *Strategies for Joint Ventures,* Lexington Books, 1985.
5. R. Phillips et al., *Auto Industries of Europe, United States, and Japan,* The Economist Intelligence Unit, 1982.
6. "Why Japanese Auto Makers Hesitate to Go the United States?" *Oriental Economist,* April 1980.
7. Ward's Automotive Reports reported 1,908,000 Japanese car imports for 1980, and the Japan Automobile Manufacturers Association reported 1,819,092. Statistics vary by source, within and between countries.

8. See N. Fujii, "The Road to the U.S.-Japan Auto Crash: Agenda-Setting for Automobile Trade Friction" in *U.S.-Japan Relations: New Attitudes for a New Era, The Program on U.S.-Japan Relations,* Harvard University, 1984, and G. R. Winham and I. Kabashima, "The Politics of U.S.-Japanese Auto Trade" in *Coping with U.S.-Japanese Economic Conflicts,* eds. I. M. Destler and H. Sato, Lexington, 1982.

9. "Toyota Motor Co., Ltd., *"Oriental Economist,* February 1980.

10. According to a report in *The Asian Wall Street Journal* cited in *The Los Angeles Reporter,* February 14, 1983.

11. In contrast, during the 1970s, according to the MVMA, US, GM's non-Canadian imports dropped: in 1971, 88,535; in 1975, 39,730; and in 1980, none . In Canada, however, GM produced 406,186 cars in 1971 and 514,396 in 1980.

12. For more details, see S. E. Weiss, "One Impasse, One Agreement: Toyota's Joint Venture Negotiations with Ford and GM," mimeo, New York University, forthcoming.

13. L. M. Apcar, "Ford Is Likely to Reject Toyota Proposal for Joint Car-Production Venture in U.S.," *The Wall Street Journal,* July 14, 1980.

14. R. D. Hershey, Jr., "Toyota Warned by FTC," *The New York Times,* October 19, 1983.

15. "How the GM-Toyota Deal Buys Time," *Business Week,* February 28, 1983.

16. J. Holusha, "Toyota on G.M. Deal: Giving Aid to Opponent," *The New York Times,* March 22, 1983. Yamamoto also stated, "For a long time GM has sent staff to visit our manufacturing facilities, and I think GM has come to understand [our system] theoretically." See also New United Motor Manufacturing, Inc., UAW, and U.S. Dept. of Labor, "New United Motor Manufacturing, Inc. and the United Automobile Workers: Partners in Training," paper for the ILO/Turin Center, May, 1986.

17. The Japanese held the largest cost advantage over other automakers. Of the Japanese companies that had the resources for a joint venture, Toyota was best known for production technology. That is presumably why Nissan and Honda were avoided as possible partners.

18. C. Reich, "The Innovator," *The New York Times Magazine,* April 21, 1985.

19. J. P. Killing, *Strategies for Joint Venture Success,* Praeger, 1983.

20. See N. B. Thayer and S. E. Weiss, "Japan: The Changing Logic of a Former Minor Power" in *National Negotiating Styles,* ed. H. Binnendijk, U.S. Dept. of State, 1987.

21. On the concept of a "single negotiating text," see R. Fisher and W. Ury, *Getting to Yes,* Houghton Mifflin, 1981. Toyota's draft agreement, which also contained notes on the company's internal discussions, would go through some 12 revisions before becoming the actual memorandum of understanding with GM.

22. Reich, "The Innovator."

23. F. C. Ikle, *How Nations Negotiate,* Harper and Row, 1964; I. W. Zartman and M. R. Berman, *The Practical Negotiator,* Yale Univ. Press, 1982.

24. Based on an interview and cited in "GM, Toyota Agree to Explore Joint Output of Small Car, A Proposal Rejected by Ford," *The Wall Street Journal,* March 9, 1982.

25. J. Koten, "GM '90% Sure' of Joint Venture Accord With Toyota in U.S. as the Talks Drag On," *The Wall Street Journal,* January 24, 1983.

26. Based on an interview. See also *Nihon Keizei Shimbun,* February 16, 1983, as reported in J. Graham and Y. Sano, *Smart Bargaining,* Ballinger, 1984.

27. J. Hartley, "GM and Toyota Trying Too Hard?" *Automotive News,* January 24, 1983.

28. J. Koten, "GM, Toyota Pact Is Expected Soon On Joint Output," *The Wall Street Journal,* January 31, 1983.

29. As reprinted in *Federal Trade Commission Decisions,* 103.

30. According to a participant, the pricing of the car was settled only a couple of days before the signing on the 17th. The market basket standard is a formula based on the weighted average of wholesale prices of 10 competitive small cars (including Toyota's Corolla).
31. One GM official said, "When you look at it closely, they [Toyota] really aren't giving up anything. All they can do is win on this," as quoted in J. Koten, "How Toyota Stands to Gain From the GM Deal," *The Wall Street Journal*, February 14, 1983.
32. According to the Dissenting Statement of FTC Commissioner Bailey, top shares in the subcompact segment of the U.S. market in 1983 were: Ford, 19.1%, Toyota, 16.06%, and GM, 14.41%.
33. "Toyota, GM reach rough accord on joint car production in US," *Japan Economic Journal*, February 8, 1983.
34. D. Henne et al., "A Case Study in Cross-Cultural Mediation: The General Motors-Toyota Joint Venture," *Arbitration Journal*, September 1986.
35. NUMMI, UAW, US DoL, op. cit.
36. As for the epilogue, contract negotiations began in April, 1984. The talks went through the national GM-UAW negotiations during Fall 1984 and reached agreement in mid-July 1985, seven months after the plant had begun production. A new UAW chapter, Local No. 2244, was established to replace No. 1364.
37. A. Fleming, "GM-Toyota: Blazing Topic," *Automotive News*, February 21, 1983.
38. One interviewee said Toyota's outside counsel informed the FTC of "discussions" between the two companies in March, 1982. An interviewee at the FTC said he heard of the talks while in Japan in September, 1982 then notified a contact at GM in October that the FTC would be looking into the negotiations.
39. Hershey, "Toyota Warned by FTC."
40. See J. Brooks and E. Brooks, "The Role of Top Management in Negotiations," *MSU Business Topics*, Summer 1979.
41. See J. Rubin, ed., *Dynamics of Third Party Intervention*, Praeger, 1981.
42. From R. Fisher, *International Conflict for Beginners*, Harper and Row, 1969.

Questionnaires

Personal Bargaining Inventory

INTRODUCTION

One way for negotiators to learn more about themselves, and about others in a negotiating context, is to clarify their own personal beliefs and values about the negotiation process and their style as negotiators. The questionnaire in this section can help you clarify perceptions of yourself on several dimensions related to negotiation—winning and losing, cooperation and competition, power and deception—and your beliefs about how a person "ought" to negotiate. Your instructor is likely to ask you to share your responses with others after you complete the questionnaire.

ADVANCE PREPARATION

Complete the Personal Bargaining Inventory questionnaire in this exercise. Bring the inventory to class.

PROCEDURE

Option 1: 60–90 Minutes

a. Pick six–eight statements from Part I (rating yourself) and six–eight statements from Part II (rating people's behavior in general) that you feel most strongly about.

b. In groups of four to five (as organized by the instructor), discuss those statements in Part I that you feel most strongly about. Working around the group, each individual should reveal (1) the statements he/she selected, and (2) whether the statements are characteristic or uncharacteristic of him/her. Other group members may then ask questions of clarification. The group as a whole then should help the individual arrive at a two or three sentence summary description of that individual's *self-image as a negotiator.*

Adapted from an exercise developed by Bert Brown and Norman Berkowitz.

Note. The role of the group is *not* to challenge, confront, or attempt to change an individual's view of himself. Group members are encouraged to be supportive of an individual's self-view and try to understand how that individual sees himself/ herself.

c. Using the same groups, members should now proceed to Part II (people's behavior in general) of the questionnaire. The same format and approach should be followed. Individuals should identify the six–eight statements that they most strongly agree or disagree with. Each individual should state these to the group, and the group should then help each individual to identify that individual's *philosophy of negotiation effectiveness.* Again, the purpose of the groups is not to talk an individual out of his/her beliefs, but to try to understand how people approach this process with very different beliefs and values. Individuals should work to understand how their own view is *similar* or *different* to other individuals in the group and class.

d. One person from the group should be selected as spokesperson to prepare a report to the class. The reporter should *not* identify individuals, but try to summarize the different "types" of individuals that were identified in the group.

Option 2: 60–90 Minutes

a. The instructor will give you six–eight 3 × 5 file cards. Select *six* statements from the first group of 23 that you feel most strongly about (statements which are either strongly characteristic or strongly uncharacteristic of you). Write each statement on a separate 3 × 5 card—statement number, full text of the statement, and whether it is characteristic or uncharacteristic of you.

b. Your instructor will give you further information on how to proceed.

Personal Bargaining Inventory Questionnaire
___

The questions in this inventory are designed to measure your responses to your perceptions of human behavior in situations of bargaining and negotiation. The first group of statements ask you about *your own behavior* in bargaining; the second group asks you to judge *people's behavior in general.*

Part I: Rating Your Own Behavior

For each statement, please indicate how much the statement is *characteristic of you* on the following scale:

1 Strongly uncharacteristic
2 Moderately uncharacteristic
3 Mildly uncharacteristic
4 Neutral; no opinion
5 Mildly characteristic
6 Moderately characteristic
7 Strongly characteristic

Rate each statement on the seven-point scale by writing in one number closest to your personal judgment of yourself:

Rating   *Statement*

_____ 1. I am sincere and trustworthy at all times. I will not lie, for whatever ends.

_____ 2. I would refuse to bug the room of my opponent.

_____ 3. I don't particularly care what people think of me. Getting what I want is more important than making friends.

_____ 4. I am uncomfortable in situations where the rules are ambiguous and there are few precedents.

_____ 5. I prefer to deal with others on a one-to-one basis rather than as a group.

_____ 6. I can lie effectively. I can maintain a poker face when I am not telling the truth.

_____ 7. I pride myself on being highly principled. I am willing to stand by those principles no matter what the cost.

_____ 8. I am a patient person. As long as an agreement is finally reached, I do not mind slow-moving arguments.

_____ 9. I am a good judge of character. When I am being deceived, I can spot it quickly.

_____ 10. My sense of humor is one of my biggest assets.

_____ 11. I have above-average empathy for the views and feelings of others.

_____ 12. I can look at emotional issues in a dispassionate way. I can argue strenuously for my point of view, but put the dispute aside when the argument is over.

_____ 13. I tend to hold grudges.

_____ 14. Criticism doesn't usually bother me. Any time you take a stand people are bound to disagree, and it's ok for them to let you know they don't like your stand.

_____ 15. I like power. I want it for myself, to do with what I want. In situations where I must share power I strive to increase my power base, and lessen that of my co-power holder.

_____ 16. I like to share power. It is better for two or more to have power than it is for power to be in just one person's hands. The balance of shared power is important to effective functioning of any organization because it forces participation in decision making.

_____ 17. I enjoy trying to persuade others to my point of view.

_____ 18. I am not effective at persuading others to my point of view when my heart isn't really in what I am trying to represent.

_____ 19. I love a good old, knockdown, drag-out verbal fight. Conflict is healthy, and open conflict where everybody's opinion is aired is the best way to resolve differences of opinion.

_____ 20. I hate conflict and will do anything to avoid it—including giving up power over a situation.

_____ 21. In any competitive situation I like to win. Not just win, but win by the biggest margin possible.

_____ 22. In any competitive situation I like to win. I don't want to clobber my opponent, just come out a little ahead.

_____ 23. The only way I could engage conscionably in bargaining would be by dealing honestly and openly with my opponents.

Part II: Rating People's Behavior in General

For each statement, please indicate how much you agree with the statement on the following scale:

1. Strongly disagree
2. Moderately disagree
3. Mildly disagree
4. Neutral; no opinion
5. Mildly agree
6. Moderately agree
7. Strongly agree

Rate each statement on the seven-point scale by writing in one number closest to your personal judgment of people's behavior in general:

Rating   *Statement*

_____   24. If you are too honest and trustworthy, most people will take advantage of you.

_____   25. Fear is a stronger persuader than trust.

_____   26. When one is easily predictable, one is easily manipulated.

_____   27. The appearance of openness in your opponent should be suspect.

_____   28. Make an early minor concession; the other side may reciprocate on something you want later on.

_____   29. Personality and the ability to judge people and persuade them to your point of view (or to an acceptable compromise) are more important than knowledge and information about the issues at hand.

_____   30. Silence is golden—it's the best reply to a totally unacceptable offer.

_____   31. Be the aggressor. You must take the initiative if you are going to accomplish your objectives.

_____   32. One should avoid frequent use of a third party.

_____   33. Honesty and openness are necessary to reach equitable agreement.

_____   34. It is important to understand one's values prior to bargaining.

_____   35. Be calm. Maintaining your cool at *all* times gives you an unquestionable advantage. Never lose your temper.

_____   36. Keep a poker face: never act pleased as terms are agreed upon.

_____   37. A good negotiator must be able to see the issues from the opponent's point of view.

_____   38. An unanswered threat will be read by your opponent as weakness.

_____   39. In bargaining, winning is the most important consideration.

_____   40. The best outcome in bargaining is one which is fair to all parties.

_____   41. Most results in bargaining can be achieved through cooperation.

_____   42. Principles are all well and good, but sometimes have to be compromised to achieve your goals.

_____   43. You should never try to exploit your adversary's personal weakness.

_____   44. A member of a bargaining team is morally responsible for the strategies and tactics employed by that team.

_____ 45. Good ends justify the means. If you know you're right and your goal is worthy, you needn't be concerned too much about *how* your goal is achieved.

_____ 46. Honesty means openness, candor, telling all and not withholding pertinent information, not exaggerating emotion. One should always be honest during bargaining.

_____ 47. Imposing personal discomfort on an opponent is not too high a price to pay for success in negotiation.

_____ 48. Regardless of personal considerations one should accept any role assigned to him by the bargaining team.

_____ 49. There is no need to deal completely openly with your adversaries. In bargaining as in life, what they don't know, won't hurt them.

_____ 50. There is nothing wrong with lying to an opponent in a bargaining situation as long as you don't get caught.

DISCUSSION QUESTIONS

Option 1

1. Which six–eight statements did you identify for Part I? What summary statement did you arrive at to characterize your self-image as a negotiator?

2. Which six–eight statements did you identify for Part II? What summary statement did you arrive at to characterize your philosophy of negotiation effectiveness?

3. How similar or different were you to other people in your group? In your class? Did this surprise you? Why?

4. What do you believe are the good and bad aspects of your self-image as a negotiator? Are there aspects that you would like to change? Which ones?

Option 2

1. Which six statements did you begin with? Which six statements did your group end with? How much do your statements still represent your own self-image?

2. How much influence do you think you had in the group meetings? If you had a lot of influence, how were you influential? If you had very little influence, how were others influential?

3. Are you comfortable with the group's statements? Do you wish you had behaved any differently in group discussions?

4. How do the groups' statements differ from one another? What does this say about personal views of negotiation?

Questionnaire on Machiavellianism

INTRODUCTION

The questionnaire in this section explores your orientation to a personality dimension known as Machiavellianism. Please complete the questionnaire, and then your instructor will explain how to score the instrument and how to interpret these scores.

ADVANCE PREPARATION

As provided by your instructor.

PROCEDURE

Complete the M–V Personality Profile.

Your instructor will hand out a scoring key. Follow the key in order to score your questionnaire.

Below are 20 sets of statements. In each set, there are three statements lettered A, B, and C.

For *each set,* you are to mark the statement that is *most descriptive* of you with an M, and to mark the statement that is *least* descriptive of you with an L. Leave the third statement blank. At the end of the test, therefore, you will have 20 statements (one in each set) marked M, 20 marked L, and 20 left blank. Even if the choices are difficult, select a "most" and "least" descriptive statement from each set.

1. _____ A. It takes more imagination to be a successful criminal than a successful businessman.

   _____ B. The phrase, "the road to hell is paved with good intentions," contains a lot of truth.

   _____ C. Most men forget more easily the death of their father than the loss of their property.

Reprinted from *Studies in Machiavellianism* by Florence Geis and Richard Christie. Reprinted with the permission of Academic Press.

2. _____ A. Men are more concerned with the car they drive than with the clothes their wives wear.

_____ B. It is very important that imagination and creativity in children be cultivated.

_____ C. People suffering from incurable diseases should have the choice of being put painlessly to death.

3. _____ A. Never tell anyone the real reason you did something unless it is useful to do so.

_____ B. The well-being of the individual is the goal that should be worked for before anything else.

_____ C. Since most people don't know what they want, it is only reasonable for ambitious people to talk them into doing things.

4. _____ A. People are getting so lazy and self-indulgent that it is bad for our country.

_____ B. The best way to handle people is to tell them what they want to hear.

_____ C. It would be a good thing if people were kinder to others less fortunate than themselves.

5. _____ A. Most people are basically good and kind.

_____ B. The best criterion for a wife or husband is compatibility—other characteristics are nice but not essential.

_____ C. Only after a man has gotten what he wants from life should he concern himself with the injustices in the world.

6. _____ A. Most people who get ahead in the world lead clean, moral lives.

_____ B. Any man worth his salt shouldn't be blamed for putting his career above his family.

_____ C. People would be better off if they were concerned less with how to do things and more with what to do.

7. _____ A. A good teacher is one who points out unanswered questions rather than gives explicit answers.

_____ B. When you ask someone to do something, it is best to give the real reasons for wanting it rather than giving reasons which might carry more weight.

_____ C. A person's job is the best single guide as to the sort of person he is.

8. _____ A. The construction of such monumental works as the Egyptian pyramids was worth the enslavement of the workers who built them.

_____ B. Once a way of handling problems has been worked out it is best to stick to it.

_____ C. One should take action only when sure it is morally right.

9. _____ A. The world would be a much better place to live in if people would let the future take care of itself and concern themselves only with enjoying the present.

_____ B. It is wise to flatter important people.

_____ C. Once a decision has been made, it is best to keep changing it as new circumstances arise.

10. _____ A. It is a good policy to act as if you are doing the things you do because you have no other choice.

_____ B. The biggest difference between most criminals and other people is that criminals are stupid enough to get caught.

_____ C. Even the most hardened and vicious criminal has a spark of decency somewhere within him.

11. _____ A. All in all, it is better to be humble and honest than to be important and dishonest.
_____ B. A man who is able and willing to work hard has a good chance of succeeding in whatever he wants to do.
_____ C. If a thing does not help us in our daily lives, it isn't very important.

12. _____ A. A person shouldn't be punished for breaking a law that he thinks is unreasonable.
_____ B. Too many criminals are not punished for their crimes.
_____ C. There is no excuse for lying to someone else.

13. _____ A. Generally speaking, men won't work hard unless they are forced to do so.
_____ B. Every person is entitled to a second chance, even after he commits a serious mistake.
_____ C. People who can't make up their minds are not worth bothering about.

14. _____ A. A man's first responsibility is to his wife, not his mother.
_____ B. Most men are brave.
_____ C. It's best to pick friends that are intellectually stimulating rather than ones it is comfortable to be around.

15. _____ A. There are very few people in the world worth concerning oneself about.
_____ B. It is hard to get ahead without cutting concerns here and there.
_____ C. A capable person motivated for his own gain is more useful to society than a well-meaning but ineffective one.

16. _____ A. It is best to give others the impression that you can change your mind easily.
_____ B. It is a good working policy to keep on good terms with everyone.
_____ C. Honesty is the best policy in all cases.

17. _____ A. It is possible to be good in all respects.
_____ B. To help oneself is good; to help others even better.
_____ C. War and threats of war are unchangeable facts of human life.

18. _____ A. Barnum was probably right when he said that there's at least one sucker born every minute.
_____ B. Life is pretty dull unless one deliberately stirs up some excitement.
_____ C. Most people would be better off if they control their emotions.

19. _____ A. Sensitivity to the feelings of others is worth more than poise in social situations.
_____ B. The ideal society is one where everybody knows his place and accepts it.
_____ C. It is safest to assume that all people have a vicious streak and it will come out when they are given a chance.

20. _____ A. People who talk about abstract problems usually don't know what they are talking about.
_____ B. Anyone who completely trusts anyone else is asking for trouble.
_____ C. It is essential for the functioning of a democracy that everyone vote.

Read, if your instructor does not cover the concepts in class, the article entitled "The Machiavellis among Us," by Richard Christie in the "Readings" section of this volume.

DISCUSSION QUESTIONS

1. What was your score?
2. How does this score compare to other students in the class? How does it compare to the national norms reported by Christie and Geis?
3. Do you think that this score is an accurate reflection of your tendencies toward Machiavellianism as described by Christie and Geis? Why or why not?
4. How might individuals who are high in Machiavellianism behave in negotiating situations? Have you seen examples of this behavior in class activities? Describe.

Ethics Questionnaires

INTRODUCTION

The purpose of the Ethics Questionnaires is to inquire about your general disposition toward questions of ethics, particularly those ethical issues related to negotiations. Please complete the two questionnaires in this activity. The instructor will explain how to score the questionnaires and interpret their results.

ADVANCE PREPARATION

None, unless specified by the instructor.

PROCEDURE

1. Complete the Ethics Position Questionnaire.
2. Complete the Incidents in Negotiation Questionnaire.
3. Your instructor will hand out a scoring key for the Ethics Position Questionnaire. Follow the key in order to score your questionnaire. A description of the questionnaire and what it measures can be found following the questionnaire.
4. Be prepared to share your answers to the Incidents in Negotiation Questionnaire with others in a small group or class discussion.

The Ethics Position Questionnaire
_____

You will find a series of general statements listed below. Each represents a commonly held opinion, and there are no right or wrong answers. You will probably agree with some items and disagree with others. We are interested in the extent to which you agree or disagree with such matters of opinion.

Please read each statement carefully. Then indicate the extent to which you agree or disagree by placing in *front* of the statement the number corresponding to your feelings, where:

The Ethics Position Questionnaire was originally published by Donelson R. Forsyth, "A Taxonomy of Ethical Ideologies," *Journal of Personality and Social Psychology,* 39, 1980, pp. 175–84. Copyright 1980 by the American Psychological Association. Reprinted by permission of the APA and the author.

1 = Completely disagree   4 = Slightly disagree   7 = Moderately agree
2 = Largely disagree   5 = Neither agree or disagree 8 = Largely agree
3 = Moderately disagree   6 = Slightly agree   9 = Completely agree

Rating

_____ 1. A person should make certain that his or her actions never intentionally harm another, even to a small degree.

_____ 2. Risks to another should never be tolerated, irrespective of how small the risks might be.

_____ 3. The existence of potential harm to others is always wrong, irrespective of the benefits to be gained.

_____ 4. One should never psychologically or physically harm another person.

_____ 5. One should not perform an action which might in any way threaten the dignity and welfare of another individual.

_____ 6. If an action could harm an innocent other, then it should not be done.

_____ 7. Deciding whether or not to perform an act by balancing the positive consequences of the act against the negative consequences is immoral.

_____ 8. The dignity and welfare of people should be the most important concern in any society.

_____ 9. It is never necessary to sacrifice the welfare of others.

_____ 10. Moral actions are those which closely match ideals of the most ''perfect'' action.

_____ 11. There are no ethical principles that are so important that they should be a part of any code of ethics.

_____ 12. What is ethical varies from one situation in society to another.

_____ 13. Moral standards should be seen as being individualistic; what one person considers to be moral may be judged to be immoral by another person.

_____ 14. Different types of moralities cannot be compared to one another as to ''rightness.''

_____ 15. Questions of what is ethical for everyone can never be resolved, since what is moral or immoral is up to the individual.

_____ 16. Moral standards are simply *personal* rules, which indicate how a person should behave, and are not to be applied in making judgments of others.

_____ 17. Ethical considerations in interpersonal relations are so complex that individuals should be allowed to formulate their own codes.

_____ 18. Rigidly codifying an ethical position that prevents certain types of actions could stand in the way of better human relations and adjustment.

_____ 19. No rule concerning lying can be formulated; whether a lie is permissible or not permissible totally depends on the situation.

_____ 20. Whether a lie is judged to be moral or immoral depends upon circumstances surrounding the action.

Ab. (1-10) _____   Rel. (11-20)_____

INCIDENTS IN NEGOTIATION QUESTIONNAIRE

Listed below you will find a number of negotiating tactics. These tactics primarily address how honest you will be in negotiation. There are no "right answers" as to what is the right or wrong thing to do, so please be candid in your answers.

You are about to enter into a negotiation. You are negotiating for something which is very important to you. Please think about each tactic, and then rate each one on the following two scales:

1. How appropriate is the tactic to use in this situation?

1	2	3	4	5	6	7
not at all appropriate			somewhat appropriate			very appropriate

2. How likely would you be to use the tactic in this negotiation?

1	2	3	4	5	6	7
not at all likely			somewhat likely			very likely

(If you have any need to explain your answer or comment on a tactic, feel free to do so in the margin or at the end of the questionnaire.)

1. Threaten to harm your opponent if he/she doesn't give you what you want, even if you know you will never follow through to carry out that threat.

   Appropriate (1–7)? _____   Likely (1–7)? _____

2. Promise that good things will happen to your opponent if he/she gives you what you want, even if you know that you can't (or won't) deliver those good things when the other's cooperation is obtained.

   Appropriate (1–7)? _____   Likely (1–7)? _____

3. Lead the other negotiators to believe that they can only get what they want by negotiating with you, when in fact they could go elsewhere and get what they want cheaper or faster.

   Appropriate (1–7)? _____   Likely (1–7)? _____

4. Hide your real bottom line from your opponent.

   Appropriate (1–7)? _____   Likely (1–7)? _____

5. Make an opening demand that is far greater than what one really hopes to settle for.

   Appropriate (1–7)? _____   Likely (1–7)? _____

6. Gain information about an opponent's negotiating position and strategy by "asking around" in a network of your own friends, associates, and contacts.

   Appropriate (1–7)? _____   Likely (1–7)? _____

7. Gain information about an opponent's negotiating position by paying friends, associates, and contacts to get this information for you.

   Appropriate (1–7)? _____   Likely (1–7)? _____

8. Gain information about an opponent's negotiating position by trying to recruit or hire one of your opponent's key subordinates (on the condition that the key subordinate bring confidential information with him/her).

   Appropriate (1–7)? _____   Likely (1–7)? _____

9. Gain information about an opponent's negotiating position by cultivating his/her friendship through expensive gifts, entertaining, or "personal favors."

   Appropriate (1–7)? _____   Likely (1–7)? _____

10. Make an opening offer or demand so high (or low) that it seriously undermine's your opponent's confidence in his/her own ability to negotiate a satisfactory settlement.

    Appropriate (1–7)? _____   Likely (1–7)? _____

11. Talk directly to the people who your opponent reports to, or is accountable to, and tell them things that will undermine their confidence in your opponent as negotiator.

    Appropriate (1–7)? _____   Likely (1–7)? _____

12. Talk directly to the people who your opponent reports to, or is accountable to, and try to encourage them to defect to your side.

    Appropriate (1–7)? _____   Likely (1–7)? _____

13. Convey a false impression that you are in absolutely no hurry to come to a negotiation agreement, thereby trying to put more time pressure on your opponent to concede quickly.

    Appropriate (1–7)? _____   Likely (1–7)? _____

14. Threaten to make your opponent look weak or foolish in front of a boss or others to whom he/she is accountable.

    Appropriate (1–7)? _____   Likely (1–7)? _____

15. Intentionally misrepresent factual information to your opponent in order to support your negotiating arguments or position.

    Appropriate (1–7)? _____   Likely (1–7)? _____

16. Intentionally misrepresent the nature of negotiations to the press or your constituency in order to protect delicate discussions that have occurred.

    Appropriate (1–7)? _____   Likely (1–7)? _____

17. Intentionally misrepresent the progress of negotiations to the press or your constituency in order to make your own position or point of view look better.

    Appropriate (1–7)? _____   Likely (1–7)? _____

18. Intentionally misrepresent factual information to your opponent when you know that he/she has already done this to you.

    Appropriate (1–7)? _____   Likely (1–7)? _____

When you have finished, review all 18 statements and pick the five which are most ethical, and the five which are most unethical. Write the numbers below, and be prepared to state how you made your choices.

Most Ethical	*Least Ethical*
1. _____	1. _____
2. _____	2. _____
3. _____	3. _____
4. _____	4. _____
5. _____	5. _____

DISCUSSION

The Ethics Position Questionnaire was developed by Donelson Forsyth, and designed to measure individual variations in approaches to making moral judgments along two major dimensions. The first dimension is the degree to which an individual makes moral judgments based on universal moral rules versus relativistic criteria. When considering moral and ethical issues, some individuals tend to rely upon "moral absolutes" (e.g., "Thou shalt not lie"), while others rely upon the circumstances of the situation to determine what to do (e.g., it's OK to lie in some situations). The second major dimension is the amount of idealism in an individual's moral judgments. Some individuals are high in idealism and believe that if one always does the "right" thing, good consequences will occur (e.g., if I always tell the truth, everything will work out OK). Others, lower in idealism, believe that doing the "right" thing will not always lead to the desirable consequences (e.g., if I always tell the truth, sometimes the truth will get me in more trouble than a lie would.)

Based on responses to the items in the questionnaire, Forsyth proposed that an individual's general ethical ideology could be described by one of four different types, depending upon whether the respondent scored high or low on the idealism and relativism scales (see Exhibit 1). In Forsyth's research, an individual's ethical ideology has been demonstrated to be related to attitudes on contemporary moral issues and on ways to deal with people who violate moral and ethical codes. Absolutists—particularly males—are much more moralistic than the other types, and wish to deal significantly more harshly with those who violate the rules. Subjectivists, on the other hand, were much more pragmatic and much more likely to judge events and actions based on the specific facts, circumstances, and outcomes that resulted, rather than on moralistic grounds.

EXHIBIT 1   Taxonomy of Ethical Ideologies

	Relativism	
	High	*Low*
Idealism	*Situationalists*	*Absolutists*
High	Rejects moral rules; advocates an individual analysis of each act in each situation to determine what is right; relativistic.	Assumes that the best possible outcome can always be achieved by following universal moral rules.
	Subjectivists	*Exceptionists*
Low	Appraises the situation based on own personal values and perspectives rather than universal moral principles; relativistic.	Moral absolutes guide personal judgments but pragmatically open to exceptions to these standards; utilitarian.

The Incidents in Negotiation Questionnaire was prepared by one of the authors of this book. The purpose of the questionnaire is to explore your beliefs about which of these negotiation tactics—all of which involve some form of "lying", "bluffing," or other forms of "dishonesty"—are ethical and appropriate to do in negotiation versus unethical and inappropriate. There are no clear "right" or "wrong" answers as to how ethical these items are; your instructor will give you some information about how other groups of students and executives have rated these items.

Class discussion will focus on your responses to these two questionnaires and your thoughts on the following discussion questions.

DISCUSSION QUESTIONS

1. What were your scores on the Relativism and Idealism scales? Based on information provided by your instructor, what is your predominant ethical ideology? Is this score consistent with the way you think you make judgments about moral or ethical issues?

2. How do your scores compare to others in your class or group? Are there differences based on age or sex? What might be some other ways to explain differences among the group?

3. How did you respond to the Incidents in Negotiation Questionnaire? Are some of these tactics ethically acceptable? Which ones? Are some ethically wrong? Which ones? Are there some that are OK depending upon the circumstances? What might those circumstances be?

4. Do you agree with the following quotation? (Think about it and then discuss with your classmates):

   There is no such thing as an "honest bluff" as distinguished from the empty promise or the treacherous falsehood. If an "honest bluff" fails, the bluffer may be forgiven for trying a legitimate stratagem, but if he has lied he may be cold shouldered out of the game.[1]

5. Do you agree with the following quotation? (Think about it and then discuss with your classmates):

   Falsehood ceases to be a falsehood when it is understood on all sides that the truth is not expected to be spoken. [attributed to Sir Henry Taylor, British statesman].[1]

---

[1] Quotations from Albert Carr, "Is Business Bluffing Ethical?" *Harvard Business Review,* January–February 1968.

Influence Tactics Inventory

INTRODUCTION

The questionnaire in this exercise is designed to measure your predisposition to use different influence tactics at work. In responding to these questions, you will learn something about the influence tactics that you use, depending upon who you want to influence.

ADVANCE PREPARATION

At the discretion of the instructor.

PROCEDURE

Step 1: 5 minutes

Identify three different people who you need to influence at work. One should be a superior, one a subordinate, and the other a co-worker.

Step 2: 20 minutes

Work completely through the questionnaire for *each* of the three people that you have chosen, keeping only one person in mind at a time. Use the following scale to respond to each of the statements below. Be sure to respond to all of the statements for each of the three people.

5: Usually use this tactic to influence him or her.

4: Frequently use this tactic to influence him or her.

3: Occasionally use this tactic to influence him or her.

2: Seldom use this tactic to influence him or her.

1: Never use this tactic to influence him or her.

Adapted from "Intraorganizational Influence Tactics: Explorations in Getting One's Way," *Journal of Applied Psychology* 65, 440–52, by David Kipnis, Stuart M. Schmidt, and Ian Wilkinson. Used with permission.

Step 3: 30 minutes

Your instructor will hand out a scoring key. Follow the key in order to score the questionnaire.

Superior	Subordinate	Co-Worker	Statement
___	___	___	1. Kept checking up on him or her.
___	___	___	2. Made him or her feel important ("only you have the brains, talent to do this").
___	___	___	3. Wrote a detailed plan that justified my ideas.
___	___	___	4. Gave no salary increase or prevented that person from getting a raise.
___	___	___	5. Offered an exchange (e.g., if you this for me, I will do something for you).
___	___	___	6. Made a formal appeal to higher levels to back up my request.
___	___	___	7. Threatened to notify an outside agency if he or she did not give in to my request.
___	___	___	8. Obtained the support of co-workers to back up my request.
___	___	___	9. Simply ordered him or her to do what I requested.
___	___	___	10. Acted very humbly to him or her while making my request.
___	___	___	11. Presented him or her with information in support of my point of view.
___	___	___	12. Threatened his or her job security (e.g., hint of firing or getting him or her fired).
___	___	___	13. Remind him or her of past favors that I had done for them.
___	___	___	14. Obtained the informal support of higher-ups.
___	___	___	15. Threatened to stop working with him or her until he or she gave in.
___	___	___	16. Had him or her come to a formal conference at which I made my request.
___	___	___	17. Demanded that he or she do what I requested.
___	___	___	18. Acted in a friendly manner prior to asking for what I wanted.
___	___	___	19. Explained the reasons for my request.

____	____	____	20. Promised (or gave) a salary request.
____	____	____	21. Offered to make a personal sacrifice if he or she would do what I wanted (e.g., work late, work harder, do his/her share of the work, etc.).
____	____	____	22. Filed a report about the other person with higher-ups (e.g., my superior).
____	____	____	23. Engaged in a work slowdown until he or she did what I wanted.
____	____	____	24. Obtained the support of my subordinates to back up my request.

DISCUSSION QUESTIONS

1. What was your score for each of the different influence tactics?

	Superior	*Subordinate*	*Co-Worker*
Assertiveness	____	____	____
Ingratiation	____	____	____
Rationality	____	____	____
Sanctions	____	____	____
Exchange	____	____	____
Upward Appeal	____	____	____
Blocking	____	____	____
Coalitions	____	____	____

2. Compare the influence tactics used with superiors, subordinates, and co-workers by your classmates. Which tactics are most frequently used with which role? Which are least frequently used? Why did this pattern occur?

3. Which is the most powerful influence tactic? Does this depend on situational factors? How?

4. When others are trying to influence you, which tactics do you think are most effective? Most ineffective? Annoying?

5. When you are trying to influence others, which tactics are you most comfortable using? Least comfortable?

Appendixes

Capital Mortgage Insurance Corporation (B)

By late afternoon on May 21, 1979, Frank Randall and Jim Dolan had finished putting together Capital Mortgage Insurance Corporation's formal offer to purchase all the outstanding stock of Corporate Transfer Services, Inc. The offer they settled on was virtually identical to the draft that Jim Dolan had already prepared, with one significant addition: an offer to retain Elliott Burr as a consultant to help build a strong relationship between the relocation company and MetroNet.

Randall considered the offer to keep Burr actively involved as a key ingredient in the total package. As he told Jim Dolan: "Burr fathered this company, and now he's putting it up for adoption. I want to give him every assurance that we'll be an adequate foster parent. Besides, he can be a key link to MetroNet for us." The consulting arrangement would also be a way to provide Burr with some extra income beyond what he stood to make by selling his stock.

In addition to the purchase offer letter, Randall also prepared a letter formally stating CMI's interest in acquiring CTS. The letter (see Exhibit 1) opened by expressing Randall's gratitude to the four stockholders for their help and cooperation during the past several months. Randall planned to distribute this letter to the four men before discussing the formal purchase offer.

Once the purchase offer details were settled, Randall telephoned Elliott Burr again to arrange the details of their meeting. At Randall's suggestion it was agreed that he and Dolan would fly to Chicago on the morning of May 24 and meet with the CTS stockholders at the Burr and Lehman Real Estate office. Again, however, Randall was intentionally vague about his agenda for the meeting.

Capital Mortgage Insurance Company (A)-(F) 9-480-057-062.

Copyright © 1980 by the President and Fellows of Harvard College.

This case was prepared by James P. Ware as a basis for class discussion rather than to illustrate either effective or ineffective handling of an administrative situation. Reprinted by permission of the Harvard Business School.

EXHIBIT 1

Board of Directors and Stockholders
Corporate Transfer Services
Chicago, IL

May 24, 1979

Gentlemen:

The purpose of this letter is to express our sincere appreciation for the help and cooperation you and your staff have provided over the past several months to enable us to understand the employee relocation service business. You have been most liberal with your time and candid in the sharing of your knowledge of the industry.

As you know, we have conducted an extensive study of the employee relocation service industry and we realize there is still much for us to learn. During our analysis, we have gained a high regard for CTS and the manner in which you have conducted your business.

Capital Mortgage Insurance Corporation would like to acquire the ownership of Corporate Transfer Services. We will make every effort to do so on a mutually fair and equitable basis. We enter these negotiations with you fully aware of your personal feelings as individuals who have created and nurtured CTS for several years.

Upon acquiring CTS, I want to assure you that we are committed to building and expanding the operations on a nationwide basis that will continue the high business standards you have established.

Sincerely,

Franklin T. Randall
President

THE MAY 24 MEETING

When Randall and Dolan arrived in Chicago, they found only Elliott Burr, William Lehman, and Tom Winder in attendance. Burr explained that Michael Kupchak, the fourth stockholder, was tied up in a meeting in Gary, Indiana, and would not be able to get back in time.

The five men sat down at a conference table in a private room in the back of the Burr and Lehman Real Estate office. Burr sat on one side of the table, flanked by Winder and Lehman. Randall and Dolan settled into the seats directly opposite. Randall opened the meeting with a brief but warm statement of thanks for all the help the CTS group had provided. He then distributed his formal letter of intent and expressed his continuing interest in developing a formal relationship with Corporate Transfer Services. Randall concluded:

> We appreciate the fact that you have created this company out of nothing, and that you care a great deal about its future. We understand those feelings, and we respect them. We are definitely interested in acquiring you, but we want to do so only on terms that will satisfy your concerns about the future of Corporate Transfer Services.

Elliott Burr then replied, ''What is your offer?'' Randall responded:

> We find it exceedingly difficult to put a price on your company. Most acquisitions are completed on the basis of a projected earnings stream; you don't have one. Most acquisitions involve a careful analysis of a company's management team; you have only one man. You have only very small exposure to the MetroNet brokers, and your business is basically self-liquidating with no residual value. But we do want to buy you on the basis of your goodwill and reputation.

Burr:

What is your offer?

Randall:

We will pay you $400,000 above your audited net worth.

Burr:

We are very disappointed in that offer price.

Randall:

What did you have in mind?

Burr:

We wanted $5 million.[1]

---

[1] All dollar figures hereafter represent the amount to be paid for goodwill only, over the agreed-upon $420,000 in the company's book value.

Capital Mortgage Insurance Corporation (C)

On hearing Elliott Burr's demand for $5 million for CTS, Frank Randall replied:

> "If you're serious, we might as well leave right now. But why don't you listen to our complete offer?"

Jim Dolan then read through CMI's formal offer letter, which spelled out all the details of the proposed agreement. Dolan took the CTS group slowly through the letter, explaining the meaning of each item in great detail.

Elliott Burr then suggested that they skip the price issue momentarily. He reviewed the offer step by step, asking questions to clarify the implications of each part of the proposal. Winder and Lehman remained silent during this exchange.

The tremendous difference in the asking and offering prices continued to be the major source of contention, however. After several minutes of open debate, Randall finally asked in exasperation, "How did you ever come up with that figure?" Tom Winder mentioned hearing that 60 percent of another employee relocation company had been sold recently for something in excess of $3 million.

Dolan:

How does that relate to us?

Winder:

Well, I guess it really isn't the same thing. I suppose we made a mistake using that as a base.

There was a long silence following Winder's comment. Finally, after several minutes, Elliott Burr said:

Capital Mortgage Insurance Company (A)-(F) 9-480-057-062

Copyright © 1980 by the President and Fellows of Harvard College.

This case was prepared by James P. Ware as a basis for class discussion rather than to illustrate either effective or ineffective handling of an administrative situation. Reprinted by permission of the Harvard Business School.

Let me tell you about Mike, who isn't here. I have his proxy, and he'll sell right now for $3.5 million.

Randall replied, "That's ridiculous."

The meeting then degenerated for several minutes, as Burr, Lehman, and Winder whispered among themselves. They finally announced their willingness to sell for $2 million.

Capital Mortgage Insurance Corporation (D)

Frank Randall paused only briefly before saying, "That's still way too high."

Burr:

But we control MetroNet.

Randall:

No you don't; you have no control there—no ability to guarantee their performance.

Burr:

You don't understand . . .

Randall:

No, you don't understand. You can't deliver MetroNet. In fact, I'll have to live down your poor performance with MetroNet.

Dolan:

Just how much time have you spent working with MetroNet?

Winder:

Well, I spoke at half a dozen regional seminars in 1976. I made up a bunch of slides, passed out brochures, and answered a lot of questions. That was a lot of work.

Dolan:

How much of that effort is still valid? Has it generated much business?

Winder:

Well, I really don't know . . . I guess we probably haven't grown as fast as we should have to satisfy MetroNet . . .

Capital Mortgage Insurance Company (A)-(F) 9-480-057-062.

Copyright © 1980 by the President and Fellows of Harvard College.

This case was prepared by James P. Ware as a basis for class discussion rather than to illustrate either effective or ineffective handling of an administrative situation. Reprinted by permission of the Harvard Business School.

Burr interrupted, cutting Winder off:

> We're still awfully far apart. Can we work out a deal giving us some now and something more in the future?

Dolan:

> If you want to take on some future risks, we'll pay you net worth now and a fixed dollar payout in the future, based on the ROE we can get. The fact is, the future performance of this company will depend a lot more on the capital we're going to put in than it will on what it's worth today.

Burr:

> That's not acceptable. But I'm still certain we can work something out. You have a John F. Kennedy stadium in Philadelphia, don't you? I remember he used to say that people of goodwill can always get things done.

Randall:

> You've got my geography misplaced. I'm originally from Missouri; you've got to show me. Besides, I preferred Harry Truman to J.F.K. I especially like one of his sayings: "If you can't stand the heat, get out of the kitchen."
>
> Look, why don't you all get together and discuss our offer in more detail. Maybe you can quantify your performance with MetroNet, and sign a written warranty or pledge to produce the business.
>
> Meanwhile, let's keep the lines of communication open. Come on, Jim, let's get back to the hotel. I want to get some dinner.

Capital Mortgage Insurance Corporation (E)

Randall and Dolan stopped only briefly at the hotel before going out for dinner; Randall was certain Elliott Burr would be trying to reach them before too long. Sure enough, when they returned to the hotel at 11:00 P.M., there were several phone messages. They ignored the messages and went to bed, since they had to get up at 6:00 A.M. to catch their flight back to Philadelphia.

Promptly at 6:00 A.M., Jim Dolan's telephone rang. As he groggily picked up the phone, a familiar voice said, "Good morning, Jim. This is your wake-up call. It's Elliott Burr. I tried to reach Frank and couldn't; but I would like to talk some more before you leave." Now fully awake, Dolan responded, "All right, I'll listen. But let's be clear that this is *not* a negotiating session."

Dolan met Burr in the hotel coffee shop at 6:30 A.M. after a quick shower and shave. Burr had CMI's offer letter with him. He had crossed out the offer to pay $400,000 over net worth and replaced it with $1 million. Jim was deliberately non-committal in responding to Burr. All he said was that he and Randall were flying back to Philadelphia immediately and, "Frank will let you know."

Capital Mortgage Insurance Company (A)-(F) 9-480-057-062.

Copyright © 1980 by the President and Fellows of Harvard College.

This case was prepared by James P. Ware as a basis for class discussion rather than to illustrate either effective or ineffective handling of an administrative situation. Reprinted by permission of the Harvard Business School.

Capital Mortgage Insurance Corporation (F)

As the big jet banked over the city and began its final approach toward the Philadelphia Airport, Frank Randall closed his briefcase and looked at Jim Dolan.

> Well, I don't know about you, Jim, but I think we're in good shape. We brought their price down into our range, and we established our feelings about CTS' intrinsic value—or lack of value.
>
> And I know my ceiling price; I won't go a dollar over it. If they won't accept it, we'll just forget them. But one way or another, we're going into the business.

FURTHER NEGOTIATIONS WITH CORPORATE TRANSFER SERVICES

Once again, Randall and Dolan let their relationship with Elliott Burr and his partners cool off a bit. There were several phone conversations over the next two weeks, but Randall often "forgot" to return calls, and he remained deliberately neutral in his discussions with Burr. The conversations that did occur tended to focus on technical matters such as alternate payout arrangements; the price issue was hardly mentioned.

Randall kept David Osgood of MetroNet up to date on the negotiations. During one of their conversations Randall told Osgood about Burr's claim that he "controlled" the MetroNet brokers and could "deliver" them. Osgood was incensed; he told Randall he was going to write a letter to Burr calling attention to CTS's failure to meet commitments the company had made to MetroNet.

During this time Randall also hired the consultant who had prepared the relocation industry report for MetroNet earlier in the spring. The consultant spent several days in Philadelphia helping Randall and Dolan think about how to structure and operate a

Capital Mortgage Insurance Company (A)-(F) 9-480-057-062.

Copyright © 1980 by the President and Fellows of Harvard College.

This case was prepared by James P. Ware as a basis for class discussion rather than to illustrate either effective or ineffective handling of an administrative situation. Reprinted by permission of the Harvard Business School.

relocation business, and suggesting the names of experienced managers they might want to recruit. The consultant also put Randall in touch with the parent organization of one of the well-established relocation companies. The consultant hinted that the parent was not satisfied with its subsidiary and might be willing to sell it, even though it was one of the largest in the industry. Randall made an appointment for early June to "discuss matters of mutual interest" with the Executive Vice President responsible for the subsidiary.

Jim Dolan was beginning to question whether they really wanted to acquire CTS. The discussions with the consultant had given him new insights into the business, and now he not only had someone to compare Elliott Burr and Tom Winder with, but there was the possibility, however remote, of buying a much bigger and clearly more successful operation.

Finally, on June 5, Burr called again. He told Randall, "We've thought about your offer and talked it over. How about $750,000 over book value?" Randall replied, "We're not even sure we want to go through with it. I'll get back to you in a day or two."

Randall and Dolan spent most of June 6 rethinking their whole assessment of Corporate Transfer Services. As Dolan later recalled:

> At that point we had a chance to do some real soul-searching. It was fully in our hands; we knew we could get the company, and get it at a price we considered reasonable. The negotiations were in a sense over; the next move was our real commitment. We talked ourselves into and out of doing it several times, and we thought about our other options as well.

Finally, late in the day, Randall called Elliott Burr and offered $600,000 over net worth. Burr, without any hesitation, agreed.

Pacific Oil Company (B)

Kelsey called Meredith the next day. They both agreed that a resale clause would be a dangerous commitment and an even more dangerous precedent for Pacific Oil. They made an appointment for a conference call to Saunders for the following morning. When they talked to him, they learned that Saunders had approved the concession, that Fontaine had already talked to Hauptmann and told him it was O.K. to include it in the revised agreement.

Olympic Television Rights (B)

The $309 Million Games[*]

William Taaffe

The setting: an ABC-TV press conference. November 17, 1987. The site: a Calgary warehouse that was rapidly being transformed into the ABC broadcast center for the Winter Olympics. The speaker: Roone Arledge, the founder of ABC Sports and the man most responsible for turning the Games, Summer and Winter, into a television institution.

Arledge, who left ABC Sports two years before to become president of the network's news division, kept clearing his throat and nervously rubbing the corner of his forehead. What, the press wanted to know, did he have to say about the price ABC paid for the rights to telecast the Calgary Olympics? Almost four years ago, Arledge had bid the astonishing sum of $309 million for those rights, more than three times the $91.5 million ABC had paid for the 1984 Winter Games in Sarajevo. "I don't know if I should use this word," Arledge replied, "but I'm going to, anyway. We were misled. . . ."

Later Arledge explained what he meant by "misled." He said that as late as the morning of the day on which bidding for the Calgary Olympics began, ABC "had been assured" by Barry Frank—senior corporate vice-president of Trans World International, a TV marketing house, and an adviser during the rights negotiations to Olympiques Canada Olympics (OCO), the committee organizing the Calgary Games—that negotiations with the three major U.S. networks wouldn't end in an auction. "There was a breach of faith . . . ," Arledge said. "The [bidding] process was ill-conceived, and I think the result showed it."

During the same press conference, Arledge and his successor as president of ABC Sports, Dennis Swanson, professed to be glad that their network had won the bidding for the Calgary Games—for the prestige—even though ABC management sources say the network will lose $20 million to $30 million on them. But as for the way the deal had been cut, well, there was still resentment in Arledge's comments.

According to Arledge, the person most responsible for the "breach of faith" was Frank, who reportedly earned a $2 million commission for his efforts. Arledge claims

---

that Frank had promised ABC that when the bidding reached the level OCO hoped to attain, the real negotiations would begin and that ABC's traditional relationship with the Olympics—it had telecast 9 of the previous 12 Winter and Summer Games—would be taken into account.

Frank and International Olympic Committee member Dick Pound, who chaired the negotiations, dispute Arledge. There was nothing left to negotiate, they say, because weeks in advance of the bidding the three networks had signed identical 60-page contracts, agreeing to all details of the deal except the final dollar figure. "They knew that what was involved was, in essence, an auction," says Pound.

"There were no assurances, verbal or otherwise," says Frank. "What Roone Arledge is saying is redolent of sour grapes."

The bidding, held in the ornate Palace Hotel in Lausanne, Switzerland, began in an atmosphere of relatively good humor. Once the network executives were nestled in their suites on Tuesday afternoon, January 24, 1984, Frank informed them of the most important ground rule: The bidding would be over when the IOC committee said it was. Whenever the committee wanted to go to a higher round of bidding, the networks would be informed of the minimum bid required to stay in the action. Each network would then have 30 minutes to deliver its bid in writing to the door of the hotel conference room where the committee was meeting.

Frank now says he limited the bidding to hard cash—there would be no dealing in the soft currency of favors—to assure fairness. NBC was particularly worried that Arledge might call in markers from the IOC. In fact, NBC's European representative stayed near the door of the conference room for 11 hours to make sure no one from ABC or CBS made a secret visit. Frank instituted a buddy system within the committee; no one from his side could leave the conference room—not even to go to the bathroom—unaccompanied.

Just before the bidding began at 2 P.M., each of the dozen committee negotiators bet $1 on what the final price would be. Frank was high man, with a figure of $287 million, and thus wound up the winner.

By the third round the minimum to stay in the bidding had reached $265 million, whereupon CBS submitted a blank piece of paper—in effect, dropping out. After the fourth round ABC and NBC were tied at $300 million. "The atmosphere in that conference room was unlike anything I've ever seen," Frank says. "People weren't talking about lunch money in there."

Bill Wardle, OCO's vice-president for marketing, recalls that he and his OCO colleagues wanted to have one more closed bid and go home—the $300 million bid had already surpassed their expectations. Frank, however, persuaded them to change the bidding to an auction. "I felt at this point, in fairness to the networks, the bidding shouldn't be open to guesswork," he said. "The more equitable solution was to allow them to eliminate themselves.

Arledge, who says ABC led the bidding in each of the first three rounds and thus was in the position of having to bid against itself, was furious at the implementation of the auction idea and even considered dropping out. But when NBC, having won a coin flip to determine which network would kick off the auction, bid $304 million, Arledge came back with the $309 million, "just to see what happened." What happened was that NBC tossed in its hand.

In the conference room there was cheering. Frank had served his client brilliantly. The difference between ABC's bid and OCO's hoped-for figure of $275 million by itself almost accounts for the $35 million profit that the Calgary organizers expect to make on the Games.

But Arledge was outraged. The next day, he skipped the traditional luncheon for the winning network and vowed to IOC President Juan Antonio Samaranch that ABC never again would enter open-ended bidding.

From a programming standpoint Arledge, who will return to ABC Sports for 16 days as the hands-on producer of the Calgary Games, has no reason to squawk. More than any previous Olympics, these Games have been tailor-made for U.S. television, which will pay an incredible 95 percent of Calgary's worldwide TV rights fees. To increase the value of the Calgary Games to American television, Frank had asked the IOC to move the Olympic schedule forward by a week and a half—so that all the competition would occur in February, one of three annual TV "sweeps" periods that determine ad rates for the ensuing four months. Also, these Winter Olympics were scheduled to extend over three weekends instead of the usual two, adding to their value in the eyes of the networks.

Still, the money paid for Calgary marked the end of an era for ABC. NBC won the bidding for the Seoul Games with a bid of $300 million and a share of advertising revenue that may add as much as another $200 million; ABC reportedly offered a bid of only $250 million. It's questionable whether ABC will ever again pay the price for exclusive rights to the Games. Two years after the Calgary deal, Capital Cities took over the network. Arledge was reassigned to the news division, and Jim Spence, his deputy that day in Lausanne, left ABC and started his own company. Spence is now writing a book that will focus in part on the Calgary bidding. He ought to call it *Shootout at the Barry Frank Corral*—and ask Arledge to write the preface.

Olympic Television Rights (C)

New King of the Hill[*]

William Taaffe

The TV networks may be lean and mean nowadays, but at least one of them still is willing to say to the Olympics, "Take me, Darling, I'm yours." With a bid that made a mockery of frugality but also made sense for the third-rated network, CBS outbid NBC to secure the U.S. broadcast rights to the 1992 Winter Olympics at Albertville, France, for a stunning $243 million.

The two networks submitted their bids in sealed envelopes to the International Olympic Committee last week in New York City. The IOC contingent, which included famed skier Jean-Claude Killy, had expected the Games to command several million dollars less, particularly after ABC shocked the IOC and the broadcast community with an eleventh-hour decision not to participate in the bidding. Because the networks aren't the money trees they once were, this was only the third-richest round of bidding in Olympic history. ABC paid $309 million for this year's Calgary Games, and September's Seoul Games cost NBC $300 million.

NBC, which bid $175 million for the Albertville Games, sweetened its tender by offering the IOC and the Albertville Organizing Committee 50 percent of all ad revenues in excess of $325 million, which, according to some estimates, could have raised the value of its bid to $220 million. Nonetheless, by the time CBS and the IOC were celebrating their agreement with a magnum of champagne, NBC Sports president Arthur Watson was needling his CBS counterpart, Neal Pilson, for overspending.

"ABC had its Calgary; this one could be CBS's Calgary," said Watson, referring to ABC's reported loss of $65 million on the Winter Games. "Pilson speaks with forked tongue. He preaches one thing [austerity] and then doesn't practice it. This shocks me. How the hell could they leave that much money on the table?"

Said Pilson, "Art Watson can manage his business and we'll manage ours. This bid reflected the value of the Games to CBS. The winner can always look back and say we could've bid less, and the loser can look back and say we should've bid more. In the end we will have the Olympics four years from now and the other guys won't.''

''We're a very strong company financially,'' said CBS president and CEO Laurence Tisch. ''We can afford to take the risk of a $10 million or $15 million loss on an event the magnitude of an Olympics.''

Still, CBS is taking a chance by spending so lavishly to land the Games. No one knows in which direction the soft sports marketplace is headed. The six- to nine-hour time difference between Albertville and the United States poses another risk: Because of it, prime-time coverage will be taped and the results of events will generally be known. To recover its costs, CBS projects carrying more than 100 hours, some 10 more than ABC aired from Calgary.

But the deal can't be considered a mistake when one takes into account how desperately CBS needed to make a statement to its affiliates, employees, advertisers and potential investors. So serious are CBS's ratings and public relations problems that it could hardly afford *not* to get the Games. Keep in mind that for all the difficulties the Calgary Games caused ABC, they pushed the network into second place in prime time last season.

If CBS delighted the IOC, ABC disappointed and angered the committee with its decision not to participate in the bidding. ABC still resents IOC TV chairman Dick Pound and agent Barry Frank, who represents the organizing committee in TV negotiations, for allegedly trapping the network into overpaying for the rights to the Calgary Games. Was this ABC's way of getting back?

''I was upset that ABC would choose to make an announcement at a time when it would not help,'' said Pound. Frank believes the announcement was ''timed to discredit [the rights] to some degree. I felt there was a little bit of dog in the manager in this.''

ABC's vague withdrawal announcement said that it feared being dragged into a ''multiround auction'' and that it had problems with certain sponsorship and ''procedural'' changes in the proposed TV contract. ABC Sports president Dennis Swanson declined to elaborate. ''They [the IOC] did what they had to do,'' he said. ''We opted not to participate and said so. Life goes on.''

The withdrawal was all the more surprising because ABC tried to obtain both the Albertville Games and the 1992 Summer Olympics at Barcelona as a package. In a move that would have deep-sixed CBS and NBC, ABC proposed to the IOC in early May that the network be awarded the rights to both Olympics for $500 million. Pound and IOC president Juan Antonio Samaranch were intrigued by the idea, because the two Games might have produced more revenue sold as a package than separately. But the deal fell through when Albertville and Barcelona couldn't agree on how the proceeds would be divided.

Since Calgary, ABC had argued that the IOC should give it ''most favored network'' status for bidding on both 1992 Games because of its Olympic contributions over the years (ABC has telecast 10 of the previous 13 Olympics). Until last week ABC's best pal in the IOC was Samaranch. In a May 18 letter to Samaranch, Swanson informed him of ABC's intention to withdraw and then tried to call in a favor.

"It would be our hope," he wrote, "that you could convince the organizing committees of the wisdom of accepting our joint financial proposal prior to next week's meeting. . . ." Swanson finished by thanking Samaranch for his "gift of the Olympic torso by Berrocal, [which] adorns my office and serves as a visual reminder to me of our friendship."

In a return letter to Swanson two days later, Samaranch made no reference to ABC's package-deal proposal and noted "how disappointed I am with the contents of your letter."

Says Pound, "Basically ABC has passed on the last two Olympic bids. Any claim it may have thought it had to a favored status has now fully exploded. There is no basis for ABC to bid [for future Games] on any footing except equal with the other two networks."

In the meantime, CBS can crow. Just before he aimed the cork at the cameras last week, Pilson jokingly said, "Is there an ABC crew here?" Then he finished his glass of champagne faster than Killy could schuss down a hill.

Olympic Television Rights (D)

Makegoods Mean Pain for Spain[*]

William Taaffe

When the final TV ratings for the Olympics came out with a thud last week, a dark cloud must have descended over Barcelona, site of the 1992 Games. The U.S. broadcast rights to the Barcelona Olympics, which will be up for bid before Thanksgiving (talk about timing!), were valued before the '88 Games at upward of $500 million. Thanks to the Seoul Olympics' poor showing on NBC, the Barcelona organizers now may get $100 million less than they expected.

NBC guaranteed major sponsors ratings of 21.2 for those portions of the Seoul Games telecast in prime time. When the dust settled, the network's average came to 16.9, or 20 percent lower than projections and 27 percent worse than ABC's average for the 1984 Olympics in Los Angeles. NBC did beat out the other major networks 14 out of the 15 nights the Games were on, and that was enough to give it the best Nielsen ratings for the month and probably for the entire fall season. The only evening NBC lost was October 2, when the closing ceremonies were upstaged by a made-for-TV movie about Liberace on ABC. Nevertheless, because NBC fell short of projections by an average of 3.8 million homes a night, it will have to give sponsors the equivalent of some $70 million in makegoods, which is televisionese for commercial time given by the networks to advertisers as compensation for not attaining guaranteed ratings.

Because of having to broadcast all those makegoods, NBC's anticipated $40 to $60 million profit from its operation in Seoul has vanished. The network will probably break even, because its seven TV stations, which had no overhead, are likely to realize a $30 million profit from the sale of local advertising. But the trend ain't pretty. Following on the heels of ABC's loss of an estimated $65 million on last winter's Games in Calgary, the Seoul Olympics was the second in a row that failed to produce a cent for the company that paid the bulk of the costs for putting on the Games.

There are many reasons that ratings suffered, chief among them the fact that these Games were the first ones to begin in September, when kids are back in school and a heavy diet of sports fare gluts the tube. One plus for the Barcelona Games: They'll begin in late July.

But there were other lessons to be learned from Seoul:

• In an age of falling ratings, the International Olympic Committee (IOC) had better negotiate the fees for the rights to future Olympics before the preceding Games begin. Hindsight is 20/20, but IOC president Juan Antonio Samaranch and the committee's TV chairman, Richard Pound, may well have blown it by now wrapping up a Barcelona deal before the ratings from Seoul came in.

• A live Olympics isn't necessarily more popular than a tape-delayed one. NBC hurt itself in the Nielsens by opting for 80 percent live coverage from Seoul. What good was having such American notables as Janet Evans and Matt Biondi on live when their events were running at 2:30 A.M. EDT? NBC should have broadcast more tapes of important events in prime time, when American viewers were ready and waiting to be engaged emotionally. But instead the network stayed live, even when that meant showing water polo for an hour, and the ratings never reached critical mass.

NBC's production was honest, immediate, and technically superb. The ratings suggest, however, that most viewers aren't willing to hunt for programming of gymnastics and other premier events during odd hours. Spain poses a time-difference problem, too. When it's early evening in New York, it's bedtime in Barcelona, and there's normally not a lot of first-class Olympics action then. Whichever network gets the TV rights in Barcelona will have to walk a narrow line between live and taped action. The 1984 Winter Games in Sarajevo, some viewers will recall, turned out to be the Sominex Olympics because many of the results were known before ABC went on the air. Look for a Hollywood-style, celebrate-America's-medals version of the Barcelona Games each night. It's also likely that the network carrying that Olympics will for the first time sell the rights to individual events to a cable service. That means subscribers to the service may get a chance to see uncut coverage of basketball or other sports from the preliminaries through the finals.

• No longer can the Games be shown as a kind of four-star track meet–basketball tournament. Purists may have loved NBC's unemotional, just give-'em-the-sports approach, but the viewers didn't. Early in the first week, for example, NBC stayed with a U.S.-Canada basketball prelim in prime time while Greg Louganis, having cut his head the night before, was making a comeback on the springboard. "It looked like they were programming Saturday-Sunday-afternoon sports," says Bill Croasdale, director of network programming for the advertising agency Backer, Spielvogel, Bates. "That was a turnoff, particularly for the female audience." Indeed, women traditionally compose at least 50 percent of the prime-time Olympics audience. That ABC did better than expected in the ratings going up against the Games with a series of sitcoms suggests that NBC never hooked the female audience.

• Madison Avenue and the networks have got to start listening to the outcry over the plethora of commercials. When NBC's Week 1 ratings came in 15 percent below projections, the network added commercials during Week 2 to get a head start on makegoods. That not only depressed ratings even further but also brought an angry response from viewers. Some ad agencies are floating the idea of eliminating 15-second spots on the Olympics to avoid clutter. In addition, the networks should run fewer ads at higher prices, which would make viewers happy while generating the same amount of revenue.

With NBC licking its wounds, CBS and ABC have emerged as the front-runners in the race for the Barcelona rights. But the networks will now have to resharpen their pencils. As NBC Sports president Arthur Watson says, "No way Barcelona can be projected at a higher rating than Seoul—all of it will have to be taped except for what's on the weekend. They can say, 'O.K., we'll do events at midnight, which is 5 P.M. in the East,' but the athletes will bitch about that, and I don't think that will fly."

CBS, which is currently the third-rated network, may be eager for an Olympics double dip. The network already has the rights to the 1992 Winter Games at Albertville, France, and company president Larry Tisch has plenty of cash to spend from the recent sale of assets. The fact that CBS will have staff and equipment on-site in Albertville, only six hours by car from Barcelona, could save the network $20 million should it get both Olympics—a savings that could give it a leg up in the bidding.

Still, when the closing ceremonies are beaten by a Liberace bio-pic, you have to wonder where the price is headed. Three hundred and fifty million, anyone?

Olympic Television Rights (E)

A Golden Opportunity*

William Oscar Johnson

When NBC pledged $401 million last week for the U.S. rights to the 1992 Summer Olympics in Barcelona—a bid that will yield the largest sum ever paid for a single TV event—both the size and the source of the figure stunned the TV sports world. For one thing, it was $92 million more than the previous-record $309 million that ABC had paid for the 1988 Winter Games in Calgary, and most insiders had reckoned that $375 million or so would be about the most Barcelona could expect. Beyond that, NBC was considered at best a dark horse behind the other two networks in the bidding.

The smart money was on CBS for several compelling reasons. First, last May CBS had obtained the rights to the Albertville Games for $243 million ($68 million more than runner-up NBC had offered) and thus held a $15 million to $20 million advantage in the Balcelona bidding because it would already have production equipment and personnel in Europe in '92, ready to move to the venues in Spain at little cost. More to the point, CBS had the wherewithal to outbid its rivals because it had recently amassed cash reserves of some $3 billion from the sale of most of its non-TV properties. Also, during the last two years CBS has been mired in third place in the Neilsen ratings. The showcasting of two Olympics in one year would be a crucial element in plans to turn around the network's fortunes.

Industry pundits also favored ABC over NBC, in part because ABC is *the* Olympic network, having telecast 10 of the 14 Games held from 1964 to '88, and many experts felt it would be unwilling to surrender the Olympic franchise completely in '92. Not only that, but ABC, the once reigning champion of TV sports, is widely expected to deal itself out of baseball's new television contract, which will be announced later this month. This would leave the network with week-to-week sports programming consisting of the NFL's less-than-splendid *Monday Night Football,* some college football, lots of golf, and a college basketball package that doesn't include the NCAA Final

Four. That's hardly a championship lineup, but a Summer Olympics would give it a big boost in class. ABC also was thought to have an advantage because it owns ESPN, America's No. 1 sports-cable company, and the Barcelona deal was going to be the first Olympics TV contract to allow a network to share the broadcast with a cable partner.

When the day of the bidding arrived, almost no one in the television business, including a lot of folks at NBC Sports, believed NBC would enter more than a token bid. The network is a solid No. 1 in the Neilsen ratings and doesn't need the kind of lift CBS does. It was also widely assumed that NBC had either lost money or, at best, had made a negligible profit on its 179½-hour coverage of the Seoul Games. Since the network is now owned by General Electric, which is known for its bottom-line management, no one figured NBC Sports would be allowed to bid seriously for an event that was already a proven loser.

So why was everyone wrong? Mainly because NBC *did* make a profit on the 1988 Summer Olympics—more than $30 million, according to sources inside and outside the network. And though that was a pittance compared with the $40 million to $60 million profit that NBC was hoping for, it wasn't a negligible amount. NBC Sports president Arthur Watson refused to divulge the size of his network's take, but he did say, "We made some money in Seoul, and what [GE's CEO] Jack Welch and [NBC president] Bob Wright care most about is profit. Believe me, it didn't take a sales talk to convince them that NBC should be very aggressive in our bid.

The showdown took place in two phases. At 10 A.M., the top executives of all three network sports divisions filed into the New York offices of O'Melveny & Myers, the counsel for the Barcelona organizing committee, and delivered their first round of bids in sealed envelopes to International Olympic Committee (IOC) vice-president Richard Pound. The IOC also submitted an envelope of its own containing the minimum amount it would accept for the rights: $360 million.

Pound, who serves as the head of the IOC's television negotiations committee, discussed the bids with other committee members and then summoned representatives of each network for another 20 minutes or so of questioning. The plan had been to reduce the competition to two networks for the second round, but because the bids were so close and difficult to understand, Pound allowed all three networks to go again.

"In the old days, the networks used to bid X dollars, and that was it," said Pound later. "But this was terribly complex. There were all sorts of revenue-sharing gimmicks and different bases for guarantees. The networks are trying to avoid having to swallow the unswallowable nut; they're much more interested in risk-sharing than revenue-sharing. We can't get involved in that. We simply told them we had to know the worst-case scenario—meaning how much money would they guarantee us with no strings attached."

The first bids of all three networks contained guarantees that were said to be between $350 and $360 million, with ABC's being the highest. "The strategy in the first bid was to put in all sorts of bells and whistles that the others might not have," said Watson. "But the psychology was to make sure you made it through to the second round. That's where the whole thing happened."

The networks were given one hour to produce a second bid. Once the envelopes were opened, it was only a matter of minutes before the winner was announced. NBC had beefed up its sum by a staggering $40 million. The others had gone up only a cautious few million.

What was NBC's thinking in doing this? "The Olympics are good for our company, good for our affiliates," Watson said. "Everybody keeps saying we didn't get the ratings we had predicted in Seoul, but even with lower ratings, the Olympics dominated American TV in the weeks they were on. We may not make a lot of money in Barcelona, but $401 million is not a money-losing bid, believe me. The big variable this time is the cable TV package. I'm convinced we will get well over $75 million for our cable commitment, which we won't have nailed down for another week or so." The most likely scenario: NBC will sell the rights to about 75 hours of lesser Olympic events to SportsChannel America, an East Coast-based division of Cablevision Systems Corp., which between now and the Barcelona Games is planning to grow into a national entity.

Whatever the profits or losses ahead, NBC made history with its Olympian dollar commitment. But this was only the first act of a high-risk, big-bucks drama that NBC Sports is playing a starring role in. Baseball's new TV package is expected to produce $1.2 billion over three years, and the high rollers from NBC will be footing a good chunk of the bill. As Watson put it after his network's splurge last week, "The fact we just spent $401 million on the Olympics has no bearing at all on our baseball bidding. They are two entirely separate issues. The Olympics is a dramatic, one-time spectacle. Baseball is a matter of serious, consistent programming for this network. Baseball has been an indelible part of the fabric of NBC for 40 years, and it will continue to be for many years more, I promise you."

Index of Readings and Cases